Kawasaki ZX-10R
Service and Repair Manual

by Matthew Coombs

Models covered

(5542-320)

ZX1000C. 998cc. 2004 and 2005
ZX1000D. 998cc. 2006 and 2007
ZX1000E. 998cc. 2008 and 2009
ZX1000F. 998cc. 2010

© Haynes Publishing 2014

ABCDE
FGHIJ
KLMNO
PQRST

A book in the Haynes Service and Repair Manual Series

ISBN 978 0 85733 542 5

Library of Congress Control Number 2013954584

Printed in the USA

Haynes Publishing
Sparkford, Yeovil, Somerset BA22 7JJ, England

Haynes North America, Inc
861 Lawrence Drive, Newbury Park, California 91320, USA

Haynes Publishing Nordiska AB
Box 1504, 751 45 Uppsala, Sweden

Contents

LIVING WITH YOUR KAWASAKI ZX-10R

Introduction

Pre-ride checks

MAINTENANCE

Routine maintenance and servicing

Contents

Kawasaki The Green Meanies

by Julian Ryder

Kawasaki Heavy Industries

Kawasaki is a company of contradictions. It is the smallest of the big four Japanese manufacturers but the biggest company, it was the last of the four to make and market motorcycles yet it owns the oldest name in the Japanese industry, and it was the first to set up a factory in the USA. Kawasaki Heavy Industries, of which the motorcycle operation is but a small component, is a massive company with its heritage firmly in the old heavy industries like shipbuilding and railways; nowadays it is as much involved in aerospace as in motorcycles.

In fact it may be because of this that Kawasaki's motorcycles have always been quirky, you get the impression that they are designed by a small group of enthusiasts who are given an admirably free hand. More realistically, it may be that Kawasaki's designers have experience with techniques and materials from other engineering disciplines. Either way, Kawasaki have managed to be the factory who surprise us more than the rest. Quite often, they do this by totally ignoring a market segment the others are scrabbling over, but more often they hit us with pure, undiluted performance.

The origins of the company, and its name, go back to 1878 when Shozo Kawasaki set up a dockyard in Tokyo. By the late 1930s, the company was making its own steel in massive steelworks and manufacturing railway locos and rolling stock. In the run up to war, the Kawasaki Aircraft Company was set up in 1937 and it was this arm of the now giant operation that would look to motorcycle engine manufacture in post-war Japan.

They bought their high-technology experience to bear first on engines which were sold on to a number of manufacturers as original equipment. Both two- and four-stroke units were made, a 58 cc and 148 cc OHC unit. One of the customer companies was Meihatsu Heavy Industries, another company within the Kawasaki group, which in 1961 was shaken up and renamed Kawasaki Auto Sales. At the same time, the Akashi factory which was to be Kawasaki's main production facility until the Kobe earthquake of 1995, was opened.

Shortly afterwards, Kawasaki took over the ailing Meguro company, Japan's oldest motorcycle maker, thus instantly obtaining a range of bigger bikes which were marketed as Kawasaki-Meguros. The following year, the first bike to be made and sold as a Kawasaki was produced, a 125 cc single called the B8 and in 1963 a motocross version, the B8M appeared.

Model development

Kawasaki's first appearance on a road-race circuit came in 1965 with a batch of disc-valve 125 twins. They were no match for the opposition from Japan in the shape of Suzuki and Yamaha or for the fading force of the factory MZs from East Germany. Only after the other Japanese factories had pulled out of the class did Kawasaki win, with British rider Dave Simmonds becoming World 125 GP Champion in 1969 on a bike that looked astonishingly similar to the original racer. That same year Kawasaki reorganised once again, this time merging three companies to form Kawasaki Heavy Industries. One of the new organisation's objectives was to take motorcycle production forward and exploit markets outside Japan.

KHI achieved that target immediately and set out their stall for the future with the astonishing and frightening H1. This three-cylinder air-cooled 500 cc two-stroke was arguably the first modern pure performance bike to hit the market. It hypnotised a whole generation of motorcyclists who'd never before encountered such a ferocious, wheelie inducing power band or such shattering straight-line speed allied to questionable handling. And as for the 750 cc version ...

The triples perfectly suited the late '60s, fitting in well with the student demonstrations of 1968 and the anti-establishment ethos of the Summer of Love. Unfortunately, the oil crisis would put an end to the thirsty strokers but Kawasaki had another high-performance ace up their corporate sleeve. Or rather they thought they did.

The 1968 Tokyo Show saw probably the single most significant new motorcycle ever made unveiled: the Honda CB750. At Kawasaki it caused a major shock, for they also had a 750 cc four, code-named New

The three cylinder two-stroke 750

The first Superbike, Kawasaki's 900 cc Z1

no major difference between that first Z1 and the air-cooled GPz range. Add water-cooling and you have the GPZ900, which in turn metamorphosed into the GPZ1000RX and then the ZX-10 and the ZZ-R1100. Indeed, the last three models share the same 58 mm stroke. The bikes are obviously very different but it's difficult to put your finger on exactly why.

Other models have remained effectively untouched for over a decade: the KH and KE single-cylinder air-cooled two-stroke learner bikes, the GT550 and 750 shaft-drive hacks favoured by big city despatch riders and the GPz305 being prime examples. It's only when they step outside the performance field that Kawasakis seems less sure. Their first factory customs were dire, you simply got the impression that the team that designed them didn't have their heart in the job. Only when the Classic range appeared in 1995 did they get it right.

Racing success

Kawasaki also have a more focused approach to racing than the other factories. The policy has always been to race the road bikes and with just a couple of exceptions that's what they've done. Even Simmonds' championship winner bore a strong resemblance to the twins they were selling in the late '60s and racing versions of the 500 and 750 cc triples were also sold as over-the-counter racers, the H1R and H2R. The 500 was in the forefront of the two-stroke assault on MV Agusta but wasn't a Grand Prix

York Steak, almost ready to roll and it was a double, rather than single, overhead cam motor. Bravely, they took the decision to go ahead - but with the motor taken out to 900 cc. The result was the Z1, unveiled at the 1972 Cologne Show. It was a bike straight out of the same mould as the H1, scare stories spread about unmanageable power, dubious straight-line stability and frightening handling, none of which stopped the sales graph

rocketing upwards and led to the coining of the term 'superbike'. While rising fuel prices cut short development of the big two-strokes, the Z1 went on to found a dynasty, indeed its genes can still be detected in Kawasaki's latest products like the ZZ-R1100 (Ninja ZX-11).

This is another characteristic of the way Kawasaki operates. Models quite often have very long lives, or gradually evolve. There is

One of the two-stroke engined KH and KE range - the KE100B

The GT750 - a favourite hack for despatch riders

The high-performance ZXR750

winner. It was the 750 that made the impact and carried the factory's image in F750 racing against the Suzuki triples and Yamaha fours.

The factory's decision to use green, usually regarded as an unlucky colour in sport, meant its bikes and personnel stood out and the phrase 'Green Meanies' fitted them perfectly. The Z1 motor soon became a full 1000 cc and powered Kawasaki's assault in F1 racing, notably in endurance which Kawasaki saw as being most closely related to its road bikes.

That didn't stop them dominating 250 and 350 cc GPs with a tandem twin two-stroke in the late '70s and early '80s, but their path-breaking monocoque 500 while a race winner never won a world title. When Superbike arrived, Kawasaki's road 750s weren't as track-friendly as the opposition's out-and-out race replicas. This makes Scott Russell's World title on the ZXR750 in 1993 even more praiseworthy, for the homologation bike, the ZXR750RR, was much heavier and

much more of a road bike than the Italian and Japanese competition.

The company's Supersport 600 contenders have similarly been more sports-tourers than race-replicas, yet they too have been competitive on the track. Indeed, the flagship bike, the ZZ-R1100, is most definitely a sports tourer capable of carrying two people and their luggage at high speed in comfort all day and then doing it again the next day. Try that on one of the race replicas and you'll be in need of a course of treatment from a chiropractor.

Through doing it their way Kawasaki developed a brand loyalty for their performance bikes that kept the Z1's derivatives in production until the mid-'80s and turned the bike into a classic in its model life. You could even argue that the Z1 lives on in the shape of the 1100 Zephyr's GPz1100-derived motor. And that's another Kawasaki invention, the retro bike. But when you look at what many commentators refer to as the retro boom, especially in Japan, you find that it is no such thing. It is the Zephyr boom. Just another example of Japan's most surprising motorcycle manufacturer getting it right again.

The ZX-10R models

Of all the big four Japanese factories, Kawasaki has always had a bit of an edge to its image. This may be because motorcycles are a small percentage of the company's business so their lines appear to be designed by enthusiasts; historically, there have been no 50cc scooters or mopeds, no commuters, and what look like cruisers that are probably better defined as muscle bikes. Yes, there have been exceptions to this generalisation along the way but when Kawasaki first made an impact it was with their legendary three-cylinder air-cooled two strokes, fire-breathing man-eating motorcycles with a reputation for punishing the most trifling of pilot errors.

The arrival of the mighty Z1 added four-stroke muscle to the range and helped set the industry standard pattern of DOHC across the frame fours that came to be known as the Universal Japanese Motorcycle. It was also the base of the factory's first Superbike racers, and there's never been a more purposeful looking racer than the one Eddie Lawson rode in American racing: stepped seat, high bars, twin shocks; four-into-one exhaust and all. Typically, Kawasaki were the first factory to fit fuel injection to a production bike on the 1980 Z1000H.

The Z1 was really a 1970s bike: in the '80s Kawasaki were the first factory to produce the equivalent of a hot hatchback by hopping up their standard UJMs and producing the GPz range. Note the lower-case 'z,' it denotes air-cooled engines. Then came the upper-case 'Z', the GPZ900R Ninja, Japan's first water-cooled superbike for the masses. Flexible enough to take you and the other half to the coast or on holiday in comfort; fast enough to win a Production TT on the Isle of

The very first ZX-10R, the 2004 C1

The ZX1000D with its distinctive under-seat exhausts

The 2010 ZX1000F

Man. Kawasaki's original ZX-10 superseded the GPZ900R at the end of 1987.

The Ninja's successors were a little more road-focussed. Superbike regulations had been rationalised world wide for the start of the world championship at 750cc capacity for four-cylinder engined bikes, so Kawasaki's GPZ then the ZXR750 did the track stuff. Despite regulations that arguably favoured the V-twins, the only four-cylinder 750 to win the World Superbike Championship was Scott Russell's ZXR.

When in 2003 the World Superbike Championship allowed all engine configurations to have a capacity of up to a litre, Kawasaki's ZX-9R was their top of the range model. It was fast, of course, but it was really a cross between the seriously sporty ZXR750 and the totally roads-orientated ZZ-R1100. What was needed was a true

superbike homologation model: enter the ZX-10R.

Here was a true super sports bike, following the lead set first by Honda with the FireBlade and then by Yamaha with the R1 – packing 1000cc performance into a package the size of a 600.

Compared to the ZX-9R, the ZX-10R's motor was lower and further back, the front wheel nearer to the front of the engine. The chassis beams went over the engine, not round it, producing a chassis that could easily perform the sort of quick changes of direction needed on a race track at the expense of straight-line stability. The motor was, of necessity, narrow with stacked gearbox shafts and the generator running piggy back behind the cylinders, not on the end of the crank. Other race-track necessities like a slipper clutch and radial brakes were present and

correct. The ZX-10R was even racier than the Suzuki GSX-R1000 and certainly much more so than the FireBlade of the time.

The most noticeable thing about the bike, apart from its sheer speed, was the narrowness of the chassis. The back of the tank was about six inches wide – even by Kawasaki standards, this was one extreme motorcycle.

And it achieved its objectives, although not instantly. The ZX-10R won the 2013 world superbike championship with Tom Sykes doing the riding and the year before won the most important domestic championship in the world, the British Superbike Championship in the hands of Shakey Byrne. Perhaps more significantly, the ZX-10R became the base bike of choice for privateer teams. That alone tells you how race ready the standard bike is.

Acknowledgements

Our thanks are due to Bransons Motorcycles of Yeovil, Frasers Motorcycles of Gloucester and SP Motorcycles of Exeter who supplied the machines featured in the illustrations throughout this manual. We would also like to thank NGK Spark Plugs (UK) Ltd for supplying the colour spark plug condition photographs, the Avon Rubber Company for supplying information on tyre fitting and Draper Tools Ltd for some of the workshop tools shown.

Thanks are also due to Julian Ryder who wrote the introduction 'Kawasaki – The Green Meanies' and to Kawasaki (UK) Ltd. who supplied model photographs.

About this Manual

The aim of this manual is to help you get the best value from your motorcycle. It can do so in several ways. It can help you decide what work must be done, even if you choose to have it done by a dealer; it provides information and procedures for routine maintenance and servicing; and it offers diagnostic and repair procedures to follow when trouble occurs.

We hope you use the manual to tackle the work yourself. For many simpler jobs, doing it yourself may be quicker than arranging an appointment to get the motorcycle into a dealer and making the trips to leave it and pick it up. More importantly, a lot of money

can be saved by avoiding the expense the shop must pass on to you to cover its labour and overhead costs. An added benefit is the sense of satisfaction and accomplishment that you feel after doing the job yourself.

References to the left or right side of the motorcycle assume you are sitting on the seat, facing forward.

We take great pride in the accuracy of information given in this manual, but motorcycle manufacturers make alterations and design changes during the production run of a particular motorcycle of which they do not inform us. No liability can be accepted by the authors or publishers for loss, damage or injury caused by any errors in, or omissions from, the information given.

ZX1000C1 and C2 (2004 and 2005) models

The ZX-10R has an in-line four cylinder liquid-cooled engine. Drive to the double overhead camshafts that actuate the four valves per cylinder is by chain from the right-hand end of the crankshaft. The clutch is a wet multi-plate unit with diaphragm springs and slipper mechanism, with cable actuation. The alternator is on top of the crankcase. The starter clutch and its associated gears are on the left-hand side of the engine. The gearbox is 6-speed. Drive to the rear wheel is by chain and sprockets.

The Mikuni fuel injection system supplies fuel and air to the engine via dual valve 43mm throttle bodies housing a single injector per cylinder. Air is drawn in via a central air duct in the fairing that leads to dual air ducts through the frame to the air filter housing. The injectors are mounted in the throttle bodies below the throttle valves. An electronic engine management system controls both the injection system and the ignition system. The exhaust system incorporates a butterfly valve for precise exhaust gas control.

The engine sits in an aluminium twin-beam frame that uses the engine as a stressed member. Front suspension is by fully adjustable oil-damped inverted 43 mm forks with cartridge dampers. Rear suspension is by a fully adjustable single shock absorber via a three-way rising rate linkage. The swingarm pivots through the frame.

The front brake system has two twin opposed-piston radially-mounted monoblock calipers with four brake pads per caliper acting on floating discs. The rear brake system has a single piston sliding caliper acting on a conventional disc.

ZX1000D6 and D7 (2006 and 2007) models

Major changes were made to both the engine and frame on the D model.

A new frame features revised steering geometry with a steering damper fitted as standard, revised engine and swingarm mounts, and a new rear sub-frame. There is a new underseat exhaust system and revised body styling overall.

Changes to the engine included modifications to the clutch, sump and crankcases, the alternator was moved onto the left-hand end of the crankshaft, and the starter clutch and its associated gears were moved to the right-hand side of the engine.

A new radial front brake master was fitted, and a new instrument cluster.

ZX1000E8 and E9 (2008 and 2009) models

On E models a Keihin fuel injection system was fitted featuring oval sub-throttles and dual fuel injectors. The primary injectors, mounted in the throttle bodies below the throttle valves, operate all the time the engine is running. The secondary injectors mounted in the top of the air filter housing, operate only at high engine speeds and wide throttle openings, and spray fuel into the air entering the throttle bodies above the throttle valves.

There was a new exhaust system and revised body styling overall. Changes were made to the air intake system to enable a more direct passage to the new air filter housing. There was a new swingarm, and the front brake calipers featured a conventional brake pad arrangement.

ZX1000FA (2010) model

A new starter motor was fitted, and some minor changes were made to the bodywork.

Dimensions and weights

	ZX1000C models	ZX1000D models	ZX1000E and F models
Overall length	2045 mm	2065 mm	2110 mm
Overall width	705 mm	705 mm	710 mm
Overall height	1115 mm	1130 mm	1135 mm
Wheelbase	1385 mm	1390 mm	1415 mm
Seat height	825 mm	825 mm	830 mm
Ground clearance	125 mm	125 mm	125 mm
Weight (dry)	170 kg	175 kg	179 kg

Engine

Type	Four-stroke in-line four
Capacity	998 cc
Bore	76.0 mm
Stroke	55.0 mm
Compression ratio	
C and D models	12.7 to 1
E and F models	12.9 to 1
Cooling system	Liquid cooled
Clutch	Wet multi-plate, cable actuation
Transmission	Six-speed constant mesh
Final drive	Chain and sprockets
Camshafts	DOHC, chain-driven
Fuel system	Fuel injection, 43 mm throttle bodies
Exhaust system	
C models	Four-into-one
D models	Four-into-two
E and F models	Four-into-one
Ignition system	Computer-controlled digital transistorised with electronic advance

Chassis

Frame type	Composite pressed and die-cast aluminium, twin beam backbone
Rake and Trail	
C models	24°, 102 mm
D models	24.5°, 102 mm
E and F models	25.5°, 110 mm
Fuel tank capacity	17 litres
Front suspension	
Type	43 mm oil-damped cartridge-type upside down telescopic forks
Travel	120 mm
Adjustment	Spring pre-load, rebound and compression damping
Rear suspension	
Type	Single shock absorber, rising rate linkage, box section aluminium swingarm
Travel (at axle)	125 mm
Adjustment	Spring pre-load, rebound and compression damping
Wheels	17 inch, 6-spoke alloys
Tyres	
Front	120/70-ZR17 (58W) Radial
Rear	
C models	190/50-ZR17 (73W) Radial
D, E and F models	190/55-ZR17 (73W) Radial
Front brake	
C and D models	Twin 300 mm floating discs with four piston calipers and four pads per caliper
E and F models	Twin 310 mm floating discs with four piston calipers and two pads per caliper
Rear brake	Single 220 mm disc with single piston sliding caliper

Identification numbers

Frame and engine numbers

The frame serial number is stamped into the right-hand side of the steering head. The engine number is stamped into the upper crankcase half at the back of the engine. Both of these numbers should be recorded and kept in a safe place so they can be given to law enforcement officials in the event of a theft. The VIN plate is on the right-hand side of the steering head. The throttle bodies also have an ID number stamped into them.

The frame serial number, engine serial number, and colour code should also be kept in a handy place (such as with your driver's licence) so they are always available when purchasing or ordering parts for your machine.

The procedures in this manual identify models by their code letter (e.g. C models) and where necessary by their production year letter (e.g. C2 model).

Model	Year
ZX1000C1	2004
ZX1000C2	2005
ZX1000D6	2006
ZX1000D7	2007
ZX1000E8	2008
ZX1000E9	2009
ZX1000FA	2010

Buying spare parts

Once you have found all the identification numbers, record them for reference when buying parts. Since the manufacturers change specifications, parts and vendors (companies that manufacture various components on the machine), providing the ID numbers is the only way to be reasonably sure that you are buying the correct parts.

Whenever possible, take the old part to the dealer so direct comparison with the new component can be made. Along the trail from the manufacturer to the parts shelf, there are numerous places that the part can end up with the wrong number or be listed incorrectly.

The two places to purchase new parts for your motorcycle – the franchised or main dealer and the parts/accessories store – differ in the type of parts they carry. While dealers can obtain every single genuine part for your motorcycle, the accessory store is usually limited to normal high wear items such as chains and sprockets, brake pads and spark plugs.

Used parts can be obtained from breakers yards for roughly half the price of new ones, but you can't always be sure of what you're getting. Once again, take your worn part to the breaker for direct comparison, or when ordering by mail order make sure that you can return it if you are not happy.

Whether buying new, used or rebuilt parts, the best course is to deal directly with someone who specialises in your particular make.

The frame number is stamped into the right-hand side of the steering head. Note the VIN plate riveted next to it.

The engine number is on the back of the crankcase

Professional mechanics are trained in safe working procedures. However enthusiastic you may be about getting on with the job at hand, take the time to ensure that your safety is not put at risk. A moment's lack of attention can result in an accident, as can failure to observe simple precautions.

There will always be new ways of having accidents, and the following is not a comprehensive list of all dangers; it is intended rather to make you aware of the risks and to encourage a safe approach to all work you carry out on your bike.

Asbestos

● Certain friction, insulating, sealing and other products - such as brake pads, clutch linings, gaskets, etc. - contain asbestos. Extreme care must be taken to avoid inhalation of dust from such products since it is hazardous to health. If in doubt, assume that they do contain asbestos.

Fire

● Remember at all times that petrol is highly flammable. Never smoke or have any kind of naked flame around, when working on the vehicle. But the risk does not end there - a spark caused by an electrical short-circuit, by two metal surfaces contacting each other, by careless use of tools, or even by static electricity built up in your body under certain conditions, can ignite petrol vapour, which in a confined space is highly explosive. Never use petrol as a cleaning solvent. Use an approved safety solvent.

● Always disconnect the battery earth terminal before working on any part of the fuel or electrical system, and never risk spilling fuel on to a hot engine or exhaust.

● It is recommended that a fire extinguisher of a type suitable for fuel and electrical fires is kept handy in the garage or workplace at all times. Never try to extinguish a fuel or electrical fire with water.

Fumes

● Certain fumes are highly toxic and can quickly cause unconsciousness and even death if inhaled to any extent. Petrol vapour comes into this category, as do the vapours from certain solvents such as trichloro-ethylene. Any draining or pouring of such volatile fluids should be done in a well ventilated area.

● When using cleaning fluids and solvents, read the instructions carefully. Never use materials from unmarked containers - they may give off poisonous vapours.

● Never run the engine of a motor vehicle in an enclosed space such as a garage. Exhaust fumes contain carbon monoxide which is extremely poisonous; if you need to run the engine, always do so in the open air or at least have the rear of the vehicle outside the workplace.

The battery

● Never cause a spark, or allow a naked light near the vehicle's battery. It will normally be giving off a certain amount of hydrogen gas, which is highly explosive.

● Always disconnect the battery ground (earth) terminal before working on the fuel or electrical systems (except where noted).

Electricity

● When using an electric power tool, inspection light etc., always ensure that the appliance is correctly connected to its plug and that, where necessary, it is properly grounded (earthed). Do not use such appliances in damp conditions and, again, beware of creating a spark or applying excessive heat in the vicinity of fuel or fuel vapour. Also ensure that the appliances meet national safety standards.

● A severe electric shock can result from touching certain parts of the electrical system, such as the spark plug wires (HT leads), when the engine is running or being cranked, particularly if components are damp or the insulation is defective. Where an electronic ignition system is used, the secondary (HT) voltage is much higher and could prove fatal.

Remember...

✗ **Don't** start the engine without first ascertaining that the transmission is in neutral.

✗ **Don't** suddenly remove the pressure cap from a hot cooling system - cover it with a cloth and release the pressure gradually first, or you may get scalded by escaping coolant.

✗ **Don't** attempt to drain oil until you are sure it has cooled sufficiently to avoid scalding you.

✗ **Don't** grasp any part of the engine or exhaust system without first ascertaining that it is cool enough not to burn you.

✗ **Don't** allow brake fluid or antifreeze to contact the machine's paintwork or plastic components.

✗ **Don't** siphon toxic liquids such as fuel, hydraulic fluid or antifreeze by mouth, or allow them to remain on your skin.

✗ **Don't** inhale dust - it may be injurious to health (see Asbestos heading).

✗ **Don't** allow any spilled oil or grease to remain on the floor - wipe it up right away, before someone slips on it.

✗ **Don't** use ill-fitting spanners or other tools which may slip and cause injury.

✗ **Don't** lift a heavy component which may be beyond your capability - get assistance.

✗ **Don't** rush to finish a job or take unverified short cuts.

✗ **Don't** allow children or animals in or around an unattended vehicle.

✗ **Don't** inflate a tyre above the recommended pressure. Apart from overstressing the carcass, in extreme cases the tyre may blow off forcibly.

✔ **Do** ensure that the machine is supported securely at all times. This is especially important when the machine is blocked up to aid wheel or fork removal.

✔ **Do** take care when attempting to loosen a stubborn nut or bolt. It is generally better to pull on a spanner, rather than push, so that if you slip, you fall away from the machine rather than onto it.

✔ **Do** wear eye protection when using power tools such as drill, sander, bench grinder etc.

✔ **Do** use a barrier cream on your hands prior to undertaking dirty jobs - it will protect your skin from infection as well as making the dirt easier to remove afterwards; but make sure your hands aren't left slippery. Note that long-term contact with used engine oil can be a health hazard.

✔ **Do** keep loose clothing (cuffs, ties etc. and long hair) well out of the way of moving mechanical parts.

✔ **Do** remove rings, wristwatch etc., before working on the vehicle - especially the electrical system.

✔ **Do** keep your work area tidy - it is only too easy to fall over articles left lying around.

✔ **Do** exercise caution when compressing springs for removal or installation. Ensure that the tension is applied and released in a controlled manner, using suitable tools which preclude the possibility of the spring escaping violently.

✔ **Do** ensure that any lifting tackle used has a safe working load rating adequate for the job.

✔ **Do** get someone to check periodically that all is well, when working alone on the vehicle.

✔ **Do** carry out work in a logical sequence and check that everything is correctly assembled and tightened afterwards.

✔ **Do** remember that your vehicle's safety affects that of yourself and others. If in doubt on any point, get professional advice.

● If in spite of following these precautions, you are unfortunate enough to injure yourself, seek medical attention as soon as possible.

Note: *The Pre-ride checks are also outlined in the owner's manual.*

Coolant level

> ⚠️ **Warning: DO NOT remove the radiator pressure cap to add coolant. Topping up is done via the coolant reservoir tank filler. DO NOT leave open containers of coolant about, as it is poisonous.**

Before you start:

✔ The coolant reservoir is located behind the left-hand fairing side panel.
✔ Make sure you have a supply of coolant available. Either a bottle of pre-mixed coolant or a prepared mixture of 50% distilled water and 50% silicate-free corrosion inhibited ethylene glycol anti-freeze or is needed.
✔ Check the coolant level when the engine is cold.
Caution: Do not run the engine in an enclosed space such as a garage or workshop.
✔ Make sure the motorcycle is on level ground. Support it upright using an auxiliary stand or by having an assistant hold it.

Bike care:

● Use only the specified coolant mixture. It is important that anti-freeze is used in the system all year round, and not just in the winter. Do not top the system up using only water, as the system will become too diluted.
● Do not overfill the reservoir tank. If the coolant is significantly above the F level line at any time, the surplus should be siphoned or drained off to prevent the possibility of it being expelled out of the overflow hose.
● If the coolant level falls steadily, check the system for leaks (see Chapter 1). If no leaks are found and the level continues to fall, it is recommended that the machine is taken to a Kawasaki dealer for a pressure test.

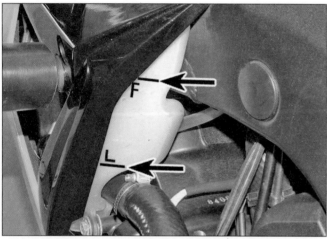

1 With the motorcycle vertical, the coolant level should lie between the F (full) and L (low) level lines (arrowed) on the reservoir.

2 If the coolant level is on or below the L line, remove the reservoir filler cap. On D models remove the left-hand fairing side panel to access the cap, and on E models remove the the left-hand fairing side cover (see Chapter 7).

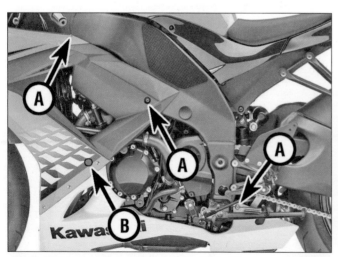

3 On F models remove the three fairing bolts (A), release the peg (B) from the grommet on the inside and ease the panel away from the frame sufficiently to access the cap.

4 Top the reservoir up with the recommended coolant mixture to the F level line, using a suitable funnel if required. Fit the cap.

Engine oil level

Before you start:

✔ Make sure the motorcycle is on level ground.
✔ Start the engine and let it idle for 3 to 5 minutes.
Caution: Do not run the engine in an enclosed space such as a garage or workshop.
✔ Stop the engine and allow the oil level to stabilise for 2 to 3 minutes. Support the motorcycle upright using an auxiliary stand or by having an assistant hold it.

Bike care:

● If you have to add oil frequently, check whether you have any oil leaks from the engine joints, oil seals and gaskets. If not, the engine could be burning oil, in which case there will be white smoke coming out of the exhaust (see *Fault Finding*).

The correct oil

● Modern, high-revving engines place great demands on their oil. It is very important that the correct oil for your bike is used. Do not use oil designed for use in car engines.
● Always top up with a good quality motorcycle oil of the specified type and viscosity and do not overfill the engine.
Caution: Do not use chemical additives or oils labelled "ENERGY CONSERVING". Such additives or oils could cause clutch slip.

Oil type	API grade: SG or higher motorcycle oil JASO grade: MA, MA1 or MA2
Oil viscosity	SAE 10W/40

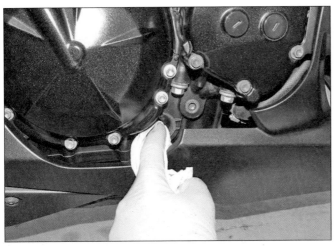

1 The oil level inspection window is on the right-hand side of the engine – wipe it clean, on C and D models via the aperture in the lower fairing.

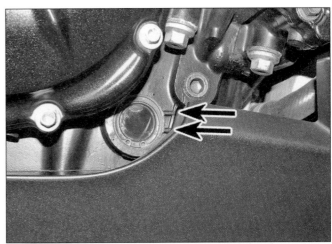

2 Check the level in the window – it must be between the upper and lower level lines (arrowed).

3 If the level is near, on or below the lower line, unscrew the filler cap.

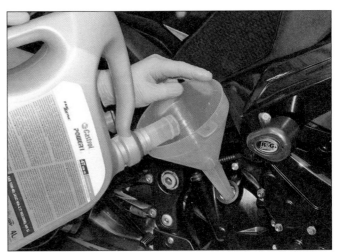

4 Top up the engine with the recommended grade and type of oil to bring the level almost up to the upper line on the window. Do not overfill. Make sure the filler cap O-ring is in good condition and correctly seated before refitting it.

Brake fluid levels

> **Warning: Brake hydraulic fluid can harm your eyes and damage painted surfaces, so use extreme caution when handling and pouring it and cover surrounding surfaces with rag. Do not use fluid that has been standing open for some time, as it is hygroscopic (absorbs moisture from the air) which can cause a dangerous loss of braking effectiveness.**

Before you start:

✔ The front brake fluid reservoir is on the right-hand handlebar. The rear brake fluid reservoir is on the right-hand side of the rear sub-frame.

✔ Make sure you have a supply of DOT 4 brake fluid.

✔ Wrap a rag around the reservoir being worked on to ensure that any spillage does not come into contact with painted surfaces.

✔ When checking the fluid in the front reservoir turn the handlebars so the reservoir is level.

✔ When checking the fluid in the rear reservoir support the motorcycle upright – on C models remove the left-hand side cover for access (see Chapter 7).

Bike care:

● The fluid in the front and rear brake master cylinder reservoirs will drop as the brake pads wear down, but at a very slow rate.

● If either fluid reservoir requires repeated topping-up there is a leak somewhere in the system. Check for signs of fluid leakage from the hydraulic hoses and/or brake system components – if found, rectify immediately (see Chapter 6).

● Check the operation of both brakes before taking the machine on the road; if there is evidence of air in the system (spongy feel to lever or pedal), it must be bled (see Chapter 6).

FRONT

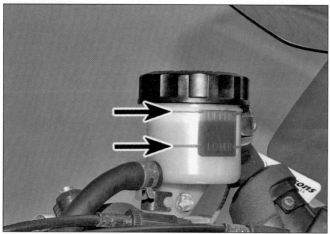

1 The front brake fluid level is visible through the window in the reservoir body – it must be between the UPPER and LOWER level lines (arrowed).

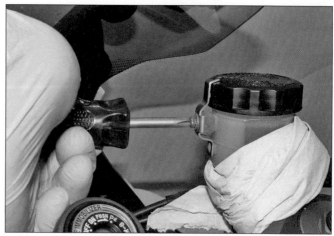

2 If the level is on or below the LOWER line, undo the cap clamp screw, then unscrew the cap and remove the diaphragm plate and diaphragm.

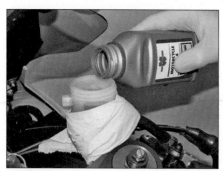

3 Top up with new clean DOT 4 hydraulic fluid, until the level is up to the UPPER line on the reservoir. Do not overfill and take care to avoid spills (see **Warning** above).

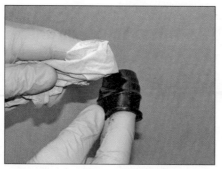

4 Wipe any moisture off the diaphragm with a tissue.

5 Ensure that the diaphragm is correctly seated before fitting the plate and cap. Secure the cap with the clamp.

REAR

1 The rear brake fluid level is visible through the reservoir body – it must be between the UPPER and LOWER level lines (arrowed).

2 If the level is on or below the LOWER line unscrew the cap and remove the diaphragm plate and diaphragm. The cap is secured by a clamp on D, E and F models.

3 Top up with new clean DOT 4 hydraulic fluid, until the level is up to the UPPER line on the reservoir. Do not overfill and take care to avoid spills (see **Warning**).

4 Wipe any moisture off the diaphragm with a tissue.

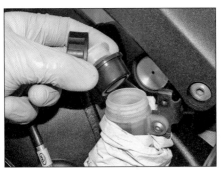

5 Ensure that the diaphragm is correctly seated before fitting the plate and cap. Secure the cap with the clamp where applicable.

Suspension, steering and drive chain checks

Suspension and Steering:

● Check that the front and rear suspension operates smoothly without binding (see Chapter 1).
● Check that the suspension is adjusted as required (see Chapter 5).
● Check that the steering moves smoothly from lock-to-lock (take into account the effect of the steering damper where fitted).

Drive chain:

● Check that the chain isn't too loose or too tight, and adjust it if necessary (see Chapter 1).
● If the chain looks dry, lubricate it (see Chapter 1).

Legal and safety checks

Lighting and signalling:

● Take a minute to check that the headlights, tail light, brake light, instrument lights and turn signals all work correctly.
● Check that the horn sounds when the button is pressed.
● A working speedometer, graduated in mph, is a statutory requirement in the UK.

Safety:

● Check that the throttle grip rotates smoothly when opened and snaps shut when released, in all steering positions. Also check for the correct amount of freeplay (see Chapter 1).
● Check that the brake lever and pedal, clutch lever and gearchange lever operate smoothly. Lubricate them at the specified intervals or when necessary (see Chapter 1).
● Check that the engine shuts off when the kill switch is operated. Check the starter interlock circuit (see Chapter 1).

● Check that the sidestand return springs hold the stand up securely when retracted.

Fuel:

● This may seem obvious, but check that you have enough fuel to complete your journey. If you notice signs of fuel leakage – rectify the cause immediately.
● Ensure you use the correct grade fuel – see Chapter 4 Specifications.

Tyres

The correct pressures:

● The tyres must be checked when **cold**, not immediately after riding. The pressure inside the tyre will increase when the tyre is hot. Note that tyre pressure will also change from one day to the next as air temperature changes.

● Use an accurate pressure gauge. Many forecourt gauges are wildly inaccurate. If you buy your own, spend as much as you can justify on a quality gauge.

● Proper air pressure will increase tyre life and provide maximum stability and ride comfort. Incorrect tyre pressures will cause abnormal tread wear and unsafe handling. Very low tyre pressures may cause the tyre to slip on the rim or come off.

Front	Rear
36 psi (2.5 Bar)	42 psi (2.9 Bar)

Tyre care:

● Check the tyres carefully for cuts, tears, embedded nails or other sharp objects and excessive wear. Operation of the motorcycle with excessively worn tyres is extremely hazardous, as traction and handling are directly affected.

● Check the condition of the tyre valve and ensure the dust cap is in place.

● Pick out any stones or nails which may have become embedded in the tyre tread. If left, they will eventually penetrate through the casing and cause a puncture.

● If tyre damage is apparent, or unexplained loss of pressure is experienced, seek the advice of a tyre fitting specialist without delay.

Tyre tread depth:

● At the time of writing UK law requires that tread depth must be at least 1 mm over 3/4 of the tread breadth all the way around the tyre, with no bald patches. Many riders, however, consider 2 mm tread depth minimum to be a safer limit. Kawasaki recommend a minimum of 1 mm on the front and 2 mm on the rear, but note that German law requires a minimum of 1.6 mm for each tyre.

● Many tyres now incorporate wear indicators in the tread. Identify the location marking on the tyre sidewall to locate the indicator bar and replace the tyre if the tread has worn down to the bar.

1 Remove the dust cap from the valve and do not forget to fit the cap after checking the pressure.

2 Check the tyre pressures when the tyres are **cold**.

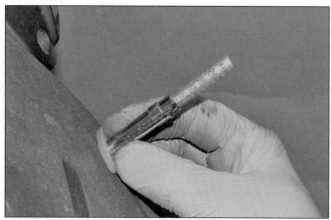

3 Measure tread depth at the centre of the tyre using a depth gauge.

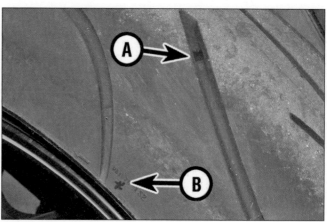

4 Tyre tread wear indicator (A) and its location marking (B) on the edge or sidewall (according to manufacturer).

Chapter 1
Routine maintenance and servicing

Contents

Degrees of difficulty

Easy, suitable for novice with little experience	Fairly easy, suitable for beginner with some experience	Fairly difficult, suitable for competent DIY mechanic	Difficult, suitable for experienced DIY mechanic	Very difficult, suitable for expert DIY or professional

Specifications

Engine

Cylinder numbering	1 to 4 from left to right
Spark plug type	NGK CR9EIA-9
Spark plug electrode gap	0.8 to 0.9 mm
Engine idle speed	1100 ± 50 rpm
Valve clearances (COLD engine)	
C and D models	
Intake valves	0.15 to 0.24 mm
Exhaust valves	0.17 to 0.22 mm
E and F models	
Intake valves	0.15 to 0.22 mm
Exhaust valves	0.17 to 0.22 mm
Throttle body vacuum range at idle speed	
C models	215 to 235 mmHg
D models	226 to 246 mmHg
E and F models	235 to 255 mmHg

Cycle parts

Drive chain slack	
C models	35 to 45 mm
D models	30 to 35 mm
E and F models..	30 to 40 mm
Drive chain 20-link length	
Standard...	317.5 to 318.2 mm
Stretch limit...	323 mm
Brake pad friction material thickness	
Standard – front pads.................................	4 mm
Standard – rear pads	5 mm
Wear limit – front and rear pads	1 mm
Throttle cable freeplay	2 to 3 mm at twistgrip flange
Clutch cable freeplay	2 to 3 mm
Tyre pressures (cold).....................................	see *Pre-ride checks*

Lubricants and fluids

Engine oil type	SAE 10W/40 motorcycle oil. API grade: SG or higher; JASO grade: MA, MA1 or MA2
Engine oil capacity	
C models	
Oil change......................................	2.7 litres
Oil and filter change............................	3.0 litres
Following engine overhaul – dry engine, new filter.............	3.7 litres
D, E and F models	
Oil change......................................	3.2 litres
Oil and filter change	3.7 litres
Following engine overhaul – dry engine, new filter.............	4.0 litres
Coolant type...	50% distilled water, 50% silicate-free corrosion inhibited ethylene glycol anti-freeze
Coolant capacity	2.5 litres
Brake fluid	DOT 4
Drive chain	Aerosol chain lubricant or SAE 90 gear oil
Steering head bearings and seals	Multi-purpose grease with EP2 rating
Swingarm pivot bearings and seal lips.....................	Multi-purpose grease with EP2 rating
Suspension linkage bearings and seal lips	Multi-purpose grease with EP2 rating
Sidestand pivot	Multi-purpose grease
Wheel bearing seal lips..................................	Multi-purpose grease
Wheel axles	Multi-purpose grease
Gearchange lever/rear brake pedal/footrest pivots	Multi-purpose grease
Clutch lever pivot	Multi-purpose grease
Throttle twistgrip.......................................	Multi-purpose grease
Front brake lever pivot and piston tip	Silicone grease
Cables	Aerosol cable lubricant

Torque settings

Cooling system drain bolts...............................	10 Nm
Engine oil drain plug	
C and D models	20 Nm
E and F models......................................	30 Nm
Engine oil filter	
C and D models	31 Nm
E and F models	17 Nm
Fork clamp bolts (top yoke)	20 Nm
Handlebar clamp bolts...................................	25 Nm
Handlebar positioning bolts..............................	10 Nm
Rear axle nut	108 Nm
Spark plugs	13 Nm
Steering stem nut – C and D models......................	78 Nm
Steering stem bolt – E and F models......................	108 Nm
Timing rotor cover bolts – C and D models	10 Nm

Note: *The Pre-ride checks outlined in the owner's manual cover those items that should be inspected before every ride. Also perform the pre-ride inspection at every maintenance interval (in addition to the procedures listed). The intervals listed below are the intervals recommended by the manufacturer for the models covered in this manual.*

Pre-ride

☐ See *'Pre-ride checks'* at the beginning of this manual.

After the initial 600 miles (1000 km)

Note: *This check is usually performed by a Kawasaki dealer after the first 600 miles (1000 km) from new. Thereafter, maintenance is carried out according to the following intervals of the schedule.*

Every 600 miles (1000 km)

☐ Check, adjust, clean and lubricate the drive chain (Section 1)

Every 3750 miles (6000 km) or 6 months

☐ Check the brake pads for wear (Section 2)
☐ Check the brake system and brake light switch operation (Section 2)
☐ Check the EVAP (evaporative emission control) system (California models only) (Section 3)

Every 7500 miles (12,000 km) or 12 months

Carry out all the items under the 3750 mile (6000 km) check, plus the following:
☐ Check the drive chain and sprocket wear and chain stretch (Section 1)
☐ Check and adjust the clutch cable (Section 4)
☐ Check and adjust the throttle cables (Section 5)
☐ Fit new spark plugs (Section 6)
☐ Change the engine oil and fit a new filter (Section 7)
☐ Check the fuel system and hoses (Section 8)
☐ Check and adjust the engine idle speed (Section 9)
☐ Check throttle body synchronisation (Section 10)
☐ Check the cooling system (Section 11)
☐ Check the air suction system (Section 12)
☐ Check the headlight beam aim (Section 13)
☐ Check the sidestand and starter safety circuit (Section 14)
☐ Check the front and rear suspension (Section 15)
☐ Check and adjust the steering head bearings (Section 16)

Every 7500 miles (12,000 km) or 12 months (continued)

☐ Check the condition of the wheels, wheel bearings and tyres (Section 17)
☐ Lubricate the clutch, gearchange and brake levers, brake pedal, sidestand pivot, and the throttle cables (Section 18)
☐ Check the tightness of all nuts, bolts and fasteners (Section 19)
☐ Check the battery (Section 20)

Every 11,250 miles (18,000 km)

Carry out all the items under the 3750 mile (6000 km) check, plus the following:
☐ Fit a new air filter element (Section 21)

Every 15,000 miles (24,000 km) or two years

Carry out all the items under the 7500 mile (12,000 km) check, plus the following:
☐ Change the brake fluid (Section 2)
☐ Check and adjust the valve clearances (Section 22)
☐ Re-grease the swingarm and suspension linkage bearings (Section 15)
☐ Re-grease the steering head bearings (Section 16)

Every 22,500 miles (36,000 km) or three years

Carry out all the items under the 11,250 mile (18,000 km) and 7500 mile (12,000 km) checks, plus the following:
☐ Change the coolant and fit new cooling system hoses (Section 11)

Every 30,000 miles (48,000 km) or four years

Carry out all the items under the 15,000 mile (24,000 km) check, plus the following:
☐ Fit new brake hoses and master cylinder and caliper seals (Section 2)
☐ Fit new fuel hoses (Section 8)

Non-scheduled maintenance

☐ Change the front fork oil (Section 15)

Component locations – ZX1000C left side

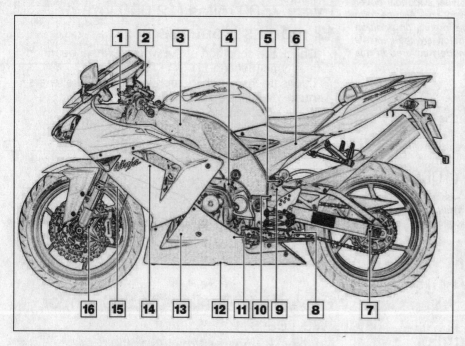

1   Clutch cable upper adjuster
2   Fork pre-load and rebound damping adjuster
3   Air filter
4   Idle speed adjuster
5   Rear shock compression damping adjuster
6   Battery
7   Drive chain adjuster
8   Rear shock rebound damping adjuster
9   Rear shock pre-load adjuster
10 Drive chain slider
11 Coolant drain bolt on water pump cover
12 Engine oil drain bolt
13 Engine oil filter
14 Coolant reservoir
15 Fork seals
16 Fork compression damping adjuster

Component locations – ZX1000C right side

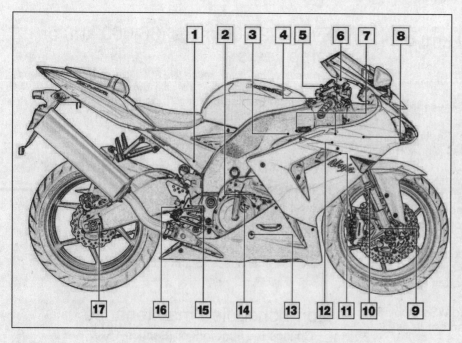

1   Rear brake fluid reservoir
2   Clutch cable lower adjuster
3   Air suction valve
4   Steering head bearing adjuster
5   Fork pre-load and rebound damping adjuster
6   Front brake fluid reservoir
7   Throttle cable upper adjusters
8   EVAP system canister
9   Fork compression damping adjuster
10 Fork seals
11 EVAP system separator
12 Radiator pressure cap
13 Engine oil level window
14 Engine oil filler cap
15 Rear brake light switch
16 Rear brake pedal height adjuster
17 Drive chain adjuster

Component locations – ZX1000D left side

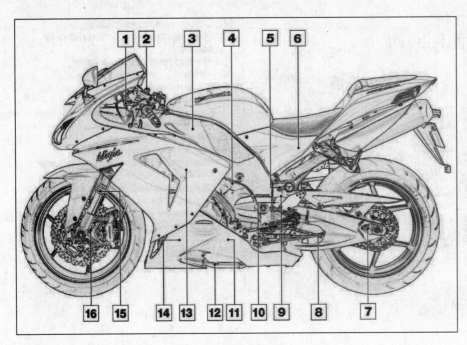

1 Clutch cable upper adjuster
2 Fork pre-load and rebound damping adjuster
3 Air filter
4 Idle speed adjuster
5 Rear shock compression damping adjuster
6 Battery
7 Drive chain adjuster
8 Rear shock rebound damping adjuster
9 Rear shock pre-load adjuster
10 Drive chain slider
11 Coolant drain bolt on water pump cover
12 Engine oil drain bolt
13 Coolant reservoir
14 Engine oil filter
15 Fork seals
16 Fork compression damping adjuster

Component locations – ZX1000D right side

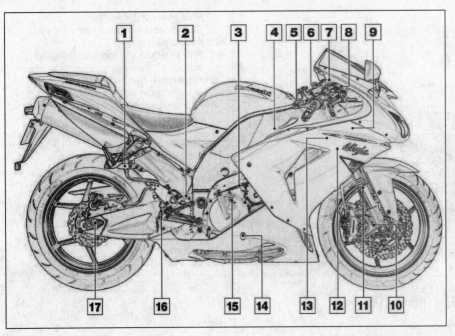

1 Rear brake fluid reservoir
2 Rear brake light switch
3 Clutch cable lower adjuster
4 Air suction valve
5 Steering head bearing adjuster
6 Fork pre-load and rebound damping adjuster
7 Front brake fluid reservoir
8 Throttle cable upper adjusters
9 EVAP system canister
10 Fork compression damping adjuster
11 Fork seals
12 EVAP system separator
13 Radiator pressure cap
14 Engine oil level window
15 Engine oil filler cap
16 Rear brake pedal height adjuster
17 Drive chain adjuster

Component locations – ZX1000E and F left side

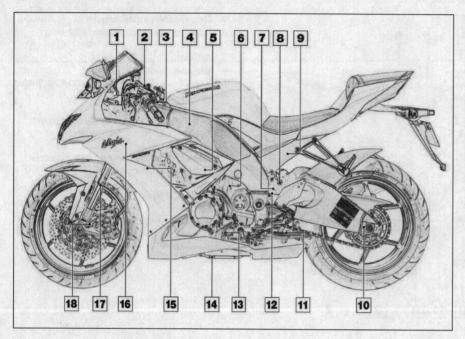

1 Clutch cable upper adjuster
2 Fork pre-load and rebound damping adjuster
3 Steering head bearing adjuster
4 Air filter
5 Coolant reservoir
6 Idle speed adjuster
7 Rear shock pre-load adjuster
8 Rear shock compression damping adjuster
9 Battery
10 Drive chain adjuster
11 Rear shock rebound damping adjuster
12 Drive chain slider
13 Coolant drain bolt on water pump cover
14 Engine oil drain bolt
15 EVAP system separator
16 EVAP system canister
17 Fork seals
18 Fork compression damping adjuster

Component locations – ZX1000E and F right side

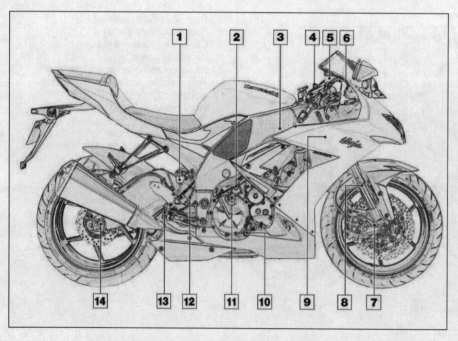

1 Rear brake fluid reservoir
2 Clutch cable lower adjuster
3 Air suction valve
4 Fork pre-load and rebound damping adjuster
5 Front brake fluid reservoir
6 Throttle cable upper adjusters
7 Fork compression damping adjuster
8 Fork seals
9 Radiator pressure cap
10 Engine oil level window
11 Engine oil filler cap
12 Rear brake light switch
13 Rear brake pedal height adjuster
14 Drive chain adjuster

1 This Chapter is designed to help the home mechanic maintain his/her motorcycle for safety, economy, long life and peak performance.

2 Deciding where to start or plug into the routine maintenance schedule depends on several factors. If your motorcycle has been maintained according to the warranty standards and has just come out of warranty, start routine maintenance as it coincides with the next mileage or calendar interval. If you have owned the machine for some time but have never performed any maintenance on it, start at the nearest interval and include some additional procedures to ensure that nothing important is overlooked. If you have just had a major engine overhaul, then start the maintenance routine from the beginning. If you have a used machine and have no knowledge of its history or maintenance record, combine all the checks into one large service initially and then settle into the specified maintenance schedule.

3 Before beginning any maintenance or repair, the machine should be cleaned thoroughly, especially around the oil filter, drive chain, suspension, wheels, etc. Cleaning will help ensure that dirt does not contaminate the engine and will allow you to detect wear and damage that could otherwise easily go unnoticed. If you use a pressure washer make sure you do not direct the jet at wheel bearing and suspension seals and at the steering head, or at any electrical/ignition components and connectors.

4 Certain maintenance information is sometimes printed on labels attached to the motorcycle. If the information on the labels differs from that included here, use the information on the label.

---

1 Drive chain and sprockets

Chain slack check

1 A neglected drive chain won't last long and will quickly damage the sprockets. Routine chain adjustment and lubrication isn't difficult and will ensure maximum chain and sprocket life.

2 To check the chain, place the bike on its sidestand and shift the transmission into neutral. Make sure the ignition switch is OFF.

3 Push up on the bottom run of the chain and measure the slack midway between the two sprockets, then compare your measurement to that listed in this Chapter's Specifications **(see illustration)**. As the chain stretches with wear, adjustment will periodically be necessary (see below). Since the chain will rarely wear evenly, roll the bike forward so that another section of chain can be checked (having an assistant to do this makes the task a lot easier); do this several times to check the entire length of chain, and mark the tightest spot.

Caution: Riding the bike with excess slack in the chain could lead to damage.

4 If the chain has been neglected, corrosion and dirt may cause the links to bind and kink, which effectively shortens the chain's length and makes it tight **(see illustration)**. Thoroughly clean and work free any such links, then highlight them with a marker pen or paint. Take the bike for a ride.

5 After the bike has been ridden, repeat the measurement for slack in the highlighted area. If the chain has kinked again and is still tight, replace it with a new one (see Chapter 6). A rusty, kinked or worn chain will damage the sprockets and can damage transmission bearings. If in any doubt as to the condition of a chain, it is far better to install a new one than risk damage to other components and possibly yourself.

6 Check the entire length of the chain for damaged rollers, loose links and pins, and missing O-rings and replace it with a new one if necessary. **Note:** *Never fit a new chain onto*

1.3 Push up on the chain and measure the slack

old sprockets, and never use the old chain if you fit new sprockets – replace the chain and sprockets as a set.

Chain slack adjustment

7 Move the bike so that the chain is positioned with the tightest point at the centre of its bottom run, then put it on the sidestand.

8 Remove the split pin, then slacken the rear axle nut **(see illustration)**.

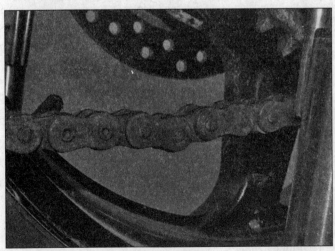

1.4 Neglect has caused the links in this chain to kink

1.8 Straighten and remove the split pin, then slacken the nut (arrowed)

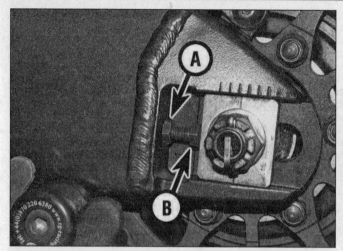

1.9a Slacken each locknut (A) and turn each adjuster bolt (B) by an equal amount...

1.9b ...then check the relative position of the adjustment marker line (arrowed) to the alignment marks

1.10 Push the wheel forwards while tightening the nut

1.11 Bend the ends around as shown

9 Slacken the locknut on each adjuster bolt **(see illustration)**. Turn the adjuster bolt on each side of the swingarm equally until the amount of freeplay specified at the beginning of the Chapter is obtained at the centre of the bottom run of the chain. Following adjustment, check that the line in the top of each adjustment marker is in the same position in relation to the marks on the swingarm **(see illustration)**. It is important the alignment is the same on each side otherwise the rear wheel will be out of alignment with the front and cause handling problems. Always make sure that the front edge of each marker is butted against the end of the adjuster bolt. If there is a difference in the positions, adjust one of them so that its position is exactly the same as the other. Check the chain freeplay again and readjust if necessary.

10 When adjustment is complete, hold the adjuster bolt and tighten locknut on each side **(see illustration 1.9a)**. Push the wheel forwards to make sure each marker is butted against the end of the adjuster bolt and keep it pushed while you tighten the axle nut to the torque setting specified at the beginning of the Chapter **(see illustration)**. Recheck the adjustment and alignment as above, then place the machine on an auxiliary stand and spin the wheel to make sure it runs freely.

11 Check the alignment of the notches in the nut and the hole in the axle for the split pin – if they do not align tighten the axle nut a little, but no more than until the next pair of notches align (i.e. no more than 30°) – if you go past, slacken the nut one full turn, then re-tighten to the specified torque and align the nut. Fit a new split pin and bend its ends around the nut a shown **(see illustration)**.

Chain cleaning and lubrication

12 If required, wash the chain using a dedicated aerosol cleaner, or in paraffin (kerosene), using a soft brush to work any dirt out if necessary **(see illustration)**. Wipe the cleaner off the chain and allow it to dry, or blow it dry using compressed air if available.

If the chain is excessively dirty remove it from the bike and allow it to soak in the paraffin or solvent (see Chapter 6).
Caution: Don't use petrol (gasoline), an unsuitable solvent or other cleaning fluids which might damage the internal sealing properties of the chain. Don't use high-pressure water to clean the chain.

1.12 Specially shaped chain cleaning brushes are commercially available

1.13 Apply the lubricant to the overlapping sections of the sideplates

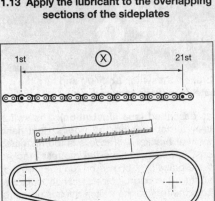

1.17 Measure a 20-link section (X) as shown to determine chain stretch

The entire process shouldn't take longer than ten minutes, otherwise the O-rings could be damaged.

13 The best time to lubricate the chain is after the motorcycle has been ridden. When the chain is warm, the lubricant will penetrate the joints between the sideplates better than when cold. **Note:** *Kawasaki specifies an*

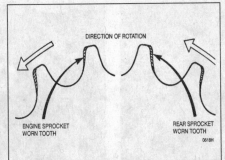

1.14 Check the sprockets in the areas indicated to see if they are worn excessively

aerosol chain lube that it is suitable for O-ring or X-ring (sealed) chains, or SAE 90 gear oil; do not use any other chain lubricants – their solvents could damage the chain's sealing rings. Apply the lubricant to the area where the sideplates overlap – not the middle of the rollers **(see illustration)**.

⚠ *Warning: Take care not to get any lubricant on the tyre or brake components. If any of the lubricant inadvertently contacts them, clean it off thoroughly using a suitable solvent or dedicated brake cleaner before riding the machine.*

Drive chain stretch check and sprocket wear check

14 Remove the front sprocket cover (see Chapter 6). Check the teeth on the front sprocket and the rear sprocket for wear **(see illustration)**. If the sprocket teeth are worn excessively, replace the chain and both sprockets with a new set.

15 With the sprocket cover removed check for wear and damage on the chain slider around the front of the swingarm – if the rubbing surfaces of the slider have worn excessively or there is evidence of damage remove the swingarm and replace the slider with a new one (see Chapter 5).

16 Measure the amount of chain stretch as follows:

17 Obtain a 10 Kg or 20 lb weight and hang it from the centre of the bottom run of the chain **(see illustration)**. Measure along the top run the length of 20 links (from the centre of the 1st pin to the centre of the 21st pin) and compare the result to the stretch limit specified at the beginning of the Chapter. Rotate the rear wheel so that several sections of the chain can be measured, then calculate the average. If the chain stretch measurement exceeds the service limit the chain must be replaced with a new one (see Chapter 6). **Note:** *Never fit a new chain onto old sprockets, and never use the old chain if you fit new sprockets – replace the chain and sprockets as a set.*

2 Brake system

Brake pad wear check

1 Each brake pad has wear indicators – on the front calipers there are grooves in the face of the friction material, and on the rear caliper there is a step or cut-out in the side of the material **(see illustrations)**. The wear indicators should be plainly visible but note that an accumulation of road dirt and brake dust could make them difficult to see.

2 If the pads are worn to the bottom of the grooves or to the beginning of the cut-outs, they must be replaced with new ones (see Chapter 6). **Note:** *Some after-market pads may use different indicators to those on the original equipment.*

3 If the indicators aren't visible, then the amount of friction material remaining should be, and it will be obvious when the pads need replacing. Kawasaki specifies a minimum thickness for the friction material of 1 mm. **Note:** *Some after-market pads may use*

2.1a Front brake pad wear indicator grooves (arrowed)

2.1b Rear brake pad wear indicator step or cut-out location (arrowed)

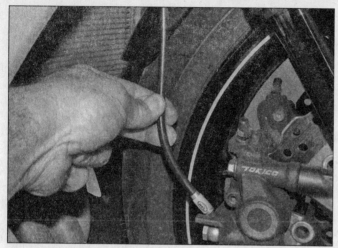

2.9 Check all hoses and unions for cracks and leaks

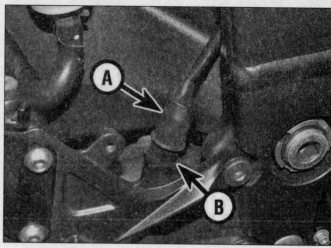

2.12 Hold the rear brake light switch body (A) and turn the adjuster ring (B) as required

different indicators to those on the original equipment.

4 On the front calipers also check for uneven wear in the brake pads, which is indicative of a sticking or seized piston. If found, the calipers must be overhauled (see Chapter 6).

5 If the pads are dirty or if you are in doubt as to the amount of friction material remaining, remove them for inspection (see Chapter 6). If the pads have worn to the backing material check the brake discs for scoring (see Chapter 6). From time to time check the thickness of each disc and replace them with new ones if worn below the service limit specified in Chapter 6 and stamped on the disc centre.

Brake system check

6 A routine general check of the brake system will ensure that any problems are discovered and remedied before the rider's safety is jeopardised.

7 Check the brake pads for wear (see above) and make sure the fluid level in the reservoirs is correct (see *Pre-ride checks*).

8 Check the brake lever and pedal pivots for sloppy or rough action, excessive play, bends, and other damage. Replace any damaged parts with new ones (see Chapter 5). Clean

and lubricate the lever and pedal pivots if their action is stiff or rough (see Section 18). If the lever or pedal is spongy, bleed the brakes (see Chapter 6).

9 Look for leaks at the hose connections and check for cracks in the unions **(see illustration)**. If a hose shows signs of deterioration it must be replaced with a new one. Make sure all brake hose and pipe fasteners are tight (see Section 19).

10 Inspect the master cylinders and calipers for any sign of fluid leakage due to failed seals. Leakage from the master cylinders is unlikely, but the caliper pistons can become corroded over a period of time, especially due to road salt over the winter, and this can lead to seal damage. Seal kits are available for the master cylinders and calipers – refer to Chapter 6.

11 Make sure the brake light comes on when the front brake lever or rear pedal is applied. If it fails to operate properly, check the connections to the LED tail light unit, then check the switch (see Chapter 8).

12 The brake light should come on at 10 mm of rear pedal travel and before the rear brake takes effect. If adjustment is necessary, hold the switch and turn the adjuster ring on the switch body until the brake light is activated

as described **(see illustration)**. The switch is mounted behind the rider's right-hand footrest bracket – if access is too restricted on C models displace the footrest bracket. If the brake light comes on too late or not at all, turn the ring clockwise (when looked at from the top) so the switch threads up out of the bracket. If the brake light comes on too soon or is permanently on, turn the ring anti-clockwise so the switch threads down into the bracket. If the switch doesn't operate the brake light, check it (see Chapter 8).

13 The front brake lever has a span adjuster that alters the distance of the lever from the handlebar. Each setting is identified by a number on the adjuster that aligns with the arrow on the lever. Push the lever away from the handlebar and turn the adjuster ring until the setting which best suits the rider is obtained **(see illustration)**. Do not set the adjuster between the defined settings.

14 The height of the end of the rear brake pedal relative to the top of the footrest can be adjusted to suit the rider's preference. Slacken the master cylinder pushrod locknut, then turn the pushrod using a spanner on the hex at the top of the rod until the pedal is at the correct or desired height **(see illustration)**. On completion tighten the locknut. Adjust the rear brake light switch after adjusting the pedal height (see Step 12).

Brake fluid change

15 The brake fluid should be changed at the prescribed interval or whenever a master cylinder or caliper overhaul is carried out. Refer to Chapter 6 for details. Ensure that all the old fluid is be pumped from the hydraulic system and that the level in the fluid reservoirs is checked and the brakes tested before riding the motorcycle.

Brake caliper and master cylinder seals

16 Brake system seals deteriorate with age and lose their effectiveness, leading to sticky

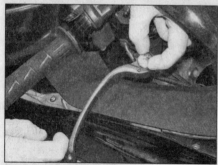

2.13 Push the lever away from the bar and turn the adjuster

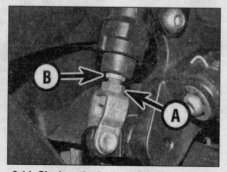

2.14 Slacken the locknut (A) and turn the pushrod using the hex (B) to adjust pedal height

operation of the brake master cylinders or the pistons in the brake calipers, or fluid loss. They should be replaced with new ones at the prescribed interval and particularly if fluid leakage or a sticking action is apparent.

17 Replace all the seals in each caliper and master cylinder as a set; master cylinder seals are supplied as a kit along with a new piston and spring (see Chapter 6).

Brake hoses

18 The brake hoses should be renewed at the specified interval.

3 EVAP (Evaporative emission control) system (California models)

1 On C and D models remove the right-hand fairing side panel (Chapter 7). On E and F models remove the fairing assembly.

2 Visually inspect all the system hoses between the fuel tank, the separator and the canister for kinks and splits and any other damage or deterioration. Make sure that the hoses are securely connected with a clamp on each end. Replace any hoses that are damaged or deteriorated.

3 Check the EVAP canister and the separator for cracks or other damage.

4 See Chapter 4 for further information on the system. Note that there is an information label and an emission control system hose routing label on the bike.

4 Clutch

1 Check that the clutch lever operates smoothly and easily.

2 If the clutch lever operation is heavy or stiff, lubricate both the cable and the lever (see Section 18). If the cable is still stiff, replace it with a new one.

3 With the cable operating smoothly, check that it is correctly adjusted. Periodic adjustment is necessary to compensate for wear in the clutch plates and stretch of the cable. Pull lightly on the clutch lever until freeplay is taken up, then measure the gap between the lever and the lever bracket as shown (see illustration). Check that the gap is as specified at the beginning of the Chapter.

4 If adjustment is required, this can be done first at the lever end of the cable. Turn the adjuster in or out until the required amount of freeplay is obtained (see illustration). To reduce freeplay, thread the adjuster out of the bracket. To increase freeplay, thread the adjuster into the lever bracket.

5 Make sure that the slot in the adjuster is not aligned with the slot in the lever bracket – these slots are to allow removal of the cable, and if they are all aligned while the bike is in use the cable could jump out. Also make sure the adjuster is not threaded too far out of the bracket so is only held by a few threads – this will leave it unstable and the threads could be damaged.

6 If all the adjustment has been taken up at the lever, thread the adjuster into the bracket until about 5 mm of thread is left exposed to give plenty of freeplay, making sure the slots are offset.

7 Now set the correct amount of freeplay using the adjuster on the clutch end of cable. The adjuster is set in a bracket on the right-hand side of the engine.

8 Draw the rubber boot back off the outer cable. Slacken the rear nut securing the cable in the holder (see illustration). Grasp the cable and pull it towards the front of the bike until all freeplay in the release mechanism arm has been taken up, then thread the front

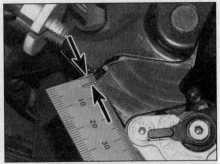

4.3 Measure the amount of freeplay at the clutch lever bracket as shown

nut down until it locates against the bracket. Tighten the rear nut against the bracket. Now reset the correct amount of freeplay using the lever adjuster (Steps 3 and 4).

9 Push the release mechanism arm forwards until freeplay is taken up and check that the angle between the arm and the cable is about 60°. If not the clutch plates could be worn and should be checked (Chapter 2).

5 Throttle cables

1 Make sure the throttle grip rotates smoothly and freely from fully closed to fully open with the front wheel turned at various angles. The grip should return automatically from fully open to fully closed when released. If the throttle sticks, lubricate the cable as described below.

Checking cable freeplay – C models

2 Check for a small amount of freeplay in the cables, measured in terms of the amount of twistgrip rotation before the throttle opens,

4.4 Turn the adjuster ring as required

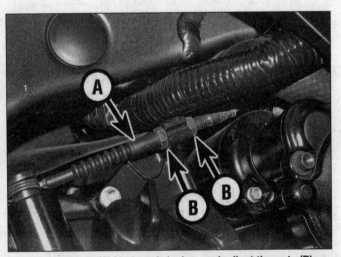

4.8 Pull the boot (A) back and slacken and adjust the nuts (B) as described

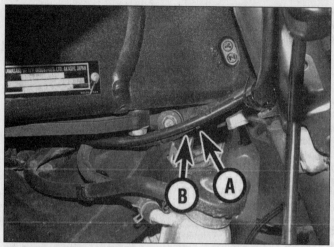

5.2 Opening cable adjuster locknut (A) and adjuster (B) – C models, shown from the side with fairing side panel removed, though access is easy with it in place from above

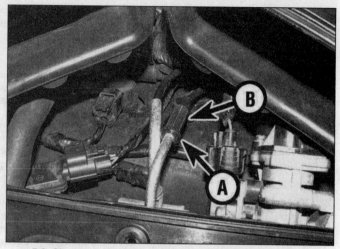

5.3 Closing cable adjuster locknut (A) and adjuster (B) – C models

and compare the amount to that listed in this Chapter's Specifications **(see illustration 5.4)**. Locate the opening (accelerator) cable and loosen its locknut **(see illustration)**. Turn the adjuster until the specified amount of freeplay is obtained in the throttle, then retighten the locknut.

5.4 Throttle cable freeplay is measured in terms of twistgrip rotation

3 If necessary, the closing (decelerator) cable can be adjusted. Remove the air filter housing (see Chapter 4) to access the adjuster **(see illustration)**. Loosen its locknut and turn the adjuster until the specified amount of freeplay is obtained in the throttle, then retighten the locknut

Checking cable freeplay – D, E and F models

4 Check for a small amount of freeplay in the cables, measured in terms of the amount of twistgrip rotation before the throttle opens, and compare the amount to that listed in this Chapter's Specifications **(see illustration)**.
5 Loosen the locknuts on the opening (accelerator) and closing (decelerator) adjusters **(see illustration)**. Turn both adjusters to create excess freeplay, then starting with the closing cable turn the adjuster to give the specified freeplay and tighten its locknut. Now do the same with the adjuster on the opening cable.

Cable and twistgrip lubrication

6 If the throttle sticks, this is probably due to a cable fault. Remove the cables (see Chapter 4) and lubricate them (see Section 18). Check that the inner cables slide freely and easily in the outer cables. If not, replace the cables with new ones.
7 With the cables removed, make sure the throttle twistgrip rotates freely on the handlebar – dirt combined with a lack of lubrication can cause the action to be stiff. If necessary, undo the handlebar end-weight and slide the twistgrip off **(see illustration)**. Clean any old grease from the bar and the inside of the tube. Smear some multi-purpose grease onto the bar, then refit the twistgrip and the end-weight.
8 Install the cables, making sure they are correctly routed (see Chapter 4). If this fails to improve the operation of the throttle, the cables must be replaced with new ones. Note that in very rare cases the fault could lie in the

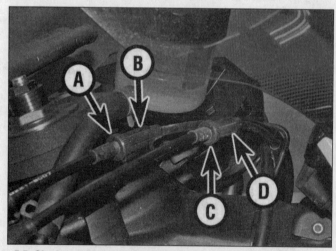

5.5 Closing cable adjuster locknut (C) and adjuster (D); opening cable adjuster locknut (A) and adjuster (B) – D, E and F models

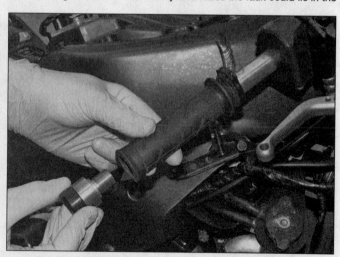

5.7 Remove the end-weight and slide the twistgrip off

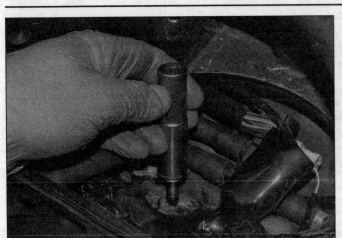

6.3a Unscrew the plug and lift it out with the tool...

6.3b ...then remove it from the tool

throttle bodies. Remove the air filter housing and check the action of the throttle pulley and linkage (see Chapter 4).

> ⚠️ **Warning: Turn the handlebars all the way through their travel with the engine idling. Idle speed should not change. If it does, the cables may be routed incorrectly. Correct this condition before riding the bike.**

6 Spark plugs

Note 1: *The spark plug caps are integral with the 'stick type' ignition coils. To avoid damaging the wiring, always disconnect the connectors before removing the coils. Do not attempt to lever the coils off the plugs or pull them off with pliers. Do not drop the coils.*

Note 2: *All models are equipped with plugs that have an iridium coated centre electrode. The plugs must be treated differently to conventional plugs – they should not be cleaned or adjusted, just replaced with new ones at the prescribed interval. Do not substitute them with conventional plugs.*

1 Remove the ignition coils (Chapter 4).

2 If compressed air is available clean around the base of each spark plug to prevent any dirt falling into the combustion chamber.

3 Using the tool provided in the bike's toolkit or the equivalent 16 mm spark plug socket, unscrew and remove the plugs from the cylinder head **(see illustrations)**. Lay each plug out in relation to its cylinder; if any plug shows up a problem it will then be easy to identify the troublesome cylinder.

4 Check the condition of the electrodes, referring to the spark plug reading chart at the end of this manual if signs of contamination are evident.

5 Fit the new plug into the end of the tool, then use the tool to insert the plug **(see illustrations 19.3b and a)**. Since the cylinder head is made of aluminium, which is soft and easily damaged, thread the plugs as far

as possible into the head turning the tool by hand. Once the plugs are finger-tight, the job can be finished with a spanner on the tool supplied or a socket drive. If a torque wrench can be applied, tighten the spark plugs to the torque setting specified at the beginning of the Chapter. Do not over-tighten them.

> **HAYNES HINT**
> *As the plugs are quite recessed, slip a short length of hose over the end of the plug to use as a tool to thread it into place. The hose will grip the plug well enough to turn it, but will start to slip if the plug begins to cross-thread in the hole – this will prevent damaged threads.*

> **HAYNES HINT**
> *Stripped plug threads in the cylinder head can be repaired with a Heli-Coil insert – see 'Tools and Workshop Tips' in the Reference section.*

6 Install the ignition coils (Chapter 4).

7 Engine oil and filter change

Special tool: *A filter socket is necessary for this job, and one can be obtained from Kawasaki dealers under part No. 57001-1249, or otherwise there are commercially available equivalents available from good accessory dealers (take a filter with you as there are several different sizes). The socket (as opposed to another type of filter removal tool) is necessary because, unlike the others, it provides the means to tighten the new filter to the correct torque.*

> ⚠️ **Warning: Be careful when draining the oil, as the exhaust pipes, the engine, and the oil itself can cause severe burns.**

1 Consistent routine oil and filter changes are the single most important maintenance procedure you can perform. The oil not only lubricates the internal parts of the engine, transmission and clutch, but it also acts as a coolant, a cleaner, a sealant, and a protector. Because of these demands, the oil takes a terrific amount of abuse and should be replaced often with new oil of the recommended grade and type. The oil filter should be changed with every oil change.

> **HAYNES HINT**
> *Saving a little money on the difference in cost between a good oil and a cheap oil won't pay off if the engine is damaged.*

2 Before changing the oil, warm up the engine so the oil will drain easily. Make sure the bike is on level ground. The oil drain plug is in the underside of the sump. Remove the left-hand lower fairing panel (see Chapter 7).

3 Position a large clean drain tray below the engine, so it is under the drain plug and the filter. Unscrew the oil filler cap from the clutch cover to vent the crankcase and to act as a reminder that there is no oil in the engine **(see illustration)**.

7.3 Unscrew the oil filler cap to act as a vent

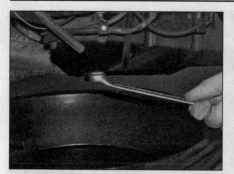

7.4a Unscrew the oil drain plug...

7.4b ...and allow the oil to completely drain

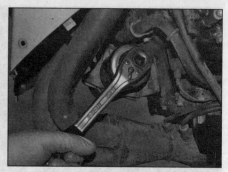

7.5a Unscrew the filter...

7.5b ...and allow the oil to drain

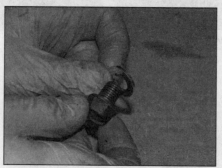

7.6a Fit a new sealing washer...

7.6b ...then fit the plug into the sump and tighten to the correct torque

4 Unscrew the oil drain plug and allow the oil to flow into the drain tray **(see illustrations)**. Remove the sealing washer from the drain plug – you may have to cut it off. A new washer must be used.
5 Unscrew the filter using a filter socket (see **Special tool** above), and tip any residual oil into the drain tray **(see illustrations)**.
6 When the oil has completely drained, fit a new sealing washer onto the drain plug, then fit the plug into the sump and tighten it to the torque setting specified at the beginning of the Chapter for your model **(see illustrations)**. Do not overtighten it as the threads in the sump are easily damaged. Clean any oil off the engine and exhaust.
7 On C and D models smear clean engine oil onto the rubber seal on the new filter **(see illustration)**. On E and F models smear grease onto the rubber seal on the new filter. Thread the filter onto the engine and tighten it to the specified torque setting for your model using the filter socket **(see illustration)**. **Note:** *Do not use a strap or chain filter removing tool to tighten the filter, as you will damage it.*
8 Support the motorcycle so it is upright. Wipe the oil level inspection window clean

7.7a Smear clean oil onto the seal...

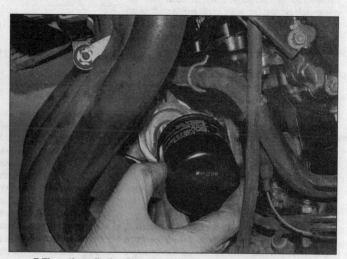

7.7b ...then fit the filter and tighten to the correct torque

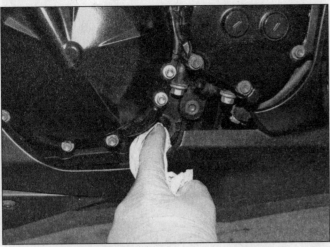

7.8a Wipe the level inspection window clean

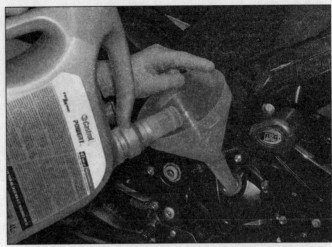

7.8b Add the correct type and amount of oil via the filler hole

7.8c Add oil to the upper level line (arrowed)

7.8d Check the O-ring (arrowed)

(see illustration). Refer to the Specifications and refill the engine to the upper level line on the inspection window using the specified type of oil (see illustrations). Check the condition of the O-ring on the filler cap and replace it with a new one if damaged or worn (see illustration).

9 Start the engine and let it run for two or three minutes (make sure that the oil pressure light extinguishes after a few seconds). Shut it off, wait a few minutes, then recheck the oil level – it will have dropped a bit as the filter holds a certain amount. If necessary, add more oil to bring the level between the lines and close to the upper line, but do not go above it (see illustration 7.8c).

10 Check around the drain plug and the oil filter for leaks – if any are evident check the plug or filter is tightened to the correct torque for your model. Install the lower fairing panel (see Chapter 7).

11 The old oil drained from the engine cannot be re-used and should be disposed of properly. Check with your local refuse disposal company, disposal facility or environmental agency to see whether they will accept the used oil for recycling. Don't pour used oil into drains or onto the ground.

HAYNES HiNT *Check the old oil carefully – if it is very metallic coloured, then the engine is experiencing wear from break-in (new engine) or from insufficient lubrication. If there are flakes or chips of metal in the oil, then something is drastically wrong internally and the engine will have to be disassembled for inspection and repair. If there are pieces of fibre-like material in the oil, the clutch is experiencing excessive wear and should be checked.*

Note: It is illegal and anti-social to dump oil down the drain. To find the location of your local oil recycling bank in the UK, call 08708 506 506 or visit www.oilbankline.org.uk

In the USA, note that any oil supplier must accept used oil for recycling.

8 Fuel system

Warning: Petrol (gasoline) is extremely flammable, so take extra precautions when you work on any part of the fuel system.

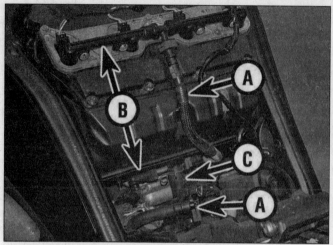

8.2 Fuel hoses (A), fuel rails (B), crankcase breather hose (C)

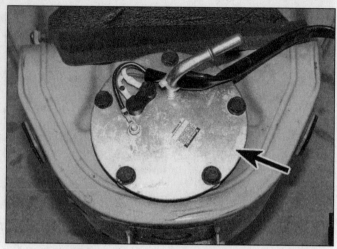

8.3 Check for leakage around the pump plate (arrowed)

Don't smoke or allow open flames or bare light bulbs near the work area, and don't work in a garage where a natural gas-type appliance is present. If you spill any fuel on your skin, rinse it off immediately with soap and water. When you perform any kind of work on the fuel system, wear safety glasses and have a fire extinguisher suitable for a Class B type fire (flammable liquids) on hand.

Check the fuel system hoses, air suction system hoses, and system components

1 Remove the fuel tank (see Chapter 4).
2 Check the tank, the fuel hose(s), the tank drain and breather hoses, and the crankcase breather hose for signs of leaks, deterioration or damage (see illustration). In particular check that there are no leaks from the fuel hoses or hose unions. Replace any hose that is cracked or deteriorated with a new one (see Chapter 4).
3 Check for signs of leakage around the fuel pump mounting plate on the underside of the tank (see illustration). If any is evident, check the mounting bolts are tightened to the specified torque setting (see Chapter 4). If the leak persists, remove the pump and fit a new seal (see Chapter 4).
4 Inspect the joints between the fuel rail, the injectors and the throttle bodies, and on E and F models similarly check the secondary fuel rail and injectors on the air filter housing (see illustration 8.2) – remove the air filter housing for best visual access to the fuel rail and injectors on the throttle bodies (see Chapter 4). If there are any leaks, remove the fuel rail(s) and injectors and fit new seals and O-rings (see Chapter 4).

Fuel filter

5 Fuel filter cleaning or replacement is not a service item. The filter is integral with the fuel pump, and is not available as a separate component. If fuel starvation is experienced,

and all other possibilities have been checked, a blocked filter could be the cause; in this event a new pump assembly must be installed (see Chapter 4).

9 Idle speed

1 The idle speed should be checked and adjusted before and after synchronising the throttle bodies and after checking the valve clearances, and when it is obviously too high or too low. Before adjusting the idle speed, make sure the valve clearances were checked at the previous prescribed interval, the spark plugs are in good condition and the air filter is clean. Also, turn the handlebars from side-to-side and check the idle speed does not change as you do. If it does, the throttle cables may not be adjusted or routed correctly, or may be worn out. This is a dangerous condition that can cause loss of control of the bike. Be sure to correct this problem before proceeding.
2 The engine should be at normal operating temperature, which is usually reached after 10 to 15 minutes of stop-and-go riding. Place the motorcycle on its sidestand, and make sure the transmission is in neutral.

9.3 Idle speed adjuster (arrowed)

3 The idle speed adjuster is a knurled knob located on the left-hand side of the bike (see illustration). With the engine running, turn the knob until the engine idles at the speed specified at the beginning of the Chapter. Turn the screw clockwise to increase idle speed, and anti-clockwise to decrease it.
4 Snap the throttle open and shut a few times, then recheck the idle speed. If necessary, repeat the adjustment procedure.
5 If a smooth, steady idle can't be achieved check the throttle body synchronisation again, and check the valve clearances (see Sections 10 and 22).

10 Throttle body synchronisation

 Warning: Petrol (gasoline) is extremely flammable, so take extra precautions when you work on any part of the fuel system. Don't smoke or allow open flames or bare light bulbs near the work area, and don't work in a garage where a natural gas-type appliance is present. If you spill any fuel on your skin, rinse it off immediately with soap and water. When you perform any kind of work on the fuel system, wear safety glasses and have a fire extinguisher suitable for a Class B type fire (flammable liquids) on hand.

Warning: Do not allow exhaust gases to build up in the work area; either perform the check outside or use an exhaust gas extraction system.

Special tool: *A set of vacuum gauges or a manometer is necessary for this job.*

1 Throttle body synchronisation ensures each throttle body passes the same amount of fuel/air mixture to each cylinder. This is done by measuring the vacuum produced in each cylinder. Throttle bodies that are out of

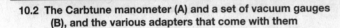

10.2 The Carbtune manometer (A) and a set of vacuum gauges (B), and the various adapters that come with them

10.4 Vacuum take-off unions (arrowed)

synchronisation will result in increased fuel consumption, higher engine temperature, less than ideal throttle response and higher vibration levels. Before synchronising the throttle bodies, make sure that the idle speed is properly adjusted (Section 9) and that the valve clearances were checked at the previous prescribed interval (Section 22).

2 To synchronise the throttle bodies, you will need a manometer, such as the Morgan Carbtune Pro4, or a set of four vacuum gauges, with the necessary hoses and adapters (if required) to fit the take-off points **(see illustration)**. When using such equipment always read the instructions supplied. The hoses usually have some form of restrictor in them for damping the movement of the manometer rod or gauge needle – make sure these are fitted correctly if not already in place otherwise it will be difficult to get an accurate reading, and that in the case of the Carbtune the hoses are connected with the restrictors closest to the take-off points on the throttle bodies.

3 Start the engine and let it run until it reaches normal operating temperature, then shut it off. Support the machine upright on level ground using an auxiliary stand. Remove the air filter

housing (see Chapter 4) – displace the intake air temperature sensor from the housing, leaving its wiring connected, rather than disconnecting it and removing the housing with the sensor attached. Plug the ends of the air suction system and crankcase breather hoses.

4 Remove the blanking cap from the vacuum take-off union on each throttle body (on California models two of the unions have the EVAP system vacuum hoses instead of caps, so pull these off instead) **(see illustration)**. Connect the vacuum gauge hose ends to the exposed vacuum take-off unions. Make sure the No. 1 gauge is attached to the No. 1 (left-hand) throttle body, and so on.

5 On E and F models position the air filter housing cover on the bike and connect the secondary fuel hose to its union on the secondary fuel rail.

6 Start the engine and let it idle, making sure the speed is still correct. If the gauges are fitted with damping adjustment, set this so that the needle/rod flutter is just eliminated but so that they can still respond to small changes in pressure.

7 The vacuum readings should all be the same and within the range specified at the

beginning of the Chapter for your model **(see illustration)**.

8 If the vacuum readings are out of the specified range, first try to synchronise them by using the screw located in the centre between the throttle body pairs – this screw will adjust Nos. 1 and 2 to Nos. 3 and 4 **(see illustration)**. If all four readings can be set within the range specified using this screw no further adjustment is necessary. If the difference between 1 and 2 or between 3 and 4 is greater than 20 mmHg, locate the air screws in the throttle bodies and adjust them as required by turning the appropriate air screw until the readings are the same and as specified **(see illustration)**.

9 When all the throttle bodies are synchronised, open and close the throttle quickly to settle the linkage, and recheck the gauge readings, readjusting if necessary.

10 When the adjustment is complete, adjust the idle speed (see Section 9). Remove the gauges and refit the blanking caps or reconnect the hoses as required according to your model **(see illustration 10.4)**. Remove the plugs from the air suction and crankcase breather hoses and install the air filter housing (see Chapter 4).

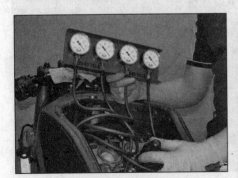

10.7 Checking synchronisation

10.8a Synchronisation adjustment screw (arrowed)

10.8b Nos. 1 and 2 synchronisation air screws (arrowed)

11.3 Check all the coolant hoses as described

11.4 Check each hose joint for leakage

11 Cooling system check and coolant change

Check

⚠️ **Warning: The engine must be cool before beginning this procedure.**

1 On C and D models remove the fairing side panels (see Chapter 7). On E and F models remove the fairing assembly (Chapter 7).

2 Check the coolant level in the reservoir (see *Pre-ride checks*).

3 Check the entire cooling system for evidence of leaks. Examine each rubber coolant hose along its entire length. Look for cracks, abrasions and other damage. Squeeze each hose at various points to see whether they are dried out or hard **(see illustration)**. They should feel firm, yet pliable, and return to their original shape when released. If necessary, replace them with new ones (see Chapter 3).

4 Check for evidence of leaks at each cooling system joint and around the pump on the left-hand side of the engine **(see illustration)**. Tighten the hose clips carefully to prevent future leaks. If the pump is leaking around the cover, check that the bolts are tight. If they are, remove the cover and replace the O-ring with a new one (see Chapter 3). If it is leaking around the crankcase, remove the pump and replace the body O-ring with a new one (see Chapter 3).

5 To prevent leakage of coolant from the cooling system to the lubrication system and vice versa, two seals are fitted on the pump shaft. The coolant seal on the water pump side is of the mechanical type and bears on the rear face of the impeller. The oil seal, mounted behind the mechanical seal, is of the normal feathered lip type. On the underside of the pump housing there is a drain hole **(see illustration)** – using a mirror makes seeing it easier. If either seal fails, the drain allows the coolant or oil to escape. If on inspection the drain shows signs of leakage, particularly of continuous leakage with the engine running, remove the pump and replace it with a new one (see Chapter 3) – it comes as an assembly and the seals are not available separately.

6 Check the radiator for leaks and other damage. Leaks leave tell-tale scale deposits or coolant stains on the outside of the core below the leak. If leaks are noted, remove the radiator (see Chapter 3) and have it repaired or replace it with a new one – do not use a liquid leak stopping compound to try to repair leaks.

7 Check the radiator fins for mud, dirt and insects, which will impede the flow of air through the radiator. If the fins are dirty, remove the radiator (see Chapter 3) and clean it using water or low pressure compressed air directed through the fins from the inner side of the radiator. If the fins are bent or distorted, straighten them carefully with a screwdriver **(see illustration)**. If airflow is restricted by bent or damaged fins over more than 20% of the radiator's surface area, replace the radiator with a new one.

⚠️ **Warning: Do not remove the pressure cap when the engine is hot. It is good practice to cover the cap with a heavy cloth and turn it slowly anti-clockwise. If you hear a hissing sound (indicating that there is still pressure in the**

11.5 The drain hole (arrowed) on the underside of the pump, shown removed

11.7 Use a small screwdriver to straighten bent fins

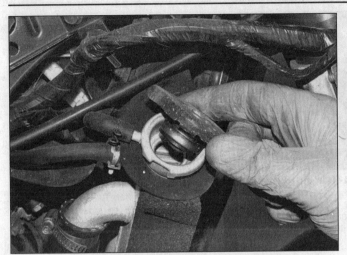

11.8 Remove the pressure cap as described

11.12 Check the oil cooler (arrowed) for leaks and damage

system), wait until it stops, then continue turning the cap until it can be removed.

8 Remove the pressure cap from the radiator filler neck by turning it anti-clockwise until it reaches the stop. Now press down on the cap and continue turning until it can be removed (see illustration).

9 Check the condition of the coolant in the system. If it is rust-coloured or if accumulations of scale are visible, drain, flush and refill the system with new coolant (see below). Check the antifreeze content of the coolant with an antifreeze hydrometer – a 50% content should give a reading of 1.084 at 5°C to 1.074 at 25°C, varying accordingly in between. The system must have the correct coolant mixture (see Specifications) – if the coolant is too weak (i.e. too little anti-freeze giving a low reading – anything below 1.07 when cold and 1.06 when hot) there will not be adequate protection against freezing and corrosion, and if it is too strong the ability to cool the engine is reduced. If the hydrometer indicates an incorrect mixture, drain and refill the system (see below).

10 The function of the pressure cap is crucial to the correct running of the cooling system. Check the cap seal for cracks and other damage. If the coolant level consistently drops and/or the bike overheats, and no evidence of leaks can be found, have the cap pressure checked by a Kawasaki dealer, or just fit a new one. If a new

cap does not cure the problem have the entire system pressure checked by a dealer.

11 Fit the cap by turning it clockwise until it reaches the first stop then push down on it and continue turning until it can turn no further. Start the engine and let it reach normal operating temperature, then check for leaks again. As the coolant temperature increases, the electric fan (mounted on the back of the radiator) should come on automatically and the temperature should begin to drop. If not, refer to Chapter 3 and check the fan and fan circuit.

12 Check the oil cooler on the front of the engine (next to the oil filter) for any signs of oil leakage between it and the engine (see illustration). If there is leakage check the cooler bolts are tight. If the leakage persists you will have to fit a new O-ring between the cooler and the engine (see Chapter 2). Check that the coolant hoses are secure on the unions, and that there is no evidence of coolant leakage from the body of the cooler. If there is, the cooler is damaged and must be replaced with a new one.

Change the coolant

⚠️ **Warning: Allow the engine to cool completely before performing this maintenance operation. Also, don't allow anti-freeze to come into contact with your skin or the painted surfaces of the motorcycle. Rinse off spills immediately**

with plenty of water. Anti-freeze is highly toxic if ingested. Never leave anti-freeze lying around in an open container or in puddles on the floor; children and pets are attracted by its sweet smell and may drink it. Check with local authorities (councils) about disposing of anti-freeze. Many communities have collection centres which will see that anti-freeze is disposed of safely. Anti-freeze is also combustible, so don't store it near open flames.

Draining

13 Make sure the engine is cold. Support the motorcycle upright on a level surface using an auxiliary stand. On C and D models remove the fairing side panels (see Chapter 7). On E and F models remove the fairing assembly (Chapter 7).

14 Remove the pressure cap from the radiator filler neck by turning it anti-clockwise until it reaches a stop (see illustration 11.8). Now press down on the cap and continue turning until it can be removed. Also remove the coolant reservoir cap (see illustration).

15 Position a suitable container beneath the water pump on the left-hand side of the engine. Unscrew the drain bolt and allow the coolant to completely drain from the system (see illustrations). A new sealing washer is needed.

16 Now position the container beneath the

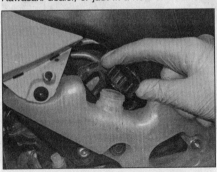

11.14 Remove the reservoir cap

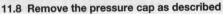

11.15a Unscrew the bolt (arrowed)...

11.15b ...and drain the coolant

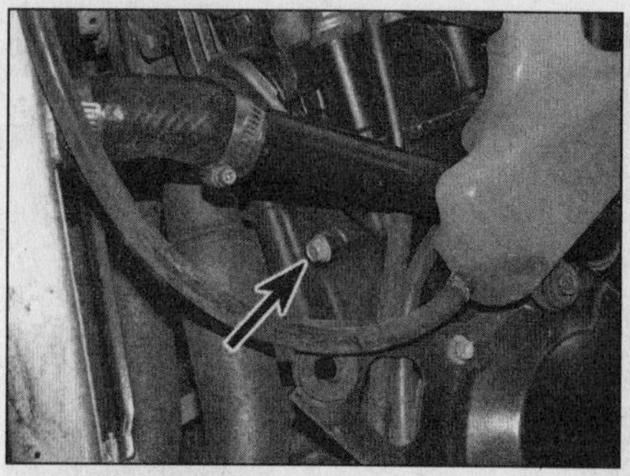

11.16 Cylinder drain bolt (arrowed)

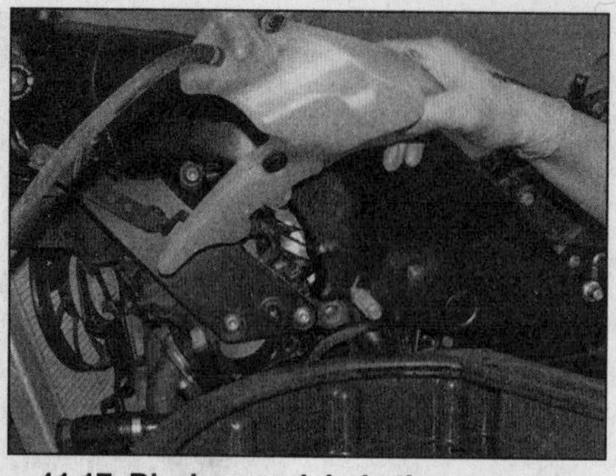

11.17 Displace and drain the reservoir

cylinder drain bolt on the front of the engine on the left-hand side. Unscrew the bolt and allow the coolant to completely drain from the cylinder jacket **(see illustration)**. A new sealing washer is needed. Wipe any spilled coolant off.

17 Detach the upper hose from the reservoir, displace the reservoir and drain the contents into the container **(see illustration)**.

Flushing

18 Flush the system with clean tap water by inserting a hose in the radiator filler neck. Allow the water to run through the system until it is clear and flows out cleanly. If the radiator is extremely corroded, remove it (see Chapter 3) and have it cleaned by a specialist. Also flush the reservoir.

Refilling

19 Fit the drain bolts using new sealing washers and tighten them to the torque setting specified at the beginning of the Chapter **(see illustration)**.

20 Fill the system to the base of the filler neck with the proper coolant mixture (see this Chapter's Specifications) **(see illustration)**. **Note:** *Pour the coolant in slowly to minimise the amount of air entering the system, and when full carefully waggle the bike from side to side and squeeze the coolant hoses to dislodge any trapped air.* Fill the reservoir to the F level line **(see illustrations)**.

21 Start the engine and allow it to idle for 2 to 3 minutes. Flick the throttle twistgrip part open 3 or 4 times, so that the engine speed rises to approximately 4000 to 5000 rpm, then

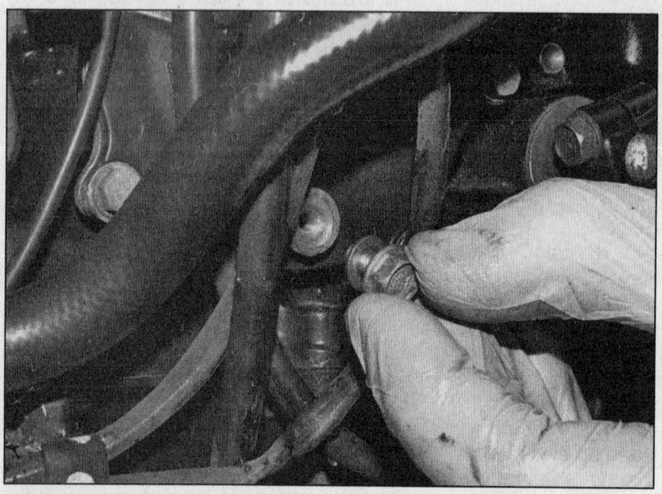

11.19 Fit each drain bolt using a new sealing washer

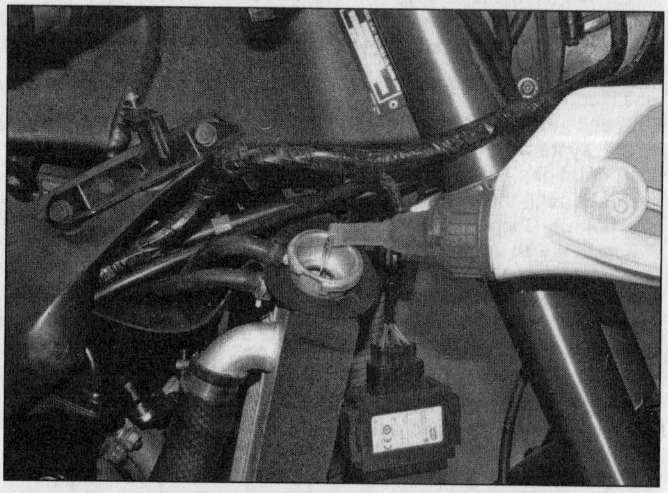

11.20a Fill the system as described

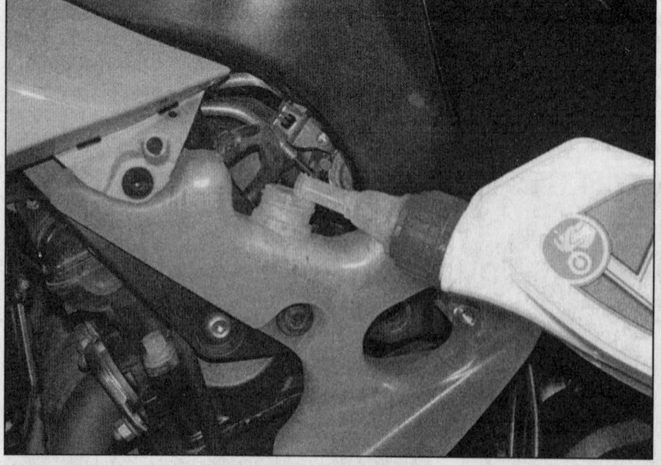

11.20b Fill the reservoir...

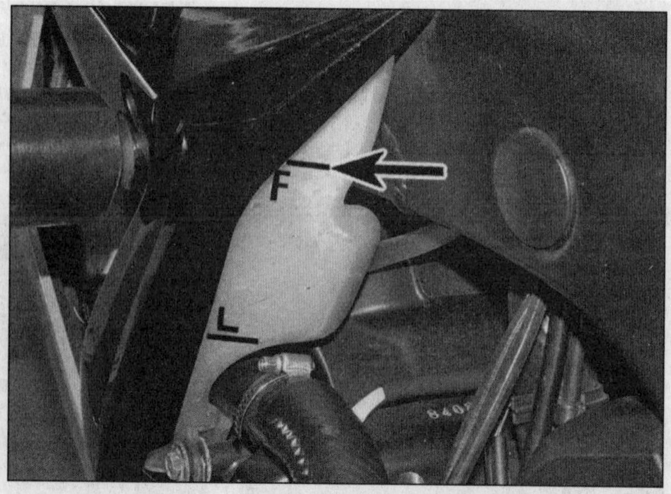

11.20c ...to the F level line (arrowed)

12.1 PAIR hoses (A), control valve (B) and reed valves (C)

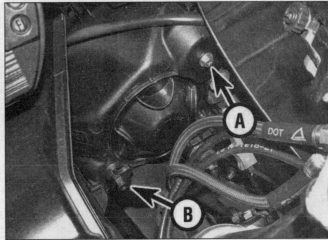

13.2a Vertical adjuster (A), horizontal adjuster (B) – C models

stop the engine. Any air trapped in the system should bleed back to the filler neck.

22 If necessary, top up the coolant level to the base of the radiator filler neck, then fit the pressure cap. Also top up the coolant reservoir to the F level line.

23 Start the engine and run it until the fan cuts in, then shut it off. Let the engine cool then remove the pressure cap as described in Step 14. Check that the coolant level is still up to the base of the radiator filler neck. If it's low, add the specified mixture until it reaches the base of the filler neck. Refit the cap.

24 Check the coolant level in the reservoir and top up if necessary.

25 Check the system for leaks. Install the fairing panels (see Chapter 7).

26 Do not dispose of the old coolant by pouring it down the drain. Instead pour it into a heavy plastic container, cap it tightly and take it into an authorised disposal site or service station – see **Warning** at the beginning of this Section.

12 Air suction system

1 To reduce the amount of unburned hydrocarbons released in the exhaust gases, an air suction system is fitted. The system consists of the control valve (mounted above the valve cover on the top of the engine), the reed valves (fitted in the valve cover) and the hoses between the air filter housing, the control valve and the reed valves **(see illustration)**. The control valve is actuated electronically by the ECM.

2 Under normal operating conditions, the valve allows filtered air to be drawn through the reed valves and cylinder head passages and into the exhaust ports. The air mixes with the exhaust gases, causing any unburned particles of the fuel in the mixture to be burnt in the exhaust port/pipes. This process changes

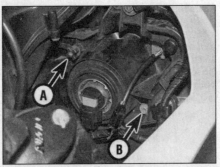

13.2b Vertical adjuster (A), horizontal adjuster (B) – D, E and F models

a considerable amount of hydrocarbons and carbon monoxide into relatively harmless carbon dioxide and water. The reed valves in the valve cover are fitted to prevent the flow of exhaust gases back up the cylinder head passages and into the air filter housing.

3 The system is not adjustable and requires little more than a visual check of the hoses. To access them remove the upper sections of the air filter housing (see Chapter 4). Check that the hoses are not kinked or pinched, are in good condition and are securely connected at each end. Replace any hoses that are cracked, split or generally deteriorated with new ones. With the air filter housing removed also check the MAP sensor vacuum hose arrangement on the throttle bodies.

4 Refer to Chapter 4 for further information on the system and for checks if it is believed to be faulty.

13 Headlight aim

Note: *An improperly adjusted headlight may cause problems for oncoming traffic or provide poor, unsafe illumination of the road ahead. Before adjusting the headlight aim, be sure to*

14.1 Check the springs (arrowed) as described

consult with local traffic laws and regulations – for UK models refer to MOT Test Checks in the Reference section.

1 The headlight beam can adjusted both horizontally and vertically. Before making any adjustment, check that the tyre pressures are correct and the suspension is adjusted as required. Make any adjustments to the headlight aim with the machine on level ground, with the fuel tank half full and with an assistant sitting on the seat. If the bike is usually ridden with a passenger on the back, have a second assistant to do this.

2 Vertical adjustment is made by turning the adjuster screw on the inner side of the relevant beam unit, and horizontal adjustment is made by turning the adjuster screw on the outer side of the relevant beam unit **(see illustrations)**.

14 Sidestand and starter safety circuit

1 Check the stand springs for damage and distortion **(see illustration)**. The springs must be capable of retracting the stand fully and holding it retracted when the motorcycle is in use. If a spring is sagged or broken it must be replaced with a new one.

2 Lubricate the stand pivot regularly (see Section 18).

3 Check the stand and its mount for bends and cracks.

4 Check the operation of the starter safety circuit according to the conditions shown in the table:

5 If the circuit does not operate as described, check the sidestand switch, neutral switch, clutch switch, starter circuit relay and diodes, and the circuit between them (see Chapter 8).

Sidestand	Gear position	Clutch lever	Engine start	Engine run
UP	NEUTRAL	RELEASED	STARTS	CONTINUES
UP	NEUTRAL	PULLED IN	STARTS	CONTINUES
UP	IN GEAR	RELEASED	DOESN'T START	CONTINUES
UP	IN GEAR	PULLED IN	STARTS	CONTINUES
DOWN	NEUTRAL	RELEASED	STARTS	CONTINUES
DOWN	NEUTRAL	PULLED IN	STARTS	CONTINUES
DOWN	IN GEAR	RELEASED	DOESN'T START	STOPS
DOWN	IN GEAR	PULLED IN	DOESN'T START	STOPS

15 Suspension

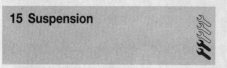

1 The suspension components must be maintained in top operating condition to ensure rider safety. Loose, worn or damaged suspension parts decrease the motorcycle's stability and control.

Front suspension check

2 While standing alongside the motorcycle, apply the front brake and push on the handlebars to compress the forks several times **(see illustration)**. See if they move up-and-down smoothly without binding.

If binding is felt, the forks should be disassembled and inspected (see Chapter 5).

3 Inspect each fork inner tube for scratches, corrosion and pitting in the area of travel through the seals, which will cause premature seal failure **(see illustration)** – if the damage is excessive, new inner tubes should be fitted (see Chapter 5), or the inner tubes must be re-chromed using hard chrome.

4 Also check the inner tubes for signs of oil leakage. Carefully lever the dust seal out using a flat-bladed screwdriver and inspect the area around the oil seal. If leakage is evident, the seals must be replaced with new ones (see Chapter 5). If there is evidence of corrosion between the oil seal retaining ring and its groove in the fork tube, spray the area with a

penetrative lubricant, otherwise the ring will be difficult to remove if needed. Press the dust seal back into the outer tube on completion.

5 The forks are adjustable for spring pre-load, rebound damping and compression damping and it is essential that both fork legs are adjusted equally. Refer to Chapter 5 and check the settings on each fork if in doubt.

6 Check the tightness of all suspension nuts and bolts to be sure none have worked loose, referring to the torque settings specified at the beginning of Chapter 5.

Rear suspension check

7 Inspect the rear shock absorber for fluid leakage and tightness of its mountings. If leakage is found, the shock must be replaced with a new one (see Chapter 5).

8 With the aid of an assistant to support the bike, compress the rear suspension several times **(see illustration)**. It should move up-and-down freely without binding. If any binding is felt, the worn or faulty component must be identified and checked (see Chapter 5). The problem could be due to the shock absorber, the suspension linkage components or the swingarm components.

9 Support the bike on an auxiliary stand (but not a paddock stand under the swingarm!) so that the rear wheel is off the ground. Grab the swingarm and rock it from side-to-side – there should be no discernible movement at the rear **(see illustration)**.

15.2 Compress the forks to check their action

15.3 Check the inner tube (arrowed) for pitting and signs of oil leakage

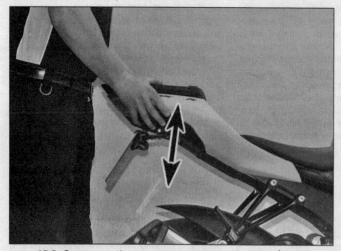

15.8 Compress the rear suspension to check its action

15.9 Checking for play in the swingarm bearings

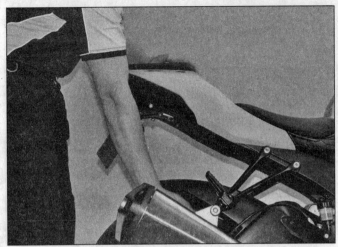

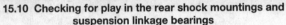

15.10 Checking for play in the rear shock mountings and suspension linkage bearings

16.4 Checking for play in the steering head bearings

10 Next, grasp the top of the rear wheel and pull it upwards – there should be no discernible freeplay before the shock absorber begins to compress **(see illustration)**.

11 If there's a little movement or a slight clicking can be heard, check the tightness of the swingarm pivot, referring to the procedure in Chapter 5, and re-check for movement. Also check the shock absorber mounting bolts/ nuts, and the suspension linkage mounting bolts/nuts. If there is still some noise or freeplay after everything has been correctly tightened then there is a worn bush, bearing or bearings in the shock absorber, swingarm or linkage. The worn component(s) must be identified and replaced with new ones (see Chapter 5).

12 You can make a more accurate assessment by isolating the swingarm from the shock absorber and linkage – remove the rear wheel (see Chapter 6) and the bolts securing the linkage to the shock absorber and swingarm (see Chapter 5).

13 Grasp the rear of the swingarm with one hand and place your other hand at the junction of the swingarm and the frame. Try to move the rear of the swingarm from side-to-side. Any wear (play) in the bearings should be felt as movement between the swingarm and the frame at the front. If there is any play, the swingarm will be felt to move forward and backward at the front (not from side-to-side). Next, move the swingarm up and down through its full travel. It should move freely, without any binding or rough spots. If there is any play in the swingarm or if it does not move freely, remove the bearings for inspection (see Chapter 5).

14 Check the bearings in the linkage arm for corrosion and wear and failure of the seals, referring to Chapter 5 for details according to model, and clean and re-grease or replace components as required.

Front fork oil change

15 Although there is no set interval for changing the fork oil, the oil will degrade over a period of time and lose its damping qualities. Refer to Chapter 5 for details of front fork removal, oil draining and refilling. The forks do not need to be completely disassembled to change the oil.

Rear suspension bearing lubrication

16 Over time the seals are likely to fail and the grease in the bearings will be washed out or will harden allowing the ingress of dirt and water.

17 At the prescribed interval remove the suspension linkage and the swingarm, clean and re-grease the bearings, and fit new seals (see Chapter 5).

16 Steering head bearings

Freeplay check and adjustment

1 This motorcycle is equipped with caged ball steering head bearings. The bearings can become dented, rough or loose during normal use of the machine and in extreme cases, worn or loose steering head bearings can cause steering wobble – a condition that is potentially dangerous.

Check

2 Remove the lower fairing panels (see Chapter 7). Where fitted detach the steering damper from the top yoke (see Chapter 5). Raise the front wheel off the ground using an auxiliary stand placed under the engine. Always make sure that the bike is properly supported and secure.

3 Point the front wheel straight-ahead and slowly move the handlebars from lock to lock.

Any dents or roughness in the bearing races will be felt and if the bearings are too tight the bars will not move smoothly and freely. Again point the wheel straight-ahead, and tap the front of the wheel to one side. The wheel should 'fall' under its own weight to the limit of its lock, indicating that the bearings are not too tight (take into account the restriction that cables and wiring may have). Check for similar movement to the other side.

4 Next, grasp the bottom of the forks and gently pull and push them forward and backward **(see illustration)**. Any looseness or freeplay in the steering head bearings will be felt as front-to-rear movement of the forks.

5 If the steering doesn't perform as described in Step 3 or there is play felt in Step 4 the bearings should be adjusted as described below. If no adjustment is need, refit the fairing panels, and where fitted the steering damper.

> **HAYNES HiNT**
>
> *Make sure you are not mistaking any movement between the bike and stand, or between the stand and the ground, for freeplay in the bearings. Do not pull and push the forks too hard – a gentle movement is all that is needed. Freeplay between the fork tubes due to worn bushes can also be misinterpreted as steering head bearing play – do not confuse the two.*

Adjustment

Special tool: *Either the Kawasaki special tool (part No. 07HMA-MR70100), equivalent peg spanner, or a suitably sized C-spanner is necessary for this procedure – see Step 11.*

6 As a precaution, remove the fuel tank (see Chapter 4) and the fairing (see Chapter 7). Though not actually necessary, this will prevent the possibility of damage should a tool slip. Where fitted remove the steering

16.7a Unscrew each handlebar positioning bolt...

16.7b ...then slacken the handlebar clamp bolt (arrowed)...

16.7c ...and the fork clamp bolt (arrowed) on each side

16.8 Unscrew the nut or bolt and remove the washer...

16.9 ...and gently ease the yoke up off the forks

16.10a Bend down the tabs securing the locknut...

16.10b ...then unscrew the locknut...

16.10c ...and remove the lockwasher

16.11 Adjust the bearings as described using a C-spanner

16.15 Fit the steering stem bolt with its washer and tighten to the specified torque

damper and its bracket from the top yoke (see Chapter 5).

7 Unscrew the handlebar positioning bolts and slacken the clamp bolts **(see illustrations)**. Slacken the fork clamp bolts in the top yoke **(see illustration)**.

8 On C and D models stick a layer of masking tape around the steering stem nut to protect its finish. On E and F models remove the plug from the centre of the steering stem bolt. Unscrew the nut or bolt and remove the washer **(see illustration)**.

9 Gently ease the top yoke up off the forks and position it clear, using a rag to protect other components **(see illustration)**.

10 Bend the upward-pointing lockwasher tabs out of the notches in the locknut **(see illustration)**. Unscrew the locknut using either your fingers (it shouldn't be tight) or a C-spanner **(see illustration)**. Remove the lockwasher, noting how the downward-pointing tabs locate in the adjuster nut **(see illustration)**. Inspect the tabs for cracks or

signs of fatigue. If there is any sign of damage, discard the lockwasher and use a new one; otherwise the old one can be re-used, but note that Kawasaki recommend using a new one as a matter of course.

11 Using a C-spanner or a suitable drift located in one of the notches, either loosen or tighten the adjuster nut slightly as required according to whether the bearings were too tight or too loose **(see illustration)**. The object is to set the adjuster nut so that the bearings are under a very light loading, just enough to remove any freeplay, but not so much that the steering does not move freely from side-to-side as described in the check procedure above. Turn the nut only a little at a time, and after each adjustment repeat the checks outlined in Steps 3 and 4.

Caution: Take great care not to apply excessive pressure because this will cause premature failure of the bearings.

12 Turn the steering from lock to lock five times to settle the bearings, then recheck the

adjustment. If the bearings cannot be correctly adjusted, disassemble the steering head and check the bearings and races (see Chapter 5).

13 With the bearings correctly adjusted, fit the lockwasher, using a new one if the tabs are weakened or cracked, onto the adjuster nut and fit the downward-pointing tabs into the slots in the adjuster nut **(see illustration 16.10c)**.

14 Fit the locknut and tighten it finger-tight **(see illustration 16.10b)**. Tighten the locknut by a further two to four notches (or by about 90°) until the notches align with the remaining lockwasher tabs, making sure the adjuster nut does not turn as well (though that is unlikely). Secure the locknut in position by bending up the horizontal tabs on the lockwasher into its notches **(see illustration 16.10a)**.

15 Fit the top yoke onto the steering stem **(see illustration 16.9)**. Fit the washer and the steering stem nut or bolt and tighten it to the torque setting specified at the beginning of the Chapter for your model **(see illustration)**.

17.3 Checking for play in the wheel bearings

16 Tighten the fork clamp bolts in the top yoke to the specified torque **(see illustration 16.7c)**. Fit the handlebar positioning bolts and tighten to the specified torque, then tighten the clamp bolts to the specified torque **(see illustrations 16.7a and b)**.
17 Check the bearing adjustment as described above and re-adjust if necessary.
18 Attach the steering damper where fitted (see Chapter 5). Install the fuel tank (see Chapter 4) and the fairing (see Chapter 7).

Lubrication

19 Over time the seals are likely to fail and the grease in the bearings will be washed out or will harden allowing the ingress of dirt and water.
20 At the prescribed interval remove the steering stem and clean and re-grease the bearings (see Chapter 5).

17 Wheels, wheel bearings and tyres

Wheels

1 Cast wheels are virtually maintenance free, but they should be kept clean and checked periodically for cracks and other damage. Also check the wheel runout and alignment (see Chapter 6). Never attempt to repair damaged cast wheels; they must be renewed if damaged. Check that the wheel balance weights are fixed firmly to the wheel rim. If you suspect that a weight has fallen off, have the wheel rebalanced by a motorcycle tyre specialist.

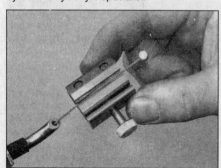

18.5a Fit the cable into the adapter...

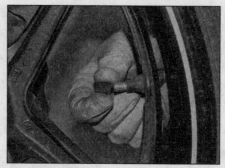

17.7 Check each valve as described and make sure a cap is fitted

Wheel bearings

2 Wheel bearings will wear over a considerable mileage and should be checked periodically to avoid handling problems.
3 Support the motorcycle upright using an auxiliary stand so that the wheel being examined is off the ground. Check for any play in the bearings by pushing and pulling the wheel against the hub **(see illustration)**. Also rotate the wheel and check that it turns smoothly and without any grating noises.
4 If any play is detected in the hub, or if the wheel does not rotate smoothly (and this is not due to brake or chain drag), the wheel should be removed and the bearings inspected for wear or damage (see Chapter 6).

Tyres

5 Check the tyre condition and tread depth thoroughly – see *Pre-ride checks*.
6 Check the valve rubber for signs of damage or deterioration and have it replaced if necessary by a tyre specialist.
7 Make sure a valve stem cap is fitted **(see illustration)**. Check the valve for signs of damage.
8 If tyre deflation occurs and it is not due to a slow puncture the valve core may be loose or it could be leaking past the seal – remove the cap and make sure the core is tight. Some valve caps double as a tool for the valve core – these caps are available in bike and automotive accessory dealers. Alternatively special tools are available, or a tool can be made quite easily by cutting a slot into the threaded end

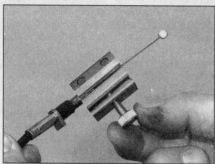

18.5b ...and tighten the screw to seal it in...

of a bolt using a hacksaw – the bolt must fit inside the valve housing and the slot must be deep enough to locate around the flat sides of the core and grip it. If the core leaks when tight fit a new one. A smear of spit or soapy water across the top of the valve will indicate if it is leaking – the leak will show as bubbles.

18 Pivot points and cable lubrication

Pivot points

1 Since the controls, cables and various other components of a motorcycle are exposed to the elements, they should be checked and lubricated periodically to ensure safe and trouble-free operation.
2 The footrest pivots, clutch and brake lever pivots, brake pedal and gearchange lever pivots and linkage and sidestand pivot should be lubricated frequently. In order for the lubricant to be applied where it will do the most good, the component should be disassembled (see Chapter 5) and multi-purpose grease applied.
3 If an aerosol lubricant is used, it can be applied to the pivot joint gaps and will usually work its way into the areas where friction occurs, so less disassembly of the component is needed. If however, the area is dirty or the pivot is stiff to operate it is preferable to dismantle it and clean off all corrosion, dirt and old lubricant first.
4 If using grease, apply it sparingly as it may attract dirt (which could cause the controls to bind or wear at an accelerated rate). **Note:** *One of the best lubricants for the control lever pivots is a dry-film lubricant (available from many sources by different names).*

Cables

Special tool: *A cable lubricating adapter is necessary for this procedure.*

5 To lubricate the cables, disconnect the relevant cable at its upper end, then lubricate it with a pressure adapter and aerosol cable lubricant **(see illustrations)**. See Chapter 4 for throttle cable removal procedures, and Chapter 2 for the clutch cable.

18.5c ...then apply the lubricant using the nozzle provided inserted in the hole in the adapter

19 Nuts and bolts

1 Since vibration of the machine tends to loosen fasteners, all nuts, bolts, screws, etc. should be periodically checked for proper tightness.

2 Pay particular attention to the fasteners for the following components, referring to the relevant Chapter:

Spark plugs
Engine oil drain plug
Levers and pedals
Footrests and sidestand
Engine mountings
Shock absorber and suspension linkage
Swingarm
Handlebars
Front fork clamps (top and bottom yoke) and fork top bolts
Steering stem nut
Steering damper
Front axle and axle clamps

Rear axle
Front and rear sprockets
Brake calipers and master cylinders
Brake hoses and caliper bleed valves
Brake discs
Exhaust system

3 If a torque wrench is available, use it along with the torque settings given at the beginning of this and other Chapters.

20 Battery

1 All models are fitted with a sealed MF (maintenance free) battery. **Note:** *Do not attempt to remove the battery caps to check the electrolyte level or battery specific gravity. Removal will damage the caps, resulting in electrolyte leakage and battery damage.* All that should be done is to check that the terminals are clean and tight and that the casing is not damaged or leaking. See Chapter 8 for further details.

2 If the machine is not in regular use, disconnect the battery and give it a refresher charge every month to six weeks (see Chapter 8).

21 Air filter

Caution: If the machine is continually ridden in wet or dusty conditions, the filter should be replaced more frequently.

1 Remove the fuel tank (see Chapter 4). On US and Canada models remove the rubber shield where fitted.

2 On C and D models undo the air filter cover screws and remove the cover **(see illustration)**. Remove the element from the housing, noting how it fits, and replace it with a new one, making sure it locates correctly and is properly seated **(see illustration)**.

3 On E and F models undo the air filter cover screws and displace the cover, noting how one screw secures a wiring clamp **(see illustrations)** – there is no need to disconnect

21.2a Air filter cover screws (arrowed)

21.2b Lift the filter out of the housing

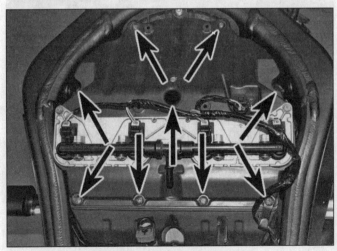

21.3a Undo the screws (arrowed)...

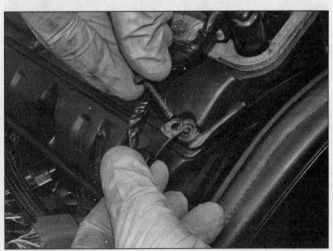

21.3b ...noting the clamp...

21.3c ...and lift the cover back

21.3d Lift the filter out of the housing

21.6 Drain the hose if necessary

the wiring or fuel hose. Remove the element from the housing, noting how it fits, and replace it with a new one, making sure it locates correctly and is properly seated **(see illustrations)**.

4 To clean the filter in between renewal intervals, tap it on a hard surface to dislodge any dirt from the folds, then check for anything stuck between them. Use compressed air

to blow through it, directing the air in the opposite way to normal flow, i.e. from the throttle body intake duct side. Do not use any solvents or cleaning agents on the element. If the element is excessively dirty or is damaged replace it with a new one.

5 Fit the cover in reverse order. Install the fuel tank (see Chapter 4).

6 Locate the clear drain pipe running from the bottom of the filter housing and check for any contents – if necessary remove the plug and drain them out **(see illustration)**.

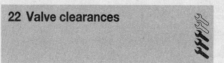

22 Valve clearances

Special tool: *A set of feeler gauges is necessary for this job* **(see illustration 22.7).**

Check

1 The engine must be completely cool for this maintenance procedure, so let the bike stand overnight before beginning.

2 Remove the spark plugs (see Section 6). Remove the valve cover (see Chapter 2).

3 Make a chart or sketch of all valve positions so that a note of each clearance can be made against the relevant valve. The cylinders are numbered 1 to 4 from left to right. The intake valves are on the back of the cylinder head and the exhaust valves are on the front.

4 To check the valve clearances the crankshaft must be turned so that the valves being checked are closed. The crankshaft can be turned using a suitable spanner or a socket on the timing rotor or starter clutch bolt (according to model) and turning it in a clockwise direction only **(see illustration 22.5a)**.

5 On C models remove the timing rotor cover (see Chapter 2). Turn the crankshaft clockwise until the line next to the numbers 1 and 4 marked on the timing rotor points back and aligns with the crankcase mating surfaces, and so that the IN mark on the intake camshaft sprocket points back parallel to the top of the cylinder head, and the EX mark on the exhaust camshaft sprocket points forwards **(see**

22.5a Turn the crankshaft clockwise using the bolt...

22.5b ...until the 1.4 line aligns with the crankcase joint (arrowed)

22.6a Unscrew the caps (arrowed)

22.6b Turn the crankshaft clockwise using the bolt...

22.6c ...until the line aligns with the notch (arrowed)...

22.6d ...and the camshaft sprocket marks (circled) are as described

illustrations and 22.6d). If the sprocket marks are upside down and facing the other way (i.e. 180° round from the desired position), rotate the engine clockwise one full turn (360°) until the line next to the 1 and 4 again aligns with the crankcase mating surfaces. The sprocket marks will now be facing correctly.

6 On D, E and F models unscrew the crankshaft end cap and timing inspection cap from the starter clutch cover (see illustration). Note that new O-rings should be used. Turn the crankshaft clockwise until the line on the starter clutch aligns with the notch in the inspection hole rim, and so that the IN mark on the intake camshaft sprocket points back parallel to the top of the cylinder head, and the EX mark on the exhaust camshaft sprocket points forwards (see illustrations). If the sprocket marks are upside down and facing the other way (i.e. 180° round from the

desired position), rotate the engine clockwise one full turn (360°) until the line again aligns with the notch. The sprocket marks will now be facing correctly.

7 With the engine in this position the No. 4 cylinder is on its compression stroke and you can check the clearances on the Nos. 4 and 2 cylinder intake valves and the Nos. 4 and 3 cylinder exhaust valves. Insert a feeler gauge of the same thickness as the correct valve clearance (see Specifications) between the camshaft lobe and the follower of each valve and check that it is a firm sliding fit – you should feel a slight drag when the you pull the gauge out (see illustration). If not, use the feeler gauges to obtain the exact clearance. Record the measured clearance on the chart.

8 Now turn the crankshaft 360° clockwise until the line on the timing rotor again aligns with the crankcase mating surfaces or the

notch, according to model (see illustration 22.5b or 22.6c). Now the IN mark on the intake camshaft sprocket points forwards parallel to

22.7 Insert the feeler gauge between the base of the cam lobe and the top of the follower as shown

22.11a Carefully lift out the follower using a magnet, a lapping tool or grips...

22.11b ...and retrieve the shim (arrowed) from inside it...

22.11c ...or from the top of the valve

the top of the cylinder head, and the EX mark on the exhaust camshaft sprocket points back, and both marks read upside down. With the engine in this position, the No. 1 cylinder is on its compression stroke, and you can check the clearances on the Nos. 1 and 3 cylinder intake valves and the Nos. 1 and 2 cylinder exhaust valves.

9 When all clearances have been measured and charted, identify whether the clearance on any valve falls outside the specified range. If any do, the shim must be replaced with one of a thickness that will restore the correct clearance.

Adjustment

10 Shim replacement requires removal of the camshafts (see Chapter 2). Place rags over the spark plug holes and the cam chain tunnel to prevent a shim from dropping into the engine on removal. Work on one valve at a time to prevent the possibility of mixing up the followers, which must be returned to their original location. If you want to remove more than one shim and follower at a time, store them in a marked container or bag, denoting which cylinder and which valve the shim and follower are from, so that they do not get mixed up.

11 With the camshaft removed, remove the cam follower of the valve in question using a magnet or the suction created by a valve lapping tool, or long nosed pliers can be used with care **(see illustration)**. Retrieve the shim from inside the follower or pick it out of the top of the valve spring retainer using either a magnet, a screwdriver with a dab of grease on it (the shim will stick to the grease), or a very small screwdriver and a pair of pliers **(see illustrations)**. Do not allow the shim to fall into the engine.

12 Measure and record the thickness of the shim using a micrometer **(see illustration)**.
13 Calculate the required replacement shim using the formula $a + b - c = d$, where a is the existing shim thickness, b is the measured valve clearance, c is the specified valve clearance, and d is the required shim size. For example:

The thickness of the existing shim is 1.600 mm, so a = 1.6
The measured clearance of the valve is 0.31 mm, so b = 0.31
The specified clearance is 0.195, so c = 0.195
Therefore, the required replacement shim a = 1.600 + 0.31 – 0.195, so a = 1.715 mm. The nearest available size is 1.725 mm (see Step 14).

Note: *If the required replacement shim is greater than 2.300 mm (the largest available), the valve is probably not seating correctly due to a build-up of carbon deposits and should be checked and cleaned or resurfaced as required (see Chapter 2).*

14 Shims are available in 0.025 mm increments from 1.300 mm to 2.300 mm. Obtain the replacement shim, then lubricate it with molybdenum disulphide oil (a 50/50 mixture of molybdenum disulphide grease and engine oil) and fit it into the recess in the top of the valve spring retainer with the size mark facing up **(see illustration 22.11c)**.

15 Check that the shim is correctly seated, then lubricate the follower with molybdenum disulphide oil and fit it onto the valve, making sure it fits squarely in its bore **(see illustration 22.11a)**. Repeat the process for any other valves until the clearances are correct, then install the camshafts (see Chapter 2).

16 Rotate the crankshaft clockwise several turns to seat the new shim(s), then check the clearances again.

17 Install the valve cover (see Section 7). Install the spark plugs (see Chapter 1).

18 On C models install the timing rotor cover (see Chapter 2).

19 On D, E and F models fit the crankshaft end cap and timing inspection cap using new O-rings smeared with grease **(see illustration)**.

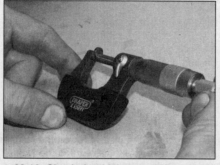

22.12 Check the thickness of the shim using a micrometer

22.19 Fit the caps

Chapter 2
Engine, clutch and transmission

Contents

Degrees of difficulty

Easy, suitable for novice with little experience	**Fairly easy,** suitable for beginner with some experience	**Fairly difficult,** suitable for competent DIY mechanic	**Difficult,** suitable for experienced DIY mechanic	**Very difficult,** suitable for expert DIY or professional

Specifications

General

Type	Four-stroke in-line four
Capacity	998 cc
Bore	76.0 mm
Stroke	55.0 mm
Compression ratio	
C and D models	12.7 to 1
E and F models	12.9 to 1
Cylinder numbering	1 to 4 from left to right
Firing order	1-2-4-3
Camshafts	DOHC, chain-driven
Cooling system	Liquid cooled
Lubrication	Wet sump, trochoid pump
Clutch	Wet multi-plate
Transmission	Six-speed constant mesh
Final drive	Chain

Camshafts

Intake cam lobe height	
C models	
Standard...	35.342 to 35.458 mm
Service limit (min)......................................	35.24 mm
D models	
Standard...	35.043 to 35.157 mm
Service limit (min)......................................	34.94 mm
E and F models	
Standard...	35.643 to 35.757 mm
Service limit (min)......................................	35.54 mm
Exhaust cam lobe height	
C models	
Standard...	34.942 to 35.058 mm
Service limit (min)......................................	34.84 mm
D, E and F models	
Standard...	34.443 to 34.557 mm
Service limit (min)......................................	34.34 mm
Camshaft journal diameter	
Standard...	23.940 to 23.962 mm
Service limit (min)......................................	23.91 mm
Camshaft holder bore diameter	
Standard...	24.000 to 24.021 mm
Service limit (min)......................................	24.08 mm
Oil clearance	
Standard...	0.038 to 0.081 mm
Service limit (max).....................................	0.17 mm
Runout (max)..	0.1 mm

Cylinder head

Cylinder compression....................................	159 to 242 psi (11.2 to 17 Bars) @ 320 rpm
Warpage (max)...	0.05 mm

Valves, guides and springs

Valve clearances.......................................	see Chapter 1
Stem diameter	
Intake valve	
Standard...	4.475 to 4.490 mm
Service limit (min)......................................	4.460 mm
Exhaust valve	
Standard...	4.470 to 4.485 mm
Service limit (min)......................................	4.460 mm
Guide bore diameter – intake and exhaust	
Standard...	4.500 to 4.512 mm
Service limit (max).....................................	4.580 mm
Stem-to-guide clearance (wobble method – see Section 12)	
C models	
Intake valve	
Standard...	0.05 to 0.11 mm
Service limit (max).....................................	0.36 mm
Exhaust valve	
Standard...	0.05 to 0.13 mm
Service limit (max).....................................	0.36 mm
D models	
Intake valve	
Standard...	0.03 to 0.10 mm
Service limit (max).....................................	0.34 mm
Exhaust valve	
Standard...	0.04 to 0.12 mm
Service limit (max).....................................	0.34 mm
E and F models	
Intake valve	
Standard...	0.03 to 0.11 mm
Service limit (max).....................................	0.30 mm
Exhaust valve	
Standard...	0.04 to 0.12 mm
Service limit (max).....................................	0.32 mm

Valves, guides and springs (continued)

Valve head thickness
  C and D models
    Intake valve
      Standard . . . .   0.5 mm
      Service limit (min) . . . .   0.25 mm
    Exhaust valve
      Standard . . . .   0.8 mm
      Service limit (min) . . . .   0.4 mm
  E and F models
    Intake valve
      Standard . . . .   1.25 mm
      Service limit (min) . . . .   0.60 mm
    Exhaust valve
      Standard . . . .   0.8 mm
      Service limit (min) . . . .   0.4 mm
Seat width
  Intake valve . . . .   0.50 to 1.00 mm
  Exhaust valve . . . .   0.80 to 1.20 mm
Valve seating surface outer diameter
  C models
    Intake valve . . . .   30.4 to 30.6 mm
    Exhaust valve . . . .   24.9 to 25.1 mm
  D models
    Intake valve . . . .   29.4 to 29.6 mm
    Exhaust valve . . . .   24.9 to 25.1 mm
  E and F models
    Intake valve . . . .   29.4 to 29.6 mm
    Exhaust valve . . . .   23.9 to 24.1 mm
Valve spring free length
  C and D models
    Intake valve
      Standard . . . .   39.15 mm
      Service limit (min) . . . .   37.5 mm
    Exhaust valve
      Standard . . . .   44.78 mm
      Service limit (min) . . . .   42.9 mm
  E and F models
    Intake valve
      Standard . . . .   39.50 mm
      Service limit (min) . . . .   37.7 mm
    Exhaust valve
      Standard . . . .   44.80 mm
      Service limit (min) . . . .   42.9 mm

Lubrication system

Oil pressure (at oil pressure switch, with engine warm) . . . .   22 to 33 psi (1.5 to 2.4 Bars) @ 4000 rpm, oil @ 90°C

Selector drum and forks

Selector fork end thickness
  Standard . . . .   5.9 to 6.0 mm
  Service limit (min) . . . .   5.8 mm
Gear groove width
  Standard . . . .   6.05 to 6.15 mm
  Service limit (max) . . . .   6.25 mm
Selector fork guide pin OD
  C models
    Standard . . . .   7.9 to 8.0 mm
    Service limit (min) . . . .   7.8 mm
  D, E and F models
    Standard . . . .   5.9 to 6.0 mm
    Service limit (min) . . . .   5.8 mm
Selector drum track width
  C models
    Standard . . . .   8.05 to 8.20 mm
    Service limit (max) . . . .   8.30 mm
  D, E and F models
    Standard . . . .   6.05 to 6.20 mm
    Service limit (max) . . . .   6.30 mm

Clutch

Friction plates.	10
Plain plates.	9

Friction plate thickness
   Standard. . . . . 2.72 to 2.88 mm
   Service limit (min) . . . . 2.6 mm
Plate warpage (max). . . . . 0.3 mm
Spring free length
   Standard. . . . . 43.5 mm
   Service limit (min) . . . . 42.1 mm
Clutch plate assembly thickness . . . . 53.5 to 53.6 mm
Outer pressure plate freeplay
   C models . . . . 0.05 to 0.35 mm
   D, E and F models . . . . 0.05 to 0.70 mm

Cylinders

Bore
   Standard. . . . . 75.990 to 76.006 mm
   Service limit (max) . . . . 76.10 mm

Pistons

Piston diameter
   Standard. . . . . 75.959 to 75.974 mm
   Service limit (min) . . . . 75.81 mm
Piston-to-bore clearance . . . . 0.020 to 0.047 mm
Piston ring groove width (top and second ring)
   Standard. . . . . 0.82 to 0.84 mm
   Service limit (max) . . . . 0.92 mm

Piston rings

Ring end gap (installed)
   Top ring
      Standard. . . . . 0.15 to 0.30 mm
      Service limit (max). . . . . 0.6 mm
   Second ring
      Standard. . . . . 0.30 to 0.45 mm
      Service limit (max). . . . . 0.8 mm
Ring thickness (top and second ring)
   Standard. . . . . 0.77 to 0.79 mm
   Service limit (max) . . . . 0.70 mm
Ring-to-groove clearance (top and second ring)
   Standard. . . . . 0.03 to 0.07 mm
   Service limit (max) . . . . 0.17 mm

Crankshaft and bearings

Crankshaft side clearance
   C and D models
      Standard. . . . . 0.05 to 0.20 mm
      Service limit (max). . . . . 0.40 mm
   E and F models
      Standard. . . . . 0.05 to 0.25 mm
      Service limit (max). . . . . 0.45 mm
Main bearing oil clearance
   Standard. . . . . 0.010 to 0.034 mm
   Service limit (max) . . . . 0.06 mm
Main bearing journal diameter
   No mark on crank web. . . . . 34.984 to 34.992 mm
   '1' mark on crank web . . . . 34.993 to 35.000 mm
   Service limit (min) . . . . 34.96 mm
Crankcase main bearing bore diameter
   'O' mark on crankcase . . . . 38.000 to 38.008 mm
   No mark on crankcase . . . . 38.009 to 38.016 mm
Connecting rod big-end journal (crankpin) diameter
   No mark on crank throw. . . . . 34.484 to 34.492 mm
   'O' mark on crank throw. . . . . 34.493 to 34.500 mm
   Service limit (min) . . . . 34.47 mm
Runout (total indicator reading)
   Standard. . . . . 0.02 mm
   Service limit (max) . . . . 0.05 mm

Connecting rods

Big-end side clearance
    Standard.. 0.13 to 0.38 mm
    Service limit (max) .... 0.58 mm
Big-end oil clearance
    Standard.. 0.030 to 0.060 mm
    Service limit (max) .... 0.10 mm
Connecting rod big-end inside diameter
    No mark on side of rod........................... 37.500 to 37.508 mm
    'O' mark on side of rod.......................... 37.509 to 37.516 mm

Transmission

Gear ratios (no. of teeth)
  C and D models
    Primary reduction .... 1.611 to 1 (87/54)
    Final reduction .... 2.294 to 1 (39/17) C models, 2.353 to 1 (40/17) D models
    1st gear.. 2.533 to 1 (38/15)
    2nd gear....................................... 2.053 to 1 (39/19)
    3rd gear....................................... 1.737 to 1 (33/19)
    4th gear....................................... 1.524 to 1 (32/21)
    5th gear....................................... 1.381 to 1 (29/21)
    6th gear....................................... 1.304 to 1 (30/23)
  E and F models
    Primary reduction .... 1.611 to 1 (87/54)
    Final reduction .... 2.412 to 1 (41/17)
    1st gear.. 2.600 to 1 (39/15)
    2nd gear....................................... 2.053 to 1 (39/19)
    3rd gear....................................... 1.737 to 1 (33/19)
    4th gear....................................... 1.550 to 1 (31/20)
    5th gear....................................... 1.400 to 1 (28/20)
    6th gear....................................... 1.304 to 1 (30/23)

Torque settings

Cam chain tensioner cap bolt .... 20 Nm
Cam chain tensioner mounting bolts .... 10 Nm
Cam chain guide blade
    Upper bolt..................................... 25 Nm
    Lower bolt..................................... 12 Nm
Camshaft holder bolts .... 12 Nm
Camshaft sprocket bolts .... 15 Nm
Clutch nut.. 130 Nm
Clutch cover bolts .... 10 Nm
Clutch spring bolts
    C models .... 10 Nm
    D, E and F models .... 11 Nm
Connecting rod bolt nuts
    Torque setting................................. 20 Nm
    Angle setting.................................. +150°
Crankcase bolts
  9 mm crankshaft journal bolts
    C models....................................... 46 Nm
    D, E and F models .... 39 Nm
  8 mm bolts .... 27 Nm
  7 mm bolts
    C models....................................... 25 Nm
    D, E and F models .... 20 Nm
  6 mm bolts .... 12 Nm
Crankcase breather plate bolts .... 10 Nm
Cylinder head 10 mm bolts
    Initial setting .... 20 Nm
  Final setting
    Used bolts..................................... 57 Nm
    New bolts .... 59 Nm
Cylinder head 6 mm bolts .... 12 Nm

Torque settings (continued)

Engine mountings

Front mounting bolts	44 Nm
Middle and lower mounting adjusters	10 Nm
Middle mounting bolt nut	44 Nm
Lower mounting bolt nut	44 Nm
Front adjuster locknut.	49 Nm
Engine bracket bolts.	44 Nm
Gearchange mechanism centralising spring locating pin	29 Nm
Gearchange mechanism pawl assembly guide plate screws (E and F models)	15 Nm
Idle gear cover bolts.	10 Nm
Oil cooler bolts	20 Nm
Oil filter and cooler holder bolts	20 Nm
Oil gallery plug	20 Nm
Oil pressure relief valve	15 Nm
Oil pump cover bolts	10 Nm
Oil pump driven gear bolts	10 Nm
Oil sump bolts	10 Nm
Oil sump front section bolts (C models)	25 Nm
Selector drum bearing retainer screws	5 Nm
Selector fork retainer bolt.	12 Nm
Selector drum cam bolt	12 Nm
Starter clutch bolt.	49 Nm
Starter clutch cover bolts.	10 Nm
Stopper arm bolt	12 Nm
Throttle body holder bolts	10 Nm
Timing rotor bolt (C models).	40 Nm
Timing rotor cover bolts (C models)	10 Nm
Transmission input shaft bearing housing bolts.	25 Nm
Valve cover bolts	10 Nm

1 General information

The engine/transmission unit is a liquid-cooled in-line four cylinder. The sixteen valves are operated by double overhead camshafts that are chain driven off the right-hand end of the crankshaft. The engine/transmission is a unit assembly constructed from aluminium alloy. The crankcase divides horizontally.

The crankcase incorporates a wet sump, pressure-fed lubrication system with a trochoid oil pump that is gear-driven off the back of the clutch. The system has an oil strainer in the pick-up, a pressure relief valve, an oil filter, an oil cooler, and an oil pressure switch. The water pump is on the left-hand side of the engine, and its driveshaft is keyed to the oil pump driveshaft.

On C models the alternator is on the top of the crankcase and is gear-driven off the clutch. The starter clutch is on the left-hand end of the crankshaft. The ignition timing triggers are on a rotor on the right-hand end of the crankshaft.

On D, E and F models the alternator is on the left-hand end of the crankshaft. The ignition timing triggers are on the outside of the starter clutch on the right-hand end of the crankshaft.

Power from the crankshaft is routed to the transmission via a clutch. The clutch is of the wet, multi-plate type and is gear-driven off the crankshaft. The clutch is operated by cable. The transmission is a six-speed constant-mesh unit. Final drive to the rear wheel is by chain and sprockets.

Note: On C models the crankcases, crankshaft, clutch housing and alternator driven gear are all matched on assembly according to various code markings. If any of the above parts are replaced with new ones the new parts must carry the same marks as those being replaced to ensure correct matching. Refer to your Kawasaki parts dealer for details.

2 Component access

Operations possible with the engine in the frame

The components and assemblies listed below can be removed without having to remove the engine/transmission assembly from the frame. If however, a number of areas require attention at the same time, removal of the engine is recommended.

Valve cover
Cam chain tensioner and blades
Camshafts and cam chain
Cylinder head

Clutch
Gearchange mechanism
Alternator
Oil filter and oil cooler
Oil sump, oil pump, oil strainer and pressure relief valve
Starter motor
Starter clutch
Water pump

Operations requiring engine removal

It is necessary to remove the engine/transmission assembly from the frame to gain access to the following components.

Pistons and piston rings
Connecting rods and bearings
Crankshaft and bearings
Transmission shafts
Selector drum and forks (although see Note in Section 20)

3 Engine wear assessment

1 Poor engine performance may be caused by leaking valves, incorrect valve clearances, a leaking head gasket, or worn pistons, piston rings or cylinders. A cylinder compression check will highlight these conditions and can also indicate the presence of excessive carbon deposits in the cylinder head, and a

3.5 Select the correct adapter and fit it onto the gauge hose

3.6 Checking cylinder compression

leakdown test (for which special equipment is needed – consult a Kawasaki dealer) will pinpoint the actual cause(s) of the problem.

Cylinder compression check

Special tool: *A compression gauge is needed. You will have to use one with a threaded hose and 10 mm dia. x 1.0 mm pitch adaptor to fit the spark plug holes (use either the Kawasaki gauge and adapter (pt. Nos. 57001-221,-1601 and -1606) or an equivalent aftermarket set-up). Depending on the outcome of the initial test, a squirt-type oil can may also be needed.*

2 Start by making sure the valve clearances are correctly set (see Chapter 1). Also make sure the battery is well charged.

3 Run the engine until it is at normal operating temperature.

4 Remove the spark plugs (see Chapter 1).

5 Make sure the gauge hose/adapter threads are the same as the spark plug **(see illustration)**. Fit the gauge into the No. 1 cylinder spark plug hole.

6 With the ignition switch ON, the kill switch set to RUN, and the throttle held fully open, turn the engine over on the starter motor until the gauge reading has built up and stabilised **(see illustration)**.

7 Compare the reading on the gauge to the cylinder compression figure specified at the beginning of the Chapter. Repeat for the remaining cylinders.

8 If a reading is low, it could be due to a worn cylinder bore, piston or rings, failure of the head gasket, or worn valve seats. To

determine which is the cause, pour a small quantity of engine oil into the spark plug hole to seal the rings, then repeat the compression test. If the figures are noticeably higher the cause is a worn cylinder, piston or rings. If there is no change the cause is a leaking head gasket or worn valve seats.

9 If the unlikely event that the reading is high there could be a build-up of carbon deposits in the combustion chamber. Remove the cylinder head and scrape all deposits off the pistons and the cylinder head (see Sections 11 and 12).

Leak-down (cylinder leakage) test

10 A leak down or 'cylinder leakage' test is similar to a compression test in that it tells you how well a cylinder is sealing, but it does so by testing how much pressure is lost through leakage, as opposed to how much pressure is created through compression. Many professionals prefer a leak test to a compression test as it more accurately pin-points the cause of the problem before any disassembly is done, as it is easy to tell where the leakage is occurring. Generally however the required equipment is more expensive than for a compression test and a source of compressed air is essential. If you think a test is needed take the bike to a suitably equipped dealer or workshop. If you decide to purchase your own equipment follow the manufacturer's instructions.

11 A leakage test can also be used in conjunction with a compression test to

diagnose other kinds of problems, such as a faulty valve train component, incorrect valve timing, faulty ignition or fuel delivery problems.

Engine oil pressure check

Special tool: *An oil pressure gauge is required to perform this test.*

12 An oil pressure check can provide useful information about the condition of the engine's lubrication system, and can also be used as an indicator of excessive wear in the engine if no specific faults with the lubrication or pressure warning system are found..

13 The oil pressure warning light should come on when the ignition switch is turned ON and extinguish a few seconds after the engine is started. If the oil pressure light stays on, or comes on whilst the engine is running, low oil pressure is indicated – stop the engine immediately and carry out an oil level check *(see Pre-ride checks)*. If the oil level is correct, remove the sump and check the oil pick-up strainer for a blockage (Section 18). Also check the drained oil for sludge, which reduces its ability to flow. Note that it is possible that the cause of the light staying on or coming on while the engine is running is an electrical fault, so make sure the oil pressure switch, warning light and circuit are all functioning correctly (see Chapter 8). If all appears good an oil pressure check must be carried out.

14 To check the oil pressure, a suitable gauge and adapter (which screws into the main oil gallery) will be needed. Kawasaki can provide a gauge and adapter (part Nos. 57001-164 and -1233) for this purpose, or they can be obtained commercially. You will also need some rags to catch and mop up any residual oil that gets lost in between removing the oil gallery plug and installing the gauge.

15 On C and D models remove the right-hand lower fairing panel (see Chapter 7). On E and F models remove the left-hand lower fairing panel (see Chapter 7). Check the oil level (see *Pre-ride checks*).

16 Unscrew the oil gallery plug **(see illustrations)**. Thread the correct adapter in its place, then connect the oil pressure gauge to the adapter **(see illustration)**.

3.16a Main oil gallery plug (arrowed) – C and D models

3.16b Main oil gallery plug (arrowed) – E and F models

3.16c Thread the correct adapter in then fit the gauge hose onto it

3.17 Run the engine and check the reading on the gauge

4.7 Unscrew the bolt (arrowed) and remove the bracket

4.9 Remove the clamps

17 Warm the engine up to normal operating temperature, then briefly increase the engine speed to 4000 rpm whilst watching the gauge reading (see illustration). The oil pressure should be within the range given in the Specifications at the start of this Chapter.

18 If the pressure is significantly lower than the standard, or there is no pressure at all, and the pick-up strainer is clean, the pressure relief valve is stuck open, the oil pump or its drive mechanism is faulty, the oil filter is blocked, or there is other engine damage causing an internal oil leak. Also make sure the correct grade oil is being used. Begin diagnosis by checking the oil filter, strainer and relief valve (see Section 18), then the oil pump (Section 19). If those items check out okay, chances are the bearing oil clearances are excessive and the engine needs to be overhauled.

19 If the pressure is too high, an oil passage is clogged, the relief valve is stuck closed or the wrong grade of oil is being used.

20 If the pressure is as it should be, and if not already done, then check the oil pressure switch, warning light and circuit (see Chapter 8).

21 Stop the engine and let it cool. Clean the threads of the gallery plug and apply some fresh threadlock. Remove the gauge and adapter, fit the gallery plug and tighten it to the torque setting specified at the beginning of the Chapter.

> ⚠ **Warning: Be careful when removing the pressure gauge adapter as the exhaust pipes, the engine and the oil itself can cause severe burns.**

22 Check the oil level (see *Pre-ride checks*).
23 Install the lower fairing panel (see Chapter 7).

4 Engine removal and installation

Caution: The engine is very heavy. Engine removal and installation should be carried out with the aid of at least one assistant; personal injury or damage could occur if the engine falls or is dropped.

Note 1: A peg spanner is required to slacken and tighten the adjuster bolt locknut on the upper rear engine mounting bolt. If the Kawasaki service tool (Part no. 57001-1450) is not available, a suitable one will have to be fabricated out of a piece of steel tubing with an ID of 24 mm and OD of 28 mm, or an old 21 mm socket (see illustration 4.26a).

Note 2: If you are removing the engine for an overhaul it is best to remove the starter motor, alternator, clutch, starter clutch, timing rotor (C models), water pump, sump, oil strainer and oil pump, with the engine still in the frame – refer to the relevant Sections in this Chapter, and to Chapter 3 for the water pump and Chapter 8 for the alternator.

Removal

1 Support the bike upright using an auxiliary stand or stands that will not interfere with engine removal – a rear paddock stand is ideal. Make sure the bike is on level ground, and tie the front brake on. Work can be made easier by raising the machine to a suitable working height on a hydraulic ramp or a suitable platform. Make sure the motorcycle is secure and will not topple over (also see *Tools and Workshop Tips* in the Reference section).

2 Remove the lower fairing and fairing side panels or fairing assembly, according to model (see Chapter 7).

3 If the engine is dirty, particularly around its mountings, wash it thoroughly. This makes work much easier and rules out the possibility of caked on lumps of dirt falling into some vital component.

4 Disconnect the negative (–ve) lead from the battery (see Chapter 8).

5 Drain the engine oil and the coolant (see Chapter 1). If required remove the oil filter (see Chapter 1).

6 Remove the radiator and the coolant reservoir along with their hoses, noting their routing (see Chapter 3). Detach and remove any coolant hoses not already removed as required depending on what work is to be carried out, noting their positions and routing.

7 Remove the exhaust system (see Chapter 4). Remove the radiator bracket (see illustration).

8 Release the clutch cable from the release arm (see Section 16). Secure the cable clear of the engine.

9 Remove the fuel tank, the air filter housing and the throttle bodies (see Chapter 4). Plug the engine intake manifolds with clean rag. Remove the throttle body clamps from the intake ducts (see illustration).

10 Note the alignment of the slit in the gearchange linkage arm clamp with the punch mark on the shaft, then unscrew the pinch bolt and slide the arm off (see illustrations and 17.3a and b).

11 Remove the front sprocket (see Chapter 6).

12 If required, remove the starter motor (see

4.10a Note the alignment (E/F models shown, others differ)...

4.10b ...then remove the bolt and slide the arm off

4.12 Unscrew the nut (arrowed) and detach the lead

4.13 Unscrew the bolt (arrowed) and detach the lead

Chapter 8). If not unscrew the terminal nut and detach the lead **(see illustration)**.

13 Unscrew the engine earth lead bolt and detach the lead **(see illustration)**.

14 Remove the air suction system control valve along with the hoses (see Chapter 4). Remove the ignition coils (see Chapter 4).

15 Pull the rubber boot off the oil pressure switch, then undo the screw and detach the wiring connector **(see illustration)**.

16 Disconnect the alternator wiring, at the connector(s) on C and D models, and from the regulator/rectifier on E and F models **(see illustrations)**.

17 On E and F models disconnect the

4.15 Undo the screw and detach the wire

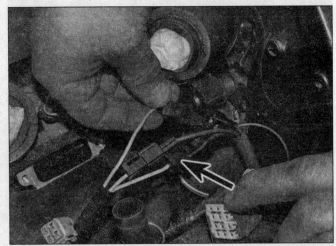

4.16a Alternator wiring connectors (arrowed) – C models

4.16b Alternator wiring connector (arrowed) – D models

4.16c Alternator wiring connector (arrowed) – E and F models

4.17a Disconnect the CKP sensor connector (E model shown)…

4.17b …the CMP sensor connector (D model shown)…

4.17c …the ECT sensor connector…

crankshaft position (CKP) sensor wiring connector **(see illustration)**. On C and D models disconnect the camshaft position (CMP) sensor wiring connector **(see illustration)**. On D, E and F models disconnect the coolant temperature (ECT) sensor wiring connector, the

speed sensor wiring connector and the gear position switch/sub-loom wiring connector **(see illustrations)**. Disconnect the sidestand switch wiring connector **(see illustrations)**.
18 Release any wiring secured to the engine and position it clear, noting its routing.

19 Position a hydraulic or mechanical jack under the engine with a block of wood between the jack head and sump **(see illustration)**. Make sure the jack is centrally positioned so the engine will not topple in any direction when the last mounting bolt is removed. Raise the

4.17d …the speed sensor connector…

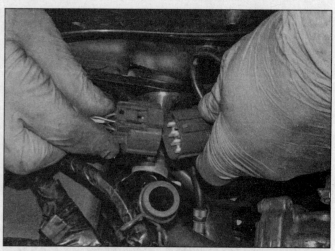

4.17e …and the gear position switch/sub-loom connector

4.17f Sidestand switch connector (arrowed) – C and D models (D shown)

4.17g Sidestand switch connector – E and F models

4.19 Place a jack under the engine

4.20a Fairing bracket bolts (arrowed) – right-hand side, E model shown

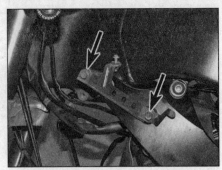

4.20b Fairing bracket bolts (arrowed) – left-hand side, E model shown

jack to take the weight of the engine, but make sure it is not lifting the bike and taking the weight of that as well. The idea is to support the engine so that there is no pressure on any of the mounting bolts once they have been slackened, so they can be easily withdrawn.

20 Unscrew the fairing bracket bolts on each side and remove the brackets (see illustrations). On E and F models remove the blanking cap from each side of the middle mounting (see illustration).
21 Unscrew the engine bracket bolts on

each side and remove the brackets (see illustrations).
22 Unscrew the front mounting bolt on the left-hand side (see illustration).
23 Counter-hold the right-hand end of the middle mounting bolt and unscrew the nut

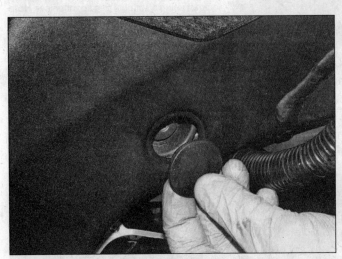

4.20c Remove the blanking caps

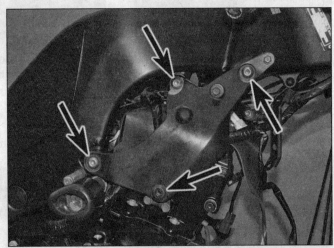

4.21a Engine bracket bolts (arrowed) – right-hand side, E model shown

4.21b Engine bracket bolts (arrowed) – left-hand side, E model shown

4.22 Unscrew the front left bolt

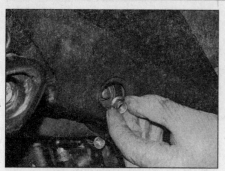

4.23a Unscrew the nut

4.23b Turn the bolt clockwise...

4.23c ...to create a gap (arrowed) between engine and frame

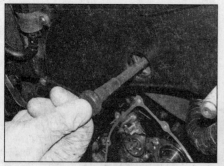

4.23d Withdraw the bolt...

4.23e ...and remove the spacer

the left-hand end (see illustration). Now turn the bolt head clockwise so that it threads the adjuster in the crankcase away from the frame to create a gap.

25 Unscrew the front mounting bolt on the right-hand side (see illustration).

26 Unscrew the front right mounting adjuster locknut using a suitable peg spanner (see Note above) (see illustration). Turn the adjuster anti-clockwise using a hex bit to create a gap between it and the engine (see illustrations).

27 Check that the engine is properly supported by the jack. Check that all wiring, cables and hoses are free and clear.

28 Hold the engine steady, then withdraw the rear mounting bolt from the right-hand side (see illustration). The engine can now be removed from the frame (see Caution above). Unhook the drive chain from the output shaft,

on the left-hand end (see illustration). Now turn the bolt head clockwise so that it threads the adjuster in the crankcase away from the frame to create a gap (see illustrations).

Withdraw the bolt and remove the spacer (see illustrations).

24 Counter-hold the right-hand end of the rear mounting bolt and unscrew the nut on

4.24 Unscrew the nut via the hole in the frame

4.25 Unscrew the front right bolt

4.26a Use a peg spanner to unscrew the locknut

4.26b Turn the adjuster anti-clockwise...

4.26c ...to create a gap (arrowed) between engine and frame

4.28 Withdraw the bolt and remove the engine

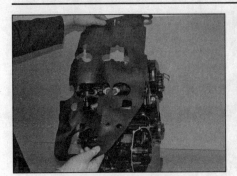

4.29 Remove the heat shield

4.30a Thread the adjusters (arrowed) all the way into the frame…

4.30b …and crankcase

lower the jack, and with the aid of assistants remove the jack from under the engine and remove the engine **(see illustration 4.31)**.

29 If required thread the adjusters out of the frame and crankcase, noting which fits where **(see illustrations 4.30a and b)**. Remove the rubber heat shield from the engine, noting how it fits **(see illustration)**.

Installation

30 Smear some engine oil onto the threads of the adjuster for the front mounting on the right-hand side and screw it into the inner side of the mounting as far as it will go **(see illustration)**. Smear some molybdenum grease onto the threads of the adjusters for the middle and lower mountings and screw them into the crankcase as far as they will go – on E and F models the longer adjuster

is for the middle mount **(see illustration)**. Fit the rubber heart shield over the engine **(see illustration)**.

31 Manoeuvre the engine into position under the frame and lift it onto the jack **(see illustration 4.19)**. Raise the engine to align all the mounting bolt holes, making sure that all cables and wiring are correctly routed and do not get trapped, and loop the drive chain over the output shaft **(see illustration)**. Note that it may be necessary to adjust the jack as some of the bolts are installed and tightened to realign the other bolt holes.

32 Slide the middle and lower rear mounting bolts through from the right-hand side, fitting the spacer with the middle bolt, and engaging the flats on the shanks of both bolts in the adjusters **(see illustrations 4.23d and e, and 4.28)**.

33 Fit the front mounting bolts and tighten

them finger-tight **(see illustrations 4.22 and 4.25)**. Tighten the front bolt on the left-hand side to the torque setting specified at the beginning of the Chapter.

34 Turn the middle and lower rear bolts anticlockwise so the adjusters thread out of the crankcase and contact the frame, then tighten them against the frame (anti-clockwise) to the specified torque setting **(see illustrations)**.

35 Thread the nuts onto the left-hand ends of the middle and lower bolts **(see illustrations 4.23a and 4.24)**. Counter-hold the head of the middle bolt and tighten the nut to the specified torque. Repeat for the lower bolt/nut.

36 Remove the front mounting bolt on the right-hand side **(see illustration 4.22)**. Turn the adjuster clockwise using a hex key until the flange just contacts the engine **(see illustrations)**. Thread the locknut onto

4.30c Fit the heat shield – E model shown

4.31 Loop the chain over the shaft

4.34a Turn the adjusters anti-clockwise…

4.34b …so they contact the frame and tighten to the specified torque

4.36a Turn the adjuster clockwise…

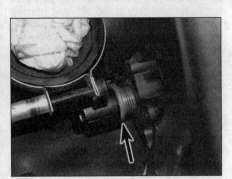

4.36b …so it contacts the engine

4.36c Tighten the locknut using the peg spanner

4.39a Thread the adjuster (arrowed) in so it does not protrude

4.39b Fit the left-hand bracket...

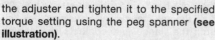

4.39c ....and the right hand bracket...

4.39d ... with the longer bolt at the lower front

the adjuster and tighten it to the specified torque setting using the peg spanner **(see illustration)**.

37 Refit the right front mounting bolt and tighten to the specified torque.

38 On C models fit the engine brackets and tighten the bolts to the specified torque.

39 On D, E and F models thread the adjuster in the right-hand engine bracket in as far as it will go **(see illustration)**. Fit both engine brackets and tighten the bolts finger-tight **(see illustrations)** – the longer bolt is for the lower front mount (with the adjuster) in the right-hand bracket **(see illustration)**. Now tighten the bracket bolts as follows: in the left-hand bracket tighten the upper front bolt to the specified torque, then the lower rear bolt, then the upper rear bolt; in the right-hand bracket tighten the upper front bolt to the specified torque, then the lower rear bolt, then the upper rear bolt; in the left-hand bracket tighten the lower front bolt to the specified torque; remove the lower front bolt from the right-hand bracket, then turn the adjuster clockwise using a hex key until the flange just contacts the engine; refit the lower front bolt and tighten to the specified torque.

40 The remainder of the installation procedure is the reverse of removal, noting the following points:

● Make sure the throttle body clamps are fitted with the screw head facing the frame **(see illustration 4.9)**.
● Use new gaskets on the exhaust pipe connections.
● Make sure all wires, cables and hoses

are correctly routed and connected, and secured by any clips or ties.
● Refill the engine with oil and coolant (see Chapter 1).
● Adjust the throttle and clutch cable freeplay.
● Adjust the drive chain (see Chapter 1).
● Start the engine and check that there are no oil or coolant leaks.

5 Engine disassembly and reassembly general information

1 Before beginning the engine overhaul, read through the related procedures to familiarise yourself with the scope and requirements of the job. Overhauling an engine is not all that difficult, but it is time consuming. Check on the availability of parts and make sure that any necessary special tools are obtained in advance.

2 Most work can be done with a decent set of typical workshop hand tools, although a number of precision measuring tools are required for inspecting parts to determine if they are worn.

3 To ensure maximum life and minimum trouble from a rebuilt engine, everything must be assembled with care in a spotlessly clean environment.

Disassembly

4 Before disassembling the engine, thoroughly clean and degrease its external surfaces.

This will prevent contamination of the engine internals, and will also make the job a lot easier and cleaner. A high flash-point solvent, such as paraffin (kerosene) can be used, or better still, a proprietary engine degreaser. Use old paintbrushes and toothbrushes to work the solvent into the various recesses of the casings. Take care to exclude solvent or water from the electrical components and intake and exhaust ports.

⚠ **Warning: The use of petrol (gasoline) as a cleaning agent should be avoided because of the risk of fire.**

5 When clean and dry, position the engine on the workbench, leaving suitable clear area for working. Gather a selection of small containers, plastic bags and some labels so that parts can be grouped together in an easily identifiable manner. Also get some paper and a pen so that notes can be taken. You will also need a supply of clean rag, which should be as absorbent as possible.

6 Before commencing work, read through the appropriate section so that some idea of the necessary procedure can be gained. When removing components note that great force is seldom required, unless specified (checking the specified torque setting of the particular bolt being removed will indicate how tight it is, and therefore how much force should be needed). In many cases, a component's reluctance to be removed is indicative of an incorrect approach or removal method – if in any doubt, re-check with the text.

7 When disassembling the engine, keep 'mated' parts that have been in contact with each other during engine operation together (i.e. pistons with their piston rings and connecting rods, valves with their followers, shims and other components, etc). These 'mated' parts must be reinstalled together and in their original location.

8 A complete engine/transmission disassembly should be done in the following general order with reference to the appropriate Sections.

Remove the valve cover
Remove the camshafts
Remove the cylinder head
Remove the starter motor (see Chapter 8)
Remove the alternator (see Chapter 8)

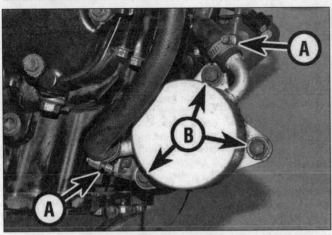

6.3 Slacken the clamps (A) and detach the hoses. Cooler mounting bolts (B)

6.6 Fit a new O-ring into the groove

Remove the starter clutch
Remove the cam chain and blades
Remove the clutch
Remove the gearchange mechanism
Remove the oil pump
Remove the oil sump
Remove the selector drum and forks
Separate the crankcase halves
Remove the transmission shafts
Remove the crankshaft
Remove the connecting rods and pistons

Reassembly

9 Reassembly is accomplished by reversing the general disassembly sequence.

6 Oil cooler

Removal

1 The cooler is located on the front of the engine next to the oil filter. Remove the lower fairing panels (see Chapter 7).
2 Drain the engine oil and coolant (see Chapter 1).

3 Slacken the clamp securing each hose to the cooler and detach the hoses (see illustration).
4 Unscrew the bolts and remove the cooler (see illustration 6.3). Remove the O-ring from the back of the cooler (see illustration 6.6) – a new one must be used.
5 Check the cooler body for cracks and dents and any evidence of coolant leakage and replace it with a new one if necessary. Also check the hoses for splits, cracks, hardening and deterioration and fit new ones if required.

Installation

6 Installation is the reverse of removal, noting the following:
● Ensure the mating surfaces of the cooler and its holder are clean and dry.
● Use a new O-ring on the cooler body and smear it with grease. Make sure it seats in its groove (see illustration).
● Tighten the bolts to the torque setting specified at the beginning of the Chapter.
● Make sure the coolant hoses are secured by the clamps (see illustration 6.3).
● Fill the engine with oil to the correct level (see Chapter 1).
● Refill the cooling system (see Chapter 1).

7 Valve cover

Removal

1 Remove the air filter housing, the air suction system control valve and hoses, and the ignition coils (see Chapter 4).
2 Remove the radiator (see Chapter 3).
3 Remove the right-hand engine bracket (see Section 4, Step 21).
4 Disconnect any wiring connectors on the top of the valve cover and move the wiring aside as required for best access and clearance according to model. Draw the rubber heat shield back, noting how it fits.
5 Unscrew the valve cover bolts, lift the cover off the cylinder head and remove it (see illustrations). If it is stuck, do not try to lever it off with a screwdriver. Tap it gently around the sides with a rubber hammer or block of wood to dislodge it. Note the thick washers for the bolts and remove them from the cover if they are loose.
6 The rubber perimeter gasket may be glued into the groove in the cover, and is best left there if re-usable. If it is in any way damaged,

7.5a Valve cover bolts (arrowed)

7.5b Lift the cover and manoeuvre it out the front to the right

7.7 Remove each plug hole gasket, and its dowel (arrowed) if loose

8.1 Slacken the clamp (arrowed), detach the hose and secure it to the rear out of the way

8 Cam chain tensioner

Removal

1 Drain the cooling system (see Chapter 1). Slacken the clamp securing the large bore coolant hose to the top of the radiator, detach the hose and secure it clear of the tensioner **(see illustration)**.

2 Unscrew the tensioner cap bolt and remove the sealing washer, the spring and the rod **(see illustrations)**.

3 Unscrew the tensioner mounting bolts and withdraw the tensioner from the engine **(see illustration)**.

4 Remove the O-ring – a new one must be used on installation **(see illustration 8.8)**. Do not attempt to dismantle the tensioner.

Inspection

5 Check that the plunger cannot be pushed into the body **(see illustration)** – if it can, fit a new tensioner.

6 Release the ratchet stopper and check that the plunger moves smoothly in and out of the tensioner **(see illustration)**.

Installation

7 Release the ratchet stopper and push the plunger almost fully into the tensioner body **(see illustration 8.6)**.

8 Make sure the tensioner mating surfaces are clean and dry. Fit a new O-ring into the groove on the tensioner body and smear it with grease **(see illustration)**.

---

deformed or deteriorated, remove it and fit a new one – note that Kawasaki specify to use a new one whatever the apparent condition.

7 Remove the plug hole gaskets, noting how they seat over the dowels that link the air suction system air passages between the valve cover and cylinder head **(see illustration)**. Remove the dowels for safekeeping if they are loose (which is unlikely), taking care not to drop them. Check the condition of the gaskets and replace them with new ones if necessary.

8 If required, remove the air suction system reed valves (see Chapter 4).

Installation

9 If removed, install the air suction system reed valves (see Chapter 4).

10 If removed, fit the air suction system dowels into the valve cover **(see illustration 7.7)**. Fit the plug hole gaskets.

11 If a new valve cover gasket is being fitted, clean all traces of the old glue from the groove in the cover and the sealant from the cut-outs in the cylinder head and clean it and the cylinder head mating surface with solvent. Fit the new gasket into the perimeter groove, using a suitable glue, sealant or grease to hold it in place. Also apply a suitable silicone sealant (ask your dealer) to the cut-outs in the cylinder head.

12 If removed, fit the washers into the cover, using new ones if required, and making sure the metal side faces up. Position the valve cover on the cylinder head, making sure the gaskets stay in place **(see illustration 7.5b)**. Fit the cover bolts and tighten them to the torque setting specified at the beginning of the Chapter **(see illustration 7.5a)**.

13 Install the remaining components in the reverse order of removal.

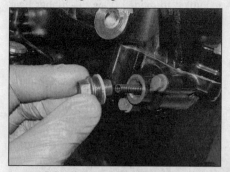

8.2a Unscrew the cap bolt...

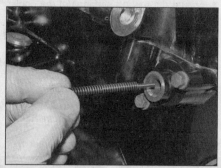

8.2b ...and remove the spring and rod

8.3 Tensioner mounting bolts (arrowed)

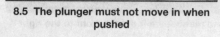

8.5 The plunger must not move in when pushed

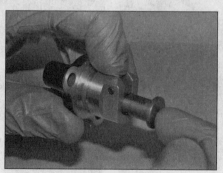

8.6 Release the ratchet and check the action of the plunger

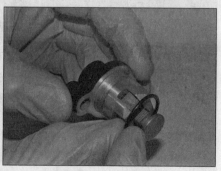

8.8 Fit a new O-ring...

8.9 ...then install the tensioner

9.3a Turn the crankshaft clockwise using the bolt...

9.3b ...until the 1.4 line aligns with the crankcase joint (arrowed)

9 Install the tensioner with the ratchet stopper facing up and tighten the mounting bolts to the torque setting specified at the beginning of the Chapter **(see illustration)**.

10 Fit the sealing washer onto the cap bolt. Fit the rod into the spring, then locate them in the tensioner **(see illustration 8.2b)**. Fit the cap bolt and tighten to the specified torque **(see illustration 8.2a)**. As you thread the cap bolt in the plunger will be pushed out against the tensioner blade.

11 Refer to Section 9, Steps 2 and 3 or 4 and turn the engine clockwise through two full turns to set the tensioner.

12 Connect the coolant hose to the radiator **(see illustration 8.1)**. Refill the cooling system (see Chapter 1).

9 Camshafts and followers

Note: *Place clean rags over the spark plug holes and the cam chain tunnel to prevent any component from dropping into the engine.*

Removal

1 Remove the spark plugs (see Chapter 1). Remove the valve cover (see Section 7).
2 To remove the camshafts the crankshaft must be turned so that the Nos. 1 and 4

pistons are at TDC (top dead centre), with No. 4 on its compression stroke. The crankshaft can be turned using a suitable spanner or a socket on the timing rotor or starter clutch bolt (according to model) and turning it in a clockwise direction only.

3 On C models remove the timing rotor cover (see Section 13). Turn the crankshaft clockwise until the line next to the numbers 1 and 4 marked on the timing rotor points back and aligns with the crankcase mating surfaces, and so that the IN mark on the intake camshaft sprocket points back parallel to the top of the cylinder head, and the EX mark on the exhaust camshaft sprocket points forwards **(see illustrations and 9.4d)**. If the sprocket marks are upside down and facing the other way (i.e.

180° round from the desired position), rotate the engine clockwise one full turn (360°) until the line next to the 1 and 4 again aligns with the crankcase mating surfaces. The sprocket marks will now be facing correctly.

4 On D, E and F models unscrew the crankshaft end cap and timing inspection cap from the starter clutch cover **(see illustration)**. Note that new O-rings should be used. Turn the crankshaft clockwise until the line marked on the starter clutch aligns with the notch in the inspection hole rim, and so that the IN mark on the intake camshaft sprocket points back parallel to the top of the cylinder head, and the EX mark on the exhaust camshaft sprocket points forwards **(see illustrations)**. If the sprocket marks are upside down and

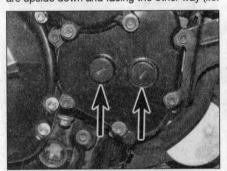

9.4a Unscrew the caps (arrowed)

9.4b Turn the crankshaft clockwise using the bolt...

9.4c ...until the line aligns with the notch (arrowed)...

9.4d ...and the camshaft sprocket marks (circled) are as described

9.7a Unscrew the bolts as described and remove the top guide...

9.7b ...the main holders...

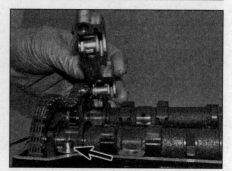

9.7c ...and the end holder, noting the dowels (arrowed)

facing the other way (i.e. 180° round from the desired position), rotate the engine clockwise one full turn (360°) until the line again aligns with the notch. The sprocket marks will now be facing correctly.

5 Remove the cam chain tensioner (see Section 8).

6 The four main camshaft holders are numbered 1 to 4, and there are corresponding numbers marked on the head in the middle, to identify which fits where **(see illustration 9.29)**. If the marks aren't clear make your own as the camshafts and their holders must be installed in their original location.

7 Unscrew the camshaft holder bolts, slackening them evenly and a very little at a time in a **reverse** of the tightening sequence shown **(see illustration 9.29)**. Remove the bolts and top cam chain guide (on the

end holder), then lift off the holders **(see illustrations)**. Note the positions of the locating dowels (2 per holder) – do not remove them unless they are loose and liable to drop out.

Caution: Make sure the holders lift up squarely and evenly and do not stick on a dowel or distort from some of the bolts being slackened more than the others as they or a camshaft could easily break.

8 Hold the cam chain and carefully lift each camshaft off the head **(see illustrations 9.28a and 9.27a)**. Secure the chain using wire or a rod of some sort to prevent it from dropping down the tunnel. The camshafts are marked for identification – the intake camshaft is marked IN and the exhaust camshaft is marked EX **(see illustration)**.

9 While the camshafts are out do not rotate

the crankshaft unless you are holding the chain taut, otherwise it could bind between the crankshaft and case, which could damage these components. Place rag over the spark plug holes and the cam chain tunnel to prevent anything from dropping into the engine.

10 If the followers and shims are being removed from the cylinder head, obtain a container that is divided into sixteen compartments, and label each compartment with the location of a valve, i.e. intake or exhaust camshaft, left or right valve. If a container is not available, use labelled plastic bags (egg cartons also do very well!). Remove the cam follower of the valve in question using a magnet or the suction created by a valve lapping tool, or long nosed pliers can be used with care **(see illustration)**. Remove the shim from inside the follower or pick it out of the top of the valve spring retainer using either a magnet, a screwdriver with a dab of grease on it (the shim will stick to the grease), or a very small screwdriver and a pair of pliers **(see illustrations)**. Do not allow the shim to fall into the engine.

11 The camshaft sprockets are identical and are therefore interchangeable, so mark them according to the camshaft they fit on if you need to remove them from the camshafts. Unscrew the sprocket bolts and remove the sprockets **(see illustration)**.

Inspection

12 Inspect the bearing surfaces of the camshaft holders and cylinder head and the

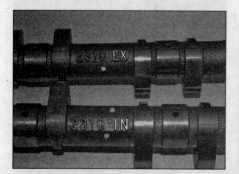

9.8 Note the ID letters on each camshaft

9.10a Carefully lift out the follower using a lapping tool, grips or a magnet...

9.10b ...and retrieve the shim from inside it...

9.10c ...or from the top of the valve

9.11 Sprocket bolts (arrowed)

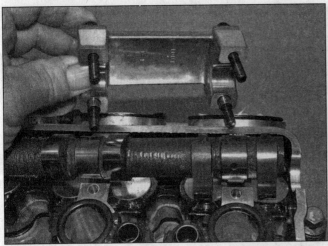

9.12 Check all related bearing surfaces

9.13 Measure the height of the camshaft lobes with a micrometer

corresponding journals on the camshafts **(see illustration)**. Look for score marks, deep scratches and evidence of spalling (a pitted appearance). Check the oil passages for clogging.

13 Check the camshaft lobes for heat discoloration (blue appearance), score marks, chipped areas, flat spots and spalling. Measure the height of each lobe with a micrometer **(see illustration)** and compare the results to the minimum height listed in this Chapter's Specifications. If damage is noted or wear is excessive, the camshaft must be replaced with a new one.

14 Check the amount of camshaft runout by supporting each end on V-blocks, and measuring any runout using a dial gauge. If the runout exceeds the specified limit the camshaft must be replaced with a new one.

 Refer to Tools and Workshop Tips in the Reference section for details of how to read a micrometer and dial gauge.

15 Next, check the camshaft journal oil clearances. In order to negate the probability of the camshafts rotating (due to the fact that some of the lobes will be depressing their valves) as the holder bolts are tightened down, which will disturb the Plastigauge and lead to a false measurement, the cylinder head should be removed and the valves removed from it (see Sections 11 and 12). Clean the camshafts and the bearing surfaces in the cylinder head and camshaft holder with a clean lint-free cloth, then lay each camshaft in its correct location in the head (see Step 8).

16 Cut some strips of Plastigauge and lay one piece on each journal, parallel with the camshaft centreline **(see illustration 24.18)**. Make sure the camshaft holder dowels are installed. If the valves are installed, fit the holders in their correct location (Step 29) and tighten the bolts as described in

Step 29. If the valves have been removed, fit the holders in their correct location (Step 29) and tighten the bolts evenly and a little at a time in a criss-cross sequence to the specified torque setting, making sure the holders are pulled down squarely onto the dowels. While doing this, don't let the camshafts rotate, or the Plastigauge will be disturbed and you will have to start again.

17 Now unscrew the camshaft holder bolts as described in Step 7 (valves installed) or evenly and a little at a time in a criss-cross sequence (valves removed), and lift off the holders.

18 To determine the oil clearance, compare the crushed Plastigauge (at its widest point) on each journal to the scale printed on the Plastigauge container **(see illustration 24.21)**. Compare the results to this Chapter's Specifications. If the oil clearance is greater than specified, measure the diameter of each camshaft journal and compare the results to the minimum listed in this Chapter's Specifications. If wear is excessive replace the camshaft with a new one and recheck the clearance. If the clearance is still too great, also replace the cylinder head and holders with new ones.

 Before replacing the camshafts, cylinder head or holders because of damage, check with motorcycle cylinder head specialists to see whether worn components can be renewed. Due to the cost of new components it is recommended that all options be explored before condemning them as trash!

19 Except in cases of oil starvation, the cam chain should wear very little. If the chain has stretched excessively, which makes it difficult to maintain proper tension, or if it is stiff or the links are binding or kinking, replace it with a new one. Refer to Section 10 for replacement.

20 Check the sprockets for wear, cracks and other damage, and replace them with new ones if necessary (Steps 11 and 23). If the sprockets are worn, the cam chain is also worn, and so probably is the sprocket on the crankshaft. If severe wear is apparent, the entire engine should be disassembled for inspection.

21 Inspect the cam chain guides and tensioner blade (see Section 10).

22 Inspect the outer surface of each cam follower for evidence of scoring or other damage. If a follower is in poor condition, it is probable that the bore in the cylinder head in which it works is also damaged. Check for clearance between each follower and its bore. If any follower or bore is worn, out-of-round or tapered, replace the follower and/or cylinder head with a new one.

Installation

23 If removed, clean the threads of the sprocket bolts. Fit each sprocket onto its camshaft according to the marks made on removal (unless new ones are being fitted), with the timing marks facing out and aligned as shown **(see illustration)**. Apply some fresh threadlock to the bolts and tighten them to the torque setting specified at the beginning of the Chapter.

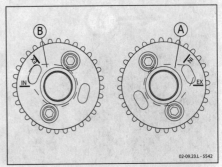

9.23 Camshaft/sprocket alignment – exhaust camshaft (A), intake camshaft (B)

9.27a Seat the exhaust camshaft...

9.27b ...with the EX mark (arrowed) as shown and described

9.28a Seat the intake camshaft...

9.28b ...with the IN mark (arrowed) as shown and described

27 Lay the exhaust camshaft (marked EX) onto the head with the EX mark on the sprocket facing forward and level with the cylinder head top mating surface, fitting the cam chain around the sprocket as you install the camshaft, pulling up on the chain to remove all slack in the front run between the crankshaft and the camshaft **(see illustrations)**.

28 Lay the intake camshaft (marked IN) onto the head with the IN mark on the sprocket facing back and level with the cylinder head top mating surface, fitting the cam chain around the sprocket as you install the camshaft, pulling on it to remove all slack from between the two sprockets **(see illustrations)**. Now count from the 1st pin that is just above the EX mark on the exhaust camshaft and make sure that the 28th pin is just above the IN mark on the intake camshaft sprocket **(see illustration)**. The slack in the chain must lie in the rear run of the chain between the intake camshaft and the crankshaft for the tensioner to take up. Secure the chain to each sprocket using a cable-tie as shown to prevent it jumping while tightening the holder bolts down **(see illustration)**.

29 Make sure the bearing surfaces in the camshaft holders are clean, then apply molybdenum disulphide oil (a 50/50 mixture of molybdenum disulphide grease and engine oil) to each of them. Make sure the camshaft holder dowels are installed. Fit the end holder **(see illustration 9.7c)**. Lay the main holders in their correct location (No. 1 holder front left, No. 2 front right, No. 3 rear left, No. 4 rear right) on the head **(see illustration 9.7b)**. Fit the bolts, not forgetting the top cam chain guide **(see illustration 9.7a)**, and tighten them finger-tight. Now tighten the bolts evenly and a little at a time to bring the holders squarely down onto the head, starting with the bolts that are above valves that will be opened by the camshaft lobes as they are tightened down so as not to create any bend in the camshaft,

24 If removed, lubricate each shim and its follower with molybdenum disulphide oil (a 50/50 mixture of molybdenum disulphide grease and engine oil). Fit each shim into its recess in the top of the valve spring retainer with the size mark facing up, making sure it is correctly seated **(see illustration 9.10c)**. **Note:** *It is most important that the shims and followers are returned to their original valves otherwise the valve clearances will be inaccurate.* Fit each follower, making sure it slides squarely in its bore **(see illustration 9.10a)**.

25 Make sure the bearing surfaces on the camshafts and in the cylinder head are clean, then apply molybdenum disulphide oil (a 50/50 mixture of molybdenum disulphide grease and engine oil) to each of them. Also apply it to the camshaft journals and lobes. Make sure that none gets on the mating surfaces between the holder and the head, or in the bolt holes.

26 Check that the line marked on the timing rotor or starter clutch (according to model) aligns as described in Step 3 or 4 **(see illustration 9.3b or 9.4c)**. If both camshafts have been removed, install the exhaust camshaft first, then the intake.

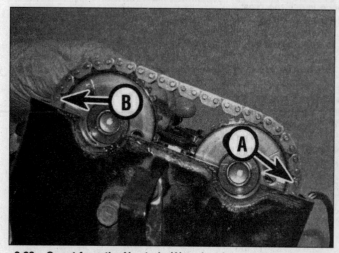

9.28c Count from the No. 1 pin (A) and make sure (B) is the 28th pin

9.28d Secure the chain on each sprocket as shown

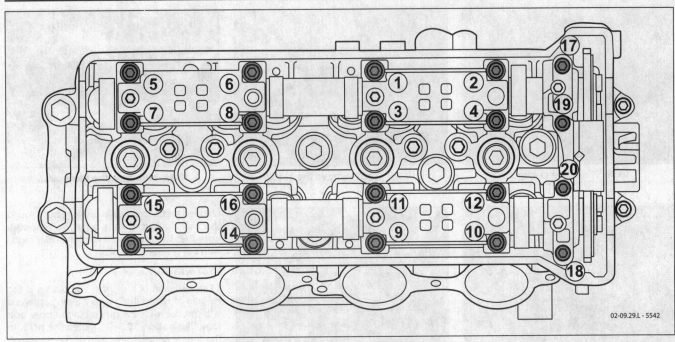

02-09.29.L - 5542

9.29 Camshaft holder bolt TIGHTENING sequence

until the dowels locate and the holders seat. Now tighten them in the numerical sequence shown and in two stages to the torque setting specified at the beginning of the Chapter (set the first stage to half the final torque setting) **(see illustration)**.

Caution: Whilst tightening the bolts, make sure the holders are being pulled evenly and squarely down and are not binding on the dowels or tilting to one side – if they do, adjust the relevant bolts until the holder is again square to the head. The holders or a camshaft is likely to break if the bolts are not tightened down evenly and squarely.

30 Use a piece of wooden dowel to press on the back of the cam chain tensioner blade via the tensioner bore to ensure that any slack in the cam chain is taken up and transferred to the rear run of the chain. At this point check that all the timing marks are still in **exact** alignment as described in Steps 3 or 4 and 27 and 28. Note that it is easy to be slightly out (one tooth on the sprocket) without the marks appearing drastically out of alignment. If the

marks are out, repeat the installation procedure and check the marks again, following correct bolt slackening and tightening procedures.

Caution: If the marks are not aligned exactly as described, the valve timing will be incorrect and the valves may strike the pistons, causing extensive damage to the engine.

31 Install the cam chain tensioner (see Section 8).

32 Turn the engine clockwise through two full turns and check again that all the timing marks still align (see Step 3 or 4).

33 Check the valve clearances and adjust them if necessary (see Chapter 1).

34 Install the valve cover (see Section 7). Install the spark plugs (see Chapter 1).

35 On C models install the timing rotor cover (see Section 13).

36 On D, E and F models fit the crankshaft end cap and timing inspection cap using new O-rings smeared with grease **(see illustration)**.

<table>
<tr><td>

10 Cam chain, tensioner blade and front guide blade

</td></tr>
</table>

Removal

Tensioner and guide blades

1 Remove the camshafts – this procedure involves removing the top guide (see Section 9).

2 On C models remove the timing rotor (Section 13). On D, E and F models remove the starter clutch (Section 14). On all models remove the crankshaft position (CKP) sensor (see Chapter 4).

3 Unscrew the front guide blade bolts, noting the washer and sleeve with the lower bolt on C models and the collar on D, E and F models, and the O-ring with the upper bolt, and draw the blade out of the top of the engine **(see illustrations)**. Discard the O-ring as a new one must be used.

9.36 Fit the caps

10.3a Unscrew the bolts (arrowed)...

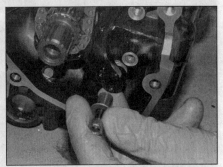

10.3b ...noting the washer/sleeve or collar...

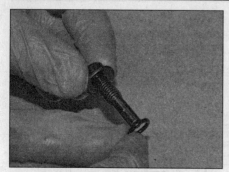

10.3c ...and the O-ring...

10.3d ...and remove the blade

10.4a Withdraw the pivot pin...

10.4b ...and remove the blade

10.6 Slide the sprocket (arrowed) along and remove the chain

chipped teeth. Damage is unlikely, but if found the camshaft sprockets must be renewed; note that the crankshaft sprocket is integral with the crankshaft itself.

Installation

11 Installation of the chain and blades is the reverse of removal. Fit a new O-ring smeared with grease with the guide blade upper bolt **(see illustration 10.3c)**. Tighten the bolts to the torque settings specified at the beginning of the Chapter.

11 Cylinder head removal and installation

Removal

1 Drain the cooling system (see Chapter 1). Remove the throttle bodies and the exhaust downpipe assembly (see Chapter 4).
2 Detach the coolant hoses from the thermostat housing **(see illustration)**. Disconnect the coolant temperature (ECT) sensor wiring connector **(see illustration 4.17c)**.
3 Refer to Section 4, Steps 20 to 22 and 25, and remove the fairing brackets and the front engine mounting brackets and bolts.
4 Remove the camshafts, followers and shims (see Section 9).

4 Withdraw the tensioner blade pivot and draw the blade out of the top of the engine **(see illustrations)**.

Cam chain – C models

5 Remove the front guide blade (Steps 1 to 3).
6 Slide the sprocket along the crankshaft until the chain is clear of the wall, then remove the chain, and if required the sprocket **(see illustration)**.

Cam chain – D, E and F models

7 Remove the engine (Section 4). Remove the front guide blade (Steps 1 to 3). Separate the crankcase halves (Section 21).

8 Slip the cam chain off the crankshaft sprocket **(see illustration)**.

Inspection

Tensioner and guide blades

9 Check the sliding surface and edges of the blades for excessive wear, deep grooves, cracking and other obvious damage, and replace them with new ones if necessary.

Cam chain

10 Check the chain for binding, kinks and any obvious damage and replace it with a new one if necessary. Check the camshaft and crankshaft sprocket teeth for wear and

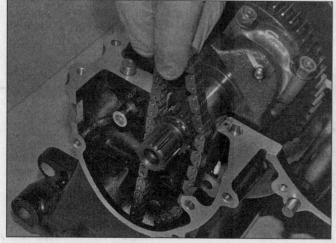

10.8 Remove the chain from the crankshaft

11.2 Release the clamps (arrowed) and detach the hoses

11.6a Cylinder head 6mm bolts (arrowed)

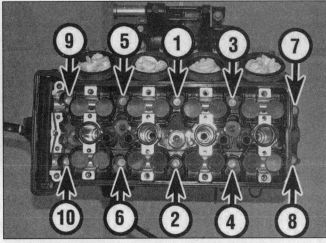

11.6b Cylinder head 10mm bolt TIGHTENING sequence

5 Remove the cam chain front guide blade (see Section 10). Displace the camshaft position (CMP) sensor (see Chapter 4).
6 The cylinder head is secured by two 6 mm bolts, and ten 10 mm bolts with washers. First unscrew and remove the 6 mm bolts **(see illustration)**. Now unscrew the 10 mm bolts, slackening them evenly and a little at a time in a **reverse** of the tightening sequence shown (i.e. working from the outside to the middle) until they are all loose **(see illustration)**. Remove the bolts with their washers, along with the bracket secured by the outer bolts on the left-hand end **(see illustrations 11.17a and b)**.
7 Let the cam chain drop into the tunnel. Lift the cylinder head up off the block **(see illustration)**. If it is stuck, tap around the joint faces with a soft-faced mallet. Do not attempt to free the head by inserting a screwdriver between the head and block mating surfaces – you'll damage them.
8 Remove the cylinder head gasket and discard it – a new one must be used **(see illustration 11.15)**. If they are loose, remove the dowels from the cylinder block or the underside of the cylinder head.
9 If required remove the intake ducts from the head – they come as two pairs, each secured by three bolts **(see illustration)**. On each pair loosen the right-hand bolt first, then the left, then the middle. Remove the O-rings – new ones must be used. Also remove the bracket from the right-hand end of the head if required, noting the wiring clamp secured with the top bolt **(see illustration)**.
10 Check the cylinder head gasket and the mating surfaces on the cylinder head and block for signs of leakage, which could indicate warpage. Refer to Section 12 and check the cylinder head gasket surface for warpage.
11 Clean all traces of old gasket material from the cylinder head and block. If a scraper is used, take care not to scratch or gouge the soft aluminium. Be careful not to let any of the gasket material fall into the cylinder bores or the oil and coolant passages.

Installation

12 If removed clean the threads of the engine bracket bolts and apply some fresh threadlock. Fit the bracket and tighten the bolts to the torque setting specified at the beginning of the Chapter, aligning the wiring clamp sides with the line of the front two bolts **(see illustration 11.9b)**.
13 If removed fit the intake ducts using new O-rings smeared with grease and tighten the bolts to the torque setting specified at the beginning of the Chapter – on each pair tighten the middle bolt first, then the left, then the right **(see illustration 11.9a)**.
14 Make sure both cylinder head and crankcase mating surfaces are clean. If removed, fit the dowels into the cylinder block **(see illustration 11.15)**.
15 Lay the new head gasket onto the block, locating it over the dowels and making sure all the holes are correctly aligned **(see illustration)**. Never reuse the old gasket.
16 Carefully fit the cylinder head onto the block, making sure it locates correctly onto the dowels **(see illustration 11.7)**. Hook the

11.7 Carefully lift the head up off the block

11.9a Intake duct bolts (arrowed)

11.9b Remove the bracket (arrowed) if required

11.15 Fit the dowels (arrowed) then lay the new gasket on the block

11.17a Make sure the washers are fitted on all 10mm bolts

11.17b Fit the bracket with the outer bolts, making sure the boss (arrowed) is positioned as shown

There is a quick way of removing valve components that avoids having to use a spring compressor: select a socket that seats on the valve retainer and give it a sharp tap with a soft hammer – this compresses the spring without moving the valve itself and unseats the collets. Note that a valve spring compressor has to be used when refitting the valve assembly.

cam chain up through the tunnel, then secure it in place with a piece of wire to prevent it from falling back down.

17 Apply some molybdenum disulphide oil (a 50/50 mixture of molybdenum disulphide grease and engine oil) to both sides of the washers on the 10 mm bolts **(see illustration)**. Install the 10 mm bolts, not forgetting the bracket on the left-hand end and fitting it with the raised boss at the front and facing out **(see illustration)**. Tighten them all finger-tight at first. Now tighten them following the numerical sequence, first to the initial torque setting specified at the beginning of the Chapter, then to the final torque setting specified, noting the different settings for new and used bolts **(see illustration 11.6b)**.

18 Fit the 6 mm bolts and tighten to the specified torque **(see illustration 11.6a)**.

19 Install the remaining components in a reverse of the removal sequence, referring to the relevant Sections or Chapters (see Steps 1 to 5).

12 Cylinder head and valve overhaul

1 Because of the complex nature of this job and the special tools and equipment required, most owners leave servicing of the valves, valve seats and valve guides to a professional. However, you can make an initial assessment of whether the valves are seating correctly, and therefore sealing, by pouring a small amount of solvent into each of the valve ports. If the solvent leaks past any valve into the combustion chamber area the valve is not seating correctly and sealing.

2 With the correct tools (a valve spring compressor is essential – make sure it is suitable for motorcycle work), you can also remove the valves and associated components from the cylinder head, clean them and check them for wear to assess the extent of the work needed, and, unless seat cutting or guide replacement is required, grind in the valves and reassemble them in the head.

3 A dealer service department or specialist can replace the guides and re-cut the valve seats. Make sure that anyone working on the valves knows that the exhaust valves on C and D models, and all the valves on E and F models, have a thin oxide coating that will be damaged if they are lapped – it is ok to lap the intake valves on C and D models.

4 After the valve service has been performed,

be sure to clean the head thoroughly before installation to remove any metal particles or abrasive grit that may still be present from the valve service operations. Use compressed air, if available, to blow out all the holes and passages.

Disassembly

5 Before proceeding, arrange to label and store the valves along with their related components in such a way that they can be returned to their original locations without getting mixed up **(see illustration)**. Either use the same container as the cam followers and shims are stored in (see Section 9), or obtain a separate container and label each compartment accordingly. Alternatively, labelled plastic bags will do just as well.

6 Compress the valve spring on the first valve with a spring compressor, making sure it is correctly located onto each end of the valve assembly **(see illustration)**. On the top of the valve the adaptor needs to be about the same size as the spring retainer – if it is too big it will contact the follower bore and mark it, and if it is too small it will be difficult to remove and install the collets **(see illustration)**. On the

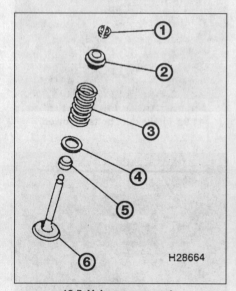

12.5 Valve components

1 Collets
2 Spring retainer
3 Spring
4 Spring seat
5 Valve stem oil seal
6 Valve

H28664

12.6a Compressing the valve springs using a valve spring compressor

12.6b Make sure the compressor locates correctly both on the top of the spring retainer...

12.6c ...and on the bottom of the valve

underside of the head make sure the tip only contacts the valve and not the soft aluminium of the head **(see illustration)**. Do not compress the springs more than is necessary to release the collets.

Caution: Take great care not to mark the cam follower bore with the spring compressor.

7 Remove the collets, using a magnet or a screwdriver with a dab of grease on it **(see illustration)**. Carefully release the valve spring compressor and remove the spring retainer, noting which way up it fits, the spring and the valve **(see illustrations)**. If the valve binds in the guide and won't pull through, push it back into the head and deburr the area around the collet groove with a very fine file or whetstone **(see illustration)**.

8 Pull the valve stem seal off the top of the valve guide with pliers and discard it (the

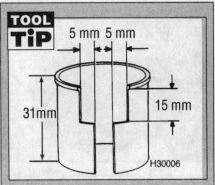

Protect the follower bore in the cylinder head from scratches by the valve spring compressor by fabricating a shield from an old 35 mm film canister cut as shown.

old seals should never be re-used), then remove the spring seat noting which way up, it fits – using a magnet is the easiest way to remove the seat from the head **(see illustrations)**.

9 Repeat the procedure for the remaining valves. Remember to keep the parts for each valve together so they can be reinstalled in the same location.

10 Clean the cylinder head with solvent and dry it thoroughly. Compressed air will speed the drying process and ensure that all holes and recessed areas are clean. **Note:** *Do not use a wire brush mounted in a drill motor to clean the combustion chambers as the head*

material is soft and may be scratched or eroded away by the wire brush.

11 Clean all of the valve springs, collets, retainers and spring seats with solvent and dry them thoroughly. Do the parts from one valve at a time so that no mixing of parts between valves occurs.

12 Scrape off any deposits that may have formed on the valve, then use a motorised wire brush to remove deposits from the valve heads and stems. Again, make sure the valves do not get mixed up.

Inspection

13 Inspect the head very carefully for cracks and other damage. If cracks are found, a new head is required. Check the camshaft bearing surfaces for wear and evidence of seizure. Check the camshafts and holders for wear as well (see Section 9).

14 Using a precision straight-edge and a feeler gauge set to the warpage limit listed in the specifications at the beginning of the Chapter, check the head gasket mating surface for warpage. Refer to *Tools and Workshop Tips* in the Reference section for details of how to use the straight-edge. If the head is warped beyond the limit specified at the beginning of this Chapter, consult a Kawasaki dealer or take it to a specialist repair shop for an opinion, though be prepared to have to buy a new one.

15 Examine the valve seats in the combustion chamber. If they are pitted, cracked or burned, the head will require work beyond the scope of the home mechanic. Measure

12.7a Remove the collets...

12.7b ...the spring retainer and spring...

12.7c ...and the valve

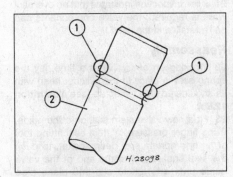

12.7d If the valve stem (2) won't pull through the guide, deburr the area (1) above the collet groove

12.8a Pull the seal off the valve stem...

12.8b ...then remove the spring seat

12.15a Measure the valve seat outer diameter...

12.15b ...and the seat width

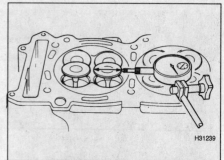

12.16a Measure the amount of wobble using a dial gauge

12.16b Measure the valve stem diameter with a micrometer

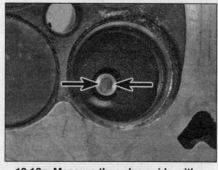

12.16c Measure the valve guide with a small bore gauge, then measure the bore gauge with a micrometer

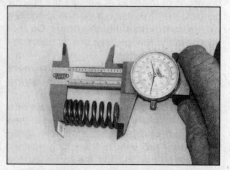

12.19 Measure the free length of each valve spring and check for bend

the outer diameter of the seating surface and compare it to this Chapter's specifications **(see illustration)**. Also measure the seat width on each valve and compare it to the Specifications **(see illustration)**. If either exceeds the service limit, or if it varies around its circumference, overhaul is required.

16 Working on one valve and guide at a time clean the guide using a reamer to remove any carbon build-up – insert the reamer from the underside of the head and turn it clockwise only. Flush and clean the guide with solvent after reaming. Fit each valve in its guide in turn so that its face is clear of the seat but as close to the head mating surface as possible. Mount a dial gauge against the side of the valve stem as close to the cylinder head as possible and measure the amount of side clearance (wobble) between the valve stem and its guide in two

perpendicular directions **(see illustration)**. If the side clearance exceeds the limit specified, remove the valve and measure the valve stem diameter **(see illustration)**. Also measure the inside diameter of the guide with a small hole gauge and micrometer, if available **(see illustration)**. Measure the guides at each end and at the centre to determine if they are worn unevenly. Replace any component that is worn beyond its specifications with a new one. If the valve guide is within specifications, but is worn unevenly, it should be replaced. Repeat for the other valves.

17 Carefully inspect each valve face, stem and collet groove area for cracks, pits and burned spots.

18 Rotate the valve and check for any obvious indication that it is bent, in which case it must be replaced with a new one. Check the end

of the stem for pitting and excessive wear. The presence of any of the above conditions indicates the need for valve servicing.

19 Check the end of each valve spring for wear and pitting. Measure the spring free length and compare it to the specifications **(see illustration)**. If any spring is shorter than specified it has sagged and must be replaced with a new one. Also place the spring upright on a flat surface and check it for bend by placing a ruler against it, or alternatively lay it against a setsquare. If the bend in any spring is excessive, it must be replaced with a new one.

20 Check the spring seats, retainers and collets for obvious wear and cracks. Any questionable parts should not be re-used, as extensive damage will occur in the event of failure during engine operation.

21 If the inspection indicates that no overhaul work is required, the valve components can be reinstalled in the head.

Reassembly

22 Working on one valve at a time, lay the spring seat in place in the cylinder head with its shouldered side facing up **(see illustration 12.8b)**.

23 Fit a new valve stem seal onto the guide, using finger pressure, a stem seal fitting tool or an appropriate size deep socket, to push the seal squarely onto the end of the valve guide until it is felt to clip into place **(see illustrations)**. Make sure the seal does not get cocked sideways as it could be damaged – using a rod as a guide as for the seat helps.

12.23a Fit a new valve stem seal...

12.23b ... and press it squarely into place

12.24 Lubricate the stem and slide the valve into its correct location

12.25a Fit the spring...

12.25b ...then fit the spring retainer

24 Coat the valve stem with molybdenum disulphide oil (a 50/50 mixture of molybdenum disulphide grease and engine oil), then slide it into its guide, rotating it slowly to avoid damaging the seal **(see illustration)**. Check that the valve moves up-and-down freely in the guide.

25 Next, fit the spring, with the closer-wound coils facing down into the cylinder head **(see illustration)**. Note that the intake valve springs are colour-coded green on C and D models, and blue on E and F models, and the exhaust valve springs are coded purple on all models, so they cannot be mixed up. Fit the spring retainer, with its shouldered side facing down so that it fits into the top of the spring **(see illustration)**.

26 Apply a small amount of grease to the collets to help hold them in place. Compress the valve spring with a spring compressor, making sure it is correctly located onto each end of the valve assembly (see Step 6) **(see illustrations 12.6a, b and c)**. Do not compress the spring any more than is necessary to slip the collets into place. Locate each collet in turn into the groove in the valve stem using a screwdriver with a dab of grease on it **(see illustration)**. Carefully release the compressor, making sure the collets seat and lock in the retaining groove.

27 Repeat the procedure for the remaining valves. Remember to keep the parts for each valve together and separate from the other valves so they can be reinstalled in the same location.

28 Support the cylinder head on blocks so

12.26 Locate each collet in its groove in the top of the valve stem

the valves can't contact the work surface, then tap the top of each valve stem lightly using a punch to seat the collets in their grooves **(see illustration)**.

29 After the cylinder head and camshafts have been installed, check the valve clearances and adjust as required (see Chapter 1).

13 Timing rotor – C models

Removal

1 Unscrew the timing rotor cover bolts, noting the routing of the wiring and the position of the clamps, and remove the cover **(see illustration)**. Note that a new O-ring must be used.

12.28 Tap the top of the valve (arrowed) to seat the collets

2 Counter-hold the rotor using a pegged holding tool in the holes and unscrew the bolt **(see illustration)** – if no suitable tool is available, engage 6th gear and hold the rear brake on, or remove the starter clutch cover and counter-hold the starter clutch bolt (see Section 14).

3 Remove the rotor from the end of the crankshaft, noting how it locates.

Installation

4 Fit the rotor onto the end of the crankshaft, aligning the wide splines, and fit the bolt **(see illustration)**.

5 Counter-hold the rotor as on removal and tighten the bolt to the torque setting specified at the beginning of the Chapter.

6 Remove all traces of old sealant from the timing rotor cover, crankcase and wiring

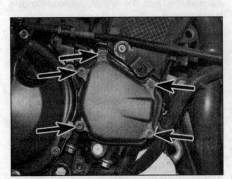

13.1 Timing rotor cover bolts (arrowed)

13.2 Timing rotor bolt (arrowed)

13.4 Align the wide splines and slide the rotor onto the shaft

13.6 Smear some sealant onto the grommet and the joints (arrowed)

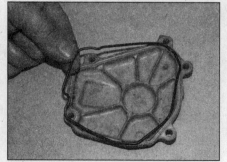

13.7a Fit a new O-ring into the groove…

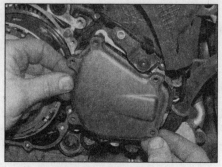

13.7b …and fit the cover

grommet. Apply a smear of a suitable silicone sealant (ask your dealer) to the grommet and the crankcase joints **(see illustration)**.

7 Clean the threads of the timing rotor cover bolts and apply some threadlock. Fit the cover using a new O-ring smeared with grease, and tighten bolts **(see illustrations)**.

14 Starter clutch and gears

C models

Removal

1 Remove the left-hand lower fairing panel and fairing side panel (see Chapter 7). Either drain the engine oil (see Chapter 1), or place a container suitable for catching some oil under

14.2 Idle gear cover bolts (arrowed)

14.4 Starter clutch cover bolts (arrowed)

the starter clutch cover – having the bike upright on an auxiliary stand will minimise oil loss.

2 Unscrew the idle gear cover bolts and remove the damper, then remove the cover **(see illustration)**. Note the dowel and remove it if loose. Remove the gasket.

3 Withdraw the idle gear shaft with its spacer and remove the gear **(see illustration)**.

4 Unscrew the starter clutch cover bolts and remove the clamps, then remove the cover **(see illustration)**. Remove the gasket. Note the dowels and remove them if loose.

5 The starter clutch bolt has left-hand threads, and so must be undone by turning it clockwise. Counter-hold the starter clutch using a pegged holding tool in the holes or a rotor strap around it, and unscrew the bolt **(see illustration)**.

6 Slide the starter clutch, driven gear, needle bearing and collar off the shaft.

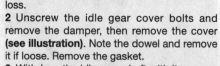

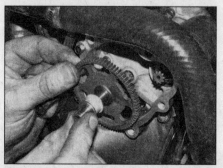

14.3 Remove the shaft with its spacer and the gear

14.5 Starter clutch bolt (arrowed)

Inspection

7 With the starter clutch face down on a workbench, check that the starter driven gear rotates freely anti-clockwise and locks against the rotor clockwise **(see illustration 14.27)**. If it doesn't, the starter clutch should be dismantled for further investigation.

8 Withdraw the collar and needle bearing if not already removed, then turn the starter driven gear anti-clockwise and withdraw it from the starter clutch.

9 Check the condition of the sprags inside the clutch body and the external surface on the driven gear hub – if they are damaged, marked or flattened at any point, the sprag assembly and/or driven gear must be replaced with a new one. To remove the sprag assembly, release the retaining circlip holding it and remove it from the housing **(see illustrations 14.29a and b)**. Fit the new assembly with the fitted circlip facing in **(see illustrations 14.29c and d)**. Secure the sprag assembly with the retaining circlip. Apply clean engine oil to the sprags.

10 Check the needle roller bearing and the bearing surfaces on the collar and the driven gear. If the bearing surfaces show signs of excessive wear or the bearing itself is worn or damaged, they should be replaced with new ones.

11 Check the teeth on the starter motor drive shaft, the idle gear and the starter driven gear. Replace the gears and/or starter motor if worn or chipped teeth are discovered on related gears. Also check the idle gear shaft for damage, and check that the gear is not a loose fit on it.

Installation

12 Remove all of the old gasket and sealant from the starter clutch cover, the idle gear cover and the crankcase.

13 Lubricate the outside of the starter driven gear hub with molybdenum disulphide oil (a 50/50 mixture of molybdenum disulphide grease and engine oil), then fit the gear into the clutch, rotating it anti-clockwise as you do so to spread the sprags and allow the hub to enter. Lubricate the needle roller bearing with molybdenum disulphide oil and fit it into the driven gear, then lubricate and fit the collar.

14 Slide the starter clutch onto the crankshaft,

14.15 Fit a new gasket onto the dowels (arrowed)...

14.15b ...then fit the cover

14.17 Fit a new gasket onto the dowel (arrowed)

engaging the splines. Thread the bolt in, turning it anti-clockwise, then counter-hold the starter clutch and tighten the bolt to the torque setting specified at the beginning of the Chapter.

15 Smear a suitable silicone sealant (ask your dealer) onto the crankcase joints. Fit the starter clutch cover dowels into the crankcase if removed. Fit a new gasket, locating it over the dowels **(see illustration)**. Fit the cover, the bolts and the guide and wiring clamps, and tighten the bolts evenly in a criss-cross pattern to the specified torque setting **(see illustration)**.

16 Lubricate the idle gear shaft with molybdenum disulphide oil then fit the gear, shaft and spacer **(see illustration 14.3)**.

17 Fit the idle gear cover dowel if removed. Fit a new gasket, locating it over the dowel **(see illustration)**. Fit the cover and secure it with the upper bolts, tightening them finger-tight only, then fit the damper and the remaining bolts, and tighten all the bolts evenly in a criss-cross pattern to the specified torque setting **(see illustration 14.2)**.

18 Replenish the engine oil as required (see Chapter 1). Install the fairing panels (see Chapter 7).

D, E and F models

Removal

19 On D models remove the right-hand

lower fairing panel and fairing side panel (see Chapter 7). On E models remove the right-hand lower fairing panel, and either remove the fairing side cover, or if preferred for best access and to reduce the possibility of damage, remove the fairing assembly (see Chapter 7). On F models remove the right-hand lower fairing panel, and for best access and to reduce the possibility of damage remove the fairing assembly (see Chapter 7).

20 On D models detach the clutch cable from the release arm (see Section 16).

21 Unscrew the upper idle gear cover bolts and remove the cover **(see illustration)**. Note the dowel and remove it if loose. Remove the gasket. The sealing washer on the lower

front bolt must be replaced with a new one on installation.

22 Remove the upper idle gear and its shaft **(see illustrations 14.37b and a)**.

23 Unscrew the starter clutch cover bolts, and on E and F models remove the bracket, then remove the cover **(see illustration)**. Note the dowel(s) and remove if loose. Remove the gasket.

24 Remove the lower idle gear and its shaft **(see illustrations 14.35b and a)**.

25 Remove the alternator cover (see Chapter 8). Counter-hold the alternator rotor using a suitable holding tool, then unscrew the starter clutch bolt and remove the washer **(see illustrations)**.

14.21 Upper idle gear cover bolts (arrowed)

14.23 Starter clutch cover bolts (arrowed)

14.25a Counter-hold the alternator rotor bolt...

14.25b ...and unscrew the starter clutch bolt

14.27 Check the operation of the starter clutch as described

14.28a Withdraw the driven gear...

14.28b ...and remove the bearing

26 Slide the starter clutch assembly off the shaft **(see illustration 14.34a)**.

Inspection

27 With the starter clutch on a workbench, check that the starter driven gear rotates freely anti-clockwise and locks against the rotor clockwise **(see illustration)**. If it doesn't, the starter clutch should be dismantled for further investigation.

28 Turn the starter driven gear anti-clockwise and withdraw it from the starter clutch **(see illustrations)**. Remove the needle bearing.

29 Check the condition of the sprags inside

the clutch body and the external surface on the driven gear hub – if they are damaged, marked or flattened at any point, the sprag assembly and/or driven gear must be replaced with a new one. To remove the sprag assembly release the retaining circlip that holds it and remove it from the housing **(see illustrations)**. Fit the new assembly with the fitted circlip facing in and push it all the way in so the retaining circlip groove is exposed **(see illustrations)**. Secure the sprag assembly with the retaining circlip **(see illustration)**. Apply clean engine oil to the sprags.

30 Check the needle roller bearing and the bearing surfaces on the starter clutch hub and the driven gear **(see illustration 14.28b)**. If the bearing surfaces show signs of excessive wear or the bearing itself is worn or damaged, they should be replaced with new ones.

31 Check the teeth on the starter motor drive shaft, the idle gears and the starter driven gear. Replace the gears and/or starter motor if worn or chipped teeth are discovered on related gears. Also check the idle gear shafts for damage, and check that the gears are not a loose fit on them.

14.29a Remove the circlip...

14.29b ...and remove the sprag assembly

14.29c Fit the assembly with the fitted circlip facing into the housing...

14.29d ...and push it all the way in...

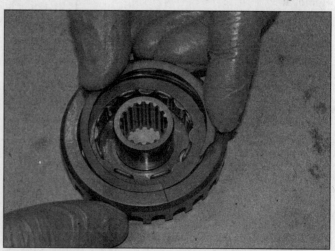

14.29e ...and secure it with the retaining circlip

14.34a Align the wide splines and slide the starter clutch on...

14.34b ...then fit the bolt with its washer

14.35a Seat the shaft pin in the cut-out...

Installation

32 Remove all of the old gasket and sealant from the starter clutch cover, the upper idle gear cover, the CKP sensor wiring grommet and the crankcase.

33 Lubricate the needle roller bearing with molybdenum disulphide oil (a 50/50 mixture of molybdenum disulphide grease and engine oil), and fit it into the clutch **(see illustration 14.28b)**. Lubricate the starter driven gear hub with molybdenum disulphide oil, then fit the gear into the clutch, rotating it anti-clockwise as you do so to spread the sprags and allow the hub to enter **(see illustration 14.28a)**.

34 Slide the starter clutch onto the crankshaft, aligning the wide splines **(see illustration)**. Thread the bolt in with its washer **(see illustration)**. Counter-hold the alternator rotor and tighten the bolt to the torque setting specified at the beginning of the Chapter **(see illustrations 14.25a and b)**.

35 Lubricate the lower idle gear shaft with molybdenum disulphide oil. Fit the shaft, locating the pin in the cut-out **(see illustration)**. Slide the gear onto the shaft **(see illustration)**.

36 Smear a suitable silicone sealant (ask your dealer) onto the crankcase joints and the CKP sensor grommet. Fit the starter clutch cover dowel(s) into the crankcase if removed. Fit a new gasket, locating it over the dowels **(see illustration)**. Fit the cover, the bolts (shorter ones top and bottom), and on E and F models the bracket, and tighten the bolts evenly in

14.35b ...and slide the gear on

14.36a Fit a new gasket onto the dowels (arrowed)

14.36b Fit the cover...

14.36c ...with the shorter bolts top and bottom...

a criss-cross pattern to the specified torque setting **(see illustrations)**.

37 Lubricate the upper idle gear shaft with molybdenum disulphide oil. Fit the shaft, locating the pin in the cut-out **(see illustration)**. Slide the gear onto the shaft **(see illustration)**.

14.36d ...and where fitted do not forget the bracket

14.37a Seat the shaft pin in the cut-out...

14.37b ...and slide the gear on

14.38a Fit a new gasket onto the dowel (arrowed)

14.38b Fit the cover...

14.38c ...with a new sealing washer on the bottom front bolt

38 Fit the upper idle gear cover dowel if removed. Fit a new gasket, locating it over the dowel **(see illustration)**. Fit the cover and the bolts, using a new sealing washer on the lower front bolt, then tighten them evenly in a criss-cross pattern to the specified torque setting **(see illustrations)**.
39 On D models connect the clutch cable to the release arm (see Section 16).
40 Install the fairing panels (see Chapter 7).

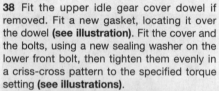

15 Clutch

Note 1: *The clutch nut must be discarded and a new one used on installation – it is best to obtain the new nut in advance.*
Note 2: *On C models the crankcases, crankshaft, clutch housing and alternator driven gear are all matched on assembly according to various code markings. If any of the above parts are replaced with new ones the new parts must carry the same marks as those being replaced to ensure correct matching. Refer to your Kawasaki parts dealer for details.*
Special tool: *A clutch centre holding tool will be required for this procedure (see Step 6).*

Removal

1 Remove the right-hand lower fairing panel

(see Chapter 7). Drain the engine oil (see Chapter 1).
2 Detach the clutch cable from the release arm (see Section 16).
3 Unscrew the clutch cover bolts evenly in a criss-cross pattern, noting which fits where as on C, E and F models there are different lengths, and also a cable holder **(see illustration)**. Remove the cover, turning the release lever arm back (anti-clockwise) as you do to disengage the shaft from the pull-rod. Be prepared to catch any residual oil. Remove the gasket. Remove the two dowels from either the cover or the crankcase if they are loose.
4 Hold the clutch and gradually slacken

15.3 Unscrew the bolts (arrowed) and remove the cover

the spring bolts in a criss-cross pattern until pressure is released **(see illustration)**. Remove the bolts, spring seats and springs. Remove the pressure plate and the pull-rod **(see illustration)**.
5 Remove the clutch friction and plain plates, hooking them as necessary, noting how they fit and keeping them in order **(see illustration)**. Note how the tabs on the outer friction plate locate in the shallow slots in the housing, while the rest sit in the deep slots. Make sure you keep the plates as a pack in the correct order. On D, E and F models remove the anti-judder spring and spring seat, noting which way round they fit, then remove the plates behind them **(see illustrations 15.26e, d, c and b)**.

15.4a Unscrew the bolts (arrowed) and remove the spring seats and springs...

15.4b ...then remove the pressure plate and the pull-rod (arrowed)

15.5 Remove the clutch plates

15.6 Commercial holding tool shown

15.9 Ease the guide and bearing out then remove the housing

6 To remove the clutch nut, the clutch centre/input shaft must be locked to prevent them turning. This can be done in two ways. If the engine is in the frame, engage 6th gear and hold the rear brake on hard with the rear tyre in firm contact with the ground. Alternatively, the Kawasaki service tool (Pt. No. 57001-1243) or a similar commercially available tool can be used to stop the clutch centre from turning whilst the nut is slackened (see illustration). *Caution: The clutch nut can be extremely tight. On the model photographed it was necessary to lock the rear wheel by fitting a piece of 4 x 2 inch wood through the rear wheel to lock it against the swingarm as the rear brake and holding tool were not sufficient. The clutch nut was then heated using a hot air gun, and a very long extension bar used to provide additional leverage.*

7 With the clutch locked unscrew the nut – a new one must be used on installation. Remove the torque limiter springs, keeping them in order and orientation as there are two different types fitted in different ways (see illustration 15.25b).

8 Remove the clutch centre, the clutch hub and the outer thrust washer from the shaft (see illustrations 15.24d, b and a).

9 Ease out the clutch guide and needle bearing from between the clutch housing and the input shaft – this can be done using a magnet, or more easily by threading a 4 mm bolt into one of the holes in the guide and using it to pull the guide out (see illustration). Remove the clutch housing. Remove the inner spacer (see illustration 15.22).

Inspection

10 After an extended period of service the clutch friction plates will wear and promote clutch slip. Measure the thickness of each friction plate using a Vernier caliper (see illustration). If any plate has worn to or beyond the service limits given in the Specifications at the beginning of the Chapter, or if any of the plates smell burnt or are glazed, the friction plates must be replaced with a new set.

11 The plain plates should not show any signs of excess heating (bluing). Check for

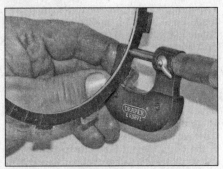

15.10 Measuring clutch friction plate thickness

15.11 Check the plain plates for warpage

warpage using a flat surface and feeler gauges (see illustration). If any plate exceeds the maximum permissible amount of warpage, or shows signs of bluing, all plain plates must be replaced with a new set.

12 If the back-torque limiter mechanism function is thought to be not working properly, for example there is too much back-torque causing rear wheel hop, or if the clutch lever feels spongy or pulsates when pulled in, the amount of pressure plate freeplay must be checked. To do this it is necessary to remove and strip the transmission input shaft, or obtain a spare from somewhere, and clamp it upright in a padded vice, then assemble the clutch on it, leaving out the torque limiter springs, the clutch nut, the springs, spring

seats and bolts. Mount a dial gauge on the top of the inner rim of the outer pressure plate. Turn the clutch housing back and forth and measure the amount of movement between the high and low points – this is the amount of freeplay (see illustration). If it is not within the usable range specified for your model, replace the friction plates with new ones, then recheck the freeplay. If it is still not as specified, adjust it as described in the following Step using different thickness plain plates.

13 Assemble the clutch hub, clutch centre, on D, E and F models the anti-judder spring seat and spring, and the complete set of friction and plain plates (using new plates if new ones are needed) in the clutch centre, then fit the pressure plate (making sure

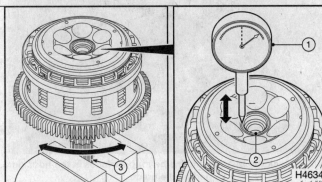

15.12 Pressure plate freeplay check set-up

1 Dial gauge
2 Inner rim of pressure plate
3 Input shaft held between padded jaws of vice

H46346

15.15a Check the friction plate tabs and housing slots...

15.15b ...and the plain plate teeth and centre slots as described

15.16 Check the back-torque limiter dogs on the bottom of the clutch centre and their slots in the hub

it locates correctly), the springs, spring seats and bolts and tighten the bolts to the torque setting specified at the beginning of the Chapter. Measure the thickness of the complete plate pack (from the underside of the innermost friction plate tab to the outside of the outermost friction plate tab, excluding the clutch hub and pressure plate) using a Vernier caliper. If the thickness is less than the service limit given in the Specifications at the beginning of the Chapter, calculate by how much it is out of specification and replace one or more of the outer plain plates with thinner or thicker ones as required to restore the assembled pack thickness. The standard plain plates fitted are 2.6 mm thick on C models, and 2.9 mm on D, E and F models. Replacements are available in 2.3 and 2.9 mm on C models, and 2.3 and 2.6 mm on D, E and F models. Note that when assembling the plates on installation the thickest and thinnest plates should not be placed together – they must be separated by a standard plate.

14 Measure the free length of each clutch spring using a Vernier caliper (**see illustration 12.19**). Place each spring upright on a flat surface and check it for bend by placing a

ruler against it, or alternatively lay it against a set square. If any spring is below the minimum free length specified or if the bend in any spring is excessive, replace all the springs as a set. On D, E and F models also check the anti-judder spring and spring seat for damage or distortion and replace them with new ones if necessary.

15 Inspect the friction plates and the clutch housing for burrs and indentations on the edges of the protruding tabs on the plates and/or the slots in the housing (**see illustration**). Similarly check for wear between the inner teeth of the plain plates and the slots in the clutch centre (**see illustration**). Wear of this nature will cause clutch drag and slow disengagement during gear changes as the plates will snag when the pressure plate is lifted. With care a small amount of wear can be corrected by dressing with a fine file, but if this is excessive the worn components should be replaced with new ones.

16 Check the mating surfaces of the back-torque mechanism dogs and slots in the clutch centre and the clutch hub for wear and damage and replace the parts with new ones if necessary (**see illustration**). Also check the torque limiter springs for sag and their tangs

for wear and replace them with new ones if necessary – no spring free height is given, but they should be all the same.

17 Inspect the needle roller bearing and the bearing surfaces in the clutch housing and on the clutch guide (**see illustration**). If there are any signs of wear, pitting or other damage the affected parts must be replaced with new ones – on C models refer to Step 20 and select the correct new bearing according to the size code marks on the clutch housing.

18 Check the pressure plate and its bearing for signs of wear or damage and roughness. Check that the bearing outer race is a good fit in the centre of the plate, and that the inner race rotates freely without any rough spots. Check the pull-rod end and the corresponding cut-out in the release lever shaft for signs of wear or damage (**see illustration**). Replace any parts necessary with new ones.

19 Check the release mechanism in the clutch cover for a smooth action. If the action is stiff or rough, withdraw the shaft, noting the washer and how the return spring ends locate (**see illustrations**). Clean and check the oil seal and the two needle bearings in the cover (**see illustrations**). If required lever the seal out with a seal hook or screwdriver. Refer

15.17 Check the bearing and the bearing surfaces in the housing and on the guide

15.18 Check the pressure plate, its bearing and the pull-rod

15.19a Withdraw the shaft...

15.19b ...noting the washer and spring

15.19c Check the seal (arrowed)...

15.19d ...and the bearings (arrowed)

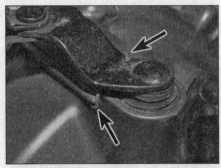

15.19e Position the return spring ends (arrowed) as shown

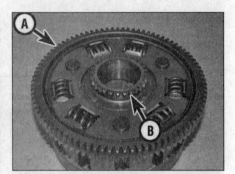

15.20a Primary drive gear (A), oil pump drive gear (B)

to *Tools and Workshop Tips* in the Reference Section for details of removing and installing needle bearings. Press the new seal in with your fingers or tap it in using a socket on the outer rim. Lubricate the bearings with oil and the seal lips with grease before installing the shaft. Make sure the return spring ends locate correctly **(see illustration)**.

20 Check the teeth of the primary driven gear on the back of the clutch housing and the corresponding teeth of the primary drive gear on the crankshaft, and on C models the alternator driven gear **(see illustration)**. Replace the clutch housing and/or crankshaft

and/or alternator gear with a new one if worn or chipped teeth are discovered. Similarly check the oil pump drive and driven gear teeth. Note that on C models the clutch housing must be matched with the needle bearing and the alternator driven gear, so if the housing or bearing is replaced with a new one select the new bearing as follows: a housing marked one must be fitted with a white coded bearing (part No. 92046-0010), a housing marked two must be fitted with a blue coded bearing (part No. 92046-0011), a housing marked three must be fitted with a red coded bearing (part No. 92046-1263) **(see illustration)**. If a new

housing is required check for any letter (A, B, C or D) marked next to the bearing number and obtain a new one with the same marking – if no letter is visible, the new one must also have no letter.

Installation

21 Remove all traces of old gasket and sealant from the crankcase and clutch cover surfaces.

22 Slide the inner spacer onto the shaft with its stepped side facing in and/or its marked side facing out, according to model **(see illustration)**.

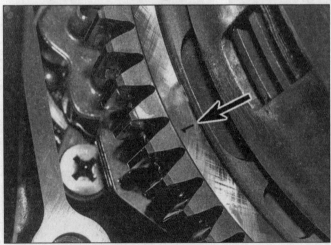

15.20b Clutch housing code number (arrowed) for fitting new bearing

15.22 Fit the inner spacer

15.23a Position the housing over the shaft and engage the gears...

15.23b ... then slide the bearing...

15.23c ...and the guide in

23 Smear the inside and outside of the clutch guide, the inside of the clutch housing and the needle bearing with molybdenum disulphide oil (a 50/50 mixture of molybdenum disulphide grease and engine oil). Position the clutch housing, engaging all related gears, hold it steady and slide the clutch guide and needle bearing onto the shaft and into the centre of the housing **(see illustrations)**. Check that the primary drive and driven gear teeth, and the alternator gear teeth on C models, and the oil pump drive and driven gear teeth engage – if required turn the oil pump driven gear using a screwdriver while pressing on the housing until the teeth are felt to engage and the housing moves in a bit further, then double-check by making sure the gear can't turn independently of the housing.

24 Slide the outer spacer onto the shaft with its stepped side facing out **(see illustration)**. Slide the clutch hub then the clutch centre onto the shaft splines **(see illustrations)** – make sure the centre is aligned with the hub so the dogs engage the slots.

25 Fit the four diaphragm springs – there are two each of two types, and each 'like pair' must be fitted together, but the small tang on all four must be offset from the rest so none are in the same position **(see illustrations)**. Hold the springs in place and thread the new clutch nut onto the shaft **(see illustration)**. Using the method employed on removal to lock the shaft (see Step 6), tighten the nut to the torque setting specified at the beginning of the Chapter **(see illustration)**.

15.24a Fit the outer spacer...

15.24b ...and the clutch hub

15.24c Align the dogs with the slots...

15.24d ...then fit the clutch centre

15.25a Assemble the springs as shown...

15.25b ...fit them onto the shaft...

15.25c ...then thread the nut on...

15.25d ...and tighten to the specified torque

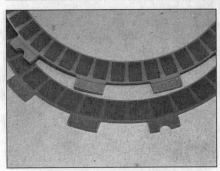

15.26a Note the difference between the sizes of friction block

15.26b Fit a small-blocked plate...

15.26c ...then a plain plate...

26 Coat each clutch plate with engine oil prior to installation, then build up the plates as follows: first fit a friction plate with the smaller friction blocks, then a plain plate (the thick circled one on C models), then on D, E and F models fit the anti-judder spring seat and the spring, so that the spring's outer edge is raised off the seat and facing outwards **(see illustrations)**.

27 Next fit a friction plate with the bigger friction blocks, on D, E and F models making sure it seats around the spring and spring seat, then fit a plain plate, then alternate friction plates with the bigger friction blocks and plain plates until all except the second friction plate with the smaller friction blocks are installed, and fit that friction plate with its tabs in the shallow slots in the housing **(see illustrations)**.

28 Lubricate the pull-rod bearing with oil and each end of the pull-rod with molybdenum grease. Fit the pull-rod into the shaft **(see illustration)**. Fit the pressure plate onto the

clutch, aligning the projections on the inner face with the wide slots in the clutch centre **(see illustration)**. Fit the springs, spring seats and the bolts, then hold the clutch housing and tighten the bolts evenly and a little at a

time in a criss-cross sequence to the specified torque setting **(see illustration)**.

29 Apply a smear of a suitable silicone sealant (ask your dealer) 10 to 15 mm either side of the crankcase joints where they contact the clutch

15.26d ...then where fitted the anti-judder spring seat...

15.26e ...and spring

15.27a Fit a large-blocked friction plate...

15.27b ...then a plain plate

15.27c Fit the tabs of the outer small-blocked friction plate into the shallow slots

15.28a Fit the pull-rod

15.28b Align each projection (A) with a slot (B)

15.28c Fit the springs, spring seats and bolts and tighten as described

15.29a Locate the gasket on the dowels (arrowed)

15.29b Fit the cover…

15.29c …making sure the release mechanism engages

cover. Fit the two dowels into the crankcase if removed. Fit a new gasket over the dowels **(see illustration)**. Fit the cover, pulling the release lever arm back (anti-clockwise) as you do then moving it forward so that it engages behind the pull-rod end as you push the cover home on the dowels and shaft ends **(see**

illustrations). Fit all the bolts finger tight, on all except D models making sure the clutch cable holder and the different length bolts are correctly positioned **(see illustrations)**. Tighten the bolts evenly and a little at a time in the sequence shown for your model, to the specified torque setting.

30 Connect the clutch cable (see Section 16).
31 Fill the engine with the correct amount and type of oil (see Chapter 1) and check the level. Adjust the clutch cable freeplay (see Chapter 1). Install the lower fairing panel (See Chapter 7).

15.29d Do not forget the cable bracket on C, E and F models

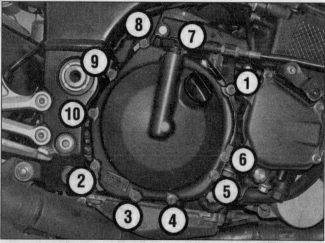

15.29e Clutch cover bolt tightening sequence – C models

Bolts 1, 7, 9 and 10 – 40 mm　　　　*Bolt 2 – 30 mm*
Bolts 3, 4, 5, 6 and 8 – 25 mm

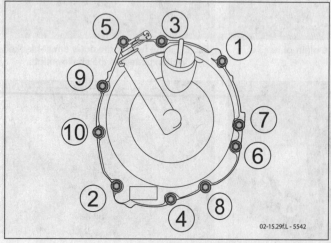

02-15.29f.L - 5542

15.29f Clutch cover bolt tightening sequence – D models

15.29g Clutch cover bolt location and tightening sequence – E and F models *(Bolt nos. 1 and 7 are longer than the others)*

16.2 Turn the adjuster in

16.3a Pull the boot off, then slacken the nuts (arrowed)…

16.3b …and thread the front nut up and the rear nut off

16 Clutch cable

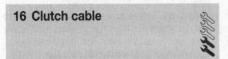

1 On C and D models remove the right-hand fairing side panel (see Chapter 7). On E models remove the right-hand fairing upper panel, or if preferred for best access and to reduce the possibility of damage, remove the fairing assembly (see Chapter 7). On F models remove the fairing assembly (see Chapter 7).
2 Thread the adjuster at the handlebar end of the cable fully in **(see illustration)**. This provides freeplay in the cable and re-sets the adjuster to the beginning of its span.
3 Carefully pull the rubber boot off the cable at the clutch end, then slacken the nuts **(see illustration)**. Thread the front nut as far up as it will go and thread the rear nut off so it is loose on the inner cable **(see illustration)**. Slide the cable into the bracket to get some freeplay and free the cable end from the release arm, noting how it fits **(see illustration)**. Draw the threaded section of the cable out of the bracket and slip the inner cable out **(see illustration)**. Secure the release arm in its forward position using some tape.
4 Align the slot in the adjuster at the handlebar end of the cable with that in the lever bracket,

16.3c Free the cable end…

then pull the outer cable end from the socket in the adjuster and release the inner cable from the lever **(see illustrations)**. Remove the cable from the machine, noting its routing.

> **HAYNES HiNT**
> *Before removing the cable from the bike, tape the lower end of the new cable to the upper end of the old cable. Slowly pull the lower end of the old cable out, guiding the new cable down into position. Using this method will ensure the cable is routed correctly.*

16.3d …then draw the cable out

5 Installation is the reverse of removal. Apply grease to the cable ends. Make sure the cable is correctly routed. Adjust the amount of clutch lever freeplay (see Chapter 1).

17 Gearchange mechanism

C and D models

Note: *If the gearchange shaft oil seal is leaking it can be removed and a new one fitted without having to remove the shaft itself – see Steps 3, 4 and 10.*

16.4a Align the slots and free the cable from the adjuster…

16.4b …and from the lever

17.3a Linkage arm/shaft alignment – C models

17.3b Linkage arm/shaft alignment – D models

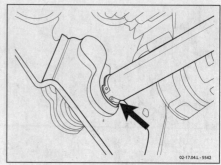

17.4 Release the circlip (arrowed)

Removal

1 Make sure the transmission is in neutral. Remove the lower fairing panels (see Chapter 7).
2 Remove the clutch (see Section 15). Remove the sump (see Section 18).
3 Note the alignment of the punch mark with the slit in the gearchange linkage arm, then unscrew the pinch bolt and slide the arm off **(see illustrations)**.
4 Release the circlip on the inner right-hand side of the crankcase and slide it to the left-hand end of the shaft, along with the inner washer **(see illustration)**.
5 Note how the gearchange shaft centralising spring ends fit on each side of the locating pin in the casing, and how the pawls on the selector arm locate onto the pins on the end of the selector drum cam. Grasp the end of the shaft and withdraw the shaft/arm assembly, retrieving the circlip and inner washer as you do **(see illustration)**. Also retrieve the outer washer from the crankcase if it didn't come with the shaft.
6 If required, note how the stopper arm spring ends locate and how the roller on the arm locates in the neutral detent on the selector drum cam, then unscrew the stopper arm bolt and remove the spacer (C models only), arm, washer and spring, noting how they fit **(see illustration 17.21)**.

Inspection

7 Check the selector arm for cracks, distortion and wear of its pawls, and check for any corresponding wear on the pins of the selector drum cam. Check the arm moves up smoothly and freely and returns under pressure of its spring. Also check the stopper arm roller and the detents in the selector drum cam for any wear or damage, and make sure the roller turns freely **(see illustration 17.22c)**. Replace any components that are worn or damaged with new ones. If required, refer to the illustrations in Section 20 and remove the selector drum cam by unscrewing the bolt in its centre. Note the locating pin in the end of the drum and remove it for safekeeping if required. On installation, locate the pin in the cut-out in the back of the cam. Clean the threads of the cam bolt and apply a suitable non-permanent thread locking compound, and tighten it to the torque setting specified at the beginning of the Chapter.
8 Inspect the shaft centralising spring and the stopper arm return spring for fatigue, wear or damage. If any is found, they must be replaced with new ones. To replace the shaft spring, slide the outer washer off the shaft, then remove the circlip, and on D models remove the other washer **(see illustration 17.5)**. Slide the spring off the shaft, noting how its ends locate. Fit the new spring, locating the ends on each side of the tab. On D models fit the washer. Fit the circlip, making sure it locates in its groove. Slide the outer washer against the circlip. Also check that the centralising spring

locating pin in the crankcase is tight. If it is loose, remove it, clean the threads and apply a non-permanent thread locking compound, then tighten it to the specified torque.
9 Check the gearchange shaft is straight and look for damage to the splines. If the shaft is bent you can attempt to straighten it, but if the splines are damaged the shaft must be replaced with a new one.
10 Check the condition of the shaft oil seal in the left-hand side of the crankcase. If it is damaged, deteriorated or shows signs of leakage it must be replaced with a new one, though it is wise to fit a new one whatever the apparent condition. Lever out the old seal with a seal hook or screwdriver **(see illustration 17.26a)**. If the shaft has been removed, check the condition of the needle bearing, and replace that with a new one as well if necessary **(see illustration 17.26b)** – refer to *Tools and Workshop Tips* in the Reference Section. Smear the lip of the new seal with grease, and fit it with the marked side facing out. Press the seal squarely into place using your fingers, a seal driver or suitable socket **(see illustration 17.26c)**.

Installation

11 If removed, fit the bolt through the spacer (C models only) and the stopper arm so the hole in the arm seats around the shoulder, then fit the washer and the return spring **(see illustration)**. Fit the arm and tighten the

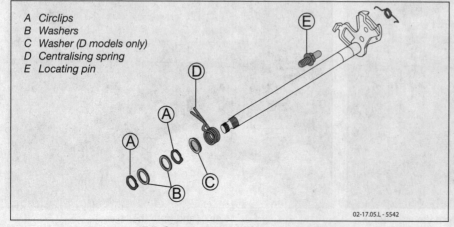

A *Circlips*
B *Washers*
C *Washer (D models only)*
D *Centralising spring*
E *Locating pin*

17.5 Gearchange shaft/arm assembly

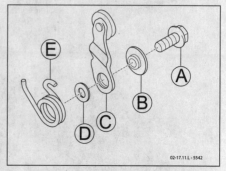

17.11 Stopper arm assembly

A *Bolt*
B *Spacer (C models only)*
C *Stopper arm*
D *Washer*
E *Spring*

bolt, making sure the arm remains seated over the shoulder on the spacer or bolt (according to model), and locating the roller onto the neutral detent on the selector drum as the bolt tightens. Tighten the bolt to the torque setting specified at the beginning of the Chapter. Check that the arm and spring ends are correctly positioned (see illustration 17.21).

12 Check that the shaft centralising spring is properly positioned and slide the outer washer onto the shaft if removed (see illustration 17.5). Apply some grease to the lips of the gearchange shaft oil seal in the left-hand side of the crankcase. Slide the shaft into place and fit the inner washer and circlip over its end as it passes through the inside of the crankcase, then push it all the way through the case until the splined end comes out the other side. Locate the selector arm pawls onto the pins on the selector drum and the centralising spring ends onto each side of the locating pin in the crankcase.

13 Slide the inner washer up against the right-hand wall of the crankcase then fit the circlip into its groove, making sure it seats correctly (see illustration 17.4).

14 Slide the gearchange linkage arm onto the shaft, aligning its slit with the mark made on the shaft (see illustration 17.3a or b). Fit the pinch bolt and tighten it.

15 Install the clutch (see Section 15). Install the sump (see Section 18).

E and F models

Note: *If the gearchange shaft oil seal is leaking it can be removed and a new one fitted without having to remove the shaft itself – see Steps 17, 18 and 26.*

Removal

16 Make sure the transmission is in neutral. Remove the clutch (see Section 15). Block the holes into the sump with clean rag.

17.18a Release the circlip...

17.18b ...and slide the washer off

17.19a Withdraw the shaft/arm assembly, noting how it fits...

17.19b ...and remove the collar

17 Note the alignment of the punch mark with the slit in the gearchange linkage arm, then unscrew pinch bolt and slide the arm off (see illustrations 4.10a and b).

18 Release the circlip and remove the washer from the left-hand end of the shaft (see illustrations).

19 Note how the gearchange shaft centralising spring ends fit on each side of the locating pin in the casing, and how the slot in the arm locates over the collar on the drum shift ratchet pin. Grasp the end of the shaft and

withdraw the shaft/arm assembly, retrieving the collar from the pin (see illustrations).

20 Undo the pawl guide plate screws, then remove the plate along with the pawl assembly, noting that the pawls are under spring pressure (see illustrations). Note the correct fitted position of all components.

21 If required, note how the stopper arm spring ends locate and how the roller on the arm locates in the neutral detent on the selector drum cam, then unscrew the stopper

17.20a Undo the screws (arrowed)...

17.20b ...and remove the guide plate and pawl assembly

17.21 Note how the spring ends locate, and how the roller sits in the neutral detent, then unscrew the bolt (arrowed) and remove the arm

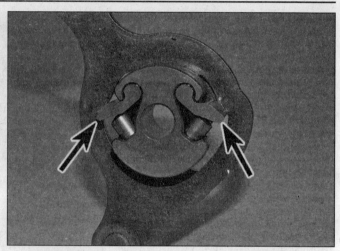

17.22a Check the pawls (arrowed) and the guide plate...

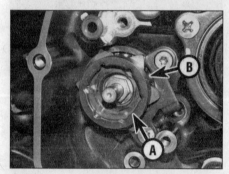

17.22b ...and the pawl cam (A). Stopper arm detents (B)

arm bolt and remove the arm, the washer and the spring, noting how they fit **(see illustration)**.

Inspection

22 Check the pawls, pins and springs, the guide plate, and the pawl cam on the end of the selector drum for wear and damage **(see illustrations)**. Also check the stopper arm roller and the detents on the back of the cam for any wear or damage, and make sure the roller turns freely **(see illustrations)**. Replace any components that are worn or damaged with new ones **(see illustrations)**. If required,

refer to the illustrations in Section 20 and remove the cam from the selector drum by unscrewing the bolt in its centre. Note the locating pin in the end of the drum and remove it for safekeeping if required. On installation, locate the pin in the cut-out in the back of the cam. Clean the threads of the cam bolt and apply a suitable non-permanent thread locking compound, and tighten it to the torque setting specified at the beginning of the Chapter.
23 Check the selector arm for cracks, distortion and wear of its slot, and check for any corresponding wear on the collar and pin **(see illustration)**.

17.22c Check the stopper arm roller

17.22d If required remove the pawl carrier from the guide plate...

17.22e ...then remove the pawls...

17.22f ...and the pins and springs

17.22g Make sure everything is correctly positioned on reassembly

17.23 Check the arm, collar and pin

17.24a Shaft centralising spring (arrowed)

17.24b Make sure the pin (arrowed) is tight

17.26a Lever the seal out

24 Inspect the shaft centralising spring and the stopper arm return spring for fatigue, wear or damage (see illustration). If any is found, they must be replaced with new ones. To replace the shaft spring, slide the collar off the shaft, then slide the spring off, noting how its ends locate. Fit the new spring, locating the ends on each side of the tab, then fit the narrow end of the collar into the spring. Also check that the centralising spring locating pin in the crankcase is tight (see illustration). If it is loose, remove it, clean the threads and apply a non-permanent thread locking compound, then tighten it to the specified torque.

25 Check the gearchange shaft is straight and look for damage to the splines. If the shaft is bent you can attempt to straighten it, but if the splines are damaged the shaft must be replaced with a new one.

26 Check the condition of the shaft oil seal in the left-hand side of the crankcase. If it is damaged, deteriorated or shows signs of leakage it must be replaced with a new one, though it is wise to fit a new one whatever the apparent condition. Lever out the old seal with a seal hook or screwdriver (see illustration). If the shaft has been removed, check the condition of the needle bearing, and replace that with a new one as well if necessary (see illustration) – refer to *Tools and Workshop Tips* in the Reference Section. Smear the lip of the new seal with grease, and fit it with the marked side facing out. Press the seal squarely into place using your fingers, a seal driver or suitable socket (see illustration).

17.26b Check the bearing (arrowed)

Installation

27 If removed, fit the bolt through the stopper arm so the hole in the arm seats around the shoulder, then fit the washer and the return spring (see illustrations). Fit the arm and tighten the bolt, making sure the arm remains seated over the shoulder on the bolt, and locating the roller onto the neutral detent on the selector drum as the bolt tightens (see illustration). Tighten the bolt to the torque setting specified at the beginning of the Chapter. Check that the arm and spring ends are correctly positioned (see illustration 17.21).

28 If the pawl assembly was disassembled, fit the springs, pins and pawls, making sure the rounded end of each pawl fits into the rounded cut-out in the pawl holder (see illustrations 17.22f and e).

29 Depress the pawls and fit the pawl assembly into the guide plate, aligning it as

17.26c Fit the new seal flush with the crankcase

shown (see illustrations 17.22d and g). Fit the assembly into the cam, locating the pin bolt through the hole in the holder (see illustration 17.20b). Make sure the pawls locate correctly in the grooves in the cam. Clean the threads of the guide plate screws, then apply a suitable non-permanent thread locking compound and tighten them to the specified torque setting (see illustration 17.20a). Make sure the pawl holder is correctly positioned – if necessary turn the holder while depressing the pawls to re-position it.

30 Check that the shaft centralising spring is properly positioned (see illustration 17.24a). Apply some grease to the lips of the gearchange shaft oil seal in the left-hand side of the crankcase. Fit the collar, narrow end facing out, onto the pawl holder pin (see illustration 17.19b). Slide the shaft into place and push it all the way through the case until the splined end comes out the other side (see

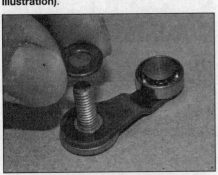

17.27a Fit the bolt, washer...

17.27b ...and spring

17.27c Make sure everything locates correctly as you tighten the bolt

17.30 Make sure everything is correctly positioned

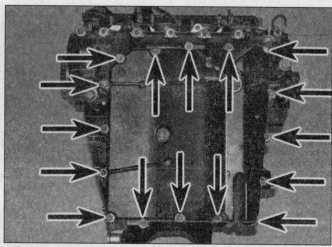

18.3 Unscrew the bolts (arrowed) and remove the sump – D, E, F model shown

illustration 17.19a). Locate the selector arm slot over the collar and the centralising spring ends onto each side of the locating pin in the crankcase **(see illustration).**

31 Slide the washer onto the left-hand end of the shaft, then fit the circlip, seating it in its groove **(see illustration 17.18b and a).**

32 Slide the gearchange linkage arm onto the shaft, aligning its slit with the mark made on the shaft **(see illustrations 4.10b and a).** Fit the pinch bolt and tighten it.

33 Remove the rag that was blocking the sump, then install the clutch (see Section 15).

18 Oil sump, strainer and pressure relief valve

Removal

1 Remove the exhaust system (see Chapter 4).

2 Drain the engine oil (see Chapter 1).

3 Slacken the sump bolts evenly in a criss-cross sequence to prevent distortion, then remove the bolts, noting the positions

of the longer bolt and the bracket on C models and of the wiring clamps on D, E and F models, and remove the sump **(see illustration).** Remove the gasket.

4 Pull the strainer out, noting how it locates **(see illustration 18.12b).** Remove the rubber seal and the relief valve damper **(see illustration)** – a new seal must be used.

5 Unscrew the pressure relief valve **(see illustration).** Remove the rubber seal.

6 On C models, if required the front section of the sump can be removed by unscrewing the bolts. Remove the O-ring – a new one must be used.

Inspection

7 Clean the oil strainer in solvent and remove any debris caught in the mesh **(see illustration).** If the strainer gauze is damaged, replace the strainer with a new one.

8 Push the relief valve plunger into the valve body and check that it moves smoothly and returns fully under spring pressure **(see illustration).** If not clean through the valve with solvent then blow it with compressed air – do not disassemble the valve. Lubricate the valve with clean oil and recheck it. If in any doubt, replace the relief valve with a new one.

Installation

9 Remove all traces of gasket from the sump and crankcase mating surfaces, and clean the inside of the sump with solvent. Blow the sump dry with compressed air if available.

10 On C models, if removed fit the front section of the sump using a new O-ring smeared with grease, and tighten the bolts to the torque setting specified at the beginning of the Chapter.

11 Clean the threads of the pressure relief valve. Apply a smear of fresh threadlock

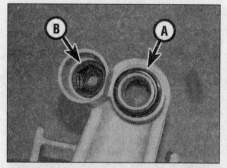

18.4 Remove the strainer seal (A) and the relief valve damper (B)

18.5 Pressure relief valve (arrowed)

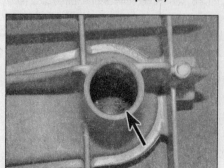

18.7 Clean the mesh (arrowed)

18.8 Push the plunger into the body and check that it moves smoothly

18.11 Apply some threadlock to the valve threads

18.12a Fit the damper onto the top of the relief valve

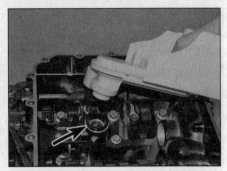

18.12b Fit the seal (arrowed) into the orifice, then fit the strainer into it

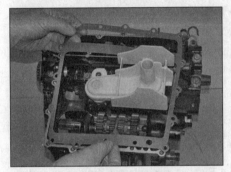

18.13a Fit a new gasket...

18.13b ...then fit the sump

18.13c Wiring clamp positions (arrowed) – D, E and F models

and tighten the valve to the torque setting specified at the beginning of the Chapter **(see illustration)**.

12 Fit the damper onto the relief valve **(see illustration)**. Fit the rubber seal into the strainer orifice, using a new one if necessary **(see illustration)**. Do not fit it onto the strainer as it will distort when the strainer is fitted. Fit the strainer over the relief valve and push it into its seal.

13 Lay a new gasket onto the sump, or onto the crankcase if the engine has been removed and is upside down **(see illustration)**. Position the sump onto the crankcase and fit the bolts, along with the bracket or wiring clamps (according to model), and tighten them finger-tight **(see illustrations)**. Tighten the bolts evenly and a little at a time in a criss-cross pattern to the specified torque setting.

14 Install the exhaust system, but do not yet fit the fairing panels.

15 Fill the engine with the correct type and quantity of oil as described in Chapter 1. Start the engine and check that there are no leaks around the sump.

16 Install the fairing panels (see Chapter 7).

19 Oil pump

Removal

1 Remove the clutch (Section 15).

2 Lock the oil pump driven gear to prevent it from turning and unscrew the bolts **(see illustration)**. Remove the gear.

3 Stuff some clean rag under the pump. Unscrew the pump cover bolts, withdraw the cover/shaft assembly and the rotors, taking care not to let the drive pin fall out of the shaft

(see illustrations). Remove the rotors, the pin and the washer **(see illustrations 19.9e, d, c and b)**.

4 Withdraw the shaft from the cover **(see illustration 19.9a)**. Remove the locating pin from the cover if loose.

Inspection

5 Clean all the components in solvent.

6 Inspect the rotors and rotor housing for scoring and wear. If any damage, scoring or uneven or excessive wear is evident, replace the rotors with a new pair. If the housing is scored the only option, if necessary, is to fit new crankcases.

7 Check the pump drive gear on the back of the clutch housing and the driven gear for wear or damage, and replace them with a new set if necessary.

8 Check the shaft for damage and wear.

19.2 Lock the gear and unscrew its bolts

19.3a Unscrew the bolts (arrowed)...

19.3b ... and remove the pump and its rotors (arrowed)

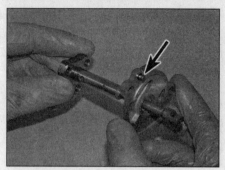

19.9a Cover locating pin (arrowed)

19.9b Fit the washer...

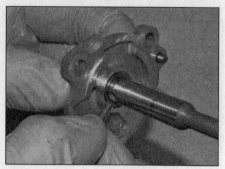

19.9c ...and the drive pin

19.9d Seat the cut-outs in the inner rotor over the drive pin

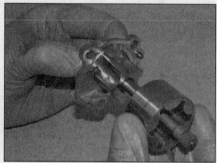

19.9e Slide the outer rotor over the inner rotor

Installation

9 Apply some molybdenum disulphide oil (a 50/50 mixture of molybdenum disulphide grease and engine oil) to the pump shaft journal sections. Fit the locating pin into the cover if removed, then slide the shaft through the cover **(see illustration)**. Fit the washer then slide the drive pin into its hole **(see illustrations)**. Slide the inner rotor onto the shaft with the cut-outs facing the cover and seat them over the drive pin **(see illustration)**. Apply some molybdenum disulphide oil to the inner rotor. Fit the outer rotor over the inner rotor **(see illustration)**.

10 Slide the shaft and rotors into the housing, aligning the tab on the shaft end with the slot in the water pump drive shaft, and seat the locating pin in its hole **(see illustration)**. Fit the cover bolts and tighten to the specified torque **(see illustration 19.3a)**.

11 Clean the threads of the pump driven gear bolts and apply a suitable non-permanent thread locking compound. Fit the gear with the bolt head recesses facing out **(see illustration)**. Lock the sprocket and tighten the bolts to the torque setting specified at the beginning of the chapter **(see illustration 19.2)**.

12 Install the clutch (Section 15).

20 Selector drum and forks

Note: *The selector drum and forks can be removed with the engine in the frame, though the procedure is considerably easier with the engine removed and placed upside-down on a bench – there is no need to separate the crankcase halves.*

Removal

1 The selector drum and forks are located in the lower crankcase half. For easiest access remove the engine (see Section 4) and rest it upside down, using blocks of wood to support it so that any projecting parts are not taking any excess weight.

2 Remove the gearchange mechanism (Section 17) and the oil sump and strainer (Section 18).

3 Remove the gear position switch (See Chapter 8).

4 Remove the selector drum bearing/fork shaft retainer(s) according to model **(see illustration)**.

5 Withdraw the input shaft fork shaft from the casing **(see illustration 20.18b)**. Remove the fork from the input shaft **(see illustration 20.18a)**.

6 Withdraw the output shaft fork shaft from the casing **(see illustration 20.17a)**. Check that the output shaft fork guide pins are clear of their tracks in the selector drum, then withdraw the drum from the right-hand side of the engine **(see illustration 20.16)**.

7 Remove the output shaft forks **(see illustrations 20.15b and a)**. Slide each one back onto its shaft to keep them the correct way round, or mark them L and R according to side.

Inspection

8 Inspect the selector forks for any signs of wear or damage, especially around the fork ends where they engage with the groove in the pinion. Check that each fork fits correctly

19.10 Fit the pump assembly into the crankcase, aligning the shaft end correctly

19.11 Make sure the bolt recesses face out

20.4 Undo the screws (arrowed) and remove the plate – E/F model shown

20.8 Check the fit of each fork in its pinion

20.9 Measure the fork end thickness

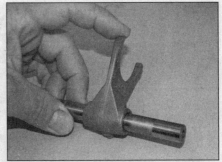

20.10 Check the fit of each fork on the shaft

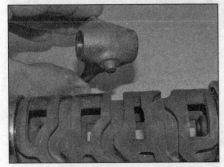

20.12 Check the guide pins and their grooves in the drum

20.13a Check the bearings (arrowed)

20.13b Unscrew the bolt (arrowed) to remove the cam – E/F model shown

in its pinion groove **(see illustration)**. If the forks are in any way damaged they must be replaced with new ones.

9 Measure the thickness of the fork ends and the width of the groove in the relative pinion and compare the readings to the specifications **(see illustration)**. Replace the forks and/or gear pinions with new ones if they are worn beyond their specifications.

10 Check closely to see if the forks are bent. Check that the forks fit correctly on their shaft **(see illustration)**. They should move freely with a light fit but no appreciable freeplay. Check that the fork shaft holes in the casing are neither worn nor damaged.

11 Check each fork shaft is straight by rolling it along a flat surface. A bent rod will cause difficulty in selecting gears and make the gearchange action heavy. Replace the shaft with a new one if it is bent.

12 Inspect the selector drum grooves and selector fork guide pins for signs of wear or damage **(see illustration)**. Measure the width of each groove and the diameter of the relative guide pin and compare the readings to the specifications. If either component shows signs of wear beyond their specifications or damage the fork(s) and/or drum must be replaced with new ones.

13 Check that the selector drum bearings rotate freely **(see illustration)**. To fit a new bearing on the cam end, remove the cam by unscrewing the bolt in its centre – fit the shaft of a screwdriver through the drum to counter-hold it **(see illustration)**. Note the locating pin in the end of the drum and remove it for safekeeping if required. Remove the old bearings using a puller if necessary and fit new ones (see *Tools and Workshop Tips* in the Reference Section if necessary). Clean the threads of the

cam bolt. Fit the cam, locating the pin in the cut-out in the back of the cam. Apply a suitable non-permanent thread locking compound to the bolt and tighten it to the torque setting specified at the beginning of the Chapter.

Installation

14 Prior to installation lubricate all moving and contacting surfaces (i.e. fork ends, pinion grooves, guide pins, selector drum grooves, fork shafts and bores) with molybdenum disulphide oil (a 50/50 mixture of molybdenum disulphide grease and engine oil).

15 Fit each output shaft fork into the groove in its pinion **(see illustrations)**. Make sure they are the correct way round so the guide pins will locate in the selector drum tracks, but position them clear at the moment to allow the drum to be inserted.

16 Slide the selector drum into position in the crankcase **(see illustration)**.

20.15a Fit each output shaft fork...

20.15b ...into its pinion groove

20.16 Slide the drum into the crankcase

20.17a Slide the shaft through and lift each fork in turn...

20.17b ...so the guide pins locate in the drum tracks

17 Slide the output fork shaft (the longer of the two shafts) into the crankcase, lifting each fork using long-nosed pliers to seat the guide pin in its groove in the selector drum and sliding the shaft through each fork and into its bore in the crankcase **(see illustrations)**.

18 Fit the input shaft fork into the groove in its pinion and seat the guide pin in its track in the drum **(see illustration)**. Slide the shaft in **(see illustration)**.

19 Clean the threads of the retainer plate screws and bolt (where fitted) and apply a suitable non-permanent thread locking compound. Fit the plate(s) and tighten the screws and bolt (where fitted) to the torque settings specified at the beginning of the Chapter **(see illustration)**.

20.18a Locate the fork...

20.18b ...then slide the shaft through

20 Install the gearchange mechanism (Section 18), the oil sump and strainer (Section 18), and the gear position switch (see Chapter 8).

21 Crankcase separation and reassembly

Separation

Note 1: *On C models the crankcases, crankshaft, clutch housing and alternator driven gear are all matched on assembly according to various code markings. If any of the above parts are replaced with new ones the new parts must carry the same marks as those being replaced to ensure correct matching. Refer to your Kawasaki parts dealer for details.*

1 To access the pistons, connecting rods, crankshaft, bearings and transmission shafts, the crankcase must be split into its two halves. To do this, remove the engine from the frame (see Section 4).

2 Before the crankcases can be separated the following components must be removed:

Valve cover (Section 7)
Camshafts (Section 9) – see Note 2
Cylinder head (Section 11) – see Note 2
Crankshaft position (CKP) sensor (see Chapter 4).
Timing rotor (C models – Section 13)

20.19 Fitting the plate – E/F model shown

Starter clutch (Section 14)
Cam chain and blades (Section 10) – see Note 2
Clutch (Section 15)
Water pump and hoses (Chapter 3)
Gearchange mechanism (Section 17)
Oil filter (Chapter 1)
Oil cooler (Section 6)
Alternator (Chapter 8)
Starter motor (Chapter 8) – see Note 2
Oil sump, strainer and pressure relief valve (Section 18)
Oil pump (Section 19)
Selector drum and forks (Section 20)
Speed sensor, gear position switch and oil pressure switch (if required – Chapter 8)

Note 2: *If the crankcases are being separated to inspect the crankshaft without removing it, the camshafts and cylinder head can remain in situ. To remove the crankshaft without removing the connecting rods and pistons, the camshafts must be removed but the head can stay. However, if removal of the connecting rod assemblies is intended, full disassembly of the top-end is necessary. To inspect or remove the transmission shafts, the camshafts and cylinder head can remain in situ.*

3 Unscrew the oil filter/cooler holder bolts and remove the holder and its O-ring **(see illustration)** – a new O-ring will be needed.

4 Unscrew and remove the upper crankcase bolts – the three 6 mm bolts first, followed

21.3 Unscrew the bolts (arrowed) and remove the holder

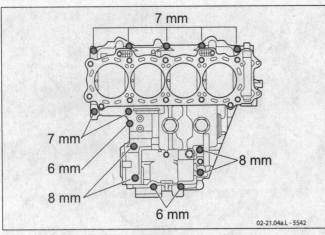

21.4a Upper crankcase bolts – C models

21.4b Upper crankcase bolts – D/E/F models
A 6 mm bolts   B 7 mm bolts   *C 8 mm bolts*

by the 7 mm bolts (seven on C models and two on all other models), followed by the four 8 mm bolts with their sealing washers **(see illustrations)**. **Note:** *As each crankcase bolt is removed, store it in its relative position in a cardboard template of the crankcase halves* **(see illustration)**. *This will ensure all bolts and washers are installed in the correct location on reassembly. New sealing washers will be needed for the 8 mm bolts.*

5 Turn the engine upside down and support it as required using wooden blocks.

6 On D, E and F models unscrew the seven 6 mm bolts along the front, working from the outsides to the centre **(see illustration)**. On all models unscrew the two 7 mm bolts. Store the bolts in the template.

7 Now unscrew the ten 9 mm crankshaft journal bolts evenly, a little at a time and in a **reverse** of the tightening sequence shown, i.e. starting from the outside and working to the centre, until they are finger-tight, then remove them **(see illustration 21.17b)**. Note that new washers are required for these bolts.

8 Carefully lift the lower crankcase half off the upper half, using a soft-faced hammer to tap around the joint to initially separate the halves if necessary **(see illustration)**. **Note:** *If the halves do not separate easily, make sure all fasteners have been removed. Do not try to separate the halves by levering against the crankcase mating surfaces as they are easily scored and will leak oil in the future if damaged. The transmission input shaft comes away with the lower crankcase half, leaving the crankshaft and transmission output shaft in the upper crankcase half.*

9 Remove the locating dowels from the crankcase if they are loose (they could be in either crankcase half) **(see illustration 21.13)**. Refer to Sections 22 to 29 for the removal and installation of the components housed within the crankcases.

Reassembly

10 Remove all traces of sealant from the crankcase mating surfaces.

11 Ensure that all components and their

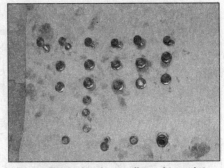

21.4c Example of a cardboard template for storing the crankcase bolts

bearings are in place in the upper and lower crankcase halves. If the transmission shafts have not been removed, remove the oil seal from the left-hand end of the output shaft and replace it with a new one **(see illustration 28.8)**.

12 Generously lubricate the crankshaft and transmission shafts, particularly around the bearings, with clean engine oil, then use a rag

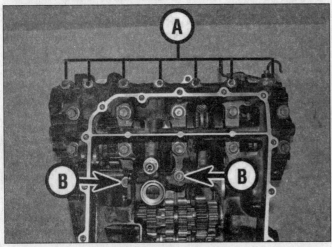

21.6 Lower crankcase 6mm bolts (A) – D/E/F models. Lower crankcase 7mm bolts (B) – all models

21.8 Carefully separate the crankcase halves

21.13 Crankcase dowels (arrowed)

21.14a Apply sealant...

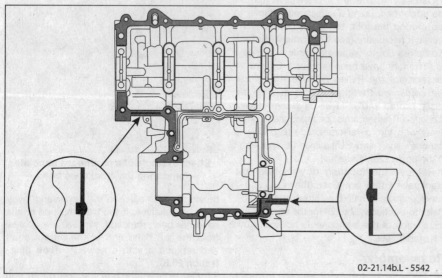

21.14b ...to the shaded area shown...

02-21.14b.L - 5542

Caution: Apply the sealant only to the shaded areas. Do not apply an excessive amount as it will ooze out when the case halves are assembled and may obstruct oil passages. Do not apply the sealant close to any of the bearing shells or surfaces, or oil passages.

15 Check again that all components are in position, particularly that the bearing shells are still correctly located in the lower crankcase half, and that the cam chain is fitted around its sprocket on the crankshaft. Carefully fit the lower crankcase half down onto the upper crankcase half, making sure the dowels all locate correctly **(see illustration 21.8)**.

16 Check that the lower crankcase half is correctly seated.

Caution: The crankcase halves should fit together without being forced. If the casings are not correctly seated, remove the lower crankcase half and investigate the problem. Do not attempt to pull them together using the crankcase bolts as the casing will crack and be ruined.

17 Clean the ten crankshaft journal 9 mm bolts and fit new copper washers **(see illustration)**. Apply molybdenum disulphide oil (a 50/50 mixture of molybdenum disulphide grease and engine oil) to the threads, under the heads and to the lower sides of the new copper washers. Secure the bolts finger-tight at first, then tighten them evenly and a little at a time in the numerical sequence shown to the torque setting specified for your model at the beginning of the Chapter **(see illustration)**.

18 Clean the threads of the 7 mm lower crankcase bolts and tighten them finger-tight at first, then tighten the bolts to the specified torque for your model **(see illustration)**. On D, E and F models fit the 6 mm bolts along the front and tighten to the specified torque setting, working from the centre outwards **(see illustration 21.6)**.

19 Turn the engine over. Clean the threads of the upper crankcase bolts (see Step 4) and

soaked in high flash-point solvent to wipe over the mating surfaces of both crankcase halves to remove all traces of oil.

13 If removed, fit the locating dowels in the upper crankcase half **(see illustration)**.

14 Apply and evenly spread a small amount of suitable sealant (Kawasaki-Bond 92104-1064 or equivalent RTV sealant) to the outer mating surface of the lower crankcase half as shown **(see illustrations)**.

21.14c ...and spread it evenly

21.17a Fit new washers

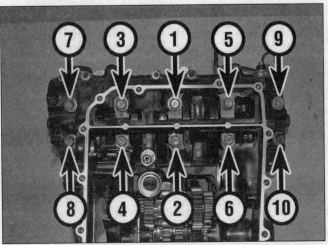

21.17b Crankshaft journal bolt tightening sequence

21.18 Fit the 7mm bolts as shown

21.19 Use a new sealing washer on each 8mm bolt

21.21a Fit a new O-ring into the groove...

21.21b ...then fit the holder

fit new sealing washers onto the 8 mm bolts **(see illustration)**. Secure the bolts finger-tight at first, then tighten the 8 mm bolts first, then the 7 mm bolts and finally the 6 mm bolts, to the specified torque settings for your model **(see illustration 21.4a or b)**.

20 With all crankcase fasteners tightened, check that the crankshaft and transmission shafts rotate smoothly and easily. Check that the transmission shafts rotate freely and independently in neutral, then when installed rotate the selector drum by hand and select each gear in turn whilst rotating the output

shaft as fast as possible – because of the positive neutral selector mechanism the output shaft has to turn fast enough to create enough centrifugal force for the steel balls to be flung out to free the 5th gear, otherwise it will remain locked to the shaft and you will not be able to select gears properly. Check that all gears can be selected and that the shafts rotate freely in every gear. If there are any signs of undue stiffness, tight or rough spots, or of any other problem, the fault must be rectified before proceeding further.

21 Fit the oil filter/cooler holder using

a new O-ring smeared with grease and tighten the bolts to the specified torque **(see illustrations)**.

22 Install all other removed assemblies in a reverse of the sequence given in Step 2.

22 Crankcases and cylinders

Crankcases

Note: *On C models the crankcases, crankshaft, clutch housing and alternator driven gear are all matched on assembly according to various code markings. If any of the above parts are replaced with new ones the new parts must carry the same marks as those being replaced to ensure correct matching. Refer to your Kawasaki parts dealer for details.*

1 After the crankcases have been separated, remove the crankshaft, connecting rods and pistons, and the transmission shafts, plus the speed sensor and oil pressure switch if not already removed. If there are any other components or assemblies that have not been removed as part of your disassembly procedure, for example the coolant inlet union, remove these as well, referring to the relevant

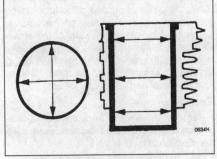

22.11a Measure the cylinder bore in the directions shown...

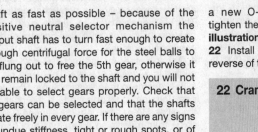

22.11b ...using a telescoping gauge, then measure the gauge with a micrometer

Chapter. Also remove the transmission input shaft bearing in the crankcase if required, but note that if you do a new one must be fitted – see Section 29.

2 If required unscrew the crankcase breather plate bolts and remove the plate.

3 Clean the crankcases and all oil passages, including the oil jets, with new solvent and dry them with compressed air, blowing it through the passages and jets.

4 Remove all traces of old gasket sealant from the mating surfaces. Clean up minor damage to the surfaces with a fine sharpening stone or grindstone.

Caution: Be very careful not to nick or gouge the crankcase mating surfaces or oil leaks will result. Check both crankcase halves very carefully for cracks and other damage.

5 Small cracks or holes in aluminium castings can be repaired with an epoxy resin adhesive as a temporary measure. Permanent repairs can only be done by argon-arc welding, and only a specialist in this process is in a position to advise on the economy or practical aspect of such a repair. If any damage is found that can't be repaired, replace the crankcase halves as a set – refer to your dealer.

6 Damaged threads can be economically reclaimed using a diamond section wire insert, for example of the Heli-Coil type (though there are other makes), which are easily fitted after drilling and re-tapping the affected thread.

7 Sheared studs or screws can be removed with extractors, which consist of a tapered, left-hand thread screw of very hard steel. These are inserted into a pre-drilled hole in the stud, and usually succeed in dislodging the most stubborn stud or screw. Otherwise the stud must be drilled out, and if necessary a thread insert fitted as in Step 6. If a stud has sheared above its bore line, it can be removed using a conventional stud extractor that avoids the need for drilling.

 HAYNES HiNT *Refer to Tools and Workshop Tips for details of installing a thread insert and using screw extractors.*

8 If removed apply a 1 to 1.5 mm bead of suitable sealant (Three-Bond (TB1207B) or equivalent sealant) to the mating surface of the crankcase breather plate, then fit the plate. Clean the threads of the breather plate bolts and apply a non-permanent thread locking compound, and tighten them to the torque setting specified at the beginning of the Chapter.

9 Install all other components and assemblies, referring to the relevant Sections of this and the other Chapters, before reassembling the crankcase halves.

Cylinders

Note: *The liners are made of aluminium and so great care must be taken not to scratch or gouge them. Do not attempt to separate the cylinder liners from the cylinder block.*

10 Check the cylinder walls carefully for scratches and score marks.

11 Using telescoping gauges and a micrometer (see *Tools and Workshop Tips*), check the dimensions of each cylinder to assess the amount of wear, taper and ovality. Measure 10 mm and 60 mm from the top of the bore, both parallel to and across the crankshaft axis **(see illustrations)**. Compare the results to the specifications at the beginning of the Chapter. If the cylinders are worn, oval or tapered beyond the service limit replace the crankcases with a new set.

12 If the precision measuring tools are not available, take the upper crankcase to a Kawasaki dealer or specialist motorcycle repair shop for assessment and advice.

23 Connecting rod and main bearing information

1 Even though new main and connecting rod bearings are generally fitted during engine overhaul, the old bearings should be retained for close examination as they may reveal valuable information about the condition of the engine.

2 Bearing failure occurs mainly because of lack of lubrication, the presence of dirt or other foreign particles, overloading the engine and/or corrosion. Regardless of the cause of bearing failure, it must be corrected before the engine is reassembled to prevent it from happening again.

3 When examining the bearings, lay them out on a clean surface in the same general position as their location on the crankshaft journals. This will enable you to match any noted bearing problems with the corresponding crankshaft journal.

4 Dirt and other foreign particles get into the engine in a variety of ways. They may be left in the engine during assembly or they may pass through filters or breathers, then get into the oil and from there into the bearings. Metal chips from machining operations and normal engine wear are often present. Abrasives are sometimes left in engine components after reconditioning operations, especially when parts are not thoroughly cleaned using the proper cleaning methods. Whatever the source, foreign objects often end up imbedded in the soft bearing material and are easily recognised. Large particles will not imbed in the bearing and will score or gouge the bearing and journal. The best prevention for this cause of bearing failure is to clean all parts thoroughly and keep everything spotlessly clean during engine reassembly. Regular oil and filter changes are also recommended.

5 Lack of lubrication or lubrication breakdown has a number of interrelated causes. Excessive heat (which thins the oil), overloading (which squeezes the oil from the bearing face) and oil leakage or throw off (from excessive bearing clearances, worn oil

pump or high engine speeds) all contribute to lubrication breakdown. Blocked oil passages will starve a bearing of lubrication and destroy it. When lack of lubrication is the cause of bearing failure, the bearing material is wiped or extruded from the steel backing of the bearing. Temperatures may increase to the point where the steel backing and the journal turn blue from overheating.

 HAYNES HiNT *Refer to Tools and Workshop Tips for bearing fault finding.*

6 Riding habits can have a definite effect on bearing life. Full throttle low speed operation, or labouring the engine, puts very high loads on bearings, which tend to squeeze out the oil film. These loads cause the bearings to flex, which produces fine cracks in the bearing face (fatigue failure). Eventually the bearing material will loosen in pieces and tear away from the steel backing. Short trip riding leads to corrosion of bearings, as insufficient engine heat is produced to drive off the condensed water and corrosive gases produced. These products collect in the engine oil, forming acid and sludge. As the oil is carried to the engine bearings, the acid attacks and corrodes the bearing material.

7 Incorrect bearing installation during engine assembly will lead to bearing failure as well. Tight fitting bearings which leave insufficient bearing oil clearances result in oil starvation. Dirt or foreign particles trapped behind a bearing shell result in high spots on the bearing which lead to failure.

8 To avoid bearing problems, clean all parts thoroughly before reassembly, double check all bearing clearance measurements and lubricate the new bearings with clean engine oil during installation.

24 Crankshaft and main bearings

Note 1: *The connecting rod nuts and bolts can only be used in a running engine once, though they can be used to do a big-end oil clearance check to prevent having to buy two sets of new bolts.*

Note 2: *On C models the crankcases, crankshaft, clutch housing and alternator driven gear are all matched on assembly according to various code markings. If any of the above parts are replaced with new ones the new parts must carry the same marks as those being replaced to ensure correct matching. Refer to your Kawasaki parts dealer for details.*

Removal

1 Remove the engine from the frame (see Section 4) and separate the crankcase halves (see Section 21).

2 On C and D models, before removing the crankshaft insert a feeler gauge between the crankshaft web and the No. 2 main

24.3a Check the side clearance...

24.3b ...then remove the thrust bearings, poking them around with a screwdriver

24.4 Check the big-end side clearance on each rod

24.5 Mark the relevant cylinder number on each connecting rod and cap

24.6a Unscrew the nuts (arrowed) and remove the connecting rod caps

26.6b Push each rod off its crankpin

bearing journal and check the side clearance. Compare the measurement with this Chapter's Specifications. If the clearance is excessive, replace the crankcase halves as a set.

3 On E and F models, before removing the crankshaft insert a feeler gauge between the thrust bearing and the No. 3 main bearing journal and check the side clearance **(see illustration)**. Compare the measurement with this Chapter's Specifications. If the clearance is excessive, replace the thrust bearings with a new set and recheck the clearance. If it is still excessive replace the crankshaft with a new one. Remove the thrust bearings by pushing the top down on one end and drawing it out by the other end **(see illustration)**.

4 Before removing the rods from the crankshaft, measure the big-end side clearance (the gap between the connecting rod big-end and the crankshaft web) with a feeler gauge **(see illustration)**. If the clearance is greater than the service limit listed in this Chapter's Specifications, replace the rods with new ones. If the clearance is still excessive, replace the crankshaft with a new one.

5 Using paint or a felt marker pen, mark the relevant cylinder identity on the front face of each connecting rod and cap to ensure that they are fitted correctly on reassembly **(see illustration)**.

6 Unscrew the connecting rod cap nuts **(see illustration)**. Pull the caps off, noting the locating pins – if a cap is difficult to remove tap the bolts on the top to push the rod down. Push the rods and pistons up to the tops of

the bores so that the bottom ends are clear of the crankshaft, taking care to keep the rods clear of the cylinder liners – it is best to protect the liners with some rag **(see illustration)**. **Note:** *Even if no work is to be carried out on the piston/connecting rod assemblies they must be removed, as new bolts must be fitted, along with new nuts – refer to Section 25.*

7 Lift the crankshaft out of the upper crankcase half, bringing the cam chain with it if it hasn't been removed, and taking care not to dislodge the main bearing shells **(see illustration)**. Wrap some rag around each connecting rod to protect the cylinder walls.

8 Remove the main bearing shells from the crankcase halves **(see illustration 24.32)**. Keep the shells in order.

9 Remove the piston/connecting rod assemblies (see Section 25).

Inspection

10 Clean the crankshaft with solvent, squirting it under pressure through all the oil passages. If available, blow the crank dry with compressed air, and blow through the oil passages. Check the primary drive gear for wear and damage **(see illustration)**. If any of the gear teeth are excessively worn, chipped or broken, the crankshaft must be replaced with a new one. If wear or damage is found, also inspect the primary driven gear on the back of the clutch housing (see Section 15).

11 Refer to Section 23 and examine the main bearing shells. If they are scored, badly scuffed or appear to have been seized, new bearings must be installed. Always replace the main bearings as a set. If they are badly damaged, check the corresponding crankshaft journals. Evidence of extreme heat, such as discoloration, indicates that lubrication failure

24.7 Lift the crankshaft out of the crankcase

24.10 Primary drive gear (arrowed)

24.18 Lay a strip (arrowed) on each journal

24.21 Measuring the squashed strip

24.29 Main bearing housing size marking location (arrowed)

has occurred. Be sure to thoroughly check the oil pump and pressure relief valve as well as all oil holes and passages before reassembling the engine.

12 Give the crankshaft journals a close visual examination, paying particular attention where damaged bearings have been discovered. If the journals are scored or pitted in any way a new crankshaft will be required. Note that undersizes are not available, precluding the option of regrinding the crankshaft.

13 Place the crankshaft on V-blocks and check the runout at the centre main bearing journal using a dial gauge. Compare the reading to the maximum specified at the beginning of the Chapter. If the runout exceeds the limit, the crankshaft must be replaced with a new one.

Oil clearance check

14 Whether new bearing shells are being fitted or the original ones are being re-used, the main bearing oil clearance should be checked before the engine is reassembled. Main bearing oil clearance is measured with a product known as Plastigauge.

15 Clean both sides of the bearing shells, the bearing housings in both crankcase halves, and the journals on the crankshaft.

16 Press the bearing shells into their correct locations. Make sure the tab on each shell engages in the notch in the casing **(see illustration 24.32)**, and that the grooved shells are fitted to journals 2, 3 and 4 (left-to-right) on C and D models, and to journals 2 and 4 (left-to-right) on E and F models **(see illustration 24.30b)**. Take care not to touch any shell's bearing surface with your fingers.

17 Make sure the shells and crankshaft are clean and dry. Lay the crankshaft in position in the upper crankcase **(see illustration 24.7)**. Fit the three crankcase dowels if removed **(see illustration 21.13)**.

18 Cut five lengths of the appropriate size Plastigauge (they should be slightly shorter than the width of the crankshaft journals). Place a strand of Plastigauge on each (cleaned) journal, avoiding the oil hole **(see illustration)**. Make sure the crankshaft is not rotated.

19 Carefully fit the lower crankcase half onto the upper half **(see illustration 21.8)**. Check that the lower half is correctly seated. **Note:** *Do not tighten the crankcase bolts if the casing is not correctly seated.* Clean the ten crankshaft journal 9 mm bolts, then apply molybdenum disulphide oil (a 50/50 mixture of molybdenum disulphide grease and engine oil) to the threads, under the heads and to the lower sides of the copper washers (use the old ones). Secure the bolts finger-tight at first, then tighten them evenly and a little at a time in the numerical sequence shown to the torque setting specified for your model at the beginning of the Chapter **(see illustration 21.17b)**.

20 Slacken the bolts evenly and a little at a time in a reverse of the tightening sequence, i.e. starting from the outside and working to the centre, until they are all finger-tight, then remove the bolts. Carefully lift off the lower crankcase half, making sure the Plastigauge is not disturbed.

21 Compare the width of the crushed Plastigauge on each crankshaft journal to the scale printed on the Plastigauge envelope to obtain the main bearing oil clearance **(see illustration)**. Compare the reading to the specifications at the beginning of the Chapter.

22 On completion carefully scrape away all traces of the Plastigauge material from the crankshaft journal and bearing shells; use a fingernail or other object which is unlikely to score them.

23 If the oil clearance falls into the specified range, no bearing replacement is required (provided they are in good shape). If the clearance is between the maximum standard specification and the service limit, replace all the old bearing shells with new shells that have blue paint marks **(see illustration 24.30a)**, then check the oil clearance once again.

24 The new clearance can slightly exceed the maximum standard clearance, but it must be not less than the minimum standard clearance.

25 If the clearance is greater than the service limit listed in this Chapter's Specifications, measure the diameter of the crankshaft

journals with a micrometer and compare your findings with this Chapter's Specifications. Also, by measuring the diameter at a number of points around each journal's circumference, you'll be able to determine whether or not the journal is out-of-round. Take the measurement at each end of the journal, near the crank throws, to determine if the journal is tapered.

26 If any crank journal has worn down past the service limit, replace the crankshaft with a new one.

27 If the diameters of the journals aren't less than the service limit but differ from the original size according to the markings on the crankshaft in relation to the specifications given at the beginning of the Chapter, apply new marks with a hammer and punch, then select new bearing shells according to the new size marks (Steps 29 and 30).

28 Remove the main bearing shells and reassemble the crankcase halves. Using a telescoping gauge and a micrometer, measure the diameters of the main bearing bores, then compare the measurements with the marks on the upper case half. They should correspond.

Main bearing shell selection

29 Replacement bearing shells for the main bearings are supplied on a selected fit basis. Code marks and numbers stamped on the crankshaft and crankcase are used to identify the correct replacement bearings. The crankshaft main bearing journal size numbers are stamped on the crankshaft webs and will be either unmarked or marked 1. The corresponding main bearing housing size marks are stamped into the front of the upper crankcase half and will be either unmarked or marked O **(see illustration)**. The left-hand mark corresponds to the left-hand bearing, and the marks correspond consecutively from left to right.

30 A range of bearing shells is available. To select the correct bearing for a particular journal, use the table below and cross-refer the main bearing journal size mark (stamped on the crank web) with the main bearing housing size mark (stamped on the crankcase) to determine the colour code of the bearing required. The colour is marked on the side of

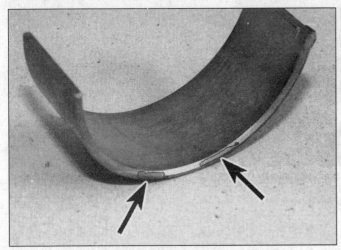

24.30a Bearing shell colour code (arrowed)

24.30b Make sure the grooved shells are correctly positioned – E/F model shown, lower crankcase

the shell **(see illustration)**. Note that the shells for journals 2, 3 and 4 (left-to-right) on C and D models, and for journals 2 and 4 (left-to-right) on E and F models have an oil groove, while the others don't **(see illustration)** – check with your dealer and make sure you obtain the correct number of each type when ordering replacement shells.

Main bearing journal code	Main bearing housing code	Replacement bearing colour
1	O	Brown
1	None	Black
None	O	Black
None	None	Blue

Installation

31 Clean both sides of the bearing shells, the bearing housings in both crankcase halves, and the journals on the crankshaft. If new shells are being fitted, ensure that all traces of the protective grease are cleaned off using paraffin (kerosene). Wipe the shells, crankcase halves and journals dry with a lint-free cloth. Make sure all the oil passages and holes are clear, and blow them through with compressed air if available and not already done.

32 Press the bearing shells into their locations **(see illustration)**. Make sure the bearings are fitted in the correct locations (Step 16) and the tab on each shell engages in the notch in the casing. Lubricate the bearing surface of each shell with molybdenum disulphide oil (a 50/50 mixture of molybdenum disulphide grease and clean engine oil).

33 Install the piston/connecting rod assemblies, making sure you fit new bolts first (Section 25).

34 Lower the crankshaft into position in the upper crankcase, making sure all bearings remain in place **(see illustration 24.7)**.

35 On E and F models, lubricate the grooved side of each thrust bearing with molybdenum disulphide oil (a 50/50 mixture of molybdenum disulphide grease and clean engine oil). Slide the thrust bearings into place on each side of the No. 3 main bearing journal with the oil grooves facing out **(see illustration)** – if the second one is difficult to fit push the crankshaft to the left or right as required to create some extra clearance.

36 Lubricate the crankpins with molybdenum disulphide oil (a 50/50 mixture of molybdenum disulphide grease and clean engine oil). Carefully pull the connecting rods onto the crankpins, taking care not to mark the cylinders **(see illustration)**. Fit the caps onto the rods **(see illustration)**. Make sure each cap is fitted the correct way around so the previously made markings align, and that the rod is facing the right way (see Step 5 and Section 25).

37 Apply some clean oil to the bolt threads and under the heads of the NEW connecting rod nuts, then fit them and tighten them

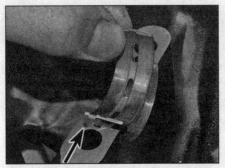

24.32 Fit the shells, locating the tab in the notch

24.35 Face the oil groove (arrowed) to the crank web

24.36a Pull each rod up onto its crankpin...

24.36b ...then fit the cap, locating the pins in the holes

24.37a Lubricate and fit the new nuts...

24.37b ...and tighten them as described first to the specified torque and then through the specified angle

25.7 Check for freeplay between the rod and pin

finger-tight **(see illustration)**. First tighten them to the torque setting specified at the beginning of the Chapter. Now, using a degree disc, tighten each bolt in turn by a further 150° **(see illustration)**. You are recommended to have an assistant to hold the crankshaft down in the crankcase while tightening the bolts as it could jump out.

If a degree disc is not available, the angle can be determined by using the points on the connecting rod cap nut. There are six points on the nut, so the angle between each point is 60°. Select one point as a reference and mark it with paint or a marker. Now mark the connecting rod cap mid-way between the second and third points clockwise from the marked point. Tighten the nut – when the mark on the first point aligns with the mark on the connecting rod cap, it will have turned through 150°.

38 Carefully turn the crankshaft to check the connecting rod is not tight – if there are any signs of roughness or tightness, try tapping the bottom of the connecting rod cap as this may relieve tightness, but if in doubt remove the rod and recheck the bearing clearance.
39 Install the other connecting rods in the same way. Check to make sure that all components have been returned to their original locations using the marks made on disassembly.
40 Reassemble the crankcase halves (see Section 21).

25 Connecting rods and bearings

Note: *The connecting rod nuts and bolts can only be used in a running engine once, though they can be used when performing the oil clearance check to prevent having to buy two new sets instead of one. If new connecting rods are fitted they will come with nuts and bolts.*

Removal

1 Remove the engine from the frame (see Section 4) and separate the crankcase halves (see Section 21). Remove the transmission input shaft (see Section 28).
2 Remove the crankshaft (see Section 24, Steps 2 to 7). Wrap some rag around each connecting rod to protect the cylinder walls.
3 Turn the crankcase on its side. Push each piston/connecting rod assembly up its bore and remove it from the top making sure the connecting rod does not mark the cylinder walls.

To ease removal of the pistons, carefully remove any ridge of carbon built up on the top of each cylinder bore using a scraper, Stanley knife blade or scouring cloth. If there is a pronounced wear ridge, remove it using a ridge reamer.

Caution: Do not try to remove the piston/connecting rod from the bottom of the cylinder bore. The piston will not pass the crankcase main bearing webs. If the piston is pulled right to the bottom of the bore the oil control ring will expand and lock the piston in position. If this happens it is likely the ring will break.

4 Keep the rod, cap, nuts and bolts, and the bearing shells (if they are to be re-used) together in their correct positions to ensure correct installation – fit the caps back onto the rods and finger-tighten the nuts to make sure.
5 Remove the pistons from the connecting rods if required (see Section 26), but note that if you are doing a big-end oil clearance check they must be on the rods to prevent them rotating on the crankpin and dislodging the Plastigauge.

Inspection

6 Check the connecting rods for cracks and other obvious damage.
7 With the piston removed, apply clean engine oil to the piston pin, insert it into the connecting rod small-end and check for any

freeplay between the two **(see illustration)**. If the clearance is excessive, replace the pin with a new one and recheck for freeplay. If it is still excessive replace the connecting rod with a new one.
8 Refer to Section 23 and examine the connecting rod bearing shells. If they are scored, badly scuffed, corroded, or appear to have seized, new shells must be installed. Remove them if required by pushing their centres out to the side then lifting them out **(see illustration 25.26)**. Always replace the shells in the connecting rods as a set. If they are badly damaged, check the corresponding crankpin. Evidence of extreme heat, such as discoloration, indicates that lubrication failure has occurred. Be sure to thoroughly check the oil pump and pressure relief valve as well as all oil holes and passages before reassembling the engine.
9 Have the rods checked for twist and bend by a Kawasaki dealer if you are in doubt about their straightness.

Oil clearance check

10 If the bearings and journals appear to be in good condition, check the oil clearances as follows:
11 Start with the rod for the number one cylinder. Wipe the bearing shells and the connecting rod and cap clean, using a lint-free cloth. Fit the bearing shells in the connecting rod and cap. Make sure the tab on the bearing engages with the notch in the rod or cap **(see illustration 25.26)**. Refer to Step 27 and fit the rod and piston into its correct cylinder, making sure it is the correct way round. Lay the crankshaft in the upper crankcase half, then pull the connecting rod onto the crankpin **(see illustration 24.36b)**.
12 Wipe off the No. 1 crankpin with a lint-free cloth. Lay a strip of Plastigauge across the top of the crankpin, parallel with the axis **(see illustration 24.18)**. Fit the connecting rod cap.
13 Fit the nuts and tighten them to the torque setting specified in this Chapter's Specifications, then tighten them further through the angle specified using a degree disc **(see illustrations 24.37a and b)**. Do not allow the connecting rod to rotate at all.

25.22 Connecting rod size mark (arrowed)

25.24a Knock the old bolts out

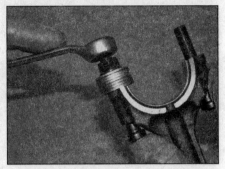

25.24b Fit washers and an old nut and tighten the nut to draw the bolt in...

14 Unscrew the nuts and remove the connecting rod and cap, being very careful not to disturb the Plastigauge. Compare the width of the crushed Plastigauge to the scale printed in the Plastigauge envelope to determine the bearing oil clearance (**see illustration 24.21**).

15 If the clearance is within the range listed in this Chapter's Specifications and the bearings are in perfect condition, they can be reused. If the clearance is between the maximum standard specification and the service limit, replace all the bearing shells with shells that have blue paint marks, then check the oil clearance once again (**see illustration 24.30a**).

16 The new clearance can slightly exceed the maximum standard clearance, but it must not be less than the minimum standard clearance.

17 If the clearance is greater than the service limit listed in this Chapter's Specifications, measure the diameter of the big-end journal (crankpin) on the crankshaft with a micrometer and compare your findings with this Chapter's Specifications. Also, by measuring the diameter at a number of points around the pin's circumference, you'll be able to determine whether or not it is out-of-round. Take the measurement at each end to determine if the journal is tapered.

18 If any crankpin has worn down past the service limit, replace the crankshaft with a new one.

19 If the diameters of the crankpins aren't less than the service limit but differ from the original size according to the markings on the crankshaft in relation to the specifications given at the beginning of the Chapter, apply new marks with a hammer and punch, then select new bearing shells according to the new size marks (Steps 22 and 23).

20 Remove the bearing shells from the connecting rod and cap, then assemble the cap to the rod. Tighten the nuts to the torque and angle listed in this Chapter's Specifications.

21 Using a telescoping gauge and a micrometer, measure the inside diameter of the connecting rod big-end. The mark on the connecting rod (if any) should coincide with the

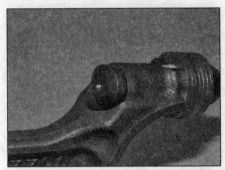

25.24c ...making sure the bolt head is correctly aligned and seated

measurement according to the specifications, but if it doesn't, make a new mark.

Bearing shell selection

22 Replacement bearing shells for the big-end bearings are supplied on a selected fit basis. Code marks stamped on the crankshaft and connecting rod are used to identify the correct replacement bearings. The big-end journal size marks are stamped on a crankshaft web adjacent to the journal and will be either unmarked or marked O. The connecting rod size mark is on the flat face of the connecting rod and cap and will be either unmarked or marked with a circle around the weight mark (**see illustration**).

23 A range of bearing shells is available. To select the correct bearings for a particular journal, use the table below and cross-refer the big-end journal size mark (stamped on the crank web) with the big-end housing size mark (stamped on the connecting rod) to determine the colour code of the bearing required. The colour is marked on the side of the shell (**see illustration 24.30a**).

Crankpin code	Connecting rod big-end code	Replacement bearing colour
O	None	Brown
None	None	Black
O	O	Black
None	O	Blue

25.26 Fit the shells, locating the tab in the notch

Installation

Caution: The connecting rod bolts are designed to stretch when they are tightened. NEVER reuse the old bolts.

24 Remove the old bolts from the rod (**see illustration**). Clean the new connecting rod nuts and bolts, and the rods themselves if new ones are being fitted, with solvent to remove the anti-rust coating, then dry them using compressed air. Draw the new bolts into the rod using the old nuts and some washers as shown until the nuts go tight, aligning their flats so the head will seat in its cut-out (**see illustrations**). Remove the old nuts and the washers.

25 Fit the pistons onto the connecting rods (see Section 26).

26 Clean both sides of the bearing shells and the bearing housings in both cap and rod. If new shells are being fitted, ensure that all traces of any protective grease are cleaned off using paraffin (kerosene). Wipe the shells, cap and rod dry with a clean lint free cloth. Fit the bearing shells in the connecting rods and caps, making sure the tab on each shell engages the notch (**see illustration**). Lubricate the shells with molybdenum disulphide oil (a 50/50 mixture of molybdenum disulphide grease and clean engine oil).

27 Lubricate the pistons, rings and cylinder bore with clean engine oil. Wrap some rag round the bottom of each connecting rod. Insert the piston/connecting rod assembly into the top of its correct bore according to the

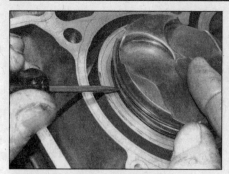

25.27a Carefully compress and feed each ring in

25.27b Fit the compressor over the piston and rings...

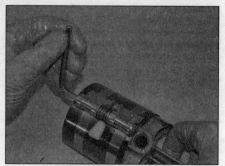

25.27c ...then compress the rings by tightening the bands on the compressor using an Allen key

25.27d Fit the rod into the bore, circle (arrowed) to the front, and rest the compressor on the crankcase...

25.27e ...then tap the top of the piston with a soft tool so that it enters

from the other side to free the piston from the connecting rod **(see illustration)**. If required remove the other circlip. New circlips must be used. When the piston has been removed, slide its pin back into its bore so that related parts do not get mixed up.

> **HAYNES HiNT** *If a piston pin is a tight fit in the piston bosses, use a heat gun to heat the piston – this will expand the alloy piston sufficiently to release its grip on the pin. If the piston pin is particularly stubborn, extract it using a drawbolt tool, but be careful to protect the piston's working surfaces.*

cylinder number marked on removal, taking care not to allow the connecting rod to mark the bore. Make sure the circle on the piston crown faces the exhaust side of the cylinder. Carefully compress and feed each piston ring into the bore until the piston crown is flush with the top of the bore **(see illustration)**. If available, a piston ring compressor makes installation a lot easier – fit the compressor around the piston and over the rings and tighten it to compress the rings, then locate the assembly on the top of the bore and tap the top of the piston using a wooden or plastic tool (such as the handle end of a hammer) until the piston is completely in the bore **(see illustrations)**.

28 Install the crankshaft (see Section 24).

29 Reassemble the crankcase halves (see Section 21).

26 Pistons

Removal

1 Remove the connecting rods (see Section 25).

2 Before removing the piston from the connecting rod, use a felt marker pen to write the cylinder identity on the skirt of each piston. The piston crown is marked with a circle that faces the exhaust side of the cylinder **(see illustration)**.

3 Carefully prise out the circlip on one side of the piston using needle-nose pliers or a small flat-bladed screwdriver inserted into the notch **(see illustration)**. Push the piston pin out

4 Using your thumbs or a piston ring removal and installation tool, carefully remove the rings from the pistons **(see illustrations 27.10b, 27.9b, 27.7c, b and a)**. Do not nick or gouge the pistons in the process. Carefully note which way up each ring fits and in which groove, as they must be installed in their original positions if being re-used. The upper surface of the top ring should be marked with the letter R at one end, and the second (middle) ring marked RN **(see illustrations 27.10a and 27.9a)**. The top and middle rings can also be identified by their different cross-section profiles **(see illustration 27.11)**.

5 Scrape all traces of carbon from the tops of the pistons. A hand-held wire brush or a piece of fine emery cloth can be used once most of

26.2 Note the circle (arrowed) on the front (exhaust) side of the piston

26.3a Prise out the circlip using a suitable tool in the notch...

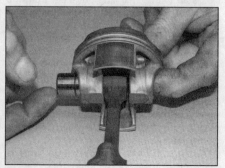

26.3b ...then push out the pin and separate the piston from the rod

26.10 Measure the piston ring-to-groove clearance with a feeler gauge

26.11 Measure the piston diameter with a micrometer at the specified distance from the bottom of the skirt

the deposits have been scraped away. Do not use a wire brush mounted in a drill motor to remove deposits from the pistons – the piston material is soft and will be eroded away by the wire brush.

6 Use a piston ring groove cleaning tool to remove any carbon deposits from the ring grooves. If a tool is not available, a piece broken off an old ring will do the job. Be very careful to remove only the carbon deposits. Do not remove any metal and do not nick or gouge the sides of the ring grooves.

7 Once the deposits have been removed, clean the pistons with solvent and dry them thoroughly. If the identification mark previously made on the piston is cleaned off, be sure to re-mark it with the correct identity. Make sure the oil return holes below the oil ring groove are clear.

Inspection

8 Carefully inspect each piston for cracks around the skirt, at the pin bosses and at the ring lands. Normal piston wear appears as even, vertical wear on the thrust surfaces of the piston. If the skirt is scored or scuffed, the engine may have been suffering from overheating and/or abnormal combustion, which caused excessively high operating temperatures. Also check that the circlip grooves are not damaged.

9 Burned areas around the edge of the piston crown, indicate that pre-ignition or knocking under load have occurred. If you find evidence of any problems the cause must be corrected

or the damage will occur again (see *Fault Finding* in the *Reference* section).

10 Measure the piston ring-to-groove clearance by laying each piston ring in its groove and slipping a feeler gauge in beside it **(see illustration)**. Make sure you have the correct ring for the groove (see Step 4). Check the clearance at three or four locations around the groove. If the clearance is greater than specified, measure the thickness of the ring and the width of its groove and replace the rings and/or piston with new ones as required, though if wear is evident it is advisable to replace all pistons and rings as a complete set.

11 Check the piston-to-bore clearance by measuring the bore (see Section 22), then measure the piston 5 mm up from the bottom of the skirt on C and D models and 8.5 mm up on E and F models, and at 90° to the piston pin axis **(see illustration)**. Make sure each piston is matched to its correct cylinder. Refer to the Specifications at the beginning of the Chapter and subtract the piston diameter from the bore diameter to obtain the clearance. If it is greater than the specified figure, the piston must be replaced with a new one (assuming the bore itself is within limits).

Installation

12 Inspect and install the piston rings (see Section 27).

13 Lubricate the piston pin, the piston pin bore and the connecting rod small-end bore

with molybdenum disulphide oil (a 50/50 mixture of molybdenum disulphide grease and clean engine oil).

14 When fitting the pistons onto the connecting rods make sure the circle on the piston crown faces the exhaust side of the cylinder, and that if fitting the old piston it is matched to its correct cylinder **(see illustration 26.2)**.

15 If both circlips were removed fit one **new** circlip into one side of the piston (do not re-use old circlips). Line up the piston on its correct connecting rod, and insert the piston pin from the other side **(see illustration)**. Secure the pin with another **new** circlip **(see illustration)**. When fitting the circlips, compress them only just enough to fit them in the piston, and make sure they are properly seated in their grooves with their open end away from the removal notch.

16 Install the connecting rods (see Section 25) and reassemble the crankcase halves (see Section 21).

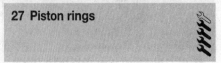

27 Piston rings

Note: *It is good practice to replace the piston rings with new ones when an engine is being overhauled.*

Removal

1 See Section 26, Steps 1 to 4.

Inspection

2 Whether re-using the old rings or fitting new ones, check the installed end gaps with the rings installed in the bore, as follows. Lay out each piston with its ring set and keep them together so the rings will be matched with the same piston and bore during the measurement procedure and engine assembly.

3 Insert the top ring into the top of the bore and square it up with the bore walls by sitting the top of the piston against the ring, then push the ring down towards the bottom of the bore, but keeping it within the area of ring travel, using the piston **(see illustration)**. Slip a feeler gauge between the ends of the ring and compare the measurement to the

26.15a Slide the pin through the piston and rod...

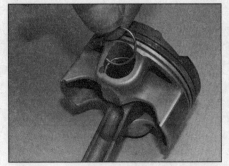

26.15b ...and secure it with new circlips

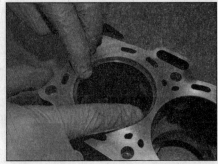

27.3a Set the ring square in its bore ...

27.3b ...and measure the end gap using a feeler gauge

27.7a Fit the oil ring expander in its groove...

27.7b ...then fit the lower side rail...

27.7c ...and the upper side rail on each side of it

27.9a Note the marking on each ring and make sure it faces up

27.9b Fit the middle ring into its groove

specifications at the beginning of the Chapter **(see illustration)**.

4 If the gap is larger or smaller than specified, double check to make sure that you have the correct rings before proceeding; excess end gap is not critical unless it exceeds the service limit.

5 If the service limit is exceeded with new rings, check the bore for wear (see Section 22). If the gap is too small, the ring ends may come in contact with each other during engine operation, which can cause serious damage.

6 Repeat the procedure for the second (middle) ring, but not the oil control ring side-rails or expander ring. Remember to keep the rings, pistons and bores matched up.

Installation

7 Fit the oil control ring (lowest on the piston) first. It is composed of three separate components, namely the expander and the

upper and lower side-rails. Slip the expander into the groove, making sure the ends don't overlap **(see illustration)**. Next fit the lower side-rail **(see illustration)**. Do not use a piston ring installation tool on the side-rails as they may be damaged. Instead, place one end of the side-rail into the groove between the expander and the ring land. Hold it firmly in place and slide a finger around the piston while pushing the rail into the groove. Next, fit the upper side-rail in the same manner **(see illustration)**. Check that the ends of the expander have not overlapped.

8 After the three oil ring components have been installed, check to make sure that both the upper and lower side-rails can be turned smoothly in the ring groove.

9 Fit the second (middle) ring next – it is marked with the letters RN at one end **(see illustration)**. Fit the ring into the middle groove in the piston with the identification

letters facing up **(see illustration)**. Do not expand the ring any more than is necessary to slide it into place. To avoid breaking the ring, use a piston ring installation tool.

10 Finally, fit the top ring, which should be marked with the letter R (though the example photographed wasn't), and has a chamfered upper inner rim, which must face up, in the same manner into the top groove in the piston **(see illustrations)**.

11 Once the rings are correctly installed, check they move freely without snagging and stagger their end gaps as shown **(see illustration)**.

27.10a Top ring has a chamfered inner upper rim (arrowed)

27.10b Fit the top ring into its groove

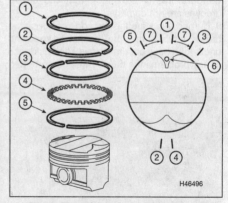

27.11 Piston ring end gap positions

1 Top	5 Oil lower rail
2 Second	6 Circle
3 Oil upper rail	7 30 to 40°
4 Expander	

28.2 Remove the output shaft

28.3a Unscrew the bolts (arrowed) and remove the housing

28.3b Draw the shaft out

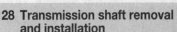

28 Transmission shaft removal and installation

Removal

1 Remove the engine from the frame (see Section 4) and separate the crankcase halves (see Section 21).

2 Lift the output shaft out of the upper crankcase (see illustration). If the shaft is stuck, use a soft-faced hammer and gently tap on the ends. Remove the oil seal and discard it as a new one must be used (see illustration 28.8). If required, remove the needle bearing locating pin and the caged-ball bearing half-ring retainer (see illustrations 28.9a and b) – if they are not in their slot or hole in the crankcase, remove them from the bearings themselves.

3 Unscrew the input shaft bearing housing bolts and remove the housing from the lower crankcase (see illustration). Draw the input shaft out (see illustration). Remove the bearing housing dowel if loose (see illustration 28.7b). Note that a new O-ring must be used when refitting the housing.

4 Referring to *Tools and Workshop Tips* (Section 5) in the Reference Section, check the bearings on the shafts and in the crankcase. Replace the bearings with new ones if necessary (see Section 29).

5 The transmission shafts can be disassembled and inspected for wear or damage (see Section 29).

Installation

6 Fit a new O-ring smeared with grease into the groove in the input shaft bearing housing (see illustration). Make sure the dowel is fitted (see illustration 28.7b).

7 Slide the input shaft into the lower crankcase (see illustration). Fit the bearing housing, making sure the dowel locates correctly, and tighten the bolts to the torque setting specified at the beginning of the Chapter (see illustration).

8 Lubricate the left-hand end of the output shaft with clean oil and slide the new oil seal on (see illustration).

9 If removed, fit the needle bearing pin into its hole in the upper crankcase half, and fit the caged-ball bearing half-ring retainer into its slot (see illustrations). Fit the output shaft (see illustration 28.2), making sure the pin and retainer locate in the hole and groove respectively and the bearing outer races are fully seated. Make sure the outer face of the oil seal is flush with the crankcase wall.

Caution: If the ring retainer or dowel do not locate correctly, the crankcase halves will not seat properly.

10 Reassemble the crankcase halves (see Section 21).

28.6 Fit a new O-ring

28.7a Slide the shaft in...

28.7b ...then fit the housing, locating it on the dowel (arrowed)

28.8 Lubricate the end of the shaft and fit the oil seal

28.9a Fit the pin (arrowed)...

28.9b ...and the ring

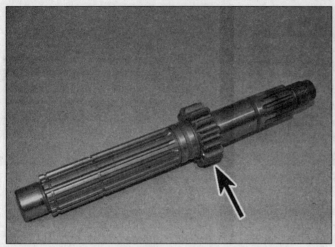

29.6 1st gear pinion (arrowed) is part of the shaft

29.8a Undo the screws (arrowed) and remove the retainer

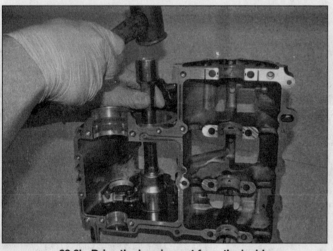

29.8b Drive the bearing out from the inside

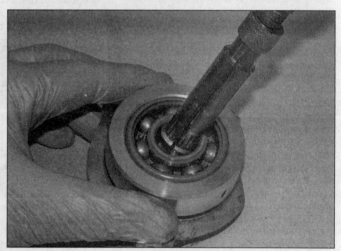

29.8c Locate the knife-end behind the inner race and expand it...

29 Transmission shaft overhaul

1 Remove the transmission shafts from the crankcase (see Section 28). Always disassemble the transmission shafts separately to avoid mixing up the components.

 HAYNES HiNT *When disassembling the transmission shafts, place the parts on a long rod or thread a wire through them to keep them in order and facing the proper direction.*

Input shaft

Disassembly

2 Remove the circlip from the left-hand end of the shaft and slide the 2nd gear pinion off **(see illustrations 29.20b and a)**.
3 Slide the 6th gear pinion off, followed its splined bush and the splined washer **(see illustrations 29.19c, b and a)**.
4 Remove the circlip securing the combined 3rd/4th gear pinion, then slide the pinion off the shaft **(see illustrations 29.18b and a)**.
5 Remove the circlip securing the 5th gear pinion, then slide the thrust washer, the pinion and its bush off the shaft **(see illustrations 29.17d, c, b and a)**.
6 The 1st gear pinion is integral with the shaft **(see illustration)**.

Inspection

7 Wash all of the components in clean solvent and dry them off.
8 Check the bearings, referring to *Tools and Workshop Tips* in the Reference Section, and replace them with new ones if necessary. To remove the input shaft right-hand bearing from the crankcase, first remove the retainer **(see illustration)**. Use a suitable socket or bearing driver located on the outer race to drive the bearing out from inside the crankcase **(see illustration)**. Heat around the bearing housing first using a hot air gun to make removal easier. Use an expanding puller with slide-hammer

attachment to remove the input shaft left-hand bearing from the housing **(see illustrations)**. Heat around the bearing housing first using a hot air gun to make removal easier. When fitting the input shaft left-hand bearing into the housing fit it with the sealed side facing into the housing. Use a suitable socket or bearing driver located on the outer race to drive the bearings in. To remove the bearing from the output shaft use a puller, draw the spacer

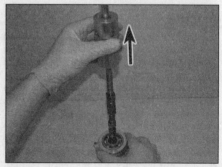

29.8d ...then use the slide-hammer to jar the bearing out

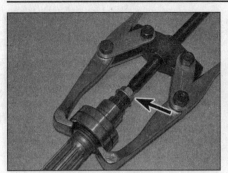

29.8e Puller set-up to draw the bearing and spacer off the output shaft – note the nut (arrowed) used to protect the end of the shaft

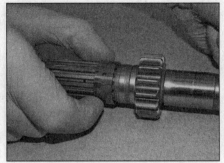

29.17a Slide the 5th gear pinion bush...

29.17b ...the 5th gear pinion...

off with the bearing (see illustration). Drive the new bearing and the spacer, on using a suitable tube or a deep socket.

9 Check the gear teeth for cracking, chipping, pitting and other obvious wear or damage. Any pinion that is damaged as such must be replaced with a new one.

10 Inspect the dogs and the dog holes in the gears for cracks, chips, and excessive wear especially in the form of rounded edges. Make sure mating gears engage properly. Replace the paired gears as a set if necessary.

11 Check for signs of scoring or bluing on the pinions, bushes and shaft. Overheating due to inadequate lubrication can cause this. Check that all the oil holes and passages are clear. Replace any damaged pinions or bushes.

12 Check that each pinion moves freely on its shaft or its bush but without undue freeplay. Check that each bush moves freely on the shaft but without undue freeplay.

13 The shaft is unlikely to sustain damage unless the engine has seized, placing an unusually high loading on the transmission, or the machine has covered a very high mileage. Check the surface of the shaft, especially where a pinion turns on it, and replace the shaft if it has scored or picked up, or if there are any cracks. Damage of any kind can only be cured by replacement.

14 Check the washers and circlips and replace any that are bent or appear weakened or worn. Use new ones if in any doubt. Note that it is good practice to renew all circlips when overhauling gearshafts.

Reassembly

15 During reassembly, apply molybdenum disulphide oil (a 50/50 mixture of molybdenum disulphide grease and clean engine oil) to the mating surfaces of the shaft, pinions and bushes.

16 When fitting the circlips, do not expand their ends any further than is necessary and position them with each end aligned with a spline (see illustration 28.17e). Make sure the round edged side of the circlip faces the direction of thrust so the sharp edged side takes the thrust of the pinion it seats against.

17 Slide the 5th gear pinion bush onto the shaft, then fit the 5th gear pinion onto the bush with its dogs facing away from the integral 1st gear (see illustrations). Slide the thrust washer onto the shaft, then fit the circlip, making sure that it locates in the groove (see illustrations).

18 Slide the combined 3rd/4th gear pinion onto the shaft with the smaller 3rd gear pinion facing the 5th gear pinion, and aligning the oil holes (see illustration). Fit the circlip, making sure it is locates correctly in its groove (see illustrations).

29.17c ...and the washer onto the shaft...

29.17d ...and secure them with the circlip...

29.17e ...making sure it locates properly in its groove

29.18a Slide the combined 3rd/4th gear pinion onto the shaft...

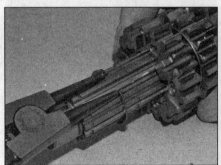

29.18b ...and secure it with the circlip...

29.18c ...making sure it locates properly in its groove

29.19a Slide the splined washer...

29.19b ...and the 6th gear pinion splined bush onto the shaft...

29.19c ...then slide the 6th gear pinion onto the bush

29.20a Slide the 2nd gear pinion on...

29.20b ...then fit the snap-ring...

29.20c ...making sure it locates properly in its groove

19 Slide the splined washer onto the shaft, followed by the 6th gear pinion splined bush, aligning the oil hole in the bush with the hole in the shaft **(see illustrations)**. Slide the 6th gear pinion onto the bush, making sure its dogs face the 3rd/4th gear pinion **(see illustration)**.
20 Slide the 2nd gear pinion onto the end of the shaft with the recessed side facing out **(see illustration)**. Fit the circlip into its groove **(see illustrations)**.
21 Check that all components have been correctly installed **(see illustration)**.

Output shaft

Disassembly

22 Remove the needle bearing outer race from the right-hand end of the shaft, then remove the circlip and slide the bearing off **(see illustrations 29.37c, b and a)**.
23 Remove the circlip securing the 1st gear pinion, then slide the thrust washer off the shaft, followed by the 1st gear pinion, its bush, and the thrust washer **(see illustrations 29.36e, d, c, b and a)**.

24 The fifth gear pinion has three steel balls in it for the positive neutral finder mechanism. These lock fifth gear to the shaft unless it is spun rapidly enough to fling the balls outward. To remove fifth gear, place the shaft vertical with 5th gear uppermost, then spin the shaft by the 3rd gear pinion while pulling fifth gear up **(see illustration)**; it may take several tries to disengage fifth gear from the shaft, but it will slide off easily once it is disengaged. After fifth gear is removed, collect the three steel balls from the slots inside it **(see illustration 29.35a)**.

29.21 The assembled input shaft should be as shown

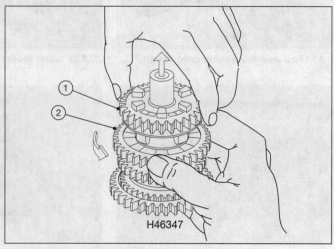

29.24 Pull up on the 5th gear pinion (1) whilst spinning the 3rd gear pinion (2)

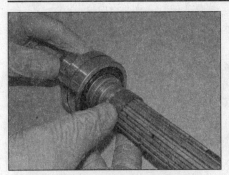

29.31a Slide the 2nd gear pinion bush...

29.31b ...the 2nd gear pinion...

29.31c ...and the washer onto the shaft...

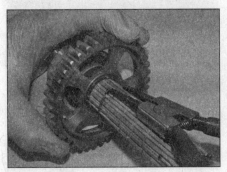

29.31d ...and secure them with the circlip...

29.31e ...making sure it locates in the groove

29.32a Slide the 6th gear pinion onto the shaft...

Caution: Don't pull the gear up too hard or fast – the balls will fly out of the gear.

25 Remove the circlip securing the 3rd gear pinion, then slide the pinion and its collared/ splined bush off the shaft together, followed by the splined washer **(see illustrations 29.34d, c, b and a)**. Remove the collar from the bush.

26 Slide the 4th gear pinion and its collared/ splined bush off the shaft **(see illustrations 29.33b and a)**.

27 Remove the circlip securing the 6th gear pinion, then slide the pinion off the shaft **(see illustrations 28.32b and a)**.

28 Remove the circlip securing the 2nd gear pinion, then slide the thrust washer, the pinion and its bush off the shaft **(see illustrations 29.31d, c, b and a)**.

Inspection

29 Refer to Steps 7 to 14 above.

Reassembly

30 During reassembly, apply molybdenum disulphide oil (a 50/50 mixture of molybdenum disulphide grease and clean engine oil) to the mating surfaces of the shaft, pinions and bushes. When installing the circlips, do not expand their ends any further than is necessary and position them with each end aligned with a spline **(see illustration 29.31e)**. Make sure the round edged side of the circlip faces the direction thrust so the sharp edged side takes the thrust of the pinion it seats against.

31 Slide the 2nd gear pinion bush onto the shaft, then slide the 2nd gear pinion onto

the bush with its shouldered side facing the bearing **(see illustrations)**. Slide the thrust washer on **(see illustration)**. Fit the circlip, making sure it is locates correctly in its groove in the shaft **(see illustrations)**.

32 Slide the 6th gear pinion onto the shaft with its selector fork groove facing away from the 2nd gear pinion, then fit the circlip, making sure it is locates correctly in its groove in the shaft **(see illustrations)**.

33 Slide the 4th gear pinion collared/ splined bush onto the shaft with the collar facing the 6th gear pinion, making sure the oil holes in the bush align with the hole in the shaft, then slide the 4th gear pinion onto its bush with its shouldered side facing away from the 6th gear pinion **(see illustration)**.

29.32b ...and secure it with the circlip

29.33a Slide the collared splined bush onto the shaft...

29.33b ...then slide the 4th gear pinion onto the bush...

29.34a Slide the splined washer onto the shaft...

29.34b ...followed by the 3rd gear pinion...

29.34c ...then slide the bush into the centre of the pinion

29.34d Secure them with the circlip...

29.34e ... making sure it locates in the groove

29.35a Fit each ball (arrowed) into a hole...

34 Slide the splined washer onto the shaft (**see illustration**). Slide the 3rd gear pinion onto the shaft with its recessed side facing away from the 4th gear pinion, making sure the oil holes in the bush align with the hole in the shaft (**see illustration**). Fit the collared/splined bush into the recessed side of the 3rd gear pinion (**see illustration**). Fit the circlip, making sure it is locates correctly in its groove in the shaft (**see illustrations**).

35 Lubricate the positive neutral finder mechanism balls with engine oil – don't use grease as it will impair the action of the mechanism. Fit the balls into the holes with the narrow outer ends in the 5th gear pinion (**see illustrations**). Stand the output shaft vertical and slide the 5th gear pinion on with its selector fork groove facing down, aligning the holes in the gear that contain the balls with the slots in the shaft spline grooves, and making sure the balls do not drop out (**see illustration**). When the gear is in place, tilt the shaft horizontal and turn it slowly, then check that the pinion cannot slide off.

36 Slide the thrust washer and the 1st gear pinion bush onto the shaft, aligning the oil holes, then slide the pinion onto the bush with its recessed side facing the 5th gear pinion (**see illustration**). Fit the thrust washer (**see**

29.35b ...with a narrow outer end (arrowed)

29.35c Slide the 5th gear pinion onto the shaft aligning the small holes with the slots (arrowed)

29.36a Slide the thrust washer...

29.36b ...and the bush onto the shaft...

29.36c ...then slide the pinion onto the bush

illustration). Fit the circlip, making sure it is locates correctly in its groove in the shaft (see illustration).

37 Slide the needle bearing on, then fit the circlip into its groove (see illustrations). Fit the outer race over the needle bearing (see illustration).

38 Check that all components have been correctly installed (see illustration).

30 Running-in procedure

1 Make sure the engine oil and coolant levels are correct (see *Pre-ride checks*). Make sure there is fuel in the tank.

2 Turn the engine kill switch to the ON position and shift the gearbox into neutral. Turn the ignition ON.

3 Start the engine and allow it to run with no throttle applied until it reaches operating temperature.

> ⚠ **Warning: If the oil pressure warning light doesn't go off, or it comes on while the engine is running, stop the engine immediately.**

4 If the oil pressure warning light does not go out, stop the engine immediately and try to find the cause – refer to Section 3. If an engine is run without oil pressure, even for a short period of time, severe damage will occur.

5 Check carefully for oil and coolant leaks and make sure the transmission and controls, especially the brakes, function properly before road testing the machine.

6 Treat the machine gently for the first few miles to make sure oil has circulated throughout the engine and any new parts installed have started to seat.

29.36d Fit the thrust washer

29.36e Secure them with the circlip

29.37a Slide the needle bearing on...

29.37b ...then fit the circlip

7 Even greater care is necessary if new pistons/rings or a new crankcase/bores have been fitted, and the bike will have to be run in as when new. This means greater use of the transmission and a restraining hand on the throttle, keeping engine speed below 4000 rpm until at least 500 miles (800 km) have been covered. There's no point in keeping to any set speed limit – the main idea is to keep from labouring the engine.

Between 500 and 1000 miles (800 and 1600 km) keep engine speeds below 6000 rpm. Experience is the best guide, since it's easy to tell when an engine is running freely.

8 Upon completion of the road test, and after the engine has cooled down completely, recheck the valve clearances (see Chapter 1) and check the engine oil and coolant levels (see *Pre-ride checks*).

29.37c Slide the race over the bearing

29.38 The assembled output shaft should be as shown

Chapter 3
Cooling system

Contents

Degrees of difficulty

Easy, suitable for novice with little experience	**Fairly easy,** suitable for beginner with some experience	**Fairly difficult,** suitable for competent DIY mechanic	**Difficult,** suitable for experienced DIY mechanic	**Very difficult,** suitable for expert DIY or professional

Specifications

Coolant

Mixture type and capacity	see Chapter 1

Temperature gauge (ECT) sensor

Resistance @ 50°C	170 to 250 ohms
Resistance @ 120°C	20 to 23 ohms

Thermostat

Opening temperature	58 to 62°C
Fully open	75°C
Valve lift	8 mm (min)

Radiator

Cap valve opening pressure	
C models	16 to 21 psi (1.15 to 1.45 Bar)
D, E and F models	14 to 18 psi (0.95 to 1.25 Bar)

Torque settings

By-pass hose union	9 Nm
Coolant inlet union bolts	10 Nm
ECT sensor	25 Nm
Thermostat cover bolts	6 Nm
Thermostat housing bolts	10 Nm
Water pump bolts	10 Nm

1 General information

The cooling system uses a water/anti-freeze coolant to carry away excess heat from the engine and maintain as constant a temperature as possible. The cylinders are surrounded by a water jacket from which the heated coolant is circulated by thermo-syphonic action in conjunction with a water pump, which is driven by the oil pump. The hot coolant passes upwards to the thermostat and through to the radiator. The coolant then flows across the core of the radiator, then to the water pump and back to the engine where the cycle is repeated.

A thermostat is fitted in the system to prevent the coolant flowing through the radiator when the engine is cold, allowing the engine to reach normal operating temperature quicker. A dual circuit engine coolant temperature (ECT) sensor mounted in the back of the cylinder head transmits information to the temperature gauge on the instrument panel, and to the ECU (electronic control unit). A cooling fan fitted to the back of the radiator aids cooling in extreme conditions by drawing extra air through. The fan motor is controlled by a relay that receives a signal from the ECU

2.2a Cooling fan wiring connector (arrowed) – D models

that in turn receives information from the ECT sensor.

The complete cooling system is partially sealed and pressurised, the pressure being controlled by a valve contained in the spring-loaded radiator cap. By pressurising the coolant the boiling point is raised, preventing premature boiling in adverse conditions. The overflow pipe from the system is connected to a reservoir into which excess coolant is expelled under pressure. The discharged coolant automatically returns to the radiator by the vacuum created when the engine cools.

⚠ *Warning: Do not remove the pressure cap from the radiator when the engine is hot. Scalding hot coolant and steam may be blown out under pressure, which could cause serious injury. When the engine has cooled, place a thick rag, like a towel, over the pressure cap; slowly rotate the cap anti-clockwise to the first stop. This procedure allows any residual pressure to escape. When the steam has stopped escaping, press down on the cap while turning it anti-clockwise and remove it.*
Caution: Do not allow anti-freeze to come in contact with your skin or painted surfaces of the motorcycle. Rinse off any spills immediately with plenty of water. Anti-freeze is highly toxic if ingested. Never leave anti-freeze lying around in an open container or in puddles on the floor; children and pets are attracted by its sweet smell and may drink it. Check with the local authorities about disposing of used anti-freeze. Many communities will have collection centres which will see that anti-freeze is disposed of safely.
Caution: At all times use the specified type of anti-freeze, and always mix it with distilled water in the correct proportion. The anti-freeze contains corrosion inhibitors which are essential to avoid damage to the cooling system. A lack of these inhibitors could lead to a build-up of corrosion which would block the coolant passages, resulting in overheating and severe engine damage.

Distilled water must be used as opposed to tap water to avoid a build-up of scale which would also block the passages.

2 Cooling fan and relay

1 The cooling fan is on the back of the radiator on the left-hand side side. The fan has its own fuse and relay. If the engine is overheating and the cooling fan isn't coming on, first check the cooling fan fuse (see Chapter 8). If the fuse is good, check the fan and the relay as described below. If the fan is on the whole time, first check the relay. If all is good check the ECT sensor. If the ECT sensor is good the electronic control unit (ECU) could be faulty (see Chapter 4).

Cooling fan

Check

2 On C models remove the fairing (see Chapter 7). On D models remove the left-hand fairing side panel (see Chapter 7). On E and F models remove the upper section of the air filter housing (see Chapter 4). Disconnect the fan wiring connector **(see illustrations)**.
3 Using a 12 volt battery and two jumper wires with suitable connectors, connect the battery positive (+) lead to the blue wire terminal on the fan side of the wiring connector, and the battery negative (–) lead to the black wire terminal on the connector. Once connected the fan should operate. If it does not, and the connector and wiring between it and the motor is good, then the fan motor is faulty.

Replacement

⚠ *Warning: The engine must be completely cool before carrying out this procedure.*
4 Remove the radiator (see Section 5).
5 Unscrew the bolts securing the fan bracket to the radiator and remove the fan assembly **(see illustration)**.
6 Installation is the reverse of removal.

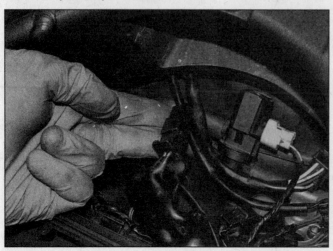

2.2b Cooling fan wiring connector – E/F models

2.5 Fan bracket bolts (arrowed)

2.8a Relay box (arrowed) – C models

2.8b Relay box – D models

2.8c Relay box – E/F models

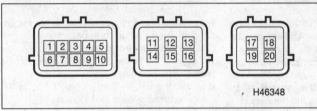

2.9a Relay test terminal ID – C models

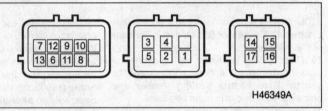

2.9b Relay test terminal ID – D/E/F models

Cooling fan relay

7 On C and D models remove the rider's seat (see Chapter 7). On E and F models remove the centre section of the seat cowling (see Chapter 7).

8 Draw the relay box out of its rubber holder and disconnect the wiring connectors **(see illustrations)**.

9 Set a multimeter to the ohms x 1 scale and connect its probes to terminals 17 and 19 on the relay box on C models, and to terminals 14 and 17 on all other models **(see illustrations)**. There should be no continuity (infinite resistance). Using a fully-charged 12 volt battery and two insulated jumper wires, connect the positive (+) terminal of the battery to terminal 18 on C models and to terminal 15 on all other models, and the negative (–) terminal to terminal 20 on C models and to terminal 16 on all other models. At this point the multimeter should read 0 ohms (continuity). If this is the case the relay is proven good. If the relay still indicates no continuity (infinite resistance) across its terminals, it is faulty and the relay box must be replaced with a new one – individual relays are not available.

3.8 ECT sensor terminal 2 (arrowed)

10 If the relay is good, refer to Section 2 at the beginning of Chapter 8 and the Wiring Diagrams at the end of it and check all the wiring and connectors in the cooling fan circuit.

11 If the fan works but is suspected of cutting in at the wrong temperature, check the ECT sensor (see Chapter 4).

3 Temperature display and ECT sensor

Temperature display

Check

1 The circuit consists of the ECT (engine coolant temperature) sensor mounted in the cylinder head and the digital temperature display in the instrument cluster. When the ignition is first switched on all the segments in the LCD display and the warning light should come on temporarily – this serves as an indication that the display is functioning correctly (if not, refer to Chapter 8).

2 Under normal operating conditions, when the coolant temperature is below 40°C the display will show '- -'. When the temperature is between 41°C and 115°C the display will show the actual temperature. If the temperature reaches between 116°C and 120°C the display will start to flash. If this occurs stop the engine and check the coolant level in the reservoir (see *Pre-ride checks*). If the temperature goes above 120°C the display will flash 'HI'.

3 If the display is not working, check the instrument cluster (see Chapter 8).

4 If the display as a whole works but the coolant function doesn't or is thought to be inaccurate, check the sensor (see below). If the sensor is good, refer to Chapter 8 and check the wiring between the sensor and the

instrument cluster connector for continuity. If the wiring is good the display is faulty.

Replacement

5 The temperature display is part of the LCD unit in the instrument cluster PCB. No individual components are available for the instrument cluster PCB. If it is faulty, replace it with a new one (see Chapter 8).

ECT sensor

Check

6 Displace or remove the throttle bodies (see Chapter 4). The sensor is mounted in the cylinder head **(see illustration 3.8)**. First make sure the connector terminals are secure and all wires are intact.

7 The resistance of the sensor changes with changes in temperature – see the Specifications at the beginning of the chapter. While in theory it is possible to bench test the sensor at those temperatures, in practice the test is difficult to set up and perform. You can, however, test the resistance of the sensor in the bike with the engine cold, warm and hot..

8 On D6, D7, E8, E9 and FA models disconnect the sensor wiring connector **(see illustration 3.10)**. Connect the positive probe of a multimeter set to read resistance to the No. 2 terminal on the sensor, and the negative (–) probe to the body of the sensor, and check that the resistance decreases as the sensor gets warmer, with the value being as specified at 50°C **(see illustration)**. If the sensor fails it is most likely to give a zero, constant value, or infinite resistance reading at all temperatures.

Replacement

 Warning: The engine must be completely cool before carrying out this procedure.

3.10 Disconnect the wiring connector

4.3 Release the clamps (arrowed) and detach the hoses

4.4 Thermostat housing bolts (arrowed)

9 Displace or remove the throttle bodies (see Chapter 4). The sensor is mounted in the back of the cylinder head.

10 Disconnect the sensor wiring connector **(see illustration)**. Unscrew and remove the sensor. Remove the sealing washer and discard it as a new one must be used.

11 Install the sensor using a new sealing washer, smear some suitable silicone sealant on the upper portion of the threads, and tighten it to the torque setting specified at the beginning of the Chapter. Connect the wiring.

12 Install the throttle bodies (see Chapter 4).

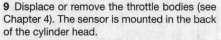

4 Thermostat housing and thermostat

1 The thermostat is automatic in operation and should give many years service without requiring attention. In the event of a failure, the valve will probably jam open, in which case the engine will take much longer than normal to warm up. Conversely, if the valve jams shut, the coolant will be unable to circulate and the engine will overheat. Neither condition is acceptable, and the fault must be investigated promptly.

Thermostat housing

Removal

⚠️ *Warning: The engine must be completely cool before carrying out this procedure.*

2 The thermostat housing is on the back of the cylinder head in the middle. Drain the cooling system (see Chapter 1). Remove the throttle bodies (see Chapter 4).

3 Release the clamps securing the hoses to the housing and detach them, noting which fits where **(see illustration)** – if they are difficult to detach do so after displacing the housing.

4 Unscrew the thermostat housing bolts and remove the housing **(see illustration)**. Remove the O-ring **(see illustration 4.6a)** – a new one must be used.

Installation

5 Check the by-pass hose union is tight **(see illustration)**. If a new housing is being installed unscrew the union from the old housing. Clean the threads of the union and apply a suitable non-permanent thread locking compound, then tighten the union to the torque setting specified at the beginning of the Chapter.

6 Fit the housing using a new O-ring smeared

4.5 By-pass hose union (arrowed)

4.6b ...then fit the housing

with grease and tighten the bolts to the torque setting specified at the beginning of the Chapter **(see illustrations)**.

7 Connect the hoses and tighten the clamps **(see illustration 4.3)**.

8 Install the throttle bodies (see Chapter 4). Fill the cooling system (see Chapter 1).

Thermostat

Removal

⚠️ *Warning: The engine must be completely cool before carrying out this procedure.*

9 Remove the thermostat housing.

10 Unscrew the thermostat cover bolts and detach it from the housing **(see illustration)**.

11 Withdraw the thermostat, noting how it fits **(see illustration)**.

Check

12 Examine the thermostat visually before

4.6a Fit a new O-ring into the groove...

4.10 Unscrew the bolts (arrowed) and detach the cover...

4.11 ...then withdraw the thermostat from the housing

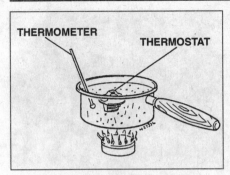

4.13 Thermostat testing set-up

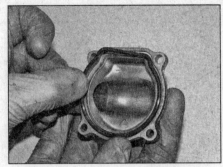

4.16a Fit a new O-ring into the groove...

4.16b ...then fit the cover

carrying out the test. If it remains in the open position at room temperature, it should be replaced with a new one. Also check the condition of the seal.

13 Suspend the thermostat by a piece of wire in a container of cold water. Place a thermometer capable of reading temperatures up to 110°C in the water so that the bulb is close to the thermostat **(see illustration)**. Heat the water, noting the temperature when the thermostat opens, and compare the result with the specifications given at the beginning of the Chapter. Also check the amount the valve opens after it has been heated for a few minutes and compare the measurement to the specifications. If the readings obtained differ from those given, the thermostat is faulty and must be replaced with a new one.

14 In the event of thermostat failure, if the thermostat is permanently closed, as an emergency measure only it can be removed and the machine used without it (this is better than leaving it in as the engine will overheat). If it is permanently open you are better to leave it in. In both cases take care when starting the engine from cold as it will take much longer than usual to warm up. Ensure that a new unit is installed as soon as possible.

Installation

15 Fit the thermostat into the housing with the bleed hole at the top **(see illustration 4.11)**.

16 Fit the cover using a new O-ring smeared with grease and tighten the bolts to the torque setting specified at the beginning of the Chapter **(see illustrations)**.

17 Install the thermostat housing.

5 Radiator

Note: *If the radiator is being removed as part of the engine removal procedure, detach the hoses from their unions on the engine rather than on the radiator and remove the radiator with the hoses attached to it. Note the routing of the hoses.*

Removal

 Warning: The engine must be completely cool before carrying out this procedure.

1 On C models remove the fairing side panels and the fairing (see Chapter 7). On D models remove the fairing side panels (see Chapter 7). On E and F models remove the fairing assembly (Chapter 7) and the upper section of the air filter housing (see Chapter 4).

2 Drain the cooling system (see Chapter 1) – on C models do not refit the reservoir after draining it.

3 Disconnect the fan wiring connector **(see illustration 2.2a or b)**.

4 On D, E and F California models displace the EVAP system separator from the radiator.

5 On D, E and F models remove the horn (see Chapter 8). Remove the pressure cap and displace the rubber shield from around the filler neck **(see illustration)**.

6 Release the clamps securing the hoses to the radiator and detach the hoses **(see illustrations)**.

5.5 Release the rubber shield from the filler neck

5.6a Release the clamps (arrowed), and detach the hoses from the right-hand side...

5.6b ...and the left-hand side'

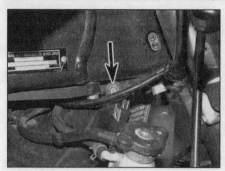

5.7a Upper mounting bolt (arrowed) – C models

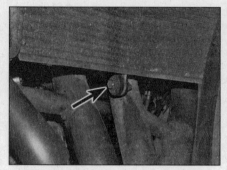

5.7b Lower mounting bolt (arrowed) – E/F model shown

5.7c Displace the radiator from its lug (arrowed) – E/F model shown

7 On C models unscrew the upper mounting bolt **(see illustration)**. On all models unscrew the lower mounting bolt **(see illustration)**. Ease the radiator to the left on C and D models and to the right on E and F models off its upper mounting lug, then remove the radiator, taking care not to catch the fins on the bracket **(see illustration)**. Note the arrangement of the collars and rubber grommets in the radiator mounts. Replace the grommets with new ones if they are damaged, deformed or deteriorated **(see illustration 5.9)**.

8 If necessary, remove the cooling fan (see Section 2). Check the radiator for signs of damage and clear any dirt or debris that might obstruct air flow and inhibit cooling. If the radiator fins are badly damaged or broken the radiator must be replaced with a new one.

Installation
9 Installation is the reverse of removal, noting the following.
● Make sure the coolant hoses and their clamps are in good condition (see Chapter 1).
● Make sure the rubber grommets are in place with the collars fitted in them **(see illustration)**.
● Push the hoses fully onto their unions and tighten the clamps.
● Make sure that the fan wiring is connected **(see illustration 2.2a or b)**.
● On completion refill the cooling system as described in Chapter 1.

Pressure cap check
10 If problems such as overheating or loss of coolant occur, check the entire system as described in Chapter 1. The radiator cap opening pressure should be checked by a Kawasaki dealer with the special tester required to do the job. If the cap is defective, replace it with a new one.

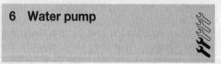

6 Water pump

Check
1 Refer to Chapter 1, Section 11.

Removal
2 Drain the engine oil and coolant (see Chapter 1).
3 On E and F models remove the front sprocket cover (see Chapter 6).
4 Slacken the clamps securing the coolant hoses to the pump and detach the outer hoses, noting which fits where **(see illustration)**.
5 Unscrew the pump mounting bolts, draw the pump out and detach the inner hose **(see illustrations)**. It may be necessary to lever it out to overcome the O-ring on the pump body. Remove the O-ring from the rear of the

5.9 Note the collars and check the condition of the grommets

6.4 Slacken the clamps (arrowed) and detach the outer two hoses from the cover

6.5a Unscrew the bolts (arrowed)...

6.5b ...withdraw the pump and detach the inner hose (arrowed)

6.6 Unscrew the bolts and remove the cover

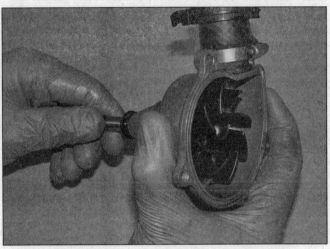
6.8 Check the pump impeller as described

6.9a Fit the new O-ring into its groove...

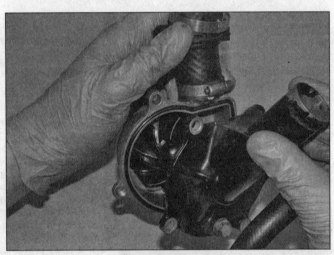
6.9b ...then fit the cover

body – a new one must be used **(see illustration 6.10)**.

6 Unscrew the cover bolts and remove the cover **(see illustration)**. Remove the O-ring – a new one should be used **(see illustration 6.9a)**. Note that a new O-ring is only listed as being available for E and F models, but check with your dealer as it may well fit all models (take the old one along as a match), and otherwise

6.10 Fit a new O-ring (arrowed) into the groove

the only alternative if the O-ring is damaged or no longer sealing is to fit a new pump.

7 Do not attempt to remove the impeller and seals – the pump comes as an assembly and no internal components are available.

8 Wiggle the water pump impeller back-and-forth and in-and-out **(see illustration)**. If there is excessive movement, replace the pump with a new one. Also check for corrosion or a build-up of scale in the pump body and clean or replace the pump as necessary.

Installation

9 Smear the new cover O-ring with grease and fit it into its groove **(see illustration)**. Fit the cover onto the pump **(see illustration)**. Fit the bolts and tighten them to the torque setting specified at the beginning of the Chapter **(see illustration 6.6)**.

10 Make sure the gear position switch wire is correctly routed around the underside of the pump hole. Apply a smear of grease to the new pump body O-ring and fit it onto the body **(see illustration)**. Slide the pump into

the crankcase, aligning the slot in the shaft end with the tab on the oil pump shaft **(see illustration 6.5b)**. Make sure the bolt holes are aligned, fit the bolts and tighten them to the torque setting specified at the beginning of the Chapter.

11 Fit the coolant hoses onto the pump and secure them with the clamps **(see illustration 6.4)**.

12 Replenish the engine oil and refill the cooling system (see Chapter 1). On E and F models install the front sprocket cover (see Chapter 6).

7 Coolant reservoir

1 The coolant reservoir is on the left-hand side. On C and D models remove the left-hand fairing side panel (see Chapter 7). On E models remove the left-hand fairing side cover (see Chapter 7). On F models remove the fairing assembly (see Chapter 7).

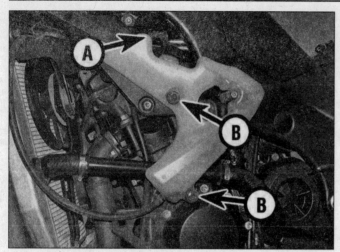

7.2a Disconnect the upper hose (A), then unscrew the bolts (B)...

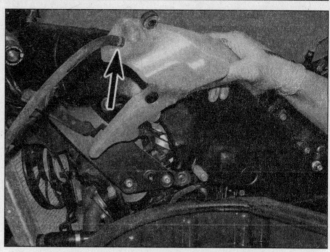

7.2b ...displace and drain the reservoir, then detach the bottom hose (arrowed) – E/F model shown

2 Detach the upper hose. Unscrew the bolts, and displace the reservoir **(see illustration)**. Remove the cap and drain the reservoir **(see illustration)**. Detach the lower hose. Note the collars in the rubber grommets.

3 Installation is the reverse of removal. Make sure the grommets are in good condition and the collars are fitted in them from behind. On completion refill the reservoir to the F level line with the specified coolant mixture (see Chapter 1).

8.4 Inlet union bolts (arrowed)

8 Coolant hoses, pipes and unions

Removal

1 Before removing a hose or pipe, drain the coolant (see Chapter 1).

2 Use a screwdriver to slacken the larger-bore hose clamps, then slide them clear. The smaller-bore hoses are secured by spring clamps that can be expanded by squeezing their ears together with pliers.

Caution: The radiator unions are fragile. Do not use excessive force when attempting to remove the hoses.

3 If a hose proves stubborn, release it by rotating it on its union before working it off. If all else fails, cut the hose with a sharp knife. Whilst this means replacing the hose with a new one, it is preferable to buying a new radiator.

4 The inlet union to the cylinder block can be removed by unscrewing its bolts **(see illustration)** – remove the throttle bodies to access the union (see Chapter 4). If the union is removed, the O-ring must be replaced with a new one. The outlet from the cylinder head

goes into the thermostat housing, which is covered in Section 4.

Installation

5 Slide the clamps onto the hose and then work the hose on to its union as far as the spigot where present.

HAYNES HiNT *If the hose is difficult to push on its union, soften it by soaking it in very hot water, or alternatively a little soapy water on the union can be used as a lubricant.*

6 Rotate the hose on its unions to settle it in position before sliding the clamps into place and tightening them securely.

7 If the inlet union to the cylinder block has been removed, fit a new O-ring into the groove, using a dab of grease to hold it in place if necessary. Fit the union and tighten the mounting bolts to the torque setting specified at the beginning of the Chapter.

8 Refill the cooling system with fresh coolant (see Chapter 1).

Chapter 4
Engine management system

Contents

Degrees of difficulty

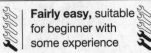

Easy, suitable for novice with little experience	**Fairly easy,** suitable for beginner with some experience	**Fairly difficult,** suitable for competent DIY mechanic	**Difficult,** suitable for experienced DIY mechanic	**Very difficult,** suitable for expert DIY or professional

Specifications

General information

Cylinder numbering	1 to 4 from left to right
Firing order	1-2-4-3
Spark plugs	See Chapter 1

Fuel

Grade	Unleaded. Minimum 95 RON (Research Octane Number)
Fuel tank capacity	17 litres

Fuel injection system

Engine idle speed	1100 ± 50 rpm
Fuel pressure with pump running or engine idling	
C and D models	44 psi (3.1 Bars)
E and F models	43 psi (3.0 Bars)
Minimum fuel flow rate	
C and D models	72 ml every 4 seconds
E and F models	67 ml every 3 seconds
Throttle body vacuum range at idle speed	see Chapter 1

Fuel injection system test data

Camshaft position (CMP) sensor resistance	400 to 460 ohms
Crankshaft position (CKP) sensor resistance.	380 to 570 ohms
Engine coolant temperature (ECT) sensor resistance	
@ 20°C	2.317 to 2.575 K-ohms
@ 80°C	0.31 to 0.33 K-ohm
@ 110°C	138.5 to 146.7 ohms
Fuel injector resistance	
C and D models	11.7 to 12.3 ohms at 20°C (68°F)
E and F models	
Primary injectors.	11.7 to 12.3 ohms at 20°C (68°F)
Secondary injectors	10.5 ohms at 20°C (68°F)
Intake air temperature (IAT) sensor resistance	
C and D models	
At 20°C (68°F)	2.09 to 2.81 K-ohms
At 80°C (176°F)	approx. 0.322 K-ohm
E and F models	
At 0°C (32°F)	5.4 to 6.6 K-ohms
At 80°C (176°F)	approx. 0.29 to 0.39 K-ohm
Oxygen (O2) sensor heater resistance	
D models	approx. 8 ohms at 20°C (68°F)
E and F models.	6.7 to 10.5 ohms at 20°C (68°F)
Secondary throttle position (STP) sensor resistance	4 to 6 K-ohms
Secondary throttle valve servo resistance	
C models	5.0 to 30 ohms
D models	approx. 5.0 to 7 ohms
E and F models.	approx. 6.3 to 9.5 ohms
Throttle position (TP) sensor resistance.	4 to 6 K-ohms

Exhaust valve

Servo sensor resistance.	4 to 6 K-ohms
Servo actuator resistance.	5 to 200 ohms

Air suction system

Control valve resistance	
C and D models	18 to 22 ohms
E and F models.	20 to 24 ohms

Ignition system

Coil primary winding resistance.	1.2 to 1.6 ohms
Coil secondary winding resistance.	8.5 to 11.5 K-ohms
Initial voltage (see text).	Battery voltage (approximately 12 volts)
Minimum peak voltage (see text)	72 volts

Immobiliser receiver

Receiver resistance	0.6 to 0.9 ohm

Torque settings

Camshaft position sensor bolt.	10 Nm
Crankshaft position sensor bolts	6 Nm
Exhaust system	
C models	
Downpipe assembly mounting bolt	25 Nm
Downpipe nuts	17 Nm
Silencer can nuts	22 Nm
Silencer clamp bolt.	17 Nm
Silencer mounting bolt nut	25 Nm
D models	
Downpipe nuts	17 Nm
Middle pipe clamp bolts	17 Nm
Middle pipe mounting bolt nut	25 Nm
Silencer nuts.	22 Nm
Silencer mounting bolt nut	25 Nm
E and F models	
Downpipe nuts	17 Nm
Middle chamber clamp bolt	25 Nm
Middle pipe mounting bolt	25 Nm
Silencer clamp bolt.	25 Nm
Silencer mounting bolt nut	25 Nm
Fuel pump bolts	10 Nm
Oxygen sensor	25 Nm

1 General information and precautions

General information

Fuel system

The fuel supply system consists of the fuel tank, an integrated fuel pump, pressure regulator, filter and level sensor, the fuel hose(s), fuel rail(s), injectors, throttle bodies, and control cables. The fuel pump is switched on and off with the engine via the fuel pump relay. The injection system supplies fuel and air to the engine via 43 mm throttle bodies. On C and D models there is a single injector per cylinder. On E and F models there are two injectors per cylinder – the primary injectors are mounted in the throttle bodies below the throttle valve and operate all the time the engine is running, and the secondary injectors are mounted in the top of the air filter housing, operate only at high engine speeds and wide throttle openings, and spray fuel into the air entering the throttle bodies above the throttle valves. The injectors are operated by the electronic control unit (ECU) using the information obtained from the sensors it monitors.

The exhaust system incorporates a valve that regulates the flow of gases according to throttle opening and engine speed for optimum performance, and a catalytic converter. Models from 2006-on have oxygen sensors in the exhaust supplying information to the ECU.

All models have a low fuel warning light incorporated in the instrument cluster LCD, actuated by a level sensor that is part of the fuel pump inside the fuel tank. The warning light comes on and 'FUEL" flashes on the LCD display when there is 3.5 to 4.0 litres of fuel left.

Ignition system

The transistorised electronic ignition system is combined with the fuel injection system, both being controlled by the electronic control unit (ECU). The ignition system timing triggers, on a rotor on the right-hand end of the crankshaft on C models, and on the starter clutch on the right-hand end of the crankshaft on all other models, a crankshaft position (CKP) sensor, the electronic control unit, ignition coils and spark plugs.

The triggers generate a signal in the CKP sensor as the crankshaft rotates. The CKP sensor sends that signal to the ECU which, in conjunction with information received from the throttle position sensor, camshaft position sensor, and engine coolant temperature sensor, calculates the ignition timing and supplies the ignition coils with the power necessary to produce a spark at the plugs. There is no provision for adjusting the ignition timing.

The system uses four HT coils, one for each cylinder. The coils are of the plug top type known as 'stick coils', with the coil windings being incorporated in the spark plug cap. This eliminates the need for HT leads and saves space.

The system incorporates a safety interlock circuit that cuts the ignition if the sidestand is extended whilst the engine is running and in gear, or if a gear is selected whilst the engine is running and the sidestand is down. It also prevents the engine from being started if the sidestand is down and the engine is in gear. The engine can be started with the sidestand up when it is in gear as long as the clutch lever is pulled in.

Models sold in certain markets are fitted with an immobiliser system that will not allow the engine to be started unless the correct key is used. The immobiliser system has its own fault diagnosis function.

Note: *Individual engine management system components can be checked but not repaired. If system troubles occur, and the faulty component can be isolated, the only cure for the problem in most cases is to replace the part with a new one. Keep in mind that most electronic parts, once purchased, cannot be returned. To avoid unnecessary expense, make very sure the faulty component has been positively identified before buying a new part.*

Precautions

Warning: Petrol (gasoline) is extremely flammable, so take extra precautions when you work on any part of the fuel system. Always remove the battery (see Chapter 8). Don't smoke or allow open flames or bare light bulbs near the work area, and don't work in a garage where a natural gas-type appliance is present. If you spill any fuel on your skin, rinse it off immediately with soap and water. When you perform any kind of work on the fuel system, wear safety glasses and have a fire extinguisher suitable for a class B type fire (flammable liquids) on hand.

With the fuel injection system, some residual pressure will remain in the fuel feed hoses and fuel rail assemblies after the motorcycle has been used. Before disconnecting any fuel hose, ensure the ignition is switched OFF. It is vital that no dirt or debris is allowed to enter the fuel tank or the fuel rail assembly whilst the fuel hoses are disconnected. Any foreign matter in the fuel system components could result in injector damage or malfunction. Ensure the ignition is switched OFF before disconnecting or reconnecting any fuel injection system wiring connector. If a connector is disconnected or reconnected with the ignition switched ON, the electronic control unit (ECU) may be damaged.

Always perform service procedures in a well-ventilated area to prevent a build-up of fumes.

Never work in a building containing a gas appliance with a pilot light, or any other form of naked flame. Ensure that there are no naked light bulbs or any sources of flame or sparks nearby.

Do not smoke (or allow anyone else to smoke) while in the vicinity of petrol (gasoline) or of components containing it. Remember the possible presence of vapor from these sources and move well clear before smoking.

Check all electrical equipment belonging to the house, garage or workshop where work is being undertaken (see the *Safety first!* section of this manual). Remember that certain electrical appliances such as drills, cutters etc, create sparks in the normal course of operation and must not be used near petrol (gasoline) or any component containing it. Again, remember the possible presence of fumes before using electrical equipment.

Always mop up any spilt fuel and safely dispose of the rag used.

Any stored fuel that is drained off during servicing work must be kept in sealed containers that are suitable for holding petrol (gasoline), and clearly marked as such; the containers themselves should be kept in a safe place. Note that this last point applies equally to the fuel tank if it is removed from the machine; also remember to keep its filler cap closed at all times.

Read the *Safety first!* section of this manual carefully before starting work.

2 Fuel tank

Warning: Refer to the precautions given in Section 1 before starting work.

Raise

1 Make sure the fuel cap is secure. Remove the rider's seat (see Chapter 7).
2 Disconnect the battery negative (–) lead (see Chapter 8).
3 Unscrew the front mounting bolts **(see illustration)**. On D, E and F models wrap the

2.3a Unscrew the bolts (arrowed)

2.3b Displace the damper bracket and rest it on the yoke

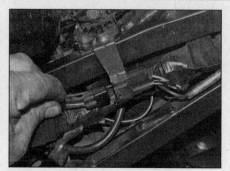

2.4a Disconnecting the pump wiring connector – C models

2.4b Fuel pump wiring connector (arrowed) – D models

steering damper in some rag and rest it on the top yoke **(see illustration)**.

4 On C and D models disconnect the fuel pump wiring connector **(see illustrations)**.

5 On E and F models detach the breather/overflow hose, and on the same California models disconnect the EVAP system hoses, noting which fits where (they are colour-coded, blue on the right, red on the left) **(see illustration)**.

6 Get a suitable piece of wood (such as a piece of 2 x 1 inch, about 12 inches long). Lift the tank and fit the wood between it and the frame to support it in the raised position

(see illustration). Note the collars fitted in the underside of the front mounting grommets **(see illustration)**.

Lower

7 Remove the prop and pivot the tank down onto the frame, making sure the hose(s) and wiring do not get squashed or kinked.

8 On D, E and F models reposition the steering damper bracket **(see illustration 2.3b)**. On all models fit and tighten the front mounting bolts **(see illustration 2.3a)**.

9 On C and D models connect the fuel pump wiring connector **(see illustration 2.4a or b)**.

10 On E and F models connect the breather/overflow hose, and on the same California models the EVAP hoses, blue to the right union, red to the left **(see illustration 2.5)**.

11 Connect the battery (see Chapter 8). If the tank was removed, make sure the kill switch is set to RUN, then turn the ignition ON to allow the fuel pump to pressurise the system, then turn it off. Repeat a couple of times and each time check for leaks at the hose connector. Install the seat.

Removal

Note: *Removing the tank may involve a small amount of unavoidable fuel spillage, which is obviously dangerous. Refer to the precautions given in Section 1 before starting work, and have plenty of rag to hand. Try to time the removal procedure with a near empty tank, which makes it much easier to lift. Once the tank has been removed, rest it on some soft rag to prevent damaging the paintwork or hose unions.*

12 Raise the tank as described above.

13 On C and D models detach the breather/overflow hose, and on the same California models disconnect the EVAP system hoses, noting which fits where (they are colour-coded, red to the front, blue to the rear) **(see illustration)**.

2.5 Detach the hose(s) from the union(s)

2.6a Tank in raised position with wood support

2.6b Make sure the collars do not drop out

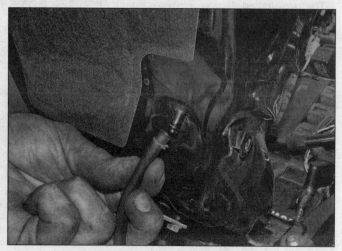

2.13 Detach the hose(s) from the union(s)

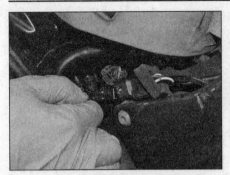

2.14 Disconnecting the pump wiring connector – E/F models

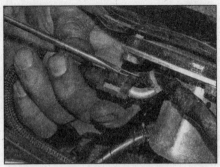

2.16a Press the tabs in and push the retainer down...

2.16b ...then pull the hose off its union

14 On E and F models disconnect the fuel pump wiring connector **(see illustration)**.

15 Clean any dirt from the fuel hose connector. Place a wad of rag for catching any residual fuel in the hose under the connector.

16 On C models press in the tabs on the fuel hose connector retainer and pull the retainer out, then pull the connector off the pipe **(see illustrations)**. Seal the pipe and the connector with a piece from a plastic bag or the finger from a latex glove, secured with an elastic band, to prevent dirt getting in.

17 On D, E and F models insert a suitable flat-bladed screwdriver in the fuel hose connector retainer, then twist the screwdriver to release the retainer, and pull the connector off the pipe **(see illustrations)**. Seal the pipe and the connector with a piece from a plastic bag or the finger from a latex glove, secured with an elastic band, to prevent dirt getting in.

18 Unscrew the rear mounting bolt **(see illustration)**. Carefully lift the tank off the frame and remove it.

19 Remove the sleeve and the rear mounting rubbers if required **(see illustration)**. Similarly remove the collars from the front **(see illustration 2.6b)**. Check all the tank rubbers and hoses for signs of damage or deterioration and replace them with new ones if necessary.

Installation

20 Fit the mounting rubbers into their mounts if removed, and fit the collars into the front rubbers and the sleeve into the rear **(see illustrations 2.6b and 2.19)**.

2.17a Twist the screwdriver to release the retainer...

2.17b ...then pull the hose off its union

21 Depending on how the tank has been stood and how full it is there is the possibility of fuel having made its way into the breather pipe which could spurt out of the hose when the tank is moved – be prepared with some rag for this. Once the tank is upright the pipe will fill itself with air.

22 Position the tank on the frame. Insert and tighten the rear bolt **(see illustration 2.18)**. Raise and support the tank.

23 Make sure the fuel hose connector retainer is in its released position. Fit the connector onto the pipe and push it until it clicks into place, then push the retainer in **(see illustration)**. Try to pull the connector off to make sure it has locked.

24 On C and D models connect the breather/overflow hose, and on the same California models the EVAP hoses, red to

the front union, blue to the rear **(see illustration 2.13)**.

25 On E and F models connect the fuel pump wiring connector **(see illustration 2.14)**.

26 Lower the tank as described above.

Repair

27 Any repairs to the fuel tank should be carried out by a professional who has experience in this critical and potentially dangerous work. Even after cleaning and flushing of the fuel system, explosive fumes can remain and ignite during repair of the tank.

28 If the fuel tank is removed from the bike, it should not be placed in an area where sparks or open flames could ignite the fumes coming out of the tank. Be especially careful inside garages where a natural gas-type appliance is located, because the pilot light could cause an explosion.

2.18 Unscrew the rear bolt and remove the tank

2.19 Withdraw the sleeve and remove the rubbers

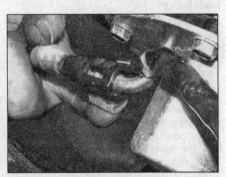

2.23 Push the retainer up to lock the hose in place

3.3 Detach the hoses (arrowed)

3.4 Disconnect the IAT sensor connector

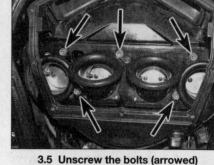

3.5 Unscrew the bolts (arrowed)

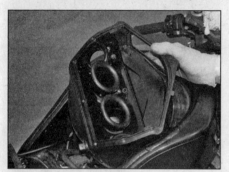

3.6 Remove the housing as described and shown

3.7a Feed the ducts into the housing...

3.7b ...making sure they seat correctly all around

3 Air filter housing

C and D models

Removal

1 Remove the fuel tank (see Section 2).
2 Remove the air filter (see Chapter 1).
3 Disconnect the drain hose and crankcase breather hose **(see illustration)**.
4 Disconnect the IAT sensor wiring connector **(see illustration)**.
5 Undo the air filter housing bolts **(see illustration)**.
6 Displace the housing from the intake ducts, twist it clockwise, lift the left side up and remove the housing **(see illustration)**. Cover the throttle bodies with a clean rag.

Installation

7 Installation is the reverse of removal, noting the following:
● Check the condition of the rim seals in the top of the housing and on the throttle body plate, and make sure they are in their grooves.
● Make sure the hoses are in good condition.
● Make sure each intake duct is seated inside the housing correctly **(see illustrations)** – the ducts are easier to locate after the housing has been bolted to the throttle bodies to prevent it moving about.
● Make sure the IAT sensor wiring connector is securely connected.

E and F models

Removal

8 Remove the fuel tank (see Section 2).
9 Disconnect the fuel hose from the secondary

fuel rail in the same way as from the fuel tank **(see illustrations)**. Disconnect the IAT sensor wiring connector and the secondary injector wiring connectors **(see illustrations)**. If required remove the secondary fuel rail and

3.9a Twist the screwdriver to release the retainer...

3.9b ...then pull the hose off its union

3.9c Disconnect the IAT sensor connector...

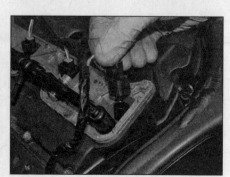

3.9d ...and the injector connectors

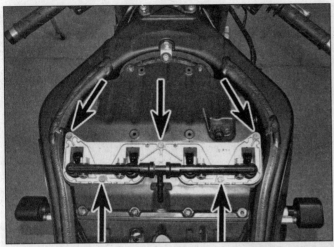

3.9e Injector mounting plate bolts (arrowed)

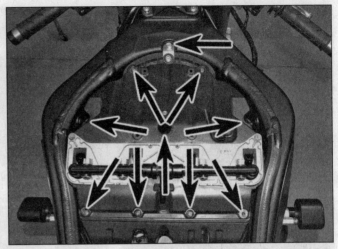

3.10a Undo the screws and bolt (arrowed)...

injector assembly by unscrewing the mounting plate bolts **(see illustration)**.

10 Undo the air filter cover screws and the bolt at the front and remove the cover and the upper section of the filter housing **(see illustrations)**.

11 Disconnect the drain hose from the back of the lower housing, and the air suction system hose from the front **(see illustrations)**.

12 Undo the air funnel screws, and if required remove the funnels, noting which fits where **(see illustration)**. Otherwise they can stay loose in the housing.

13 Lift the lower housing up off the throttle bodies, disconnect the crankcase breather hose from the back, and remove the housing **(see illustration)**. Remove the O-rings from the throttle bodies **(see illustration 3.14b)** – new ones should be used. Cover the throttle bodies with a clean rag.

Installation

14 Installation is the reverse of removal, noting the following:

● Check the condition of the rim seals in the top of each section of the housing, and make sure they are in their grooves **(see illustration 3.14a)**.

3.10b ...and remove the cover...

3.10c ...and the upper section

3.11a Disconnect the drain hose (arrowed)...

3.11b ...and the air hose

3.12 Air funnel screws (arrowed)

3.13 Disconnect the breather hose and remove the housing

3.14a Check the rim seals

3.14b Use new O-rings

3.14c The taller funnels fit in the middle

3.14d Do not forget the wiring clamp

3.14e Push the retainer down to lock the hose in place

- Fit a new O-ring into the groove around each throttle **(see illustration 3.14b)**.
- Make sure the crankcase breather, air system and drain hoses are in good condition. Connect the crankcase hose before seating the lower housing on the throttle bodies **(see illustration 3.13)**.
- Fit the air intake funnels so the taller funnels are above the middle (Nos. 2 and 3) throttle bodies **(see illustration 3.14c)**.
- Fit the wiring clamp with its screw and secure the wiring in it **(see illustration 3.14d)**. Make sure the secondary injector and IAT sensor wiring connectors are securely connected.
- Make sure the fuel hose connector retainer is in its released position. Fit the connector onto the pipe and push it until it clicks into place, then push the retainer down **(see illustration 3.14e)**. Try to pull the connector off to make sure it has locked.

4 Engine management system description

1 The engine management system consists of three main component groups, the fuel circuit, the ignition circuit and the electronic control circuit.

2 The fuel circuit consists of the tank, the integrated pump/filter/pressure regulator, the throttle bodies and the injectors. On all models there is an injector for each cylinder mounted in the throttle bodies below the throttle valve. On E and F models there are also secondary injectors mounted in the top of the air filter housing, operating only at high engine speeds and wide throttle openings, and spraying fuel into the air entering the throttle bodies above the throttle valves. Fuel is pumped under pressure from the tank to the fuel rail(s), from which the individual injectors are fed. Operating pressure is maintained by the pressure regulator. The injectors spray pressurised fuel into the throttle bodies where it mixes with air and vaporises, before entering the cylinder where it is compressed and ignited.

3 The ignition circuit consists of the stick type ignition coils and the spark plugs.

4 The electronic control circuit consists of the electronic control unit (ECU), which operates and co-ordinates both the fuel injection and ignition systems, and the various sensors which provide the ECU with information on engine operating conditions.

5 The electronic control unit (ECU) monitors signals from the following sensors.

- Intake air temperature (IAT) sensor
- Intake air pressure (IAP) sensor
- Throttle position (TP) sensor
- Secondary throttle position (STP) sensor
- Camshaft position (CMP) sensor
- Crankshaft position (CKP) sensor
- Coolant temperature (ECT) sensor
- Atmospheric pressure (AP) sensor
- Tip-over (TO) sensor
- Oxygen (O2) sensors (where fitted)

6 Based on the information it receives, the ECU calculates the appropriate ignition and fuel requirements of the engine. By varying the length of the electronic pulse it sends to each injector, the ECU controls the length of time the injectors are held open and thereby the amount of fuel that is supplied to the engine. Fuel supply varies according to the engine's needs for starting, warming-up, idling, cruising and acceleration.

7 On C models, the FI warning light should come on briefly when the ignition is switched ON, then go out – this serves as a check that the circuit is working correctly. If the light comes on and stays on a fault has occurred. If the light does not come on at all check the instrument cluster (see Chapter 8).

8 On D, E and F models the FI warning light and all segments in the LCD display should come on briefly when the ignition is switched ON, then go out – this serves as a check that the circuit is working correctly. If the warning light and the FI letters in the display flash a fault has occurred. If the light and/or LCD display do not come on at all check the instrument cluster (see Chapter 8).

9 In the event of an abnormality in any of the sensor signals, the ECU will determine whether the engine can still be run safely. If it can, a back-up mode substitutes the sensor signal with a fixed signal, restricting performance but allowing the bike to be ridden home or to a dealer. In some cases the engine will continue to run after a fault has been registered, but once stopped the engine will not be able to be restarted. If the fault is serious, the fuel injection system will be shut down and the engine will not run.

10 After the engine has been stopped, the appropriate self-diagnostic fault code can be accessed.

5 Engine management system fault diagnosis

C models

1 The self-diagnosis system has two modes: user mode (the standard mode), in which the fuel injection system (FI) warning light will come on and stay on to warn the rider that a fault has occurred; dealer mode, in which the FI light will emit a series of flashes to denote the current fault code or codes.

2 If the FI warning light comes on, enter dealer mode as follows to read the fault code: remove the rider's seat (see Chapter 7). Identify the self-diagnosis single female bullet connector **(see illustration)**. Prepare an auxiliary lead

5.2 Self-diagnosis bullet connector – C models

with male bullet connector on one end and a crocodile clip at the other. Connect the auxiliary lead male bullet connector into the self-diagnosis female bullet connector. Turn the ignition ON. Connect the crocodile clip end of the auxiliary lead to the battery negative (-) terminal or lead end and keep it there – the FI light should start to flash the fault code (see Step 3). Keep the lead earthed (grounded) until you have finished reading the fault code.

3 The FI warning light emits long (1 second) and short (0.3 second) flashes to give out the fault code. One or more long flashes are used to indicate the first digit of the fault code, and one or more short flashes are used to indicate the second digit (all codes are double digit). There is a 1.0 second gap between long (1 sec) flashes and a 0.3 second gap between the short (0.3 sec) flashes. For example, two long (1 sec) flashes followed by four short (0.3 sec) flashes indicates the fault code number 24. If there is more than one fault code, there will be a 3 second gap before the other codes are revealed, and the codes will be revealed in numerical order, lowest to highest. Once all codes have been revealed, the ECU will

continuously run through the code(s) stored in its memory, revealing each one in turn with a 3 second gap between them.

4 Once all the codes have been revealed and recorded, return to user mode by switching off the ignition and removing the auxiliary lead.

5 Refer to the table below to determine the faulty component or circuit according to the fault code(s) shown, then refer to the Check procedures at the end of this Section. When the fault has been repaired the code will no longer be displayed, but will be stored in the ECU memory.

Fault code	Faulty component – ECU response	Possible causes
11	Throttle position sensor – engine will continue to run but with reduced performance	Faulty wiring or wiring connector Faulty, damaged or improperly installed sensor Faulty ECU
12	Intake air pressure sensor – engine will run	Faulty wiring or wiring connector Faulty, damaged or improperly installed sensor Detached, pinched or blocked hose Faulty ECU
13	Intake air temperature sensor – engine will run, intake temperature signal fixed at 30°C	Faulty wiring or wiring connector Faulty, damaged or improperly installed sensor Faulty ECU
14	Coolant temperature sensor – engine will run, coolant temperature signal fixed at 80°C	Faulty wiring or wiring connector Faulty, damaged or improperly installed sensor Faulty ECU
15	Atmospheric pressure sensor – engine will run, air pressure signal fixed at 760 mmHg	Faulty wiring or wiring connector Faulty sensor Faulty ECU
21	Crankshaft position sensor – engine will not run	Faulty wiring or wiring connector Faulty, damaged or improperly installed sensor or timing rotor Faulty ECU
23	Camshaft position sensor – engine will continue to run, ECU uses last good signal	Faulty wiring or wiring connector Faulty, damaged or improperly installed sensor Faulty ECU
24	Speed sensor – engine will run, no reading on instrument cluster	Faulty wiring or wiring connector Faulty damaged or improperly installed speed sensor Faulty ECU
25	Gear position switch – gear position signal fixed at 6th	Faulty wiring or wiring connector Faulty damaged or improperly installed switch Faulty ECU
31	Tip-over sensor – engine will not run, fuel and ignition systems turned OFF	Machine overturned Faulty wiring or wiring connector Faulty damaged or improperly installed speed sensor Faulty ECU
32	Secondary throttle position sensor – engine will run, sensor signal and secondary throttle fixed fully open	Faulty wiring or wiring connector Faulty, damaged or improperly installed sensor Faulty ECU
34	Exhaust valve sensor – engine will run, valve fixed fully open	Faulty wiring or wiring connector Broken or detached cable(s) Faulty servo
35*	Immobiliser amplifier – engine will not run	Faulty wiring or wiring connector Faulty amplifier
36*	Ignition key – engine will not run	Faulty or unregistered key
41	No. 1 cylinder injector – engine will run on other 3 cylinders, ECU signal to No. 1 injector cut	Faulty wiring or wiring connector Faulty or damaged injector Faulty ECU
42	No. 2 cylinder injector – engine will run on other 3 cylinders, ECU signal to No. 2 injector cut	Faulty wiring or wiring connector Faulty or damaged injector Faulty ECU

Fault code	Faulty component – ECU response	Possible causes
43	No. 3 cylinder injector – engine will run on other 3 cylinders, ECU signal to No. 3 injector cut	Faulty wiring or wiring connector Faulty or damaged injector Faulty ECU
44	No. 4 cylinder injector – engine will run on other 3 cylinders, ECU signal to No. 4 injector cut	Faulty wiring or wiring connector Faulty or damaged injector Faulty ECU
45	Fuel pump relay	Faulty wiring or wiring connector
46	Fuel pump relay	Relay stuck
51	No. 1 cylinder ignition coil – engine will run on other 3 cylinders, fuel supply to No. 1 cylinder cut	Faulty wiring or wiring connector Faulty or damaged ignition coil Faulty ECU
52	No. 2 cylinder ignition coil – engine will run on other 3 cylinders, fuel supply to No. 2 cylinder cut	Faulty wiring or wiring connector Faulty or damaged ignition coil Faulty ECU
53	No. 3 cylinder ignition coil – engine will run on other 3 cylinders, fuel supply to No. 3 cylinder cut	Faulty wiring or wiring connector Faulty or damaged ignition coil Faulty ECU
54	No. 4 cylinder ignition coil – engine will run on other 3 cylinders, fuel supply to No. 4 cylinder cut	Faulty wiring or wiring connector Faulty or damaged ignition coil Faulty ECU
62	Secondary throttle servo – engine will run, servo disabled	Faulty wiring or wiring connector Faulty, damaged or improperly installed servo Faulty ECU
63	Exhaust valve servo – engine will run, servo disabled	Faulty wiring or wiring connector Faulty, damaged or improperly installed servo Faulty ECU
75	ECU main relay	Relay stuck

* Models with an immobiliser

D, E and F models

6 The self-diagnosis system has two modes: user mode (the standard mode), in which the warning light and the FI letters in the LCD display flash to warn the rider that a fault has occurred; dealer mode, in which the LCD display shows the current fault code or codes.

7 If the warning light and the FI letters in the display flash, enter dealer mode as follows to read the fault code: turn the ignition switch ON and push the Mode button on the left side of the instrument cluster to display the odometer. Now push the Reset button on the right side for more than 2 seconds – the fault code is now shown on the LCD display. If there is more than one fault the codes are displayed sequentially in numerical order. Once all codes have been revealed, the ECU will continuously run through the code(s) stored in its memory, revealing each one in turn with a 3 second gap between them.

8 Once all the codes have been revealed and recorded, return to user mode either by pressing the Reset button for more than two seconds or by turning the ignition switch OFF.

9 Refer to the table below to determine the faulty component or circuit according to the fault code(s) shown, then refer to the Check procedures at the end of this Section. When the fault has been repaired the code will no longer be displayed, but will be stored in the ECU memory.

Fault code	Faulty component – ECU response	Possible causes
11	Throttle position sensor – engine will continue to run but with reduced performance	Faulty wiring or wiring connector Faulty, damaged or improperly installed sensor Faulty ECU
12	Intake air pressure sensor – engine will run	Faulty wiring or wiring connector Faulty, damaged or improperly installed sensor Detached, pinched or blocked hose Faulty ECU
13	Intake air temperature sensor – engine will run, intake temperature signal fixed at 30°C	Faulty wiring or wiring connector Faulty, damaged or improperly installed sensor Faulty ECU
14	Coolant temperature sensor – engine will run, coolant temperature signal fixed at 80°C or 120°C if fan is running	Faulty wiring or wiring connector Faulty, damaged or improperly installed sensor Faulty ECU
15	Atmospheric pressure sensor – engine will run, air pressure signal fixed at 760 mmHg	Faulty wiring or wiring connector Faulty sensor Faulty ECU
21	Crankshaft position sensor – engine will not run	Faulty wiring or wiring connector Faulty, damaged or improperly installed sensor or timing rotor Faulty ECU

Fault code	Faulty component – ECU response	Possible causes
23	Camshaft position sensor – engine will continue to run, ECU uses last good signal	Faulty wiring or wiring connector Faulty, damaged or improperly installed sensor Faulty ECU
24	Speed sensor – engine will run, no reading on instrument cluster	Faulty wiring or wiring connector Faulty damaged or improperly installed speed sensor Faulty ECU
25	Gear position switch – gear position signal fixed at 6th	Faulty wiring or wiring connector Faulty damaged or improperly installed switch Faulty ECU
31	Tip-over sensor – engine will not run, fuel and ignition systems turned OFF	Machine overturned Faulty wiring or wiring connector Faulty damaged or improperly installed speed sensor Faulty ECU
32	Secondary throttle position sensor – engine will run, sensor signal and secondary throttle fixed fully open	Faulty wiring or wiring connector Faulty, damaged or improperly installed sensor Faulty ECU
33*	Oxygen sensor No. 1 not activated – engine will run, ECU stops feedback mode of both oxygen sensors	Faulty wiring or wiring connector Faulty, damaged or improperly installed sensor Faulty ECU
34	Exhaust valve sensor – engine will run, valve fixed fully open	Faulty wiring or wiring connector Broken or detached cable(s) Faulty servo
35**	Immobiliser amplifier – engine will not run	Faulty wiring or wiring connector Faulty amplifier
36**	Ignition key – engine will not run	Faulty or unregistered key
39***	ECU – if no signal is sent by the ECU to the instrument cluster for more than 30 seconds	Faulty wiring or wiring connector Faulty ECU Faulty instrument cluster
46	Fuel pump relay	Relay stuck
51	No. 1 cylinder ignition coil – engine will run on other 3 cylinders, fuel supply to No. 1 cylinder cut	Faulty wiring or wiring connector Faulty or damaged ignition coil Faulty ECU
52	N.o 2 cylinder ignition coil – engine will run on other 3 cylinders, fuel supply to No. 2 cylinder cut	Faulty wiring or wiring connector Faulty or damaged ignition coil Faulty ECU
53	No. 3 cylinder ignition coil – engine will run on other 3 cylinders, fuel supply to No. 3 cylinder cut	Faulty wiring or wiring connector Faulty or damaged ignition coil Faulty ECU
54	No. 4 cylinder ignition coil – engine will run on other 3 cylinders, fuel supply to No. 4 cylinder cut	Faulty wiring or wiring connector Faulty or damaged ignition coil Faulty ECU
56***	Cooling fan relay	Faulty wiring or wiring connector Faulty relay
62	Secondary throttle servo – engine will run, servo disabled	Faulty wiring or wiring connector Faulty, damaged or improperly installed servo Faulty ECU
63	Exhaust valve servo – engine will run, servo disabled	Faulty wiring or wiring connector Faulty, damaged or improperly installed servo Faulty ECU
64***	Air system control valve	Faulty wiring or wiring connector Faulty valve Faulty ECU
67*	Oxygen sensor heater – engine will run, ECU stops feedback mode to sensor	Faulty wiring or wiring connector Faulty, damaged or improperly installed sensor Faulty ECU
75****	ECU main relay	Relay stuck
83*	Oxygen sensor No. 2 not activated – engine will run, ECU stops feedback mode of both oxygen sensors	Faulty wiring or wiring connector Faulty, damaged or improperly installed sensor Faulty ECU

* Models with oxygen sensors   ** Models with an immobiliser   *** E and F models   **** D models

Check procedures

10 If a fault appears, use the fault code table above to identify which component or circuit is faulty. First ensure that the relevant wiring connectors are securely connected and free of corrosion – poor connections are the cause of the majority of problems. Also check the wiring itself for any obvious faults or breaks, and use a continuity tester to check the wiring between the component, its connectors and the ECU, referring to Section 2 at the beginning of Chapter 8 and the wiring diagrams at the end of Chapter 8 (but note that needle probes will be required to test certain connectors and that on some models a security bracket is fitted to the ECU which denies access to the connectors).

11 Next refer to the relevant Section in this Chapter or to other Chapters as required to see if there are any other specific checks that can be made on that particular component or its circuit using home equipment. Where relevant it is also worth removing the sensor(s) in question and checking that the sensing head is clean and not obstructed by anything. If this fails to reveal the cause of the problem, the motorcycle should be taken to a Kawasaki dealer for testing. They will have the special tools that should locate the fault quickly and simply.

6 Engine management system sensors

Caution: Ensure the ignition is switched OFF before disconnecting/reconnecting any fuel injection system wiring connector. If a connector is disconnected/reconnected with the ignition switched ON the ECU could be damaged.

Throttle position (TP) sensor

Check

1 Check the sensor resistance as follows: remove the air filter housing (see Section 3). Disconnect the sensor wiring

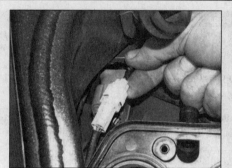

6.1a TP sensor wiring connector – C models

connector **(see illustrations)**. Connect the positive (+) probe of an ohmmeter to the blue wire terminal on the sensor, then connect the negative (–) lead to the black wire terminal on C models and to the brown/black wire terminal on all other models. The resistance should be 4 to 6 K-ohms. If not, the sensor is faulty.

Removal and installation

2 The throttle sensor is an integral part of the throttle body assembly and is not available separately. If the sensor is faulty, a complete new throttle body assembly will have to be installed, though it is worth checking with a Kawasaki dealer to see if anything can be done to avoid this.

Intake air pressure (IAP) sensor

Check

3 Remove the air filter housing (see Section 3). Make sure all the vacuum hoses between the sensor and throttle bodies are securely connected and in good condition **(see illustration)**.

Removal and installation

4 Remove the air filter housing (see Section 3).

5 On C models disconnect the wiring connector, then undo the sensor screw and detach the vacuum hose from the underside **(see illustration)**.

6.1b TP sensor wiring connector (arrowed) – D/E/F models

6 On D, E and F models disconnect the wiring connector, then displace the sensor from its bracket and detach the vacuum hose from the underside, and remove the sensor **(see illustration 6.3)**.

7 Installation is the reverse of removal.

Intake air temperature (IAT) sensor

Check

8 The resistance of the sensor changes with changes in temperature – see the Specifications at the beginning of the chapter. Remove the sensor (see below). Connect a multimeter set to the K-ohm range to the sensor terminals.

9 Test the resistance of the sensor at room temperature, then use a hair dryer directed at the sensor tip and check that the resistance decreases as the sensor gets warmer. If the sensor fails it is most likely to give a zero, constant value, or infinite resistance reading at all temperatures.

Removal and installation

10 Remove the fuel tank (see Section 2).

11 On C and D models, disconnect the sensor wiring connector **(see illustration 3.4)**. Pull the sensor out of the air filter housing **(see illustration)**.

12 On E and F models, disconnect the sensor wiring connector **(see illustration 3.9c)**.

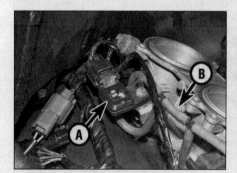

6.3 IAP sensor (A) and its hoses (B) – E models shown

6.5 IAP sensor (arrowed)

6.11 Carefully pull the sensor out

6.12 IAT sensor screw (arrowed)

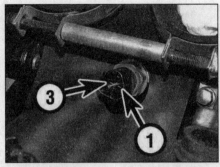

6.14 ECT sensor terminal ID

6.18a AP sensor (arrowed) – C models

Undo the screw and draw the sensor out of the air filter housing **(see illustration)**.

13 Installation is the reverse of removal.

Engine coolant temperature (ECT) sensor

Note: *The sensor also operates the coolant temperature gauge (see Chapter 3).*

Check

14 Refer to Chapter 3, Section 3, Steps 6 to 8 and check the resistance of the sensor, but connect the probes of the ohmmeter between the Nos. 1 and 3 terminals and check the resistances are as given at the beginning of this Chapter at the specified temperatures **(see illustration)**.

Removal and installation

15 Refer to Chapter 3, Section 3, Steps 9 to 12.

Atmospheric pressure (AP) sensor

Check

16 See Step 17 for sensor location. Displace the sensor and make sure the air intake port is not blocked.

Removal and installation

17 On C models remove the passenger seat and the centre section of the seat cowling (see Chapter 7). On D models remove the seat cowling (see Chapter 7). On E and F models remove the left-hand side of the seat cowling (see Chapter 7).

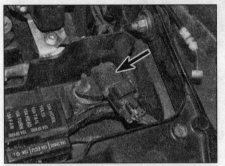

6.18b AP sensor (arrowed) – D models

18 Displace the sensor from its mount then disconnect the wiring connector **(see illustrations)**.

19 Installation is the reverse of removal.

Crankshaft position (CKP) sensor

Check

20 Remove the fuel tank (see Section 2). Trace the CKP sensor wiring from the timing rotor cover and disconnect it at the wiring connector – if access is too restricted remove the air filter housing **(see illustrations)**.

21 Using an ohmmeter check for continuity between each wire terminal on the sensor side of the connector and earth (ground). If there is continuity in either case the sensor is faulty. Measure the resistance of the sensor by

6.18c AP sensor (arrowed) – E/F models

connecting the meter, set to the ohms x 100 scale, to the terminals and compare the reading to that specified at the beginning of the chapter. If the value obtained differs greatly or is zero or infinity the sensor is faulty.

Removal

22 Refer to Step 20 and disconnect the wiring connector. Release the wiring from any clips and feed it down to the cover, noting its routing.

23 Refer to Chapter 2, Section 13 on C models, and Section 14 on all other models, and remove the timing rotor cover (C models) or starter clutch cover (all other models).

24 Free the wiring grommet from the cut-out, then undo the sensor mounting bolts, and remove the sensor along with the wiring **(see illustrations)**.

6.20a CKP sensor wiring connector (arrowed) – C/D models

6.20b CKP sensor wiring connector – E/F models

6.24 CKP sensor bolts (arrowed)

6.25 Smear sealant into the cut-out

6.26 Fit the sensor, seating the grommet

Installation

25 Remove all traces of old sealant and gasket from the cover, crankcase and wiring grommet. Apply some fresh sealant to the cut-out for the grommet **(see illustration)**.

26 Fit the sensor, seating the grommet in the cut-out, and tighten the bolts to the torque setting specified at the beginning of the chapter **(see illustration)**.

27 Install the timing rotor cover (C models) or starter clutch cover (all other models).

28 Route the wiring back to the connector and reconnect it **(see illustrations 6.20a or b)**. Install the remaining components.

Camshaft position (CMP) sensor

Check

29 Remove the air filter housing (see Section 3) – remove the upper section only on E and F models.

30 Disconnect the sensor wiring connector **(see illustration)**.

31 Using an ohmmeter check for continuity between each terminal on the sensor side of the connector and earth (ground). If there is continuity in either case the camshaft position sensor is faulty. Measure the resistance of the sensor by connecting the meter, set to the ohms x 100 scale, to the terminals and compare the reading to that specified at the beginning of the chapter. If the value obtained

differs greatly or is zero or infinity the sensor is faulty.

Removal

32 Refer to Steps 29 and 30 and disconnect the sensor wiring connector. Feed the wiring to the sensor, noting its routing.

33 Unscrew the bolt securing the sensor and draw it out of the head **(see illustration)**.

Installation

34 Clean the sensor. Smear the O-ring with oil or grease, then fit the sensor into the cylinder head and tighten the bolt to the torque setting specified at the beginning of the chapter.

35 Reconnect the wiring connector **(see illustration 6.30)**. Install the remaining components.

6.30 CMP sensor wiring connector – E/F models

6.33 CMP sensor bolt (arrowed)

Speed sensor

36 See Chapter 8, Section 16.

Gear position switch

37 See Chapter 8, Section 20.

Tip-over (TO) sensor

38 On C models remove the fuel tank (see Section 2). On D models remove the seat cowling (see Chapter 7). On E and F models remove the right-hand side of the seat cowling (see Chapter 7).

39 Disconnect the sensor wiring connector then unscrew the bolts and remove the sensor **(see illustrations)**.

40 Installation is the reverse of removal. Make

6.39a TO sensor (arrowed) – C models

6.39b TO sensor (arrowed) – D models

6.39c TO sensor (arrowed) – E/F models

sure the sensor is fitted with its UP arrow pointing upwards.

Secondary throttle position (STP) sensor

Check

41 Check the sensor resistance as follows. Remove the air filter housing (see Section 3). Disconnect the sensor wiring connector **(see illustrations)**. Connect the positive (+) probe of an ohmmeter to the blue wire terminal on the sensor, then connect the negative (–) lead to the brown/black wire terminal. The resistance should be 4 to 6 K-ohms. If not, the sensor is faulty.

Removal and installation

42 The secondary throttle sensor is an integral part of the throttle body assembly and is not available separately. If the sensor is faulty, a complete new throttle body assembly will have to be installed, though it is worth checking with a Kawasaki dealer to see if anything can be done to avoid this.

Secondary throttle valve servo

Check

43 Remove the air filter housing (see Section 3). Turn the ignition ON and check that the secondary throttle valves (the upper set of valves in the throttle bodies) open and close. If they don't move disconnect the servo wiring connector **(see illustrations)**. Check the servo resistance between the following wires:

C models – black/blue and green wire terminals
D models – yellow and pink wire terminals
D models – black and green wire terminals
E/F models – yellow/black and pink wire terminals
E/F models – green and black/blue wire terminals

The resistance should be as specified at the beginning of the Chapter for your model in each case. If not the sensor is faulty.

Removal and installation

44 The secondary throttle servo is an integral part of the throttle body assembly and is not available separately. If the servo is faulty, a

6.41a STP sensor wiring connector (arrowed) – C models

6.41b STP sensor wiring connector (arrowed) – D/E/F models

6.43a STV servo wiring connector (arrowed) – C models

6.43b STV servo wiring connector (arrowed) – D/E/F models

complete new throttle body assembly will have to be installed, though it is worth checking with a Kawasaki dealer to see if anything can be done to avoid this.

Oxygen sensors

Check

45 First check the oxygen sensor heater fuse (see Chapter 8).
46 Disconnect the wiring connector for the sensor being checked **(see illustrations)** – on D models remove the left-hand fairing side panel to access them (see Chapter 7); on E and F models you may be able to access them from above the front sprocket cover, but if necessary remove the fuel tank (see Section 2).
47 Connect an ohmmeter set to the ohms x 10 scale, to the white wire terminals on the sensor side of the connector and measure the resistance of the sensor heater. Compare the

reading to that specified at the beginning of the chapter. If the value obtained differs greatly or is zero or infinity the sensor is faulty.

Removal and installation

48 The sensor in the left-hand downpipe pair can be removed with the exhaust system in place – access the wiring connector as described in Step 46, and on E and F models remove the left-hand section of the lower fairing (see Chapter 7). Feed the wiring down to the sensor noting its routing and freeing it from its clamp(s).
49 To remove the sensor from the right-hand downpipe pair remove the downpipe assembly (see Section 16).
50 Unscrew and remove the sensor **(see illustration)**. Take care not to drop the sensor, and keep the sensing portion on the bottom and the filter holes on the top free of dirt and dust.

6.46a Oxygen sensor wiring connectors (arrowed) – D models

6.46b Oxygen sensor wiring connectors – E/F models

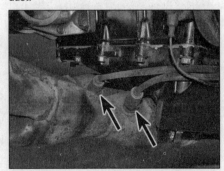
6.50 Oxygen sensors (arrowed)

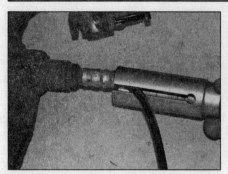

6.51 This is a purpose built socket that fits over the wiring

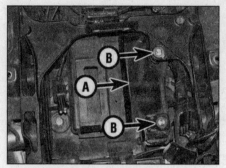

7.3a Metal security cage (A) as fitted to UK D models – drift the bolts (B) round using a cold chisel

7.3b Displace the ECU and disconnect the wiring

51 Installation is the reverse of removal. If the correct socket with a cut-out for the wiring is available tighten the sensor to the torque setting specified at the beginning of the Chapter **(see illustration)**.

7 Electronic control unit (ECU) and ECU main relay

ECU

Check

1 The electronic control unit (ECU) itself cannot be checked, but a process of elimination of other possible faulty components can point to it being faulty. First check the ECU fuse (see Chapter 8), and on C models the relay (see below). Next disconnect the ECU wiring connectors (see Steps 2 and 3) and check for loose or broken terminal pins in the connectors or ECU sockets. Check for continuity in each wire to/from the ECU and to its related component or connector, or to earth (ground) as appropriate, referring to Section 2 and the wiring diagrams in Chapter 8. If any wire does not show continuity check the connectors and terminals in the circuit before assuming there is a break in the wire.

Removal and installation

2 On C and D models remove the rider's seat.

On E and F models remove the centre section of the seat cowling (see Chapter 7). Make sure the ignition is OFF then disconnect the battery leads (see Chapter 8).

3 Displace the relay unit **(see illustration 13.2a, b or c)**. A metal security cage is fitted to some models, and this has to be removed before the wiring can be disconnected **(see illustration)**. Security bolts that can be done up using a special tool, but not undone, are fitted to secure the cage. To remove the bolts, drift them round carefully using a cold chisel. Lift the ECU and disconnect its wiring connectors **(see illustration)**.

4 Installation is the reverse of removal. Do not forget to fit the rubber sleeve.

ECU main relay – C models

Note: *The main relay is integrated into the ECU itself on other models.*

5 Remove the rider's seat (see Chapter 7). Draw the relay box out of its rubber holder and disconnect the wiring connectors **(see illustration 13.2a)**.

6 Set a multimeter to the ohms x 1 scale and connect its probes to terminals 12 and 13 **(see illustration 13.3a)**. There should be no continuity (infinite resistance). Using a fully-charged 12 volt battery and two insulated jumper wires, connect the positive (+) terminal of the battery to terminal 5, and the negative (–) terminal to terminal 10. At this point the multimeter should read 0 ohms (continuity).

If this is the case the relay is proven good. If the relay still indicates no continuity (infinite resistance) across its terminals, it is faulty and the relay box must be replaced with a new one – individual relays are not available.

8 Throttle bodies

Warning: Refer to the precautions given in Section 1 before starting work.

Removal

1 On C and D models remove the fairing side panels (see Chapter 7). On E models remove the fairing side covers (see Chapter 7). On FA (2010) models remove the fairing assembly (see Chapter 7).

2 Remove the air filter housing (see Section 3). On E and F models displace and support the coolant reservoir (see Chapter 3).

3 On C models disconnect the throttle body loom wiring connector and the crankshaft position sensor wiring connector **(see illustration)**, the IAP sensor wiring connector **(see illustration)**, the throttle position sensor wiring connectors and the throttle servo wiring connector **(see illustrations 6.1a, 6.41a and 6.43a)**, and the gear position switch and oil pressure switch sub-loom wiring

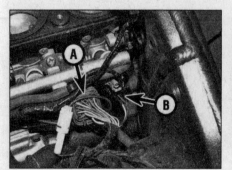

8.3a TP sensor sub-loom connector (A), CKP sensor connector (B)

8.3b IAP sensor connector

8.3c Gear position and oil pressure switch connectors (arrowed)

8.3d Detach the air hose (arrowed)

8.4a TP sensor sub-loom connector (A),
CKP sensor connector (B)

8.4b Detach the air hose (arrowed)

8.5 Disconnect the sub-loom connector

8.7 Release the idle speed adjuster

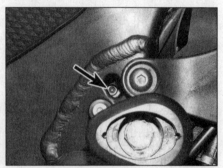

8.9a Slacken the clamp screw (arrowed)
on each side...

connectors **(see illustration)**. Disconnect the air suction system hose **(see illustration)**.

4 On D models disconnect the throttle body loom wiring connector and the crankshaft position sensor wiring connector **(see illustration)**. Disconnect the air suction system hose **(see illustration)**.

5 On E and F models disconnect the throttle body loom wiring connector **(see illustration)** and the camshaft position sensor wiring connector **(see illustration 6.30)**.

6 On California models, disconnect the EVAP system vacuum hose(s).

7 Release the idle speed adjuster from its clip **(see illustration)**.

8 Disconnect the throttle cables from the twistgrip (see Section 10).

9 Fully slacken the throttle body clamps using a long hex driver inserted through the hole in each side of the frame **(see illustrations)**. Ease the throttle body assembly up off the cylinder head – do not use the fuel rail as a handle for removal **(see illustration)**. On C models disconnect the ECT sensor wiring connector **(see illustration)**. Disconnect the throttle cables (see Section 10).

8.9b ...using a screwdriver through the hole...

8.9c ...and displace the throttle bodies

8.9d ECT sensor connector (arrowed) – C models

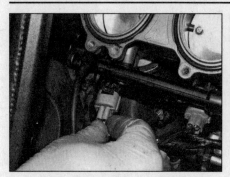

9.3a Disconnect the wiring

9.3b Checking injector resistance

9.6 Disconnect the wiring

Caution: Do not snap the throttle cam/valves from fully open to fully closed once the cables have been disconnected because this can lead to engine idle speed problems.

10 If required on C and D models remove the air filter housing base by slackening the clamps.

11 If required remove the fuel rail and injectors (Section 9).

Caution: Tape over or stuff clean rag into each cylinder head intake after removing the throttle body assembly or intake adapters to prevent anything from falling in.

Caution: The throttle body assembly must be treated as a sealed unit. NEVER loosen any of the green-painted nuts/bolts/screws on the assembly as these are pre-set at the factory to ensure correct synchronisation of the throttle valves.

Caution: NEVER use a solvent-based cleaner to clean the throttle body components. The throttle bores are covered with a molybdenum coating that could be removed by the cleaner.

Installation

12 If removed install the fuel rail and injectors (Section 9). If removed on C and D models fit the air filter housing base and tighten the clamps.

13 Remove the tape/plugs from the intake ducts. Lubricate the inside of each duct with a light smear of engine oil to aid installation.

14 Connect the throttle cable ends to the throttle bodies (see Section 10). On C models connect the ECT sensor wiring connector **(see illustration 8.9d)**.

15 Ease the throttle body assembly into the ducts and push them down until they are fully engaged – do not use the fuel rail as a handle **(see illustration 8.9c)**. Tighten the clamps **(see illustration 8.9b)**.

16 Connect the throttle cables to the twistgrip (see Section 10).

17 Connect and install all remaining components as required according to model in reverse order of removal (see Steps 7 to 1).

9 Fuel rail(s) and injectors

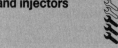

Caution: Ensure the ignition is switched OFF before disconnecting/reconnecting any fuel injection system wiring connector. If a connector is disconnected/reconnected with the ignition switched ON the ECU could be damaged.

⚠ *Warning: Refer to the precautions given in Section 1 before starting work.*

Check

1 Remove the fuel tank (see Section 2).

2 If the engine runs, start it and allow it to idle. Check the operation of each primary injector in the throttle bodies using a stethoscope or sounding rod; an injector will emit a 'clicking' noise when functioning. If any injector is silent, either the injector or its wiring harness is faulty. On E and F models check the secondary injectors in the top of the air filter housing in the same way, but note that these injectors are only active at high engine speeds and wide throttle openings.

3 If the engine does not run, disconnect the wiring connector from the injector in question **(see illustration)**. Connect an ohmmeter between the terminals of each injector in turn and measure the resistance **(see illustration)**. Compare the reading for each injector to that given in the Specifications.

4 If the injector resistance is good check the wiring and connectors to the injectors, referring to Chapter 8, Section 2, and to the wiring diagrams.

Removal

5 Remove the air filter housing (see Section 3). On E and F models, and for best access on all other models, remove the throttle bodies (see Section 8).

6 Disconnect the wiring connector from each injector **(see illustration)**. Release the wiring and/or hoses from the fuel rail.

7 Undo the fuel rail screws **(see illustration)**. Carefully lift off the fuel rail assembly and injectors **(see illustration)**. Remove the seals from the injectors, or from the injector seats in the throttle bodies **(see illustration)**. New seals must be used.

9.7a Undo the screws (arrowed)...

9.7b ...and remove the fuel rail and injectors

9.7c Remove the seals

9.8a Ease the injector out...

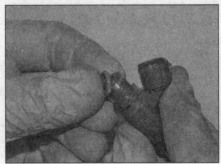

9.8b ...and remove its O-ring

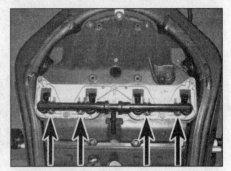

9.13a Undo the screws (arrowed)...

8 If required pull the injectors out of the fuel rail **(see illustration)**. Remove the O-rings **(see illustration)** – new ones must be used.

9 If required detach the fuel hose(s) as described in Section 2.

Secondary rail and injectors – E and F models

10 Remove the fuel tank (see Section 2).

11 Detach the fuel hose from the rail **(see illustration 3.9a and b)**.

12 Disconnect the IAT sensor wiring connector and the secondary injector wiring connectors **(see illustration 3.9c and d)**. Release the wiring from the clamp.

13 Undo the fuel rail screws **(see illustration)**. Carefully lift off the fuel rail assembly and injectors **(see illustration)**. Remove the seals

from the injector seats **(see illustration)**. New seals must be used.

14 If required pull the injectors out of the fuel rail **(see illustration)**. Remove the O-rings **(see illustration)** – new ones must be used.

15 If required pull each fuel rail off the centre joint piece **(see illustration)**. Remove the O-rings **(see illustration)** – new ones must be used.

Installation

16 On E and F models, if the secondary fuel rails have been separated from the joint piece, fit a new O-ring lubricated with clean engine oil into the groove in the end of each rail **(see illustration 9.15b)**. Push each rail onto the joint, making sure the O-ring stays in place **(see illustration 9.15a)**. **Note:** *The primary*

injectors have green bodies and the secondary injectors have black bodies

17 Make sure all components are spotlessly clean.

18 If the injectors have been removed from their rail, fit a new O-ring lubricated with clean engine oil into the groove in the top of each injector **(see illustration 9.8b or 9.14b)**.

19 Align the injector connector and ease the injector into place, taking care not to dislodge the O-ring **(see illustration 9.8a or 9.14a)**.

20 Fit a new seal onto each injector seat **(see illustration 9.7c or 9.13c)**.

21 Fit the fuel rail assembly, making sure each injector enters its seat and the seals stay in place and locate correctly **(see illustration 9.7b or 9.13b)**. Fit and tighten the screws **(see illustration 9.7a or 9.13a)**.

9.13b ...and remove the fuel rail and secondary injectors

9.13c Remove the seals

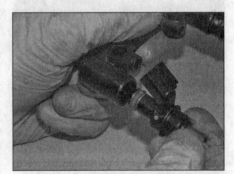

9.14a Ease the injector out...

9.14b ...and remove its O-ring

9.15a Ease the rail off...

9.15b ...and remove its O-ring

22 Refer to Section 2 for connection of the fuel hose(s).
23 Reconnect the wiring connectors and secure the wiring and/or hoses **(see illustration 9.6 or 3.9d and c)**.
24 Install the remaining components in reverse order of removal. Run the engine and check that the fuel system is working correctly and there is no leakage before taking the bike out on the road.

10 Throttle cables

> ⚠ **Warning: Refer to the precautions given in Section 1 before proceeding.**

Removal

1 Remove the air filter housing (see Section 3). Mark each cable according to its location.
2 Pull the rubber boot off the cable housing at the throttle pulley **(see illustration)**. Undo the housing screws **(see illustration)**. Separate the housing halves, then detach the cable ends from the pulley **(see illustrations 10.7d, c, b and a)**. Mark each cable to ensure it is connected correctly on installation.
3 Refer to Section 8 and displace the throttle bodies.
4 Release the cable retaining clip, draw the

10.2a Pull the boot back

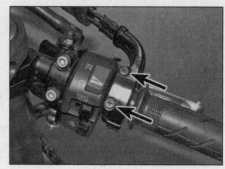

10.2b Undo the housing screws (arrowed)

cables out of the bracket and detach the ends from the pulley **(see illustrations 10.6d, c, b and a)**. Withdraw the cables from the frame noting their correct routing. Mark each cable to ensure it is connected correctly on installation.

Installation

5 Route the cables correctly between the handlebar and the throttle bodies. The cables must not interfere with any other component and should not be kinked or bent sharply. Lubricate the cable ends with multi-purpose grease.
6 The throttle opening cable is the one with the adjuster that is closest to the upper end

elbow. Fit the throttle opening cable end around the underside of the pulley on the throttle bodies and into the lower socket, then seat the elbow in the lower holder on the bracket **(see illustration)**. Fit the closing cable in the same way around the top and into the upper socket and holder **(see illustrations)**. Fit the retaining clip **(see illustration)**.
7 Position the twistgrip as shown and fit the closing cable end into the upper socket, then twist the grip forwards so the cable feeds around the underside until the sockets are on top, and fit the opening cable into the front socket **(see illustrations)**. Fit the elbows into the housing halves then assemble the housing onto the handlebar, making sure the pin in the bottom half locates in the hole, then fit the

10.6a Fit the opening cable end into the lower socket and the elbow into the lower holder

10.6b Fit the closing cable end into the upper socket...

10.6c ...and the elbow into the upper holder

10.6d Secure the elbows with the retaining clip

10.7a Position the twistgrip as shown and fit the closing cable end...

10.7b ...then turn the pulley and fit the opening cable end

10.7c Seat the elbows in the housing halves...

10.7d ...then join them

screws and tighten them **(see illustrations)**. Fit the rubber boot **(see illustration 10.2a)**.
8 Refer to Section 8 and install the throttle bodies.
9 Operate the throttle to check that it opens and closes freely.
10 Check and adjust the throttle cable freeplay (see Chapter 1). Turn the handlebars back-and-forth to make sure the cable doesn't cause the steering to bind.
11 Install the air filter housing (see Section 3).
12 Start the engine and check that the idle speed does not rise as the handlebars are turned. If it does, the throttle cables are routed incorrectly. Correct the problem before riding the motorcycle.

11 Fuel pressure check

Special Tool: *A fuel pressure gauge is required for this procedure.*

1 To check the fuel pressure, a suitable gauge, gauge adapter and hoses are needed. Kawasaki provides service tools (Pt. Nos. 57001-1593, 57001-1607 and 57001-125) for this purpose.
2 Raise the fuel tank, then disconnect the fuel hose from the pump union and throttle body union (see Section 2). Use the hoses and adapter to connect the gauge between the fuel tank and the fuel rail **(see illustration)**.
3 Turn the ignition switch ON and check the

pressure reading on the gauge as the pump runs for a few seconds and pressurises the system – when the system is pressurised the reading will drop a few psi. Start the engine and check the pressure with the engine idling. In each case the pressure should be as specified at the beginning of this Chapter.
4 Turn the ignition OFF and disconnect the gauge and adapters. Use a rag to catch any residual fuel as before. Connect the fuel hoses (see Section 2).
5 If the pressure is too low, check for a leak in the fuel supply system, including the fuel rails and injectors. If there is no leakage the pick-up or filter in the pump could be blocked, or the pump could be faulty. Check the pump (Section 12).
6 If the pressure is too high, either the pressure regulator or the fuel pump check valve is faulty or the fuel hose or injector(s) is/are clogged. Check the pump, fuel hose and injectors.

12 Fuel pump

⚠️ **Warning: Refer to the precautions given in Section 1 before starting work.**

Check

1 The fuel pump is located inside the fuel tank. When the ignition is switched ON, it should be possible to hear the pump run for a few seconds until the system is up to pressure. If

you can't hear anything, check the relay (see Section 13). If it is good, check the wiring, connectors and terminals for physical damage or loose or corroded connections and rectify as necessary (see the Chapter 8, Section 2, and the *Wiring Diagrams* at the end). If the pump still will not run, proceed as follows.
2 Remove the left-hand side cover (see Chapter 7).
3 Ensure the ignition is switched OFF. Disconnect the fuel pump wiring connector **(see illustration 2.4a or b or 2.14)**.
4 Connector the positive (+) lead of a voltmeter to the white/red wire terminal on the loom side of the connector and the negative (–) lead to the black/yellow wire terminal. Switch the ignition ON whilst noting the reading obtained on the meter.
5 If battery voltage is present for a few seconds, the fuel pump circuit is operating correctly and the fuel pump itself is faulty and must be replaced with a new one.
6 If no reading is obtained, check the white/red wire and connectors between the fuel tank and the pump relay for continuity using the wiring diagrams at the end of Chapter 8, and check for continuity to earth in the black/yellow wire. If continuity (zero resistance) is not present, locate the break in the wire or faulty connector and repair or replace as required. Make sure all the connectors are free from corrosion and are securely connected. Repair/replace the wiring as necessary and clean the connectors using electrical contact cleaner. If this fails to reveal the fault, check the following components.
● Engine stop switch (see Chapter 8).
● ECU relay – C models (see Section 7).
● Tip over sensor (see Section 6).
● ECU (see Section 7).

Removal

7 If possible drain the tank before removal using a suitable hand pump, storing the fuel in a suitable container.
8 Remove the fuel tank (see Section 2), then place it upside down on some clean rag. Note the orientation of the fuel hose union.
9 Unscrew the fuel pump mounting plate bolts **(see illustration)**. Carefully withdraw the pump assembly from the tank **(see illustration)**. Remove the O-ring and discard

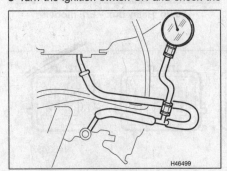

11.2 Fuel pressure test set-up

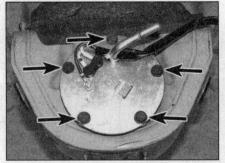

12.9a Unscrew the bolts (arrowed)...

12.9b ...and carefully withdraw the pump assembly, noting its orientation

it – a new one must be used on installation **(see illustration 12.11)**. The pump comes as a complete assembly and no individual components are available.

Installation

10 Make sure the wiring terminal screws and nuts are tight. Clean the threads of the pump bolts.

11 Ensure the mounting plate and tank surfaces are clean and dry, then fit the new O-ring **(see illustration)**.

12 Carefully manoeuvre the pump assembly into the tank **(see illustration 12.9b)**.

13 Apply a suitable non-permanent thread locking compound to the bolts and tighten them in the sequence shown and in two stages to the torque setting specified at the beginning of the Chapter **(see illustration)**.

14 Install the fuel tank (see Section 2).

12.11 Fit a new O-ring

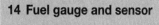

12.13 Fuel pump bolt tightening sequence

13 Fuel pump relay

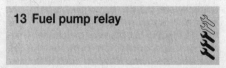

Check

1 On C and D models remove the rider's seat (see Chapter 7). On E and F models remove the centre section of the seat cowling (see Chapter 7).

2 Draw the relay box out of its rubber holder and disconnect the wiring connectors **(see illustrations)**.

3 Set a multimeter to the ohms x 1 scale and connect its probes to terminals 12 and 14 on the relay box on C models, and to terminals 4 and 5 on all other models **(see illustrations)**.

There should be no continuity (infinite resistance).

4 Leaving the meter in place, use a fully-charged 12 volt battery and two insulated jumper wires to connect the positive (+) terminal of the battery to terminal 7 on C models and to terminal 6 on all other models, and the negative (–) terminal to terminal 1 on C models and to terminal 7 on all other models.

5 With the battery connected, the multimeter should read 0 ohms (continuity). If this is the case the relay is proven good. If the relay still indicates no continuity (infinite resistance) across its terminals, it is faulty and the relay box must be replaced with a new one – individual relays are not available.

6 If the relay is good, refer to Section 2 at the beginning of Chapter 8 and the Wiring Diagrams at the end of it and check all the wiring and connectors in the fuel pump relay circuit.

Replacement

7 The fuel pump relay is an integral part of the relay box – if it is faulty replace the box with a new one.

14 Fuel gauge and sensor

Check

1 The circuit consists of the sensor, which is an integral part of the fuel pump assembly in the fuel tank, and the low fuel warning LED and display, which are part of the instrument cluster printed circuit board. The LED should come on for a few seconds when the ignition is switched on, then go out if there is sufficient fuel in the tank. When the amount of fuel reaches 3.5 litres on C models, 4 litres on D models, and 3.7 litres on E and F models, the LED should come on, and FUEL is displayed.

2 If the system malfunctions raise the fuel tank (see Section 2). Check the wiring and

13.2a Relay box (arrowed) – C models

13.2b Relay box – D models

13.2c Relay box – E/F models

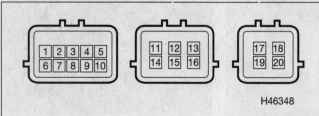
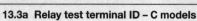

13.3a Relay test terminal ID – C models

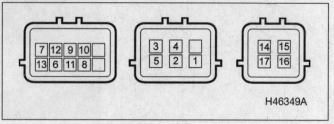

13.3b Relay test terminal ID – D/E/F models

connectors between the fuel tank and the instrument cluster for continuity referring to Section 2 at the beginning of Chapter 8 and the Wiring Diagrams at the end of it, and check for continuity to earth in the black/yellow wire. If continuity (zero resistance) is not present, locate the break in the wire or faulty connector and repair or replace as required. Make sure all the connectors are free from corrosion and are securely connected.

3 To check the sensor connect a continuity tester between the red/black and black/yellow wire terminals in the pump side of the connector. Lower the tank. With the tank full there should be no continuity, and with the tank empty there should be continuity. If not, remove the pump and check the wiring and terminals. If all is good replace the pump assembly with a new one.

4 If no faults are found, check the instruments (see Chapter 8).

Removal and installation

5 If the warning light is faulty refer to Chapter 8 for replacement of the instrument cluster PCB.

6 If the sensor is faulty replace the fuel pump assembly with a new one (see Section 12) – the sensor is not available separately.

15 Fuel system hoses

1 The fuel delivery, vacuum, and air suction system hoses should be replaced with new ones at the first sign of deterioration. On US models, also replace the EVAP system hoses.

2 Refer to the relevant Sections of this Chapter for further details and illustrations. Raise or remove the fuel tank as required, and if required remove the air filter housing (see Sections 2 and 3).

3 Note the routing of each hose and how it is secured – where necessary it is advisable to photograph the hose positions and routing before removing them to ensure they are correctly installed. Make sure each new hose is fully pushed onto its union. Use new clamps if necessary where fitted.

4 Details of how to remove and install the fuel supply hose(s) are in Section 2.

5 Run the engine and check that the fuel system is working correctly before taking the machine out on the road.

16 Exhaust system

> ⚠ **Warning: If the engine has been running the exhaust system will be very hot. Allow the system to cool before carrying out any work.**

> **HAYNES HINT** *Exhaust system clamp bolts tend to become corroded and seized. It is advisable to spray them with WD40 or a similar product before attempting to slacken them.*

Note: *Refer to the information in Section 18 regarding the catalytic converter.*

C models

Silencer

1 To remove the silencer can on its own unscrew the three nuts securing it to the pipe and remove the washers. Unscrew the nut on the silencer mounting bolt, noting the washer **(see illustration)**. Withdraw the bolt with its washer and remove the silencer. Remove the gasket – a new one must be used.

2 To remove the silencer with its pipe slacken the silencer clamp bolt **(see illustration)**. Unscrew the nut on the silencer mounting bolt, noting the washer **(see illustration 16.1)**. Withdraw the bolt with its washer and ease the silencer back off the downpipe assembly.

3 Check the condition of the downpipe-to-silencer sealing ring and replace it with a new one if it is damaged or deformed or no longer sealing correctly **(see illustration 16.39)** – note that Kawasaki specify to always use a new one. If fitting a new sealing ring, slide the clamp off, noting its orientation, and expand the tangs on the end of the pipe slightly to make it easier to fit.

4 Check the condition of the clamp, bolt, nuts, washers, collars and rubbers and replace them with new ones if necessary.

5 Installation is the reverse of removal, noting the following:

● Clean up rusted threads. Replace any excessively corroded or deformed mounting hardware with new ones. Apply a smear of copper grease to all threads.
● Make sure the collars are fitted in the rubbers.
● Use a new sealing ring between the downpipe assembly and the silencer pipe if necessary – see Step 3.
● Use a new gasket between the silencer can and the silencer pipe.
● Tighten the silencer can nuts, silencer mounting bolt nut and the clamp bolt to the torque settings specified at the beginning of the Chapter.
● Run the engine and check the system for leaks.

Downpipe assembly

6 Remove the radiator (see Chapter 3).

7 Remove the silencer with its pipe (see above).

8 Disconnect the exhaust valve cables from the downpipe assembly (see Section 17, Steps 23 and 24).

9 Unscrew the nuts securing the header pipes to the cylinder head **(see illustration 16.51)**.

10 Unscrew the downpipe mounting bolt, noting the washer **(see illustration)**.

11 Draw the flanges off the studs and manoeuvre the downpipe assembly off the head and remove it **(see illustration 16.52)**.

12 Remove the sealing ring from each port in the cylinder head and discard them as new ones must be used **(see illustration 16.53)**.

13 Refer to Step 3 and check the downpipe-to-silencer sealing ring.

14 Check the condition of the nuts, bolt, washer, collars and rubber and replace them with new ones if necessary.

15 Installation is the reverse of removal, noting the following:

● Clean up rusted threads. Replace any excessively corroded or deformed mounting hardware with new ones. Apply a smear of copper grease to all threads.
● Make sure the collars are fitted in the rubbers.
● Use a new sealing ring in each cylinder head port, and dab them with grease to stick them in place **(see illustration 16.56)**.

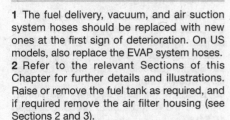

16.1 Unscrew the nut (arrowed) and withdraw the bolt

16.2 Silencer clamp bolt (arrowed)

16.10 Unscrew the bolt (arrowed)

16.16 Unscrew the bolts (arrowed) and remove the footrest assembly

- Use a new sealing ring between the downpipe assembly and the silencer if necessary – see Step 3.
- Locate the downpipes in the cylinder head and loosely fit the mounting bolt and washer. Tighten the downpipe nuts first, tightening them to the torque setting specified at the beginning of the Chapter, then tighten the downpipe bolt to the specified torque.
- Install the radiator and the refill the cooling system (see Chapter 3). Install the silencer.
- Run the engine and check the system for leaks. Check the operation of the exhaust valve (see Section 17).

D models

Silencers

16 Remove the seat cowling (see Chapter 7). Remove the passenger footrest assembly **(see illustration)**.
17 Unscrew the three nuts securing the silencer to the middle pipe and remove the washers **(see illustration)**. Unscrew the nut on the silencer mounting bolt, noting the washer **(see illustration)**. Withdraw the bolt with its washer and remove the silencer. Remove the gasket – a new one must be used.
18 Check the condition of the bolt, nuts, washers, collars and rubbers and replace them with new ones if necessary.
19 Installation is the reverse of removal, noting the following:
- Clean up rusted threads. Replace any excessively corroded or deformed mounting hardware with new ones. Apply

16.21 Left-hand pipe clamp bolt (arrowed)

16.17a Unscrew the nuts (arrowed)

a smear of copper grease to all threads.
- Make sure the collars are fitted in the rubbers.
- Use a new gasket between the silencer can and the silencer pipe.
- Tighten the silencer nuts to the torque setting specified at the beginning of the Chapter.
- Run the engine and check the system for leaks.

Middle pipes

20 Remove the silencers.
21 Slacken the left-hand pipe clamp bolt **(see illustration)**. Ease the pipe out of the main middle pipe assembly.
22 Disconnect the exhaust valve cables from the middle pipe assembly (see Section 17, Steps 23 and 24).
23 Slacken the middle pipe clamp bolt **(see illustration)**. Unscrew the nut on the middle pipe mounting bolt, noting the washer. Withdraw the bolt with its washer and ease the middle pipe back off the downpipe assembly.
24 Check the condition of the middle pipe sealing rings and replace them with new ones if they are damaged or deformed or no longer sealing correctly **(see illustration 16.39)** – note that Kawasaki specify to always use new ones. If fitting new sealing rings, slide the clamps off, noting their orientation and how the slot aligns with the tab, and expand the tangs on the end of the pipe slightly to make them easier to fit.
25 Check the condition of the clamp, bolt, nut, washers, collars and rubbers and replace them with new ones if necessary.

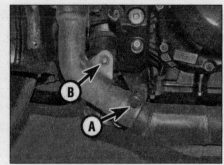

16.23 Middle pipe clamp bolt (A) and mounting bolt (B)

16.17b Unscrew the nut (arrowed) and withdraw the bolt

26 Installation is the reverse of removal, noting the following:
- Clean up rusted threads. Replace any excessively corroded or deformed mounting hardware with new ones. Apply a smear of copper grease to all threads.
- Use a new sealing ring between the downpipe assembly and the middle pipe if necessary – see Step 24.
- Make sure the collars are fitted in the rubbers.
- Tighten the middle pipe mounting bolt nut and the clamp bolts to the torque settings specified at the beginning of the Chapter.
- Run the engine and check the system for leaks. Check the operation of the exhaust valve (see Section 17).

Downpipe assembly

27 Remove the radiator (see Chapter 3).
28 Disconnect the oxygen sensor wiring connectors and draw them out of the guide **(see illustration 6.46a)**.
29 Slacken the middle pipe clamp bolt **(see illustration 16.23)**.
30 Unscrew the nuts securing the header pipes to the cylinder head **(see illustration 16.51)**.
31 Draw the flanges off the studs and manoeuvre the downpipe assembly off the head and the middle pipe and remove it **(see illustration 16.52)**.
32 Remove the sealing ring from each port in the cylinder head and discard them as new ones must be used **(see illustration 16.53)**.
33 Check the condition of the middle pipe sealing ring and replace it with a new one if it is damaged or deformed or no longer sealing correctly **(see illustration 16.39)** – note that Kawasaki specify to always use a new one. If fitting a new sealing ring, slide the clamp off, noting its orientation and how the slot aligns with the tab, and expand the tangs on the end of the pipe slightly to make it easier to fit.
34 Check the condition of the clamp and nuts and replace them with new ones if necessary.
35 Installation is the reverse of removal, noting the following:
- Clean up rusted threads. Replace any excessively corroded or deformed mounting hardware with new ones. Apply a smear of copper grease to all threads.

16.37 Silencer clamp bolt (arrowed)

16.38a Unscrew the nut, withdraw the bolt...

16.38b ...and remove the silencer

● Use a new sealing ring in each cylinder head port, and dab them with grease to stick them in place (see illustration 16.56).
● Use a new sealing ring between the downpipe assembly and the middle pipe if necessary – see Step 33.
● Tighten the downpipe nuts first, tightening them to the torque setting specified at the beginning of the Chapter, then tighten the clamp bolt to the specified torque.
● Make sure the oxygen sensor wiring is correctly routed and connected.
● Install the radiator and the refill the cooling system (see Chapter 3).
● Run the engine and check the system for leaks.

E and F models

Silencer

36 Disconnect the exhaust valve cables from the silencer (see Section 17, Steps 23 and 24).
37 Slacken the silencer clamp bolt (see illustration).
38 Unscrew the nut on the silencer mounting bolt (see illustration). Withdraw the bolt with its washer and ease the silencer back off the middle chamber (see illustration).
39 Check the condition of the middle chamber rear sealing ring and replace it with a new one if it is damaged or deformed or no longer sealing correctly (see illustration) – note that Kawasaki specify to always use a new one. If fitting a new sealing ring, slide the clamp off, noting its orientation and how the slot aligns with the tab, and expand the tangs on the end of the pipe slightly to make it easier to fit.
40 Check the condition of the clamp, bolt, nut, washer, collars and rubbers and replace them with new ones if necessary.
41 Installation is the reverse of removal, noting the following:
● Clean up rusted threads. Replace any excessively corroded or deformed mounting hardware with new ones. Apply a smear of copper grease to all threads.
● Make sure the collars are fitted in the rubbers.
● Use a new sealing ring between the silencer and the middle chamber if necessary – see Step 39.
● Tighten the silencer mounting bolt and

clamp to the torque settings specified at the beginning of the Chapter.
● Run the engine and check the system for leaks.

Middle chamber

42 Remove the silencer.
43 If required, and to give best access to the clamp and mounting bolts, remove the shield, but note that it is likely the screws securing it will be seized (see illustration).
44 Slacken the middle chamber clamp bolt (see illustration). Unscrew the mounting bolt, noting the washer (see illustration). Ease the middle chamber back off the downpipe assembly. Remove the nut plate from the mount if loose.
45 Check the condition of the middle chamber front sealing ring and replace it with a new one if it is damaged or deformed or no longer sealing correctly (see illustration

16.39 Check the sealing ring (arrowed)

16.44a Middle chamber clamp bolt (arrowed)

16.39) – note that Kawasaki specify to always use a new one. If fitting a new sealing ring, slide the clamp off, noting its orientation and how the slot aligns with the tab, and expand the tangs on the end of the pipe slightly to make it easier to fit.
46 Check the condition of the clamp, bolt, washer, nut plate, collars and rubbers and replace them with new ones if necessary.
47 Installation is the reverse of removal, noting the following:
● Clean up rusted threads. Replace any excessively corroded or deformed mounting hardware with new ones. Apply a smear of copper grease to all threads.
● Use a new sealing ring between the downpipe assembly and the middle chamber if necessary – see Step 45.
● Make sure the collars are fitted in the rubbers, and the nut plate is correctly in place.

16.43 Undo the screws (arrowed) and remove the shield

16.44b Middle chamber mounting bolt (arrowed)

16.51 Unscrew the nuts...

16.52 ...and remove the downpipe assembly

● Tighten the chamber mounting bolt and the clamp bolt to the torque settings specified at the beginning of the Chapter.
● Run the engine and check the system for leaks.

Downpipe assembly

48 Remove the radiator (see Chapter 3).
49 Disconnect the oxygen sensor wiring connectors and release the wiring from the clamps **(see illustration 6.46b)** – you may be able to access the connectors from above the front sprocket cover, but if necessary remove the fuel tank (see Section 2)..
50 Slacken the middle chamber clamp bolt **(see illustration 16.44a)**.
51 Unscrew the nuts securing the header pipes to the cylinder head **(see illustration)**.
52 Draw the flanges off the studs and manoeuvre the downpipe assembly off the head and the middle chamber and remove it **(see illustration)**.
53 Remove the sealing ring from each port in the cylinder head and discard them as new ones must be used **(see illustration)**.

54 Check the condition of the middle chamber front sealing ring and replace it with a new one if it is damaged or deformed or no longer sealing correctly **(see illustration 16.39)** – note that Kawasaki specify to always use a new one. If fitting a new sealing ring, slide the clamp off, noting its orientation and how the slot aligns with the tab, and expand the tangs on the end of the pipe slightly to make it easier to fit.
55 Check the condition of the clamp and nuts and replace them with new ones if necessary.
56 Installation is the reverse of removal, noting the following:
● Clean up the cylinder head stud threads using a wire brush if necessary. Apply a smear of copper grease to all threads.
● Use a new sealing ring in each cylinder head port, and dab them with grease to stick them in place **(see illustration)**.
● Use a new sealing ring between the downpipe assembly and the middle chamber if necessary – see Step 54.
● Tighten the downpipe nuts first, tightening

them to the torque setting specified at the beginning of the Chapter, then tighten the clamp bolt to the specified torque.
● Make sure the oxygen sensor wiring is correctly routed and connected.
● Install the radiator and the refill the cooling system (see Chapter 3).
● Run the engine and check the system for leaks.

17 Exhaust valve

Check

1 The system controls the flow of gases through the exhaust using a butterfly valve. The valve is actuated by cables from a servo motor that is controlled by the ECU.
2 On C, E and F models remove the rider's seat (see Chapter 7). On D models remove the seat cowling (see Chapter 7).
3 Check that the pulley is in its original

16.53 Remove the old sealing rings and discard them

16.56 Use a new sealing ring in each port

17.3 The point of the pulley between the cable ends should align with the casing screw (arrowed)

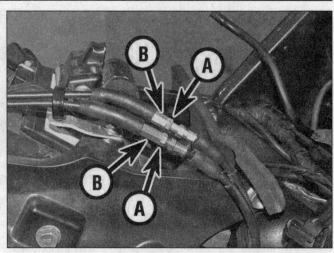

17.4 Cable adjuster locknuts (A) and adjusters (B) – D model shown

position as shown **(see illustration)**. Turn the ignition ON and check that the servo pulley rotates clockwise, then anti-clockwise, then clockwise again, so it ends up back in its original position. Turn the ignition OFF. If not, check the cables are not detached, seized or broken, and check the servo wiring connectors.

4 Check there is not excessive slack in the cables at the pulley. If there is, locate the adjusters and draw the boots off **(see illustration)**. Slacken the locknut on the valve opening cable adjuster (the opening cable has a yellow or white elbow at the servo end, the closing cable has a dark green or black elbow) and turn the adjuster away from the locknut until the excess slack is taken up. Tighten the locknut. Repeat for the closing cable adjuster.

Servo motor sensor

5 Disconnect the servo's 3-pin wiring connector **(see illustrations)**. Using an ohmmeter or multimeter set to the K-ohms scale check the resistance between the white and black wire terminals on the servo side of the connector. Compare the reading to that specified at the beginning of the Chapter and replace the servo with a new one if the reading differs.

Servo motor actuator

6 Disconnect the servo's 2-pin wiring

connector **(see illustration 17.5a or b)**. Using an ohmmeter or multimeter set to the ohms scale check there is a resistance between the terminals on the servo side of the connector. The reading obtained could be 5 to 200 ohms or more – the important thing is that there is a resistance, and that a reading of either zero ohms or infinite resistance is not shown. If it is, replace the servo with a new one.

Exhaust valve

7 Detach the cables from the valve (see below).

8 Turn the valve pulley by hand. If it doesn't turn smoothly or has seized the relevant section of the exhaust (according to model) must be replaced with a new one.

Removal

Servo motor

9 On C, E and F models remove the rider's seat (see Chapter 7). On D models remove the seat cowling (see Chapter 7).

10 Pull the rubber boots off the exhaust valve cable adjusters **(see illustration 17.4)**. Fully slacken the adjuster locknuts then thread the adjusters fully in to give maximum freeplay.

11 Disconnect the servo wiring connectors **(see illustration 17.5a or b)**.

12 Remove the cable clamp from the holder on the servo, noting how it fits **(see illustration)**. Free the outer cables from the holder and detach the cables from the pulley **(see illustrations)**.

17.5a Servo wiring connectors (arrowed) – C models

17.5b Servo wiring connectors (arrowed) – D models

17.12a Release the clamp...

17.12b ...free the outer cables...

17.12c ...and detach the cable ends

17.13a Servo nuts (arrowed) – C models

17.13b Servo bolts (arrowed) – D models

17.21 Unscrew the bolts (arrowed) and remove the cover

13 Unscrew the servo mounting nuts or bolts and remove the servo, retrieving the washers **(see illustrations)**. On C models note the collars.

14 Counter-hold the pulley and unscrew its bolt, then detach the pulley – make sure the pulley does not turn as you unscrew the bolt as the servo could be damaged.

Exhaust valve

15 Remove the relevant section of the exhaust system according to model and replace it with a new one (see Section 16).

Installation

16 Installation is the reverse of removal, noting the following:
● If the pulley was removed, make sure you counter-hold it while tightening the bolt or the servo will be damaged.

● The opening cable has a yellow or white elbow at the servo end, the closing cable has a dark green or black elbow.
● After installation turn the ignition ON and check the pulley rotates as it should (Step 3).

Cable renewal

17 The opening cable has a yellow or white elbow at the servo end, the closing cable has a dark green or black elbow.

18 On C models and E and F models remove the rider's seat (see Chapter 7). On D models remove the seat cowling (see Chapter 7).

19 Pull the rubber boots off the exhaust valve cable adjusters **(see illustration 17.4)**. Fully slacken the adjuster locknuts then thread the adjusters fully in to give maximum freeplay.

20 Remove the cable clamp from the holder

on the servo, noting how it fits **(see illustration 17.12a)**. Free the outer cables from the holder and detach the cables from the pulley **(see illustrations 17.12b and c)**.

21 On C, E and F models remove the cover from the exhaust valve **(see illustration)**.

22 On D models displace the rear brake fluid reservoir **(see illustration)**. Remove the upper cover and the exhaust shield **(see illustrations)**. Unscrew the rider's footrest bracket bolts and displace the bracket, then unhook the brake light switch spring, depress the switch retaining tabs and draw the switch out of the bracket, then tie or support the footrest bracket assembly clear **(see illustrations)**. Remove the lower cover **(see illustration)**.

23 Mark each cable according to its location in the exhaust valve bracket as a guide for fitting the new cables.

17.22a Displace the reservoir

17.22b Undo the screws (arrowed) and remove the cover...

17.22c ...then undo the screw (arrowed) and remove the shield

17.22d Unscrew the bolts (arrowed)...

17.22e ...unhook the spring (arrowed)

17.22f ...and release the switch

17.22g Undo the screws (arrowed) and remove the cover

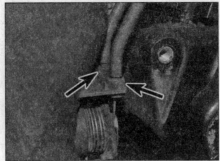

17.24a Slacken the nuts (arrowed)...

17.24b ...and detach the cables

24 Slacken the locknuts securing the cables in the bracket, then free them and detach the ends from the valve pulley (see illustrations).
25 Withdraw the cables from the machine, noting the routing.
26 On installation lubricate the cable ends with multi-purpose grease. Make sure the cables are correctly routed. Set the cables in the bracket on the exhaust so there is 6 mm of the threaded section of each cable elbow (including that covered by the nut) protruding from the lower face of the bracket (see illustration). Now set the cable adjusters so all freeplay is just about taken up, then tighten the locknuts (see illustration 17.4). Check the operation of the system.

18 Catalytic converter

General information

1 A catalytic converter is incorporated in the silencer to minimise the level of exhaust pollutants released into the atmosphere.
2 The catalytic converter consists of a canister containing a fine mesh impregnated with a catalyst material, over which the hot exhaust gases pass. The catalyst speeds up the oxidation of harmful carbon monoxide, unburned hydrocarbons and soot, effectively reducing the quantity of harmful products released into the atmosphere via the exhaust gases.

3 On all except C models the catalytic converter is of the closed-loop type with exhaust gas oxygen content information being fed back to the ECU by the oxygen sensors.
4 The oxygen sensors (where fitted) contain a heating element that is controlled by the ECU. When the engine is cold, the ECU switches on the heating element, which warms the exhaust gases as they pass over the sensor. This brings the catalytic converter quickly up to its normal operating temperature and decreases the level of exhaust pollutants emitted whilst the engine warms up. Once the engine is sufficiently warmed up, the ECU switches off the heating element.
5 Refer to Section 16 for exhaust system removal and installation, and Section 6 for oxygen sensor removal and installation information.

Precautions

6 The catalytic converter is a reliable and simple device which needs no maintenance in itself, but there are some facts of which an owner should be aware if the converter is to function properly for its full service life.
● DO NOT use leaded or lead replacement petrol (gasoline) – the additives will coat the precious metals, reducing their converting efficiency and will eventually destroy the catalytic converter.
● Always keep the ignition and fuel systems well-maintained in accordance with the manufacturer's schedule – if the fuel/air mixture is suspected of being incorrect have it checked on an exhaust gas analyser.

● If the engine develops a misfire, do not ride the bike at all (or at least as little as possible) until the fault is cured.
● DO NOT use fuel or engine oil additives – these may contain substances harmful to the catalytic converter.
● DO NOT continue to use the bike if the engine burns oil to the extent of leaving a visible trail of blue smoke.
● Remember that the catalytic converter and oxygen sensor are FRAGILE – do not strike them with tools during servicing work.

19 Air suction system

General information

1 To reduce the amount of unburned hydrocarbons released in the exhaust gases, a pulse secondary air (PAIR) system is fitted. The system consists of the control valve (mounted above the engine valve cover), the reed valves (fitted in the engine valve cover) and the hoses linking them. The control valve is actuated electronically by the ECU.
2 Under normal operating conditions the valve is open allowing filtered air to be drawn through the reed valves and cylinder head passages and into the exhaust ports. The air mixes with the exhaust gases, causing any unburned particles of the fuel in the mixture to be burnt in the exhaust port/pipes. This process changes a considerable amount of hydrocarbons and carbon monoxide into relatively harmless carbon dioxide and water. The reed valves in the valve cover are fitted to prevent the flow of exhaust gases back up the cylinder head passages and into the air filter housing.

Testing

3 On C and D models remove the air filter housing (see Section 3). On E and F models remove the upper section of the air filter housing (see Section 3).
4 Disconnect the air suction system hose from the filter housing base or lower section, according to model (see illustration). Clean the end of the hose.

17.26 Set the cables in the bracket as described

19.4 Detach the hose

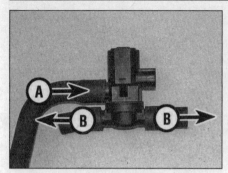

19.5a When blowing into hose (A) air should flow out of hoses (B)

19.5b Connect battery voltage to the terminals (arrowed)

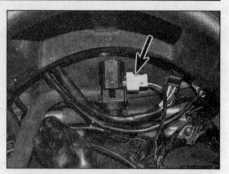

19.9 Disconnect the wiring (arrowed)...

5 Disconnect the control valve wiring connector **(see illustration 19.9)**. Manually check the operation of the system by blowing through the hose – air should flow through the control valve and reed valves **(see illustration)**. Apply battery voltage (12 volts) across the control valve terminals and repeat the check **(see illustration)** – no air should flow through the control valve. Disconnect the battery. If the valve does not behave as described check its resistance (Step 7).

6 Now suck on the air filter hose union; you should not be able to suck air back up the

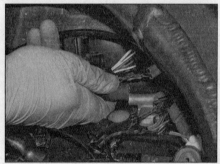

19.10 ...then detach the hoses

hose, indicating the reed valves are closing and sealing correctly. If you can suck air through, first identify which reed valve is faulty by blocking one hose, then the other. Having identified the faulty valve remove it for cleaning, then test it again. Replace the valve with a new one if necessary.

7 Check the resistance of the control valve solenoid by connecting an ohmmeter between its connector terminals and compare the reading obtained to that given in the Specifications. Replace the valve with a new one if faulty.

Component renewal

Control valve

8 On C and D models remove the air filter housing (see Section 3). On E and F models remove the upper section of the air filter housing (see Section 3).

9 Disconnect the control valve wiring connector **(see illustration)**.

10 Detach the hoses from the reed valve housings **(see illustration)**.

11 Disconnect the air suction system hose from the filter housing base or lower section, according to model **(see illustration 19.4)**.

12 Remove the valve with the hoses, then detach them if required.

13 Installation is the reverse of removal.

Reed valves

14 On C and D models remove the air filter housing (see Section 3). On E and F models remove the upper section of the air filter housing (see Section 3).

15 If required either detach the air hose from the reed valve cover, or for best access remove the control valve (see above).

16 Unscrew the bolts and remove the cover **(see illustration)**. Remove the reed valve, noting which way around it fits **(see illustration)**.

17 Gently push each reed off its seat from the underside to check they are not stuck **(see illustration)**. Release the reed and make sure there is no gap between it and its seat **(see illustration)**. Check the condition of the rubber around the valve. Replace the valve with a new one if necessary.

18 Installation is the reverse of removal. Make sure the reed valve components and housings are clean and free of carbon deposits, and they seat correctly.

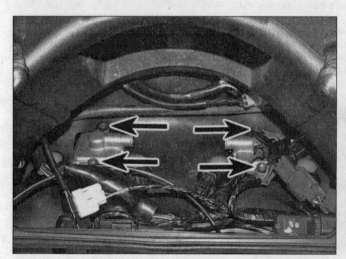

19.16a Reed valve cover bolts (arrowed)

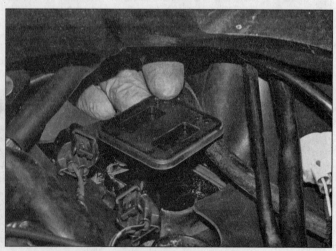

19.16b Lift the valve out of the housing

19.17a Check each reed is not stuck to its seat

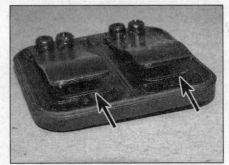

19.17b Make sure there is no gap between each reed (arrowed) and its seat

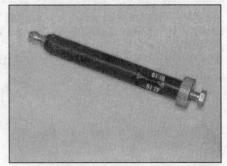

21.4 Ignition spark gap testing tool

20 Evaporative emission control (EVAP) system

Note: *This system is fitted to California market models only.*

1 The evaporative emission control system (EVAP) is fitted to minimise the escape of fuel vapour into the atmosphere. The fuel tank is sealed and a charcoal canister collects the fuel vapours generated when the motorcycle is parked and stores them until they can be cleared from the canister, via the separator valve, to be burned by the engine during normal combustion. The separator valve (which controls the flow of the vapour according to whether the engine is running or not) is controlled by a vacuum sourced from the throttle bodies.

2 The storage canister and separator valve are maintenance free and are designed to operate throughout the life of the motorcycle. Inspection and replacement of the hoses should be carried out according to the service schedule in Chapter 1.

21 Ignition system check

⚠ *Warning: The energy levels in electronic systems can be very high. On no account should the ignition be switched on whilst the plugs are being held. Shocks from the HT circuit can be most unpleasant. Secondly, it is vital that the engine is not turned over or run with any of the coils disconnected from the plugs, and that the plugs are soundly earthed (grounded) when the system is checked for sparking. The ignition system components can be seriously damaged if the HT circuit becomes isolated.*

1 As no means of adjustment is available, any failure of the system can be traced to failure of a system component or a simple wiring fault. Of the two possibilities, the latter is by far the most likely. The first step in checking the ignition system is to see whether there is

a spark at the plug. If the engine does not run at all test each plug in turn, starting with the No. 1 (left-hand) plug, and work across the engine. If the engine runs but not on all cylinders, first identify the non-firing cylinder by seeing which exhaust downpipe remains cold.

2 Make sure the ignition is switched off. Refer to Chapter 1 and remove the spark plug being tested. Reconnect the wiring connector to the removed coil. Disconnect the wiring connector from the other three coils. Fit the spark plug into the removed coil, then hold the coil so the plug threads are pressed against the cylinder head to earth it – do not hold the plug against the valve cover, and do not hold it against the inside of the plug bore (see **Warning** below). If it is difficult to contact the cylinder head use a length of fairly thick insulated wire with crocodile clips at each end to link the plug threads to the cylinder head, or some other known good earth point.

⚠ *Warning: Do not earth the plug by holding it against the side of its bore in the cylinder head – atomised fuel being pumped out of the open spark plug hole could ignite, causing severe injury! Make sure the plugs are securely held against the earth point – if they are not earthed when the engine is turned over, the ECU could be damaged.*

3 Having observed the above precautions, check that the kill switch is in the RUN position and the transmission is in neutral, then turn the ignition switch ON and turn the engine over on the starter motor. If the system is in good condition a regular, fat blue spark should be evident at the plug electrodes. If the spark appears thin or yellowish, or is non-existent, further investigation is necessary. Turn the ignition OFF and repeat the check for each coil.

4 The ignition system must be able to produce a spark that is capable of jumping at least a 6 mm gap. Simple ignition spark gap testing tools are commercially available **(see illustration)** – follow the manufacturer's instructions.

5 If the test results are good the entire ignition system can be considered good. If the spark appears thin or yellowish, or is non-existent, further investigation is necessary.

6 Ignition faults can be divided into two categories, namely those where the ignition

system has failed completely, and those that are due to a partial failure. The likely faults are listed below, starting with the most probable source of failure. Work through the list systematically, referring to the subsequent sections for full details of the necessary checks and tests. **Note:** *Before checking the following items ensure that the battery is fully charged and that the FI system fuses are in good condition.*

● Loose, corroded or damaged wiring connections, broken or shorted wiring between any of the component parts of the ignition system (see Chapter 8).
● Faulty coil connection, faulty spark plug, dirty, worn or corroded plug electrodes.
● Faulty gear position, clutch or sidestand switch (see Chapter 8).
● Faulty ignition coil(s) (Section 22).
● Faulty ignition switch or engine kill switch (see Chapter 8).
● Faulty crankshaft position (CKP) sensor (Section 6) or damaged timing trigger (Chapter 8).
● Faulty throttle position sensor (Section 6).
● Faulty tip-over sensor (Section 6).
● Faulty ECU or ECU relay (Section 7).

7 If the above checks don't reveal the cause of the problem, have the ignition system tested by a Kawasaki dealer.

22 Ignition coils

1 On C and D models, to access all the coil wiring connectors and to remove the inner cylinder (Nos. 2 and 3) coils, remove the fairing side panels and the fairing (see Chapter 7), and the air filter housing (see Section 3). Unscrew the air duct bolts and remove the air duct assembly.

2 On E and F models, to access all the coil wiring connectors and to remove the inner cylinder (Nos. 2 and 3) coils remove the fairing assembly (Chapter 7), and the upper section of the air filter housing (see Section 3).

3 To remove the No.1 cylinder coil, remove the coolant reservoir (see Chapter 3), then remove the left-hand engine bracket (see Chapter 2, Section 4). To remove the No. 4 cylinder coil,

22.5a Disconnect the wiring connector...

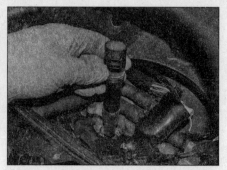

22.5b ...and pull the coil off the spark plug

remove the right-hand engine bracket (see Chapter 2, Section 4).

4 Check the coils visually for loose or damaged connectors and terminals, cracks and other damage. Clean the area around each coil to prevent any dirt falling into the spark plug channels.

5 Disconnect the coil wiring connector (see illustration). Pull the coil off the spark plug (see illustration) – if the coil is difficult to remove spray some penetrating lubricant around the seal.

6 To check the condition of the primary windings, set a multimeter to the ohms x 1 scale. Connect one meter probe to one terminal in the coil socket and the other probe to the other terminal and measure the resistance (see illustration). If the reading obtained is not within the range given in the Specifications, it is likely that the coil is defective.

7 To check the resistance of the secondary windings, set the meter to the K-ohm scale. Remove the insulating rubber from the bottom of the coil (see illustration). Connect one meter probe to the left-hand terminal in the coil socket, and the other to the spark plug contact (see illustration). If the reading obtained is not within the range given in the Specifications, it is likely that the coil is defective.

8 To confirm a coil is defective have it peak voltage tested by a Kawasaki dealer.

9 Fit the insulating rubber back onto the coil.

10 Smear some grease around the seal on the top of the coil. Fit the coil onto the spark plug and push it down to seat it fully. Connect the wiring connector.

11 Install all remaining components in reverse order (Steps 3 to 1).

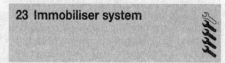

23 Immobiliser system

General information

1 An immobiliser system is fitted as standard to some models, according to country. Other models have facility in the wiring loom for connection of an immobiliser as optional equipment. The system will only allow the machine to be started if the correct registered key is used to turn the ignition ON. The system consists of a transponder, which is part of the ignition key, a receiver, which is fitted around the ignition switch, an amplifier and the ECU.

2 On C models, when the ignition is switched ON the FI warning light comes on for two seconds and extinguishes when the ECU matches the code of the key being used with that stored in the ECU memory. If the key code signal is not recognised, the engine cannot be started and the FI light flashes. If there is a fault in the system, the FI warning light will flash. In either case refer to Section 5 to identify the fault code, then perform the checks given in this Section on the components as required.

3 On D, E and F models, when the ignition is switched ON the warning light and the key symbol in the LCD display come on briefly and extinguish when the ECU matches the code of the key being used with that stored in the

ECU memory. If the key code signal is not recognised, the engine cannot be started and the light and symbol flash. If there is a fault in the system, the warning light and symbol will flash. In either case refer to Section 5 to identify the fault code, then perform the checks given in this Section on the components as required.

4 When the ignition is turned OFF the warning light flashes for a period of 24 hours before switching itself off, though the immobiliser system is still functional. To turn this flashing function off or on, press the mode and reset buttons on the instrument cluster down simultaneously for more than 2 seconds within 20 seconds of turning the ignition off. If the battery is low the flashing function automatically switches off. If the battery is disconnected the flashing function is automatically set on when the battery is reconnected.

5 The ECU stores the codes for the registered master key (which has a red head) and up to five user keys (which have black heads). The master key should be kept in a safe place and not be used – if it is lost it is not possible to register any new user keys, so in the event they are also lost a new ECU must be installed. The user keys should be kept separately (i.e. not on the same key-ring) as the proximity of another key to the one being used in the switch can lead to the signal from it being jammed, and the bike will not start. The key has a built in transponder which can be damaged if the key is dropped or knocked, gets too hot, is too close to a magnetic object, or is submerged in water for too long. Always make sure you have at least one spare key. If a new key is obtained, it must be registered into the system before the bike can be started. For additional security if a key is lost it is best to have the key registration invalidated in the ECU – take along your master key and a spare key.

Key registration procedure

With old ignition switch

Note: To do this you will need either the Kawasaki special tool(s) (Part No. 57001-1582, and also 57001-1746 on FA (2010) models), or a commercially available equivalent. The tool is a wiring loom adapter that connects to

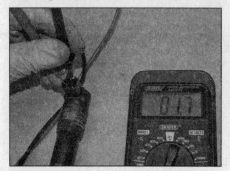

22.6 To test the coil primary resistance, connect the multimeter leads between the connector socket terminals

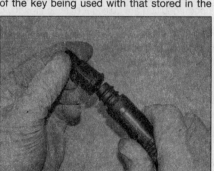

22.7a Remove the insulating rubber from the coil

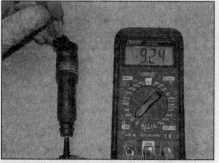

22.7b To test the coil secondary resistance, connect the multimeter leads between one terminal and the spark plug socket

23.7a Immobiliser diagnosis wiring connector (arrowed) – C models

23.7b Immobiliser diagnosis wiring connector (arrowed) – D models

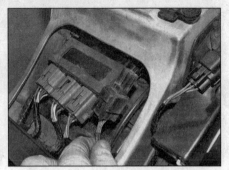

23.7c Immobiliser diagnosis wiring connector – E/F models

a wiring connector under the seat. Otherwise registration must be carried out by a Kawasaki dealer with the special tool.

6 Obtain a new key from a Kawasaki dealer, and have it cut to match the original key.

7 On C and D models remove the rider's seat (see Chapter 7). On E and F models remove the centre section of the seat cowling (see Chapter 7). Locate the immobiliser diagnosis wiring connector **(see illustrations)**. Remove the blanked side of the connector and connect the special tool(s) in its place.

8 Turn the ignition switch ON using the master key. The warning light in the instrument cluster should flash at 0.5 second intervals. If the light flashes at 0.2 second intervals check the immobiliser amplifier, and if it flashes at 0.3 second intervals the master key has not been recognised.

9 Turn the ignition OFF and remove the master key, placing it well away from the receiver – the light should flash at 0.5 second intervals, indicating that the system is in registration mode.

10 Within 15 seconds insert the new key into the switch and turn it ON. The light should now flash (twice for the first key being registered, three times for the second key, four times for the third key and so on for up to five keys) at 0.3 second intervals, then go out for 1 second, then repeat this pattern. This indicates that the system has registered the new key. If the light flashes continuously at 0.2 second intervals check the immobiliser amplifier (see below), if it flashes at 0.3 second intervals the key has not been registered, if it flashes at 0.5 second intervals the key is already registered.

11 Turn the ignition OFF and remove the key – the FI light should flash at 0.5 second intervals, indicating that the system is still in registration mode. To register any other keys, repeat Step 10 within 15 seconds. After 15 seconds the system leaves registration mode.

12 On completion turn the ignition OFF, wait 15 seconds until the system is no longer in registration mode, then remove the special tool and fit the blank in its place.

13 Check that all registered keys can start the motorcycle.

With a new ignition switch

Note: *To do this you will need either the*

Kawasaki special tool(s) (Part No. 57001-1582, and also 57001-1746 on FA (2010) models), or a commercially available equivalent. The tool is a wiring loom adapter that connects to a wiring connector under the seat. Otherwise registration must be carried at a Kawasaki dealer with the special tool.

14 Obtain a new switch, which comes with two new keys.

15 Remove the faulty switch (see Chapter 8), but retain the receiver to fit with the new switch.

16 On C and D models remove the rider's seat (see Chapter 7). On E and F models remove the centre section of the seat cowling (see Chapter 7). Locate the immobiliser diagnosis wiring connector **(see illustration 23.7a, b or c)**. Remove the blanked side of the connector and connect the special tool(s) in its place.

17 Connect the new ignition switch and the original receiver to their connectors, but keep them at least 15 cm apart. Place the master key next to the receiver.

18 Turn the new switch ON with one of the new keys. The warning light in the instrument cluster should flash at 0.5 second intervals. If the light flashes at 0.2 second intervals check the immobiliser amplifier, and if it flashes at 0.3 second intervals the master key has not been recognised.

19 Turn the ignition OFF and remove the new key. Within fifteen seconds fit the receiver onto the new switch. Insert the new key into the switch and turn it ON. The light should now flash (twice for the first key being registered, three times for the second key, four times for the third key and so on for up to five keys) at 0.3 second intervals, then go out for 1 second, then repeat this pattern. This indicates that the system has registered the new key. If the light flashes continuously at 0.2 second intervals check the immobiliser amplifier (see below), if it flashes at 0.3 second intervals the key has not been registered, if it flashes at 0.5 second intervals the key is already registered.

20 Turn the ignition OFF and remove the key – the light should flash at 0.5 second intervals, indicating that the system is still in registration mode. To register any other keys, repeat Step 19 within 15 seconds. After 15 seconds the system leaves registration mode.

21 On completion turn the ignition OFF, wait

15 seconds until the system is no longer in registration mode, then remove the special tool and fit the blank in its place.

22 Check that all registered keys can start the motorcycle.

With a new ECU (electronic control unit)

23 Obtain and install a new ECU (see Section 7).

24 Insert the master key into the switch and turn it ON. The warning light in the instrument cluster should flash once, then go out for 1 second, then repeat this pattern. This indicates that the system has registered the master key. If the light flashes continuously at 0.2 second intervals check the immobiliser amplifier (see below), if it flashes at 0.3 second intervals the key has not been registered.

25 Turn the ignition OFF and remove the master key. The immobiliser indicator light should flash at 0.5 second intervals.

26 Insert the first user key within 15 seconds and turn the ignition ON. The light should now flash (twice for the first user key being registered, three times for the second key, four times for the third key and so on for up to five keys) at 0.3 second intervals, then go out for 1 second, then repeat this pattern. This indicates that the system has registered the new key. If the light flashes continuously at 0.2 second intervals check the immobiliser amplifier (see below), if it flashes at 0.3 second intervals the key has not been registered, if it flashes at 0.5 second intervals the key is already registered.

27 Turn the ignition OFF and remove the key – the light should flash at 0.5 second intervals, indicating that the system is still in registration mode. To register any other keys, repeat Step 26 within 15 seconds. After 15 seconds the system leaves registration mode.

28 On completion turn the ignition OFF, wait 15 seconds until the system is no longer in registration mode.

29 Check that all registered keys can start the motorcycle.

Fault code 35

30 If fault code 35 is displayed (see Section 5), first check the receiver, then the amplifier (see below)

23.33a Immobiliser receiver wiring connector (arrowed) – C models

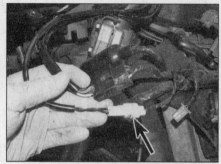

23.33b Immobiliser receiver wiring connector (arrowed) – D models

23.33c Immobiliser receiver wiring connector (arrowed) – E/F models

Fault code 36

31 If fault code 36 is displayed (see Section 5), either the transponder in the registered key being used has failed, or the key being used has not been registered. First try the key registration procedure above (Steps 6 to 13), and if the fault code still appears then replace the key with a new one and register it.

Receiver

Check

32 On C models remove the left-hand fairing side panel (see Chapter 7). On D models remove the left-hand cockpit trim panel (see Chapter 7). On E and F models remove the right-hand cockpit trim panel (see Chapter 7).
33 Disconnect the receiver wiring connector **(see illustrations)**. Connect the probes of an ohmmeter to the terminals in the receiver side of the wiring connector and check the resistance. If it is not as specified at the beginning of the Chapter replace the receiver with a new one.

Removal and installation

34 Remove the ignition switch from the top yoke (see Chapter 8).
35 Cut the cable-tie securing the receiver wiring. Undo the screws securing the receiver to the switch, then release the shroud from the tabs on the switch and remove the receiver and shroud **(see illustration)**.
36 Fit a new receiver to the switch along with

the shroud, making sure the wiring is routed down the channel. Install the switch (see Chapter 8).

Amplifier

Check

37 On C and D models remove the left-hand fairing side panel (see Chapter 7). On E and F models remove the right-hand cockpit trim panel (see Chapter 7).
38 If needle probes are available, check for battery voltage at the brown/white wire terminal in the amplifier connector with the connector connected and the ignition ON **(see illustrations)**. Also check for continuity to earth in the black/yellow wire. If needle probes are not available check for continuity in all the wiring and connectors, referring to the wiring diagrams in Chapter 8.

23.35 Receiver screws (arrowed)

39 If all the wiring is good check the receiver. If that is good replace the amplifier with a new one.

Removal and installation

40 On C models remove the left-hand fairing side panel and inner panel (see Chapter 7). Release the wiring from the clamp. Undo the screws, free the amplifier from its bracket and disconnect the wiring connector **(see illustration)**.
41 On D models remove the left-hand fairing side panel (see Chapter 7). Disconnect the wiring connector and release the amplifier from its bracket **(see illustration 23.38b)**.
42 On E and F models remove the right-hand cockpit trim panel (see Chapter 7). Free the amplifier from its bracket and disconnect the wiring connector **(see illustration 23.38c)**.
43 Installation is the reverse of removal.

23.38a Immobiliser amplifier wiring connector (arrowed) – C models

23.38b Immobiliser amplifier wiring connector (arrowed) – D models

23.38c Immobiliser amplifier wiring connector (arrowed) – E/F models

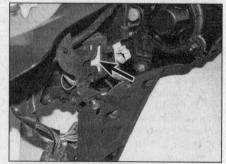

23.40 Immobiliser amplifier (arrowed) – C models

Chapter 5
Frame and suspension

Contents

Degrees of difficulty

Easy, suitable for novice with little experience 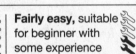	Fairly easy, suitable for beginner with some experience 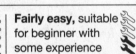	Fairly difficult, suitable for competent DIY mechanic 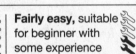	Difficult, suitable for experienced DIY mechanic 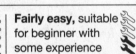	Very difficult, suitable for expert DIY or professional

Specifications

Front forks

Fork oil type	Kayaba KHL 15-10 fork oil or equivalent 5W fork oil
Fork oil capacity	
Oil change	
C1, E and F models	490 ml
C2 and D models	480 ml
Fork stripdown	
C1 model	576 ± 4 ml
C2 model	565 ± 4 ml
D models	567 ± 4 ml
E and F models	575 ± 4 ml
Fork oil level*	
C1 model	91 ± 2.0 mm
C2 model	101 ± 2.0 mm
D models	111 ± 2.0 mm
E and F models	107 ± 2.0 mm
Fork spring free length (min)	
C models	
Standard	245.3 mm
Service limit	243 mm
D models	
Standard	232.1 mm
Service limit	227 mm
E and F models	
Standard	232.3 mm
Service limit	228 mm
Fork tube runout limit	0.2 mm

*Oil level is measured from the top of the tube, with the fork spring removed.

Torque settings

Clutch lever bracket clamp bolts	8 Nm
Fork damper cartridge bolt.	23 Nm
Fork top bolt.	23 Nm
Fork yoke clamp bolts	
Top yoke bolts	20 Nm
Bottom yoke bolts	30 Nm
Front brake master cylinder clamp bolts	
C and D models	9 Nm
E and F models.	11 Nm
Gearchange lever pivot bolt	25 Nm
Handlebar clamp bolts.	25 Nm
Handlebar positioning bolts	10 Nm
Front brake lever pivot bolt	1 Nm
Front brake lever pivot bolt nut	6 Nm
Rider's footrest bracket bolts	25 Nm
Shock absorber bolt nuts.	34 Nm
Sidestand pivot bolt	44 Nm
Steering damper mounting bolts	
D6 model	16 Nm
D7, E and F models	11 Nm
Steering head bearing adjuster nut	
Initial setting	
Using torque wrench and pegged socket	55 Nm
Using Kawasaki C-spanner and spring balance.	305 N
Final setting	
Using torque wrench and pegged socket	20 Nm
Using Kawasaki C-spanner and spring balance.	101 N
Steering stem nut	
C and D models	78 Nm
E and F models.	108 Nm
Suspension linkage	
Linkage rod-to arm and swingarm bolt nuts	59 Nm
Linkage arm-to-frame bolt nut	34 Nm
Swingarm	
Pivot bolt nut	108 Nm
Adjuster	20 Nm
Adjuster locknut	98 Nm

1 General information

All models have a composite pressed and die-cast aluminium, twin beam backbone frame that uses the engine as a stressed member.

Front suspension is by a pair of 43 mm oil-damped upside-down telescopic forks with a cartridge damper, and are adjustable for spring pre-load and both rebound and compression damping.

At the rear, a box-section aluminium swingarm acts on a single shock absorber via a three-way linkage. The swingarm pivots through the frame. The shock absorber is adjustable for spring pre-load and both rebound and compression damping.

2 Frame inspection and repair

1 The frame should not require attention unless accident damage has occurred. In most cases, fitting a new frame is the only satisfactory remedy for such damage. A few frame specialists have the jigs and other equipment necessary for straightening frames to the required standard of accuracy, but even then there is no simple way of assessing to what extent the frame may have been over stressed.

2 After a high mileage, the frame should be examined closely for signs of cracking or splitting at the welded joints. Loose engine mounting bolts can cause ovaling or fracturing of the mounting points. Minor damage can often be repaired by specialised welding, depending on the extent and nature of the damage.

3 Remember that a frame that is out of alignment will cause handling problems. If, as the result of an accident, misalignment is suspected, it will be necessary to strip the machine completely so the frame can be thoroughly checked.

3 Footrests, brake pedal and gearchange lever

Footrests

1 Remove the E-clip from the bottom of the footrest pivot pin, then withdraw the pivot pin

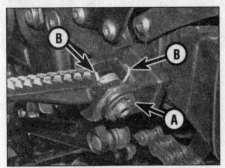

3.1a E-clip (A), return spring ends (B) – rider's footrests

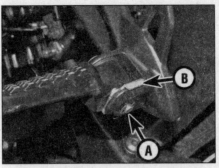

3.1b E-clip (A), detent plate, balls and springs (B) – passenger footrests

3.3 Unscrew the bolts (arrowed)

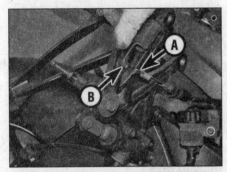

3.4 Unhook the switch spring (A) first, then the pedal spring (B)

3.5 Remove the split pin then withdraw the clevis pin (arrowed)

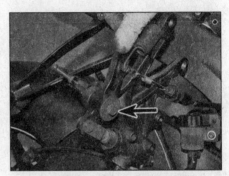

3.6 Brake pedal bolt (arrowed)

3.7 Correct fitting of the split pin

3.8 Hold the rod and slacken the locknuts (arrowed)

3.9 Unscrew the bolt (arrowed) and remove the lever

and remove the footrest **(see illustration)**. On the rider's footrests, note the fitting of the return spring. On the passenger footrests, note the fitting of the washer, detent plate, balls and springs, and take care not to let the balls and springs ping away when removing the footrest **(see illustration)**.

2 Installation is the reverse of removal. Apply a small amount of grease to the pivot pin.

Brake pedal

Removal

3 Unscrew the rider's footrest bracket bolts and displace the bracket so that you can access the back **(see illustration)**.

4 Unhook the brake light switch spring and the pedal return spring **(see illustration)**.

5 Remove the split pin from the clevis pin securing the brake pedal to the master cylinder pushrod, then withdraw the clevis pin and detach the pushrod from the pedal **(see illustration)**.

6 Unscrew the bolt securing the brake pedal and remove the thrust washer **(see illustration)**. Slide the pedal off its pivot. Remove the washer from the pivot.

Installation

7 Installation is the reverse of removal, noting the following:
● Clean any old grease off the pedal and pivot, then apply fresh grease.
● Slide the washer onto the pivot, then slide the pedal on, then the thrust washer.
● Use a new split pin on the master cylinder pushrod clevis pin and bend its ends round as shown **(see illustration)**.
● Make sure the springs are correctly located **(see illustration 3.4)**.

● Tighten the rider's footrest bracket bolts to the torque setting specified at the beginning of the Chapter.
● Check the operation of the rear brake light switch (see Chapter 1).

Gearchange lever and linkage

Removal

8 Counter-hold the gearchange lever linkage rod using a spanner on its flats and slacken the locknuts **(see illustration)**. Unscrew the rod and separate it from the lever and the arm – the rod is reverse-threaded on one end and so will simultaneously unscrew from both lever and arm when turned in the one direction. Note how far the rod is threaded onto the lever and arm as this determines the height of the lever relative to the footrest.

9 Unscrew the gearchange lever pivot bolt

3.10a Linkage arm/shaft alignment –
C models

3.10b Linkage arm/shaft alignment –
D models

3.10c Linkage arm/shaft alignment –
E/F models

and remove the lever and thrust washer **(see illustration)**.

10 Note the alignment of the punch mark on the gearchange shaft with the slit in the linkage arm **(see illustrations)**. Unscrew the linkage arm bolt and slide the arm off the shaft.

Installation

11 Installation is the reverse of removal, noting the following:

● Align the slit in the linkage arm clamp with the mark on the shaft **(see illustration 3.10a, b or c)**.
● The washer fits between the lever and the footrest bracket.
● Apply grease to the pivot section on the

4.3 Unhook the springs (arrowed)

lever bolt. Tighten the bolt to the torque setting specified at the beginning of the Chapter.
● Adjust the gear lever height as required by screwing the linkage rod in or out of the lever and arm. Tighten the locknuts.

4 Sidestand

Removal

1 Remove the left-hand lower fairing (see Chapter 7).

4.4a Sidestand switch bolt (arrowed) –
C/D models

2 Support the bike using an auxiliary stand.
3 Carefully unhook and remove the stand springs **(see illustration)**.
4 Unscrew the sidestand switch bolt and displace the switch, noting how it locates **(see illustrations)** – there is no need to disconnect its wiring connector or remove it completely, just let it hang from its wiring.
5 Unscrew the nut from the pivot bolt **(see illustration)**. Unscrew the pivot bolt and remove the stand.

Installation

6 Apply grease to the pivot bolt shank and the sliding surfaces of the stand. Tighten the pivot bolt to the torque setting specified at the beginning of the Chapter. Fit the nut, then counter-hold the bolt and tighten the nut.
7 Fit the sidestand switch **(see illustration 4.4a or b)**.
8 Reconnect the springs and check that they hold the stand securely up when not in use – an accident is almost certain to occur if the stand extends while the machine is in motion **(see illustration 4.3)**.
9 Check the operation of the stand and switch (see Chapter 1).
10 Install the left-hand lower fairing (see Chapter 7).

4.4b Sidestand switch bolt (arrowed) – E/F models

4.5 Sidestand pivot nut (arrowed)

5.2a Unscrew the bolt (arrowed)

5.2b Unscrew the clamp bolts (arrowed) and displace the master cylinder...

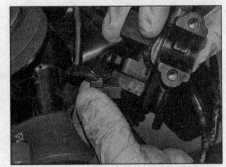

5.2c ...then disconnect the wiring

5.4 Switch housing screws (arrowed)

5.5 Remove the handlebar end-weight and twistgrip

5.7 Slacken the clamp bolt (arrowed) and remove the handlebar bolt on each side

5 Handlebars and levers

1 As a precaution, remove the fuel tank and the fairing (see Chapter 7). Though not actually necessary, this will prevent the possibility of damage should a tool slip.

Right handlebar removal

2 Displace the front brake fluid reservoir from its bracket **(see illustration)**. Unscrew the master cylinder assembly clamp bolts, displace the master cylinder and disconnect the brake light switch wiring connector **(see illustrations)**. Support the assembly clear of

the handlebar, making sure no strain is placed on the hydraulic hose. Keep the master cylinder reservoir upright to prevent possible fluid leakage.
3 Disconnect the throttle cables (see Chapter 4).
4 Undo the handlebar switch housing screws and separate the halves **(see illustration)**.
5 Undo the handlebar end-weight screw and remove the weight **(see illustration)**. Slide the throttle twistgrip off
6 Where fitted remove the steering damper, then remove the bracket from the yoke (see Section 11).
7 Slacken the fork clamp bolts in the top yoke and unscrew the handlebar positioning bolts **(see illustration)**.

8 On C and D models, wrap a layer of masking tape around the steering stem nut to protect its finish. On E and F models, remove the blanking plug from the steering stem bolt. Unscrew the nut or bolt and remove the washer **(see illustration)**. Ease the yoke up and off the forks and lay it aside on some rag **(see illustration)**.
9 Slacken the handlebar clamp bolt. Ease the handlebar up and off the fork **(see illustration 5.14)**.

Left handlebar removal

10 Disconnect the clutch switch wiring connector **(see illustration)**. Unscrew the clutch lever bracket clamp bolts and displace

5.8a Unscrew the steering stem nut or bolt...

5.8b ...and ease the yoke up and off the forks

5.10a Disconnect the wiring connector

5.10b Clutch lever bracket clamp bolts (arrowed)

5.11 Switch housing screws (arrowed)

5.14 Slacken the clamp bolt and lift the handlebar off

the bracket **(see illustration)**. Support the assembly clear of the handlebar.

11 Undo the handlebar switch housing screws and separate the halves **(see illustration)**.

12 Undo the handlebar end-weight retaining screw, then remove the weight from the end of the handlebar and prise off the grip **(see illustration 5.5)**.

13 Refer to Steps 6, 7 and 8 and displace the top yoke.

14 Slacken the handlebar clamp bolt. Ease the handlebar up and off the fork **(see illustration)**.

Handlebar installation

15 Installation is the reverse of removal, noting the following.

● Do not tighten the handlebar clamp bolts until the top yoke and positioning bolts have been installed and tightened. Tighten the steering stem nut first, then the top yoke clamp bolts, then the handlebar positioning bolts, then the handlebar clamp bolts, tightening them all to the torque settings specified at the beginning of the Chapter.

● Smear some grease onto the right handlebar before sliding the throttle twistgrip on.

● If new grips are being fitted, secure them using a suitable adhesive, and rotate the grip as you fit it to spread the glue evenly.

● Make sure the switch housing locating pin fits in its hole in the handlebar. Do not overtighten the switch screws.

● Reconnect the front brake light switch wiring connector before fitting the master cylinder **(see illustration 5.2c)**.

● Fit the front brake master cylinder clamp with the UP mark facing up **(see illustration 5.2b)**, and align the clamp mating surfaces with the punch mark on the top of the handlebar **(see illustration 5.15a)**. Tighten the master cylinder clamp bolts to the specified torque setting, tightening the top bolt first.

● Align the clutch lever bracket clamp mating surfaces with the punch mark on the top of the handlebar **(see illustration 5.15b)**. Tighten the clamp bolts to the specified torque setting, tightening the top bolt first. Reconnect the clutch switch wiring connector **(see illustration 5.10a)**.

● Refer to Chapter 4 to install the throttle cables.

Levers

16 To remove the front brake lever, undo the lever pivot bolt locknut, then undo the bolt and remove the lever **(see illustrations)**.

17 To remove the clutch lever turn the cable adjuster into the bracket to provide freeplay in the cable **(see illustration)**. Undo the lever pivot nut, then remove the pivot by tapping it up from the bottom, and remove the lever, detaching the cable nipple as you do **(see illustration)**.

5.15a Align the master cylinder clamp mating surfaces with the punch mark (arrowed)

5.15b Align the clutch bracket clamp mating surfaces with the punch mark (arrowed)

5.16a Unscrew the nut...

5.16b ...then unscrew the bolt and remove the lever

5.17a Turn the adjuster in

5.17b Clutch lever nut (arrowed)

5.18 Hold the bolt and tighten the nut

6.5a Slacken the fork clamp bolt (arrowed)...

6.5b ...and the handlebar clamp bolt

18 Installation is the reverse of removal. Apply silicone grease to the contact area between the front brake master cylinder pushrod tip and the brake lever, and to the lever pivot bolt. Apply lithium grease to the clutch lever pivot screw shaft and the contact areas between the lever and its bracket. Tighten the brake lever pivot bolt lightly (to the torque setting specified at the beginning of the Chapter if the correct tools are available), then hold it and tighten the locknut to the specified torque (see illustration). Adjust clutch cable freeplay (see Chapter 1).

6 Fork removal and installation

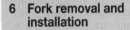

Caution: Although not strictly necessary, before removing the forks it is recommended that the fairing and fairing panels are removed (see Chapter 7). This will prevent accidental damage to the paintwork.

Removal

1 On C and D models remove the fairing side panels (see Chapter 7). On E and F models remove the fairing assembly (see Chapter 7).

2 Remove the front wheel (see Chapter 6). Tie the front brake calipers back so that they are out of the way.
3 Remove the front mudguard (see Chapter 7).
4 Note the routing of all cables, hoses and wiring around the forks. Note the amount of protrusion of the fork above the top yoke – as standard the mating surface of the outer tube and the top bolt is flush with the upper surface of the top yoke (see illustration 6.8).
5 Working on one fork at a time, slacken the fork clamp bolt in the top yoke and the handlebar clamp bolt (see illustrations). If the fork is to be disassembled, or if the fork oil is being changed, slacken the fork top bolt now (see illustration 7.3) – wrapping some masking tape round the hex helps preserve the finish.
6 Hold the fork, then slacken the clamp bolts in the bottom yoke, and remove the fork by twisting it and pulling it downwards, guiding the handlebar off as you do (see illustration).

Installation

7 Remove all traces of dirt and corrosion from the fork tube and in the yokes. Slide the fork up through the bottom yoke and the handlebar clamp and into the top yoke, making sure all

HAYNES HINT *If the fork legs are seized in the yokes, spray the area with penetrating oil and allow time for it to soak in before trying again.*

cables, hoses and wiring are routed on the correct side of the fork.
8 Make sure the fork is set so the joint between the outer tube and the top bolt is flush with the upper surface of the top yoke (see illustration). Tighten the fork clamp bolts in the bottom yoke to the torque setting specified at the beginning of the Chapter.
9 If the fork has been dismantled or if the fork oil was changed, tighten the fork top bolt to the specified torque setting.
10 Tighten the fork clamp bolt in the top yoke to the specified torque setting (see illustration 6.5a). Tighten the handlebar clamp bolt to the specified torque (see illustration 6.5b).
11 Install the front mudguard (see Chapter 7), the front wheel (see Chapter 6), and the fairing side panels (see Chapter 7).
12 Check the operation of the front forks and brakes before taking the machine out on the road.

6.6 Slacken the bolts (arrowed) then draw the fork down

6.8 Set the tube/top bolt joint flush with the yoke

7.3 Thread the top bolt out of the tube

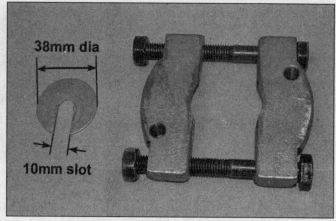

38mm dia

10mm slot

7.4a Bearing separator and slotted washer

7 Fork oil change

Special tool: *A holding tool and stopper plate are required for this procedure – see Step 4 for details.*

1 After a high mileage the fork oil will deteriorate and its damping and lubrication qualities will be impaired. Always change the oil in both fork legs.

2 Remove the fork – make sure you loosen the top bolt while the leg is still clamped in the bottom yoke (see Section 6).

3 Unscrew the fork top bolt from the top of the outer tube **(see illustration)**. The top bolt will remain on the damper rod, held by the locknut. Slide the outer tube down gently until it seats on the bottom.

4 Next you need either the Kawasaki service tools (Pt. Nos. 57001-1540 and 57001-1587), or an equivalent home-made set-up as follows: If you can have an assistant to help you all you need is a commercially available bearing separator as shown, and a 38 to 40 mm plate washer with a 10 mm slot cut so it will fit around the damper rod **(see illustration)**. If you do not have an assistant then you will also need two ratchet straps. Fit the puller clamp so it fits over the shaped washer on the top of the fork spacer and tighten the clamp bolts so it is secure as shown **(see illustration)**. Now, if you have the help of an assistant, have one person press down on the tool to compress the spring and expose the locknut on the damper rod, while you hold the top bolt up and insert the slotted washer under the locknut and on top of the tool **(see illustration)**. Carefully release the pressure on the tool and allow it to rest against the underside of the locknut under spring pressure. If you don't have an assistant fit the puller clamp as described and shown, then fit the front axle through the bottom of the fork and fit a ratchet strap around each exposed end of the axle and the exposed section of bolt between the clamp halves and take up the slack. Now tighten the ratchet straps evenly to compress the spring, and when the locknut is exposed (pull the top bolt up to check as you tighten the straps) fit the slotted washer under it. The Kawasaki tools use the same principal as the ratchet strap method, but use threaded rods and nuts and a pre-drilled bar instead of the ratchet straps and axle, with the top ends of the rods fitting through their clamping tool. Tightening nuts on the tops of the threaded rods compresses the spring.

5 Counter-hold the locknut using one spanner and loosen the top bolt assembly using another spanner, then thread the top bolt off and draw the damping adjuster rod out **(see illustrations)**. **Note:** *The top bolt should not be disassembled.*

7.4b Fit the tool onto the fork as shown and tighten the nuts/bolts to secure it

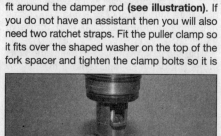

7.4c Push down on the holder and slip the washer (arrowed) under the nut

7.5a Hold the locknut and loosen the top bolt...

7.5b ...then unscrew the top bolt...

7.5c ...and draw the adjuster rod out

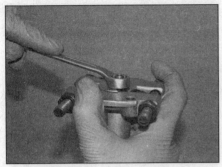

7.6a Thread the locknut to the top of the rod

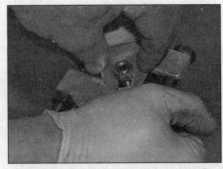

7.6b Push the tool down and remove the slotted washer

7.6c Remove the shaped washer and the spacer (arrowed)

7.7a Tip the fork to drain the oil and remove the spring...

7.7b ...then pump the damper rod

7.8a Add the oil slowly to prevent air bubbles

6 Thread the locknut up to the top of the rod to reduce spring pressure, but do not thread it off **(see illustration)**. Push down on the tool and remove the plate or slotted washer, then carefully allow the spring to relax **(see illustration)**. Remove the shaped washer and spacer **(see illustration)**. On E and F models note the spring seat on the bottom of the spacer.

7 Tip the fork leg over a suitable container to catch the oil. Remove the spring and pump the fork and damper rod several times to expel as much fork oil as possible **(see illustrations)**. Support the fork upside down in the container for a while to allow as much oil as possible to drain, then pump the fork and rod again. If the fork oil contains metal particles inspect the fork bushes for wear (see Section 8). Wipe any excess oil off the spring and spacer.

8 Stand the fork upright and slide the outer tube down gently until it seats on the bottom. Slowly pour in the specified quantity of the specified grade of fork oil **(see illustration)**. Pump the outer tube up and down several times, then draw the damper rod up and slowly pump it up and down at least ten times **(see illustration)** – this distributes the oil and expels all air from the damper. Slide the outer tube down gently until it seats on the bottom, and let the damper rod sink down. Leave the fork to stand for five minutes. After this measure the oil level from the top of the tube **(see illustration)**. Add or subtract oil until it is at the level specified at the beginning of this Chapter.

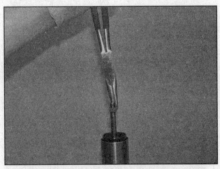

7.8b Draw the rod out and pump it to distribute the oil

9 Pull the damper rod out as far as possible, then fit the spring **(see illustration)** – Kawasaki specify to fit it with the tapered end at the top,

7.9a Insert the spring...

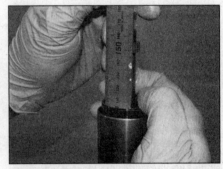

7.8c Measure the distance from the top of the tube to the oil

but on the fork photographed the spring was the same at each end. Insert the damping adjuster rod **(see illustration)**. Fit a piece of

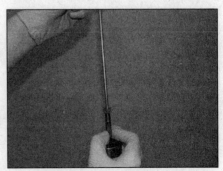

7.9b ...and the adjuster rod

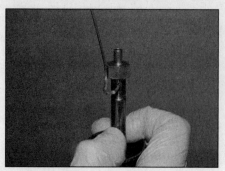

7.9c Tie some wire under the locknut

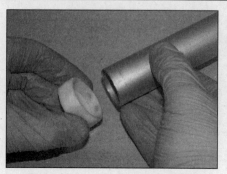

7.10a Make sure the seat is fitted

7.10b Insert the spacer...

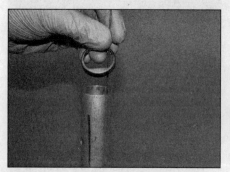

7.10c ...then fit the shaped washer on its top

7.12 Thread the nut down the rod

7.13 Check and lubricate the O-ring (arrowed)

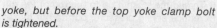
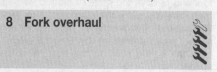

wire around the rod under the locknut to help keep it extended **(see illustration)**.

10 On E and F models fit the spring seat onto the bottom of the spacer if removed **(see illustration)**. On all models fit the spacer, sliding it down over the wire **(see illustration)**. Fit the shaped washer on the top of the spacer **(see illustration)**.

11 Fit the tool used earlier onto the top of the spacer (see Step 4). Keeping the damper rod extended, push down on the spacer to compress the spring, then insert the slotted washer under the locknut **(see illustration 7.12)**. Remove the wire.

12 Set the locknut so there is a minimum of 12 mm of thread exposed above it **(see illustration)**. Thread the top bolt onto the damper rod and down to the locknut,

making sure the nut does not move **(see illustration 7.5b)**. Counter-hold the locknut and tighten the top bolt assembly securely against it **(see illustration 7.5a)**. Press down on the spacer to compress the spring and remove the slotted washer, then carefully release the spring pressure. Remove the tool.

13 If the top bolt O-ring is damaged or deteriorated fit a new one **(see illustration)**. Smear some fork oil onto the O-ring. Extend the outer tube and thread the top bolt into it, making sure it does not cross-thread, and tighten it as much as possible holding the inner tube by hand **(see illustration 7.3)**. **Note:** *Tighten the top bolt to the specified torque setting when the fork has been installed in the bike and is held in the bottom*

yoke, but before the top yoke clamp bolt is tightened.

14 Install the fork (see Section 6).

8 Fork overhaul

Disassembly

1 Remove the fork – make sure you loosen the top bolt while the leg is still clamped in the bottom yoke (see Section 6). Always dismantle the fork legs separately to avoid interchanging parts and thus causing an accelerated rate of wear. Store all components in separate, clearly marked containers.

2 Lay the fork flat on the bench with the caliper mounting lugs to the left. Hold the fork down and slacken the damper cartridge bolt in the base of the fork **(see illustration)**. If the damper cartridge rotates inside the fork whilst attempting to unscrew the bolt, compress the fork so that the spring exerts pressure on the cartridge body whilst the bolt is unscrewed. Alternatively, use an air wrench.

3 Drain the fork oil (see Section 7, Steps 3 to 7).

4 Draw the inner and outer tubes fully apart **(see illustration)**.

5 Remove the previously loosened damper cartridge bolt and its sealing washer from the bottom of the fork **(see illustration 8.18b)**. Discard the washer as a new one must be fitted on reassembly.

8.2 Slacken the damper cartridge bolt

8.4 Draw the tubes apart

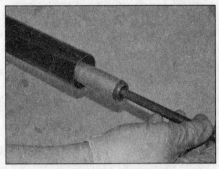

8.6 Withdraw the damper

8.7a Remove the dust seal...

8.7b ...and the retaining clip

6 Withdraw the damper cartridge assembly from the inner tube **(see illustration)**.

7 Carefully prise the dust seal from the bottom of the outer tube **(see illustration)**. Remove the oil seal retaining clip **(see illustration)**.

8 Carefully prise out the oil seal using either a seal hook or an internal puller with slide-hammer attachment, or the Kawasaki tool (part No.09913-50121), taking great care not to damage the rim of the tube **(see illustrations)**. Remove the oil seal washer if it doesn't come away with the seal. Discard the seals as new ones must be fitted on reassembly.

Inspection

9 Clean all parts in a suitable solvent and blow them dry with compressed air, if available.

10 Check the outer surface of the inner tube for score marks, scratches, flaking of the finish and excessive or abnormal wear. Look for creases and dents. Check the tube for runout using V-blocks and a dial gauge - no limits are specified, but anything above 0.2 mm should be considered excessive for runout. If necessary have the tube checked by a Kawasaki dealer or suspension specialist. Replace the inner tubes in both forks with new ones if any defects are found.

 Warning: If the inner tube is bent, replace it with a new one - it should not be straightened.

11 Inspect the working surface of each bush inside the outer tube for score marks, scratches and signs of excessive wear **(see illustrations)**. Fit the inner tube into the outer tube and check for any freeplay between them. If the bushes are worn the outer tube must be replaced with a new one.

8.8a Fit the puller under the seal and washer...

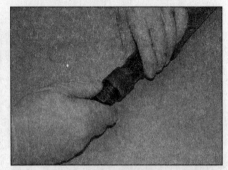

8.8b ...and expand it...

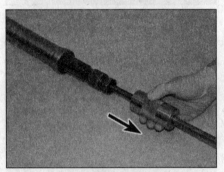

8.8c ...then attach the slide-hammer...

8.8d ...and use it to jar the seal and washer out

12 Check the fork oil seal housing for nicks, gouges and scratches. If damage is evident, leaks will occur. Also check the oil seal washer for damage or distortion and replace it with a new one if necessary.

13 Check the spring for cracks and other damage. Measure the spring free length and compare the measurement to the specifications at the beginning of this Chapter **(see illustration)**. If the spring is defective or has sagged below the service limit, fit new springs in both forks. Never fit only one new spring.

8.11a Check the top bush (arrowed)...

8.11b ...and the bottom bush for wear of its grey coating

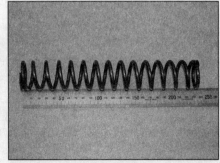

8.13 Measure the free length of the spring

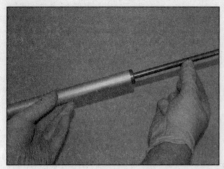

8.14 Check the rod for a smooth action

8.15a Fit the washer...

8.15b ...then the seal...

8.15c ...and push or tap it in using a socket...

8.15d ...until the retaining clip groove (arrowed) is fully exposed

14 Check the damper cartridge assembly for damage and wear. Hold the cartridge and gently pump the rod in and out **(see illustration)**. If the rod does not move smoothly the assembly must be replaced with a new one.

Reassembly

15 Fit the oil seal washer into the outer tube **(see illustration)**. Fit the new oil seal into the tube and tap it into place until it seats and the retaining clip groove is visible – tap it in using a suitable socket with walls thin enough so it sits only on the hard outer rim of the seal and not on the spring rim on the top **(see illustrations)**. If necessary you can use the old seal as an interface between the socket and the new seal, especially if your socket is not the ideal size.

16 Fit the retaining clip, making sure it locates correctly in its groove **(see illustration)**.

17 Lubricate the inner surface of the oil seal and the outer surface of the inner tube with the specified fork oil. Slide the dust seal onto and all the way down the inner tube, making sure it is the correct way round **(see illustration)**. Carefully insert the inner tube into the outer tube using a twisting motion – it is important to keep the tubes parallel or the seal lips could be damaged and leak **(see illustration)**. After inserting the tube check the seal lips have not turned inside **(see illustration)**. Slide the inner tube fully into the outer tube so the dust seal is pushed into place **(see illustration)**.

8.16 Fit the clip into its groove

8.17a Slide the dust seal all the way down the inner tube

8.17b Slide the inner tube into the outer...

8.17c ...then check the seal lips

8.17d Push the dust seal into place

18 Insert the damper cartridge assembly into the fork until it contacts the bottom of the inner tube (see illustration). Fit a new sealing washer onto the damper cartridge bolt and apply a few drops of a suitable non-permanent thread locking compound, then fit the bolt into the damper cartridge and tighten it to the torque setting specified at the beginning of this Chapter (see illustration). Note: If the damper cartridge assembly rotates inside the slider, either fit the slotted washer under the damper rod locknut and use it pull up on the rod, or fit the spring and spacer and press down on the spacer – either method should help the bolt to tighten, or if one doesn't work try the other. Remove the spacer and spring after tightening the bolt.

19 Pour in the correct quantity and type of fork oil, and finish assembling the fork (see Section 7, Steps 8 to 13).

20 Install the fork leg (see Section 6).

9 Steering stem

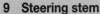
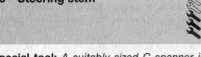

Special tool: A suitably sized C-spanner is necessary for this procedure – the Kawasaki tool (part No. 57001-1100) can be used with a spring balance to apply the torque setting for the bearing adjuster nut. If you use any other C-spanner the handle length will be different and so you cannot apply the torque setting, but you can easily set the bearings by feel. The torque settings can also be applied using a pegged socket, which can be made by cutting pegs out of the rim of an old socket that is the same diameter as the nut.

Removal

1 On C and D models remove the fairing side panels and the fairing (see Chapter 7). On E and F models remove the fairing assembly (see Chapter 7). To prevent the possibility of damage should a tool slip remove the fuel tank (see Chapter 4).

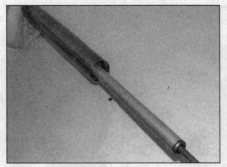

8.18a Insert the damper...

2 Where fitted remove the steering damper, then remove the bracket from the yoke (see Section 11).

3 Unscrew the brake hose guide bolt on the bottom yoke (see illustration).

4 Remove the front forks (see Section 6).

5 Unscrew the handlebar positioning bolts and support the handlebars to each side (see illustration 5.7).

6 On C and D models, wrap a layer of masking tape around the steering stem nut to protect its finish. On E and F models, remove the blanking plug from the steering stem nut. Unscrew the nut and remove the washer (see illustration). Ease the yoke up and off the

9.3 Unscrew the bolt (arrowed)

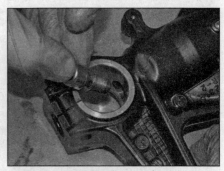

8.18b ...then fit and tighten the bolt

steering stem and lay it aside on some rag (see illustration).

7 Check for any corrosion on the steering stem threads above the locknut, and if there is any clean it off using a wire brush, then spray with a lubricant. A build up of corrosion in this area will make the locknut and adjuster nut difficult to remove and most likely damage their threads.

8 Bend the lockwasher tabs out of the notches in the locknut (see illustration). Unscrew the locknut using your fingers (see illustration 9.20) – if necessary use a C-spanner located in one of the notches. Remove the lockwasher (see illustration 9.19). Inspect

9.6a Unscrew the nut or bolt and remove the washer...

9.6b ...then lift the yoke off

9.8 Bend the tabs down

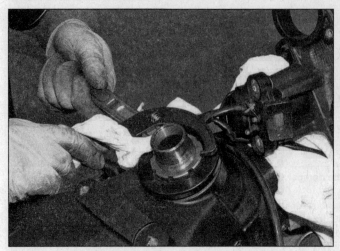

9.10a Unscrew the adjuster nut...

9.10b ...then draw the bottom yoke/steering stem out of the steering head

the tabs for cracks or signs of fatigue and get a new one if necessary.

9 Make an alignment mark between the adjuster nut and the frame – this can serve as a rough guide for the tightness of the adjuster nut on installation. As you unscrew the nut count the number of turns.

10 Support the bottom yoke then loosen the adjuster nut using a C-spanner **(see illustration)**. Thread the nut off and lower the bottom yoke and steering stem out of the frame **(see illustration)**. Check the condition of the grease seal around the nut and discard it if it is damaged.

11 Remove the inner race and bearing from the top of the steering head **(see illustration)**. Remove the bearing from the base of the steering stem **(see illustration)**.

12 Remove all traces of old grease from the bearings and races and check them for wear or damage as described in Section 10. **Note:** *Do not attempt to remove the races from the steering head or the steering stem unless they are to be replaced with new ones.*

Installation

13 Smear a liberal quantity of multi-purpose grease with EP2 rating onto the bearing races,

and work some grease well into both the upper and lower bearings **(see illustrations)**.

14 Fit the lower bearing onto the steering stem **(see illustration 9.11b)**. Fit the upper bearing and its inner race into the top of the steering head **(see illustration 9.11a)**. If separated fit the adjuster nut into the top cap **(see illustration)**.

15 Carefully lift the steering stem/bottom yoke up through the steering head and support it there **(see illustration 9.10b)**. Thread the adjuster nut onto the stem and tighten it finger-tight **(see illustration)**.

16 If you are using the Kawasaki service

9.11a Remove the inner race and upper bearing...

9.11b ...and the lower bearing

9.13a Lubricate the races...

9.13b ...and the bearings

9.14 Fit the nut into the cap

9.15 Thread the adjuster nut on finger-tight

tools (see above), with the spring balance fitted to the hole in the end of the handle and pulled at 90° to the line between the centre of the steering stem and the centre of the nut (see illustration), or a suitable peg spanner (see illustration), tighten the adjuster nut to the initial torque setting specified at the beginning of the Chapter, then loosen the nut, then tighten it to the final torque setting specified. Check that the steering stem is able to move smoothly (though it may feel a bit tight, but this is normal as the weight of the forks and wheel is not influencing the feel) from lock-to-lock following adjustment – note that it is best to check and if necessary reset the bearing adjustment as described in Chapter 1 after the forks and front wheel and all other components have been installed.

17 If you are not using the special tools and are refitting the original bearings, tighten the nut the number of turns recorded on removal using a C-spanner until the marks align (see illustration). Turn the steering from lock-to-lock five times, then slacken the nut, and tighten it again until the marks align.

18 If are not using the special tools and are fitting new bearings, tighten the nut using a C-spanner so that bearing play is eliminated, then tighten it a bit more to pre-load the bearings, then slacken the nut and then re-tighten it until freeplay is just eliminated but the steering stem is able to move smoothly from lock-to-lock (though it may feel a bit tight, but this is normal as the weight of the forks and wheel is not influencing the feel) (see illustration 9.17).

Caution: Take great care not to apply excessive pressure because this will cause premature failure of the bearings.

19 Fit the lockwasher with its angled tabs pointing down and seating them into the notches in the adjuster nut (see illustration).

20 Fit the locknut and tighten it finger-tight (see illustration). Tighten the locknut further until its notches align with the remaining lockwasher tabs. Bend these tabs up into the notches in the locknut.

21 Fit the top yoke onto the steering stem (see illustration 9.6b). Fit the steering stem washer and nut and tighten it finger-tight (see illustration 9.6a). Install the forks to align the yokes, seating the handlebars over them,

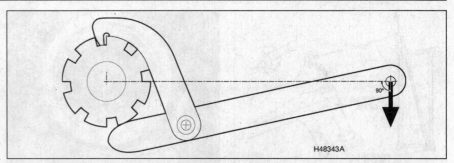

9.16a Kawasaki tool fitted to nut, showing direction of pull using spring balance

9.16b Home-made peg spanner

9.17 Tighten the adjuster nut as described

and secure them by tightening the bottom yoke clamp bolts only (see Section 6). Now tighten the steering stem nut to the torque setting specified at the beginning of the Chapter.

22 Working on one fork at a time slacken the clamp bolts in the bottom yoke and position the forks correctly in the top yoke so the joint between the outer tube and the top bolt is flush with the upper surface of the top yoke (see illustration 6.8). Tighten the clamp bolts in the bottom yoke to the torque setting specified at the beginning of the Chapter. Tighten the clamp bolts in the top yoke to the specified torque setting.

23 Align the handlebars, fit the positioning bolts and tighten them to the specified torque, followed by the handlebar clamp bolts (see illustration 5.7).

24 Install the front mudguard (see Chapter 7), the front wheel (see Chapter 6), and the brake hose guide (see illustration 9.3).

25 Carry out a final check of the steering

head bearing freeplay as described in Chapter 1, and if necessary re-adjust.

26 Install the steering damper, fuel tank and fairing panels.

10 Steering head bearings

Inspection

1 Remove the steering stem (see Section 9).

2 Remove all traces of old grease from the bearings and races and check them for wear or damage – the outer races are in the top and bottom of the steering head, and the lower bearing inner race is on the bottom of the steering stem.

3 The races should be polished and free from indentations (see illustration). Inspect the bearing balls for signs of wear, damage or

9.19 Fit the lockwasher

9.20 Thread the locknut on and tighten as described

10.3 Check the outer races in the top and bottom of the steering head

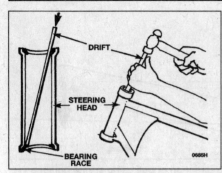

10.4a Drive the bearing races out with a brass drift...

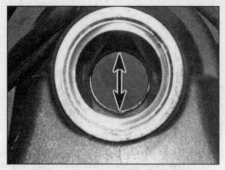

10.4b ...locating it in the cut-outs (arrowed)

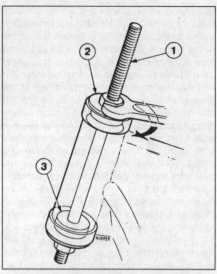

10.5 Drawbolt arrangement for fitting steering stem bearing races

1 *Long bolt or threaded bar*
2 *Thick washer*
3 *Guide for lower race*

discoloration, and examine the ball retainer cage for signs of cracks or splits. If there are any signs of wear on any of the above components both upper and lower bearing assemblies must be renewed as a set. Only remove the outer races in the steering head and the lower bearing inner race on the steering stem if they need to be replaced with new ones – do not re-use them once they have been removed.

Replacement

4 The outer races are an interference fit in the steering head – tap them from position using a suitable drift located in the recesses provided in the steering head that expose the lip of the race **(see illustrations)**. Tap firmly and evenly around each race to ensure that it is driven out squarely. Curve the end of the drift slightly to improve access if necessary.
5 Press the new outer races into the

head using a drawbolt arrangement **(see illustration)**, or drive them in using a large diameter tubular drift. Ensure that the drawbolt washer or drift (as applicable) bears only on the outer edge of the race and does not contact the working surface. Alternatively, have the races installed by a Kawasaki dealer equipped with the bearing race installation tools.

> **HAYNES HINT** *Installation of new bearing outer races is made much easier if the races are left overnight in the freezer. This causes them to contract slightly making them a looser fit. Alternatively, use a freeze spray. You can also heat the race seat in the steering stem using a hot air gun.*

6 Only remove the lower bearing inner race from the steering stem if a new one is being fitted. To remove the race, first thread the steering stem nut onto the top then position the yoke on its front and up against something solid for stability – the nut will protect the threads. Tap under the race using a cold chisel to displace it, and if required use two screwdrivers placed on opposite sides to work it free, using blocks of wood to improve leverage and protect the yoke **(see illustration)**. If the race is firmly in place it will be necessary to use a puller **(see illustration)**. Take the steering stem to a Kawasaki dealer if required.
7 Remove the seal from the bottom of the

stem and replace it with a new one **(see illustration)**. Smear the new one with grease then fit it onto the stem.
8 Fit the new lower race onto the steering stem. Drive the new race into position using a length of tubing with an internal diameter slightly larger than the steering stem **(see illustration)** – heating the race and cooling the steering stem will make installation easier, or use an hydraulic press if necessary.
9 Install the steering stem (see Section 9).

11 Steering damper

Removal

1 Using a security Torx bit unscrew the bolt securing the damper arm to the top yoke and

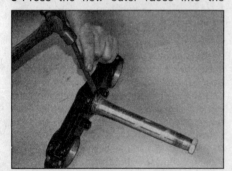

10.6a Dislodge the lower bearing using a cold chisel and/or screwdrivers...

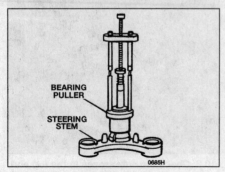

10.6b ...or using a puller if necessary

10.7 Fit a new seal (arrowed)

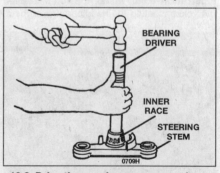

10.8 Drive the new inner race on using a suitable bearing driver or a length of pipe that bears only against the inner rim and not the bearing surface

11.1a Steering damper bolts (arrowed)

11.1b Note the washer

11.3a Unscrew the bolt (arrowed)...

11.3b ...and remove the arm bracket

11.3c Damper body bracket bolts (arrowed)

11.6 Seat the head of the bolt in the hole (arrowed)

remove the washer from between the arm and the yoke **(see illustrations)**.

2 Unscrew the bolt securing the damper body to the bracket and remove the washer, collar and the damper.

3 If required unscrew the damper arm and body bracket bolts and remove the brackets **(see illustrations)**.

Inspection

4 Check for any oil leakage on the damper arm and replace the damper with a new one if any is found.

5 Make sure the arm moves smoothly in and out of the body, and that the amount of resistance varies as you turn the adjuster (note how much you turn it so it can be reset to its original position after the check).

Installation

6 Installation is the reverse of removal, noting the following:

● Clean the threads of the damper bracket bolts and apply some fresh threadlock.

● Seat the hole in the upper side of the damper bracket over the handlebar positioning bolt **(see illustration)**.

● Clean the threads of the damper mounting bolts and apply some fresh threadlock. Tighten the damper mounting bolts to the torque setting specified at the beginning of the Chapter for your model.

● Make sure there is a bit of up and down movement in the damper body after tightening the bolts.

Adjustment

7 The amount of damping can be adjusted

by turning the knurled knob on the left-hand end of the damper body. Turn it clockwise to increase damping and anti-clockwise to decrease it. The standard position is with the adjuster turned fully anti-clockwise, i.e. at its minimum setting.

12 Rear shock absorber

Warning: Do not attempt to disassemble this shock absorber. It is nitrogen-charged under high pressure. Improper disassembly could result in serious injury. No individual components are available for it.

Removal

Note: *If you are removing the suspension linkage as well, do so first (see Section 13).*

1 On D models remove the exhaust system

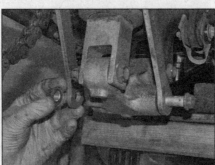

12.3 Remove the linkage rod-to-linkage arm bolt

silencers and middle pipes (see Chapter 4). On E and F models remove the exhaust system silencer and middle chamber (see Chapter 4).

2 Support the motorcycle so that no weight is transmitted through any part of the rear suspension – one way to do this is to place a block of wood under the sidestand so the bike will be upright and an axle stand under the bottom of the frame on the right-hand side. Tie the front brake lever to the handlebar to ensure the bike can't roll forward. Position a support under the rear wheel or swingarm so that it does not drop when the shock absorber is removed, but also making sure that the weight of the machine is off the rear suspension so that the shock is not compressed.

3 Unscrew the nut and withdraw the bolt securing the linkage rods to the linkage arm **(see illustration)**.

4 Unscrew the nut and withdraw the bolt securing the shock absorber to the linkage arm and pivot the arm down **(see illustration)**.

12.4 Remove the shock absorber-to-linkage arm bolt

12.5a Unscrew the nut, withdraw the bolt...

12.5b ...and remove the shock absorber

12.8 Drill a hole into the centre point (arrowed)

5 Unscrew the nut on the bolt securing the top of the shock absorber to the swingarm **(see illustration)**. Support the shock from the bottom and withdraw the bolt, then lower the shock absorber and remove it, twisting it as required **(see illustration)**.

Inspection

Note: *Refer to Tools and Workshop Tips in the Reference Section for information on bearing removal and installation methods using a suitable driver or socket or a drawbolt. Note that applying some heat to the bearing housing using a hot air gun will ease removal and installation.*

6 Inspect the shock absorber for obvious physical damage and oil leakage, and the coil spring for looseness, cracks or signs of fatigue.

7 Inspect the bush in the top of the shock absorber for wear or damage.

8 Parts are not available for the shock absorber. If it is worn or damaged, it must be replaced with a new one. Before disposing of an old shock absorber, you should release the nitrogen gas from the reservoir as follows: on C models remove the cap from the release valve on the right-hand end of the reservoir and depress the centre of the valve using a nail, making sure the valve is pointed away from you; on D, E and F models drill a 2 mm hole into the centre of the right-hand end of the reservoir, making sure it is pointed away from you **(see illustration)**.

⚠ *Warning: Be very careful when releasing the gas pressure – it is possible for fine debris particles to be released with it, and as the pressure is high these could damage your eyes if done carelessly. Always wear eye protection and point the valve well away.*

Installation

9 Installation is the reverse of removal, noting the following:
● Install the shock absorber with the reservoir facing back.
● Install all bolts from the right-hand side **(see illustrations 12.5a, 12.4 and 12.3)**.
● Tighten the nuts to the torque settings specified at the beginning of the Chapter.

13 Rear suspension linkage

Removal

1 On D models remove the exhaust system silencers and middle pipes (see Chapter 4). On E and F models remove the exhaust system silencer and middle chamber (see Chapter 4).

2 Support the motorcycle so that no weight is transmitted through any part of the rear suspension – one way to do this is to place a block of wood under the sidestand so the bike will be upright and an axle stand under the bottom of the frame on the right-hand side. Tie the front brake lever to the handlebar to ensure the bike can't roll forward. Position a support under the rear wheel or swingarm so that it does not drop when the shock absorber is removed, but also making sure that the weight of the machine is off the rear suspension so that the shock is not compressed.

3 Unscrew the nut and withdraw the bolt securing the linkage rods to the linkage arm **(see illustration 12.3)**.

4 Unscrew the nut and withdraw the bolt securing the linkage rods to the swingarm and remove the rods **(see illustration)**.

5 Unscrew the nut and withdraw the bolt securing the shock absorber to the linkage arm **(see illustration 12.4)**.

6 Unscrew the nut and withdraw bolt securing the linkage arm to the frame and remove the arm **(see illustration)**.

Inspection

7 Withdraw the sleeves from the linkage arm and the linkage rod mount on the swingarm **(see illustrations)**.

13.4 Unscrew the nut, withdraw the bolt and remove the linkage rods

13.6 Unscrew the nut, withdraw the bolt and remove the linkage arm

13.7a Withdraw the sleeves from the linkage arm...

13.7b ...and the swingarm

8 Thoroughly clean all components, removing all traces of dirt, corrosion and grease.

9 Check the linkage arm and rods and their swingarm mount, looking for obvious signs of wear such as heavy scoring, or for damage such as cracks or distortion. Replace worn or damaged components with new ones as required.

10 Check the condition of the grease seals and bearings. Fit the sleeves back in and check for play between them and the bearings. Refer to *Tools and Workshop Tips* (Section 5) in the Reference section for more information on bearings. Inspect all components closely, looking for corrosion and obvious signs of wear such as heavy scoring, or for damage such as cracks or distortion. Replace worn or damaged components with new ones as required.

11 If required, lever out the grease seals using a seal hook or screwdriver, noting which size/type fits where **(see illustration)**. Discard them – new ones must be used.

12 Worn bearings can be driven or drawn out of their bores, but note that removal will destroy them; new bearings should be obtained before work commences. The new bearings should be pressed or drawn into their bores rather than driven into position. In the absence of a

press, a suitable drawbolt tool can be made up as described in *Tools and Workshop Tips* in the Reference section. When fitting the new bearings make sure the marked side faces out, and all bearings are set to the specified depths as follows **(see illustration)**:

Single bearing in the linkage arm-to-frame mount – 7.5 mm depth on each side.
Single bearing in the linkage arm-to-shock absorber mount – 6 mm depth (C models) or 5.5 mm depth (D, E, F models) on each side.
Double bearings in the linkage arm-to-linkage rods mount – 5 mm depth on each side.
Double bearings in the swingarm-to-linkage rods mount – 5 mm depth on each side.

13 Lubricate the needle bearings, sleeves and seals with a multi-purpose grease with EP2 rating.

14 Press the new seals squarely into place, fitting the plain seals with the marked side facing out into the shock absorber mount in the linkage arm, and noting that the collared seals for the arm-to-frame mount are different to those for the linkage rod mounts **(see illustration)**. Fit the sleeves **(see illustrations 13.7a and b)**.

Installation

15 Installation is the reverse of removal, noting the following:
● Apply multi-purpose grease to the bearings, seals and sleeves.
● Make sure the marked side of each linkage rod faces out.
● Insert all bolts from the right-hand side **(see illustrations 13.6, 12.4, 13.4 and 12.3)**.
● Tighten the nuts/bolts to the torque settings specified at the beginning of the Chapter.

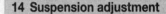

14 Suspension adjustment

Front forks

1 The front forks are adjustable for spring pre-load and both rebound and compression damping. Always make sure both forks are set equally.

2 Spring pre-load is adjusted using a spanner on the adjuster flats **(see illustration)** – one should be provided in the toolkit. Turn the adjuster clockwise to increase pre-load and anti-clockwise to decrease it. The amount of pre-load is indicated by the height of the adjuster above the top bolt hex (measured from the top of the top bolt hex to the top of the adjuster hex). The adjustment range is 4 to 19 mm, and the standard setting is 17 mm on D models, and 14 mm on all other models.

3 Rebound damping is adjusted using a screwdriver in the slot in the top of the adjuster protruding from the pre-load adjuster **(see illustration 14.2)**. Turn it clockwise to increase damping and anti-clockwise to decrease it. The amount of damping is measured by counting the number of clicks when turned anti-clockwise from the fully turned-in (clockwise) setting. The adjustment range is 11 clicks on C and D models and 13

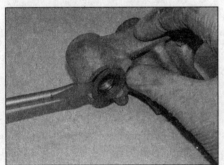
13.11 Lever the seals out

13.12 Set the bearings in their bores as described

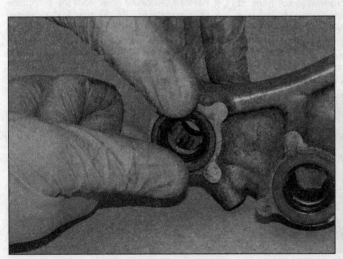
13.14 Press the new seals in

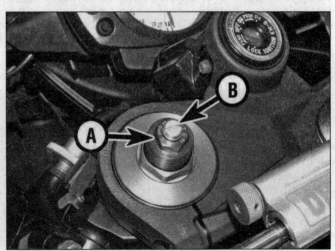
14.2 Spring pre-load adjuster (A); rebound damping adjuster (B)

14.4 Compression damping adjuster (arrowed)

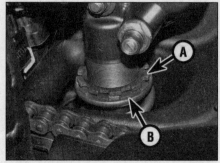

14.6 Spring pre-load adjuster locknut (A) and adjuster (B)

14.7 Rebound damping adjuster (arrowed)

clicks on E and F models, and the standard setting is 9 clicks out on C models and 10 clicks out on D, E and F models.

4 Compression damping is adjusted using a screwdriver in the slot in the adjuster in the bottom of the fork **(see illustration)**. Turn it clockwise to increase damping and anti-clockwise to decrease it. The amount of damping is measured by counting the number of clicks when turned anti-clockwise from the fully turned-in (clockwise) setting. The adjustment range is 13 clicks and the standard setting is 7 clicks out on C models and 10 clicks out on D, E and F models.

Rear shock absorber

5 The shock absorber is adjustable for spring pre-load and both rebound and compression damping, with both high and low speed compression damping on E and F models.
6 Spring pre-load is adjusted using a suitable C-spanner (one is provided in the toolkit) to slacken the locknut and turn the adjuster on the top of the spring **(see illustration)**. For best access remove the heel guard and the chainguard. Turn the adjuster clockwise to increase pre-load and anti-clockwise to reduce it. The amount of pre-load is determined by the length of the spring – the longer the spring the less pre-load. The usable range is from 191.5 mm (min. pre-load) to 173.5 mm (max. pre-load). The standard setting is 178 mm on C models and 179 mm on D, E and F models. With access to the rear shock being restricted on C models you may find it easier to remove

the shock in order to measure the spring length and make adjustment.
7 Rebound damping is adjusted using a screwdriver to turn the adjuster on the bottom of the shock absorber on the left-hand side **(see illustration)**. Turn it clockwise to increase damping and anti-clockwise to decrease it. The amount of damping is measured by counting the number of turns when turned anti-clockwise from the fully turned-in (clockwise) setting. The adjustment range is 4 ½ turns on C models and 2 ½ turns on D, E and F models, and the standard setting is 1 ¾ turns out on C models and 2 turns out on D, E and F models.
8 Compression damping on C and D models is adjusted using a screwdriver to turn the adjuster on the top of the shock absorber on the left-hand side. Turn it clockwise to increase damping and anti-clockwise to decrease it. The amount of damping is measured by counting the number of turns when turned anti-clockwise from the fully turned-in (clockwise) setting. The adjustment range is 4 turns, and the standard setting is 3 turns out on C models and 4 turns out on D models.
9 High speed compression damping on E and F models is adjusted using a 14 mm spanner to turn the outer adjuster on the top of the shock absorber on the left-hand side **(see illustration)**. Turn it clockwise to increase damping and anti-clockwise to decrease it (when you turn it the low speed adjuster screw will turn as well, but this does not alter the low speed setting). The amount of damping is measured by counting the number of turns when turned anti-clockwise from the fully

turned-in (clockwise) setting. The adjustment range is 5 ½ turns, and the standard setting is 2 ¾ turns out.
10 Low speed compression damping on E and F models is adjusted using a screwdriver to turn the inner adjuster **(see illustration 14.9)**. Turn it clockwise to increase damping and anti-clockwise to decrease it. The amount of damping is measured by counting the number of turns when turned anti-clockwise from the fully turned-in (clockwise) setting. The adjustment range is 4 ½ turns, and the standard setting is 2 ¼ turns out.

15 Swingarm

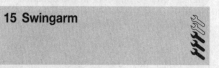

Special Tool: *A peg spanner is needed to slacken and tighten the pivot bolt locknut (Step 6).*

Removal

1 Remove the front sprocket (see Chapter 6).
2 Remove the rear wheel (see Chapter 6).
3 Remove the shock absorber, but detach the linkage rods from the swingarm instead of the linkage arm (Section 12).
4 Release the brake hose from the swingarm **(see illustration)**. Tie the rear brake caliper up or hook the bracket over a footrest or the brake pedal.
5 Unscrew the nut on the left-hand end of the pivot bolt **(see illustration)**.
6 Unscrew the locknut on the right-hand side

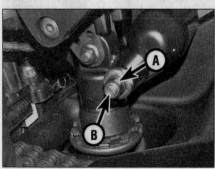

14.9 High speed compression damping adjuster (A), low speed adjuster (B)

15.4 Release the brake hose

15.5 Unscrew the nut

15.6 Unscrew the locknut (arrowed) using a peg spanner

15.7a Turn the pivot bolt head anti-clockwise a few turns

15.7b Withdraw the pivot bolt, draw the swingarm back...

15.7c ...and unhook the chain

using a suitable peg spanner (Kawasaki part no. 57001-1597), or alternatively fabricate one by cutting castellations into an old 29 mm socket or a piece of steel tube with an ID of 32 mm and OD of 36 mm **(see illustration)**.

7 Unscrew the pivot bolt a few turns using a hex key – the head of the bolt engages an adjuster collar in the frame, which needs to be clear of the swingarm **(see illustration)**. Withdraw the bolt and manoeuvre the swingarm out of the frame, detaching the drive chain from the sprocket when there is enough free movement **(see illustrations)**.

8 Remove the hugger, the chainguard and the chain slider from the swingarm if required **(see illustrations)**. If the slider is badly worn or damaged, it should be replaced with a new one.

Inspection

9 Thoroughly clean the swingarm, removing all traces of dirt, corrosion and grease.
10 Inspect the swingarm closely, looking for

obvious signs of wear such as heavy scoring, and cracks or distortion due to accident damage. Any damaged or worn component must be replaced.

11 Check the swingarm pivot bolt is straight by rolling it on a flat surface such as a piece of plate glass (first wipe off all old grease

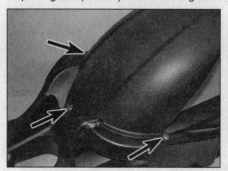

15.8a Rear hugger screws (arrowed)

and remove any corrosion using steel wool). Replace the pivot bolt with a new one if it is bent.

Bearing check, replacement and lubrication

12 Remove the collar from the left-hand side

15.8b Chainguard and slider screws (arrowed)

15.12a Remove the collar

15.12b Lever the seal out from each side of each pivot

15.12c Withdraw the long sleeve

15.13 A circlip (arrowed) secures the right-hand bearings

(see illustration). Lever the grease seal out from each side, noting which size fits where (see illustration). New seals must be used, but keep the old ones laid out in order so the new seals can be matched for position. Withdraw the sleeve from the left-hand side (see illustration).

13 Refer to *Tools and Workshop Tips* in the Reference section and check the bearings – there is a needle bearing and a caged ball bearing in the right-hand pivot, and two needle bearings in the left-hand pivot. Clean them and inspect them for corrosion, wear and damage. If the bearings do not run smoothly and freely or if there is excessive freeplay between them and the collars, they must be replaced with new ones – refer to the Reference Section for removal and installation

methods. The bearings in the right-hand pivot are held by a circlip (see illustration). The bearings must be replaced with new ones if removed – they cannot be reused.

14 When installing the new bearings, pack them with multi-purpose grease with EP2 rating and fit them with the marked side facing out. The needle bearings are installed at specific depths, measured from the outside edge of the swingarm pivot (see illustration). Study the diagram before installing the bearings and check the installed depths with a Vernier caliper. The new needle bearings should be pressed or drawn into their bores rather than driven into position. In the absence of a press, a suitable drawbolt tool can be made up as described in *Tools and WorkshopTips*.

15 The ball bearing fits against a shoulder

inside the swingarm pivot. Do not forget to fit the circlip into the groove in the right-hand side, using a new one if the old one deformed on removal (see illustration 15.13)

16 Lubricate the sleeve, collar, and grease seal lips with multi-purpose grease. Slide the sleeve into the swingarm from the left (see illustration 15.12c). Press the new seals into place (see illustration). Fit the collar (see illustration 15.12a).

Installation

16 If removed, clean the threads of the chain slider bolts and apply a suitable non-permanent thread locking compound, then fit the slider, the chainguard and the hugger as required (see illustrations 15.b and a).

17 If not already done remove the collar from the left-hand pivot (see illustration 15.12a). Clean off all old grease, then lubricate the grease seals, bearings, collar, adjuster end and the pivot bolt with multi-purpose grease. Fit the collar.

18 Offer up the swingarm, loop the drive chain over the front sprocket, and slide the pivot bolt through from the right-hand side, engaging the flats on its head in the adjuster collar (see illustrations 15.7c and b).

19 Tighten the adjuster collar by turning the pivot bolt head using a hex key to the torque setting specified at the beginning of the Chapter (see illustration 15.7a).

20 Thread the locknut onto the adjuster and tighten to the specified torque setting using the peg spanner (see illustration 15.6).

21 Thread the nut onto the left-hand end of the pivot bolt and tighten to the specified torque setting (see illustration 15.5).

22 Secure the brake hose on the swingarm (see illustration 15.4).

23 Install the shock absorber (see Section 12).

24 Install the rear wheel (see Chapter 6).

25 Install the front sprocket (see Chapter 6).

26 Check and adjust the drive chain slack (see Chapter 1). Check the operation of the rear suspension and brake before taking the machine on the road.

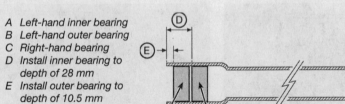

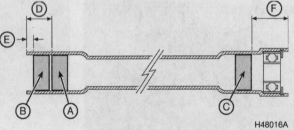

A Left-hand inner bearing
B Left-hand outer bearing
C Right-hand bearing
D Install inner bearing to depth of 28 mm
E Install outer bearing to depth of 10.5 mm
F Install bearing to depth of 32 mm

H48016A

15.14 Fitted position of swingarm needle roller bearings

15.16 Make sure you select the correct seal for each pivot

Chapter 6
Brakes, wheels and final drive

Contents

Degrees of difficulty

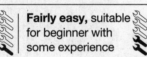

Easy, suitable for novice with little experience	**Fairly easy,** suitable for beginner with some experience	**Fairly difficult,** suitable for competent DIY mechanic	**Difficult,** suitable for experienced DIY mechanic	**Very difficult,** suitable for expert DIY or professional

Specifications

Brake fluid
Brake fluid type . . . . DOT 4

Front brake discs
Disc thickness
  C and D models
    Standard . . . . 6.0 mm
    Service limit . . . . 5.5 mm
  E and F models
    Standard . . . . 5.5 mm
    Service limit . . . . 5.0 mm
Disc maximum runout . . . . 0.3 mm

Rear brake disc
Disc thickness
  Standard . . . . 5.0 mm
  Service limit . . . . 4.5 mm
Disc maximum runout . . . . 0.3 mm

Wheels
Maximum wheel runout (front and rear)
  Axial (side-to-side) . . . . 1.0 mm
  Radial (out-of-round) . . . . 1.0 mm
Maximum axle runout (front and rear) . . . . 0.2 mm

Tyres

Tyre pressures and tread depth	see *Pre-ride* checks
Tyre sizes*	
Front	120/70-ZR17 (58W) Radial
Rear	
C models	190/50-ZR17 (73W) Radial
D, E and F models	190/55-ZR17 (73W) Radial

Refer to the owners handbook or the tyre information label on the swingarm for approved tyre brands.

Final drive

Drive chain slack and lubricant	see Chapter 1
Drive chain	
Make	RK
Type	
C and D models	RK 525MFO
E and F models	RK 525MFOZ
Links	
C, E and F models	110
D models	108
Joining link staked ends diameter	5.6 to 5.9 mm
Joining link plate width	19.7 to 20.0 mm
Sprocket sizes (No. of teeth)	
Front (engine) sprocket	17
Rear (wheel) sprocket	
C models	39
D models	40
E and F models	41
Maximum rear sprocket warp	0.5 mm

Torque settings

Brake caliper bleed valves	
Front and rear calipers	8 Nm
Front master cylinder	5.5 Nm
Brake disc bolts	27 Nm
Brake hose banjo bolts	25 Nm
Front axle nut	
C models	108 Nm
D, E and F models	127 Nm
Front axle clamp bolts	20 Nm
Front brake caliper mounting bolts	34 Nm
Front brake caliper body joining bolts	22 Nm
Front brake master cylinder clamp bolts	
C and D models	9 Nm
E and F models	11 Nm
Front brake pad retaining pins	15 Nm
Front sprocket nut	125 Nm
Rear axle nut	108 Nm
Rear brake caliper mounting bolts	25 Nm
Rear brake master cylinder mounting bolts	25 Nm
Rear sprocket nuts	59 Nm
Rider's footrest bracket bolts	25 Nm

1 General information

All models covered in this manual are fitted with cast alloy wheels designed for tubeless tyres only. Both front and rear brakes are hydraulically operated disc brakes.

The front brake system has two radial calipers with four opposed pistons, with 300 mm floating discs on C and D models, and 310 mm floating discs on all other models. The rear brake system has a single piston sliding caliper acting on a 220 mm disc.

Final drive is by chain and sprockets.

Caution: Disc brake components rarely require disassembly. Do not disassemble components unless absolutely necessary. If an hydraulic brake hose is loosened or disconnected, the banjo union sealing washers must be replaced with new ones and the system must be bled upon reassembly. Do not use solvents on internal brake components. Solvents will cause the seals to swell and distort. Use only clean DOT 4 brake fluid for cleaning. Use care when working with brake fluid as it can injure your eyes and it will damage painted surfaces and plastic parts.

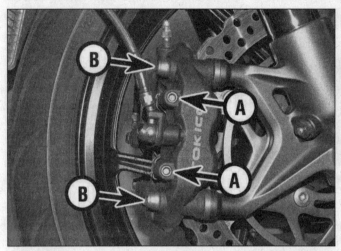

2.1a Brake pad pins (A), caliper mounting bolts (B) – C/D models

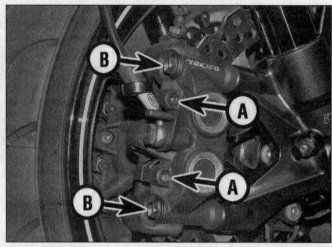

2.1b Brake pad pins (A), caliper mounting bolts (B) – E/F models

2 Front brake pads

Caution: Do not operate the brakes while a caliper is off the disc.

1 Slacken the pad retaining pins **(see illustrations)**.

2 Unscrew the caliper mounting bolts and slide the caliper off the disc **(see illustration 2.17)**. Remove the caliper locating dowels if loose.

3 On C and D models, working on one set of pads at a time unscrew and remove the pad pin, then remove the pad spring and drop the pads from the caliper.

4 On E and F models unscrew and remove the pad pins, then remove the pads from the bottom of the caliper **(see illustrations)**. The pad spring can stay in place unless you are overhauling the caliper – to remove the spring the pistons must be pushed all the way back into their bores to give clearance (see Step 8) **(see illustration 2.12)**.

5 Where fitted and if required remove the shim from the back of each pad, noting how it fits **(see illustration 2.13)** – note that new pads should come with new shims where applicable.

6 Inspect the surface of each pad for contamination and check that the friction material has not worn to or beyond its service limit (see Chapter 1, Section 2). If any pad is worn, is fouled with oil or grease, or is heavily scored or damaged, fit a complete set of new pads. Also check for even wear in each pad on C and D models, and across each pad on E and F models – uneven wear is indicative of a sticking or seized piston (see Steps 8 and 9). **Note:** *It is not possible to degrease the friction material; if the pads are contaminated in any way they must be replaced with new ones.*

7 If the pads are in good condition clean them carefully using a fine wire brush that is

2.4a Remove the pad pins...

completely free of oil and grease to remove all dirt and dust. Using a pointed instrument, clean the grooves and dig out any embedded particles of foreign matter. Spray with a dedicated brake cleaner.

8 Clean around the exposed section of each piston to remove any dirt or debris that could cause the seals to be damaged **(see illustration)**. If new pads are being fitted check the fluid level in the reservoir (see *Pre-ride checks*) – if the level is much above the LOWER level line remove the master cylinder reservoir cap, plate and diaphragm

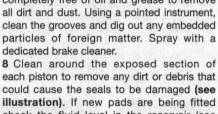

2.4b ...then remove the pads

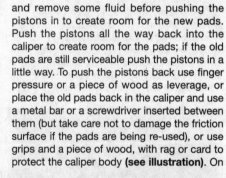

and remove some fluid before pushing the pistons in to create room for the new pads. Push the pistons all the way back into the caliper to create room for the pads; if the old pads are still serviceable push the pistons in a little way. To push the pistons back use finger pressure or a piece of wood as leverage, or place the old pads back in the caliper and use a metal bar or a screwdriver inserted between them (but take care not to damage the friction surface if the pads are being re-used), or use grips and a piece of wood, with rag or card to protect the caliper body **(see illustration)**. On

2.8a Clean off any dirt from around the pistons

2.8b Press the pistons in as described to make clearance for new pads

2.8c **This is a commercially available piston pushing tool**

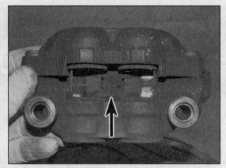

2.12 **Make sure the pad spring (arrowed) is correctly in place**

2.13 **Make sure the shims are correctly seated**

E and F models you can use a proper piston-pushing tool that you can get from a good tool supplier **(see illustration)**. If the pistons are difficult to push back, remove the bleed valve cap, then attach a length of clear hose to the bleed valve and place the open end in a suitable container, then open the valve and try again (see Section 11). Take great care not to draw any air into the system. If in doubt, bleed the brakes afterwards.

9 If any of the pistons appear seized, first block or hold the other pistons using wood or cable-ties, then apply the brake lever and check whether the piston in question moves at all. If it moves out but can't be pushed back in the chances are there is some hidden corrosion stopping it. If it doesn't move at all, or to fully clean and inspect the pistons, disassemble the caliper and overhaul it (see Section 3).

10 Remove all dirt and corrosion from the pad pins and check for wear and damage.

11 Check the condition of the brake disc (see Section 4).

12 On E and F models, if the pad spring was removed fit it into the caliper, making sure it locates correctly **(see illustration)**.

13 Where fitted and if removed fit the shim onto the back of each pad, making sure it locates correctly **(see illustration)**. Clean the outer face of each shim so it is shiny.

14 Lightly smear the edges of the backing material where it contacts the caliper body with copper-based grease, making sure that none gets on the friction material. Also smear the pad pins.

15 On C and D models fit the pads up into the caliper so the friction material on each pad faces the other. Seat the pad spring, then slide the pad pin through and tighten it finger-tight **(see illustration)**. Repeat for the other set of pads.

16 On E and F models fit the pads into the caliper so the friction material on each pad faces the other **(see illustration 2.4b)**. Press them up against the spring to align the holes, then insert the pad pins and tighten them finger-tight **(see illustration 2.4a)**.

17 Make sure the caliper locating dowels are fitted. Slide the caliper onto the disc making sure the pads locate correctly on each side **(see illustration)**. Fit the caliper mounting bolts and tighten them to the torque setting specified at the beginning of the Chapter.

18 Tighten the pad pins to the torque setting specified at the beginning of this Chapter.

19 Operate the brake lever until the pads contact the disc. Check the level of fluid in the reservoir and top-up if necessary (see *Pre-ride checks*).

20 Check the operation of the brakes before riding the motorcycle.

3 Front brake calipers

⚠ *Warning: Overhaul of the brake calipers must be done in a spotlessly clean work area to avoid contamination and possible failure of the brake hydraulic system components. Do not, under any circumstances, use petroleum-based solvents to clean brake parts. Use clean DOT 4 brake fluid, dedicated brake cleaner or denatured alcohol only, as described. To prevent damage from spilled brake fluid, always cover paintwork when working on the braking system, and have plenty of absorbent rag to hand to catch and wipe off any spilled fluid.*

Removal

Note: *If the caliper is being overhauled (usually due to sticking pistons or fluid leaks) read through the entire procedure first and make sure that you have obtained all the new parts required, including some new DOT 4 brake fluid. Caution: Do not operate the brakes while a caliper is off the disc.*

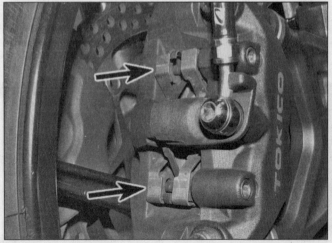

2.15 **Make sure the pad springs (arrowed) are correctly in place**

2.17 **Slide the caliper onto the disc and fit the bolts**

3.2a Brake hose banjo bolt (arrowed)

3.2b Seal the banjo using a nut and bolt and the sealing washers

3.6 Caliper body joining bolts (arrowed)

3.7a Block the fluid inlet using a suitable bolt

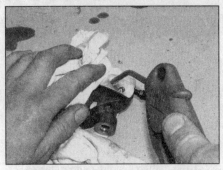

3.7b Apply compressed air to the fluid passage...

3.7c ...until the pistons are displaced

1 Drain the brake fluid from the system (see Section 11).

2 Unscrew the brake hose banjo bolt and detach the banjo union, noting its alignment with the caliper **(see illustration)**. Seal the banjo union to prevent any dirt getting in **(see illustration)**. Note that new sealing washers will be required later.

3 Refer to Section 2, Steps 1 to 4, and remove the brake pads – this involves removing the caliper from the disc.

Overhaul

4 Clean the exterior of the caliper with denatured alcohol or brake system cleaner. Have some clean rag ready to catch any spilled brake fluid.

5 To remove the pistons you need either a supply of compressed air, or a piston removal tool, or if neither are available a good pair of external circlip removal pliers.

6 Unscrew the caliper body joining bolts and separate the body halves, catching any residual fluid with the rag **(see illustration)**. Remove the O-ring from whichever body half it is in and discard it – you must fit a new one on reassembly **(see illustration 3.16a)**.

7 If you are using compressed air place one of the caliper halves piston-up on the bench. When working on the outer caliper half, make sure the bleed valve is tight, and find a suitable bolt to block the fluid inlet banjo bolt bore and thread it in **(see illustration)**. Get a wad of rag and hold it against the pistons as a cushion to protect your hand as the pistons are forced out. Apply compressed

air gradually and progressively, starting with a fairly low pressure, to the fluid passage on the caliper joint and allow the pistons to ease out of their bores, controlling them with hand pressure and the rag **(see illustration)**. Make sure the pistons are displaced evenly, using pressure to block one while the other moves if necessary **(see illustration)**. Repeat the procedure for the other caliper half. Lay the pistons out so that they can be matched to their original bores on installation.

8 If you are using a dedicated tool or the circlip pliers, grip the inner wall of the piston then twist and pull the piston out, keeping it square to the bore wall until it is free. Do not try to remove a piston by levering it out or by using pliers or other grips that may scratch the outer wall, unless you are prepared to fit a new piston, and possibly a new caliper.

9 If a piston is stuck in its bore due to

corrosion the caliper should be replaced with a new one.

10 Remove the dust seals and the piston seals from the bores using a plastic tool to avoid scratching the bores **(see illustration)**. Discard the seals – new ones must be fitted on reassembly.

11 Clean the pistons and bores with clean brake fluid. If compressed air is available, blow it through the fluid passages to ensure they are clear (make sure it is filtered and unlubricated).

Caution: Do not, under any circumstances, use a petroleum-based solvent to clean brake parts.

12 Inspect the caliper bores and pistons for signs of corrosion, nicks and burrs and loss of plating **(see illustration)**. If surface defects are present, the pistons and/or the caliper assembly must be replaced with new ones. If

3.10 Remove the seals and discard them

3.12 Check the pistons for damage – on this example the plating is peeling off

3.13 Fit the new piston seals...

3.14 ...and new dust seals...

3.15 ...then fit the pistons

3.16a Fit the O-ring into its recess...

3.16b ...then join the caliper halves

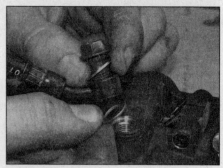

3.18 Always use new sealing washers

one caliper is in poor condition, the other front caliper and the master cylinder should also be checked.

13 Lubricate the new piston seals with clean brake fluid and fit them into their grooves in the caliper bores **(see illustration)**. Note that there are two sizes of bore in each caliper in each caliper half on E and F models and care must therefore be taken to ensure that the correct size seals are fitted to the correct bores (see Specifications). The same applies when fitting the new dust seals and pistons.

14 Lubricate the new dust seals with silicone grease and fit them into their grooves in the caliper bores **(see illustration)**.

15 Lubricate the pistons with clean brake fluid and fit them, closed-end first, into the caliper bores, taking care not to displace the seals **(see illustration)**. Using your thumbs, push the pistons all the way in, making sure they enter the bore squarely.

16 Lubricate the new caliper body O-ring with clean DOT 4 brake fluid and fit it into its recess **(see illustration)**. Join the two halves of the caliper body together, ensuring that the O-ring stays in place **(see illustration)**. Fit the caliper body joining bolts and tighten them evenly to the torque setting specified at the beginning of the Chapter **(see illustration 3.6)**.

Installation

17 Refer to Section 2 and if not already done clean and check the pads and pad spring. Fit the brake pads into the caliper and the caliper onto the disc following the procedure in Section 2, Steps 12 to 20.

18 Connect the brake hose to the caliper, using new sealing washers on each side of the banjo fitting **(see illustration)**. Align the hose as noted on removal **(see illustration 3.2a)**. Tighten the banjo bolt to the torque setting specified at the beginning of the Chapter.

19 Refer to Section 11 to fill and bleed the system.

20 Check that there are no fluid leaks and test the operation of the brakes before riding the motorcycle.

4 Front brake discs

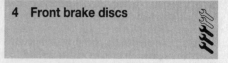

Inspection

1 Inspect the surface of the disc for score marks and other damage. Light scratches are normal after use and won't affect brake operation, but deep grooves and heavy score marks will reduce braking efficiency and accelerate pad wear. If a disc is badly grooved it must be replaced with a new one.

2 The disc must not be allowed to wear down to a thickness less than the service limit listed in this Chapter's Specifications. Check the thickness of the disc in the middle of the pad contact area using a micrometer **(see illustration)** – do not measure across the rim of the disc with a ruler. Replace the disc with a new one if necessary.

3 To check if the disc is warped, position the bike on an auxiliary stand with the front wheel raised off the ground and the handlebar turned fully to one side. Mount a dial gauge to the fork leg, with the gauge plunger touching the surface of the disc close to the inner rim so there is no chance of the plunger going into any of the holes **(see illustration)**. Rotate the wheel and watch the gauge needle,

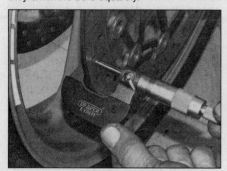

4.2 Measuring disc thickness using a micrometer

4.3 Checking disc runout with a dial gauge

4.5 The disc is secured by five bolts

5.3 Brake hose banjo bolt (arrowed)

comparing the reading with the limit listed in the Specifications at the beginning of this Chapter. If the runout is greater than the service limit, check the wheel bearings for play (see Chapter 1), and also check the wheel itself for runout before assuming the disc is warped (see Section 12). If the bearings are worn, fit new ones (see Section 16) and repeat this check. If the disc runout is still excessive, remove the disc (Steps 4 and 5) and check for corrosion where it seats on the hub and clean it up if necessary. You can also try moving the disc around the wheel one bolt hole at a time and after each movement rechecking for runout. In most cases a new disc will have to be fitted.

Removal

4 Remove the wheel (see Section 14).
Caution: Don't lay the wheel down and allow it to rest on a disc – set the wheel on wood blocks so the wheel rim supports the weight of the wheel.
5 If you are not replacing the disc with a new one, mark the alignment of the disc to the wheel, so it can be installed in the same position. Unscrew the disc bolts, loosening them evenly and a little at a time in a criss-cross pattern to avoid distorting the disc, then remove the disc **(see illustration)**.

Installation

6 Before fitting the disc, make sure there

is no dirt or corrosion where it seats on the hub. If the disc does not sit flat when it is bolted down, it will appear to be warped when checked or when the front brake is used.
7 Fit the disc on the wheel with its marked side facing out, aligning the previously applied marks (if you're reinstalling the original disc), and making sure any arrow points in the direction of normal rotation, matching the arrows on both the wheel and the tyre.
8 Clean the threads of the bolts and apply fresh thread locking compound, and tighten them evenly and a little at a time in a criss-cross pattern to the torque setting specified at the beginning of this Chapter. Clean the disc using acetone or brake system cleaner. If a new disc has been installed, remove any protective coating from its working surfaces and fit new brake pads.
9 Install the wheel (see Section 14).
10 Operate the brake lever until the pads contact the disc.
11 Check the operation of the brakes before riding the motorcycle.

5 Front brake master cylinder

> ⚠ *Warning: Overhaul must be done in a spotlessly clean work area to avoid contamination and possible failure*

of the brake hydraulic system components. Do not, under any circumstances, use petroleum-based solvents to clean brake parts. Use clean DOT 4 brake fluid, dedicated brake cleaner or denatured alcohol only, as described. To prevent damage from spilled brake fluid, always cover paintwork when working on the braking system, and have plenty of absorbent rag to hand to catch and wipe off any spilled fluid.
Note: *If the master cylinder is being overhauled (usually due to sticking or poor action, or fluid leaks) read through the entire procedure first and make sure that you have obtained all the new parts required, including some new DOT 4 brake fluid.*

Removal

1 Drain the brake fluid from the system (see Section 11).
2 Remove the brake lever (see Chapter 5).
3 Unscrew the brake hose banjo bolt and detach the banjo union, noting its alignment with the master cylinder **(see illustration)**. Seal the banjo union to prevent any dirt getting in **(see illustration 3.2b)**. Note that new sealing washers will be required later.
4 Displace the brake fluid reservoir from its bracket **(see illustration)**.
5 Unscrew the two master cylinder assembly clamp bolts, displace the master cylinder and disconnect the brake light switch wiring connector **(see illustrations)**.

5.4 Unscrew the bolt (arrowed)

5.5a Unscrew the clamp bolts (arrowed) and displace the master cylinder...

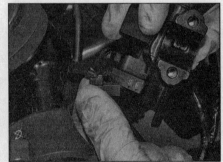

5.5b ...then disconnect the wiring

1 Rubber boot
2 Circlip
3 Piston
4 Seal
5 Cup
6 Spring
7 Reservoir hose union
8 Dust cap
9 Circlip
10 Reservoir union O-ring

06-05.08.L - 5542

5.8 Front brake master cylinder – C models

on reassembly. Inspect the reservoir hose for cracks or splits and replace it with a new one if necessary.

8 On C models remove the rubber boot from the master cylinder **(see illustration)**. Depress the piston and use circlip pliers to remove the circlip, then slide out the piston assembly and spring, noting how they fit. Lay the parts out in the proper order to prevent confusion during reassembly.

9 On D, E and F models remove the pushrod and the rubber boot from the master cylinder **(see illustration)**. Depress the piston and use circlip pliers to remove the circlip, then slide out the piston assembly, the spring and the spring guide, noting how they fit **(see illustrations)**. Lay the parts out in the proper order to prevent confusion during reassembly.

10 Clean the master cylinder and reservoir with clean brake fluid. If compressed air is available, blow it through the fluid galleries to ensure they are clear (make sure the air is filtered and unlubricated).

Caution: Do not, under any circumstances, use a petroleum-based solvent to clean brake parts.

11 Check the master cylinder bore for corrosion, scratches, nicks and score marks. If damage or wear is evident, the master cylinder must be replaced with a new one. If the master cylinder is in poor condition, then the calipers should be checked as well.

12 The rubber boot, circlip, piston and its cup and seal, and the spring must all be replaced with new ones. On C models the piston, cup, seal and spring come as a kit, with the circlip and boot available separately. On D, E and F models the piston, cup, seal, spring, spring guide, pushrod and rubber boot come as a kit with the circlip available separately. Use all of the new parts, regardless of the apparent condition of the old ones.

13 Lubricate the piston, cup seal and master cylinder bore with new brake fluid.

14 On C models fit the cup onto the narrow end of the spring, locating the peg in the hole **(see illustration)**. Fit the seal onto the piston with its lips facing the inner end **(see**

6 If required, undo the screw securing the brake light switch to the bottom of the master cylinder and remove the switch.

Overhaul

7 If required release the reservoir hose clamp and detach the hose from its union on the master cylinder. If required lift the dust cap from the fluid reservoir hose union, then remove the circlip and detach the union from the master cylinder **(see illustration 5.8)**. Remove the O-ring – a new one must be fitted

5.9a Remove the pushrod and boot

5.9b Release the circlip...

5.9c ...and remove the piston assembly...

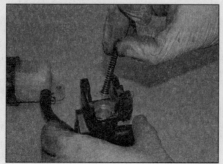

5.9d ...and the spring with its guide

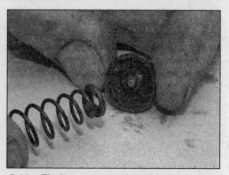

5.14a Fit the cup onto the spring, locating the peg in the hole

5.14b Fit the seal onto the piston as shown

5.15a Make sure the cup and seal are correctly installed

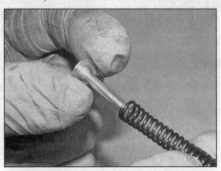

5.15b Fit the guide into the spring...

illustration). Slide the spring wide end first into the master cylinder and ease the cup in, making sure the lips do not turn inside out. Slide the piston in up against the cup. Push the piston in to compress the spring and fit the new circlip, making sure it locates in the groove. Smear inside the rubber boot with silicone grease. Fit the boot over the end of the piston and locate its narrow end lips in the groove. Carefully push the wide rim of the boot onto its seat in the master cylinder.

15 On D, E and F models carefully fit the cup and seal onto the piston as shown (see illustration). Fit the spring guide into the wide end of the spring and locate the spring end on the lip (see illustration). Fit the spring into the piston (see illustration). Slide the piston assembly into the master cylinder – make sure the lips on the cup and seal do not turn inside out (see illustrations). Push the piston in to compress the spring and fit the new circlip, making sure it locates in the groove (see illustration). Fit the boot onto the pushrod so its narrow end lips locate in the groove (see illustration). Smear the inner end of the pushrod and inside the rubber boot with silicone grease (see illustration). Locate the inner end of the pushrod in the end of the piston and carefully push the wide rim of the boot onto its seat in the master cylinder (see illustration).

16 If removed fit a new O-ring smeared with brake fluid onto the fluid reservoir hose union, then press the union into the master cylinder and secure it with the circlip. Fit the dust cap

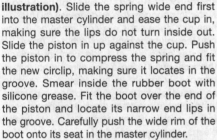

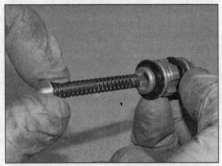

5.15c ...then fit the spring into the piston

5.15d Fit the assembly into the master cylinder...

5.15e ...and push the piston in, checking the cup and seal lips...

5.15f ...and fit the circlip in its groove

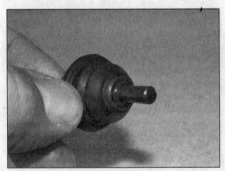

5.15g Correct fitting of pushrod in boot

5.15h Apply silicone grease as described

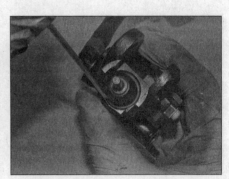

5.15i Seat the inner rim of the boot

5.18 Align the mating surfaces with the punch mark (arrowed)

6.1 Caliper mounting bolts (arrowed)

over the circlip. Do not fit the reservoir hose onto the union until both are installed on the handlebar to ensure correct alignment.

Installation

17 If removed, fit the brake light switch onto the bottom of the master cylinder, making sure the pin locates in the hole, and tighten the screw.
18 Connect the brake light switch wiring connector and attach the master cylinder to the handlebar, aligning the clamp joint with the punch mark on the top of the handlebar, then fit the clamp with its UP mark facing up **(see illustration)**. Tighten the upper bolt to the torque setting specified at the beginning of this Chapter, followed by the lower bolt.
19 Fit the brake fluid reservoir onto its bracket **(see illustration 5.4)**. If required connect the hose to the union on the master cylinder and secure it with the clamp.

20 Connect the brake hose to the master cylinder, using new sealing washers on each side of the banjo fitting **(see illustration 3.18)**. Align the hose as noted on removal **(see illustration 5.3)**. Tighten the banjo bolt to the torque setting specified at the beginning of the Chapter.
21 Install the brake lever (see Chapter 5).
22 Refer to Section 11 to fill and bleed the system.
23 Check that there are no fluid leaks and test the operation of the brakes before riding the motorcycle.

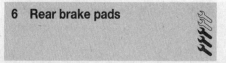

6   Rear brake pads

Note: *Do not operate the brake pedal with the caliper off the disc.*

1 Unscrew the caliper mounting bolts and slide the caliper off the disc **(see illustration)**.
2 Remove the clip from the pad pin, then withdraw the pin and remove the pads, noting how they fit **(see illustrations)**.
3 Slide the caliper off the bracket **(see illustration)**. Note the pad spring in the top of caliper and the pad guide on the caliper bracket and remove them if required for cleaning or replacement, noting how they fit **(see illustrations 6.12 and 6.14)**.
4 Inspect the surface of each pad for contamination and check that the friction material has not worn beyond its service limit (see Chapter 1, Section 2). If either pad is worn, is fouled with oil or grease, or heavily scored or damaged, fit a set of new pads. **Note:** *It is not possible to degrease the friction material; if the pads are contaminated in any way they must be replaced with new ones.*
5 If the pads are in good condition clean them carefully using a fine wire brush that is completely free of oil and grease to remove all traces of dirt and dust. Using a pointed instrument, dig out any embedded particles of foreign matter. Spray with a dedicated brake cleaner to remove any dust.
6 Clean off all traces of corrosion and hardened grease from the slider pins on the bracket and from the rubber boots **(see illustration)**. Check the boots for cracks and splits and replace them with new ones if necessary, making sure they locate correctly.
7 Clean around the exposed section of the piston to remove any dirt or debris that could cause the seals to be damaged. If new pads

6.2a Remove the clip…

6.2b …and withdraw the pin

6.2c Pivot the inner pad up and slide it off the post…

6.2d …then remove the outer pad

6.3 Slide the caliper and bracket apart

6.6 Clean and check the pins (A) and the boots (B)

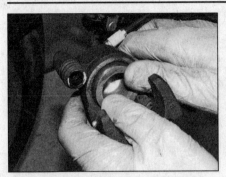

6.7 Press the piston in as described to make clearance for the new pads

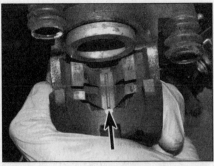
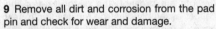

6.12 Make sure the pad spring (arrowed) is correctly in place

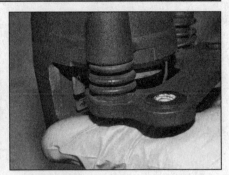
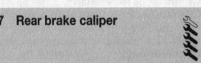

6.13 Check the boot lips are correctly seated

are being fitted check the fluid level in the reservoir (see *Pre-ride checks*) – if the level is much above the LOWER level line remove the master cylinder reservoir cap, plate and diaphragm and remove some fluid before pushing the pistons in to create room for the new pads. If new pads are being fitted, push the piston all the way back into the caliper to create room for them; if the old pads are still serviceable push the piston in a little way. To push the piston back use finger pressure or a piece of wood as leverage, or place the old pads back in the caliper and use a metal bar or a screwdriver inserted between them (but take care not to damage the friction surface if the pads are being re-used), or use grips and a piece of wood, with rag or card to protect the caliper body **(see illustration)**. Alternatively you can use a proper piston-pushing tool that you can get from a good tool supplier **(see illustration 2.8c)**. If the piston is difficult to push back, remove the bleed valve cap, then attach a length of clear hose to the bleed valve and place the open end in a suitable container, then open the valve and try again (see Section 11). Take great care not to draw any air into the system. If in doubt, bleed the brake afterwards.

8 If the piston appears seized, apply the brake pedal and check whether the piston moves at all. If it moves out but can't be pushed back in, it is likely there is some hidden corrosion stopping it. If it doesn't move at all, or to fully clean and inspect the piston, disassemble the caliper and overhaul it (see Section 7).

9 Remove all dirt and corrosion from the pad pin and check for wear and damage.
10 Check the condition of the brake disc (see Section 4).
11 Lightly smear the edges of the pad backing material where it contacts the caliper body with copper-based grease, making sure that none gets on the friction material. Also smear the pad pin.
12 If removed fit the pad spring into the caliper and the guide onto the bracket **(see illustration)**. Apply some silicone grease to the slider pins and inside the boots.
13 Slide the caliper onto the bracket **(see illustration 6.3)**, making sure the boots locate correctly to provide a seal **(see illustration)**.
14 Fit the outer pad into the caliper, making sure it locates correctly in the bracket **(see illustration)**. Fit the eye on the inner pad over the post on the bracket then pivot the pad into the caliper and onto the spring **(see illustration 6.2c)**. Press the inner pad against the spring to align the holes and slide the pin through, aligning it so the hole is at the bottom **(see illustration 6.2b)**. Fit the clip into the hole to secure the pin **(see illustration 6.2a)**.
15 Slide the caliper onto the disc making sure the pads locate correctly on each side **(see illustration)**. Fit the caliper mounting bolts and tighten them to the torque setting specified at the beginning of the Chapter.
16 Operate the brake pedal until the pads contact with the disc. Check the level of fluid in the reservoir and top-up if necessary (see *Pre-ride checks*).

17 Check the operation of the rear brake before riding the motorcycle.

7 Rear brake caliper

⚠ *Warning: Overhaul must be done in a spotlessly clean work area to avoid contamination and possible failure of the brake hydraulic system components. Do not, under any circumstances, use petroleum-based solvents to clean brake parts. Use clean DOT 4 brake fluid, dedicated brake cleaner or denatured alcohol only, as described. To prevent damage from spilled brake fluid, always cover paintwork when working on the braking system.*

Removal

Note: *If the caliper is being overhauled (usually due to a sticking piston or fluid leaks) read through the entire procedure first and make sure that you have obtained all the new parts required, including some new DOT 4 brake fluid.*
Caution: Do not operate the brake while the caliper is off the disc.
1 Drain the brake fluid from the system (see Section 11).
2 Unscrew the brake hose banjo bolt and detach the banjo union, noting its alignment with the caliper **(see illustration)**. Seal the

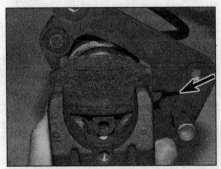

6.14 Make sure the outer pad locates correctly in the bracket against the guide (arrowed)

6.15 Slide the caliper onto the disc and fit the bolts

7.2 Brake hose banjo bolt (arrowed)

7.5 Carefully push the piston out of the caliper

7.7 Remove the seals and discard them

7.10 Fit the new piston seal...

banjo union to prevent any dirt getting in **(see illustration 3.2b)**. Note that new sealing washers will be required later.

3 Refer to Section 6, Steps 1 to 3, and remove the brake pads – this involves removing the caliper from the disc and sliding the caliper and bracket apart.

Overhaul

4 Clean the exterior of the caliper with denatured alcohol or brake system cleaner. Have some clean rag ready to catch any spilled brake fluid.

5 Support the caliper as shown and push the piston out of the bore using a suitable tool inserted through the banjo bolt hole **(see illustration)**.

6 If the piston is stuck in its bore due to corrosion the caliper should be replaced with a new one.

7 Remove the dust seal and the piston seal from the piston bore using a plastic tool to avoid scratching the bores **(see illustration)**. Discard the seals – new ones must be fitted on reassembly.

8 Clean the piston and bore with clean brake fluid. If compressed air is available, blow it through the fluid passages to ensure they are clear (make sure it is filtered and unlubricated).

Caution: Do not, under any circumstances, use a petroleum-based solvent to clean brake parts.

9 Inspect the caliper bore and piston for signs of corrosion, nicks and burrs and loss of plating **(see illustration 3.12)**. If surface

defects are present, the piston and/or the caliper assembly must be replaced with new ones. If the caliper is in poor condition, the master cylinder should also be checked.

10 Lubricate the new piston seal with clean brake fluid and fit it into the inner groove in the caliper bore **(see illustration)**.

11 Lubricate the new dust seal with silicone grease and fit it into the outer groove in the caliper bore **(see illustration)**.

12 Lubricate the piston with clean brake fluid and fit it, closed-end first, into the caliper bore, taking care not to displace the seals **(see illustration)**. Using your thumbs, push the piston all the way in, making sure it enters the bore squarely.

Installation

13 Refer to Section 6 and if not already done clean and check the pads, the pad pin, spring and guide, and the slider pins and boots. Fit the brake pads into the caliper and the caliper onto the disc following the procedure in Section 6, Steps 11 to 15.

14 If detached, connect the brake hose to the caliper, using new sealing washers on each side of the banjo fitting **(see illustration 3.18)**. Align the hose as noted on removal **(see illustration 7.2)**. Tighten the banjo bolt to the torque setting specified at the beginning of the Chapter.

15 Refer to Section 11 to fill and bleed the system.

16 Check that there are no fluid leaks and test the operation of the brakes before riding the motorcycle.

8 Rear brake disc

Inspection

1 Refer to Section 4 of this Chapter, noting that the dial gauge should be attached to the swingarm.

Removal

2 Remove the wheel (see Section 15).
Caution: Don't lay the wheel down and allow it to rest on the disc or sprocket – set the wheel on wood blocks so the wheel rim supports the weight of the wheel.

3 If you are not replacing the disc with a new one, mark the relationship of the disc to the wheel so it can be installed in the same position. Unscrew the disc bolts, loosening them evenly and a little at a time in a criss-cross pattern to avoid distorting the disc, then remove the disc **(see illustration)**.

Installation

4 Before installing the disc, make sure there is no dirt or corrosion where the disc seats on the hub. If the disc does not sit flat when it is bolted down, it will appear to be warped when checked or when the rear brake is used.

5 Fit the disc on the wheel with its marked side facing out, aligning the previously applied marks (if you're reinstalling the original disc), and making sure any arrow points in the direction of normal rotation, matching the arrows on both the wheel and the tyre.

7.11 ...and the new dust seal...

7.12 ...then fit the piston

8.3 Rear brake disc bolts (arrowed)

9.2 Brake hose banjo bolt (arrowed)

9.3a Unscrew the bolts (arrowed)

9.3b Remove the split pin then withdraw the clevis pin (arrowed)

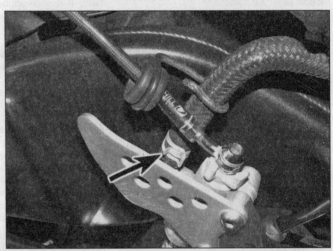

9.4a Release the clamp (arrowed) and detach the hose

6 Clean the threads of the bolts and apply fresh thread locking compound. Tighten the bolts evenly and a little at a time in a criss-cross pattern to the torque setting specified at the beginning of this Chapter. Clean the disc using acetone or brake system cleaner. If a new disc has been installed, remove any protective coating from its working surfaces and fit new brake pads.
7 Install the wheel (see Section 15).
8 Operate the brake pedal until the pads contact the disc.
9 Check the operation of the brake before riding the motorcycle.

9 Rear brake master cylinder

Warning: Overhaul must be done in a spotlessly clean work area to avoid contamination and possible failure of the brake hydraulic system components. Do not, under any circumstances, use petroleum-based solvents to clean brake parts. Use clean DOT 4 brake fluid, dedicated brake cleaner or denatured alcohol only, as described. To prevent damage from spilled brake fluid, always cover paintwork when working on the braking system.

Removal

Note: *If the master cylinder is being overhauled (usually due to sticking or poor action, or fluid leaks) read through the entire procedure first and make sure that you have obtained all the new parts required, including some new DOT 4 brake fluid.*

1 Drain the brake fluid from the system (see Section 11).
2 Unscrew the brake hose banjo bolt and detach the banjo union, noting its alignment with the master cylinder **(see illustration)**. Seal the banjo union to prevent any dirt getting in **(see illustration 3.2b)**. Note that new sealing washers will be required later.
3 Unscrew the rider's footrest bracket mounting bolts and displace the bracket so that you can access the back **(see**

illustrations). Remove the split pin from the clevis pin securing the brake pedal to the master cylinder pushrod, then withdraw the clevis pin and detach the pushrod from the pedal **(see illustration)**. Refit the footrest bracket and tighten the bolts finger-tight.
4 On C models detach the reservoir hose from the master cylinder **(see illustration)**. On D, E and F models displace the fluid reservoir from its bracket **(see illustration)**.

9.4b Displace the reservoir

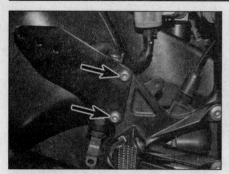

9.5 Unscrew the bolts (arrowed)

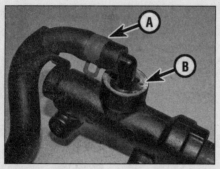

9.6 Reservoir hose clamp (A), hose union circlip (B)

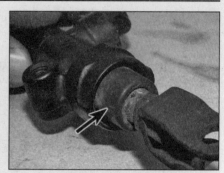

9.7 Dislodge the rubber boot (arrowed)

5 Unscrew the two master cylinder assembly bolts and remove the heel guard and the master cylinder, along with the reservoir hose on C models and the reservoir on all other models **(see illustration)**.

Overhaul

6 If required on D, E and F models release the reservoir hose clamp and detach the hose from its union on the master cylinder **(see illustration)**. If required on all models remove the circlip and detach the union from the master cylinder. Remove the O-ring – a new one must be fitted on reassembly. Inspect the reservoir hose for cracks or splits and replace it with a new one if necessary.

7 Dislodge the rubber boot from the base of the master cylinder and from around the pushrod, noting how it locates, and remove it **(see illustration)**. Push the pushrod in and, using circlip pliers, remove the circlip from its groove in the master cylinder and remove the

pushrod, piston and spring, noting how they fit. Lay the parts out in order as you remove them to prevent confusion during reassembly.
8 Clean the master cylinder with clean brake fluid. If compressed air is available, blow it through the fluid galleries to ensure they are clear (make sure the air is filtered and unlubricated).
Caution: Do not, under any circumstances, use a petroleum-based solvent to clean brake parts.
9 Check the master cylinder bore for corrosion, scratches, nicks and score marks. If damage or wear is evident, the master cylinder must be replaced with a new one. If the master cylinder is in poor condition, then the caliper should be checked as well.
10 The rubber boot, circlip, piston and its cup and seal, and the spring must all be replaced with new ones. The piston, seal, cup and spring are all included in a master cylinder rebuild kit, and should come pre-assembled

as shown **(see illustration)**. The circlip can be obtained separately, but the rubber boot comes as part of the complete pushrod assembly. Use all of the new parts, regardless of the apparent condition of the old ones.
11 If the rubber boot is not already on the pushrod, fit it over the top and seat the lower lip in the groove above the hex. Fit the circlip loosely between the boot and the washer.
12 Smear the master cylinder bore and the cup and seal with new brake fluid.
13 Fit the spring wide-end first into the master cylinder and push the piston assembly in, making sure the cup and seal lips do not turn inside out.
14 Smear some silicone grease onto the rounded end of the pushrod and around the lips of the boot. Push the piston in using the pushrod until the washer is beyond the circlip groove, then locate the circlip in the groove. Carefully push the upper lip of the boot into the master cylinder, making sure it is seated correctly, and that the lower lip is still in its groove in pushrod.
15 If removed fit a new fluid reservoir hose union O-ring smeared with brake fluid, then press the union into the master cylinder and secure it with a new circlip **(see illustration 9.6)**. Connect the hose to the union on the master cylinder and secure it with the clamp.

Installation

16 Fit the master cylinder and heel guard onto the bracket and tighten the bolts to the torque setting specified at the beginning of the Chapter **(see illustration)**.
17 On C models connect the reservoir hose to the master cylinder **(see illustration 9.4a)**. On D, E and F models fit the fluid reservoir onto its bracket **(see illustration 9.4b)**.
18 Displace the rider's footrest bracket **(see illustration 9.3a)**. Fit the pushrod onto the pedal and slide the clevis pin through. Fit a new split pin and bend its ends round as shown **(see illustration)**. Refit the footrest bracket and tighten the bolts to the specified torque.
19 Align the brake hose as noted on removal and connect the hose to the master cylinder, using a new sealing washer on each side of the banjo fitting **(see illustration)**. Tighten the

9.10 Piston, seal, cup and spring assembly

9.16 Fit the master cylinder and heel guard

9.18 Correct fitting of the split pin

9.19 Always use new sealing washers

banjo bolt to the torque setting specified at the beginning of this Chapter.

20 Refer to Section 11 to fill and bleed the system.

21 Check that there are no fluid leaks and test the operation of the brakes before riding the motorcycle.

10 Brake hoses and fittings

Inspection

1 Check brake hose condition regularly (see Chapter 1). Twist and flex the hoses while looking for cracks, bulges and seeping hydraulic fluid. Check extra carefully around the areas where the hoses connect with the banjo fittings, as these are common areas for hose failure.

Removal and installation

2 Drain the brake fluid from the system (see Section 11).

3 The brake hoses have banjo fittings on each end. Cover the surrounding area with plenty of rags and unscrew the banjo bolt at each end of the hose, noting the alignment of the fitting with the master cylinder or brake caliper **(see illustrations 3.2a, 5.3, 7.2 and 9.2)**. Free the hose from any clips or guides and remove it, noting its routing. Discard the sealing washers. **Note:** *Do not operate the brake lever or pedal while a brake hose is disconnected.*

4 Position the new hose, making sure it isn't twisted or otherwise strained, and ensure that it is correctly routed through any clips or guides and is clear of all moving components.

5 Check that the fittings align correctly, then install the banjo bolts, using new sealing washers on both sides of the fittings **(see illustration 3.18 and 9.19)**. Tighten the banjo bolts to the torque setting specified at the beginning of this Chapter.

6 Refill the system with new DOT 4 brake fluid (see *Pre-ride checks*) and bleed the air from it (see Section 11).

7 Check the operation of the brakes before riding the motorcycle.

11 Brake system bleeding and fluid change

Bleeding principles

1 Bleeding a brake is the process of removing aerated brake fluid from the master cylinder, the hose(s) and the brake caliper(s). Bleeding is necessary whenever a brake system hydraulic connection is loosened, after a component or hose is replaced with a new one, when a master cylinder or a caliper is overhauled, or when there is a spongy feel to the lever or pedal and it travels all the way to its stop, and where braking force is less than it should be, and it is not due to any mechanical fault in the system (i.e. a sticking piston in the caliper, or a pad that is not moving as it should due to corrosion, for example on the pad pin). Leaks in the system may also allow air to enter, but leaking brake fluid will reveal their presence and warn you of the need for repair.

2 Brake bleeding is considered by some as a bit of a black art – seasoned professionals sometimes have trouble getting a good firm feel in the brake lever, while a first timer may have no trouble at all. One of the problems, particularly with the front brake system, is that you are working against natural principles – science dictates that air bubbles in a liquid will rise to the top, but the process entails pumping the brake fluid and any air bubbles it contains down, from the master cylinder at the top to the bleed valve in the caliper at the bottom, so while the fluid is moving down the air bubbles will try to rise. Air bubbles can also get trapped, particularly where there are high points in its path.

3 To bleed the brakes using the conventional method, you will need some new DOT 4 brake fluid, a length of clear flexible hose, a small container partially filled with clean brake fluid, some rags, and a spanner to fit the brake caliper bleed valve. Bleeding kits that include the hose, a one-way valve and a container are available relatively cheaply from a good auto store, and simplify the task.

4 Cover painted components to prevent damage in the event that brake fluid is spilled.

Caution: Brake fluid attacks painted finishes and some plastics – to prevent damage from spilled fluid, always cover paintwork when working on the braking system, and clean up any spills immediately using brake cleaner.

Bleeding the front brake system

Note: *On C models bleed the right-hand caliper first, then the left. On D, E and F models bleed the master cylinder first, then the right-hand caliper, then the left.*

5 Turn the handlebars so the brake fluid reservoir is level. Remove the reservoir cap clamp, cap, diaphragm plate and diaphragm **(see illustrations)**. Slowly pump the brake lever a few times to dislodge any air bubbles from the holes in the bottom of the reservoir.

6 Pull the dust cap off the bleed valve **(see**

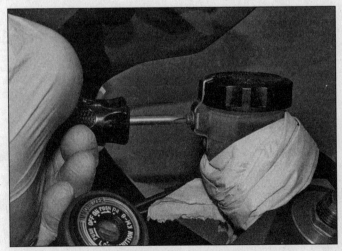

11.5a Undo the clamp screw

11.5b Remove the cap, diaphragm plate and diaphragm

11.6a Master cylinder bleed valve (arrowed) on D/E/F models

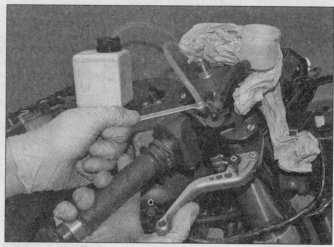

11.6b Fitting the ring spanner and hose onto the front caliper bleed valve

illustration). If using a ring spanner (which is preferable to an open-ended one) fit it onto the valve **(see illustration).** Attach one end of the bleed hose to the bleed valve and, if not using a kit, submerge the other end in the clean brake fluid in the container.

11.7 Keep the reservoir topped up

7 Check the fluid level in the reservoir – keep it topped up and do not allow the level to drop below the bottom of the window during the procedure **(see illustration).**

8 Slowly pump the brake lever three or four times, then hold it in and open the bleed valve a quarter turn **(see illustrations).** When the valve is opened, brake fluid will flow out into the clear tubing, and the lever will move toward the handlebar. Tighten the bleed valve, then release the brake lever gradually.

9 If there is air in the system there will be air bubbles visible in the brake fluid, but not necessarily on the first pump. Repeat the process until no air bubbles have been seen for a few pumps, and the lever is firm when applied, topping the reservoir up when necessary.

10 Now transfer the equipment to the next bleed valve, and repeat the bleeding procedure.

11 When the system has been successfully bled there should be a good and progressively firm feel as the lever is applied, and the lever should not be able to travel all the way back to the handlebar.

12 On completion remove the equipment and make sure the bleed valve is tight (to the torque setting specified at the beginning of the Chapter if you have a suitable torque wrench for small units), then fit the dust cap. Top-up the reservoir, then fit the diaphragm, diaphragm plate, cap and clamp **(see illustrations 11.5b and a).** Check for spilled brake fluid and clean up as required. Check that there are no fluid leaks from the system and check the operation of the brake before riding the motorcycle.

Bleeding the rear brake system

13 On C models remove the left-hand side cover (see Chapter 7). On D, E and F models,

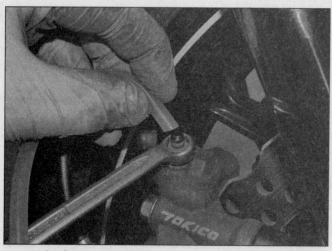

11.8a Connect the bleed tube to the caliper bleed valve

11.8b Bleeding a front caliper

undo the cap clamp screw **(see illustration)**. Unscrew the cap and remove the diaphragm plate and diaphragm **(see illustration)**. Slowly pump the brake pedal a few times to dislodge any air bubbles from the holes in the bottom of the reservoir.

14 Pull the dust cap off the caliper bleed valve **(see illustration)**. If using a ring spanner (which is preferable to an open-ended one) fit it onto the valve. Attach one end of the bleed hose to the bleed valve and, if not using a kit, submerge the other end in the clean brake fluid in the container **(see illustration)**.

15 Check the fluid level in the reservoir – keep it topped up and do not allow the level to drop below the bottom of the window during the procedure **(see illustration)**.

16 Slowly pump the brake pedal three or four times, then hold it down and open the bleed valve a quarter turn **(see illustration)**. When the valve is opened, brake fluid will flow out into the clear tubing, and the pedal will move

down. Tighten the bleed valve, then release the brake pedal gradually.

17 If there is air in the system there will be air bubbles visible in the brake fluid, but not necessarily on the first pump. Repeat the process until no air bubbles have been seen for a few pumps, and the pedal is firm

when applied, topping the reservoir up when necessary.

18 When the system has been successfully bled there should be a good and progressively firm feel as the pedal is applied.

19 On completion remove the equipment used and make sure the bleed valve is tight (to

11.13a Undo the clamp screw...

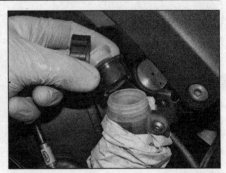
11.13b ...and remove the cap, diaphragm plate and diaphragm

11.14a Pull the cap off the bleed valve, fit the ring spanner and connect the hose

11.14b Support the container at a suitable height

11.15 Keep the reservoir topped up

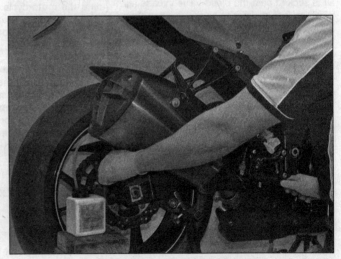
11.16 Bleeding the rear brake

the torque setting specified at the beginning of the Chapter if you have a suitable torque wrench for small units), then fit the dust cap. Top-up the reservoir, then fit the diaphragm, diaphragm plate and cap, and on D, E and F models secure the cap with the clamp. Check for spilled brake fluid and clean up as required. Check that there are no fluid leaks from the system and check the operation of the brake before riding the motorcycle.

Bleeding problems

20 If it is not possible to produce a firm feel to the lever or pedal look for any high point in the system in which a pocket of air may become trapped. Displace and move the hose so the bubble can be dislodged – tapping it may help. If necessary displace the master cylinder and/or the caliper(s), and free the brake hose(s) from its guides and move the parts around to dislodge the air and encourage it towards a bleed valve – refer to the relevant Sections as required to displace components.

21 If you are still having trouble the fluid may be full of many tiny air bubbles rather than a few big ones. To remedy this apply some pressure to the system, for the front brake by tying the front brake lever lightly back to the handlebar, and for the rear by tying a weight to the brake pedal – do not apply too much pressure to the system or the cup and seals in the master cylinder and caliper may fail. Let the fluid stabilise for a few hours, after which the tiny bubbles should either have risen to the top in the reservoir, or have formed into one or more big bubbles that can be more easily bled out by repeating the bleeding procedure.

22 If bleeding the system using the conventional tools and methods stated does not give satisfactory results, you can use a vacuum-type brake bleeding tool, such as the Mity-vac shown, following the manufacturer's instructions (see illustration). This type of tool literally sucks the fluid out by creating a vacuum at the bleed valve. You may find that air is sucked past the bleed valve threads (air provides less resistance to the vacuum than the brake fluid) where it mixes with the fluid being drawn out. If this is the case the vacuum applied may be too great, or the bleed valve may have been loosened too much. One way to get round this is to remove the bleed

valve and thread some PTFE tape around its threads, but note that doing so will be a bit messy, so have some rag to hand. Also make sure the hose from the brake bleeding tool forms an air-tight fit over the bleed valve head, otherwise air will be drawn in from around the valve head.

Fluid change

23 Changing the brake fluid is a similar process to bleeding the brake and requires the same materials plus a suitable tool (such as a syringe, or alternatively lots of absorbent rag or paper) for siphoning the fluid out of the reservoir.

24 Remove the reservoir cap or cover, diaphragm plate and diaphragm and siphon the old fluid out of the reservoir (see illustrations 11.5a and b (front) or 11.13a and b (rear)). Wipe the reservoir clean. Fill the reservoir with new brake fluid (see illustration 11.7 (front) or 11.15 (rear)).

25 Connect the brake bleeding hose to the bleed valve (see Step 6 (front) and Step 14 (rear)). Slowly pump the brake lever or pedal three or four times then hold it in and open the bleed valve. When the valve is opened, brake fluid will flow out of the valve into the clear tubing, and the lever will move toward the handlebar, or the pedal will move down.

26 Tighten the bleed valve, then release the brake lever or pedal gradually. Keep the reservoir topped-up with new fluid at all times or air may enter the system and greatly increase the length of the task. Repeat the process until new fluid can be seen emerging from the caliper bleed valve.

 HAYNES HINT *Old brake fluid is invariably much darker in colour than new fluid, making it easy to see when all old fluid has been expelled from the system.*

27 Check the operation of the brakes before riding the motorcycle. If the lever or pedal action is spongy, carry out the bleeding operation as described above.

Draining the system for overhaul

28 Draining the brake fluid is again a similar process to bleeding the brakes. The quickest and easiest way is to use a vacuum-type brake bleeding tool (see Step 22). Otherwise follow the procedure described above for changing the fluid, but quite simply do not put any new fluid into the reservoir – the system fills itself with air instead.

12 Wheel inspection and repair

1 In order to carry out a proper inspection of the wheels, support the bike on an auxiliary stand. Clean the wheels thoroughly to remove

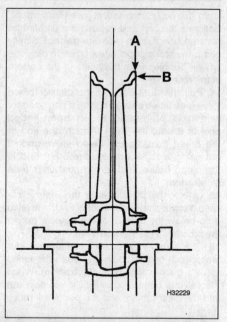

12.3 Check the wheel for radial (out-of-round) runout (A) and axial (side-to-side) runout (B)

mud and dirt that may interfere with the inspection procedure or mask defects. Make a general check of the wheels (see Chapter 1) and tyres (see *Pre-ride checks*).

2 Inspect the wheels for cracks, flat spots on the rim and other damage. Look very closely for dents in the area where the tyre bead contacts the rim. Dents in this area may prevent complete sealing of the tyre against the rim, which leads to deflation of the tyre over a period of time. If damage is evident, or if runout in either direction is excessive, the wheel will have to be renewed. Never attempt to repair a damaged alloy wheel.

3 To check axial (side-to-side) runout of the wheel rim attach a dial gauge to the fork or the swingarm and position its tip against the side of the wheel rim. Spin the wheel slowly and check the amount of run-out, comparing it to the specification listed at the beginning of the Chapter (see illustration).

4 In order to accurately check radial (out of round) runout with the dial gauge, remove the wheel from the machine, and the tyre from the wheel. With the axle clamped in a vice and the dial gauge positioned on the top of the rim, the wheel can be rotated to check the runout (see illustration 12.3).

5 An easier, though slightly less accurate, method is to attach a stiff wire pointer to the fork or the swingarm and position the end a fraction of an inch from the wheel rim where the wheel and tyre join. If the wheel is true, the distance from the pointer to the rim will be constant as the wheel is rotated. **Note:** *If wheel runout is excessive, check the wheel bearings very carefully before renewing the wheel.*

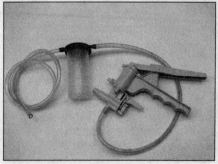

11.22 Vacuum-type brake bleeding tool

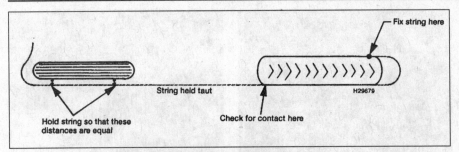

13.5 Wheel alignment check using string

13 Wheel alignment check

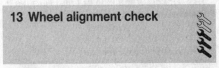

1 Misalignment of the wheels due to a bent frame or forks can cause strange and possibly serious handling problems. If the frame or forks are at fault, repair by a frame specialist or renewal are the only options. Note that failure to set the drive chain adjustment markers to the same setting on each side can cause poor wheel alignment (see Chapter 1, Section 1).

2 To check wheel alignment you will need an assistant, a length of string or a perfectly straight piece of wood and a ruler. A plumb bob or spirit level for checking that the wheels are vertical will also be required.

3 Support the bike upright on an auxiliary stand. Measure the width of both tyres at their widest points. Subtract the smaller measurement from the larger measurement, then divide the difference by two. The result is the amount of offset that should exist between the front and rear tyres on both sides of the machine.

4 If the string method is used, have your assistant hold one end of it about halfway between the floor and the rear axle, with the string touching the back edge of the rear tyre sidewall.

5 Run the other end of the string forward and pull it tight so that it is roughly parallel to the floor **(see illustration)**. Slowly bring the string into contact with the front edge of the rear tyre sidewall, then turn the front wheel until it is parallel with the string. Measure the distance from the front tyre sidewall to the string.

6 Repeat the procedure on the other side of the motorcycle. The distance from the front tyre sidewall to the string should be equal on both sides.

7 As previously mentioned, a perfectly straight length of wood or metal bar may be substituted for the string **(see illustration)**.

8 If the distance between the string and tyre is greater on one side, or if the rear wheel appears to be out of alignment, have your machine checked by a Kawasaki dealer or frame specialist.

9 If the front-to-back alignment is correct, the wheels still may be out of alignment vertically.

10 Using a plumb bob or spirit level, check the rear wheel to make sure it is vertical. To do this, hold the string of the plumb bob against the tyre upper sidewall and allow the weight to settle just off the floor. If the string touches both the upper and lower tyre sidewalls and is perfectly straight, the wheel is vertical. If it is not, adjust the stand until it is.

11 Once the rear wheel is vertical, check the front wheel in the same manner. If both wheels are not perfectly vertical, the frame and/or major suspension components are bent.

14 Front wheel

Removal

1 Support the motorcycle on an auxiliary stand so that the front wheel is off the ground. Always make sure the motorcycle is properly supported. If a support is being placed under the exhaust, remove the lower fairing (see Chapter 7).

2 Unscrew the caliper mounting bolts and

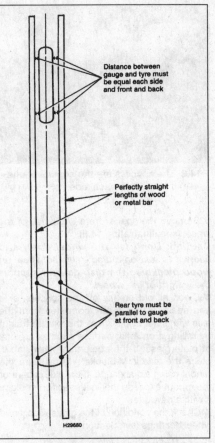

13.7 Wheel alignment check using a straight-edge

slide the calipers off the discs **(see illustration 2.1a or b)**. Tie the calipers back so that they are out of the way, making sure the hoses are not strained. Remove the locating dowels if loose. **Note:** *Do not operate the brakes with the calipers removed.*

3 Slacken the axle clamp bolts on the bottom of the left-hand fork, then unscrew the axle nut **(see illustration)**.

4 Slacken the axle clamp bolts on the bottom of the right-hand fork **(see illustration)**. Take the weight of the wheel, then push the axle through from the left-hand side and withdraw it from the right **(see illustration)**. Carefully lower the wheel and draw it forwards.

14.3 Slacken the axle clamp bolts (arrowed), then unscrew the axle nut

14.4a Slacken the axle clamp bolts (arrowed)...

14.4b ...then withdraw the axle and remove the wheel

14.8 The spacers are the same – fit one into each side

14.11 Counter-hold the axle head and tighten the nut to the specified torque

15.4 Unscrew the axle nut and remove the washer and the adjustment marker (arrowed)

5 Remove the spacer from each side of the wheel **(see illustration 14.8)**.
Caution: Don't lay the wheel down and allow it to rest on a disc – set the wheel on wood blocks so the disc doesn't support the weight of the wheel.
6 Clean all old grease off the spacers, axle and seals. Remove any corrosion from the axle with steel wool. Check the axle is straight by rolling it on a flat surface such as a piece of plate glass; if the equipment is available, place the axle in V-blocks and measure the runout using a dial gauge. If the axle is bent or the runout exceeds the limit specified, replace it with a new one.
7 Check the condition of the grease seals and wheel bearings (see Section 16).

Installation

8 Apply a smear of grease to the inside and outside of the wheel spacers. Fit the spacers into each side of the wheel **(see illustration)**. Apply a thin coat of grease to the axle.
9 Manoeuvre the wheel into position between the forks, making sure the directional arrows on the tyre and wheel are pointing in the normal direction of rotation.
10 Lift the wheel, making sure the spacers stay in place, and slide the axle in from the right **(see illustration 14.4b)**.
11 Fit the axle nut **(see illustration 14.3)**. Counter-hold the axle head and tighten the nut to the torque setting specified at the beginning of the Chapter **(see illustration)**.
12 Lower the front wheel to the ground. Place

a block of wood in front of the wheel so the bike can't roll forward. Pump the front forks a few times to settle the forks in position.
13 Tighten the axle clamp bolts on the bottom of the right-hand fork to the specified torque setting, then tighten the left-hand clamp bolts **(see illustrations 14.4a and 14.3)**.
14 Make sure the caliper locating dowels are fitted, then slide the calipers onto the discs, making sure the pads locate correctly on each side **(see illustration 2.17)**. Fit the caliper mounting bolts and tighten them to the torque setting specified at the beginning of the Chapter.
15 Apply the front brake a few times to bring the pads back into contact with the discs. Check the operation of the brake carefully before riding the bike.

15 Rear wheel

Removal

1 Support the motorcycle on an auxiliary stand or stands so that the rear wheel is off the ground. Always make sure the motorcycle is properly supported.
2 Unscrew the caliper mounting bolts and slide the caliper off the disc **(see illustration 6.1)**. Tie or support the caliper so it is out of the way, making sure the hose is not strained.
Note: *Do not operate the brake with the caliper removed.*

3 Create maximum slack in the chain (see Chapter 1, Section 1).
4 Unscrew the axle nut and remove the washer and the left-hand chain adjustment marker **(see illustration)**.
5 Push the wheel forwards and disengage the chain from the sprocket **(see illustration)**. Take the weight of the wheel, then withdraw the axle from the right-hand side, bringing the chain adjustment marker with it, and lower the wheel to the ground **(see illustration)**. If the axle is difficult to withdraw, drive it out using a soft mallet to prevent damage to the threads.
6 Draw the wheel back until the brake caliper bracket is clear of its guide on the swingarm, then remove the bracket **(see illustration)**. Remove the wheel.
Caution: Do not lay the wheel down and allow it to rest on the disc or the sprocket – set the wheel on wood blocks so neither the disc nor the sprocket supports the weight of the wheel.
7 Remove the spacer from each side of the wheel **(see illustrations 15.10a and b)**.
8 Clean all old grease of the spacers, axle and seals. Remove any corrosion from the axle using steel wool. Check the axle is straight by rolling it on a flat surface such as a piece of plate glass; if the equipment is available, place the axle in V-blocks and measure the runout using a dial gauge. If the axle is bent or the runout exceeds the limit specified, replace it with a new one.
9 Check the condition of the grease seals and wheel bearings (see Section 16).

15.5a Slip the chain off the sprocket

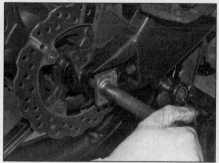

15.5b Withdraw the axle and lower the wheel

15.6 Draw the wheel back and displace the caliper bracket when clear

15.10a Fit the bevelled spacer...

15.10b ...and the plain spacer

15.13 Seat the axle head in the marker as shown

15.14 Make sure the marker is the correct way round

Installation

10 Apply a smear of grease to the inside and outside of the wheel spacers. Fit the bevel-edged spacer into the left-hand side and the plain-edge spacer into the right **(see illustrations)**. Apply a thin coat of grease to the axle.

11 Manoeuvre the wheel into position between the ends of the swingarm, making sure the directional arrows on the wheel and tyre are pointing in the normal direction of rotation. Slide the brake caliper bracket between the wheel and the swingarm and locate it in its guide **(see illustration 15.6)**.

12 Slide the right-hand chain adjustment marker onto the axle with the raised sections vertical and facing the axle head, and so the thicker edge faces forwards.

13 Lift the wheel into position and slide the axle in from the right, making sure the spacers and caliper bracket remain in place **(see illustration 15.5b)**. Align the flat edges

of the axle head vertically between the raised sections of the adjustment marker **(see illustration)**. Check that everything is correctly aligned.

14 Push the wheel forwards and fit the chain around the sprocket **(see illustration 15.5a)**. Fit the left-hand adjustment marker onto the end of the axle with the index lines vertical **(see illustration)**. Fit the washer and axle nut but leave it loose **(see illustration 15.4)**.

15 Refer to Chapter 1 and check and adjust the drive chain slack, then tighten the axle nut and fit a new split pin as described.

16 Slide the caliper onto the disc making sure the pads locate correctly on each side **(see illustration 6.15)**. Fit the caliper mounting bolts and tighten them to the torque setting specified at the beginning of the Chapter.

17 Apply the brake pedal a few times to bring the pads into contact with the disc. Check the operation of the brake carefully before riding the bike.

16 Wheel bearings

Note: *Always replace the wheel bearings in sets, never individually. Avoid using a high pressure cleaner on the wheel bearing area.*

Front wheel bearings

1 Remove the wheel (see Section 14). Support the wheel rim (not the discs) on wood blocks.

2 Inspect the seals and bearings – check that the bearing inner race turns smoothly and that the outer race is a tight fit in the hub (see *Tools and Workshop Tips* (Section 5) in the Reference Section). **Note:** *Do not remove the bearings unless they are going to be replaced with new ones.*

3 If new bearings are needed lever out the seal from each side of the hub using a flat-bladed

16.3 Lever out the bearing seals

16.4a Push the spacer aside...

16.4b ...to expose the inner race (arrowed)

screwdriver or a seal hook **(see illustration)**. Take care not to damage the hub. Discard the seals – new ones must be fitted.

4 Move the centre spacer to one side to expose the inner race of the lower bearing, then locate a drift on it and drive the bearing out **(see illustrations)**. If you can't get sufficient purchase, turn the wheel over and remove the bearing using an internal expanding puller with slide-hammer attachment, which can be obtained commercially – select the correct attachment and locate it behind the inner race of the bearing, then tighten the inner bolt to expand and lock the puller **(see illustration)**. Attach the slide-hammer, hold the wheel

firmly down and jar the bearing out **(see illustration)**. Having removed the first bearing, remove the spacer that fits between the bearings.

5 Turn the wheel over and remove the other bearing using a suitable drift (such as a socket on an extension) inserted from the opposite side to the bearing.

6 Thoroughly clean the hub area of the wheel with a suitable solvent and inspect the bearing housing for scoring and wear.

7 Drive the new bearings into the hub with the marked side facing outwards using a bearing driver or suitable socket **(see illustration)**. Make sure that the driver or socket bears only

on the outer race and the bearing fits squarely and all the way into its seat.

8 Turn the wheel over and fit the bearing spacer. Fit the second bearing in the same way as the first.

9 Fit the new seals into the hub using finger pressure or a socket on a piece of wood, setting them flush with the rim **(see illustration)**. Smear the seal lips with grease.

10 Clean the discs using brake system cleaner, then install the wheel (see Section 14).

Rear wheel bearings

11 Remove the wheel (see Section 15). Support the wheel rim (not the disc or

16.4c Drive the bearing out using a drift...

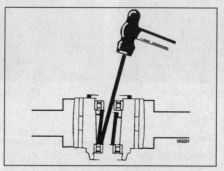

16.4d ...locating it as shown

16.4e Fit the attachment behind the bearing...

16.4f ...then fit the slide-hammer and jar the bearing out

16.7 Using a socket to drive the bearing in

16.9 Fit the seal, setting it flush with the rim

16.11a Lift the sprocket coupling off the wheel...

16.11b ...and remove the spacer

16.13 Lever out the bearing seal

sprocket) on wood blocks. Lift the sprocket coupling out of the hub and remove the spacer **(see illustrations)**.

12 Inspect the seal and the bearings in both sides of the hub – check that the bearing inner race turns smoothly and that the outer race is a tight fit in the hub (see *Tools and Workshop Tips* (Section 5) in the Reference section). **Note:** *Do not remove the bearings unless they are going to be replaced with new ones.*

13 If new bearings are needed lever out the seal from the right-hand side of the hub using a flat-bladed screwdriver or a seal hook **(see illustration)**. Take care not to damage the hub. Discard the seal – a new one must be fitted.

14 Move the centre spacer to one side to expose the inner race of the lower bearing, then locate a drift on it and drive the bearing out **(see illustrations 16.4a, b, c and d)**. If you can't get sufficient purchase, turn the wheel over and remove the bearing using an internal expanding puller with slide-hammer attachment – select the correct attachment and locate it behind the inner race of the bearing, then tighten the inner bolt to expand and lock the puller **(see illustration 16.4e)**. Attach the slide-hammer, hold the wheel firmly down and jar the bearing out **(see illustration 16.4f)**. Having removed the first bearing, remove the spacer that fits between the bearings.

15 Turn the wheel over and remove the other bearing using a suitable drift (such as a socket on an extension) inserted from the opposite side to the bearing.

16 Thoroughly clean the hub area of the wheel with a suitable solvent and inspect the bearing housing for scoring and wear.

17 Drive the new bearings into the hub with the marked side facing outwards using a bearing driver or suitable socket **(see illustration 16.7)**. Make sure that the driver or socket bears only on the outer race and the bearing fits squarely and all the way into its seat.

18 Turn the wheel over and fit the bearing spacer. Fit the second bearing in the same way as the first.

19 Fit the new seal it into the right-hand side of the hub using finger pressure or a socket on a piece of wood. Smear the seal lips with grease.

20 Check the sprocket coupling/rubber dampers (see Section 20). Check the condition of the hub O-ring and clean it or replace it with a new one if necessary **(see illustration)**. Smear the O-ring with oil. Fit the spacer into the sprocket coupling **(see illustration 16.11b)**. Fit the coupling into the wheel **(see illustration 16.11a)**. Clean the brake disc using acetone or brake system cleaner, then install the wheel (see Section 15).

Sprocket coupling bearing

21 Remove the wheel (see Section 15). Lift the sprocket coupling out of the hub and remove the spacer **(see illustrations 16.11a and b)**.

22 Inspect the seal and bearing – check that the bearing inner race turns smoothly and that the outer race is a tight fit in the coupling (see *Tools and Workshop Tips (Section 5)* in the Reference Section). **Note:** *Do not remove the bearing unless it is being replaced with a new one.*

23 If a new bearing is needed lever out the seal using a flat-bladed screwdriver or a seal hook **(see illustration)**. Take care not to damage the rim of the coupling. Discard the seal – a new one must be fitted.

24 Remove the circlip **(see illustration)**. Support the coupling on blocks of wood, sprocket side down, and drive the bearing out from the inside using a bearing driver or socket **(see illustration)**.

16.20 Fit a new O-ring if necessary

16.23 Lever out the bearing seal

16.24a Remove the circlip (arrowed)

16.24b Drive the bearing out from the inside

16.26 Using a socket to drive the bearing in

16.27 Press the new seal into the hub

25 Thoroughly clean the coupling with a suitable solvent and inspect the bearing housing for scoring and wear.

26 Drive the new bearing into the hub with the marked side facing outwards using a bearing driver or suitable socket **(see illustration)**. Make sure that the driver or socket bears only on the outer race and the bearing fits squarely and all the way into its seat. Fit the circlip, making sure it locates in the groove **(see illustration 16.24a)**.

27 Fit the new seal it into the coupling using finger pressure or a socket on a piece of wood **(see illustration)**. Smear the seal lips with grease.

28 Check the sprocket coupling/rubber dampers (see Section 20). Check the condition of the hub O-ring and clean it or replace it with a new one if necessary **(see illustration 16.20)**. Smear the O-ring with oil. Fit the spacer into the sprocket coupling **(see illustration 16.11b)**. Fit the coupling into the wheel **(see illustration 16.11a)**. Install the wheel (see Section 15).

17 Tyres

General information

1 The wheels are designed to take tubeless tyres only. Tyre sizes are given in the Specifications at the beginning of this chapter.

2 Refer to the *Pre-ride checks* listed at the beginning of this manual for tyre maintenance and pressures.

Fitting new tyres

3 When selecting new tyres, refer to the tyre information in the Owner's Handbook. Ensure that front and rear tyre types are compatible, the correct size and correct speed rating; if necessary seek advice from a Kawasaki dealer or tyre fitting specialist **(see illustration)**.

4 It is recommended that tyres are fitted by a motorcycle tyre specialist rather than attempted in the home workshop. This is particularly relevant in the case of tubeless tyres because the force required to break the seal between the wheel rim and tyre bead is substantial, and is

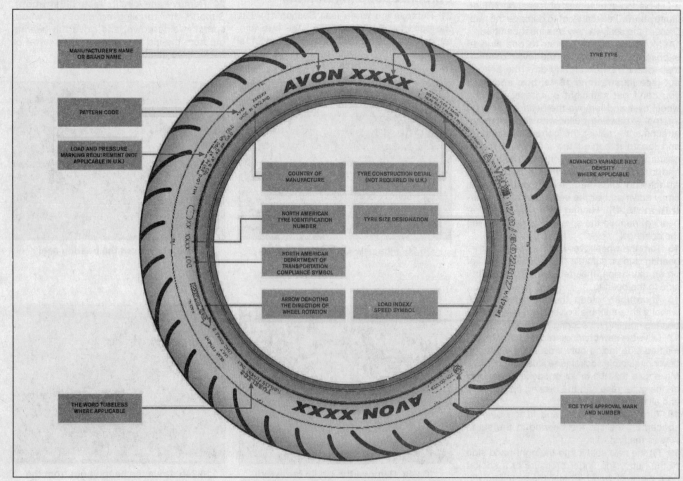

17.3 Common tyre sidewall markings

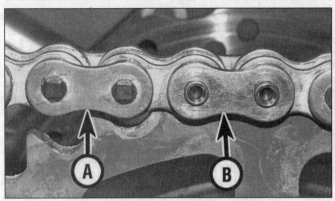

18.1 Standard chain link (A) and soft link (B)

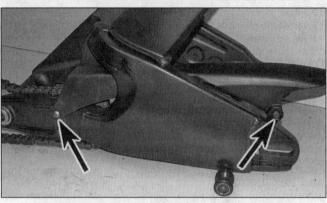

18.2 Chainguard screws (arrowed) – E/F model shown

usually beyond the capabilities of an individual working with normal tyre levers. Additionally, the specialist will be able to balance the wheels after tyre fitting.

5 Note that punctured tubeless tyres can in some cases be repaired. External repairs made using a repair kit should only ever be considered as a temporary measure to get you to a dealer for a new tyre, and riding at speed or with any extra load should be avoided. Internal repairs carried out by a motorcycle tyre fitting specialist are better. Make sure a wheel with a repaired tyre is balanced before it is fitted back on the bike. Kawasaki advise that a repaired tyre should not be used at speeds above 50 mph (80 kmh) for the first 24 hours, and not above 80 mph (130 kmh) thereafter, and carrying heavy loads should be avoided.

18 Drive chain

Note: *The drive chain has a staked-type soft link which can be disassembled using one of several commercially-available drive chain cutting/staking tools (but the cheap ones are best avoided) – Kawasaki recommend the RK Excel 70 or 90 (RK-700 or RK-90).. The soft link can be recognised by the staked ends of its two pins which look as if they have been deeply centre-punched, instead of peened over as with all the other pins.*

Removal

1 Support the motorcycle on an auxiliary stand so that the rear wheel is off the ground. Locate the soft link in a suitable position to work on by rotating the back wheel **(see illustration)**. Slacken the drive chain as described in Chapter 1.

2 If required, remove the chainguard **(see illustration)**.

3 Remove the front sprocket cover (see Section 19).

4 Split the chain at the soft link using the chain tool, following carefully the manufacturer's operating instructions (see also Section 8 in *Tools and Workshop Tips* in the Reference Section). Remove the chain from the bike, noting its routing through the swingarm.

Cleaning

5 Refer to Chapter 1, Section 1, for details of routine cleaning with the chain installed on the sprockets.

6 If the chain is extremely dirty remove it from the motorcycle and soak it in paraffin (kerosene) for approximately five or six minutes, then clean it using a soft brush. *Caution: Don't use petrol (gasoline), solvent or other cleaning fluids that might damage its internal sealing properties. Don't use high-pressure water. Remove the chain, wipe it off, then blow dry it with compressed air immediately. The entire process shouldn't take longer than ten minutes – if it does, the O-rings in the chain rollers could be damaged.*

Installation

⚠ *Warning: NEVER install a drive chain which uses a clip-type master (split) link. Use ONLY the correct service tools to secure the staked-type of master link – if you do not have access to such tools, have the chain replaced by a dealer service department to be sure of having it securely installed.*

7 Route the drive chain around the sprockets and through the swingarm, leaving the two ends mid-way between the sprockets along the bottom run.

8 Referring to Section 8 in *Tools and Workshop Tips* in the Reference Section, install the new soft link from the inside using new O-rings. Fit the new sideplate using new O-rings and with its identification marks facing out and press it on using the tool. Stake the new link using the tool, following carefully the instructions of both the chain manufacturer and the tool manufacturer. DO NOT re-use old soft link components.

9 After staking, check the soft link and staking for any signs of cracking **(see illustration)**. If there is any evidence of cracking, the link, O-rings and sideplate must be replaced. Check the width of the soft link by measuring from the outer side of each sideplate, and make sure it is within the measurements specified **(see illustration)**. Measure the diameter of the staked ends in two directions and check that it is evenly staked **(see illustration)**. Check that the link pivots freely.

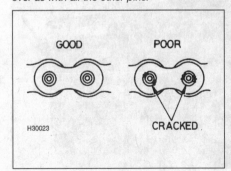

18.9a Check staking for any signs of cracking

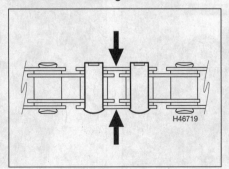

18.9b Check the width across the outer edges of the sideplates

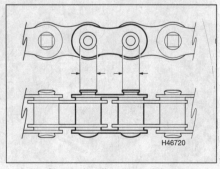

18.9c Check the diameter of the staked pin ends

10 Install the sprocket cover (see Section 19).
11 Install the chainguard if removed.
12 On completion, adjust and lubricate the chain following the procedures described in Chapter 1.

19 Sprockets
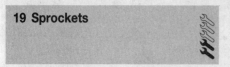

Front sprocket cover removal and installation

1 On C models unscrew the speed sensor bolt and displace it from the sprocket cover **(see illustration)**.
2 On D models remove the left-hand section of the lower fairing (see Chapter 7). Note the alignment of the punch mark on the gearchange shaft with the slit in the linkage arm clamp **(see illustration)**. Unscrew the linkage arm bolt and slide the arm off the shaft.
3 Unscrew the bolts and remove the cover, noting the dowels **(see illustration)**. On D, E and F models note the guide plate fitted in the cover and remove it if required **(see illustration 19.4)**. On C models a similar guide plate is secured to the crankcase by two bolts – remove it if required.
4 Clean all old road dirt and grease from the inside of the cover and from the guide plate. Fit the guide plate **(see illustration)**. Make sure the dowels are in place, then fit the cover and tighten its bolts.
5 On D models slide the gearchange linkage arm onto the shaft, aligning the punch mark with the slit in the clamp, then tighten the pinch bolt **(see illustration 19.2)**. Install the left-hand section of the lower fairing (see Chapter 7).
6 On C models clean the threads of the speed sensor bolt and apply some fresh threadlock.

Fit the sensor and tighten the bolt **(see illustration 19.1)**.

Sprocket check

7 Check the wear pattern on both sprockets (see Chapter 1, Section 1). If the sprocket teeth are worn excessively, replace the chain and both sprockets as a set. Whenever the sprockets are inspected, the drive chain should be inspected also (see Chapter 1). Always renew the chain and sprockets as a set – worn sprockets can ruin a new drive chain and *vice versa*.
8 Adjust and lubricate the chain following the procedures described in Chapter 1.

Sprocket removal and installation

Front sprocket

9 Remove the front sprocket cover (see Steps 1 to 3).

19.1 Speed sensor bolt (arrowed)

19.2 Note the alignment then unscrew the bolt and slide the arm off the shaft

19.3 Front sprocket cover bolts (arrowed) – E/F model shown

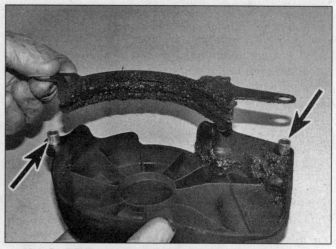

19.4 On D/E/F models seat the guide plate over the dowels (arrowed)

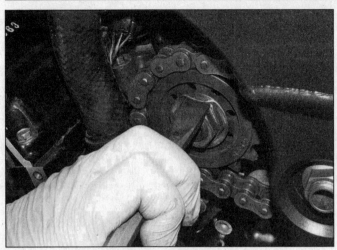

19.10 Bend the tab back off the nut

19.11 Unscrew the nut and remove the washer

10 Bend the raised tab on the lockwasher off the nut **(see illustration)**.

11 Shift the transmission into a high gear and have an assistant apply the rear brake, then unscrew the sprocket nut and remove the washer **(see illustration)**. Note that a new washer should be used on installation

12 Fully slacken the drive chain as described in Chapter 1. If the rear sprocket is being removed as well, remove the rear wheel now to give full slack (see Section 15).

13 Lift the chain off the sprocket and slide the sprocket off **(see illustration)**.

14 Engage the new sprocket with the chain, making sure the marked side is facing out, and slide it on the shaft **(see illustration 19.13)**.

15 If removed, fit the rear sprocket now, and install the wheel (see Section 15). Take up the slack in the chain.

16 Smear some molybdenum disulphide oil (a 50/50 mix of molybdenum disulphide grease and engine oil) onto the threads on the shaft and the seating surface of the nut. Fit the sprocket nut with a new washer **(see illustration 19.11)**. Tighten the nut to the torque setting specified at the beginning of

the Chapter, using the rear brake to prevent the sprocket turning.

17 Bend the lockwasher tab up against the nut **(see illustration)**.

18 Fit the sprocket cover (see Steps 3 and 4). Adjust and lubricate the chain following the procedures described in Chapter 1.

Rear sprocket

19 Remove the rear wheel (see Section 15). Support the wheel rim (not the disc) on some blocks of wood with the sprocket side up.

20 Unscrew the nuts and lift the sprocket off the studs.

21 Fit the sprocket onto the hub with the marked side facing out. Fit the nuts and tighten them evenly and in a criss-cross sequence to the torque setting specified at the beginning of the Chapter.

22 Install the rear wheel (see Section 15).

20 Rear sprocket coupling/ rubber dampers

1 Remove the rear wheel (see Section 15). Check for play between the sprocket coupling

and the wheel hub by turning the sprocket. Any play indicates worn rubber damper segments.

Caution: Do not lay the wheel down on the disc as it could become warped. Lay the wheel on wooden blocks so that the disc is off the ground.

2 Lift the sprocket coupling off the wheel leaving the rubber dampers in position **(see illustration 16.11a)**. Check the coupling for cracks or any obvious signs of damage.

3 Lift the rubber damper segments from the wheel and check them for cracks, hardening and general deterioration **(see illustration)**. Replace them with a new set if necessary.

4 Check the condition of the hub O-ring and clean it or replace it with a new one if necessary **(see illustration 16.20)**. Smear the O-ring with oil.

5 Checking and replacement procedures for the sprocket coupling bearing are in Section 16.

6 Installation is the reverse of removal. Make sure the spacer is in the coupling **(see illustration 16.11b)**. Align the coupling correctly with the rubber dampers and press it fully into the hub **(see illustration 16.11a)**.

7 Install the rear wheel (see Section 15).

19.13 Disengage the chain and draw the sprocket off the shaft

19.17 Bend the tab up against the nut

20.3 Check the rubber dampers as described

Chapter 7
Bodywork

Contents

Degrees of difficulty

Easy, suitable for novice with little experience

Fairly easy, suitable for beginner with some experience

Fairly difficult, suitable for competent DIY mechanic

Difficult, suitable for experienced DIY mechanic

Very difficult, suitable for expert DIY or professional

1 General information

This Chapter covers the procedures necessary to remove and install the bodywork.

In the case of damage to the bodywork, it is usually necessary to remove the broken component and replace it with a new (or used) one. The material that the body panels are composed of doesn't lend itself to conventional repair techniques, but there are some companies that specialise in 'plastic welding' and there are a number of bodywork repair kits now available for motorcycles.

When attempting to remove any body panel, first study it closely, noting any fasteners and associated fittings, to be sure of returning everything to its correct place on installation. Refer to Section 2 for more information on the types of trim clip used and how to release and refit them. In some cases the aid of an assistant may be useful when removing panels, to help avoid the risk of damage to paintwork. Once the evident fasteners have been removed, try to remove the panel as described but DO NOT FORCE IT – if it will not release the chances are a locating tab is stuck, but first check that all fasteners have been removed before trying again.

When installing a body panel, be sure of returning every fastener to its correct place. Check that all fasteners are in good condition, including the trim clips and damping/rubber mounts; replace any faulty fasteners with new ones before the panel is reassembled. Check also that all mounting brackets are straight and repair them or replace them with new ones if necessary before attempting to install the panel.

Make sure all locating tabs engage correctly with their related panel. Tighten the fasteners securely, but be careful not to overtighten any of them or the panel may break (not always immediately) due to the uneven stress.

2 Trim clips

1 Three types of plastic trim clip are used, so carefully note which fits where when removing the fairing panels.
2 The first type has a centre pin with a small

2.2a Push the centre pin (arrowed)...

2.2b ...into the body to release the clip

2.2c Push the centre pin out before installing the clip, then push it in when installed to lock it

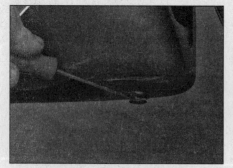

2.3a Lever the centre pin out...

2.3b ...then pull the body out of the panel

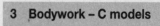

2.3c Fit the body into the panel then push the centre pin in

round head. To release them push the head of the pin into the body of the clip then draw the clip out of the panel (see illustration). To install them, push the centre pin fully out, then fit the body into its hole and push the centre pin in so that it is flush with the body (see illustrations). The clip should now be locked in place.

3 The second type has a centre pin with a large round head. To release them lever the head up using a small flat-bladed screwdriver inserted in the slot then draw the clip out of the panel (see illustrations). To install them, fit the body into its hole and push the centre

pin in so that it is flush with the body (see illustration). The clip should now be locked in place.

4 The third type has a centre pin with a Phillips screw head. To release them unscrew the centre pin using a screwdriver then pull the body of the clip out of the panel (see illustration). To install them, fit the body into its hole then screw the centre pin in so that it is flush with the body (see illustration). You can push the centre pin in instead of screwing it in, but as they are made of plastic the threads easily become worn in which case after a while the centre pin may not unscrew again.

If this happens, carefully lever the centre pin out of the body using a small screwdriver and replace the trim clip with a new one.

3 Bodywork – C models

Side covers

1 Undo the screw (see illustration 4.1).
2 Carefully pull the cover away to release the pegs from the grommets (see illustration 4.2).
3 Installation is the reverse of removal.

2.4a Undo the centre screw then pull the clip out

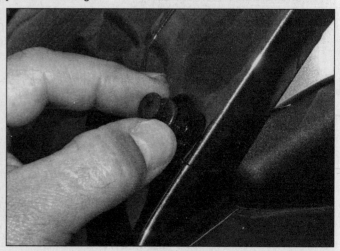

2.4b Fit the clip in the hole then push the centre in to lock it

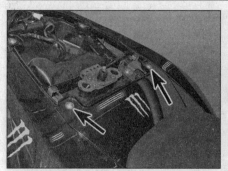

3.5a Undo the screws (arrowed)...

3.5b ...and draw the panel back

3.6 Unscrew the bolt (arrowed) and draw the seat back

Seats

Rider's seat removal

4 Remove the passenger seat (see Step 7).

5 Undo the screws securing the centre section of the seat cowling, then draw it back and up to release the tabs (see illustrations).

6 Unscrew the bolt, lift the rear of the seat and draw it back to disengage the tab from the tank bracket (see illustration).

Passenger seat removal

7 Insert the ignition key into the seat lock and turn it clockwise to unlock the seat (see illustration). Lift the front of the seat and draw it forward to disengage the tab from the bracket.

Installation

8 Installation is the reverse of removal. Make sure the tab on the front of the rider's seat locates correctly (see illustration). Make sure the tab at the back of the passenger seat locates correctly, and push down on the front to engage the latch (see illustration).

Seat cowling

9 Remove both seats.

10 Undo the screws securing the rear section of the cowling, then the Velcro patch at the back and release the hooks from their slots (see illustrations).

11 Disconnect the tail light, turn signal and licence plate light wiring connectors (see illustration).

3.7 Unlock and remove the seat

12 Unscrew the bolts and the nuts and remove the turn signal/licence plate assembly, drawing the wiring through the hole (see illustration).

3.8a Locate the tab under the bracket

3.8b Locate the hook around the bar

3.10a Undo the screws (arrowed)...

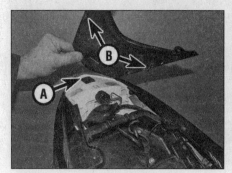

3.10b ...and release the Velcro patch (A) and the hooks (B)

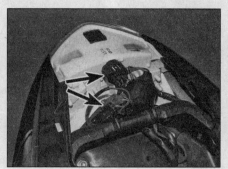

3.11 Disconnect all the wiring connectors

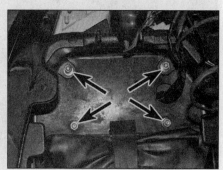

3.12 Turn signal/licence plate holder bolts and nuts (arrowed)

3.13 Undo the screws (arrowed)

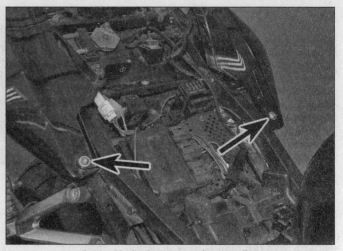

3.14a Undo the screws (arrowed)...

3.14b ...and remove the cowling

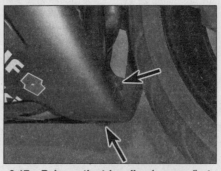

3.17a Release the trim clips (arrowed) at the front...

3.17b ...and at the back

13 Undo the seat lock screws **(see illustration)**.
14 Undo the two screws at the front and draw the cowling off the bike **(see illustrations)** – do not worry about the amount the cowling has to flex to be removed as it is designed to do so, but do not flex it more than necessary.
15 If required detach the seat lock cable. If required remove the tail light (see Chapter 8).

16 Installation is the reverse of removal.

Lower fairing panels

17 Release the five trim clips joining the two panels together **(see illustration)**.
18 Undo the screws securing the panel being removed **(see illustration)**.
19 Release the tabs from the other lower

fairing panel and from the fairing side panel.
20 Installation is the reverse of removal.

Fairing side panels

21 Remove the lower fairing panel.
22 Undo the five screws **(see illustration)**.
23 Carefully pull the panel away to release

3.18 Lower fairing panel screws (arrowed)

3.22 Fairing side panel screws (arrowed)

3.23a Release the pegs from the inner panel grommets…

3.23b …and the tabs from the slots in the fairing

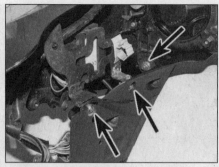

3.26 Undo the screws and nut (arrowed)

3.27 Release the panel and disconnect the wiring

3.29 Undo the screw (arrowed)…

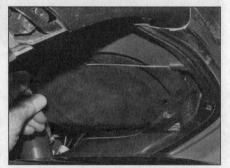

3.30 …then slide the panel back

the pegs from the grommets in the inner panel, and release the tabs from the fairing **(see illustrations)**.

24 Installation is the reverse of removal.

Fairing inner panels

25 Remove the fairing side panel.
26 Undo the two screws and the nut **(see illustration)**.
27 Carefully slide the panel rearwards to release the tabs and the peg from the grommet, then disconnect the turn signal wiring connector **(see illustration)**.
28 Installation is the reverse of removal.

Fairing centre panel

29 Undo the screw **(see illustration)**.
30 Carefully slide the panel rearwards to release the tabs from the headlight **(see illustration)**.
31 Installation is the reverse of removal.

Mirrors

32 Undo the nuts and remove the mirror **(see illustration)**.
33 Installation is the reverse of removal.

Windshield

34 Undo the six screws and remove the windshield, noting how the tabs locate **(see illustration)**.
35 Installation is the reverse of removal. Make sure the tabs locate correctly **(see illustration)** – the side tabs locate between the fairing and the bracket.

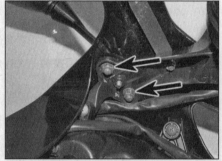

3.32 Mirror nuts (arrowed)

Fairing

36 Remove the fairing side panels and windshield (see above).
37 Unscrew the bolt on the left-hand side

3.35 Seat the front tab in the slot

3.34 Windshield screws (arrowed)

side to release the connector bracket and disconnect the front loom wiring connectors **(see illustration)**. Release the wiring clamp on each side.

3.37 Displace the bracket and disconnect the wiring

3.38 Unscrew the bolts (arrowed)...

3.39 ...and remove the fairing

38 Unscrew the three bolts on the top **(see illustration)**.

39 Draw the fairing forwards and remove it **(see illustration)**.

40 If required remove the mirrors and the inner and centre panels (see above). If required remove the instruments and headlight (see Chapter 8).

41 Installation is the reverse of removal.

Front mudguard

42 Undo the screws on each side, noting the washers **(see illustration 5.43a)**. Lift the mudguard up and release the brake hoses **(see illustrations 5.43b and c)**.

43 Installation is the reverse of removal.

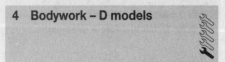

4 Bodywork – D models

Side covers

1 Undo the screw **(see illustration)**.

2 Carefully pull the cover away to release the pegs from the grommets **(see illustration)**.

3 Installation is the reverse of removal.

Seats

Rider's seat

4 Remove the side covers.

5 Unscrew the bolt on each side, lift the front of the seat and draw it forwards to disengage the tab at the back from the bracket **(see illustration 5.5)**.

Passenger seat

6 Insert the ignition key into the seat lock and turn it clockwise to unlock the seat **(see illustration)**. Lift the front of the seat and draw it forward to disengage the tab.

Installation

7 Installation is the reverse of removal. Make sure the tab on the back of the rider's seat locates correctly **(see illustration 5.7a)**. Make sure the tab at the back of the passenger seat locates correctly, and push down on the front to engage the latch **(see illustration)**.

Seat cowling

8 Remove both seats.

9 Disconnect the turn signal wiring connectors **(see illustration)**.

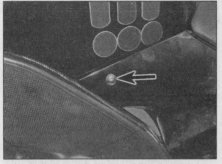

4.1 Undo the screw (arrowed)...

4.2 ...then pull the pegs from the grommets (arrowed)

4.6 Unlock and remove the seat

4.7 Locate the tab under the bracket

4.9 Disconnect the turn signal connectors (arrowed)

4.10a Release the trim clips (arrowed) on each side

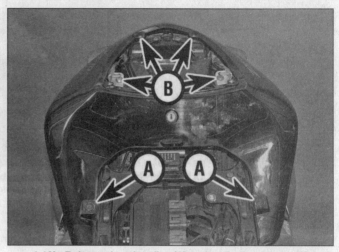

4.10b Release the trim clips (A) and undo the screws (B)

4.10c Draw the cowling back and disconnect the tail light connector...

4.10d ...and the cable

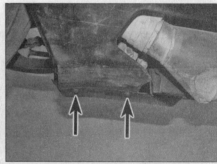

4.13a Undo the screws (arrowed)

10 Release the trim clips and undo the four screws **(see illustrations)**. Draw the cowling back and disconnect the tail light wiring connector and the seat lock cable **(see illustrations)**.

11 If required remove the tail light and turn signals (see Chapter 8).
12 Installation is the reverse of removal.

Lower fairing panels
13 Undo the screws on the underside at the back **(see illustration)**. Release the trim clips on the left-hand side and at the front **(see illustration)**.
14 Undo the screws securing the panel being removed **(see illustrations)**.

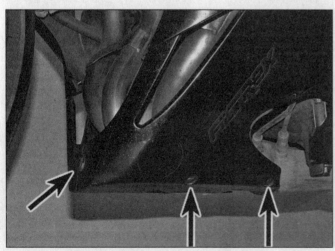

4.13b Release the trim clips (arrowed)

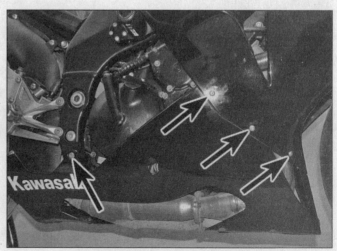

4.14 Undo the screws (arrowed)...

4.15a ...release the slot from the hook (arrowed)...

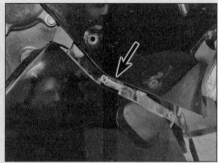

4.15b ...and the tab (arrowed) from the slot

4.19 Disconnect and release the wiring (arrowed)

15 Release the lower fairing panel from the fairing side panel **(see illustrations)**.
16 Installation is the reverse of removal.

Fairing side panels

17 Remove the lower fairing panel.
18 Remove the cockpit trim panel.
19 Disconnect the turn signal wiring

connector and free the wiring from the clamp **(see illustration)**.
20 Release the inner panel trim clips **(see illustration)**.
21 Undo the screws **(see illustration)**.
22 Carefully draw the panel back to release the tabs from the fairing.
23 Installation is the reverse of removal.

Fairing inner panels

24 Undo the two screws, release the trim clips and remove the panel **(see illustrations)**.
25 Installation is the reverse of removal.

Fairing centre panel

26 Remove the fairing.
27 Undo the screw, release the trim clips, and

4.20 Release the trim clips (arrowed)

4.21 Undo the screws (arrowed)

4.24a Undo the screws (arrowed)...

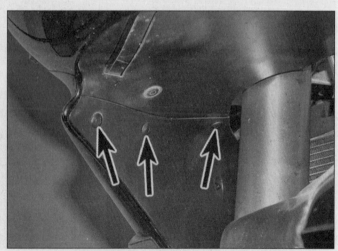

4.24b ...and release the trim clips (arrowed)

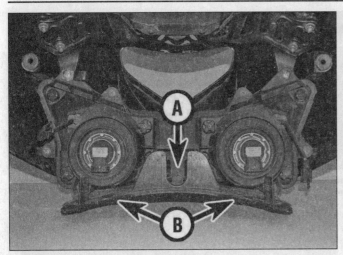

4.27 Undo the screw (A) and release the trim clips (B) on the underside

4.29a Undo the trim panel screws (arrowed)…

draw the panel back to release the tabs (see illustration).

28 Installation is the reverse of removal.

Cockpit trim panels

29 Undo the screws (see illustration). Also undo the fairing side panel rear screw to give more freedom of movement (see illustration).
30 Carefully draw the panel up to release the rear peg from the grommet, then draw the rear edge out from under the fairing side panel, then release the side hooks, then pull the front peg from its grommet (see illustrations).
31 Installation is the reverse of removal.

Mirrors

32 Remove the cockpit trim panel.
33 Undo the nuts and remove the mirror (see illustration).
34 Installation is the reverse of removal.

Windshield

35 Undo the six screws and remove the windshield, noting how the tab locates (see illustration).
36 Installation is the reverse of removal.

Fairing

37 Remove the fairing side panels and windshield (see above).

4.29b …and the side panel screw (arrowed)

4.30a Release the rear peg from the grommet (arrowed)…

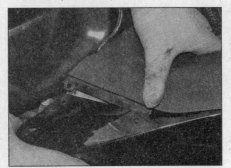

4.30b …then the rear edge…

4.30c …then the side tabs…

4.30d …then the front peg

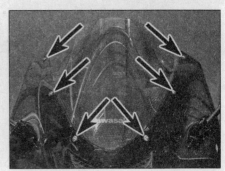

4.33 Mirror nuts (arrowed)

4.35 Windshield screws (arrowed)

4.38a Disconnect the instrument wiring connector...

4.38b ...and the headlight and sidelight connectors (arrowed) on each side...

4.38c ...and release the clamp (arrowed)

4.39 Unscrew the bolts (arrowed)...

4.40 ...and remove the fairing

5.1 Undo the screw (arrowed)...

38 Disconnect the instrument, headlight and sidelight wiring connectors, and release the wiring clamp on the left-hand side **(see illustrations)**.

39 Unscrew the three bolts on the top **(see illustration)**.

40 Draw the fairing forwards and remove it **(see illustration)**.

41 If required remove the mirrors (see above). If required remove the instruments and headlight (see Chapter 8).

42 Installation is the reverse of removal.

Front mudguard

43 Undo the screws on each side, noting the washers **(see illustration 5.43a)**. Lift the mudguard up and release the brake hoses **(see illustrations 5.43b and c)**.

44 Installation is the reverse of removal.

5 Bodywork – E and F models

Side covers

1 Undo the screw **(see illustration)**.

2 Carefully pull the cover away to release the Velcro patch in the centre and the peg from the grommet at the back **(see illustration)**.

3 Installation is the reverse of removal.

Seats

Rider's seat

4 Remove the side covers.

5 Unscrew the bolt on each side, lift the front of the seat and draw it forwards to disengage the tab at the back from the bracket **(see illustration)**.

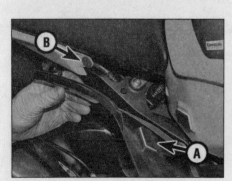

5.2 ...then release the Velcro (A) and pull the peg from the grommet (B)

5.5 Unscrew the bolt (arrowed) on each side and draw the seat back

5.6 Unlock and remove the seat

5.7a Locate the tab under the bracket

5.7b Locate the hook around the bar

Passenger seat

6 Insert the ignition key into the seat lock and turn it clockwise to unlock the seat **(see illustration)**. Lift the front of the seat and draw it forward to disengage the tab.

Installation

7 Installation is the reverse of removal. Make sure the tabs on the back of the rider's seat locate correctly **(see illustration)**. Make sure the tab at the back of the passenger seat locates correctly, and push down on the front to engage the latch **(see illustration)**.

Seat cowlings

8 Remove both seats.
9 Undo the two screws securing the centre section then lift it up to release the hooks **(see illustrations)**.
10 Release the trim clip and undo the screw **(see illustrations)**.
11 Carefully pull the front away to release the peg from the grommet, then disengage the tabs at the back **(see illustrations)**.
12 Installation is the reverse of removal.

Lower fairing panels

13 Release the trim clips at the front **(see illustration)**.

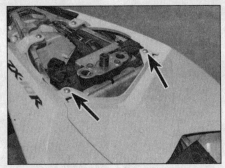

5.9a Undo the screws (arrowed)…

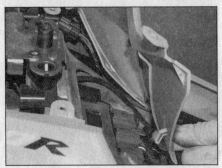

5.9b …and release the hooks

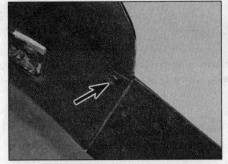

5.10a Release the trim clip (arrowed)…

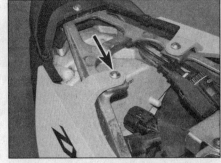

5.10b …and undo the screw (arrowed)

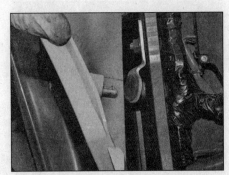

5.11a Release the peg at the front and the tabs…

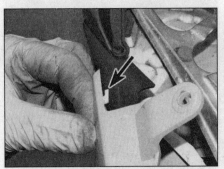

5.11b …and the hook (arrowed) at the back

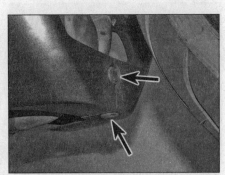

5.13 Release the trim clips (arrowed)

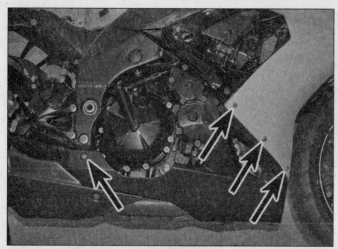

5.14 Undo the screws (arrowed)...

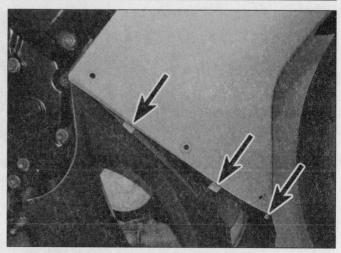

5.15 ...and release the tabs (arrowed)

5.17 Undo the screws (arrowed)...

5.18 ...and release the tabs

14 Undo the screws securing the panel being removed (see illustration).
15 Release the lower fairing panel from the fairing side panel (see illustration).
16 Installation is the reverse of removal.

Fairing side covers (E models)

17 Undo the three screws (see illustration).
18 Carefully draw the panel back to release the tabs from the fairing (see illustration).
19 Installation is the reverse of removal.

Cockpit trim panels

20 Undo the screw(s) (see illustration).
21 Carefully pull the panel in to release the grommet from the peg, then draw it back to release the tab(s) at the front (see illustrations).

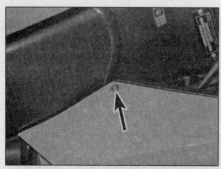

5.20 Cockpit trim panel screw (arrowed) – E models shown, F models also have two at the front

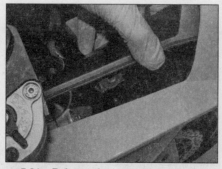

5.21a Release the grommet from the peg ...

5.21b ...and the tab(s) at the front from the slot(s) (arrowed) – E model shown

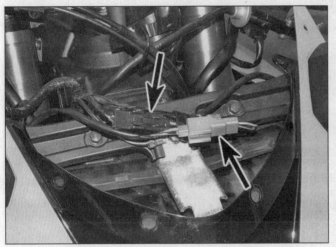

5.24 Turn signal wiring connectors (arrowed)

5.25 Mirror nuts (arrowed)

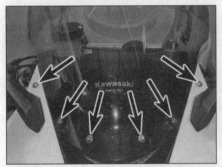

5.28a Undo the screws (arrowed)...

5.28b ...and draw the windshield back, noting how it locates

5.35a Disconnect the wiring and release the clamp (arrowed) on each side...

22 Installation is the reverse of removal.

Mirrors

23 Remove the instruments (see Chapter 8).
24 Release and disconnect the turn signal wiring connectors (see illustration).
25 Undo the nuts and remove the mirror, taking care as you draw the wiring through (see illustration).
26 Remove the turn signal if required.
27 Installation is the reverse of removal.

Windshield

28 Undo the six screws and remove the windshield, noting how it seats in relation to the fairing (see illustration).
29 Installation is the reverse of removal.

Fairing assembly

30 Remove the lower fairing panels.
31 Remove the cockpit trim panels.
32 On E models remove the fairing side covers.
33 Remove the instruments (see Chapter 8).

34 Where fitted displace the immobiliser amplifier (see Chapter 4).
35 Disconnect the headlight and sidelight wiring connectors, and release the wiring clamp on each side (see illustration). Release the wiring loom clip on each side (see illustration).
36 Release and disconnect the turn signal wiring connectors (see illustration 5.24).
37 Carefully pull the lower end away to release the peg from the grommet (see illustration).
38 Unscrew the three bolts on the top, noting the earth wire and clamp, and remove the bracket (see illustrations).

5.35b ...and release the clips

5.37 Release the peg (arrowed) on each side

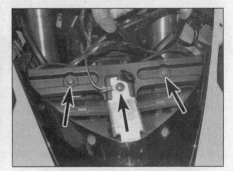

5.38a Unscrew the bolts (arrowed)...

5.38b ...and remove the bracket, noting the clamp and earth wire...

5.39 ...and remove the fairing

5.41a Release all the trim clips (arrowed) on both sides...

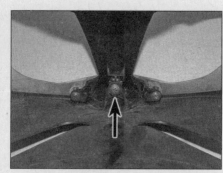

5.41b ...and undo the centre screw (arrowed)

39 Draw the fairing forwards and remove it (see illustration).
40 If required remove the mirrors. If required remove the headlight (see Chapter 8).
41 If required release the trim clips, undo the screw, release the tabs and remove the inner panel (see illustrations).
42 Installation is the reverse of removal.

Front mudguard

43 Undo the screws on each side, noting the washers (see illustration). Lift the mudguard up and release the brake hoses (see illustrations).
44 Installation is the reverse of removal.

5.43a Undo the screws (arrowed)...

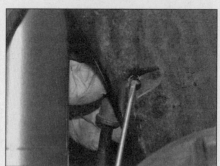

5.43b ...release the hose clips...

5.43c ...and remove the mudguard

Chapter 8
Electrical system

Contents

Degrees of difficulty

Easy, suitable for novice with little experience 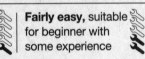	**Fairly easy,** suitable for beginner with some experience	**Fairly difficult,** suitable for competent DIY mechanic	**Difficult,** suitable for experienced DIY mechanic	**Very difficult,** suitable for expert DIY or professional

Specifications

Battery

Type	YT12B-BS
Capacity	12 V, 10 Ah
Voltage	
Fully-charged	12.8 to 13.2 V
Uncharged	below 12.4 V
Charging rate	
Normal	1.2 A for 5 to 10 hrs
Quick	5 A for 1 hr
Current leakage	2 mA (max)

Charging system

Regulated voltage output	14.2 to 15.2 V
Unregulated voltage output	
C models	min. 42 V @ 4000 rpm
D models	min. 60 V @ 4000 rpm
E and F models	min. 46 V @ 4000 rpm
Alternator stator coil resistance	
C models	0.05 to 0.5 ohm
D, E and F models	0.1 to 0.2 ohm

Starter motor

Brush length

  C models

    Standard . . . . 7.0 mm

    Service limit (min) . . . . 3.5 mm

  D models, E and F models up to engine No. ZXT00D043311

    Standard . . . . 10.0 mm

    Service limit (min) . . . . 5.0 mm

  E and F models from engine No. ZXT00D043312

    Standard . . . . 12.0 mm

    Service limit (min) . . . . 6.5 mm

Commutator diameter

  C models

    Standard . . . . 24 mm

    Service limit (min) . . . . 23 mm

  D models, E and F models up to engine No. ZXT00D043311

    Standard . . . . 28 mm

    Service limit (min) . . . . 27 mm

Fuses

Fuse numbers relate to wiring diagrams

C models

  Main fuse . . . . 30 A

  Fan fuse (1) . . . . 15 A

  ECU fuse (2) . . . . 15 A

  Turn signal relay fuse (3) . . . . 10 A

  Healight fuse (4) . . . . 10 A

  Tail light fuse (5) . . . . 10 A

  Ignition fuse (6) . . . . 10 A

  Horn fuse (7) . . . . 10 A

D models

  Main fuse . . . . 30 A

  Oxygen sensor heater fuse (Europe) (1) . . . . 10 A

  Fan fuse (2) . . . . 15 A

  ECU fuse (3) . . . . 15 A

  Turn signal relay fuse (4) . . . . 10 A

  Healight fuse (5) . . . . 10 A

  Tail light fuse (6) . . . . 10 A

  Ignition fuse (7) . . . . 15 A

  Horn fuse (8) . . . . 10 A

E and F models

  Main fuse . . . . 30 A

  Oxygen sensor heater fuse (Europe) (1) . . . . 10 A

  Fan fuse (2) . . . . 15 A

  ECU fuse (3) . . . . 10 A

  Turn signal relay fuse (4) . . . . 10 A

  Healight fuse (5) . . . . 15 A

  Tail light fuse (6) . . . . 10 A

  Ignition fuse (7) . . . . 15 A

  Horn fuse (8) . . . . 10 A

Bulbs

Headlights

  C models

    High beam . . . . 55 W H7

    Low beam . . . . 55 W H7

  D, E and F models

    High beam . . . . 65 W H9

    Low beam . . . . 55 W H11

Sidelights . . . . 5 W x 2

Brake/tail light . . . . LED

Licence plate light . . . . 5 W

Turn signal lights

  C, E and F models . . . . 10 W x 4

  D models . . . . 21 W x 4

Instrument and warning lights . . . . LED

Torque settings

Alternator
  C models
    Cover bolts . . . .   25 Nm
    Shaft clamp mounting bolt . . . .   25 Nm
    Shaft clamp pinch bolt . . . .   12 Nm
    Shaft spring bolt . . . .   10 Nm
    Stator bolts . . . .   8 Nm
  D, E and F models
    Alternator cover bolts . . . .   10 Nm
    Alternator rotor bolt
      Initial setting . . . .   70 Nm
      Final setting . . . .   155 Nm
    Alternator stator bolts . . . .   12 Nm
    Wiring clamp bolt . . . .   10 Nm
Oil pressure switch . . . .   15 Nm
Starter motor mounting bolts . . . .   10 Nm

1 General information

All models have a 12 volt electrical system charged by a three-phase alternator with a separate regulator/rectifier.

The regulator maintains the charging system output within the specified range to prevent overcharging, and the rectifier converts the ac (alternating current) output of the alternator to dc (direct current) to power the lights and other components and to charge the battery. On C models the alternator is mounted on the top of the crankcase. On all other models the alternator rotor is mounted on the left-hand end of the crankshaft.

The starter motor is mounted on the top of the crankcase. The starting system includes the motor, the battery, the relay and the various wires and switches. Some of the switches are part of a starter interlock system that prevents the engine from being started if the sidestand is down and the engine is in gear. The engine can be started with the sidestand up when it is in gear as long as the clutch lever is pulled in. The system will also cut the engine should the sidestand extend while the engine is running and in gear – see Chapter 1 for further information and checks on the system.

Note: *Keep in mind that electrical parts, once purchased, often cannot be returned. To avoid unnecessary expense, make very sure the faulty component has been positively identified before buying a replacement part.*

2 Electrical system fault finding

1 A typical electrical circuit consists of an electrical component, the switches, relays, etc, related to that component and the wiring and connectors that link the component to the battery and the frame.

2 Before tackling any troublesome electrical circuit, first study the wiring diagram thoroughly to get a complete picture of what makes up that individual circuit. Trouble spots can often be located by noting if other components related to that circuit are operating properly or not. If several components or circuits fail at one time, chances are the fault lies either in the fuse or in a common earth (ground) connection, as several circuits are often routed through the same fuse and earth (ground) connections **(see illustration)**.

3 Electrical problems often stem from simple causes, such as loose or corroded connections or a blown fuse. Prior to any electrical fault finding, always visually check the condition of the fuse, wires and connections in the problem circuit. Intermittent failures can be especially frustrating, since you can't always duplicate the failure when it's convenient to test. In such situations, a good practice is to clean all connections in the affected circuit, whether or not they appear to be good – where possible use a dedicated electrical cleaning spray along with sandpaper, wire wool or other abrasive material to remove corrosion, and a dedicated electrical protection spray to prevent further problems. All of the connections and wires should also be wiggled to check for looseness that can cause intermittent failure.

4 If you don't have a multimeter it is highly advisable to obtain one – they are not expensive and will enable a full range of electrical tests to be made **(see illustration)**. Go for a modern digital one with an LCD display, as they are easier to use. A continuity tester and/or test light are useful for certain electrical checks as an alternative, though are limited in their usefulness compared to a multimeter **(see illustrations)**.

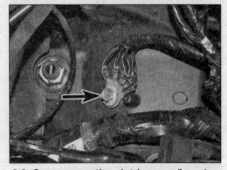

2.2 Common earth point (arrowed) – raise the fuel tank to check it

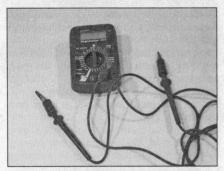

2.4a A digital multimeter can be used for all electrical tests

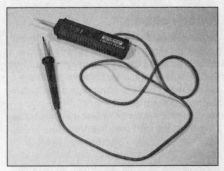

2.4b A battery-powered continuity tester

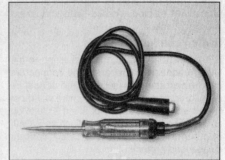

2.4c A simple test light is useful for voltage tests

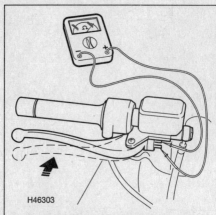

2.10 Continuity should be indicated across switch terminals when lever is operated

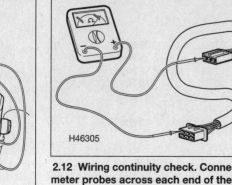

2.12 Wiring continuity check. Connect the meter probes across each end of the same wire

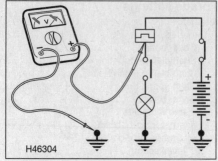

2.15 Voltage check. Connect the meter positive probe to the component and the negative probe to earth

Continuity checks

5 The term continuity describes the uninterrupted flow of electricity through an electrical circuit. Continuity can be checked with a multimeter set either to its continuity function (a beep is emitted when continuity is found), or to the resistance (ohms / Ω) function, or with a dedicated continuity tester. Both instruments are powered by an internal battery, therefore the checks are made with the ignition OFF. As a safety precaution, always disconnect the battery negative (-) lead before making continuity checks, particularly if ignition switch checks are being made.

6 If using a multimeter, select the continuity function if it has one, or the resistance (ohms) function. Touch the meter probes together and check that a beep is emitted or the meter reads zero, which indicates continuity. If there is no continuity there will be no beep or the meter will show infinite resistance. After using the meter, always switch it OFF to conserve its battery.

7 A continuity tester can be used in the same way – its light should come on or it should beep to indicate continuity in the switch ON position, but should be off or silent in the OFF position.

8 Note that the polarity of the test probes doesn't matter for continuity checks, although care should be taken to follow specific test procedures if a diode or solid-state component is being checked.

Switch continuity checks

9 If a switch is at fault, trace its wiring to the wiring connectors. Separate the connectors and inspect them for security and condition. A build-up of dirt or corrosion here will most likely be the cause of the problem – clean up and apply a water dispersant such as WD40, or alternatively use a dedicated contact cleaner and protection spray.

10 If using a multimeter, select the continuity function if it has one, or the resistance (ohms) function, and connect its probes to the terminals in the connector (see illustration). Simple ON/OFF type switches, such as brake light switches, only have two wires whereas combination switches, like the handlebar switches, have many wires. Study the wiring diagram to ensure that you are connecting to the correct pair of wires. Continuity should be indicated with the switch ON and no continuity with it OFF.

Wiring continuity checks

11 Many electrical faults are caused by damaged wiring, often due to incorrect routing or chaffing on frame components. Loose, wet or corroded wire connectors can also be the cause of electrical problems.

12 A continuity check can be made on a single length of wire by disconnecting it at each end and connecting the meter or continuity tester probes to each end of the wire (see illustration). Continuity (low or no resistance – 0 ohms) should be indicated if the wire is good. If no continuity (high resistance) is shown, suspect a broken wire.

13 To check for continuity to earth in any earth wire connect one probe of your meter or tester to the earth wire terminal in the connector and the other to the frame, engine, or battery earth (-) terminal. Continuity (low or no resistance – 0 ohms) should be indicated if the wire is good. If no continuity (high resistance) is shown, suspect a broken wire or corroded or loose earth point (see below).

Voltage checks

14 A voltage check can determine whether power is reaching a component. Use a multimeter set to the dc voltage scale, or a test light. The test light is the cheaper component, but the meter has the advantage of being able to give a voltage reading.

15 Connect the meter or test light in parallel, i.e. across the load (see illustration).

16 First identify the relevant wiring circuit by referring to the wiring diagram at the end of this manual. If other electrical components share the same power supply (i.e. are fed from the same fuse), take note whether they are working correctly – this is useful information in deciding where to start checking the circuit.

17 If using a meter, check first that the meter leads are plugged into the correct terminals on the meter (red to positive (+), black to negative (-). Set the meter to the dc volts function, where necessary at a range suitable for the battery voltage – 0 to 20 vdc. Connect the meter red probe (+) to the power supply wire and the black probe to a good metal earth (ground) on the bike's frame or directly to the battery negative terminal. Battery voltage should be shown on the meter with the ignition switch, and if necessary any other relevant switch, ON.

18 If using a test light, connect its positive (+) probe to the power supply terminal and its negative (-) probe to a good earth (ground) on the bike's frame. With the switch, and if necessary any other relevant switch, ON, the test light should illuminate.

19 If no voltage is indicated, work back towards the fuse continuing to check for voltage. When you reach a point where there is voltage, you know the problem lies between that point and your last check point.

Earth (ground) checks

20 Earth connections are made either directly to the engine or frame via the mounting of the component, or by a separate wire into the earth circuit of the wiring harness. Alternatively a short earth wire is sometimes run from the component directly to the bike's frame.

21 Corrosion is a common cause of a poor earth connection, as is a loose earth terminal fastener.

22 If total or multiple component failure is experienced, check the security of the main earth lead from the negative (-) terminal of the battery, the earth lead bolted to the engine, and the main earth point(s) on the frame (see illustration 2.2). If corroded, dismantle the connection and clean all surfaces back to bare metal. Remake the connection and prevent further corrosion from forming by smearing battery terminal grease over the connection.

23 To check the earth of a component, use an insulated jumper wire to temporarily bypass its

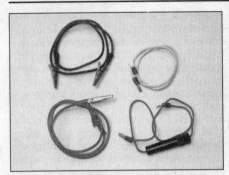

2.23 A selection of insulated jumper wires

3.2 Unscrew the bolts (arrowed)

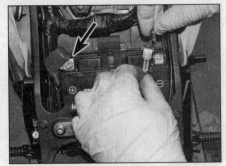

3.3 Disconnect the negative lead first then disconnect the positive lead (arrowed)

earth connection **(see illustration)** – connect one end of the jumper wire to the earth terminal or metal body of the component and the other end to the bike's frame. If the circuit works with the jumper wire installed, the earth circuit is faulty.

24 To check an earth wire first check for corroded or loose connections, then check the wiring for continuity (Step 13) between each connector in the circuit in turn, and then to its earth point, to locate the break.

3 Battery removal and maintenance

Caution: Be extremely careful when handling or working around the battery. The electrolyte is very caustic and an explosive gas (hydrogen) is given off when the battery is charging.

Removal and installation

1 Make sure the ignition is switched OFF.
2 Remove the rider's seat (see Chapter 7). On C models unscrew the fuel tank bracket bolts **(see illustration)**. On D models displace the relay box **(see illustration 6.3b)**.
3 Unscrew the negative (–) terminal bolt first and disconnect the lead from the battery **(see illustration)**. Lift up the red insulating cover to access the positive (+) terminal, then unscrew the bolt and disconnect the lead.
4 Release the retaining strap then lift the battery out **(see illustrations)** – on C models

lift the back of the fuel tank a little for clearance.
5 Installation is the reverse of removal. Clean the battery terminals and lead ends with a wire brush, emery paper or steel wool. Reconnect the leads, connecting the positive (+) terminal first.

> **HAYNES HiNT** *Battery corrosion can be kept to a minimum by applying a layer of battery terminal grease or petroleum jelly (Vaseline) to the terminals after the leads have been connected. DO NOT use a mineral based grease.*

Inspection and maintenance

6 The battery is of the maintenance free (sealed) type, therefore requiring no regular maintenance. However, the following checks should still be performed.
7 Check the state of charge by measuring the voltage at the battery terminals **(see illustration)**. Connect the voltmeter positive (+) probe to the battery positive (+) terminal, and the negative (–) probe to the battery negative (–) terminal. When fully-charged there should be 12.8 to 13.2 volts present. If the voltage falls below 12.4 volts remove the battery (see above), and recharge it as described in Section 4.
8 Check the battery terminals and leads are tight and free of corrosion. If corrosion is evident, clean the terminals as described

in Step 5, then protect them from further corrosion (see **Haynes Hint**).
9 Keep the battery case clean to prevent current leakage, which can discharge the battery over a period of time (especially when it sits unused). Wash the outside of the case with a solution of baking soda and water. Rinse the battery thoroughly, then dry it.
10 Look for cracks in the case and replace the battery with a new one if any are found. If acid has been spilled on the frame or battery box, neutralise it with a baking soda and water solution, then dry it thoroughly.
11 If the motorcycle sits unused for long periods of time, disconnect the leads from the battery terminals, negative (–) terminal first. Refer to Section 4 and charge the battery once every month to six weeks.

4 Battery charging

Caution: Be extremely careful when handling or working around the battery. The electrolyte is very caustic and an explosive gas (hydrogen) is given off when the battery is charging.

1 Remove the battery (see Section 3). Connect the charger to the battery, making sure that the positive (+) lead on the charger is connected to the positive (+) terminal on the battery, and the negative (–) lead is connected to the negative (–) terminal.
2 Kawasaki recommend that the battery is

3.4a Release the strap...

3.4b ...and remove the battery

3.7 Checking battery voltage

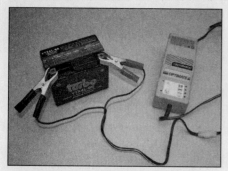

4.2 Battery connected to a charger

5.2a Starter relay (arrowed – C/D model shown)

5.2b Disconnect the wiring connector to access the main fuse (arrowed – E/F model shown)

5.2c Draw the relay out...

5.2d ...and displace the holder to access the spare (arrowed)

5.3a Fuseboxes (arrowed) – C models

5.3b Fuseboxes (arrowed) – D models

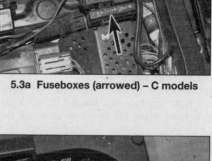

5.3c Fuseboxes (arrowed) – E/F models

5.3d Unclip the lid to access the fuses

charged at the normal rate specified at the beginning of the Chapter. A higher 'quick charge' rate that can be used if absolutely necessary is also specified, but note that exceeding this could cause the battery to overheat, buckling the plates and rendering it useless. If a normal domestic charger is used check that after a possible initial peak, the charge rate falls to a safe level. If the battery becomes hot during charging **stop**. Further charging will cause damage. Note that there are many bike-specific chargers available from good suppliers that are designed for the maintenance and recovery of motorcycle batteries, in particular catering for the requirements of heavily discharged MF batteries **(see illustration)**. They are a worthwhile investment, especially if the bike is not used over winter. Follow the manufacturer's instructions.

3 If the recharged battery discharges rapidly when left disconnected it is likely that an internal short caused by physical damage or sulphation has occurred. A new battery will be required. A sound item will tend to lose its charge at about 1% per day.

4 Install the battery (see Section 3).

5 If the motorcycle sits unused for long periods of time, charge the battery once every month to six weeks and leave it disconnected, or use a trickle charger.

5 Fuses

1 The electrical system as a whole is protected by the main fuse, and individual circuits are protected by other fuses of different ratings.

2 The main fuse is housed in the starter relay – to access it remove the fuel tank (see Chapter 4) **(see illustration)**. Disconnect the wiring connector **(see illustration)**. A spare main fuse is hosed in the bottom of the starter relay holder – to access it draw the relay out then lift the holder off the bracket **(see illustrations)**.

3 All other fuses are housed in two fuseboxes, located under the rider's seat **(see illustrations)**. The location, identity and rating of each fuse are marked on the box lid. Unclip the lid to access the fuses **(see illustrations)**. A spare fuse of each rating is provided.

4 The fuses can be removed and checked visually – if you can't pull the fuse out with your fingertips, use a pair of suitable pliers **(see illustration)**. A blown fuse is easily identified by a break in the element **(see illustration)**, but if there is any doubt check the fuse for continuity (see Section 2). Each fuse is clearly marked with its rating and must only be replaced by a fuse of the correct rating. If a spare fuse is used, always replace it with a new one so that a spare of each rating is carried on the bike at all times.

⚠️ *Warning: Never put in a fuse of a higher rating or bridge the terminals with any other substitute, however temporary it may be. Serious damage may be done to the circuit, or a fire may start.*

5 If the new fuse blows immediately check the wiring circuit very carefully for evidence of a short-circuit. Look for bare wires and chafed, melted or burned insulation.

6 Occasionally a fuse will blow or cause an open-circuit for no obvious reason. Corrosion of the fuse ends and fusebox terminals may occur and cause poor fuse contact. If this happens, remove the corrosion with a wire brush or emery paper, then spray the fuse end and terminals with electrical contact cleaner.

5.4a Pull the fuse out

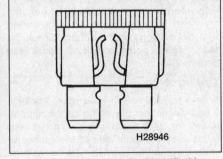

5.4b A blown fuse can be identified by a break in its element

6 Lighting system check

Note: *Refer to electrical system fault finding in Section 2 and to the wiring diagram for your model at the end of this Chapter.*
1 If a light fails first check the bulb (see relevant Section), and the bulb terminals in the connector or holder. If none of the lights work, check the battery (see Section 3). Low battery voltage indicates either a faulty battery or a defective charging system. Refer to Section 3 for battery checks and Section 28 for charging system tests. Also, check the fuses (Section 5) – if there is more than one problem at the same time, it is likely to be a fault relating to a multi-function component, such as one of the fuses governing more than one circuit, or the ignition switch. When checking for a blown filament in a bulb, it is advisable to back up a visual check with a continuity test as it is not always apparent that a bulb has blown.

Headlights
2 All models have two single filament bulbs – one bulb works on LO beam and both bulbs work on HI beam. If one headlight beam fails to work, first check the bulb (see Section 7). If both headlight beams fail to work,

first check the fuse (see Section 5), and then the bulbs (see Section 7), and then the relay (Step 3-on). If the HI beam does not work the problem could be in the dimmer switch. If they are good, the problem lies in the wiring or connectors – refer to Section 2 for continuity testing procedures, and also to the wiring diagrams at the end of this Chapter.

3 To test the relay, on C and D models remove the rider's seat (see Chapter 7). On E and F models remove the centre section of the seat cowling (see Chapter 7). Draw the relay box out of its rubber holder and disconnect the wiring connectors **(see illustrations)**.

4 Set a multimeter to the ohms x 1 scale and connect its probes to terminals 11 and 16 on the relay box on C models, and to terminals 1 and 3 on all other models **(see illustrations)**. There should be no continuity (infinite resistance). If not, replace the relay box with a new one.

5 If the relay tests are good, the problem

6.3a Relay box (arrowed) – C models

6.3b Relay box – D models

6.3c Relay box – E/F models

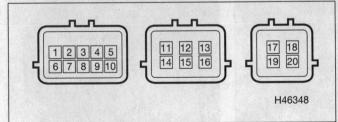

6.4a Relay test terminal ID – C models

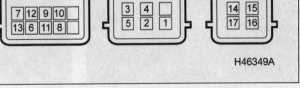

6.4b Relay test terminal ID – D/E/F models

could lie elsewhere in the starter circuit – the purpose of the relay is to turn the headlights out when the bike is being started to avoid overloading the battery. Check the starter safety circuit relay and diodes (see Section 23).

Tail light

6 If the tail light fails to work, refer to Section 9 and disconnect the wiring connector, and check for battery voltage at the red wire terminal on the loom side of the connector with the ignition switch ON. If voltage is present check for continuity to earth (ground) in the black/yellow wire from the wiring connector. If no voltage is indicated, check the wiring and connectors between the connector and the fuse box. Refer to the wiring diagrams at the end of this Chapter.

7 If the power, wiring and connectors are good, or if only one or some of the tail light LEDs have failed leaving others working, then the tail light unit is faulty and must be replaced with a new one – individual LEDs are not available.

Brake light

8 If the brake light fails to work, refer to Section 9 and disconnect the tail light wiring connector, and check for battery voltage at the blue/red wire terminal on the loom side of the connector, first with the front brake lever on, then with the rear brake pedal on. If voltage is present with one brake on but not the other,

then the switch or its wiring is faulty. If voltage is present in both cases, check for continuity to earth (ground) in the black/yellow wire from the wiring connector. If no voltage is indicated, check the wiring and connectors between the brake light and the brake switches, and the fusebox, then check the switches themselves (Section 14).

9 If the power, wiring and connectors are good, or if only one or some of the brake light LEDs have failed leaving others working, then the tail light unit is faulty and must be replaced with a new one – individual LEDs are not available.

Licence plate light

10 If the licence plate light fails to work, refer to Section 10 and check the bulb. If that is good disconnect the wiring connector, and check for battery voltage at the red wire terminal on the loom side of the connector with the ignition switch ON. If voltage is present, check for continuity to earth (ground) in the black/yellow wire from the wiring connector. If no voltage is indicated, check the wiring and connectors between the connector and the fusebox. Refer to the wiring diagrams at the end of this Chapter.

Sidelight

11 If a sidelight fails to work, refer to Section 7 and check the bulb. If that is good check there is battery voltage at the brown wire terminal on the loom side of the connector on C models, and the red wire terminal on

all other models, with the ignition switch ON. If voltage is present, check there is continuity to earth (ground) in the black or black/yellow wire (according to model) from the wiring connector. If no voltage is indicated, check the wiring and connectors between the sidelight connector and the fusebox.

Turn signals

12 See Section 11.

7 Headlight bulbs and sidelights

Note: *The headlight bulbs are of the quartz-halogen type. Do not touch the bulb glass as skin acids will shorten the bulb's service life. If the bulb is accidentally touched, it should be wiped carefully when cold with a rag soaked in methylated spirit and dried before fitting.*

Headlight bulbs

C models

1 Turn the relevant cover anti-clockwise to release it **(see illustration)**.
2 Disconnect the wiring connector from the bulb **(see illustration)**.
3 Release the bulb retaining clip, noting how it fits, then remove the bulb, **(see illustrations)**.
4 Fit the new bulb into the headlight, bearing in mind the information in the **Note** above, and make sure it locates correctly. Secure the bulb with the retaining clip **(see illustrations 7.3b and a)**.
5 Connect the wiring connector **(see illustrations 7.2)**.
6 Fit the cover, aligning the marks, and turn it clockwise **(see illustration 7.1)**.
7 Check the operation of the headlight.

D, E and F models

8 Remove the cockpit trim panel (see Chapter 7).
9 Disconnect the wiring connector from the bulb **(see illustration)**.

7.1 Remove the cover...

7.2 ...then disconnect the wiring connector

7.3a Release the clip...

7.3b ...and remove the bulb (C models)

7.9 Disconnect the connector

7.10a Release the bulb unit...

7.10b ...and withdraw it (D/E/F models)

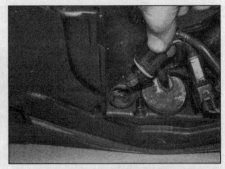

7.15a Release the bulbholder...

7.15b ...and remove the sidelight bulb (C models)

7.16a Release the bulbholder...

7.16b ...and remove the sidelight bulb (D/E/F models)

10 Turn the bulb unit anti-clockwise and remove it (see illustrations).

11 Fit the new bulb unit into the headlight, bearing in mind the information in the Note above, and make sure it locates correctly. Turn the bulb clockwise to secure it (see illustrations 7.10b and a). Note that both H9 and H11 bulbs are supplied as a unit with the plastic holder.

12 Connect the wiring connector (see illustrations 7.9).

13 Check the operation of the headlight.

14 Install the cockpit trim panel (see Chapter 7).

Sidelights

15 On C models remove the fairing centre panel (see Chapter 7). Turn the bulbholder anti-clockwise and remove it from the headlight (see illustration). Carefully pull the bulb out of the holder (see illustration).

16 On D, E and F models remove the cockpit trim panel (see Chapter 7). Pull the bulbholder out of the headlight (see illustration). Carefully pull the bulb out of the holder (see illustration).

17 Fit the new bulb into the bulbholder then fit the holder into the headlight.

18 Check the operation of the sidelight. Fit the panel.

8 Headlight

C models

1 Remove the fairing, then remove the mirrors and the inner and centre panels from it (see Chapter 7).

2 Unscrew the stud on each side using a pair of pliers or other grips on the body, not the threads, noting the washer (see illustrations).

3 Unscrew the bolt securing each side section and remove them (see illustration).

HAYNES HiNT *Always use a paper towel or dry cloth when handling new bulbs to prevent injury if the bulb should break and to increase bulb life.*

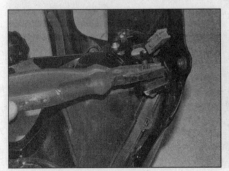

8.2a Unscrew the studs...

8.2b ...noting the washers and which way up they fit

8.3 Fairing side section bolt (arrowed)

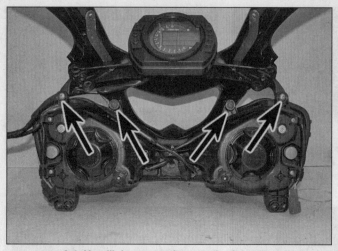

8.4 Headlight screws (arrowed) – C models

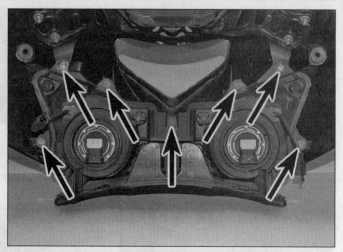

8.9 Headlight screws (arrowed) – D models

4 Undo the screws and remove the headlight **(see illustration)**.
5 If required remove the bulbs (see Section 7).
6 Installation is the reverse of removal. Check

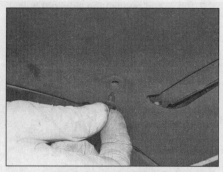

8.13a Release the trim clip...

the operation of the headlights. Check the headlight aim (see Chapter 1).

D models

8 Remove the fairing, then remove the centre panel from it (see Chapter 7).
9 Undo the screws and remove the headlight from the fairing, noting the position of the wiring clamp **(see illustration)**.
10 If required remove the bulbs (see Section 7).
11 Installation is the reverse of removal. Check the operation of the headlights. Check the headlight aim (see Chapter 1).

E and F models

12 Remove the fairing (see Chapter 7).
13 Release the trim clip, then undo the screws and remove the headlight from the fairing, noting the positions of the wiring clamps **(see illustrations)**.

14 If required remove the bulbs (see Section 7).
15 Installation is the reverse of removal. Check the operation of the headlights. Check the headlight aim (see Chapter 1).

9 Brake/tail light

1 The tail light contains LEDs rather than a conventional bulb.
2 If one or more of the LEDs within the unit has failed, replace the unit with a new one – individual LEDs are not available.

C models

3 Remove the seat cowling (see Chapter 7).
4 Unscrew the bolts and remove the tail light, noting the position of the wiring clamp **(see illustrations)**.

8.13b ...then undo the screws (arrowed) – E/F models

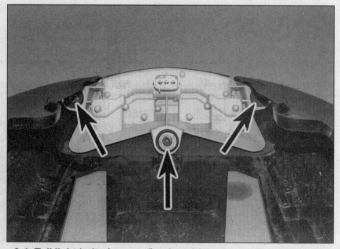

9.4 Tail light bolts (arrowed) – the wiring clamp should be fitted with the middle bolt

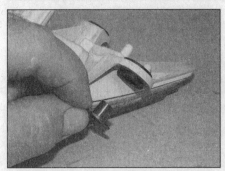

9.5 The collars fit from the back

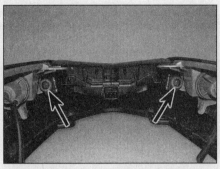

9.7a Undo the screws (arrowed)...

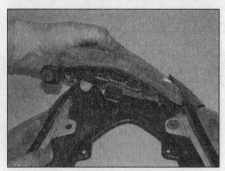

9.7b ...remove the tail light...

9.7c ...and if required the damper

9.10 Displace the relay box then the ECU

9.11a Tail light wiring connector (arrowed)

9.11b Turn signal and licence plate light connectors (arrowed)

5 Installation is the reverse of removal. Make sure the rubber grommets are in good condition and the collars are fitted in them (see illustration). Check the operation of the tail and brake lights.

D models

6 Remove the seat cowling (see Chapter 7).
7 Undo the screws and remove the tail light (see illustrations). Remove the rubber damper from the seat cowl if required (see illustration).
8 Installation is the reverse of removal. Make sure the rubber grommets are in good

condition and the collars are fitted in them. Make sure the rubber damper is in good condition and correctly in place over the tabs on the seat cowl (see illustration 9.7c). Check the operation of the tail and brake lights.

E and F models

9 Remove the seat cowling (see Chapter 7).
10 Displace the relay box and ECU (see illustration).
11 Disconnect the tail light, turn signal, licence plate light, tip-over sensor and AP sensor wiring connectors (see illustrations).

9.11c TO sensor connector (arrowed)

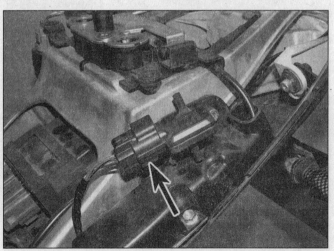

9.11d AP sensor connector (arrowed)

9.12a Unscrew the bolt (arrowed) and displace the cover...

9.12b ...detach the cable...

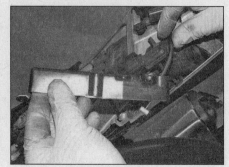

9.12c ...and draw it out

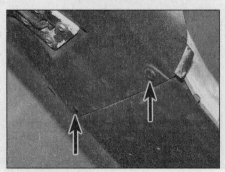

9.13 Release the trim clips (arrowed)

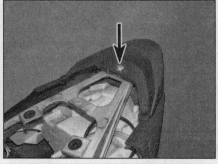

9.14 Unscrew the bolt (arrowed)

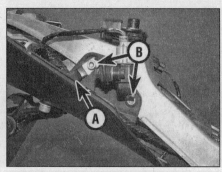

9.15 Release the clamp (A). Unscrew the bolts (B) on each side

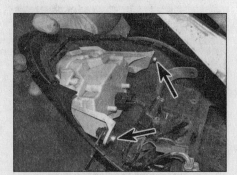

9.17 Tail light bolts (arrowed)

12 Displace the seat lock cover **(see illustration)**. Detach the cable and draw it out of the cover **(see illustrations)**.
13 Release the trim clips on the underside **(see illustration)**.
14 Unscrew the bolt at the back **(see illustration)**.
15 Release the wiring from the clamp on the right-hand side, then unscrew the two bolts on each side **(see illustration)**.
16 Draw the undertray back off the rear sub-frame and remove it.
17 Unscrew the bolts and remove the tail light **(see illustration)**. Remove the rubber damper if required.

18 Installation is the reverse of removal, noting the following:
● Make sure the rubber grommets are in good condition and the collars are fitted in them.
● Make sure the rubber damper is in good condition and correctly in place, and the posts on the undertray locate correctly in it **(see illustration 9.18a)**.
● Make sure the front edge of the undertray locates correctly **(see illustration 9.13)**.
● Make sure the bracket and tray seat on each side of the rear sub-frame **(see illustration 9.18b)**.
● Check the operation of the tail and brake lights.

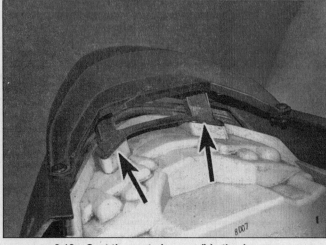

9.18a Seat the posts (arrowed) in the damper

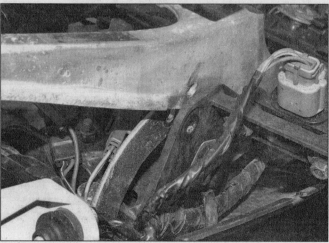

9.18b Check the sub-frame seats between the bracket and tray wall

10.1 Undo the screws and remove the cover

10.2 Push the bulb in and turn it anti-clockwise

11.3a Turn signal relay (arrowed) – C models

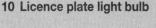

10 Licence plate light bulb

1 Undo the two screws and remove the cover **(see illustration)**.
2 On C and D models carefully push the bulb in and turn it anti-clockwise to release it, and replace with a new one **(see illustration)**.
3 On E and F models carefully pull the bulb out and replace with a new one.
4 Do not overtighten the cover screws. Check the operation of the tail and brake lights.

11 Turn signal circuit check

Note: *Refer to electrical system fault finding in Section 2 and to the wiring diagram for your model at the end of this Chapter.*
1 Most turn signal problems are the result of a burned out bulb or corroded socket. This is especially true when the turn signals function properly in one direction (although possibly too quickly), but fail to flash in the other direction. If this is the case, first check the bulbs, the sockets and the wiring connectors (see Sections 12 and 13). If all the turn signals fail to work, check the fuse (see Section 5), and then the relay (see Steps 2 to 4). If they

11.3b Turn signal relay (arrowed) – D models

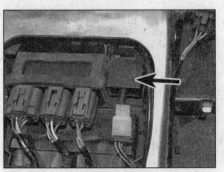

11.3c Turn signal relay (arrowed) – E/F models

are good, the problem lies in the wiring or connectors, or the switch. Refer to Section 19 for the switch testing procedures, and also to the wiring diagrams at the end of this Chapter.
2 To access the relay, on C models remove the rider's seat, on D models remove the seat cowling, and on E and F models remove the centre section of the seat cowling (see Chapter 7).
3 Displace the relay and disconnect the wiring connector **(see illustrations)**. Check for battery voltage at the brown/yellow wire terminal on the loom side of the connector with the ignition ON. If no voltage is present, check the wiring from the relay to the ignition switch (via the fuse) for continuity.
4 If voltage was present, short between the wire terminals on the connector using a

jumper wire. Turn the ignition ON and operate the turn signal switch. If the lights come on (they will not flash), the relay is faulty and must be replaced with a new one.
5 If the lights do not come on, check the orange wire for continuity to the left-hand switch housing, and repair or renew the wiring or connectors as required.
6 If all is good so far, or if the lights work on one side but not the other, check the wiring between the left-hand switch housing and the turn signals themselves. Repair or renew the wiring or connectors as necessary.

12 Turn signal bulbs

Front turn signals

C models

1 Remove the fairing side panel (see Chapter 7).
2 Undo the screws and remove the lens **(see illustration)**.
3 Push the bulb in and twist it anti-clockwise to release it **(see illustration)**. Check the socket terminals for corrosion and clean them if necessary.
4 Line up the pins of the new bulb with the slots in the socket, then push the bulb in and turn it clockwise until it locks into place.
5 Make sure the seal is seated in its groove, then fit the lens – do not overtighten the

12.2 Undo the screws (arrowed)

12.3 Push the bulb in and turn it anti-clockwise – C models

12.8 Release the bulbholder...

12.9 ...then remove the bulb – D models

12.13 Remove the lens...

screws as it is easy to strip the threads or crack the lens.

6 Install the fairing side panel.

D models

7 Remove the fairing inner panel (see Chapter 7).

8 Turn the bulbholder anti-clockwise and draw it out (see illustration).

9 Push the bulb in and twist it anti-clockwise to release it (see illustration). Check the socket terminals for corrosion and clean them if necessary.

10 Line up the pins of the new bulb with the slots in the socket, then push the bulb in and turn it clockwise until it locks into place. Note that the amber bulbs have offset pins to prevent replacement with clear lens bulbs.

11 Fit the bulbholder and turn it clockwise until it locks into place.

12 Install the fairing inner panel (see Chapter 7).

E and F models

13 Undo the screw on the underside and remove the lens (see illustration).

14 Push the bulb in and twist it anti-clockwise to release it (see illustration). Check the socket terminals for corrosion and clean them if necessary.

15 Line up the pins of the new bulb with the slots in the socket, then push the bulb in and turn it clockwise until it locks into place. Note that the amber bulbs have offset pins to prevent replacement with clear lens bulbs.

16 Fit the lens, locating the tab in the groove – do not overtighten the screw as it is easy to strip the threads or crack the lens.

Rear turn signals

C models

17 Undo the screw and displace the turn signal (see illustration).

18 Undo the screw and remove the lens (see illustrations).

19 Push the bulb in and twist it anti-clockwise to release it (see illustration). Check the socket terminals for corrosion and clean them if necessary.

20 Line up the pins of the new bulb with the slots in the socket, then push the bulb in and turn it clockwise until it locks into place.

21 Fit the lens, locating the tab in the cut-out (see illustration 12.18b) – do not overtighten the screw as it is easy to strip the threads or crack the lens.

22 Fit the turn signal, locating the tab behind the bracket (see illustration).

12.14 ...then remove the bulb – E/F models

12.17 Undo the screw (arrowed)

12.18a Undo the screw (arrowed)...

12.18b ...and remove the rear lens...

12.19 ...then remove the bulb – C models

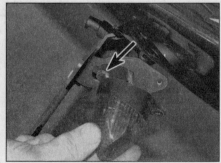

12.22 Seat the tab (arrowed) behind the bracket

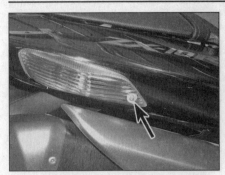

12.23 Undo the screw (arrowed) and remove the rear lens...

12.24 ...then remove the bulb – D models

12.26 Seat the tab in the groove

D models

23 Undo the screw and remove the lens **(see illustration)**.

24 Push the bulb in and twist it anti-clockwise to release it **(see illustration)**. Check the socket terminals for corrosion and clean them if necessary.

25 Line up the pins of the new bulb with the slots in the socket, then push the bulb in and turn it clockwise until it locks into place. Note that the amber bulbs have offset pins to prevent replacement with clear lens bulbs.

26 Fit the lens, locating the tab in the groove **(see illustration)** – do not overtighten the screw as it is easy to strip the threads or crack the lens.

E and F models

27 Undo the screw on the underside and remove the lens.

28 Push the bulb in and twist it anti-clockwise

to release it. Check the socket terminals for corrosion and clean them if necessary.

29 Line up the pins of the new bulb with the slots in the socket, then push the bulb in and turn it clockwise until it locks into place. Note that the amber bulbs have offset pins to prevent replacement with clear lens bulbs.

30 Fit the lens, locating the tab in the groove – do not overtighten the screw as it is easy to strip the threads or crack the lens.

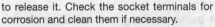

13 Turn signal assemblies

Front turn signals

C models

1 Remove the fairing inner panel (see Chapter 7).

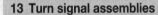

2 Undo the screws and remove the turn signal **(see illustration)**.

3 Installation is the reverse of removal. Check the operation of the turn signals.

D models

4 Remove the fairing inner panel (see Chapter 7).

5 Turn the bulbholder anti-clockwise and draw it out **(see illustration 12.8)**.

6 Undo the screws and remove the turn signal **(see illustration)**.

7 Installation is the reverse of removal. Check the operation of the turn signals.

E and F models

8 Remove the instruments (see Section 15).

9 Release and disconnect the turn signal wiring connector **(see illustration)**.

10 Undo the screws and remove the turn signal, taking care as you draw the wiring through **(see illustration)**.

11 Installation is the reverse of removal. Check the operation of the turn signals.

Rear turn signals

C models

12 Remove the passenger seat and the rear section of the seat cowling (see Chapter 7).

13 Disconnect the turn signal wiring connector **(see illustration)**.

14 Undo the screw and remove the turn signal, taking care as you draw the wire through **(see illustration 12.17)**.

15 Installation is the reverse of removal. Check the operation of the turn signals.

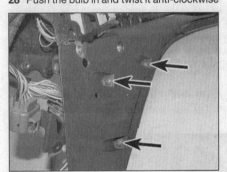

13.2 Front turn signal screws (arrowed) – C models

13.6 Front turn signal screws (arrowed) – D models

13.9 Turn signal wiring connectors (arrowed)

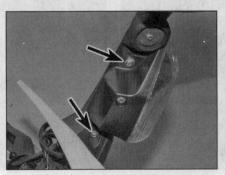

13.10 Front turn signal screws (arrowed) – E/F models

13.13 Rear turn signal wiring connectors (arrowed) – C models

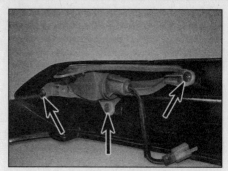

**13.17 Rear turn signal screws (arrowed) –
D models**

**14.3a Rear brake switch wiring connector
(arrowed) – C models**

**14.3b Rear brake switch wiring connector
– D/E/F models**

D models

16 Remove the tail light (see Section 9).
17 Undo the screws and remove the turn signal **(see illustration)**.
18 Installation is the reverse of removal. Check the operation of the turn signals.

E and F models

19 Remove the passenger seat (see Chapter 7).
20 Disconnect the turn signal wiring connector **(see illustration 9.11b)**.
21 Support the turn signal, undo the screw and remove the mounting plates, then remove the turn signal, taking care as you draw the wire through.
22 Installation is the reverse of removal. Check the operation of the turn signals.

14 Brake light switches

Circuit check

Note: *Refer to electrical system fault finding in Section 2 and to the wiring diagram for your model at the end of this Chapter.*

1 Before checking the switches, and if not already done, check the brake light circuit (see Section 6).
2 The front brake light switch is mounted on the underside of the brake master cylinder. Remove the switch (see Step 5). Using a continuity tester, connect the probes to the terminals of the switch. With the switch button pushed in, there should be no continuity. With the switch button out, there should be continuity. If the switch does not behave as described, replace it with a new one.
3 The rear brake light switch is mounted on the inside of the rider's right-hand footrest bracket. To access the wiring connector, on C models remove the right-hand side cover (see Chapter 7), and on all other models remove the fuel tank (see Chapter 4). Disconnect the wiring connector **(see illustrations)**. Using a continuity tester, connect the probes to the terminals on the switch side of the wiring connector. With the brake pedal at rest, there should be no continuity. With the brake pedal applied, there should be continuity. If the switch does not behave as described, replace it with a new one, although check first that the spring has not become detached or broken,

and the switch is adjusted correctly (see Chapter 1).
4 If the switch is good, check for voltage at one of the terminals in the front brake light switch connector, and in the red/blue wire on the loom side of the connector for the rear switch, in each case with the ignition switch ON – there should be battery voltage. If there's no voltage present, check the wiring between the connector and the fusebox (see the wiring diagrams at the end of this Chapter). If voltage is present, check the blue/red wire for continuity to the brake light, referring to the relevant wiring diagram. Repair or renew the wiring as necessary.

Switch replacement

Front brake lever switch

5 The switch is mounted on the underside of the brake master cylinder. Undo the single screw and displace the switch, then disconnect the wiring connector **(see illustrations)**.
6 Installation is the reverse of removal. Make sure the peg on the switch is correctly located in its hole before tightening the screw.

Rear brake pedal switch

7 The rear brake light switch is mounted on

14.5a Undo the screw (arrowed)...

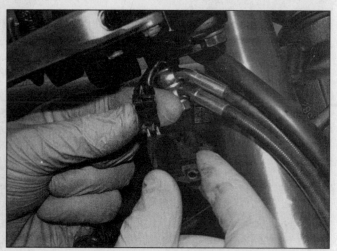

14.5b ...then disconnect the wiring

14.7 Rear brake light switch (arrowed)

14.8a Unscrew the bolts (arrowed)

14.8b Unhook the spring (arrowed)...

the inside of the rider's right-hand footrest bracket (see illustration). Refer to Step 3 and disconnect the wiring connector. Feed the wiring down to the switch, noting its routing and releasing it from any ties.

8 For best access unscrew the footrest bracket bolts and displace the bracket (see illustration). Detach the end of the switch spring from the brake pedal (see illustration). Release the switch from its bracket (see illustration).

9 Installation is the reverse of removal. Make sure the brake light is activated just before the rear brake pedal takes effect. If adjustment is necessary, refer to Chapter 1, Section 2.

15 Instruments

Check

1 To check the individual functions special electrical testing equipment and a harness adapter are needed. Take the cluster to a Kawasaki dealer for assessment.

2 Before doing this check the relevant wiring between the instrument cluster wiring connector and its sensor or switch for continuity, and check the sensor or switch itself, referring to Section 2 and to the wiring

14.8c ...and remove the switch

diagrams, and the relevant Section of this Chapter, or to Chapter 3 for the temperature display and Chapter 4 for the fuel display.

Removal

C models

3 Remove the fairing (see Chapter 7).
4 Disconnect the wiring connector (see illustration).
5 Undo the screws, noting the washers, and remove the instrument cluster.
6 Installation is the reverse of removal. Check the rubber grommets in the bracket and replace them with new ones if necessary.

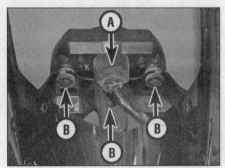

15.4 Instrument wiring connector (A) and screws (B)

D models

7 Remove the fairing (see Chapter 7).
8 Undo the screws, noting the washers, and remove the instrument cluster (see illustration).
9 Installation is the reverse of removal. Check the rubber grommets in the bracket and replace them with new ones if necessary.

E and F models

10 Remove the windshield (see Chapter 7).
11 Release the trim clip and unscrew the bolt on each side (see illustration).
12 Remove the instrument assembly, feeding

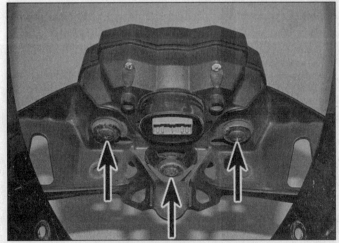

15.8 Instrument screws (arrowed)

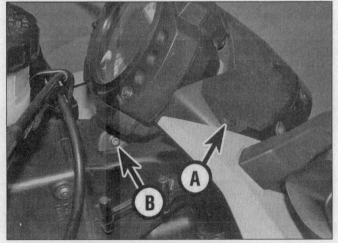

15.11 Trim clip (A) and bolt (B) on each side

15.12a Draw the assembly back...

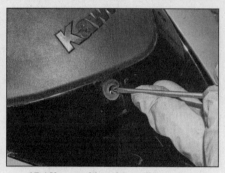

15.12b ...poking the well-nut rims through...

15.12c ...and disconnect the wiring

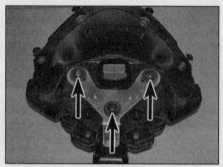

15.13a Undo the screws (arrowed)...

15.13b ...and remove the instrument cluster

15.15a Position the instrument assembly...

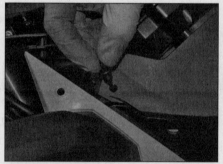

15.15b ...and fit the trim clips and bolts

the well-nut rims through the holes as you do, then disconnect the wiring (see illustrations).
13 Undo the screws, noting the washers, and remove the instrument cluster from its cowl (see illustrations).
14 Thread a windshield screw part-way back into each of the well-nuts, then push down on the head of the screw to stretch the crease of the well-nut so it can then be drawn out of its hole in the instrument cowl (see illustrations 15.15c and d). Make sure the well-nuts are in good condition and replace them with new ones if necessary, but

do not fit them until the instrument cowl is in place.
15 Installation is the reverse of removal. Seat the instrument cowl under the rim of the fairing and secure it with the trim clips and bolts (see illustrations). Smear some oil onto the body of each well-nut to help ease it into its hole and stretch it out using a screw as on removal (see illustration).

Instrument disassembly and PCB replacement

16 Remove the instruments.

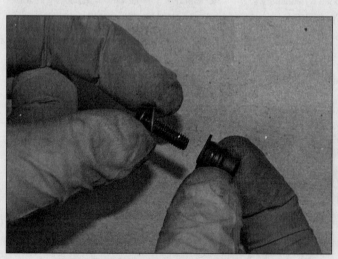

15.15c To fit the well-nuts thread a screw in...

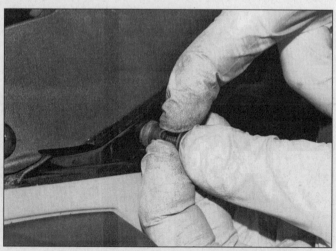

15.15d ...then stretch it out and ease it into its hole

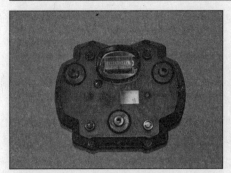

15.17a Undo the screws on the back (E/F model shown)...

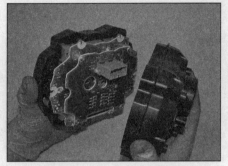

15.17b ...remove the cover...

15.17c ...and lift the PCB out

17 Undo the screws on the back and remove the rear cover, then remove the PCB from the front cover **(see illustrations)**.

18 Installation is the reverse of removal. Do not over-tighten the screws.

Instrument and warning lights

19 All instrument and warning lights are LEDs, which are part of the instrument cluster printed circuit board and are not available individually. If one of the LEDs fails disassemble the instrument cluster and replace the PCB with a new one (Steps 16 to 18).

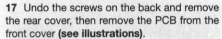

16 Speed sensor

Check

1 To check the speed sensor special electrical testing equipment and/or a harness adapter are needed. Take the bike to a Kawasaki dealer for assessment.

2 Before doing this check the wiring and connectors between the sensor and the instruments for continuity, referring to Section 2 and to the wiring diagrams.

Removal and installation

C models

3 The speed sensor is mounted in the front sprocket cover. To access the wiring connector, remove the left-hand lower fairing (see Chapter 7).

16.8 Slacken the clamp (arrowed) and detach the hose

4 Disconnect the wiring connector and feed it back to the sensor, releasing it from the clamp and noting its routing **(see illustration)**.

5 Unscrew the bolt and remove the sensor **(see illustration)**.

6 Installation is the reverse of removal – clean the threads of the bolt and apply some fresh threadlock.

D, E and F models

7 The speed sensor is mounted in the top of the crankcase near the front sprocket. Drain the cooling system (see Chapter 1). Remove the front sprocket cover (see Chapter 6).

8 Slacken the clamp securing the inner of the two large bore hoses to the water pump and detach the hose **(see illustration)**.

9 Disconnect the wiring connector from the sensor **(see illustration)**.

10 Unscrew the bolt and remove the sensor **(see illustration)**. Check the condition of

16.4 Speed sensor wiring connector (arrowed)

16.9 Disconnect the wiring connector

its O-ring and replace it with a new one if it is damaged or there is evidence of leakage around it, but note that Kawasaki do not list it as being available separately. While the sensor is removed plug the orifice with clean rag.

11 Installation is the reverse of removal – smear the O-ring with grease.

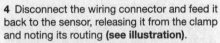

17 Oil pressure switch

Check

Note: *Refer to electrical system fault finding in Section 2 and to the wiring diagram for your model at the end of this Chapter.*

1 The oil pressure warning light should come on when the ignition switch is turned ON and go out a few seconds after the engine is

16.5 Unscrew the bolt (arrowed) and remove the sensor

16.10 Speed sensor bolt (arrowed)

17.2a On C models insert a screwdriver between the exhaust and the sump extension to undo the terminal screw (arrowed)

17.2b Access is easy on D/E/F models

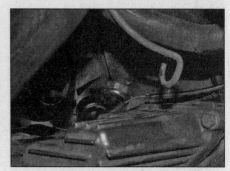

17.7 On C models access is best using a spanner from the left-hand side

started. If the oil pressure warning light does not go out or comes on whilst the engine is running, stop the engine immediately and carry out an oil level check (see *Pre-ride checks*), and if the level is correct, an oil pressure check (see Chapter 2).

2 If the oil pressure warning light does not come on when the ignition is turned ON, but all other instrument functions work, remove the left-hand side of the lower fairing (see Chapter 7). Pull the rubber cover off the oil pressure switch and undo the screw securing the wiring connector **(see illustrations)**. With the ignition switched ON, earth (ground) the wire on the crankcase and check that the warning light comes on. If the light comes on, the switch is defective and must be replaced with a new one. To confirm the switch is faulty check for continuity between the terminal and the crankcase – with the engine off there should be continuity, with the engine running there should be no continuity.

3 If the light still does not come on, check for voltage at the wire terminal with the ignition ON. If there is no voltage present check there is continuity in the wire between the switch and the instrument connector, referring to Section 15 for access. Repair the wiring if necessary. If the wiring is all good and the switch is good the instrument PCB could be faulty.

4 If the warning light does not go out when the

engine is started or comes on whilst the engine is running, yet the oil pressure is satisfactory, detach the wire from the oil pressure switch (see above). With the wire detached and the ignition switched ON the light should be out. If it is illuminated, the wire between the switch and instrument cluster is earthed (grounded) at some point. If the wiring is good, the switch must be assumed faulty and replaced with a new one.

Removal

5 The oil pressure switch is screwed into the front of the crankcase on the left-hand side. Drain the engine oil (see Chapter 1).

6 Pull the rubber cover off the switch, then undo the screw securing the wiring connector **(see illustrations 17.2a or b)**.

7 Unscrew and remove the switch **(see illustration)** – be prepared to catch any residual oil with a rag.

Installation

8 Apply a suitable sealant to the upper portion of the switch threads near the switch body, leaving the bottom 3 to 4 mm of thread clean. Thread the switch into the crankcase and tighten to the torque setting specified at the beginning of the Chapter.

9 Attach the wiring connector and secure it with the screw, then fit the rubber cover.

10 Replenish the engine oil (see Chapter 1). Run the engine and check that the switch operates correctly and without leakage.

18 Ignition switch

⚠ *Warning: To prevent the risk of short circuits, disconnect the battery negative (–) lead before making any ignition switch checks.*

Check

Note: *Refer to electrical system fault finding in Section 2 and to the wiring diagram for your model at the end of this Chapter.*

1 The switch can be checked for continuity using an ohmmeter or a continuity test light. Disconnect the battery negative (–) lead, which will prevent the possibility of a short circuit, before making the checks (see Section 3).

2 To access the connector, on C and D models remove the left-hand fairing side panel (see Chapter 7), on E and F models remove the upper section of the air filter housing (see Chapter 4). Disconnect the switch, and where fitted the immobiliser receiver, wiring connector(s) **(see illustrations)**.

3 Using an ohmmeter or a continuity tester, check the continuity of the connector terminal pairs (see the wiring diagrams at the end of this Chapter). Continuity should exist between the terminals connected by a solid line on the diagram when the switch is in the indicated position.

18.2a Ignition switch and immobiliser wiring connector (arrowed) – C models

18.2b Ignition switch and immobiliser wiring connector (arrowed) – D models

18.2c Ignition switch and immobiliser wiring connector (arrowed) – E/F models

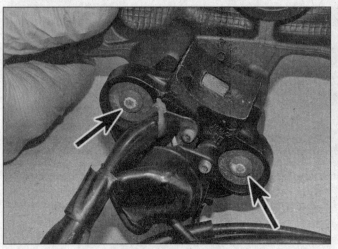

18.8 Ignition switch bolts (arrowed)

19.3a Handlebar switch wiring connectors (arrowed) – C models

4 If the switch fails any of the tests, replace it with a new one.

Removal

5 Disconnect the battery negative (–) lead (see Section 3).

6 Refer to Step 2 to access the connector(s) and disconnect it/them. Feed the wiring back to the switch, noting the routing and releasing any guides.

7 Refer to Chapter 1, Section 16, and remove the top yoke.

8 Shear-head security bolts are fitted **(see illustration)** – to remove them drive the heads around using a small cold chisel, making sure the yoke is adequately protected and secured. When loose unscrew the bolts by hand and remove the switch. On models with an immobiliser refer to Chapter 4 and remove the receiver.

Installation

9 Installation is the reverse of removal. Use new ignition switch bolts and tighten them until the heads shear off. Refer to Chapter 1 to install the top yoke. Make sure the wiring is correctly routed and securely connected.

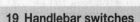

19 Handlebar switches

Check

Note: *Refer to electrical system fault finding in Section 2 and to the wiring diagram for your model at the end of this Chapter.*

1 Generally speaking, the switches are reliable and trouble-free. Most troubles, when they do occur, are caused by dirty or corroded contacts, but wear and breakage of internal parts is a possibility that should not be overlooked. If breakage does occur, the entire switch and related wiring harness will have

to be replaced with a new one, as individual parts are not available.

2 The switches can be checked for continuity using an ohmmeter or a continuity test light. Disconnect the battery negative (–) lead, which will prevent the possibility of a short circuit, before making the checks (see Section 3).

3 To access the connectors, on C models remove the fairing centre panel (see Chapter 7), on D models remove the fairing side panel on the side of the switch being tested (see Chapter 7), on E and F models remove the upper section of the air filter housing (see

Chapter 4). Disconnect the relevant switch wiring connector **(see illustrations)**.

4 Check for continuity between the terminals of the switch connector with the switch in the various positions (i.e. switch off – no continuity, switch on – continuity) – see the wiring diagram for your model at the end of this Chapter. Continuity should exist between the terminals connected by a solid line on the diagram when the switch is in the indicated position.

5 If the continuity check indicates a problem exists, displace the switch housing (Step 8),

19.3b Right-hand switch wiring connector – D models

19.3c Left-hand switch wiring connector (arrowed) – D models

19.3d Right-hand switch wiring connectors – E/F models

19.3e Left-hand switch wiring connector – E/F models

19.8a Right-hand switch housing screws (arrowed)

19.8b Left-hand switch housing screws (arrowed)

20.2a GP switch connector (arrowed) – C models

20.2b GP switch/sub-loom connector – D/E/F models

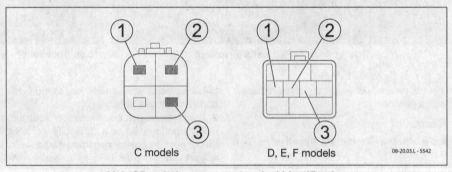

C models   D, E, F models

08-20.03.L - 5542

20.3 GP switch connector terminal identification

and spray the switch contacts with electrical contact cleaner (there is no need to remove the switch completely). If they are accessible, the contacts can be scraped clean with a knife or polished with crocus cloth. If switch components are damaged or broken, it will be obvious when the switch is disassembled.

Removal and installation

6 Refer to Step 3 to access the connectors and disconnect the relevant one. Feed the wiring back to the switch, freeing it from any clips and ties and noting the routing.
7 If removing the right-hand switch remove the brake light switch (see Section 14). If removing the left-hand switch disconnect the clutch switch wiring connector (**see illustration 22.2**).
8 Undo the switch housing screws and separate the halves from the handlebar (**see illustrations**).
9 Installation is the reverse of removal. Do not overtighten the screws.

20 Gear position switch

Note: *Refer to electrical system fault finding in Section 2 and to the wiring diagram for your model at the end of this Chapter.*

Check

1 The gear position switch is located in the left-hand side of the engine below the front sprocket. The neutral light should come on whenever the ignition switch is ON and the transmission is in neutral. The switch is part of the starter safety circuit that prevents or stops the engine running if the transmission is in gear whilst the sidestand is down, and prevents the engine from starting if the transmission is in gear unless the sidestand is up and the clutch is pulled in.

2 To access the wiring connector remove the fuel tank (see Chapter 4). Disconnect the wiring connector (**see illustrations**).
3 Refer to the table for your model and, using a multimeter set to read K-ohms, check the resistances between the relevant terminal in the wiring connector and a good earth on the crankcase with the transmission in the gear position indicated (**see illustration**). If not, replace the switch with a new one.

C and D models

GEAR POSITION	Terminal 1	Terminal 2	Terminal 3
Neutral	approx. 0	-	-
1st	-	3.0 to 3.32	11.63 to 12.87
2nd	-	1.70 to 1.89	10.33 to 11.44
3rd	-	1.07 to 1.19	9.70 to 10.74
4th	-	0.695 to 0.769	9.32 to 10.32
5th	-	0.430 to 0.476	9.06 to 10.03
6th	-	0.248 to 0.274	8.89 to 9.81

E and F models

GEAR POSITION	Terminal 1	Terminal 2	Terminal 3
Neutral	approx. 0	8.64 to 9.54	approx. 0
1st	-	2.22 to 2.46	approx. 0
2nd	-	1.42 to 1.58	approx. 0
3rd	-	0.954 to 1.055	approx. 0
4th	-	0.643 to 0.711	approx. 0
5th	-	0.410 to 0.453	approx. 0
6th	-	0.241 to 0.266	approx. 0

20.7a Disconnect the ECT sensor connector...

20.7b ...and the GP switch/sub-loom connector

4 If the switch is good check for continuity in each wire from the main loom side of the switch connector.

Removal and installation

5 Remove the left-hand side of the lower fairing (see Chapter 7). Remove the front sprocket cover (see Chapter 6). Remove the fuel tank (see Chapter 4).
6 On C models disconnect the wire from the oil pressure switch **(see illustration 17.2a)**. Disconnect the gear position switch wiring connector **(see illustration 20.2a)**. Feed the wiring to the switch, releasing it from any clamps and noting its routing.
7 On D, E and F models remove the water pump (see Chapter 3). Remove the air filter housing (see Chapter 4). Disconnect the wire from the oil pressure switch **(see illustration 17.2b)**. Disconnect the speed sensor wiring connector **(see illustration 16.9)**. Disconnect the ECT sensor wiring connector **(see illustration)**. Disconnect the GP switch/sub-loom wiring connector **(see illustration)**. Feed all the wiring to the switch, releasing it from any clamps and noting its routing.
8 Make sure the transmission is in neutral. Clean the area around the switch, then undo the screws and carefully remove the switch,

noting that there are two sprung plungers in the end of the selector drum behind it **(see illustration)**. Remove the plungers and springs **(see illustration)**. Remove the switch O-ring – a new one must be used.
9 Check the contacts on the switch and the plunger ends for wear and damage **(see illustration)**. Check the springs for distortion. Replace parts with new ones as required.
10 Fit the springs and plungers into their holes **(see illustration 20.8b)**. Fit the switch using a new O-ring smeared with grease **(see illustrations)**. Align the screw holes by turning the switch body if required. Clean the

threads of the screws and apply some fresh threadlock, then fit the screws.
11 Connect the wiring connectors and check the operation of the switch. Install all disturbed components in reverse order.

21 Sidestand switch

1 The sidestand switch is mounted on the stand pivot. The switch is part of the starter interlock safety circuit that prevents or stops

20.8a Undo the screws (arrowed) and remove the switch...

20.8b ...and the plungers and springs

20.9 Check the plunger ends and their contacts on the switch

20.10a Fit a new O-ring...

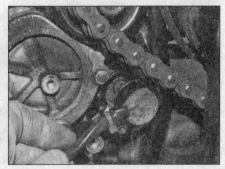

20.10b ...then fit the switch and align the holes

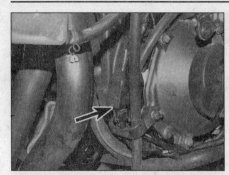

21.2a Sidestand switch wiring connector (arrowed) – C models

21.2b Sidestand switch wiring connector (arrowed) – D models

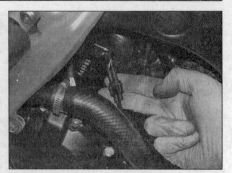

21.2c Sidestand switch wiring connector – E/F models

21.8a Sidestand switch bolt (arrowed) – C/D models

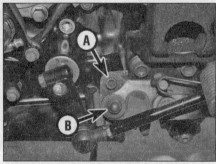

21.8b Sidestand switch bolt (A) and bracket nut (B) – E/F models

the engine running if the transmission is in gear whilst the sidestand is down, and prevents the engine from starting if the transmission is in gear unless the sidestand is up and the clutch is pulled in.

Check

Note: *Refer to electrical system fault finding in Section 2 and to the wiring diagram for your model at the end of this Chapter.*

2 Remove the left-hand lower fairing panel (see Chapter 7). Disconnect the sidestand switch wiring connector **(see illustrations)**.

3 Check the operation of the switch using an ohmmeter or continuity tester. Connect the meter between the terminals on the switch side of the connector. With the sidestand up there should be continuity (zero resistance) between the terminals, and with the stand down there should be no continuity (infinite resistance).

4 If the switch does not perform as expected, it is faulty and must be replaced with a new one.

5 If the switch is good, check the other components (clutch switch, neutral switch,

starter circuit relay and diodes) in the starter safety circuit, and check the wiring between them for continuity, and the connectors for loose or broken connections.

Removal

6 Remove the left-hand lower fairing panel (see Chapter 7).

7 Disconnect the sidestand switch wiring connector **(see illustration 21.2a, b or c)**. Feed the wiring back to the switch, releasing it from the clamps and noting its routing.

8 Unscrew the switch bolt and remove the switch from the stand, noting how it fits **(see illustrations)**.

9 If required unscrew the nut and remove the switch bracket, pivoting it round until the bracket arm is clear then drawing the stud out of the collar **(see illustrations)**. Check the condition of the three rubber dampers and replace them with new ones if necessary.

Installation

10 Make sure the rubber dampers are correctly in place and the collar is fitted. Fit the bracket stud into the collar, then pivot it round so the arm seats over the damper without distorting its rim **(see illustration 21.9b)**. Fit the nut **(see illustration 21.9a or 21.8b)**.

21.9a Sidestand bracket nut (arrowed) – C/D models

21.9b Pivot the bracket round then remove it – C/D model shown

21.11a Seat the peg in the damper…

21.11b …and the arm around the lug – C/D model shown

21.11c Fitting the switch on E/F models

11 Clean the threads of the bolt and apply a suitable non-permanent thread locking compound. Fit the switch onto the bracket, making sure the peg locates through the hole in the bracket and into the damper, and the cut-out in the switch arm locates around the lug on the stand **(see illustrations)**. Secure the switch with the bolt.

12 Feed the wiring to its connector, making sure it is correctly routed and secured, and connect it **(see illustration 21.2a, b or c)**.

13 Check the operation of the sidestand switch. Install the lower fairing panel.

22 Clutch switch

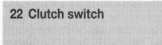

1 The clutch switch is mounted on the underside of the clutch lever bracket. The switch is part of the starter interlock safety circuit that prevents or stops the engine running if the transmission is in gear whilst the sidestand is down, and prevents the engine from starting if the transmission is in gear unless the sidestand is up and the clutch lever is pulled in. The switch isn't adjustable.

Check

Note: *Refer to electrical system fault finding in Section 2 and to the wiring diagram for your model at the end of this Chapter.*

2 To check the switch, disconnect the wiring connector from it **(see illustration)**. Connect the probes of an ohmmeter or a continuity tester to the two switch terminals. With the clutch lever pulled in, there should be continuity. With the clutch lever out, there should be no continuity (infinite resistance).

3 If the switch is good, check the other components (sidestand switch, neutral switch, diode block) in the starter safety circuit, and check the wiring between them for continuity, and the connectors for loose or broken connections.

Removal and installation

4 Disconnect the wiring connector from the switch **(see illustration 22.2)**.

5 Undo the screws and remove the switch, noting how it fits **(see illustration)**.

6 Installation is the reverse of removal.

23 Starter circuit relay and diodes

Note: *Refer to electrical system fault finding in Section 2 and to the wiring diagram for your model at the end of this Chapter.*

1 The relay and diodes are housed in the relay box. The diodes are part of the starter safety circuit that prevents or stops the engine running if the transmission is in gear whilst the sidestand is down, and prevents the engine from starting if the transmission is in gear unless the sidestand is up and the clutch lever is pulled in.

2 To check the relay and diodes, On C and D models remove the rider's seat (see Chapter 7). On E and F models remove the centre section of the seat cowling (see Chapter 7).

3 Draw the relay box out of its rubber holder and disconnect the wiring connectors **(see illustration 6.3a, b or c)**.

C models

4 Set a multimeter to the ohms x 1 scale and connect its probes to terminals 6 and 9 on the relay box **(see illustration 6.4a)**. There should be no continuity (infinite resistance).

5 Now connect to terminals 3 and 9 on. There should be no continuity (infinite resistance).

6 Using a fully-charged 12 volt battery and two insulated jumper wires, connect the positive (+) terminal of the battery to terminal 6 and the negative (–) terminal to terminal 3. Now connect the multimeter set to read DC

22.2 Disconnect the wiring

volts to terminals 9 (positive) and 3 (negative) – there should be battery voltage. If this is the case the relay is proven good. If not, it is faulty and must be replaced with a new one – individual relays are not available.

7 If the relay is good, now check the diodes in the circuit using an ohmmeter or diode tester. Connect the meter probes to the following terminal pairs, then reverse the probes – a diode should show a very small resistance in one direction and a much larger (more than ten times) resistance with the probes connected the other way round. Test terminal pairs:

     2 and 3
     2 and 4
     3 and 4
     3 and 6
     4 and 8
     9 and 15
     9 and 16

If the diodes don't behave as stated, replace the relay box with a new one.

8 If the diodes are good, check the other components (sidestand switch, neutral switch, clutch switch) in the starter safety circuit, and check the wiring between them for continuity, and the connectors for loose or broken connections.

D, E and F models

9 Set a multimeter to the ohms x 1 scale and connect its probes to terminals 8 and 13 on the relay box **(see illustration 6.4b)**. There should be no continuity (infinite resistance).

10 Now connect to terminals 8 and 9. There should be no continuity (infinite resistance).

22.5 Clutch switch screws (arrowed)

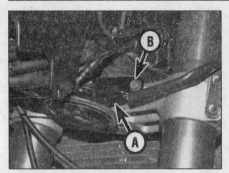

24.4a Horn wiring connectors (A) and mounting bolt (B) – C models

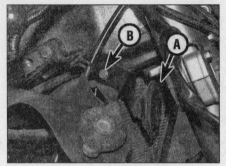

24.4b Horn wiring connectors (A) and mounting bolt (B) – D models

24.4c Horn wiring connectors (A) and mounting bolt (B) – E/F models

11 Using a fully-charged 12 volt battery and two insulated jumper wires, connect the positive (+) terminal of the battery to terminal 13 and the negative (–) terminal to terminal 9. Now connect the multimeter set to read DC volts to terminals 8 (positive) and 9 (negative) – there should be battery voltage. If this is the case the relay is proven good. If not, it is faulty and must be replaced with a new one – individual relays are not available.

12 If the relay is good, now check the diodes in the circuit using an ohmmeter or diode tester. Connect the meter probes to the following terminal pairs, then reverse the probes – a diode should show a very small resistance in one direction and a much larger (more than ten times) resistance with the probes connected the other way round. Test terminal pairs:

    1 and 8
    2 and 8
    9 and 10
    9 and 12
    9 and 13
    10 and 11
    10 and 12

If the diodes don't behave as stated, replace the relay box with a new one.

13 If the diodes are good, check the other components (sidestand switch, neutral switch, clutch switch) in the starter safety circuit, and check the wiring between them for continuity, and the connectors for loose or broken connections.

24 Horn

1 The horn is mounted on the bottom yoke on C models and on the top of the radiator on all other models.

Check

Note: *Refer to electrical system fault finding in Section 2 and to the wiring diagram for your model at the end of this Chapter.*

2 If the horn doesn't work first check the fuse (see Section 5).

3 If the fuse is good, remove one of the fairing side panels on C models, the right-hand

fairing side panel on D models, and the fairing assembly on E and F models (see Chapter 7).

4 Disconnect the wiring connectors from the horn **(see illustrations)**. Check them for loose wires. Using two jumper wires, apply voltage from a fully-charged 12V battery directly to the terminals on the horn. If the horn doesn't sound, replace it with a new one.

5 If the horn sounds, check for voltage at the brown/black wire connector with the ignition ON. If no voltage was present, check the brown/black wire for continuity to the fusebox.

6 If voltage is present, check the black/white wire for continuity to the horn button. If there is, check the black/yellow wire from the button to earth, then check the button contacts in the switch housing (see Section 19).

Replacement

7 Refer to Step 3 for access and disconnect the wiring connectors from the horn **(see illustration 24.4a, b or c)**.

8 Unscrew the bolt and remove the horn.

9 Installation is the reverse of removal. Check the horn works.

25 Starter relay

Check

1 If the starter circuit is faulty, first check the fuses (see Section 5).

2 To access the relay remove the fuel tank (see Chapter 4) **(see illustration 5.2a)**.

3 Make sure the transmission is in neutral.

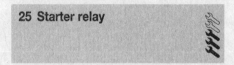

25.3 Starter motor lead terminal (arrowed)

Lift the rubber cover and unscrew the bolt securing the starter motor lead (marked M) **(see illustration)** – be careful not to touch the battery lead with the tool while unscrewing the starter motor lead, and then position the lead away from the relay.

4 With the ignition switch ON, the engine kill switch in the RUN position, and the transmission in neutral, press the starter switch. The relay should be heard to click.

5 If the relay doesn't click, switch off the ignition, remove the relay as described below, and test it as follows:

6 Set a multimeter to the ohms x 1 scale and connect it across the relay's starter motor and battery lead terminals **(see illustration)**. There should be no continuity. Connect a fully-charged 12 volt battery to the wiring terminals on the relay as shown using two insulated jumper wires. At this point the relay should be heard to click and the multimeter read 0 ohms (continuity). If this is the case the relay is proved good. If the relay does not click when battery voltage is applied and indicates no continuity (infinite resistance) across its terminals, it is faulty and must be replaced with a new one.

7 If the relay is good, check for continuity in the main power lead from the battery to the relay. Also check that the terminals and connectors at each end of the lead are tight and corrosion-free.

8 Next check for battery voltage at the yellow/red wire terminal in the relay wiring connector

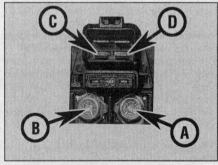

25.6 Connect the meter leads to the terminals A and B, the battery negative (-) lead to C and the positive (+) lead to D – typical relay shown

with the transmission in neutral, the kill switch in the RUN position, the ignition ON, and the starter button pressed. If there is no voltage, check the wiring between the relay wiring connector and the starter circuit relay, then if that is good check the starter circuit relay and diodes (see Section 23).

9 If voltage is present, check that there is continuity to earth in the black/yellow or black wire (according to model). If not check the wiring and connectors.

Replacement

10 Disconnect the battery (see Section 3).

11 Remove the fuel tank (see Chapter 4).

12 Disconnect the relay wiring connector **(see illustration)**. Lift the rubber cover and unscrew the bolts securing the starter motor and battery leads to the relay **(see illustration)**. Draw the relay out of its holder, then remove the holder.

13 If the relay is being replaced with a new one, remove the main fuse from the relay and its spare from the holder and keep them as spares **(see illustrations 5.2b and d)** – the new relay should come with the fuses fitted.

14 Installation is the reverse of removal. Connect the lead from the battery to the terminal marked B and the lead from the starter motor to the terminal marked M, and make sure the terminal bolts are securely tightened **(see illustration 25.12b)**. Do not forget to fit the fuses, if removed **(see illustrations 5.2b and d)**. Connect the negative (–) lead last when reconnecting the battery.

25.12a Disconnect the wiring connector...

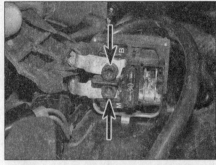

25.12b ...then unscrew the bolts (arrowed)

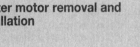

26 Starter motor removal and installation

Removal

1 Disconnect the battery negative (–) lead (see Section 3).

2 Drain the cooling system (see Chapter 1).

3 Remove the throttle bodies (see Chapter 4).

4 Remove the starter clutch cover (see Chapter 2).

5 On C models refer to Chapter 3, Section 8 and remove the coolant inlet union. Draw the hose out of the way. Unscrew the two bolts securing the starter motor to the crankcase **(see illustration)**. Draw the starter motor out, then peel back the rubber terminal cover on

the starter motor **(see illustration)**. Unscrew the nut and detach the lead.

6 On D, E and F models detach the large bore hose from the thermostat housing **(see illustration)**. Peel back the rubber terminal cover on the starter motor **(see illustration)**. Unscrew the nut and detach the lead. Unscrew the two bolts securing the starter motor to the crankcase **(see illustration)**. Slide the starter motor out **(see illustration)**.

7 Remove the O-ring(s) from the end of the starter motor – a new one(s) must be used **(see illustration 26.9)**.

Installation

8 Make sure the motor mounting base and the corresponding surface on the crankcase are clean.

9 Fit new O-ring(s) onto the end of the starter

26.5a Unscrew the bolts (arrowed)

26.5b Pull back the terminal cover then unscrew the nut (arrowed) and detach the lead

26.6a Slacken the clamp (arrowed) and detach the hose

26.6b Pull back the terminal cover then unscrew the nut (arrowed) and detach the lead

26.6c Unscrew the two bolts (arrowed)...

26.6d ...and remove the motor

26.9 Fit new O-ring(s) and lubricate it/them

27.4 Note the alignment marks (highlighted) between the housing and the covers

motor **(see illustration)**. Apply a smear of grease to the O-ring(s).

10 On C models manoeuvre the motor into position and connect the lead, making sure it points up **(see illustration 26.5b)**. Fit the rubber cover over the terminal. Fit the mounting bolts and tighten them finger-tight only at this stage **(see illustration 26.5a)**.

11 On D, E and F models manoeuvre the motor into position. Fit the mounting bolts and tighten them finger-tight only at this stage **(see illustration 26.6c)**. Connect the lead and tighten the nut **(see illustration 26.6b)**. Fit the rubber cover over the terminal.

12 Install the starter clutch cover (see Chapter 2).

13 Tighten the starter motor mounting bolts to the torque setting specified at the beginning of the Chapter.

14 On C models install the coolant inlet union and connect the hose (see Chapter 3). On D, E and F models connect the coolant hose and tighten the clamp **(see illustration 26.6a)**. Install the throttle bodies. Refer to Chapter 1 and fill the cooling system.

15 Connect the battery then check the operation of the starter. Run the engine and check for any coolant leakage.

27 Starter motor overhaul

Check

1 Remove the starter motor (see Section 26).

2 Using a fully-charged 12 volt battery and two insulated jumper wires, connect the lead from the positive (+) terminal of the battery to the protruding terminal on the starter motor, then hold the motor down on a bench, keeping your fingers clear of the shaft, and touch the lead from the negative (–) jumper terminal to one of the motor's mounting lugs. At this point the starter motor should spin. If this is the case the motor is proved good, though it is worth disassembling it and checking it if you suspect it of not working properly under load. If the motor does not spin, disassemble it for inspection.

C and D models, E and F models up to engine No. ZXT00DE043311

Disassembly

3 Remove the starter motor (see Section 26).

4 Note any alignment marks between the main housing and the front and rear covers, or make your own if they aren't clear **(see illustration)**.

5 Unscrew the two long bolts, noting the O-rings, then remove the rear cover from the motor along with its sealing ring **(see illustrations)**. Remove the washer(s) **(see illustration)**.

6 Remove the front cover **(see illustration)**. Remove the tabbed washer (from the cover or the armature shaft) and slide the insulating washer and shim(s) off the shaft **(see illustration)**.

7 Draw the main housing off the armature – it is held in by the attraction of the magnets, so hold the armature in place while you remove the housing **(see illustration)**.

8 At this stage check for continuity between the terminal bolt and the positive brush **(see**

27.5a Unscrew the bolts (arrowed)...

27.5b ...and remove the rear cover...

27.5c ...and the washer(s)

27.6a Remove the front cover

27.6b ...and the various washers/shims

27.7 Withdraw the armature

illustration) – there should be continuity (zero resistance). Check for continuity between the terminal bolt and the metal part of the brushplate – there should be no continuity (infinite resistance). Also check for continuity between the negative brush and the brushplate **(see illustration)** – there should be continuity (zero resistance). If there is no continuity when there should be or *vice versa*, replace the brushplate assembly and/or terminal bolt assembly with a new one.

9 Unscrew the nut on the terminal bolt and remove the washers, noting their fitted order **(see illustration 27.17e)**. Remove the brushplate from the rear cover noting how it locates **(see illustration 27.17c)**.

Inspection

10 The parts of the starter motor that are most likely to require attention are the brushes. Push the brush springs aside and draw the brushes out of their housings **(see illustration)**. Measure the length of each brush and compare the results to the length listed in this Chapter's Specifications **(see illustration)**. If any of the brushes are worn beyond the service limit, replace the rear brushplate and terminal bolt assemblies with new ones – individual components (with the exception of the brush springs) are not available. If the brushes are not worn excessively, nor cracked, chipped, or otherwise damaged, they may be reused.

11 Inspect the commutator bars on the armature for scoring, scratches and discoloration. The commutator can be cleaned and polished with crocus cloth, but do not use sandpaper or emery paper. After cleaning, wipe away any residue with a cloth soaked in electrical system

27.8a Checking for continuity between the bolt and its brush

cleaner or denatured alcohol. Use a Vernier caliper to measure the commutator diameter across the area which is in contact with the brushes; compare the reading with that in the Specifications and renew the armature if worn below the service limit.

12 Using an ohmmeter or a continuity test light, check for continuity between the commutator bars **(see illustration)**. Continuity should exist between each bar and all of the others. Also, check for continuity between the commutator bars and the armature shaft **(see illustration)**. There should be no continuity (infinite resistance) between the commutator and the shaft. If the checks indicate otherwise, the armature is defective and a new starter motor must be obtained – the armature is not available separately.

13 Check the front end of the armature shaft for worn, cracked, chipped and broken teeth. If the shaft is damaged or worn, a new starter

27.8b Checking for continuity between the negative brush and the plate

motor must be obtained – the armature is not available separately.

14 Inspect the front and rear covers for signs of cracks or wear. Check the oil seal and bearing in the front cover and the bush in the rear cover for wear and damage **(see illustration)** – the seal, bearing, front cover, rear cover and bush are not listed as being available separately, so if necessary a new starter motor must be fitted, but note that after-market seals and bearings are readily available from good suppliers, you just need to remove the old ones and note the size markings.

15 Inspect the magnets in the main housing and the housing itself for cracks.

16 Inspect the terminal bolt and assembly bolt O-rings and the cover sealing rings for signs of damage, deformation and deterioration and replace them with new ones if necessary **(see illustration)** – Kawasaki specifies that new ones should be used as a matter of course.

27.10a Draw the brushes out...

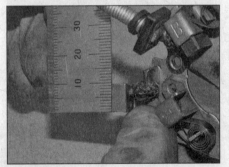

27.10b ...and measure them

27.12a There should be continuity between the bars ...

27.12b ... and no continuity between the bars and the shaft

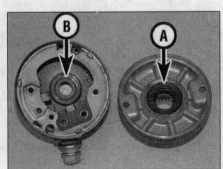

27.14 Check the bearing and seal (A) and the bush (B)

27.16 Main housing sealing rings

27.17a Make sure the spring ends are correctly seated

27.17b Insulator (A) and O-ring (B)

27.17c Fit the brushplate...

27.17d ...seating the O-ring (arrowed)

27.17e Fit the washers and nut

Reassembly

17 Fit each brush into its housing and seat the spring on its end **(see illustration)**. Make sure the insulator and O-ring are on the terminal bolt **(see illustration)**. Fit the brushplate assembly into the rear cover, making sure the O-ring seats between the bolt and its hole to insulate it from the cover **(see illustrations)**. Fit the insulating washers and plain washer as shown, then fit the nut and tighten it **(see illustration)**.

18 Fit the sealing rings onto the housing **(see illustration 27.16)**. Slide the armature into the housing so the cut-out in the housing rim is at the rear of the armature **(see illustration)**.

19 Apply a smear of grease to the front cover oil seal lip. Locate the tabbed washer into the cover so that its teeth are correctly engaged with the cover ribs **(see illustration)**. Slide the shim(s) and insulating washer onto the front end of the armature shaft **(see illustration)**. Slide the front cover into position, aligning the marks **(see illustration)**.

20 Fit the washer(s) onto the rear end of the shaft **(see illustration 27.5c)**. Align the marks on the housing and rear cover and insert the armature into the cover at an angle so the brushes locate against the commutator, then push the brushes back into their housings and

27.18 Housing rim cut-out (arrowed)

27.19a Fit the tabbed washer...

27.19b ...the shim (A) and insulating washer (B)

27.19c Align the marks when fitting the cover

27.20 Fit the cover as described

27.21 Make sure the O-ring is on each bolt

27.24 Note the alignment marks (highlighted) between the housing and the covers

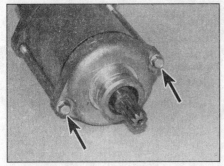

27.25a Unscrew the bolts (arrowed)...

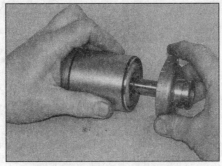

27.25b ...remove the front cover...

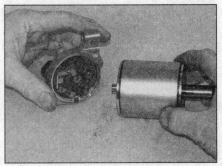

27.26 ...and the rear cover

locate the end of the shaft in the bush and the raised tab on the brushplate in the cutout in the housing rim **(see illustration)**.

21 Check the marks made on removal are correctly aligned then fit the long bolts with their O-rings (using new ones if necessary) and tighten them **(see illustration)**.

22 Install the starter motor (see Section 26).

E and F models from engine No. ZXT00DE043312-on

Disassembly

23 Remove the starter motor (see Section 26).

24 Note any alignment marks between the main housing and the front and rear covers, or make your own if they aren't clear **(see illustration)**.

25 Unscrew the two long bolts and remove the front cover from the motor **(see illustrations)**.

26 Remove the rear cover **(see illustration)**.

27 Withdraw the armature from the main housing **(see illustration)** – it is held in by the attraction of the magnets, so take care not to lose your grip on the armature before the magnets lose theirs.

28 At this stage check for continuity between the terminal bolt and the positive brushes (see

illustration) – there should be continuity (zero resistance). Check for continuity between the terminal bolt and the cover – there should be no continuity (infinite resistance). Also check for continuity between the negative and positive brushes – there should be no continuity (infinite resistance). If there is no continuity when there should be or *vice versa*, identify the faulty component and replace it with a new one.

29 Noting the correct fitted location of each component, unscrew the nut from the terminal bolt and remove the plain washer, the insulator,

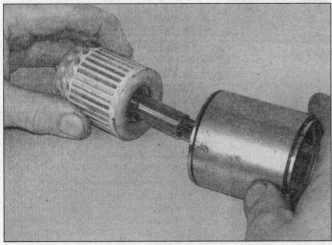

27.27 Withdraw the armature

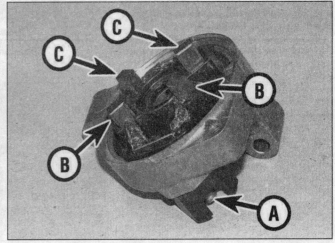

27.28 Terminal bolt (A), positive brushes (B), negative brushes (C)

27.29a Undo the nut and remove the plain washer (arrowed)...

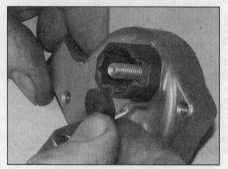

27.29b ...the insulator...

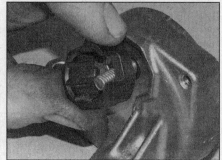

27.29c ...the shield (where fitted)...

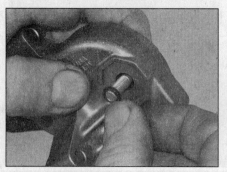

27.29d ...and the O-ring

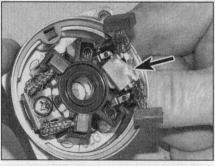

27.29e Withdraw the terminal bolt and brush assembly (arrowed)...

27.29f ...and remove the brush springs

the terminal shield where fitted, and the O-ring **(see illustrations)**. Remove the positive brush and terminal bolt assembly, then remove the positive brush springs **(see illustrations)**.

30 Undo the screw and remove the negative brush assembly **(see illustration)**. Remove the brush springs, then remove the holder **(see illustrations)**.

Inspection

31 The parts of the starter motor that are most likely to require attention are the brushes. Measure the length of each brush and compare the results to the length listed in this Chapter's Specifications **(see illustration)**. If worn replace the brushes with new ones. If the brushes are not worn excessively, nor cracked, chipped, or otherwise damaged, they can be re-used.

32 Inspect the commutator bars on the armature for scoring, scratches and discoloration. The commutator can be cleaned and polished with crocus cloth, but do not use sandpaper or emery paper. After cleaning, wipe away any residue with a cloth soaked in electrical system cleaner or denatured alcohol.

33 Using an ohmmeter or a continuity test light, check for continuity between the commutator bars **(see illustration)**.

27.30a Undo the screw and remove the negative brush assembly...

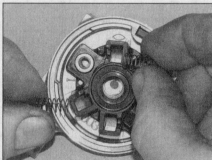

27.30b ...and springs...

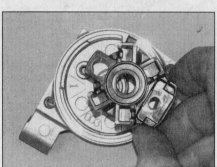

27.30c ...then remove the brushholder

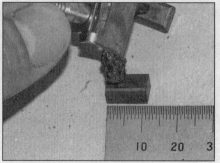

27.31 Measure the length of each brush

27.33a There should be continuity between the bars...

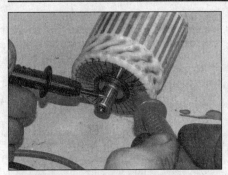

27.33b ...and no continuity between the bars and the shaft

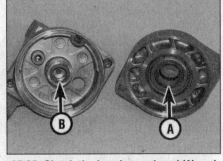

27.35 Check the bearing and seal (A) and the bush (B)

27.39 Fit the O-ring between the bolt and the cover

Continuity should exist between each bar and all of the others. Also, check for continuity between the commutator bars and the armature shaft **(see illustration)**. There should be no continuity (infinite resistance) between the commutator and the shaft. If the checks indicate otherwise, the armature is defective and a new starter motor must be obtained – the armature is not available separately.

34 Check the front end of the armature shaft for worn, cracked, chipped and broken teeth. If the shaft is damaged or worn, a new starter motor must be obtained – the armature is not available separately.

35 Inspect the front and rear covers for signs of cracks or wear. Check the oil seal and the needle bearing in the front cover and the bush in the rear cover for wear and damage **(see illustration)** – the seal, bearing, bush and covers are not listed as being available separately so if necessary a new starter motor must be fitted.

36 Inspect the magnets in the main housing and the housing itself for cracks.

37 Inspect the terminal bolt shield, insulator, and O-ring, and the sealing rings on the housing, for signs of damage, deformation and deterioration and replace them with new ones if necessary.

Reassembly

38 Locate the brush holder on the rear cover **(see illustration 27.30c)**. Fit the negative brush springs and brush assembly and secure it and the holder with the screw **(see illustrations 27.30b and a)**.

39 Fit the positive brush springs into their housings **(see illustration 27.29f)**. Fit the terminal bolt through the holder and rear cover **(see illustration 27.29e)**. Roll the O-ring down the bolt and press it into the gap between the bolt and the cover **(see illustration)**. Where removed fit the shield, aligning it as shown **(see illustration 27.29c)**. Fit the insulator and the washer, then tighten the nut **(see illustrations 27.29b and a)**. Locate the brushes in their housings against the springs, with the wires in the slots **(see illustration 27.28)**.

40 To check for correct installation do the continuity checks described in Step 8.

41 If removed fit the sealing rings onto the main housing **(see illustration)**.

42 Grasp the housing and carefully allow the armature to be drawn in, making sure the cut-out in the housing is at the same end as the commutator bars **(see illustration 27.27)**.

43 Apply a smear of grease to the short end of the shaft. Fit the rear cover, aligning the marks, and making sure the brushes remain square and seat against the commutator **(see illustration)**.

44 Apply a smear of grease to the front cover oil seal lip. Slide the front cover on, aligning the marks **(see illustration 27.25b)**.

45 Check the marks made on removal are correctly aligned then fit the long bolts and tighten them **(see illustration 27.25a)**.

46 Install the starter motor (see Section 26).

28 Charging system testing

1 If the performance of the charging system is suspect, the system as a whole should be checked first, followed by testing of the individual components. **Note:** *Before beginning the checks, make sure the battery is in good condition and fully charged, and that all system connections are clean and tight.*

2 Checking the output of the charging system and the performance of the various components within the charging system requires the use of a multimeter (with voltage, current and resistance checking facilities). If a multimeter is not available, the job of checking the charging system should be left to a Kawasaki dealer.

3 When making the checks, follow the procedures carefully to prevent incorrect connections or short circuits resulting in irreparable damage to electrical system components.

Output test

4 Remove the rider's seat (see Chapter 7). Start the engine and warm it up.

5 To check the regulated (DC) voltage output, allow the engine to idle. Connect a multimeter set to the 0-20 volts DC scale across the terminals of the battery with the positive (+) meter probe to battery positive (+) terminal and the negative (-) meter probe to battery negative (-) terminal (see Section 3) **(see illustration)**.

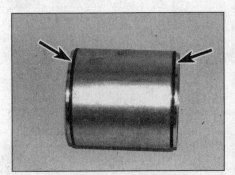

27.41 Main housing sealing rings (arrowed)

27.43 Align the marks when fitting the cover

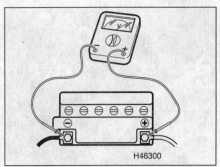

28.5 Checking the charging rate – connect the meter as shown

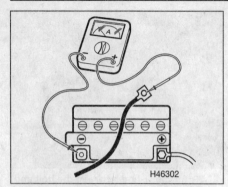

28.8 Checking the charging system leakage rate – connect the meter as shown

6 Slowly increase the engine speed to 5000 rpm and note the reading obtained. Compare the result with the Specification at the beginning of this Chapter. If the regulated voltage output is outside the specification, check the alternator and the regulator/rectifier (Sections 29 and 30).

 HAYNES HINT *Clues to a faulty regulator are constantly blowing bulbs, with brightness varying considerably with engine speed, and battery overheating.*

Leakage test

Caution: Always connect an ammeter in series, never in parallel with the battery, otherwise it will be damaged. Do not turn the ignition ON or operate the starter motor when the ammeter is connected – a sudden surge in current will blow the meter's fuse.

7 ·Make sure the ignition is OFF. Remove the rider's seat (see Chapter 7). Disconnect the battery negative (-) lead (see Section 3).
8 Set the multimeter to the Amps function and connect its negative (-) probe to the battery negative (-) terminal, and positive (+) probe to the disconnected negative (-) lead (see illustration). Always set the meter to a high amps range initially and then bring it down to the mA (milli Amps) range; if there is a high current flow in the circuit it may blow the meter's fuse.

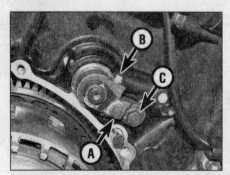

29.8a Shaft spring bolt (A), pinch bolt (B), mounting bolt (C)

9 Battery current leakage should not exceed the maximum limit (see Specifications). If a higher leakage rate is shown there is a short circuit in the wiring, although if an alarm is fitted, its current draw should be taken into account. Disconnect the meter and reconnect the battery negative (-) lead.
10 If leakage is indicated, refer to the Wiring Diagrams at the end of this Chapter to systematically disconnect individual electrical components and repeat the test until the source is identified.

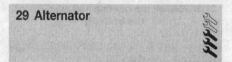

29 Alternator

C models
Check

1 Remove the fuel tank (see Chapter 4).
2 Disconnect the 3 alternator wiring connectors with the black wires (see illustration). Check the connector terminals for corrosion and security.
3 Using a multimeter set to the ohms x 1 (ohmmeter) scale measure the resistance between each of the black wires on the alternator side of the connectors, taking a total of three readings, then check for continuity between each terminal and ground (earth). If the stator coil windings are in good condition the three readings should be within the range shown in the Specifications at the start of this Chapter, and there should be no continuity (infinite resistance) between any of

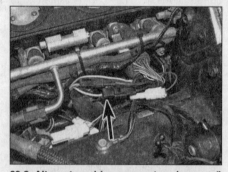

29.2 Alternator wiring connectors (arrowed)

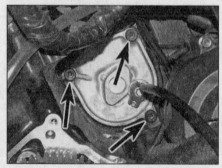

29.8b Unscrew the bolts (arrowed)...

the terminals and ground (earth). If not, the alternator stator coil assembly is at fault and should be replaced with a new one.
4 Fit the fuel tank in the raised position. Set the multimeter to read AC voltage. With the engine running at 4000 rpm, check the unregulated voltage output of the alternator between each of the black wires on the alternator side of the connectors, taking a total of three readings. If the stator coil windings are in good condition the three readings should be within the range shown in the Specifications at the start of this Chapter. If not, the alternator stator coil assembly is at fault and should be replaced with a new one. **Note:** *Before condemning the stator coils, check the fault is not due to damaged wiring between the connector and the coils.*

Removal

5 Remove the throttle bodies (see Chapter 4). Remove the thermostat housing and coolant inlet union (see Chapter 3). Remove the starter motor (see Section 26).
6 Disconnect the 3 alternator wiring connectors with the black wires (see illustration 29.2).
7 Unscrew the clutch cable bracket bolts then detach the cable end from the release arm (see illustration).
8 Unscrew the shaft spring bolt and remove the spring (see illustration). Slacken the shaft clamp pinch bolt. Unscrew the three cover bolts (see illustration). Push the end of the shaft in and remove the alternator assembly from the left (see illustrations). Remove the O-ring – a new one must be used (see illustration 29.9). Unscrew the clamp mounting bolt and remove

29.7 Clutch cable bracket bolts (arrowed)

29.8c ...push the end of the shaft in...

29.8d ...and remove the alternator

29.8e Remove the clamp...

29.8f ...and the seal

the clamp **(see illustration)**. Remove the oil seal **(see illustration)**.

Disassembly and inspection

9 Draw the stator out with the cover **(see illustration)**.

10 To remove the stator, undo the wiring plate bolt and remove the plate **(see illustration)**.

Undo the stator bolts and remove it from the cover, drawing the wiring through the hole **(see illustration)**.

11 Release the circlip and remove the toothed washer and spacer **(see illustrations)**. Withdraw the shaft from the opposite end **(see illustration)**. A new circlip must be used on reassembly.

12 Check for any rotational play in the gear by turning it from side to side – if there is any play new dampers are needed. On C2 models release the circlip and remove the washer **(see illustrations)**. Remove the gear and the rubber dampers **(see illustration)**. Check the condition of the dampers and replace them with new ones if necessary.

29.9 Draw the stator out. Note the O-ring (arrowed)

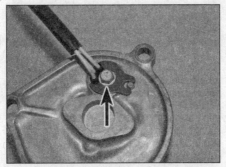

29.10a Wiring plate bolt (arrowed)

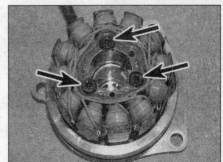

29.10b Stator bolts (arrowed)

29.11a Release the circlip...

29.11b ...remove the washers...

29.11c ...and withdraw the shaft

29.12a Release the circlip...

29.12b ...and remove the washer

29.12c Remove the gear coupling and the dampers (arrowed)

29.13 Code letter (arrowed)

29.15a Seat the tooth in the groove

29.15b Check the clearance

13 Check the condition of the gear teeth, and of the corresponding drive teeth on the clutch housing. If a new gear is required check for any letter (A, B, C or D on C1 models, or A, B, E or F on C2 models) marked on the gear and obtain a new gear with the same marking **(see illustration)** – if no letter is visible, the new gear must also have no letter.

Reassembly

14 Seat each damper pair over the ribs. Smear some oil onto the vanes of the gear assembly and fit them into the dampers, making sure they seat fully **(see illustration 29.12c)**. On C2 models fit the washer and the circlip, making sure it is seated in the groove **(see illustrations 29.12b and a)**.

15 Smear some molybdenum disulphide oil (a 50/50 mix of molybdenum disulphide grease and engine oil) onto the shaft and slide it through from the stator end **(see**

illustration 29.11c). Fit the spacer and toothed washer **(see illustration 29.11b)**, aligning the tooth with the groove in the shaft **(see illustration)**. Secure them with a new circlip, making sure it is seated in the groove **(see illustration 29.11a)**. Using a feeler gauge check the clearance between the toothed washer and the spacer **(see illustration)** – if it is not between 0.6 and 0.9 mm replace the toothed washer with a thicker or thinner one as required to bring the clearance within the specified range. On C1 models the standard washer is 1.6 mm thick, and replacements are available in increments of 0.2 mm from 1.0 to 2.0 mm, and there is also one of 2.3 mm. On C2 models replacements are available in increments of 0.1 mm from 1.0 to 2.3 mm. Only use one washer.

16 Fit the stator onto the cover, feeding the wiring through the hole and the grommet into it. Clean the threads of the bolts and apply

a strong non-permanent threadlock, then tighten them to the torque setting specified at the beginning of the Chapter **(see illustration 29.10b)**. Secure the wiring with its plate, locating the cut-out around the pin **(see illustration 29.10a)**.

17 Make sure that no metal objects have attached themselves to the magnet on the inside of the rotor. Fit the stator assembly **(see illustration 29.9)**.

Installation

18 Fit the new shaft seal with the flared rim facing in flush with the rim of its housing **(see illustration 29.8f)**. Smear the seal lips with grease. Clean the threads of the shaft clamp mounting bolt and apply a non-permanent threadlock. Fit the clamp and tighten the mounting bolt lightly, so the clamp can move for alignment if necessary **(see illustration 29.8e)**.

19 Fit a new O-ring smeared with grease onto the cover **(see illustration)**. Slide the alternator assembly into place **(see illustration 29.8d)** – as the gear has an offset sprung section you need to align it with the main gear using a screwdriver as you engage the teeth with the drive gear on the clutch, and make sure the teeth fully engage and the cover seats against the crankcase **(see illustrations)**. Tighten the cover bolts to the torque specified at the beginning of the Chapter **(see illustration 29.8b)**. Tighten the shaft clamp mounting bolt to the specified torque **(see illustration 29.8a)**. Fit the shaft spring and tighten its bolt to the specified torque. Fit the pinch bolt and tighten to the specified torque.

20 Route the wiring and connect the connectors **(see illustration 29.2)**. Connect the clutch cable and fit the bracket **(see illustration 29.7)**.

21 Install the remaining components in reverse order (see Step 5).

D, E and F models

Check

22 On D models raise the fuel tank (see Chapter 4).

23 Disconnect the 3-pin alternator wiring connector with the three white wires **(see illustrations)**. Check the connector terminals for corrosion and security.

29.19a Align the teeth using a screwdriver...

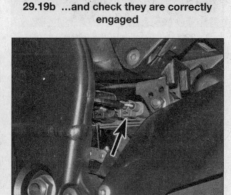

29.19b ...and check they are correctly engaged

29.23a Alternator wiring connector (arrowed) – D models

29.23b Alternator wiring connector (arrowed) – E/F models

29.30 Alternator cover bolts (arrowed)

29.31 Using a rotor strap to hold the rotor while unscrewing the bolt

24 Using a multimeter set to the ohms x 1 (ohmmeter) scale measure the resistance between each of the white wires on the alternator side of the connector, taking a total of three readings, then check for continuity between each terminal and ground (earth). If the stator coil windings are in good condition the three readings should be within the range shown in the Specifications at the start of this Chapter, and there should be no continuity (infinite resistance) between any of the terminals and ground (earth). If not, the alternator stator coil assembly is at fault and should be replaced with a new one.

25 Set the multimeter to read AC voltage. With the engine running at 4000 rpm, check the unregulated voltage output of the alternator between each of the white wires on the alternator side of the connector, taking a total of three readings. If the stator coil windings are in good condition the three readings should be within the range shown in the Specifications at the start of this Chapter. If not, the alternator stator coil assembly is at fault and should be replaced

with a new one. **Note:** *Before condemning the stator coils, check the fault is not due to damaged wiring between the connector and the coils.*

Removal

Special tools: *A rotor holding strap and rotor puller are needed (see Steps 31 and 32).*
26 Remove the coolant reservoir (see Chapter 3).
27 Remove the fuel tank (see Chapter 4).
28 If you have an auxiliary stand place the bike on it so that it is level – this minimises oil loss. If you do not have an auxiliary stand either drain the oil or place a container under the engine to catch the oil that will come out when the alternator cover is removed.
29 Disconnect the 3-pin alternator wiring connector with the three white wires **(see illustration 29.23a or b)**. Feed the wiring down to the alternator cover, releasing it from any ties and noting its routing.
30 Working in a criss-cross pattern, evenly slacken then remove the alternator cover

bolts and the bracket, noting its position **(see illustration)**. Draw the cover off the engine, noting that it will be restrained by the force of the rotor magnets, and be prepared to catch the residual oil. Remove the gasket. Remove the dowels from either the cover or the crankcase if they are loose.
31 To remove the rotor bolt it is necessary to stop the rotor from turning using a commercially available rotor strap. Clean the outside of the rotor with solvent to remove all oil, then fit the strap **(see illustration)**. Slacken the bolt and unscrew it a few turns, but do not remove it.
32 To remove the rotor from the shaft it is necessary to use a rotor puller – use either the Kawasaki tool (part No. 57001-1405) or a commercially available equivalent designed for this bike. Thread the pulley body onto the centre of the rotor and turn the centre bolt until the rotor is displaced from the shaft, holding the rotor to prevent the engine turning **(see illustrations)**. If the rotor doesn't come off easily use some extra leverage on the tool, and/or tap the end of the tool when it is tight,

29.32a Thread the puller onto the rotor...

29.32b ...then hold the rotor and turn the puller bolt

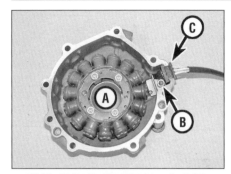

29.33 Stator bolts (A), clamp bolt (B), grommet (C)

29.36 Slide the rotor onto the shaft

29.37a Fit the bolt with its washer...

29.37b ...and tighten it to the specified torque

and if necessary heat the rotor hub using a hot air gun. Remove the puller, then unscrew the bolt with its washer and remove the rotor.

33 To remove the stator from the cover, unscrew its bolts and the wiring clamp bolt, then remove the assembly, noting how the rubber wiring grommet fits **(see illustration)**.

Installation

34 Fit the stator into the cover, aligning the rubber wiring grommet with the groove **(see illustration 29.33)**. Fit the bolts and tighten them to the torque setting specified at the beginning of the Chapter. Apply a suitable sealant to the wiring grommet then press it into the cut-out in the cover. Clean the threads of the clamp bolt and apply a non-permanent threadlock. Secure the wiring with its clamp and tighten the bolt to the specified torque.

35 Clean all old sealant and gasket off the cover and crankcase mating surfaces and wipe

them with a suitable solvent. Clean the tapered end of the crankshaft and the corresponding mating surface on the inside of the rotor, and both sides of the bolt washer, with solvent.

36 Make sure that no metal objects have attached themselves to the magnet on the inside of the rotor. Slide the rotor fully onto the shaft **(see illustration)**.

37 Fit the bolt with its washer and tighten it to the initial torque setting specified at the beginning of the Chapter, holding the rotor as on removal **(see illustrations)**. Now partially unscrew the bolt and check the rotor is firmly on the shaft by fitting the puller used on removal and making sure the bolt can be tightened to 20 Nm without the rotor coming loose. If it does come loose, remove it and clean again as before, then refit it.

38 With the rotor secure tighten the bolt to the final torque setting specified.

39 Apply a smear of suitable sealant to the mating surface of the alternator cover and 10 to 15 mm either side of the crankcase joints. Fit the dowels into the cover or crankcase if removed. Fit the new gasket over the dowels **(see illustration)**. Fit the alternator cover, noting that the rotor magnets will forcibly draw the cover/stator on, making sure the dowels locate **(see illustration)**. Fit the cover bolts, along with the bracket, and tighten them evenly in a criss-cross sequence to the specified torque **(see illustration)**.

40 Route, secure and connect the wiring **(see illustration 29.23a or b)**.

41 Fill the engine with the correct quantity of oil, or top it up to the correct level, as required according to your removal method (see Chapter 1). Install the fuel tank, coolant reservoir and fairing panels.

30 Regulator/rectifier

Check

1 Remove the regulator/rectifier (see below). Check the connector terminals for corrosion and security.

2 Set the multimeter to the 0 to 20 dc volts setting. Connect the meter positive (+) probe to the white/black (C models) or white (all other models) wire terminal on the loom side of the black connector and the negative (–) probe to a suitable ground (earth) and check for voltage. Full battery voltage should be present at all times.

3 Switch the multimeter to the resistance (ohms) scale. Check for continuity between the black/yellow (C and D models) or black (E and F models) wire terminal on the loom side of the black connector and ground (earth). There should be continuity to earth.

4 Set the multimeter to the ohms x 1 (ohmmeter) scale and measure the resistance between each of the wires in the loom side of the grey connector, taking a total of three readings, then check for continuity between each terminal and ground (earth). The three readings should be within the range shown in

29.39a Seat the gasket on the dowels (arrowed)...

29.39b ...then fit the cover

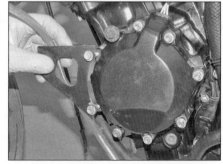

29.39c Do not forget the bracket

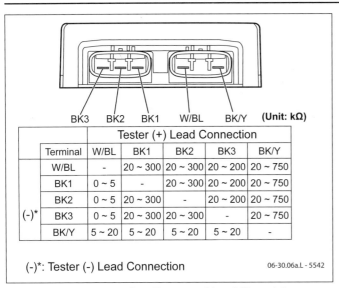

BK3 BK2 BK1 W/BL BK/Y **(Unit: kΩ)**

		Tester (+) Lead Connection				
	Terminal	W/BL	BK1	BK2	BK3	BK/Y
	W/BL	-	20 ~ 300	20 ~ 300	20 ~ 200	20 ~ 750
	BK1	0 ~ 5	-	20 ~ 300	20 ~ 200	20 ~ 750
	BK2	0 ~ 5	20 ~ 300	-	20 ~ 200	20 ~ 750
(-)*	BK3	0 ~ 5	20 ~ 300	20 ~ 300	-	20 ~ 750
	BK/Y	5 ~ 20	5 ~ 20	5 ~ 20	5 ~ 20	-

(-)*: Tester (-) Lead Connection

06-30.06a.L - 5542

30.6a Regulator/rectifier test table – C/D models

BK1	Black 1	BK/Y	Black and yellow
BK2	Black 2	W/BL	White and blue (white on
BK3	Black 3		D models)

W1 W2 W3 W4 BK/G BK **(Unit: kΩ)**

		Tester (+) Lead Connection					
	Terminal	W1	W2	W3	W4	BK/G	BK
	W1	–	∞	∞	3 ~ 11	∞	∞
	W2	∞	–	∞	3 ~ 11	∞	∞
	W3	∞	∞	–	3 ~ 11	∞	∞
(-)*	W4	∞	∞	∞	–	∞	∞
	BK/G	∞	∞	∞	3 ~ 11	–	∞
	BK	3 ~ 11	3 ~ 11	3 ~ 11	6 ~ 18	3 ~ 11	–

(-)*: Tester (-) Lead Connection

06-30.06b.L - 5542

30.6b Regulator/rectifier test table – E/F models

W1	White 1	W4	White 4
W2	White 2	BK	Black
W3	White 3	BK/G	Black and green

the Specifications for the alternator stator coil at the start of this Chapter, and there should be no continuity (infinite resistance) between any of the terminals and ground (earth).

5 If the above checks do not provide the expected results check the wiring and connectors between the battery, regulator/ rectifier and alternator for shorts, breaks, and loose or corroded terminals (see the wiring diagrams at the end of this chapter).

6 Switch the multimeter to the resistance (K-ohms) scale. Check the resistances between the terminals on the regulator/rectifier as shown **(see illustrations)**. If the results are not as specified the regulator/rectifier unit is faulty.

 Clues to a faulty regulator are constantly blowing bulbs, with brightness varying considerably with engine speed, and battery overheating.

Removal and installation

7 On C and D models unscrew the two bolts and displace the regulator/rectifier, then disconnect the wiring connectors **(see illustration)**.

8 On E and F models disconnect the regulator/rectifier wiring connectors **(see illustration 29.23b)**. Displace the rear brake

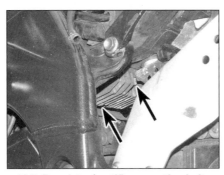

30.7 Regulator/rectifier mounting bolts (arrowed) – C/D models

fluid reservoir **(see illustration)**. Unscrew the regulator/rectifier bracket bolts and remove the regulator/rectifier/bracket assembly. Note the collar in each side of each grommet. Check the condition of the grommets and replace them with new ones if necessary. If required unscrew the bolts and detach the regulator/rectifier from the bracket.

9 Installation is the reverse of removal.

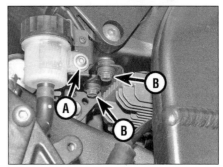

30.8 Reservoir bolt (A), regulator/rectifier bracket bolts (B) – E/F models

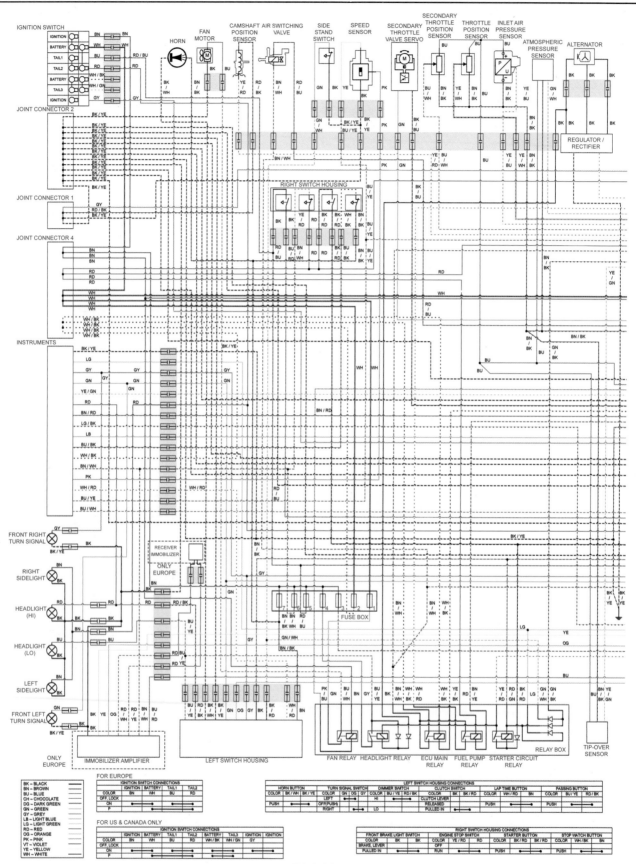

ZX1000C

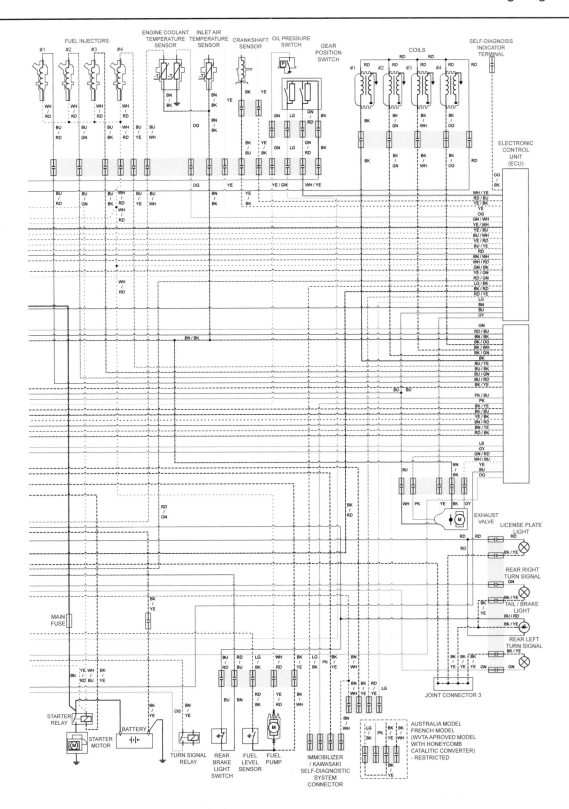

ZX1000C

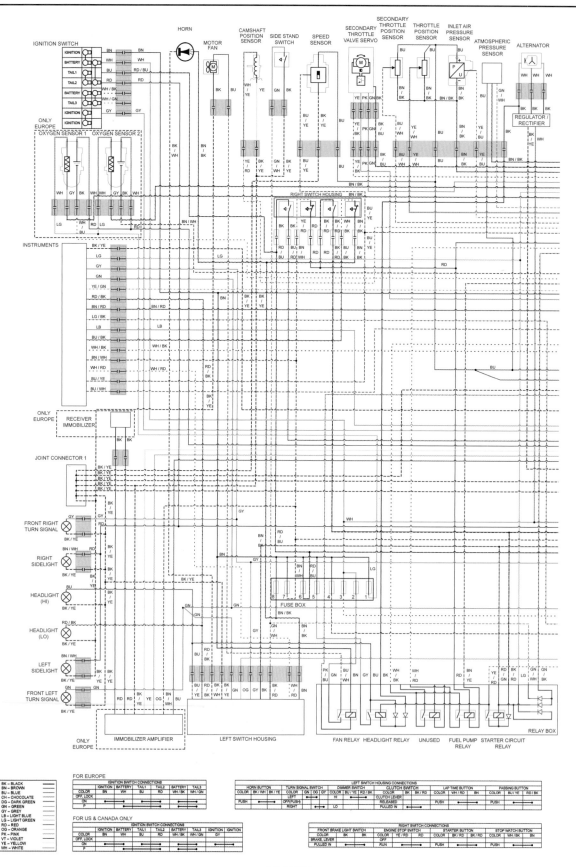

ZX1000D

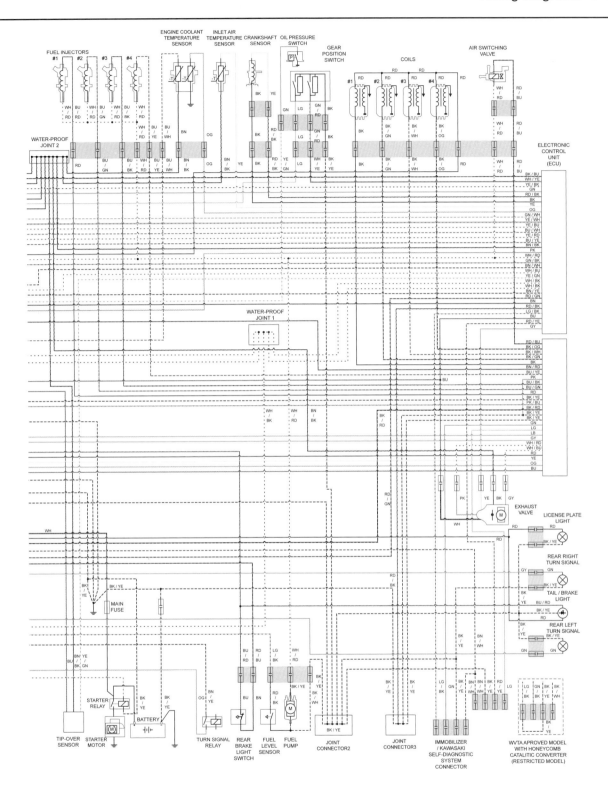

ZX1000D

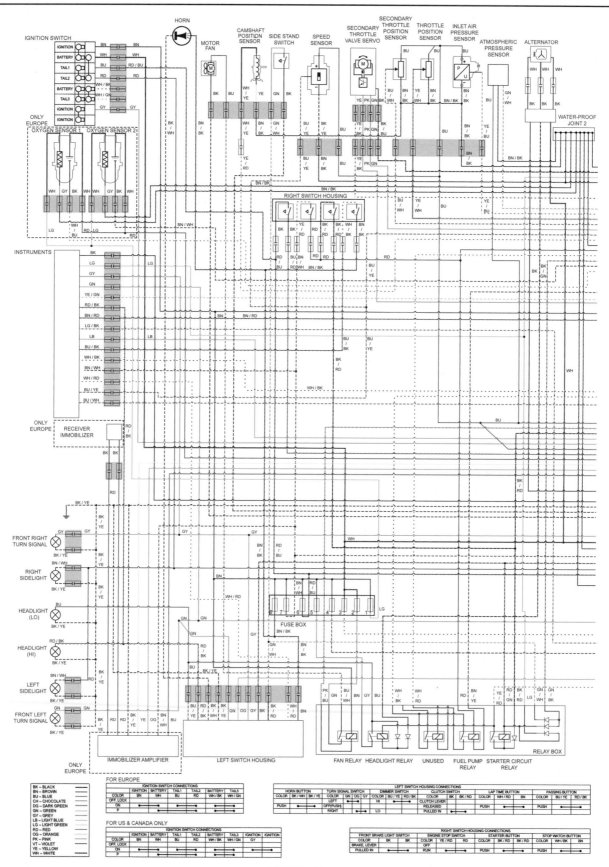

ZX1000E/F

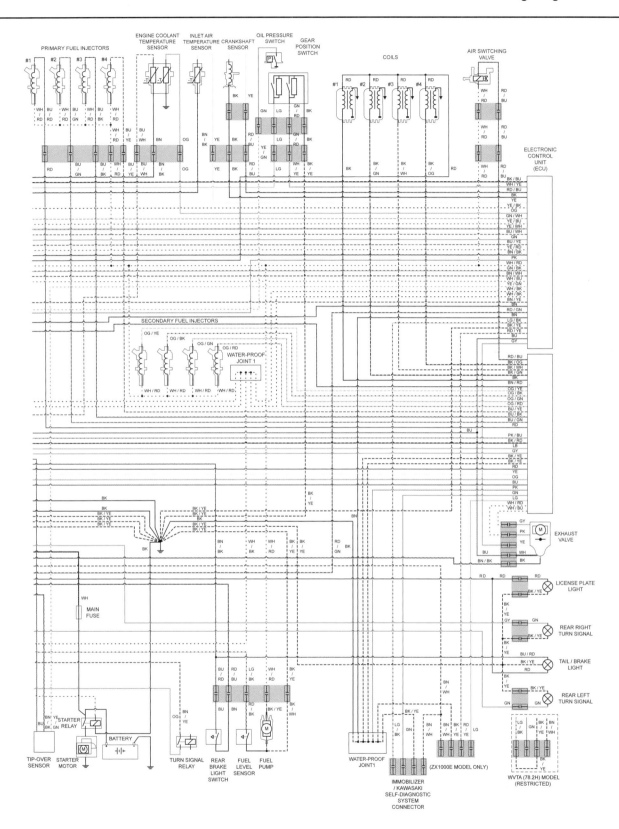

ZX1000E/F

Notes

Reference

Tools and Workshop Tips

● Building up a tool kit and equipping your workshop ● Using tools ● Understanding bearing, seal, fastener and chain sizes and markings ● Repair techniques

Security

● Locks and chains ● U-locks ● Disc locks ● Alarms and immobilisers ● Security marking systems ● Tips on how to prevent bike theft

Lubricants and fluids

● Engine oils ● Transmission (gear) oils ● Coolant/anti-freeze ● Fork oils and suspension fluids ● Brake/clutch fluids ● Spray lubes, degreasers and solvents

Conversion Factors

$$34 \text{ Nm} \times 0.738 = 25 \text{ lbf ft}$$

● Formulae for conversion of the metric (SI) units used throughout the manual into Imperial measures

MOT Test Checks

● A guide to the UK MOT test ● Which items are tested ● How to prepare your motorcycle for the test and perform a pre-test check

Storage

● How to prepare your motorcycle for going into storage and protect essential systems ● How to get the motorcycle back on the road

Fault Finding

● Common faults and their likely causes ● Links to main chapters for testing and repair procedures

Technical Terms Explained

● Component names, technical terms and common abbreviations explained

Index

Buying tools

A toolkit is a fundamental requirement for servicing and repairing a motorcycle. Although there will be an initial expense in building up enough tools for servicing, this will soon be offset by the savings made by doing the job yourself. As experience and confidence grow, additional tools can be added to enable the repair and overhaul of the motorcycle. Many of the specialist tools are expensive and not often used so it may be preferable to hire them, or for a group of friends or motorcycle club to join in the purchase.

As a rule, it is better to buy more expensive, good quality tools. Cheaper tools are likely to wear out faster and need to be renewed more often, nullifying the original saving.

> ⚠️ **Warning: To avoid the risk of a poor quality tool breaking in use, causing injury or damage to the component being worked on, always aim to purchase tools which meet the relevant national safety standards.**

The following lists of tools do not represent the manufacturer's service tools, but serve as a guide to help the owner decide which tools are needed for this level of work. In addition, items such as an electric drill, hacksaw, files, soldering iron and a workbench equipped with a vice, may be needed. Although not classed as tools, a selection of bolts, screws, nuts, washers and pieces of tubing always come in useful.

For more information about tools, refer to the Haynes *Motorcycle Workshop Practice Techbook* (Bk. No. 3470).

Manufacturer's service tools

Inevitably certain tasks require the use of a service tool. Where possible an alternative tool or method of approach is recommended, but sometimes there is no option if personal injury or damage to the component is to be avoided. Where required, service tools are referred to in the relevant procedure.

Service tools can usually only be purchased from a motorcycle dealer and are identified by a part number. Some of the commonly-used tools, such as rotor pullers, are available in aftermarket form from mail-order motorcycle tool and accessory suppliers.

Maintenance and minor repair tools

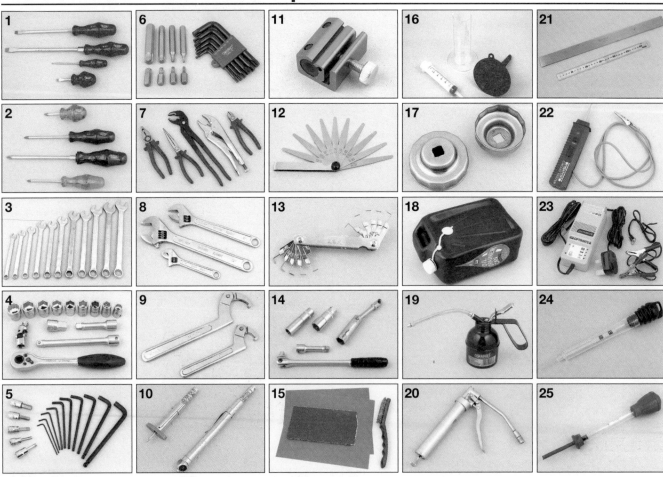

1 Set of flat-bladed screwdrivers
2 Set of Phillips head screwdrivers
3 Combination open-end and ring spanners
4 Socket set (3/8 inch or 1/2 inch drive)
5 Set of Allen keys or bits
6 Set of Torx keys or bits
7 Pliers, cutters and self-locking grips (Mole grips)
8 Adjustable spanners
9 C-spanners
10 Tread depth gauge and tyre pressure gauge
11 Cable oiler clamp
12 Feeler gauges
13 Spark plug gap measuring tool
14 Spark plug spanner or deep plug sockets
15 Wire brush and emery paper
16 Calibrated syringe, measuring vessel and funnel
17 Oil filter adapters
18 Oil drainer can or tray
19 Pump type oil can
20 Grease gun
21 Straight-edge and steel rule
22 Continuity tester
23 Battery charger
24 Hydrometer (for battery specific gravity check)
25 Anti-freeze tester (for liquid-cooled engines)

Repair and overhaul tools

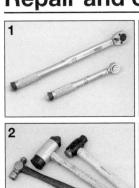

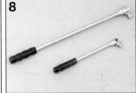

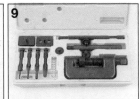

1 Torque wrench (small and mid-ranges)
2 Conventional, plastic or soft-faced hammers
3 Impact driver set
4 Vernier gauge
5 Circlip pliers (internal and external, or combination)
6 Set of cold chisels and punches
7 Selection of pullers
8 Breaker bars
9 Chain breaking/riveting tool set
10 Wire stripper and crimper tool
11 Multimeter (measures amps, volts and ohms)
12 Stroboscope (for dynamic timing checks)
13 Hose clamp (wingnut type shown)
14 Clutch holding tool
15 One-man brake/clutch bleeder kit

Specialist tools

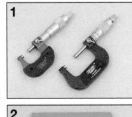
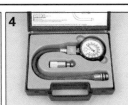

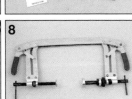
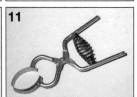

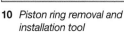
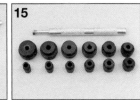

1 Micrometers (external type)
2 Telescoping gauges
3 Dial gauge
4 Cylinder compression gauge
5 Vacuum gauges (left) or manometer (right)
6 Oil pressure gauge
7 Plastigauge kit
8 Valve spring compressor (4-stroke engines)
9 Piston pin drawbolt tool
10 Piston ring removal and installation tool
11 Piston ring clamp
12 Cylinder bore hone (stone type shown)
13 Stud extractor
14 Screw extractor set
15 Bearing driver set

1 Workshop equipment and facilities

The workbench

● Work is made much easier by raising the bike up on a ramp - components are much more accessible if raised to waist level. The hydraulic or pneumatic types seen in the dealer's workshop are a sound investment if you undertake a lot of repairs or overhauls **(see illustration 1.1)**.

1.1 **Hydraulic motorcycle ramp**

● If raised off ground level, the bike must be supported on the ramp to avoid it falling. Most ramps incorporate a front wheel locating clamp which can be adjusted to suit different diameter wheels. When tightening the clamp, take care not to mark the wheel rim or damage the tyre - use wood blocks on each side to prevent this.
● Secure the bike to the ramp using tie-downs **(see illustration 1.2)**. If the bike has only a sidestand, and hence leans at a dangerous angle when raised, support the bike on an auxiliary stand.

1.2 **Tie-downs are used around the passenger footrests to secure the bike**

● Auxiliary (paddock) stands are widely available from mail order companies or motorcycle dealers and attach either to the wheel axle or swingarm pivot **(see illustration 1.3)**. If the motorcycle has a centrestand, you can support it under the crankcase to prevent it toppling whilst either wheel is removed **(see illustration 1.4)**.

1.3 **This auxiliary stand attaches to the swingarm pivot**

1.4 **Always use a block of wood between the engine and jack head when supporting the engine in this way**

Fumes and fire

● Refer to the Safety first! page at the beginning of the manual for full details. Make sure your workshop is equipped with a fire extinguisher suitable for fuel-related fires (Class B fire - flammable liquids) - it is not sufficient to have a water-filled extinguisher.
● Always ensure adequate ventilation is available. Unless an exhaust gas extraction system is available for use, ensure that the engine is run outside of the workshop.
● If working on the fuel system, make sure the workshop is ventilated to avoid a build-up of fumes. This applies equally to fume build-up when charging a battery. Do not smoke or allow anyone else to smoke in the workshop.

Fluids

● If you need to drain fuel from the tank, store it in an approved container marked as suitable for the storage of petrol (gasoline) **(see illustration 1.5)**. Do not store fuel in glass jars or bottles.

1.5 **Use an approved can only for storing petrol (gasoline)**

● Use proprietary engine degreasers or solvents which have a high flash-point, such as paraffin (kerosene), for cleaning off oil, grease and dirt - never use petrol (gasoline) for cleaning. Wear rubber gloves when handling solvent and engine degreaser. The fumes from certain solvents can be dangerous - always work in a well-ventilated area.

Dust, eye and hand protection

● Protect your lungs from inhalation of dust particles by wearing a filtering mask over the nose and mouth. Many frictional materials still contain asbestos which is dangerous to your health. Protect your eyes from spouts of liquid and sprung components by wearing a pair of protective goggles **(see illustration 1.6)**.

1.6 **A fire extinguisher, goggles, mask and protective gloves should be at hand in the workshop**

● Protect your hands from contact with solvents, fuel and oils by wearing rubber gloves. Alternatively apply a barrier cream to your hands before starting work. If handling hot components or fluids, wear suitable gloves to protect your hands from scalding and burns.

What to do with old fluids

● Old cleaning solvent, fuel, coolant and oils should not be poured down domestic drains or onto the ground. Package the fluid up in old oil containers, label it accordingly, and take it to a garage or disposal facility. Contact your local authority for location of such sites or ring the oil care hotline.

OIL CARE FOLLOW THE CODE

Note: It is antisocial and illegal to dump oil down the drain. To find the location of your local oil recycling bank in the UK, call 08708 506 506 or visit www.oilbankline.org.uk

In the USA, note that any oil supplier must accept used oil for recycling.

2 Fasteners - screws, bolts and nuts

Fastener types and applications

Bolts and screws

● Fastener head types are either of hexagonal, Torx or splined design, with internal and external versions of each type **(see illustrations 2.1 and 2.2)**; splined head fasteners are not in common use on motorcycles. The conventional slotted or Phillips head design is used for certain screws. Bolt or screw length is always measured from the underside of the head to the end of the item **(see illustration 2.11)**.

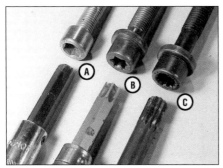

2.1 Internal hexagon/Allen (A), Torx (B) and splined (C) fasteners, with corresponding bits

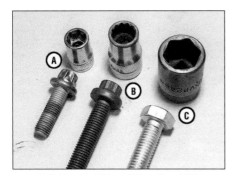

2.2 External Torx (A), splined (B) and hexagon (C) fasteners, with corresponding sockets

● Certain fasteners on the motorcycle have a tensile marking on their heads, the higher the marking the stronger the fastener. High tensile fasteners generally carry a 10 or higher marking. Never replace a high tensile fastener with one of a lower tensile strength.

Washers (see illustration 2.3)

● Plain washers are used between a fastener head and a component to prevent damage to the component or to spread the load when torque is applied. Plain washers can also be used as spacers or shims in certain assemblies. Copper or aluminium plain washers are often used as sealing washers on drain plugs.

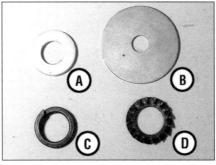

2.3 Plain washer (A), penny washer (B), spring washer (C) and serrated washer (D)

● The split-ring spring washer works by applying axial tension between the fastener head and component. If flattened, it is fatigued and must be renewed. If a plain (flat) washer is used on the fastener, position the spring washer between the fastener and the plain washer.

● Serrated star type washers dig into the fastener and component faces, preventing loosening. They are often used on electrical earth (ground) connections to the frame.

● Cone type washers (sometimes called Belleville) are conical and when tightened apply axial tension between the fastener head and component. They must be installed with the dished side against the component and often carry an OUTSIDE marking on their outer face. If flattened, they are fatigued and must be renewed.

● Tab washers are used to lock plain nuts or bolts on a shaft. A portion of the tab washer is bent up hard against one flat of the nut or bolt to prevent it loosening. Due to the tab washer being deformed in use, a new tab washer should be used every time it is disturbed.

● Wave washers are used to take up endfloat on a shaft. They provide light springing and prevent excessive side-to-side play of a component. Can be found on rocker arm shafts.

Nuts and split pins

● Conventional plain nuts are usually six-sided **(see illustration 2.4)**. They are sized by thread diameter and pitch. High tensile nuts carry a number on one end to denote their tensile strength.

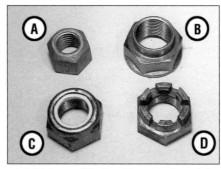

2.4 Plain nut (A), shouldered locknut (B), nylon insert nut (C) and castellated nut (D)

● Self-locking nuts either have a nylon insert, or two spring metal tabs, or a shoulder which is staked into a groove in the shaft - their advantage over conventional plain nuts is a resistance to loosening due to vibration. The nylon insert type can be used a number of times, but must be renewed when the friction of the nylon insert is reduced, ie when the nut spins freely on the shaft. The spring tab type can be reused unless the tabs are damaged. The shouldered type must be renewed every time it is disturbed.

● Split pins (cotter pins) are used to lock a castellated nut to a shaft or to prevent slackening of a plain nut. Common applications are wheel axles and brake torque arms. Because the split pin arms are deformed to lock around the nut a new split pin must always be used on installation - always fit the correct size split pin which will fit snugly in the shaft hole. Make sure the split pin arms are correctly located around the nut **(see illustrations 2.5 and 2.6)**.

2.5 Bend split pin (cotter pin) arms as shown (arrows) to secure a castellated nut

2.6 Bend split pin (cotter pin) arms as shown to secure a plain nut

Caution: If the castellated nut slots do not align with the shaft hole after tightening to the torque setting, tighten the nut until the next slot aligns with the hole - never slacken the nut to align its slot.

● R-pins (shaped like the letter R), or slip pins as they are sometimes called, are sprung and can be reused if they are otherwise in good condition. Always install R-pins with their closed end facing forwards **(see illustration 2.7)**.

2.7 Correct fitting of R-pin. Arrow indicates forward direction

Circlips (see illustration 2.8)

● Circlips (sometimes called snap-rings) are used to retain components on a shaft or in a housing and have corresponding external or internal ears to permit removal. Parallel-sided (machined) circlips can be installed either way round in their groove, whereas stamped circlips (which have a chamfered edge on one face) must be installed with the chamfer facing away from the direction of thrust load **(see illustration 2.9)**.

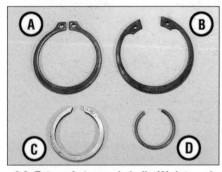

2.8 External stamped circlip (A), internal stamped circlip (B), machined circlip (C) and wire circlip (D)

● Always use circlip pliers to remove and install circlips; expand or compress them just enough to remove them. After installation, rotate the circlip in its groove to ensure it is securely seated. If installing a circlip on a splined shaft, always align its opening with a shaft channel to ensure the circlip ends are well supported and unlikely to catch **(see illustration 2.10)**.

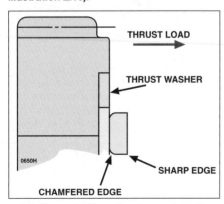

THRUST LOAD

THRUST WASHER

SHARP EDGE

CHAMFERED EDGE

0650H

2.9 Correct fitting of a stamped circlip

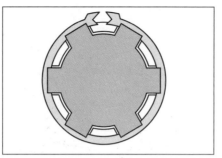

2.10 Align circlip opening with shaft channel

● Circlips can wear due to the thrust of components and become loose in their grooves, with the subsequent danger of becoming dislodged in operation. For this reason, renewal is advised every time a circlip is disturbed.

● Wire circlips are commonly used as piston pin retaining clips. If a removal tang is provided, long-nosed pliers can be used to dislodge them, otherwise careful use of a small flat-bladed screwdriver is necessary. Wire circlips should be renewed every time they are disturbed.

Thread diameter and pitch

● Diameter of a male thread (screw, bolt or stud) is the outside diameter of the threaded portion **(see illustration 2.11)**. Most motorcycle manufacturers use the ISO (International Standards Organisation) metric system expressed in millimetres, eg M6 refers to a 6 mm diameter thread. Sizing is the same for nuts, except that the thread diameter is measured across the valleys of the nut.

● Pitch is the distance between the peaks of the thread **(see illustration 2.11)**. It is expressed in millimetres, thus a common bolt size may be expressed as 6.0 x 1.0 mm (6 mm thread diameter and 1 mm pitch). Generally pitch increases in proportion to thread diameter, although there are always exceptions.

● Thread diameter and pitch are related for conventional fastener applications and the accompanying table can be used as a guide. Additionally, the AF (Across Flats), spanner or socket size dimension of the bolt or nut **(see illustration 2.11)** is linked to thread and pitch specification. Thread pitch can be measured with a thread gauge **(see illustration 2.12)**.

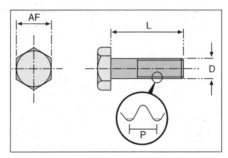

AF

L

D

P

2.11 Fastener length (L), thread diameter (D), thread pitch (P) and head size (AF)

2.12 Using a thread gauge to measure pitch

AF size	Thread diameter x pitch (mm)
8 mm	M5 x 0.8
8 mm	M6 x 1.0
10 mm	M6 x 1.0
12 mm	M8 x 1.25
14 mm	M10 x 1.25
17 mm	M12 x 1.25

● The threads of most fasteners are of the right-hand type, ie they are turned clockwise to tighten and anti-clockwise to loosen. The reverse situation applies to left-hand thread fasteners, which are turned anti-clockwise to tighten and clockwise to loosen. Left-hand threads are used where rotation of a component might loosen a conventional right-hand thread fastener.

Seized fasteners

● Corrosion of external fasteners due to water or reaction between two dissimilar metals can occur over a period of time. It will build up sooner in wet conditions or in countries where salt is used on the roads during the winter. If a fastener is severely corroded it is likely that normal methods of removal will fail and result in its head being ruined. When you attempt removal, the fastener thread should be heard to crack free and unscrew easily - if it doesn't, stop there before damaging something.

● A smart tap on the head of the fastener will often succeed in breaking free corrosion which has occurred in the threads **(see illustration 2.13)**.

● An aerosol penetrating fluid (such as WD-40) applied the night beforehand may work its way down into the thread and ease removal. Depending on the location, you may be able to make up a Plasticine well around the fastener head and fill it with penetrating fluid.

2.13 A sharp tap on the head of a fastener will often break free a corroded thread

● If you are working on an engine internal component, corrosion will most likely not be a problem due to the well lubricated environment. However, components can be very tight and an impact driver is a useful tool in freeing them **(see illustration 2.14)**.

2.14 Using an impact driver to free a fastener

● Where corrosion has occurred between dissimilar metals (eg steel and aluminium alloy), the application of heat to the fastener head will create a disproportionate expansion rate between the two metals and break the seizure caused by the corrosion. Whether heat can be applied depends on the location of the fastener - any surrounding components likely to be damaged must first be removed **(see illustration 2.15)**. Heat can be applied using a paint stripper heat gun or clothes iron, or by immersing the component in boiling water - wear protective gloves to prevent scalding or burns to the hands.

2.15 Using heat to free a seized fastener

● As a last resort, it is possible to use a hammer and cold chisel to work the fastener head unscrewed **(see illustration 2.16)**. This will damage the fastener, but more importantly extreme care must be taken not to damage the surrounding component.

> *Caution: Remember that the component being secured is generally of more value than the bolt, nut or screw - when the fastener is freed, do not unscrew it with force, instead work the fastener back and forth when resistance is felt to prevent thread damage.*

2.16 Using a hammer and chisel to free a seized fastener

Broken fasteners and damaged heads

● If the shank of a broken bolt or screw is accessible you can grip it with self-locking grips. The knurled wheel type stud extractor tool or self-gripping stud puller tool is particularly useful for removing the long studs which screw into the cylinder mouth surface of the crankcase or bolts and screws from which the head has broken off **(see illustration 2.17)**. Studs can also be removed by locking two nuts together on the threaded end of the stud and using a spanner on the lower nut **(see illustration 2.18)**.

2.17 Using a stud extractor tool to remove a broken crankcase stud

2.18 Two nuts can be locked together to unscrew a stud from a component

● A bolt or screw which has broken off below or level with the casing must be extracted using a screw extractor set. Centre punch the fastener to centralise the drill bit, then drill a hole in the fastener **(see illustration 2.19)**. Select a drill bit which is approximately half to three-quarters the diameter of the fastener

2.19 When using a screw extractor, first drill a hole in the fastener . . .

and drill to a depth which will accommodate the extractor. Use the largest size extractor possible, but avoid leaving too small a wall thickness otherwise the extractor will merely force the fastener walls outwards wedging it in the casing thread.

● If a spiral type extractor is used, thread it anti-clockwise into the fastener. As it is screwed in, it will grip the fastener and unscrew it from the casing **(see illustration 2.20)**.

2.20 . . . then thread the extractor anti-clockwise into the fastener

● If a taper type extractor is used, tap it into the fastener so that it is firmly wedged in place. Unscrew the extractor (anti-clockwise) to draw the fastener out.

> *Warning: Stud extractors are very hard and may break off in the fastener if care is not taken - ask an engineer about spark erosion if this happens.*

● Alternatively, the broken bolt/screw can be drilled out and the hole retapped for an oversize bolt/screw or a diamond-section thread insert. It is essential that the drilling is carried out squarely and to the correct depth, otherwise the casing may be ruined - if in doubt, entrust the work to an engineer.

● Bolts and nuts with rounded corners cause the correct size spanner or socket to slip when force is applied. Of the types of spanner/socket available always use a six-point type rather than an eight or twelve-point type - better grip

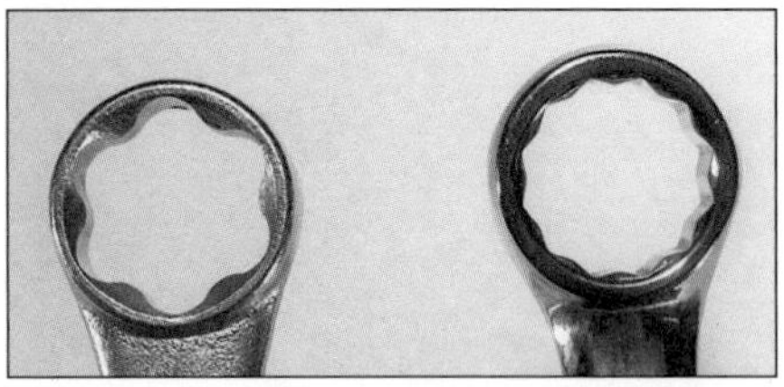

2.21 Comparison of surface drive ring spanner (left) with 12-point type (right)

is obtained. Surface drive spanners grip the middle of the hex flats, rather than the corners, and are thus good in cases of damaged heads **(see illustration 2.21)**.

- Slotted-head or Phillips-head screws are often damaged by the use of the wrong size screwdriver. Allen-head and Torx-head screws are much less likely to sustain damage. If enough of the screw head is exposed you can use a hacksaw to cut a slot in its head and then use a conventional flat-bladed screwdriver to remove it. Alternatively use a hammer and cold chisel to tap the head of the fastener around to slacken it. Always replace damaged fasteners with new ones, preferably Torx or Allen-head type.

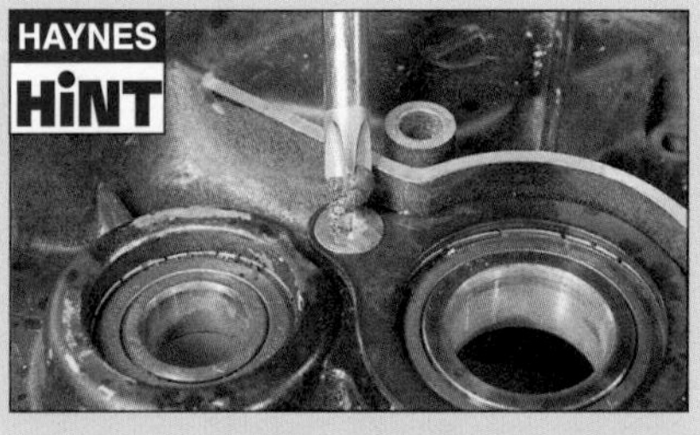

A dab of valve grinding compound between the screw head and screw-driver tip will often give a good grip.

Thread repair

- Threads (particularly those in aluminium alloy components) can be damaged by overtightening, being assembled with dirt in the threads, or from a component working loose and vibrating. Eventually the thread will fail completely, and it will be impossible to tighten the fastener.
- If a thread is damaged or clogged with old locking compound it can be renovated with a thread repair tool (thread chaser) **(see illustrations 2.22 and 2.23)**; special thread chasers are available for spark plug hole threads. The tool will not cut a new thread, but clean and true the original thread. Make sure that you use the correct diameter and pitch tool. Similarly, external threads can be cleaned up with a die or a thread restorer file **(see illustration 2.24)**.

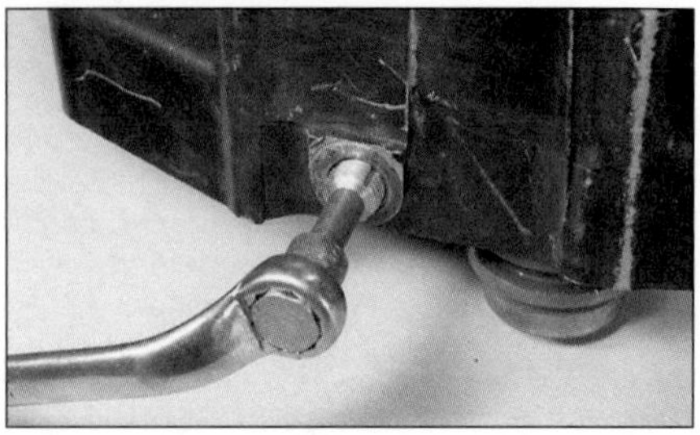

2.22 A thread repair tool being used to correct an internal thread

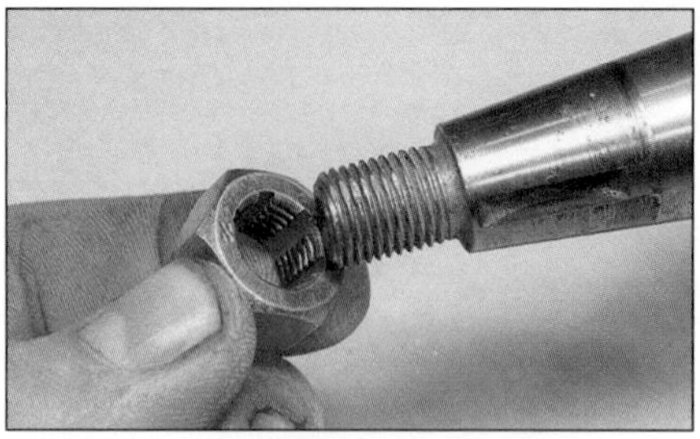

2.23 A thread repair tool being used to correct an external thread

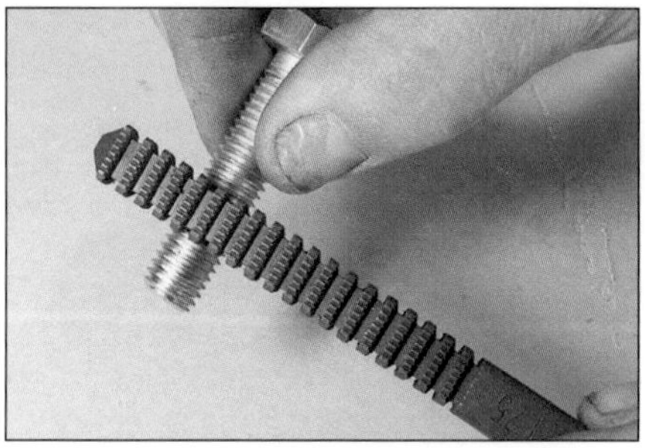

2.24 Using a thread restorer file

- It is possible to drill out the old thread and retap the component to the next thread size. This will work where there is enough surrounding material and a new bolt or screw can be obtained. Sometimes, however, this is not possible - such as where the bolt/screw passes through another component which must also be suitably modified, also in cases where a spark plug or oil drain plug cannot be obtained in a larger diameter thread size.
- The diamond-section thread insert (often known by its popular trade name of Heli-Coil) is a simple and effective method of renewing the thread and retaining the original size. A kit can be purchased which contains the tap, insert and installing tool **(see illustration 2.25)**. Drill out the damaged thread with the size drill specified **(see illustration 2.26)**. Carefully retap the thread **(see illustration 2.27)**. Install the insert on the installing tool and thread it slowly into place using a light downward pressure **(see illustrations 2.28 and 2.29)**. When positioned between a 1/4 and 1/2 turn below the surface withdraw the installing tool and use the break-off tool to press down on the tang, breaking it off **(see illustration 2.30)**.
- There are epoxy thread repair kits on the market which can rebuild stripped internal threads, although this repair should not be used on high load-bearing components.

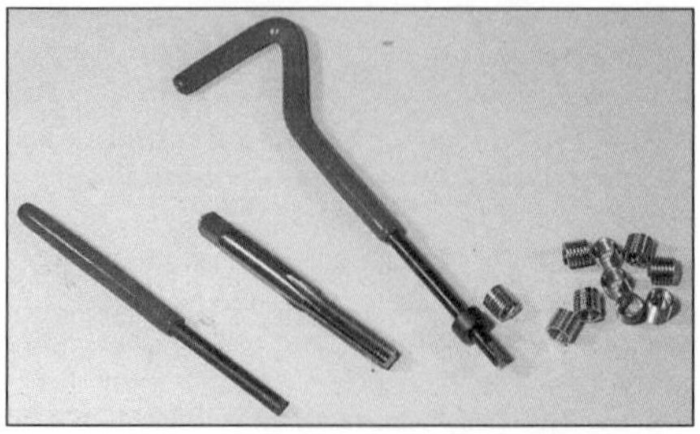

2.25 Obtain a thread insert kit to suit the thread diameter and pitch required

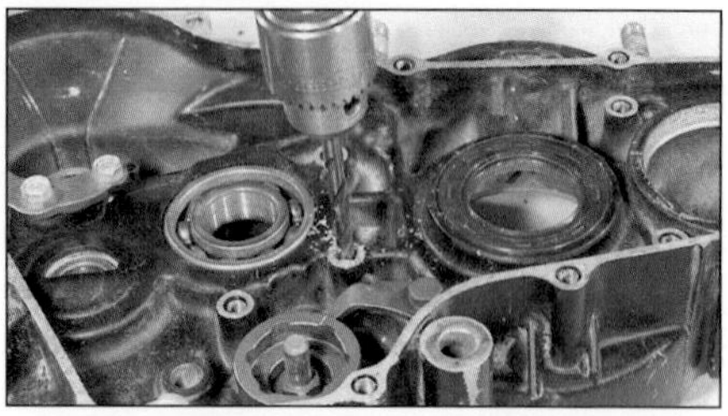

2.26 To install a thread insert, first drill out the original thread . . .

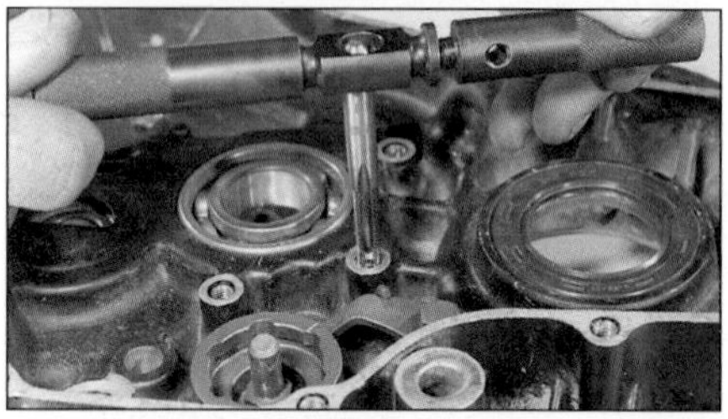

2.27 . . . tap a new thread . . .

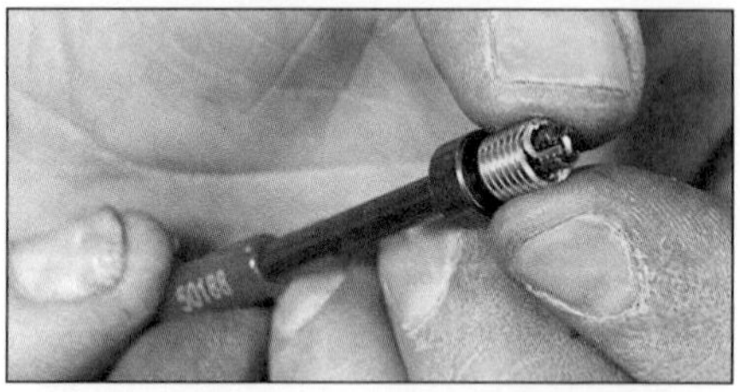

2.28 . . . fit insert on the installing tool . . .

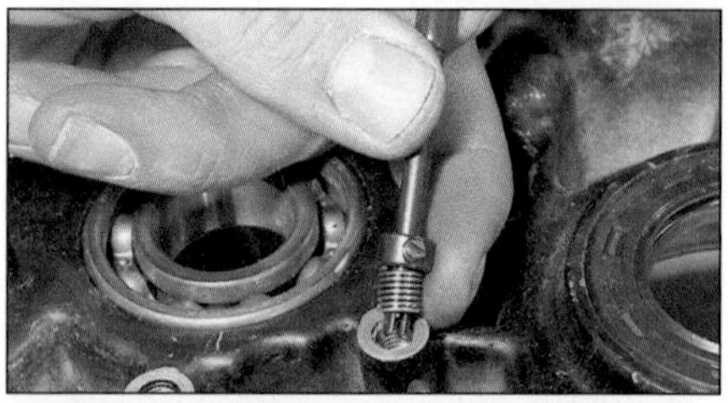

2.29 . . . and thread into the component . . .

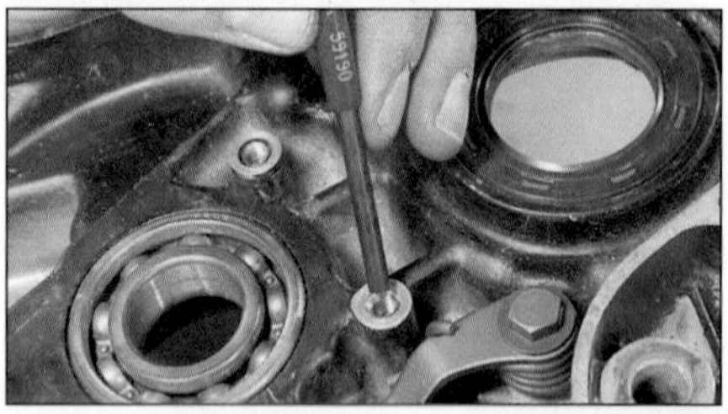

2.30 . . . break off the tang when complete

Thread locking and sealing compounds

● Locking compounds are used in locations where the fastener is prone to loosening due to vibration or on important safety-related items which might cause loss of control of the motorcycle if they fail. It is also used where important fasteners cannot be secured by other means such as lockwashers or split pins.

● Before applying locking compound, make sure that the threads (internal and external) are clean and dry with all old compound removed. Select a compound to suit the component being secured - a non-permanent general locking and sealing type is suitable for most applications, but a high strength type is needed for permanent fixing of studs in castings. Apply a drop or two of the compound to the first few threads of the fastener, then thread it into place and tighten to the specified torque. Do not apply excessive thread locking compound otherwise the thread may be damaged on subsequent removal.

● Certain fasteners are impregnated with a dry film type coating of locking compound on their threads. Always renew this type of fastener if disturbed.

● Anti-seize compounds, such as copper-based greases, can be applied to protect threads from seizure due to extreme heat and corrosion. A common instance is spark plug threads and exhaust system fasteners.

3 Measuring tools and gauges

Feeler gauges

● Feeler gauges (or blades) are used for measuring small gaps and clearances **(see illustration 3.1)**. They can also be used to measure endfloat (sideplay) of a component on a shaft where access is not possible with a dial gauge.

● Feeler gauge sets should be treated with care and not bent or damaged. They are etched with their size on one face. Keep them clean and very lightly oiled to prevent corrosion build-up.

3.1 Feeler gauges are used for measuring small gaps and clearances - thickness is marked on one face of gauge

● When measuring a clearance, select a gauge which is a light sliding fit between the two components. You may need to use two gauges together to measure the clearance accurately.

Micrometers

● A micrometer is a precision tool capable of measuring to 0.01 or 0.001 of a millimetre. It should always be stored in its case and not in the general toolbox. It must be kept clean and never dropped, otherwise its frame or measuring anvils could be distorted resulting in inaccurate readings.

● External micrometers are used for measuring outside diameters of components and have many more applications than internal micrometers. Micrometers are available in different size ranges, eg 0 to 25 mm, 25 to 50 mm, and upwards in 25 mm steps; some large micrometers have interchangeable anvils to allow a range of measurements to be taken. Generally the largest precision measurement you are likely to take on a motorcycle is the piston diameter.

● Internal micrometers (or bore micrometers) are used for measuring inside diameters, such as valve guides and cylinder bores. Telescoping gauges and small hole gauges are used in conjunction with an external micrometer, whereas the more expensive internal micrometers have their own measuring device.

External micrometer

Note: *The conventional analogue type instrument is described. Although much easier to read, digital micrometers are considerably more expensive.*

● Always check the calibration of the micrometer before use. With the anvils closed (0 to 25 mm type) or set over a test gauge

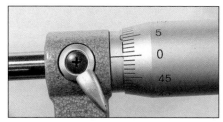

3.2 Check micrometer calibration before use

(for the larger types) the scale should read zero **(see illustration 3.2)**; make sure that the anvils (and test piece) are clean first. Any discrepancy can be adjusted by referring to the instructions supplied with the tool. Remember that the micrometer is a precision measuring tool - don't force the anvils closed, use the ratchet (4) on the end of the micrometer to close it. In this way, a measured force is always applied.

● To use, first make sure that the item being measured is clean. Place the anvil of the micrometer (1) against the item and use the thimble (2) to bring the spindle (3) lightly into contact with the other side of the item **(see illustration 3.3)**. Don't tighten the thimble down because this will damage the micrometer - instead use the ratchet (4) on the end of the micrometer. The ratchet mechanism applies a measured force preventing damage to the instrument.

● The micrometer is read by referring to the linear scale on the sleeve and the annular scale on the thimble. Read off the sleeve first to obtain the base measurement, then add the fine measurement from the thimble to obtain the overall reading. The linear scale on the sleeve represents the measuring range of the micrometer (eg 0 to 25 mm). The annular scale

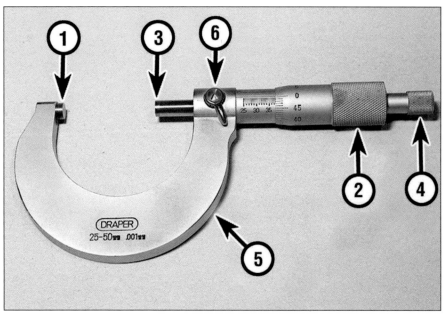

3.3 Micrometer component parts

1 Anvil	3 Spindle	5 Frame
2 Thimble	4 Ratchet	6 Locking lever

on the thimble will be in graduations of 0.01 mm (or as marked on the frame) - one full revolution of the thimble will move 0.5 mm on the linear scale. Take the reading where the datum line on the sleeve intersects the thimble's scale. Always position the eye directly above the scale otherwise an inaccurate reading will result.

In the example shown the item measures 2.95 mm (see illustration 3.4):

Linear scale	2.00 mm
Linear scale	0.50 mm
Annular scale	0.45 mm
Total figure	2.95 mm

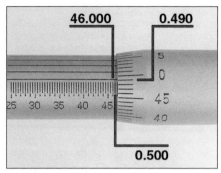

3.5 Micrometer reading of 46.99 mm on linear and annular scales . . .

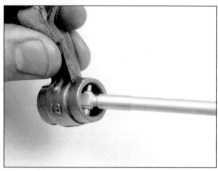

3.7 Expand the telescoping gauge in the bore, lock its position . . .

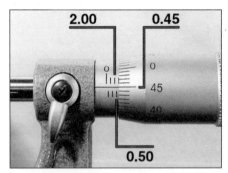

3.4 Micrometer reading of 2.95 mm

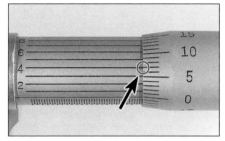

3.6 . . . and 0.004 mm on vernier scale

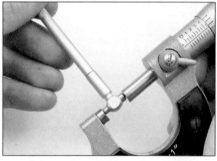

3.8 . . . then measure the gauge with a micrometer

Most micrometers have a locking lever (6) on the frame to hold the setting in place, allowing the item to be removed from the micrometer.
● Some micrometers have a vernier scale on their sleeve, providing an even finer measurement to be taken, in 0.001 increments of a millimetre. Take the sleeve and thimble measurement as described above, then check which graduation on the vernier scale aligns with that of the annular scale on the thimble **Note:** *The eye must be perpendicular to the scale when taking the vernier reading - if necessary rotate the body of the micrometer to ensure this.* Multiply the vernier scale figure by 0.001 and add it to the base and fine measurement figures.

In the example shown the item measures 46.994 mm (see illustrations 3.5 and 3.6):

Linear scale (base)	46.000 mm
Linear scale (base)	00.500 mm
Annular scale (fine)	00.490 mm
Vernier scale	00.004 mm
Total figure	46.994 mm

Internal micrometer

● Internal micrometers are available for measuring bore diameters, but are expensive and unlikely to be available for home use. It is suggested that a set of telescoping gauges and small hole gauges, both of which must be used with an external micrometer, will suffice for taking internal measurements on a motorcycle.
● Telescoping gauges can be used to

measure internal diameters of components. Select a gauge with the correct size range, make sure its ends are clean and insert it into the bore. Expand the gauge, then lock its position and withdraw it from the bore (see illustration 3.7). Measure across the gauge ends with a micrometer (see illustration 3.8).
● Very small diameter bores (such as valve guides) are measured with a small hole gauge. Once adjusted to a slip-fit inside the component, its position is locked and the gauge withdrawn for measurement with a micrometer (see illustrations 3.9 and 3.10).

Vernier caliper

Note: *The conventional linear and dial gauge type instruments are described. Digital types are easier to read, but are far more expensive.*
● The vernier caliper does not provide the precision of a micrometer, but is versatile in being able to measure internal and external diameters. Some types also incorporate a depth gauge. It is ideal for measuring clutch plate friction material and spring free lengths.
● To use the conventional linear scale vernier, slacken off the vernier clamp screws (1) and set its jaws over (2), or inside (3), the item to be measured (see illustration 3.11). Slide the jaw into contact, using the thumbwheel (4) for fine movement of the sliding scale (5) then tighten the clamp screws (1). Read off the main scale (6) where the zero on the sliding scale (5) intersects it, taking the whole number to the left of the zero; this provides the base measurement. View along the sliding scale and select the division which

3.9 Expand the small hole gauge in the bore, lock its position . . .

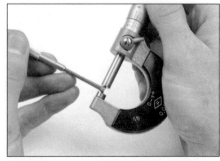

3.10 . . . then measure the gauge with a micrometer

lines up exactly with any of the divisions on the main scale, noting that the divisions usually represents 0.02 of a millimetre. Add this fine measurement to the base measurement to obtain the total reading.

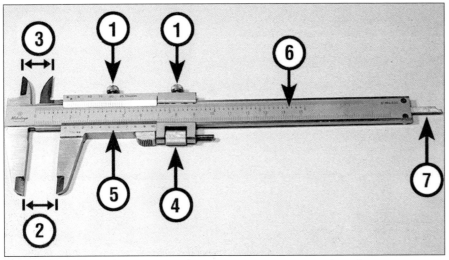

3.11 Vernier component parts (linear gauge)

1	Clamp screws	3	Internal jaws	5	Sliding scale	7	Depth gauge
2	External jaws	4	Thumbwheel	6	Main scale		

In the example shown the item measures 55.92 mm **(see illustration 3.12)**:

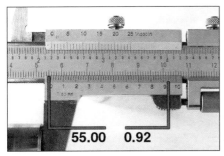

3.12 Vernier gauge reading of 55.92 mm

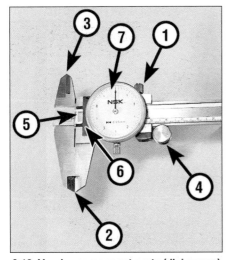

3.13 Vernier component parts (dial gauge)

1	Clamp screw	5	Main scale
2	External jaws	6	Sliding scale
3	Internal jaws	7	Dial gauge
4	Thumbwheel		

Base measurement	55.00 mm
Fine measurement	00.92 mm
Total figure	55.92 mm

● Some vernier calipers are equipped with a dial gauge for fine measurement. Before use, check that the jaws are clean, then close them fully and check that the dial gauge reads zero. If necessary adjust the gauge ring accordingly. Slacken the vernier clamp screw (1) and set its jaws over (2), or inside (3), the item to be measured **(see illustration 3.13)**. Slide the jaws into contact, using the thumbwheel (4) for fine movement. Read off the main scale (5) where the edge of the sliding scale (6) intersects it, taking the whole number to the left of the zero; this provides the base measurement. Read off the needle position on the dial gauge (7) scale to provide the fine measurement; each division represents 0.05 of a millimetre. Add this fine measurement to the base measurement to obtain the total reading.

In the example shown the item measures 55.95 mm **(see illustration 3.14)**:

Base measurement	55.00 mm
Fine measurement	00.95 mm
Total figure	55.95 mm

3.14 Vernier gauge reading of 55.95 mm

Plastigauge

● Plastigauge is a plastic material which can be compressed between two surfaces to measure the oil clearance between them. The width of the compressed Plastigauge is measured against a calibrated scale to determine the clearance.

● Common uses of Plastigauge are for measuring the clearance between crankshaft journal and main bearing inserts, between crankshaft journal and big-end bearing inserts, and between camshaft and bearing surfaces. The following example describes big-end oil clearance measurement.

● Handle the Plastigauge material carefully to prevent distortion. Using a sharp knife, cut a length which corresponds with the width of the bearing being measured and place it carefully across the journal so that it is parallel with the shaft **(see illustration 3.15)**. Carefully install both bearing shells and the connecting rod. Without rotating the rod on the journal tighten its bolts or nuts (as applicable) to the specified torque. The connecting rod and bearings are then disassembled and the crushed Plastigauge examined.

3.15 Plastigauge placed across shaft journal

● Using the scale provided in the Plastigauge kit, measure the width of the material to determine the oil clearance **(see illustration 3.16)**. Always remove all traces of Plastigauge after use using your fingernails.

Caution: Arriving at the correct clearance demands that the assembly is torqued correctly, according to the settings and sequence (where applicable) provided by the motorcycle manufacturer.

3.16 Measuring the width of the crushed Plastigauge

Dial gauge or DTI (Dial Test Indicator)

● A dial gauge can be used to accurately measure small amounts of movement. Typical uses are measuring shaft runout or shaft endfloat (sideplay) and setting piston position for ignition timing on two-strokes. A dial gauge set usually comes with a range of different probes and adapters and mounting equipment.

● The gauge needle must point to zero when at rest. Rotate the ring around its periphery to zero the gauge.

● Check that the gauge is capable of reading the extent of movement in the work. Most gauges have a small dial set in the face which records whole millimetres of movement as well as the fine scale around the face periphery which is calibrated in 0.01 mm divisions. Read off the small dial first to obtain the base measurement, then add the measurement from the fine scale to obtain the total reading.

In the example shown the gauge reads 1.48 mm **(see illustration 3.17)**:

Base measurement	1.00 mm
Fine measurement	0.48 mm
Total figure	**1.48 mm**

3.17 Dial gauge reading of 1.48 mm

● If measuring shaft runout, the shaft must be supported in vee-blocks and the gauge mounted on a stand perpendicular to the shaft. Rest the tip of the gauge against the centre of the shaft and rotate the shaft slowly whilst watching the gauge reading **(see illustration 3.18)**. Take several measurements along the length of the shaft and record the

3.18 Using a dial gauge to measure shaft runout

maximum gauge reading as the amount of runout in the shaft. **Note:** *The reading obtained will be total runout at that point - some manufacturers specify that the runout figure is halved to compare with their specified runout limit.*

● Endfloat (sideplay) measurement requires that the gauge is mounted securely to the surrounding component with its probe touching the end of the shaft. Using hand pressure, push and pull on the shaft noting the maximum endfloat recorded on the gauge **(see illustration 3.19)**.

3.19 Using a dial gauge to measure shaft endfloat

● A dial gauge with suitable adapters can be used to determine piston position BTDC on two-stroke engines for the purposes of ignition timing. The gauge, adapter and suitable length probe are installed in the place of the spark plug and the gauge zeroed at TDC. If the piston position is specified as 1.14 mm BTDC, rotate the engine back to 2.00 mm BTDC, then slowly forwards to 1.14 mm BTDC.

Cylinder compression gauges

● A compression gauge is used for measuring cylinder compression. Either the rubber-cone type or the threaded adapter type can be used. The latter is preferred to ensure a perfect seal against the cylinder head. A 0 to 300 psi (0 to 20 Bar) type gauge (for petrol/gasoline engines) will be suitable for motorcycles.

● The spark plug is removed and the gauge either held hard against the cylinder head (cone type) or the gauge adapter screwed into the cylinder head (threaded type) **(see illustration 3.20)**. Cylinder compression is measured with the engine turning over, but not running. The

3.20 Using a rubber-cone type cylinder compression gauge

gauge will hold the reading until manually released.

Oil pressure gauge

● An oil pressure gauge is used for measuring engine oil pressure. Most gauges come with a set of adapters to fit the thread of the take-off point **(see illustration 3.21)**. If the take-off point specified by the motorcycle manufacturer is an external oil pipe union, make sure that the specified replacement union is used to prevent oil starvation.

3.21 Oil pressure gauge and take-off point adapter (arrow)

● Oil pressure is measured with the engine running (at a specific rpm) and often the manufacturer will specify pressure limits for a cold and hot engine.

Straight-edge and surface plate

● If checking the gasket face of a component for warpage, place a steel rule or precision straight-edge across the gasket face and measure any gap between the straight-edge and component with feeler gauges **(see illustration 3.22)**. Check diagonally across the component and between mounting holes **(see illustration 3.23)**.

3.22 Use a straight-edge and feeler gauges to check for warpage

3.23 Check for warpage in these directions

● Checking individual components for warpage, such as clutch plain (metal) plates, requires a perfectly flat plate or piece or plate glass and feeler gauges.

4 Torque and leverage

What is torque?

● Torque describes the twisting force about a shaft. The amount of torque applied is determined by the distance from the centre of the shaft to the end of the lever and the amount of force being applied to the end of the lever; distance multiplied by force equals torque.

● The manufacturer applies a measured torque to a bolt or nut to ensure that it will not slacken in use and to hold two components securely together without movement in the joint. The actual torque setting depends on the thread size, bolt or nut material and the composition of the components being held.

● Too little torque may cause the fastener to loosen due to vibration, whereas too much torque will distort the joint faces of the component or cause the fastener to shear off. Always stick to the specified torque setting.

Using a torque wrench

● Check the calibration of the torque wrench and make sure it has a suitable range for the job. Torque wrenches are available in Nm (Newton-metres), kgf m (kilograms-force metre), lbf ft (pounds-feet), lbf in (inch-pounds). Do not confuse lbf ft with lbf in.

● Adjust the tool to the desired torque on the scale **(see illustration 4.1)**. If your torque wrench is not calibrated in the units specified, carefully convert the figure (see Conversion Factors). A manufacturer sometimes gives a torque setting as a range (8 to 10 Nm) rather than a single figure - in this case set the tool midway between the two settings. The same torque may be expressed as 9 Nm ± 1 Nm. Some torque wrenches have a method of locking the setting so that it isn't inadvertently altered during use.

4.1 Set the torque wrench index mark to the setting required, in this case 12 Nm

● Install the bolts/nuts in their correct location and secure them lightly. Their threads must be clean and free of any old locking compound. Unless specified the threads and flange should be dry - oiled threads are necessary in certain circumstances and the manufacturer will take this into account in the specified torque figure. Similarly, the manufacturer may also specify the application of thread-locking compound.

● Tighten the fasteners in the specified sequence until the torque wrench clicks, indicating that the torque setting has been reached. Apply the torque again to double-check the setting. Where different thread diameter fasteners secure the component, as a rule tighten the larger diameter ones first.

● When the torque wrench has been finished with, release the lock (where applicable) and fully back off its setting to zero - do not leave the torque wrench tensioned. Also, do not use a torque wrench for slackening a fastener.

Angle-tightening

● Manufacturers often specify a figure in degrees for final tightening of a fastener. This usually follows tightening to a specific torque setting.

● A degree disc can be set and attached to the socket **(see illustration 4.2)** or a protractor can be used to mark the angle of movement on the bolt/nut head and the surrounding casting **(see illustration 4.3)**.

4.2 Angle tightening can be accomplished with a torque-angle gauge . . .

4.3 . . . or by marking the angle on the surrounding component

Loosening sequences

● Where more than one bolt/nut secures a component, loosen each fastener evenly a little at a time. In this way, not all the stress of the joint is held by one fastener and the components are not likely to distort.

● If a tightening sequence is provided, work in the REVERSE of this, but if not, work from the outside in, in a criss-cross sequence **(see illustration 4.4)**.

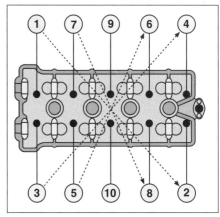

4.4 When slackening, work from the outside inwards

Tightening sequences

● If a component is held by more than one fastener it is important that the retaining bolts/nuts are tightened evenly to prevent uneven stress build-up and distortion of sealing faces. This is especially important on high-compression joints such as the cylinder head.

● A sequence is usually provided by the manufacturer, either in a diagram or actually marked in the casting. If not, always start in the centre and work outwards in a criss-cross pattern **(see illustration 4.5)**. Start off by securing all bolts/nuts finger-tight, then set the torque wrench and tighten each fastener by a small amount in sequence until the final torque is reached. By following this practice,

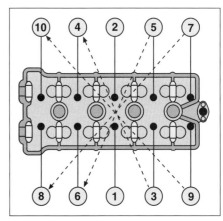

4.5 When tightening, work from the inside outwards

the joint will be held evenly and will not be distorted. Important joints, such as the cylinder head and big-end fasteners often have two- or three-stage torque settings.

Applying leverage

● Use tools at the correct angle. Position a socket wrench or spanner on the bolt/nut so that you pull it towards you when loosening. If this can't be done, push the spanner without curling your fingers around it **(see illustration 4.6)** - the spanner may slip or the fastener loosen suddenly, resulting in your fingers being crushed against a component.

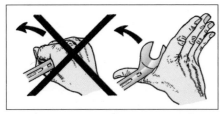

4.6 If you can't pull on the spanner to loosen a fastener, push with your hand open

● Additional leverage is gained by extending the length of the lever. The best way to do this is to use a breaker bar instead of the regular length tool, or to slip a length of tubing over the end of the spanner or socket wrench.
● If additional leverage will not work, the fastener head is either damaged or firmly corroded in place (see Fasteners).

5 Bearings

Bearing removal and installation

Drivers and sockets

● Before removing a bearing, always inspect the casing to see which way it must be driven out - some casings will have retaining plates or a cast step. Also check for any identifying markings on the bearing and if installed to a certain depth, measure this at this stage. Some roller bearings are sealed on one side - take note of the original fitted position.
● Bearings can be driven out of a casing using a bearing driver tool (with the correct size head) or a socket of the correct diameter. Select the driver head or socket so that it contacts the outer race of the bearing, not the balls/rollers or inner race. Always support the casing around the bearing housing with wood blocks, otherwise there is a risk of fracture. The bearing is driven out with a few blows on the driver or socket from a heavy mallet. Unless access is severely restricted (as with wheel bearings), a pin-punch is not recommended unless it is moved around the bearing to keep it square in its housing.

● The same equipment can be used to install bearings. Make sure the bearing housing is supported on wood blocks and line up the bearing in its housing. Fit the bearing as noted on removal - generally they are installed with their marked side facing outwards. Tap the bearing squarely into its housing using a driver or socket which bears only on the bearing's outer race - contact with the bearing balls/rollers or inner race will destroy it **(see illustrations 5.1 and 5.2)**.
● Check that the bearing inner race and balls/rollers rotate freely.

5.1 Using a bearing driver against the bearing's outer race

5.2 Using a large socket against the bearing's outer race

Pullers and slide-hammers

● Where a bearing is pressed on a shaft a puller will be required to extract it **(see illustration 5.3)**. Make sure that the puller clamp or legs fit securely behind the bearing and are unlikely to slip out. If pulling a bearing

off a gear shaft for example, you may have to locate the puller behind a gear pinion if there is no access to the race and draw the gear pinion off the shaft as well **(see illustration 5.4)**.

> **Caution: Ensure that the puller's centre bolt locates securely against the end of the shaft and will not slip when pressure is applied. Also ensure that puller does not damage the shaft end.**

5.4 Where no access is available to the rear of the bearing, it is sometimes possible to draw off the adjacent component

● Operate the puller so that its centre bolt exerts pressure on the shaft end and draws the bearing off the shaft.
● When installing the bearing on the shaft, tap only on the bearing's inner race - contact with the balls/rollers or outer race with destroy the bearing. Use a socket or length of tubing as a drift which fits over the shaft end **(see illustration 5.5)**.

5.5 When installing a bearing on a shaft use a piece of tubing which bears only on the bearing's inner race

● Where a bearing locates in a blind hole in a casing, it cannot be driven or pulled out as described above. A slide-hammer with knife-edged bearing puller attachment will be required. The puller attachment passes through the bearing and when tightened expands to fit firmly behind the bearing **(see illustration 5.6)**. By operating the slide-hammer part of the tool the bearing is jarred out of its housing **(see illustration 5.7)**.
● It is possible, if the bearing is of reasonable weight, for it to drop out of its housing if the casing is heated as described opposite.

5.3 This bearing puller clamps behind the bearing and pressure is applied to the shaft end to draw the bearing off

5.6 Expand the bearing puller so that it locks behind the bearing . . .

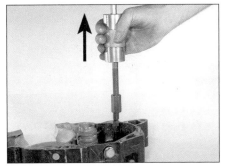

5.7 . . . attach the slide hammer to the bearing puller

If this method is attempted, first prepare a work surface which will enable the casing to be tapped face down to help dislodge the bearing - a wood surface is ideal since it will not damage the casing's gasket surface. Wearing protective gloves, tap the heated casing several times against the work surface to dislodge the bearing under its own weight **(see illustration 5.8)**.

5.8 Tapping a casing face down on wood blocks can often dislodge a bearing

● Bearings can be installed in blind holes using the driver or socket method described above.

Drawbolts

● Where a bearing or bush is set in the eye of a component, such as a suspension linkage arm or connecting rod small-end, removal by drift may damage the component. Furthermore, a rubber bushing in a shock absorber eye cannot successfully be driven out of position. If access is available to a engineering press, the task is straightforward. If not, a drawbolt can be fabricated to extract the bearing or bush.

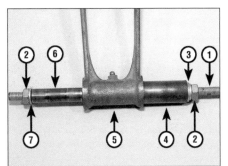

5.9 Drawbolt component parts assembled on a suspension arm

1 Bolt or length of threaded bar
2 Nuts
3 Washer (external diameter greater than tubing internal diameter)
4 Tubing (internal diameter sufficient to accommodate bearing)
5 Suspension arm with bearing
6 Tubing (external diameter slightly smaller than bearing)
7 Washer (external diameter slightly smaller than bearing)

5.10 Drawing the bearing out of the suspension arm

● To extract the bearing/bush you will need a long bolt with nut (or piece of threaded bar with two nuts), a piece of tubing which has an internal diameter larger than the bearing/bush, another piece of tubing which has an external diameter slightly smaller than the bearing/bush, and a selection of washers **(see illustrations 5.9 and 5.10)**. Note that the pieces of tubing must be of the same length, or longer, than the bearing/bush.
● The same kit (without the pieces of tubing) can be used to draw the new bearing/bush back into place **(see illustration 5.11)**.

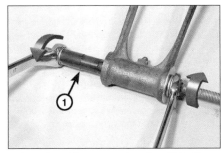

5.11 Installing a new bearing (1) in the suspension arm

Temperature change

● If the bearing's outer race is a tight fit in the casing, the aluminium casing can be heated to release its grip on the bearing. Aluminium will expand at a greater rate than the steel bearing outer race. There are several ways to do this, but avoid any localised extreme heat (such as a blow torch) - aluminium alloy has a low melting point.
● Approved methods of heating a casing are using a domestic oven (heated to 100°C) or immersing the casing in boiling water **(see illustration 5.12)**. Low temperature range localised heat sources such as a paint stripper heat gun or clothes iron can also be used **(see illustration 5.13)**. Alternatively, soak a rag in boiling water, wring it out and wrap it around the bearing housing.

> ⚠ **Warning: All of these methods require care in use to prevent scalding and burns to the hands. Wear protective gloves when handling hot components.**

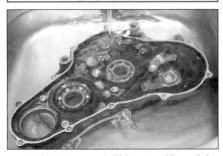

5.12 A casing can be immersed in a sink of boiling water to aid bearing removal

5.13 Using a localised heat source to aid bearing removal

● If heating the whole casing note that plastic components, such as the neutral switch, may suffer - remove them beforehand.
● After heating, remove the bearing as described above. You may find that the expansion is sufficient for the bearing to fall out of the casing under its own weight or with a light tap on the driver or socket.
● If necessary, the casing can be heated to aid bearing installation, and this is sometimes the recommended procedure if the motorcycle manufacturer has designed the housing and bearing fit with this intention.

● Installation of bearings can be eased by placing them in a freezer the night before installation. The steel bearing will contract slightly, allowing easy insertion in its housing. This is often useful when installing steering head outer races in the frame.

Bearing types and markings

● Plain shell bearings, ball bearings, needle roller bearings and tapered roller bearings will all be found on motorcycles **(see illustrations 5.14 and 5.15)**. The ball and roller types are usually caged between an inner and outer race, but uncaged variations may be found.

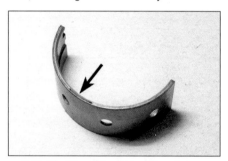

5.14 Shell bearings are either plain or grooved. They are usually identified by colour code (arrow)

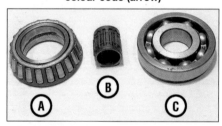

5.15 Tapered roller bearing (A), needle roller bearing (B) and ball journal bearing (C)

● Shell bearings (often called inserts) are usually found at the crankshaft main and connecting rod big-end where they are good at coping with high loads. They are made of a phosphor-bronze material and are impregnated with self-lubricating properties.
● Ball bearings and needle roller bearings consist of a steel inner and outer race with the balls or rollers between the races. They require constant lubrication by oil or grease and are good at coping with axial loads. Taper roller bearings consist of rollers set in a tapered cage set on the inner race; the outer race is separate. They are good at coping with axial loads and prevent movement along the shaft - a typical application is in the steering head.
● Bearing manufacturers produce bearings to ISO size standards and stamp one face of the bearing to indicate its internal and external diameter, load capacity and type **(see illustration 5.16)**.
● Metal bushes are usually of phosphor-bronze material. Rubber bushes are used in suspension mounting eyes. Fibre bushes have also been used in suspension pivots.

5.16 Typical bearing marking

Bearing fault finding

● If a bearing outer race has spun in its housing, the housing material will be damaged. You can use a bearing locking compound to bond the outer race in place if damage is not too severe.
● Shell bearings will fail due to damage of their working surface, as a result of lack of lubrication, corrosion or abrasive particles in the oil **(see illustration 5.17)**. Small particles of dirt in the oil may embed in the bearing material whereas larger particles will score the bearing and shaft journal. If a number of short journeys are made, insufficient heat will be generated to drive off condensation which has built up on the bearings.

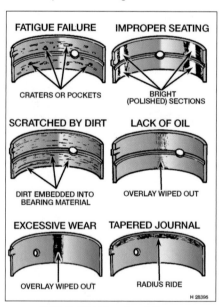

5.17 Typical bearing failures

● Ball and roller bearings will fail due to lack of lubrication or damage to the balls or rollers. Tapered-roller bearings can be damaged by overloading them. Unless the bearing is sealed on both sides, wash it in paraffin (kerosene) to remove all old grease then allow it to dry. Make a visual inspection looking to dented balls or rollers, damaged cages and worn or pitted races **(see illustration 5.18)**.
● A ball bearing can be checked for wear by listening to it when spun. Apply a film of light oil to the bearing and hold it close to the ear - hold the outer race with one hand and spin the

5.18 Example of ball journal bearing with damaged balls and cages

5.19 Hold outer race and listen to inner race when spun

inner race with the other hand **(see illustration 5.19)**. The bearing should be almost silent when spun; if it grates or rattles it is worn.

6 Oil seals

Oil seal removal and installation

● Oil seals should be renewed every time a component is dismantled. This is because the seal lips will become set to the sealing surface and will not necessarily reseal.
● Oil seals can be prised out of position using a large flat-bladed screwdriver **(see illustration 6.1)**. In the case of crankcase seals, check first that the seal is not lipped on the inside, preventing its removal with the crankcases joined.

6.1 Prise out oil seals with a large flat-bladed screwdriver

● New seals are usually installed with their marked face (containing the seal reference code) outwards and the spring side towards the fluid being retained. In certain cases, such as a two-stroke engine crankshaft seal, a double lipped seal may be used due to there being fluid or gas on each side of the joint.

● Use a bearing driver or socket which bears only on the outer hard edge of the seal to install it in the casing - tapping on the inner edge will damage the sealing lip.

Oil seal types and markings

● Oil seals are usually of the single-lipped type. Double-lipped seals are found where a liquid or gas is on both sides of the joint.
● Oil seals can harden and lose their sealing ability if the motorcycle has been in storage for a long period - renewal is the only solution.
● Oil seal manufacturers also conform to the ISO markings for seal size - these are moulded into the outer face of the seal (see illustration 6.2).

6.2 These oil seal markings indicate inside diameter, outside diameter and seal thickness

7 Gaskets and sealants

Types of gasket and sealant

● Gaskets are used to seal the mating surfaces between components and keep lubricants, fluids, vacuum or pressure contained within the assembly. Aluminium gaskets are sometimes found at the cylinder joints, but most gaskets are paper-based. If the mating surfaces of the components being joined are undamaged the gasket can be installed dry, although a dab of sealant or grease will be useful to hold it in place during assembly.
● RTV (Room Temperature Vulcanising) silicone rubber sealants cure when exposed to moisture in the atmosphere. These sealants are good at filling pits or irregular gasket faces, but will tend to be forced out of the joint under very high torque. They can be used to replace a paper gasket, but first make sure that the width of the paper gasket is not essential to the shimming of internal components. RTV sealants should not be used on components containing petrol (gasoline).
● Non-hardening, semi-hardening and hard setting liquid gasket compounds can be used with a gasket or between a metal-to-metal joint. Select the sealant to suit the application: universal non-hardening sealant can be used on virtually all joints; semi-hardening on joint faces which are rough or damaged; hard setting sealant on joints which require a permanent bond and are subjected to high temperature and pressure. **Note:** *Check first if the paper gasket has a bead of sealant*

impregnated in its surface before applying additional sealant.
● When choosing a sealant, make sure it is suitable for the application, particularly if being applied in a high-temperature area or in the vicinity of fuel. Certain manufacturers produce sealants in either clear, silver or black colours to match the finish of the engine. This has a particular application on motorcycles where much of the engine is exposed.
● Do not over-apply sealant. That which is squeezed out on the outside of the joint can be wiped off, whereas an excess of sealant on the inside can break off and clog oilways.

Breaking a sealed joint

● Age, heat, pressure and the use of hard setting sealant can cause two components to stick together so tightly that they are difficult to separate using finger pressure alone. Do not resort to using levers unless there is a pry point provided for this purpose (see illustration 7.1) or else the gasket surfaces will be damaged.
● Use a soft-faced hammer (see illustration 7.2) or a wood block and conventional hammer to strike the component near the mating surface. Avoid hammering against cast extremities since they may break off. If this method fails, try using a wood wedge between the two components.

Caution: If the joint will not separate, double-check that you have removed all the fasteners.

7.1 If a pry point is provided, apply gently pressure with a flat-bladed screwdriver

7.2 Tap around the joint with a soft-faced mallet if necessary - don't strike cooling fins

Removal of old gasket and sealant

● Paper gaskets will most likely come away complete, leaving only a few traces stuck

Most components have one or two hollow locating dowels between the two gasket faces. If a dowel cannot be removed, do not resort to gripping it with pliers - it will almost certainly be distorted. Install a close-fitting socket or Phillips screwdriver into the dowel and then grip the outer edge of the dowel to free it.

on the sealing faces of the components. It is imperative that all traces are removed to ensure correct sealing of the new gasket.
● Very carefully scrape all traces of gasket away making sure that the sealing surfaces are not gouged or scored by the scraper (see illustrations 7.3, 7.4 and 7.5). Stubborn deposits can be removed by spraying with an aerosol gasket remover. Final preparation of

7.3 Paper gaskets can be scraped off with a gasket scraper tool . . .

7.4 . . . a knife blade . . .

7.5 . . . or a household scraper

7.6 Fine abrasive paper is wrapped around a flat file to clean up the gasket face

7.7 A kitchen scourer can be used on stubborn deposits

the gasket surface can be made with very fine abrasive paper or a plastic kitchen scourer **(see illustrations 7.6 and 7.7)**.

● Old sealant can be scraped or peeled off components, depending on the type originally used. Note that gasket removal compounds are available to avoid scraping the components clean; make sure the gasket remover suits the type of sealant used.

8 Chains

Breaking and joining final drive chains

● Drive chains for all but small bikes are continuous and do not have a clip-type connecting link. The chain must be broken using a chain breaker tool and the new chain securely riveted together using a new soft rivet-type link. Never use a clip-type connecting link instead of a rivet-type link, except in an emergency. Various chain breaking and riveting tools are available, either as separate tools or combined as illustrated in the accompanying photographs - read the instructions supplied with the tool carefully.

> ⚠ **Warning: The need to rivet the new link pins correctly cannot be overstressed - loss of control of the motorcycle is very likely to result if the chain breaks in use.**

● Rotate the chain and look for the soft link. The soft link pins look like they have been

8.1 Tighten the chain breaker to push the pin out of the link . . .

8.2 . . . withdraw the pin, remove the tool . . .

8.3 . . . and separate the chain link

deeply centre-punched instead of peened over like all the other pins **(see illustration 8.9)** and its sideplate may be a different colour. Position the soft link midway between the sprockets and assemble the chain breaker tool over one of the soft link pins **(see illustration 8.1)**. Operate the tool to push the pin out through the chain **(see illustration 8.2)**. On an O-ring chain, remove the O-rings **(see illustration 8.3)**. Carry out the same procedure on the other soft link pin.

> *Caution: Certain soft link pins (particularly on the larger chains) may require their ends to be filed or ground off before they can be pressed out using the tool.*

● Check that you have the correct size and strength (standard or heavy duty) new soft link - do not reuse the old link. Look for the size marking on the chain sideplates **(see illustration 8.10)**.

● Position the chain ends so that they are engaged over the rear sprocket. On an O-ring

8.4 Insert the new soft link, with O-rings, through the chain ends . . .

8.5 . . . install the O-rings over the pin ends . . .

8.6 . . . followed by the sideplate

chain, install a new O-ring over each pin of the link and insert the link through the two chain ends **(see illustration 8.4)**. Install a new O-ring over the end of each pin, followed by the sideplate (with the chain manufacturer's marking facing outwards) **(see illustrations 8.5 and 8.6)**. On an unsealed chain, insert the link through the two chain ends, then install the sideplate with the chain manufacturer's marking facing outwards.

● Note that it may not be possible to install the sideplate using finger pressure alone. If using a joining tool, assemble it so that the plates of the tool clamp the link and press the sideplate over the pins **(see illustration 8.7)**. Otherwise, use two small sockets placed over

8.7 Push the sideplate into position using a clamp

8.8 Assemble the chain riveting tool over one pin at a time and tighten it fully

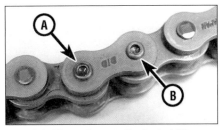

8.9 Pin end correctly riveted (A), pin end unriveted (B)

the rivet ends and two pieces of the wood between a G-clamp. Operate the clamp to press the sideplate over the pins.

● Assemble the joining tool over one pin (following the maker's instructions) and tighten the tool down to spread the pin end securely **(see illustrations 8.8 and 8.9)**. Do the same on the other pin.

> ⚠️ **Warning: Check that the pin ends are secure and that there is no danger of the sideplate coming loose. If the pin ends are cracked the soft link must be renewed.**

Final drive chain sizing

● Chains are sized using a three digit number, followed by a suffix to denote the chain type **(see illustration 8.10)**. Chain type is either standard or heavy duty (thicker sideplates), and also unsealed or O-ring/X-ring type.

● The first digit of the number relates to the pitch of the chain, ie the distance from the centre of one pin to the centre of the next pin **(see illustration 8.11)**. Pitch is expressed in eighths of an inch, as follows:

8.10 Typical chain size and type marking

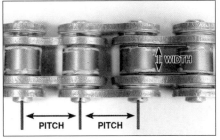

8.11 Chain dimensions

Sizes commencing with a 4 (eg 428) have a pitch of 1/2 inch (12.7 mm)

Sizes commencing with a 5 (eg 520) have a pitch of 5/8 inch (15.9 mm)

Sizes commencing with a 6 (eg 630) have a pitch of 3/4 inch (19.1 mm)

● The second and third digits of the chain size relate to the width of the rollers, again in imperial units, eg the 525 shown has 5/16 inch (7.94 mm) rollers **(see illustration 8.11)**.

9 Hoses

Clamping to prevent flow

● Small-bore flexible hoses can be clamped to prevent fluid flow whilst a component is worked on. Whichever method is used, ensure that the hose material is not permanently distorted or damaged by the clamp.

a) A brake hose clamp available from auto accessory shops **(see illustration 9.1)**.
b) A wingnut type hose clamp **(see illustration 9.2)**.

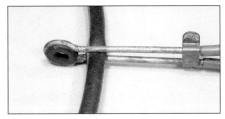

9.1 Hoses can be clamped with an automotive brake hose clamp . . .

9.2 . . . a wingnut type hose clamp . . .

c) Two sockets placed each side of the hose and held with straight-jawed self-locking grips **(see illustration 9.3)**.
d) Thick card each side of the hose held between straight-jawed self-locking grips **(see illustration 9.4)**.

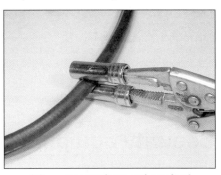

9.3 . . . two sockets and a pair of self-locking grips . . .

9.4 . . . or thick card and self-locking grips

Freeing and fitting hoses

● Always make sure the hose clamp is moved well clear of the hose end. Grip the hose with your hand and rotate it whilst pulling it off the union. If the hose has hardened due to age and will not move, slit it with a sharp knife and peel its ends off the union **(see illustration 9.5)**.

● Resist the temptation to use grease or soap on the unions to aid installation; although it helps the hose slip over the union it will equally aid the escape of fluid from the joint. It is preferable to soften the hose ends in hot water and wet the inside surface of the hose with water or a fluid which will evaporate.

9.5 Cutting a coolant hose free with a sharp knife

Introduction

In less time than it takes to read this introduction, a thief could steal your motorcycle. Returning only to find your bike has gone is one of the worst feelings in the world. Even if the motorcycle is insured against theft, once you've got over the initial shock, you will have the inconvenience of dealing with the police and your insurance company.

The motorcycle is an easy target for the professional thief and the joyrider alike and the official figures on motorcycle theft make for depressing reading; on average a motor-cycle is stolen every 16 minutes in the UK!

Motorcycle thefts fall into two categories, those stolen 'to order' and those taken by opportunists. The thief stealing to order will be on the look out for a specific make and model and will go to extraordinary lengths to obtain that motorcycle. The opportunist thief on the other hand will look for easy targets which can be stolen with the minimum of effort and risk.

Whilst it is never going to be possible to make your machine 100% secure, it is estimated that around half of all stolen motorcycles are taken by opportunist thieves. Remember that the opportunist thief is always on the look out for the easy option: if there are two similar motorcycles parked side-by-side, they will target the one with the lowest level of security. By taking a few precautions, you can reduce the chances of your motorcycle being stolen.

Security equipment

There are many specialised motorcycle security devices available and the following text summarises their applications and their good and bad points.

Once you have decided on the type of security equipment which best suits your needs, we recommended that you read one of the many equipment tests regularly carried out by the motorcycle press. These tests compare the products from all the major manufacturers and give impartial ratings on their effectiveness, value-for-money and ease of use.

No one item of security equipment can provide complete protection. It is highly recommended that two or more of the items described below are combined to increase the security of your motorcycle (a lock and chain plus an alarm system is just about ideal). The more security measures fitted to the bike, the less likely it is to be stolen.

Lock and chain

Pros: *Very flexible to use; can be used to secure the motorcycle to almost any immovable object. On some locks and chains, the lock can be used on its own as a disc lock (see below).*

Cons: *Can be very heavy and awkward to carry on the motorcycle, although some types* will be supplied with a carry bag which can be strapped to the pillion seat.

● Heavy-duty chains and locks are an excellent security measure **(see illustration 1).** Whenever the motorcycle is parked, use the lock and chain to secure the machine to a solid, immovable object such as a post or railings. This will prevent the machine from being ridden away or being lifted into the back of a van.

● When fitting the chain, always ensure the chain is routed around the motorcycle frame or swingarm **(see illustrations 2 and 3).** Never merely pass the chain around one of the wheel rims; a thief may unbolt the wheel and lift the rest of the machine into a van, leaving you with just the wheel! Try to avoid having excess chain free, thus making it difficult to use cutting tools, and keep the chain and lock off the ground to prevent thieves attacking it with a cold chisel. Position the lock so that its lock barrel is facing downwards; this will make it harder for the thief to attack the lock mechanism.

Ensure the lock and chain you buy is of good quality and long enough to shackle your bike to a solid object

Pass the chain through the bike's frame, rather than just through a wheel . . .

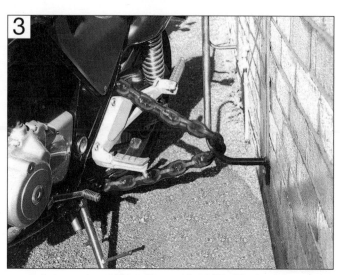

. . . and loop it around a solid object

U-locks

Pros: *Highly effective deterrent which can be used to secure the bike to a post or railings. Most U-locks come with a carrier which allows the lock to be easily carried on the bike.*

Cons: *Not as flexible to use as a lock and chain.*

● These are solid locks which are similar in use to a lock and chain. U-locks are lighter than a lock and chain but not so flexible to use. The length and shape of the lock shackle limit the objects to which the bike can be secured **(see illustration 4)**.

Disc locks

Pros: *Small, light and very easy to carry; most can be stored underneath the seat.*

Cons: *Does not prevent the motorcycle being lifted into a van. Can be very embarrassing if*

U-locks can be used to secure the bike to a solid object – ensure you purchase one which is long enough

you forget to remove the lock before attempting to ride off!

● Disc locks are designed to be attached to the front brake disc. The lock passes through one of the holes in the disc and prevents the wheel rotating by jamming against the fork/brake caliper **(see illustration 5)**. Some are equipped with an alarm siren which sounds if the disc lock is moved; this not only acts as a theft deterrent but also as a handy reminder if you try to move the bike with the lock still fitted.

● Combining the disc lock with a length of cable which can be looped around a post or railings provides an additional measure of security **(see illustration 6)**.

Alarms and immobilisers

Pros: *Once installed it is completely hassle-free to use. If the system is 'Thatcham' or 'Sold Secure-approved', insurance companies may give you a discount.*

Cons: *Can be expensive to buy and complex to install. No system will prevent the motorcycle from being lifted into a van and taken away.*

● Electronic alarms and immobilisers are available to suit a variety of budgets. There are three different types of system available: pure alarms, pure immobilisers, and the more expensive systems which are combined alarm/immobilisers **(see illustration 7)**.
● An alarm system is designed to emit an audible warning if the motorcycle is being tampered with.
● An immobiliser prevents the motorcycle being started and ridden away by disabling its electrical systems.
● When purchasing an alarm/immobiliser system, check the cost of installing the system unless you are able to do it yourself. If the motorcycle is not used regularly, another consideration is the current drain of the system. All alarm/immobiliser systems are powered by the motorcycle's battery; purchasing a system with a very low current drain could prevent the battery losing its charge whilst the motorcycle is not being used.

A typical disc lock attached through one of the holes in the disc

A disc lock combined with a security cable provides additional protection

A typical alarm/immobiliser system

Indelible markings can be applied to most areas of the bike – always apply the manufacturer's sticker to warn off thieves

Chemically-etched code numbers can be applied to main body panels . . .

. . . again, always ensure that the kit manufacturer's sticker is applied in a prominent position

Security marking kits

Pros: *Very cheap and effective deterrent. Many insurance companies will give you a discount on your insurance premium if a recognised security marking kit is used on your motorcycle.*

Cons: *Does not prevent the motorcycle being stolen by joyriders.*

● There are many different types of security marking kits available. The idea is to mark as many parts of the motorcycle as possible with a unique security number **(see illustrations 8, 9 and 10)**. A form will be included with the kit to register your personal details and those of the motorcycle with the kit manufacturer. This register is made available to the police to help them trace the rightful owner of any motorcycle or components which they recover should all other forms of identification have been removed. Always apply the warning stickers provided with the kit to deter thieves.

Ground anchors, wheel clamps and security posts

Pros: *An excellent form of security which will deter all but the most determined of thieves.*

Cons: *Awkward to install and can be expensive.*

● Whilst the motorcycle is at home, it is a good idea to attach it securely to the floor or a solid wall, even if it is kept in a securely locked garage. Various types of ground anchors, security posts and wheel clamps are available for this purpose **(see illustration 11)**. These security devices are either bolted to a solid concrete or brick structure or can be cemented into the ground.

Permanent ground anchors provide an excellent level of security when the bike is at home

Security at home

A high percentage of motorcycle thefts are from the owner's home. Here are some things to consider whenever your motorcycle is at home:
● Where possible, always keep the motorcycle in a securely locked garage. Never rely solely on the standard lock on the garage door, these are usual hopelessly inadequate. Fit an additional locking mechanism to the door and consider having the garage alarmed. A security light, activated by a movement sensor, is also a good investment.

● Always secure the motorcycle to the ground or a wall, even if it is inside a securely locked garage.
● Do not regularly leave the motorcycle outside your home, try to keep it out of sight wherever possible. If a garage is not available, fit a motorcycle cover over the bike to disguise its true identity.
● It is not uncommon for thieves to follow a motorcyclist home to find out where the bike is kept. They will then return at a later date. Be aware of this whenever you are returning

home on your motorcycle. If you suspect you are being followed, do not return home, instead ride to a garage or shop and stop as a precaution.
● When selling a motorcycle, do not provide your home address or the location where the bike is normally kept. Arrange to meet the buyer at a location away from your home. Thieves have been known to pose as potential buyers to find out where motorcycles are kept and then return later to steal them.

Security away from the home

As well as fitting security equipment to your motorcycle here are a few general rules to follow whenever you park your motorcycle.
● Park in a busy, public place.
● Use car parks which incorporate security features, such as CCTV.

● At night, park in a well-lit area, preferably directly underneath a street light.
● Engage the steering lock.
● Secure the motorcycle to a solid, immovable object such as a post or railings with an additional lock. If this is not possible,

secure the bike to a friend's motorcycle. Some public parking places provide security loops for motorcycles.
● Never leave your helmet or luggage attached to the motorcycle. Take them with you at all times.

Lubricants and fluids

A wide range of lubricants, fluids and cleaning agents is available for motor-cycles. This is a guide as to what is available, its applications and properties.

Four-stroke engine oil

● Engine oil is without doubt the most important component of any four-stroke engine. Modern motorcycle engines place a lot of demands on their oil and choosing the right type is essential. Using an unsuitable oil will lead to an increased rate of engine wear and could result in serious engine damage. Before purchasing oil, always check the recommended oil specification given by the manufacturer. The manufacturer will state a recommended 'type or classification' and also a specific 'viscosity' range for engine oil.

● The oil 'type or classification' is identified by its API (American Petroleum Institute) rating. The API rating will be in the form of two letters, e.g. SG. The S identifies the oil as being suitable for use in a petrol (gasoline) engine (S stands for spark ignition) and the second letter, ranging from A to J, identifies the oil's performance rating. The later this letter, the higher the specification of the oil; for example API SG oil exceeds the requirements of API SF oil. **Note:** *On some oils there may also be a second rating consisting of another two letters, the first letter being C, e.g. API SF/CD. This rating indicates the oil is also suitable for use in a diesel engines (the C stands for compression ignition) and is thus of no relevance for motorcycle use.*

● The 'viscosity' of the oil is identified by its SAE (Society of Automotive Engineers) rating. All modern engines require multigrade oils and the SAE rating will consist of two numbers, the first followed by a W, e.g. 10W/40. The first number indicates the viscosity rating of the oil at low temperatures (W stands for winter – tested at –20°C) and the second number represents the viscosity of the oil at high temperatures (tested at 100°C). The lower the number, the thinner the oil. For example an oil with an SAE 10W/40 rating will give better cold starting and running than an SAE 15W/40 oil.

● As well as ensuring the 'type' and 'viscosity' of the oil match the recommendations, another consideration to make when buying engine oil is whether to purchase a standard mineral-based oil, a semi-synthetic oil (also known as a synthetic blend or synthetic-based oil) or a fully-synthetic oil. Although all oils will have a similar rating and viscosity, their cost will vary considerably; mineral-based oils are the cheapest, the fully-synthetic oils the most expensive with the semi-synthetic oils falling somewhere in-between. This decision is very much up to the owner, but it should be noted that modern synthetic oils have far better lubricating and cleaning qualities than traditional mineral-based oils and tend to retain these properties for far longer. Bearing in mind the operating conditions inside a modern, high-revving motorcycle engine it is highly recommended that a fully synthetic oil is used. The extra expense at each service could save you money in the long term by preventing premature engine wear.

● As a final note always ensure that the oil is specifically designed for use in motorcycle engines. Engine oils designed primarily for use in car engines sometimes contain additives or friction modifiers which could cause clutch slip on a motorcycle fitted with a wet-clutch.

Two-stroke engine oil

● Modern two-stroke engines, with their high power outputs, place high demands on their oil. If engine seizure is to be avoided it is essential that a high-quality oil is used. Two-stroke oils differ hugely from four-stroke oils. The oil lubricates only the crankshaft and piston(s) (the transmission has its own lubricating oil) and is used on a total-loss basis where it is burnt completely during the combustion process.

● The Japanese have recently introduced a classification system for two-stroke oils, the JASO rating. This rating is in the form of two letters, either FA, FB or FC – FA is the lowest classification and FC the highest. Ensure the oil being used meets or exceeds the recommended rating specified by the manufacturer.

● As well as ensuring the oil rating matches the recommendation, another consideration to make when buying engine oil is whether to purchase a standard mineral-based oil, a semi-synthetic oil (also known as a synthetic blend or synthetic-based oil) or a fully-synthetic oil. The cost of each type of oil varies considerably; mineral-based oils are the cheapest, the fully-synthetic oils the most expensive with the semi-synthetic oils falling somewhere in-between. This decision is very much up to the owner, but it should be noted that modern synthetic oils have far better lubricating properties and burn cleaner than traditional mineral-based oils. It is therefore recommended that a fully synthetic oil is used. The extra expense could save you money in the long term by preventing premature engine wear, engine performance will be improved, carbon deposits and exhaust smoke will be reduced.

● Always ensure that the oil is specifically designed for use in an injector system. Many high quality two-stroke oils are designed for competition use and need to be pre-mixed with fuel. These oils are of a much higher viscosity and are not designed to flow through the injector pumps used on road-going two-stroke motorcycles.

Transmission (gear) oil

● On a two-stroke engine, the transmission and clutch are lubricated by their own separate oil bath which must be changed in accordance with the Maintenance Schedule.
● Although the engine and transmission units of most four-strokes use a common lubrication supply, there are some exceptions where the engine and gearbox have separate oil reservoirs and a dry clutch is used.
● Motorcycle manufacturers will either recommend a monograde transmission oil or a four-stroke multigrade engine oil to lubricate the transmission.
● Transmission oils, or gear oils as they are often called, are designed specifically for use in transmission systems. The viscosity of these oils is represented by an SAE number, but the scale of measurement applied is different to that used to grade engine oils. As a rough guide a SAE90 gear oil will be of the same viscosity as an SAE50 engine oil.

Shaft drive oil

● On models equipped with shaft final drive, the shaft drive gears are will have their own oil supply. The manufacturer will state a recommended 'type or classification' and also a specific 'viscosity' range in the same manner as for four-stroke engine oil.
● Gear oil classification is given by the number which follows the API GL (GL standing for gear lubricant) rating, the higher the number, the higher the specification of the oil, e.g. API GL5 oil is a higher specification than API GL4 oil. Ensure the oil meets or

exceeds the classification specified and is of the correct viscosity. The viscosity of gear oils is also represented by an SAE number but the scale of measurement used is different to that used to grade engine oils. As a rough guide an SAE90 gear oil will be of the same viscosity as an SAE50 engine oil.
● If the use of an EP (Extreme Pressure) gear oil is specified, ensure the oil purchased is suitable.

Fork oil and suspension fluid

● Conventional telescopic front forks are hydraulic and require fork oil to work. To ensure the forks function correctly, the fork oil must be changed in accordance with the Maintenance Schedule.
● Fork oil is available in a variety of viscosities, identified by their SAE rating; fork oil ratings vary from light (SAE 5) to heavy (SAE 30). When purchasing fork oil, ensure the viscosity rating matches that specified by the manufacturer.
● Some lubricant manufacturers also produce a range of high-quality suspension fluids which are very similar to fork oil but are designed mainly for competition use. These fluids may have a different viscosity rating system which is not to be confused with the SAE rating of normal fork oil. Refer to the manufacturer's instructions if in any doubt.

Brake and clutch fluid

● All disc brake systems and some clutch systems are hydraulically operated. To ensure correct operation, the hydraulic fluid must be changed in accordance with the Maintenance Schedule.
● Brake and clutch fluid is classified by its DOT rating with most motorcycle manufacturers specifying DOT 3 or 4 fluid. Both fluid types are glycol-based and can be mixed together without adverse effect; DOT 4 fluid exceeds the requirements of DOT 3

fluid. Although it is safe to use DOT 4 fluid in a system designed for use with DOT 3 fluid, never use DOT 3 fluid in a system which specifies the use of DOT 4 as this will adversely affect the system's performance. The type required for the system will be marked on the fluid reservoir cap.
● Some manufacturers also produce a DOT 5 hydraulic fluid. DOT 5 hydraulic fluid is silicone-based and is not compatible with the glycol-based DOT 3 and 4 fluids. Never mix DOT 5 fluid with DOT 3 or 4 fluid as this will seriously affect the performance of the hydraulic system.

Coolant/antifreeze

● When purchasing coolant/antifreeze, always ensure it is suitable for use in an aluminium engine and contains corrosion inhibitors to prevent possible blockages of the internal coolant passages of the system. As a general rule, most coolants are designed to be used neat and should not be diluted whereas antifreeze can be mixed with distilled water to provide a coolant solution of the required strength. Refer to the manufacturer's instructions on the bottle.
● Ensure the coolant is changed in accordance with the Maintenance Schedule.

Chain lube

● Chain lube is an aerosol-type spray lubricant specifically designed for use on motorcycle final drive chains. Chain lube has two functions, to minimise friction between the final drive chain and sprockets and to prevent corrosion of the chain. Regular use of a good-quality chain lube will extend the life of the drive chain and sprockets and thus maximise the power being transmitted from the transmission to the rear wheel.
● When using chain lube, always allow some time for the solvents in the lube to evaporate before riding the motorcycle. This will minimise the amount of lube which will

'fling' off from the chain when the motorcycle is used. If the motorcycle is equipped with an 'O-ring' chain, ensure the chain lube is labelled as being suitable for use on 'O-ring' chains.

Degreasers and solvents

● There are many different types of solvents and degreasers available to remove the grime and grease which accumulate around the motorcycle during normal use. Degreasers and solvents are usually available as an aerosol-type spray or as a liquid which you apply with a brush. Always closely follow the manufacturer's instructions and wear eye protection during use. Be aware that many solvents are flammable and may give off noxious fumes; take adequate precautions when using them (see Safety First!).
● For general cleaning, use one of the many solvents or degreasers available from most motorcycle accessory shops. These solvents are usually applied then left for a certain time before being washed off with water.

Brake cleaner is a solvent specifically designed to remove all traces of oil, grease and dust from braking system components. Brake cleaner is designed to evaporate quickly and leaves behind no residue.

Carburettor cleaner is an aerosol-type solvent specifically designed to clear carburettor blockages and break down the hard deposits and gum often found inside carburettors during overhaul.

Contact cleaner is an aerosol-type solvent designed for cleaning electrical components. The cleaner will remove all traces of oil and dirt from components such as switch contacts or fouled spark plugs and then dry, leaving behind no residue.

Gasket remover is an aerosol-type solvent designed for removing stubborn gaskets from engine components during overhaul. Gasket remover will minimise the amount of scraping required to remove the gasket and therefore reduce the risk of damage to the mating surface.

Spray lubricants

● Aerosol-based spray lubricants are widely available and are excellent for lubricating lever pivots and exposed cables and switches. Try to use a lubricant which is of the dry-film type as the fluid evaporates, leaving behind a dry-film of lubricant. Lubricants which leave behind an oily residue will attract dust and dirt which will increase the rate of wear of the cable/lever.

● Most lubricants also act as a moisture dispersant and a penetrating fluid. This means they can also be used to 'dry out' electrical components such as wiring connectors or switches as well as helping to free seized fasteners.

Greases

● Grease is used to lubricate many of the pivot-points. A good-quality multi-purpose grease is suitable for most applications but some manufacturers will specify the use of specialist greases for use on components such as swingarm and suspension linkage bushes. These specialist greases can be purchased from most motorcycle (or car) accessory shops; commonly specified types include molybdenum disulphide grease, lithium-based grease, graphite-based grease, silicone-based grease and high-temperature copper-based grease.

Gasket sealing compounds

● Gasket sealing compounds can be used in conjunction with gaskets, to improve their sealing capabilities, or on their own to seal metal-to-metal joints. Depending on their type, sealing compounds either set hard or stay relatively soft and pliable.

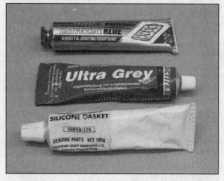

● When purchasing a gasket sealing compound, ensure that it is designed specifically for use on an internal combustion engine. General multi-purpose sealants available from DIY stores may appear visibly similar but they are not designed to withstand the extreme heat or contact with fuel and oil encountered when used on an engine (see 'Tools and Workshop Tips' for further information).

Thread locking compound

● Thread locking compounds are used to secure certain threaded fasteners in position to prevent them from loosening due to vibration. Thread locking compounds can be purchased from most motorcycle (and car) accessory shops. Ensure the threads of the both components are completely clean and dry before sparingly applying the locking compound (see 'Tools and Workshop Tips' for further information).

Fuel additives

● Fuel additives which protect and clean the fuel system components are widely available. These additives are designed to remove all traces of deposits that build up on the carburettors/injectors and prevent wear, helping the fuel system to operate more efficiently. If a fuel additive is being used, check that it is suitable for use with your motorcycle, especially if your motorcycle is equipped with a catalytic converter.

● Octane boosters are also available. These additives are designed to improve the performance of highly-tuned engines being run on normal pump-fuel and are of no real use on standard motorcycles.

Conversion factors

Length (distance)

Inches (in)	x 25.4	= Millimetres (mm)	x 0.0394	= Inches (in)	
Feet (ft)	x 0.305	= Metres (m)	x 3.281	= Feet (ft)	
Miles	x 1.609	= Kilometres (km)	x 0.621	= Miles	

Volume (capacity)

Cubic inches (cu in; in³)	x 16.387	= Cubic centimetres (cc; cm³)	x 0.061	= Cubic inches (cu in; in³)	
Imperial pints (Imp pt)	x 0.568	= Litres (l)	x 1.76	= Imperial pints (Imp pt)	
Imperial quarts (Imp qt)	x 1.137	= Litres (l)	x 0.88	= Imperial quarts (Imp qt)	
Imperial quarts (Imp qt)	x 1.201	= US quarts (US qt)	x 0.833	= Imperial quarts (Imp qt)	
US quarts (US qt)	x 0.946	= Litres (l)	x 1.057	= US quarts (US qt)	
Imperial gallons (Imp gal)	x 4.546	= Litres (l)	x 0.22	= Imperial gallons (Imp gal)	
Imperial gallons (Imp gal)	x 1.201	= US gallons (US gal)	x 0.833	= Imperial gallons (Imp gal)	
US gallons (US gal)	x 3.785	= Litres (l)	x 0.264	= US gallons (US gal)	

Mass (weight)

Ounces (oz)	x 28.35	= Grams (g)	x 0.035	= Ounces (oz)
Pounds (lb)	x 0.454	= Kilograms (kg)	x 2.205	= Pounds (lb)

Force

Ounces-force (ozf; oz)	x 0.278	= Newtons (N)	x 3.6	= Ounces-force (ozf; oz)
Pounds-force (lbf; lb)	x 4.448	= Newtons (N)	x 0.225	= Pounds-force (lbf; lb)
Newtons (N)	x 0.1	= Kilograms-force (kgf; kg)	x 9.81	= Newtons (N)

Pressure

Pounds-force per square inch (psi; lbf/in²; lb/in²)	x 0.070	= Kilograms-force per square centimetre (kgf/cm²; kg/cm²)	x 14.223	= Pounds-force per square inch (psi; lbf/in²; lb/in²)
Pounds-force per square inch (psi; lbf/in²; lb/in²)	x 0.068	= Atmospheres (atm)	x 14.696	= Pounds-force per square inch (psi; lbf/in²; lb/in²)
Pounds-force per square inch (psi; lbf/in²; lb/in²)	x 0.069	= Bars	x 14.5	= Pounds-force per square inch (psi; lbf/in²; lb/in²)
Pounds-force per square inch (psi; lbf/in²; lb/in²)	x 6.895	= Kilopascals (kPa)	x 0.145	= Pounds-force per square inch (psi; lbf/in²; lb/in²)
Kilopascals (kPa)	x 0.01	= Kilograms-force per square centimetre (kgf/cm²; kg/cm²)	x 98.1	= Kilopascals (kPa)
Millibar (mbar)	x 100	= Pascals (Pa)	x 0.01	= Millibar (mbar)
Millibar (mbar)	x 0.0145	= Pounds-force per square inch (psi; lbf/in²; lb/in²)	x 68.947	= Millibar (mbar)
Millibar (mbar)	x 0.75	= Millimetres of mercury (mmHg)	x 1.333	= Millibar (mbar)
Millibar (mbar)	x 0.401	= Inches of water (inH₂O)	x 2.491	= Millibar (mbar)
Millimetres of mercury (mmHg)	x 0.535	= Inches of water (inH₂O)	x 1.868	= Millimetres of mercury (mmHg)
Inches of water (inH₂O)	x 0.036	= Pounds-force per square inch (psi; lbf/in²; lb/in²)	x 27.68	= Inches of water (inH₂O)

Torque (moment of force)

Pounds-force inches (lbf in; lb in)	x 1.152	= Kilograms-force centimetre (kgf cm; kg cm)	x 0.868	= Pounds-force inches (lbf in; lb in)
Pounds-force inches (lbf in; lb in)	x 0.113	= Newton metres (Nm)	x 8.85	= Pounds-force inches (lbf in; lb in)
Pounds-force inches (lbf in; lb in)	x 0.083	= Pounds-force feet (lbf ft; lb ft)	x 12	= Pounds-force inches (lbf in; lb in)
Pounds-force feet (lbf ft; lb ft)	x 0.138	= Kilograms-force metres (kgf m; kg m)	x 7.233	= Pounds-force feet (lbf ft; lb ft)
Pounds-force feet (lbf ft; lb ft)	x 1.356	= Newton metres (Nm)	x 0.738	= Pounds-force feet (lbf ft; lb ft)
Newton metres (Nm)	x 0.102	= Kilograms-force metres (kgf m; kg m)	x 9.804	= Newton metres (Nm)

Power

Horsepower (hp)	x 745.7	= Watts (W)	x 0.0013	= Horsepower (hp)

Velocity (speed)

Miles per hour (miles/hr; mph)	x 1.609	= Kilometres per hour (km/hr; kph)	x 0.621	= Miles per hour (miles/hr; mph)

Fuel consumption*

Miles per gallon, Imperial (mpg)	x 0.354	= Kilometres per litre (km/l)	x 2.825	= Miles per gallon, Imperial (mpg)
Miles per gallon, US (mpg)	x 0.425	= Kilometres per litre (km/l)	x 2.352	= Miles per gallon, US (mpg)

Temperature

Degrees Fahrenheit = (°C x 1.8) + 32   Degrees Celsius (Degrees Centigrade; °C) = (°F - 32) x 0.56

It is common practice to convert from miles per gallon (mpg) to litres/100 kilometres (l/100km), where mpg x l/100 km = 282

About the MOT Test

In the UK, all vehicles more than three years old are subject to an annual test to ensure that they meet minimum safety requirements. A current test certificate must be issued before a machine can be used on public roads, and is required before a road fund licence can be issued. Riding without a current test certificate will also invalidate your insurance.

For most owners, the MOT test is an annual cause for anxiety, and this is largely due to owners not being sure what needs to be checked prior to submitting the motorcycle for testing. The simple answer is that a fully roadworthy motorcycle will have no difficulty in passing the test.

This is a guide to getting your motorcycle through the MOT test. Obviously it will not be possible to examine the motorcycle to the same standard as the professional MOT tester, particularly in view of the equipment required for some of the checks. However, working through the following procedures will enable you to identify any problem areas before submitting the motorcycle for the test.

It has only been possible to summarise the test requirements here, based on the regulations in force at the time of printing. Test standards are becoming increasingly stringent, although there are some exemptions for older vehicles. More information about the MOT test can be

obtained from the TSO publications, *How Safe is your Motorcycle* and *The MOT Inspection Manual for Motorcycle Testing*.

Many of the checks require that one of the wheels is raised off the ground. If the motorcycle doesn't have a centre stand, note that an auxiliary stand will be required. Additionally, the help of an assistant may prove useful.

Certain exceptions apply to machines under 50 cc, machines without a lighting system, and Classic bikes - if in doubt about any of the requirements listed below seek confirmation from an MOT tester prior to submitting the motorcycle for the test.

Check that the frame number is clearly visible.

Electrical System

Lights, turn signals, horn and reflector

● With the ignition on, check the operation of the following electrical components. **Note:** *The electrical components on certain small-capacity machines are powered by the generator, requiring that the engine is run for this check.*

a) *Headlight and tail light. Check that both illuminate in the low and high beam switch positions.*

b) *Position lights. Check that the front position (or sidelight) and tail light illuminate in this switch position.*

c) *Turn signals. Check that all flash at the correct rate, and that the warning light(s) function correctly. Check that the turn signal switch works correctly.*

d) *Hazard warning system (where fitted). Check that all four turn signals flash in this switch position.*

e) *Brake stop light. Check that the light comes on when the front and rear brakes are independently applied. Models first used on or after 1st April 1986 must have a brake light switch on each brake.*

f) *Horn. Check that the sound is continuous and of reasonable volume.*

● Check that there is a red reflector on the rear of the machine, either mounted separately or as part of the tail light lens.

● Check the condition of the headlight, tail light and turn signal lenses.

Headlight beam height

● The MOT tester will perform a headlight beam height check using specialised beam setting equipment **(see illustration 1)**. This equipment will not be available to the home mechanic, but if you suspect that the headlight is incorrectly set or may have been maladjusted in the past, you can perform a rough test as follows.

● Position the bike in a straight line facing a brick wall. The bike must be off its stand, upright and with a rider seated. Measure the height from the ground to the centre of the headlight and mark a horizontal line on the wall at this height. Position the motorcycle 3.8 metres from the wall and draw a vertical

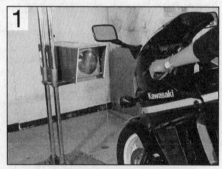

Headlight beam height checking equipment

line up the wall central to the centreline of the motorcycle. Switch to dipped beam and check that the beam pattern falls slightly lower than the horizontal line and to the left of the vertical line **(see illustration 2)**.

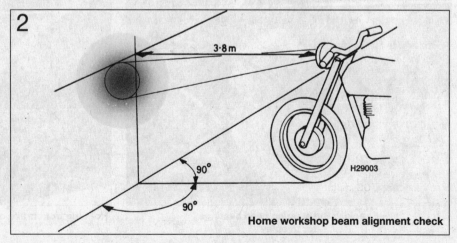

Home workshop beam alignment check

Exhaust System and Final Drive

Exhaust

● Check that the exhaust mountings are secure and that the system does not foul any of the rear suspension components.
● Start the motorcycle. When the revs are increased, check that the exhaust is neither holed nor leaking from any of its joints. On a linked system, check that the collector box is not leaking due to corrosion.

● Note that the exhaust decibel level ("loudness" of the exhaust) is assessed at the discretion of the tester. If the motorcycle was first used on or after 1st January 1985 the silencer must carry the BSAU 193 stamp, or a marking relating to its make and model, or be of OE (original equipment) manufacture. If the silencer is marked NOT FOR ROAD USE, RACING USE ONLY or similar, it will fail the MOT.

Final drive

● On chain or belt drive machines, check that the chain/belt is in good condition and does not have excessive slack. Also check that the sprocket is securely mounted on the rear wheel hub. Check that the chain/belt guard is in place.
● On shaft drive bikes, check for oil leaking from the drive unit and fouling the rear tyre.

Steering and Suspension

Steering

● With the front wheel raised off the ground, rotate the steering from lock to lock. The handlebar or switches must not contact the fuel tank or be close enough to trap the rider's hand. Problems can be caused by damaged lock stops on the lower yoke and frame, or by the fitting of non-standard handlebars.
● When performing the lock to lock check, also ensure that the steering moves freely without drag or notchiness. Steering movement can be impaired by poorly routed cables, or by overtight head bearings or worn bvearings. The tester will perform a check of the steering head bearing lower race by mounting the front wheel on a surface plate, then performing a lock to

lock check with the weight of the machine on the lower bearing **(see illustration 3)**.
● Grasp the fork sliders (lower legs) and attempt to push and pull on the forks

3

Front wheel mounted on a surface plate for steering head bearing lower race check

(see illustration 4). Any play in the steering head bearings will be felt. Note that in extreme cases, wear of the front fork bushes can be misinterpreted for head bearing play.
● Check that the handlebars are securely mounted.
● Check that the handlebar grip rubbers are secure. They should by bonded to the bar left end and to the throttle cable pulley on the right end.

Front suspension

● With the motorcycle off the stand, hold the front brake on and pump the front forks up and down **(see illustration 5)**. Check that they are adequately damped.

4

Checking the steering head bearings for freeplay

5

Hold the front brake on and pump the front forks up and down to check operation

Inspect the area around the fork dust seal for oil leakage (arrow)

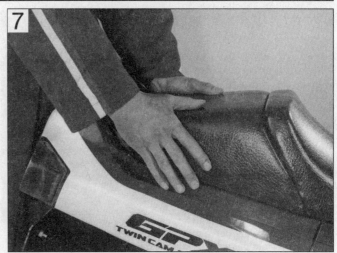

Bounce the rear of the motorcycle to check rear suspension operation

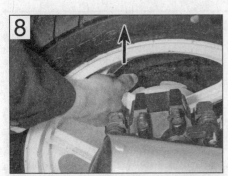

Checking for rear suspension linkage play

● Inspect the area above and around the front fork oil seals (see illustration 6). There should be no sign of oil on the fork tube (stanchion) nor leaking down the slider (lower leg). On models so equipped, check that there is no oil leaking from the anti-dive units.

● On models with swingarm front suspension, check that there is no freeplay in the linkage when moved from side to side.

Rear suspension

● With the motorcycle off the stand and an assistant supporting the motorcycle by its handlebars, bounce the rear suspension (see illustration 7). Check that the suspension components do not foul on any of the cycle parts and check that the shock absorber(s) provide adequate damping.

● Visually inspect the shock absorber(s) and check that there is no sign of oil leakage from its damper. This is somewhat restricted on certain single shock models due to the location of the shock absorber.

● With the rear wheel raised off the ground, grasp the wheel at the highest point and attempt to pull it up (see illustration 8). Any play in the swingarm pivot or suspension linkage bearings will be felt as movement. **Note:** *Do not confuse play with actual suspension movement.* Failure to lubricate suspension linkage bearings can lead to bearing failure (see illustration 9).

● With the rear wheel raised off the ground, grasp the swingarm ends and attempt to move the swingarm from side to side and forwards and backwards - any play indicates wear of the swingarm pivot bearings (see illustration 10).

Worn suspension linkage pivots (arrows) are usually the cause of play in the rear suspension

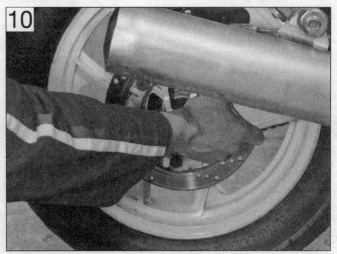

Grasp the swingarm at the ends to check for play in its pivot bearings

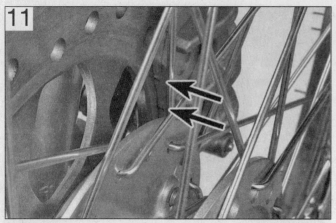

Brake pad wear can usually be viewed without removing the caliper. Most pads have wear indicator grooves (arrowed) and some also have indicator tangs or cut-outs.

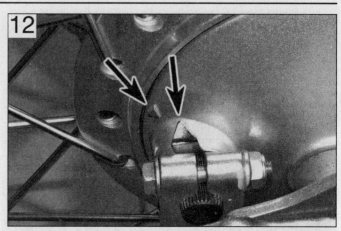

On drum brakes, check the angle of the operating lever with the brake fully applied. Most drum brakes have a wear indicator pointer or scale.

Brakes, Wheels and Tyres

Brakes

● With the wheel raised off the ground, apply the brake then free it off, and check that the wheel is about to revolve freely without brake drag.

● On disc brakes, examine the disc itself. Check that it is securely mounted and not cracked.

● On disc brakes, view the pad material through the caliper mouth and check that the pads are not worn down beyond the limit (see illustration 11).

● On drum brakes, check that when the brake is applied the angle between the operating lever and cable or rod is not too great (see illustration 12). Check also that the operating lever doesn't foul any other components.

● On disc brakes, examine the flexible hoses from top to bottom. Have an assistant hold the brake on so that the fluid in the hose is under pressure, and check that there is no sign of fluid leakage, bulges or cracking. If there are any metal brake pipes or unions, check that these are free from corrosion and damage. Where a brake-linked anti-dive system is fitted, check the hoses to the anti-dive in a similar manner.

● Check that the rear brake torque arm is secure and that its fasteners are secured by self-locking nuts or castellated nuts with split-pins or R-pins (see illustration 13).

● On models with ABS, check that the self-check warning light in the instrument panel works.

● The MOT tester will perform a test of the motorcycle's braking efficiency based on a calculation of rider and motorcycle weight. Although this cannot be carried out at home, you can at least ensure that the braking systems are properly maintained. For hydraulic disc brakes, check the fluid level, lever/pedal feel (bleed of air if its spongy) and pad material. For drum brakes, check adjustment, cable or rod operation and shoe lining thickness.

Wheels and tyres

● Check the wheel condition. Cast wheels should be free from cracks and if of the built-up design, all fasteners should be secure. Spoked wheels should be checked for broken, corroded, loose or bent spokes.

● With the wheel raised off the ground, spin the wheel and visually check that the tyre and wheel run true. Check that the tyre does not foul the suspension or mudguards.

● With the wheel raised off the ground, grasp the wheel and attempt to move it about the axle (spindle) (see illustration 14). Any play felt here indicates wheel bearing failure.

Brake torque arm must be properly secured at both ends

Check for wheel bearing play by trying to move the wheel about the axle (spindle)

Checking the tyre tread depth

Tyre direction of rotation arrow can be found on tyre sidewall

Castellated type wheel axle (spindle) nut must be secured by a split pin or R-pin

Two straightedges are used to check wheel alignment

● Check the tyre tread depth, tread condition and sidewall condition **(see illustration 15)**.
● Check the tyre type. Front and rear tyre types must be compatible and be suitable for road use. Tyres marked NOT FOR ROAD USE, COMPETITION USE ONLY or similar, will fail the MOT.

● If the tyre sidewall carries a direction of rotation arrow, this must be pointing in the direction of normal wheel rotation **(see illustration 16)**.
● Check that the wheel axle (spindle) nuts (where applicable) are properly secured. A self-locking nut or castellated nut with a split-pin or R-pin can be used **(see illustration 17)**.
● Wheel alignment is checked with the motorcycle off the stand and a rider seated. With the front wheel pointing straight ahead, two perfectly straight lengths of metal or wood and placed against the sidewalls of both tyres **(see illustration 18)**. The gap each side of the front tyre must be equidistant on both sides. Incorrect wheel alignment may be due to a cocked rear wheel (often as the result of poor chain adjustment) or in extreme cases, a bent frame.

General checks and condition

● Check the security of all major fasteners, bodypanels, seat, fairings (where fitted) and mudguards.

● Check that the rider and pillion footrests, handlebar levers and brake pedal are securely mounted.

● Check for corrosion on the frame or any load-bearing components. If severe, this may affect the structure, particularly under stress.

Sidecars

A motorcycle fitted with a sidecar requires additional checks relating to the stability of the machine and security of attachment and swivel joints, plus specific wheel alignment (toe-in) requirements. Additionally, tyre and lighting requirements differ from conventional motorcycle use. Owners are advised to check MOT test requirements with an official test centre.

Preparing for storage

Before you start

If repairs or an overhaul is needed, see that this is carried out now rather than left until you want to ride the bike again.

Give the bike a good wash and scrub all dirt from its underside. Make sure the bike dries completely before preparing for storage.

Engine

● Remove the spark plug(s) and lubricate the cylinder bores with approximately a teaspoon of motor oil using a spout-type oil can **(see illustration 1)**. Reinstall the spark plug(s). Crank the engine over a couple of times to coat the piston rings and bores with oil. If the bike has a kickstart, use this to turn the engine over. If not, flick the kill switch to the OFF position and crank the engine over on the starter **(see illustration 2)**. If the nature on the ignition system prevents the starter operating with the kill switch in the OFF position, remove the spark plugs and fit them back in their caps; ensure that the plugs are earthed (grounded) against the cylinder head when the starter is operated **(see illustration 3)**.

⚠️ *Warning: It is important that the plugs are earthed (grounded) away from the spark plug holes otherwise there is a risk of atomised fuel from the cylinders igniting.*

HAYNES HiNT *On a single cylinder four-stroke engine, you can seal the combustion chamber completely by positioning the piston at TDC on the compression stroke.*

● Drain the carburettor(s) otherwise there is a risk of jets becoming blocked by gum deposits from the fuel **(see illustration 4)**.

● If the bike is going into long-term storage, consider adding a fuel stabiliser to the fuel in the tank. If the tank is drained completely, corrosion of its internal surfaces may occur if left unprotected for a long period. The tank can be treated with a rust preventative especially for this purpose. Alternatively, remove the tank and pour half a litre of motor oil into it, install the filler cap and shake the tank to coat its internals with oil before draining off the excess. The same effect can also be achieved by spraying WD40 or a similar water-dispersant around the inside of the tank via its flexible nozzle.

● Make sure the cooling system contains the correct mix of antifreeze. Antifreeze also contains important corrosion inhibitors.

● The air intakes and exhaust can be sealed off by covering or plugging the openings. Ensure that you do not seal in any condensation; run the engine until it is hot,

Squirt a drop of motor oil into each cylinder

Flick the kill switch to OFF . . .

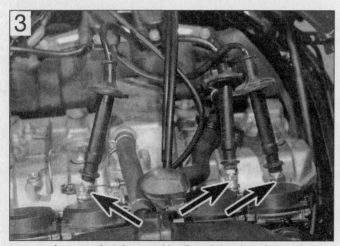

. . . and ensure that the metal bodies of the plugs (arrows) are earthed against the cylinder head

Connect a hose to the carburettor float chamber drain stub (arrow) and unscrew the drain screw

Exhausts can be sealed off with a plastic bag

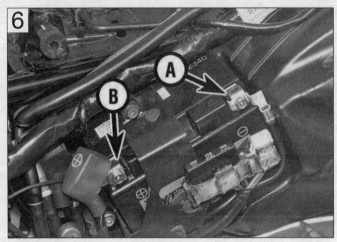
Disconnect the negative lead (A) first, followed by the positive lead (B)

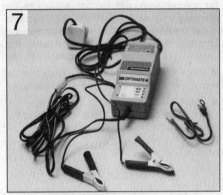
Use a suitable battery charger - this kit also assess battery condition

then switch off and allow to cool. Tape a piece of thick plastic over the silencer end(s) **(see illustration 5)**. Note that some advocate pouring a tablespoon of motor oil into the silencer(s) before sealing them off.

Battery

● Remove it from the bike - in extreme cases of cold the battery may freeze and crack its case **(see illustration 6)**.

● Check the electrolyte level and top up if necessary (conventional refillable batteries). Clean the terminals.
● Store the battery off the motorcycle and away from any sources of fire. Position a wooden block under the battery if it is to sit on the ground.
● Give the battery a trickle charge for a few hours every month **(see illustration 7)**.

Tyres

● Place the bike on its centrestand or an auxiliary stand which will support the motorcycle in an upright position. Position wood blocks under the tyres to keep them off the ground and to provide insulation from damp. If the bike is being put into long-term storage, ideally both tyres should be off the ground; not only will this protect the tyres, but will also ensure that no load is placed on the steering head or wheel bearings.
● Deflate each tyre by 5 to 10 psi, no more or the beads may unseat from the rim, making subsequent inflation difficult on tubeless tyres.

Pivots and controls

● Lubricate all lever, pedal, stand and footrest

pivot points. If grease nipples are fitted to the rear suspension components, apply lubricant to the pivots.
● Lubricate all control cables.

Cycle components

● Apply a wax protectant to all painted and plastic components. Wipe off any excess, but don't polish to a shine. Where fitted, clean the screen with soap and water.
● Coat metal parts with Vaseline (petroleum jelly). When applying this to the fork tubes, do not compress the forks otherwise the seals will rot from contact with the Vaseline.
● Apply a vinyl cleaner to the seat.

Storage conditions

● Aim to store the bike in a shed or garage which does not leak and is free from damp.
● Drape an old blanket or bedspread over the bike to protect it from dust and direct contact with sunlight (which will fade paint). This also hides the bike from prying eyes. Beware of tight-fitting plastic covers which may allow condensation to form and settle on the bike.

Getting back on the road

Engine and transmission

● Change the oil and replace the oil filter. If this was done prior to storage, check that the oil hasn't emulsified - a thick whitish substance which occurs through condensation.
● Remove the spark plugs. Using a spout-type oil can, squirt a few drops of oil into the cylinder(s). This will provide initial lubrication as the piston rings and bores comes back into contact. Service the spark plugs, or fit new ones, and install them in the engine.

● Check that the clutch isn't stuck on. The plates can stick together if left standing for some time, preventing clutch operation. Engage a gear and try rocking the bike back and forth with the clutch lever held against the handlebar. If this doesn't work on cable-operated clutches, hold the clutch lever back against the handlebar with a strong elastic band or cable tie for a couple of hours **(see illustration 8)**.
● If the air intakes or silencer end(s) were blocked off, remove the bung or cover used.
● If the fuel tank was coated with a rust

Hold clutch lever back against the handlebar with elastic bands or a cable tie

preventative, oil or a stabiliser added to the fuel, drain and flush the tank and dispose of the fuel sensibly. If no action was taken with the fuel tank prior to storage, it is advised that the old fuel is disposed of since it will go off over a period of time. Refill the fuel tank with fresh fuel.

Frame and running gear

● Oil all pivot points and cables.
● Check the tyre pressures. They will definitely need inflating if pressures were reduced for storage.
● Lubricate the final drive chain (where applicable).
● Remove any protective coating applied to the fork tubes (stanchions) since this may well destroy the fork seals. If the fork tubes weren't protected and have picked up rust spots, remove them with very fine abrasive paper and refinish with metal polish.
● Check that both brakes operate correctly. Apply each brake hard and check that it's not possible to move the motorcycle forwards, then check that the brake frees off again once released. Brake caliper pistons can stick due to corrosion around the piston head, or on the sliding caliper types, due to corrosion of the slider pins. If the brake doesn't free after repeated operation, take the caliper off for examination. Similarly drum brakes can stick due to a seized operating cam, cable or rod linkage.
● If the motorcycle has been in long-term storage, renew the brake fluid and clutch fluid (where applicable).
● Depending on where the bike has been stored, the wiring, cables and hoses may have been nibbled by rodents. Make a visual check and investigate disturbed wiring loom tape.

Battery

● If the battery has been previously removal and given top up charges it can simply be reconnected. Remember to connect the positive cable first and the negative cable last.
● On conventional refillable batteries, if the battery has not received any attention, remove it from the motorcycle and check its electrolyte level. Top up if necessary then charge the battery. If the battery fails to hold a charge and a visual checks show heavy white sulphation of the plates, the battery is probably defective and must be renewed. This is particularly likely if the battery is old. Confirm battery condition with a specific gravity check.
● On sealed (MF) batteries, if the battery has not received any attention, remove it from the motorcycle and charge it according to the information on the battery case - if the battery fails to hold a charge it must be renewed.

Starting procedure

● If a kickstart is fitted, turn the engine over a couple of times with the ignition OFF to distribute oil around the engine. If no kickstart is fitted, flick the engine kill switch OFF and the ignition ON and crank the engine over a couple of times to work oil around the upper cylinder components. If the nature of the ignition system is such that the starter won't work with the kill switch OFF, remove the spark plugs, fit them back into their caps and earth (ground) their bodies on the cylinder head. Reinstall the spark plugs afterwards.
● Switch the kill switch to RUN, operate the choke and start the engine. If the engine won't start don't continue cranking the engine - not only will this flatten the battery, but the starter motor will overheat. Switch the ignition off and try again later. If the engine refuses to start, go through the fault finding procedures in this manual. **Note:** *If the bike has been in storage for a long time, old fuel or a carburettor blockage may be the problem. Gum deposits in carburettors can block jets - if a carburettor cleaner doesn't prove successful the carburettors must be dismantled for cleaning.*
● Once the engine has started, check that the lights, turn signals and horn work properly.
● Treat the bike gently for the first ride and check all fluid levels on completion. Settle the bike back into the maintenance schedule.

This Section provides an easy reference-guide to the more common faults that are likely to afflict your machine. Obviously, the opportunities are almost limitless for faults to occur as a result of obscure failures, and to try and cover all eventualities would require a book. Indeed, a number have been written on the subject.

Successful troubleshooting is not a mysterious 'black art' but the application of a bit of knowledge combined with a systematic and logical approach to the problem. Approach any troubleshooting by first accurately identifying the symptom and then checking through the list of possible causes, starting with the simplest or most obvious and progressing in stages to the most complex.

Take nothing for granted, but above all apply liberal quantities of common sense.

The main symptom of a fault is given in the text as a major heading below which are listed the various systems or areas which may contain the fault. Details of each possible cause for a fault and the remedial action to be taken are given, in brief, in the paragraphs below each heading. Further information should be sought in the relevant Chapter.

1 Engine doesn't start or is difficult to start

- [ ] Starter motor doesn't rotate
- [ ] Starter motor rotates but engine does not turn over
- [ ] Starter works but engine won't turn over (seized)
- [ ] No fuel flow
- [ ] Engine flooded
- [ ] No spark or weak spark
- [ ] Compression low
- [ ] Stalls after starting
- [ ] Rough idle

2 Poor running at low speed

- [ ] Spark weak
- [ ] Fuel/air mixture incorrect
- [ ] Compression low
- [ ] Poor acceleration

3 Poor running or no power at high speed

- [ ] Firing incorrect
- [ ] Fuel/air mixture incorrect
- [ ] Compression low
- [ ] Knocking or pinking
- [ ] Miscellaneous causes

4 Overheating

- [ ] Engine overheats
- [ ] Firing incorrect
- [ ] Fuel/air mixture incorrect
- [ ] Compression too high
- [ ] Engine load excessive
- [ ] Lubrication inadequate
- [ ] Miscellaneous causes

5 Clutch problems

- [ ] Clutch slipping
- [ ] Clutch not disengaging completely

6 Gearchange problems

- [ ] Doesn't go into gear, or lever doesn't return
- [ ] Jumps out of gear
- [ ] Overselects

7 Abnormal engine noise

- [ ] Knocking or pinking
- [ ] Piston slap or rattling
- [ ] Valve noise
- [ ] Other noise

8 Abnormal driveline noise

- [ ] Clutch noise
- [ ] Transmission noise
- [ ] Final drive noise

9 Abnormal frame and suspension noise

- [ ] Front end noise
- [ ] Shock absorber noise
- [ ] Brake noise

10 Oil pressure low

- [ ] Engine lubrication system

11 Excessive exhaust smoke

- [ ] White smoke
- [ ] Black smoke
- [ ] Brown smoke

12 Poor handling or stability

- [ ] Handlebar hard to turn
- [ ] Handlebar shakes or vibrates excessively
- [ ] Handlebar pulls to one side
- [ ] Poor shock absorbing qualities

13 Braking problems

- [ ] Brakes are spongy, don't hold
- [ ] Brake lever or pedal pulsates
- [ ] Brakes drag

14 Electrical problems

- [ ] Battery dead or weak
- [ ] Battery overcharged

1 Engine doesn't start or is difficult to start

Starter motor doesn't rotate

☐ Engine kill switch OFF.

☐ Fuse blown. Check main fuse and IG fuse (Chapter 8).

☐ Battery voltage low. Check battery condition and recharge or replace battery (Chapter 8).

☐ Loose or corroded battery connections/terminals. Tighten or clean connections.

☐ Starter motor defective. Make sure the wiring to the starter is secure and free of corrosion. Replace or repair the motor if defective (Chapter 8).

☐ Starter relay defective. Make sure the wiring to relay is secure and free of corrosion. Test the operation of the relay, internal corrosion or arcing can cause the relay to not pass sufficient current to the starter motor even if it clicks when the start button is operated (Chapter 8).

☐ Starter button not contacting. The contacts could be wet, corroded or dirty. Disassemble and clean the switch (Chapter 8).

☐ Wiring open or shorted. Check all wiring connections and harnesses to make sure that they are dry, tight and not corroded. Also check for broken or frayed wires that can cause a short to earth (see *Wiring diagrams*, Chapter 8).

☐ Ignition or kill switch defective. This is usually caused by water, corrosion, damage or excessive wear. The switches can be disassembled and cleaned with electrical contact cleaner. If cleaning does not help, replace the switches (Chapter 8).

☐ Faulty neutral switch, sidestand switch or clutch switch. Check the wiring to each switch and the switch itself (Chapter 8).

☐ Faulty starter safety circuit relay or diodes (Chapter 8).

☐ Fuel injection system shutdown due to system fault (Chapter 4).

Starter motor rotates but engine does not turn over

☐ Starter clutch defective. Inspect and repair or replace with a new one (Chapter 2).

☐ Damaged idler or starter gears. Inspect and replace the damaged parts (Chapter 2).

Starter works but engine won't turn over (seized)

☐ Seized engine caused by one or more internally damaged components. Failure due to wear, abuse or lack of lubrication. Damage can include seized valves, followers, camshafts, pistons, crankshaft, connecting rod bearings, or transmission gears or bearings. Refer to Chapter 2 for engine disassembly.

No fuel flow

☐ No fuel in tank.

☐ Fuel tank breather hose obstructed.

☐ Faulty fuel pump relay. Check the relay (Chapter 4).

☐ Fuel pump faulty or blocked fuel filter. Replace faulty pump - the filter is not available separately (Chapter 4).

☐ Electronic control unit (ECU) or its relay defective (Chapter 4).

☐ Ignition key not recognised by immobiliser system.

☐ Fuel hose kinked. Replace the fuel hose.

☐ Fuel injector clogged. For all the injectors to be clogged, either a very bad batch of fuel with an unusual additive has been used, or some other foreign material has entered the tank. In some cases, if a machine has been unused for several months, the fuel turns to a varnish-like liquid which can cause an injector needle to stick to its seat. Drain the tank and fuel system, ultrasonically clean or replace fuel injectors (Chapter 4).

Engine flooded

☐ Injector needle valve worn or stuck open causing excess fuel to be admitted to the throttle body. In this case, the injectors should be renewed.

☐ Starting technique incorrect. Under normal circumstances (i.e. if all the components of the fuel injection system are good) the machine should start with the throttle closed.

No spark or weak spark

☐ Ignition switch OFF.

☐ Engine kill switch turned to the OFF position.

☐ Ignition or kill switch shorted. This is usually caused by water, corrosion, damage or excessive wear. The switches can be disassembled and cleaned with electrical contact cleaner. If cleaning does not help, replace the switches (Chapter 8).

☐ Battery voltage low. Check battery condition and recharge or replace battery (Chapter 8).

☐ Spark plug socket in ignition coil not making good contact. Make sure that the coils are pushed fully onto the spark plugs.

☐ Spark plugs dirty, defective or worn out. Locate reason for fouled plugs using spark plug condition chart on the inside back cover and follow the plug maintenance procedures (Chapter 1).

☐ Incorrect spark plugs. Wrong type or heat range. Check and install correct plugs (Chapter 1).

☐ Ignition coil defective. Test and replace if necessary (Chapter 4).

☐ Fuel injection system shutdown due to system fault (Chapter 4).

☐ Crankshaft position (CKP) sensor defective (Chapter 4).

☐ Faulty tip-over sensor (Chapter 4).

☐ Electronic control unit (ECU) defective (Chapter 4).

☐ Faulty sidestand switch (Chapter 8).

☐ Ignition key not recognised by immobiliser system.

☐ Wiring shorted or broken between:
  a) *Ignition switch and engine kill switch (or blown fuse)*
  b) *ECU and engine kill switch*
  c) *ECU and ignition coils*
  d) *ECU and CKP sensor*

☐ Make sure that all wiring connections are clean, dry and tight. Look for chafed and broken wires (Chapters 4 and 8).

Compression low

☐ Spark plug loose. Remove the plugs and inspect their threads. Reinstall and tighten securely (Chapter 1).

☐ Improper valve clearance. This means that the valve is not closing completely and compression pressure is leaking past the valve. Check and adjust the valve clearances (Chapter 1).

☐ Cylinder and/or piston worn. Excessive wear will cause compression pressure to leak past the rings. This is usually accompanied by worn rings as well. A top-end overhaul is necessary (Chapter 2).

☐ Piston rings worn, weak, broken, or sticking. Broken or sticking piston rings usually indicate a lubrication or fuelling problem that causes excess carbon deposits to form on the pistons and rings. Top-end overhaul is necessary (Chapter 2).

☐ Piston ring-to-groove clearance excessive. This is caused by excessive wear of the piston ring lands. Piston renewal is necessary (Chapter 2).

☐ Cylinder head gasket damaged. If a head is allowed to become loose, or if excessive carbon build-up on the piston crown and combustion chamber causes extremely high compression, the head gasket may leak. Retorquing the head is not always sufficient to restore the seal, so a new gasket is necessary (Chapter 2).

☐ Cylinder head warped. This is caused by overheating or improperly tightened head bolts. Machine shop resurfacing or head renewal is necessary (Chapter 2).

☐ Valve spring broken or weak. Caused by component failure or wear; the springs must be renewed (Chapter 2).

☐ Valve not seating properly. This is caused by a bent valve (from over-revving or improper valve adjustment), burned valve or seat (improper fuelling) or an accumulation of carbon deposits on the seat. The valves must be cleaned and/or renewed and the seats serviced (Chapter 2).

1 Engine doesn't start or is difficult to start (continued)

Stalls after starting

- ☐ Engine idle speed incorrect.
- ☐ Ignition malfunction (Chapter 4).
- ☐ Fuel injection system malfunction (Chapter 4).
- ☐ Fuel contaminated. The fuel can be contaminated with either dirt or water, or can change chemically if the machine has been unused for several months. Drain the tank and fuel system (Chapter 4).
- ☐ Intake air leak. Check for loose throttle body-to-intake duct connections or a loose or damaged vacuum hose (Chapter 4).

Rough idle

- ☐ Idle speed incorrect (Chapter 4).
- ☐ Vacuum hose detached or split.
- ☐ Ignition fault (Chapter 4).
- ☐ Fuel injection system malfunction (Chapter 4).
- ☐ Fuel contaminated. The fuel can be contaminated with either dirt or water, or can change chemically if the machine has been unused for several months. Drain the tank and the fuel system (Chapter 4).
- ☐ Intake air leak. Check for loose throttle body-to-intake duct connections (Chapter 4).
- ☐ Air filter clogged. Clean the air filter element or replace it with a new one (Chapter 1).

2 Poor running at low speeds

Spark weak

- ☐ Battery voltage low. Check battery condition and recharge or replace battery (Chapter 8).
- ☐ Spark plug socket in ignition coil not making good contact. Make sure that the coils are pushed fully onto the spark plugs.
- ☐ Spark plugs dirty, defective or worn out. Locate reason for fouled plugs using spark plug condition chart on the inside back cover and follow the plug maintenance procedures (Chapter 1).
- ☐ Incorrect spark plugs. Wrong type or heat range. Check and install correct plugs (Chapter 1).
- ☐ Ignition coil defective. Test and renew if necessary (Chapter 4).
- ☐ Loose or corroded connections in coil wiring connector. Check security and clean connections.

Fuel/air mixture incorrect

- ☐ Fuel tank breather hose obstructed.
- ☐ Fuel pump faulty or blocked fuel filter. Replace faulty pump - the filter is not available separately (Chapter 4).
- ☐ Fuel hose kinked. Replace the fuel hose.
- ☐ Fuel injector clogged. For all the injectors to be clogged, either a very bad batch of fuel with an unusual additive has been used, or some other foreign material has entered the tank. In some cases, if a machine has been unused for several months, the fuel turns to a varnish-like liquid which can cause an injector needle to stick to its seat. Drain the tank and fuel system, ultrasonically clean or replace fuel injectors (Chapter 4).
- ☐ Intake air leak. Check for loose throttle body-to-intake duct connections and loose or damaged vacuum hoses (Chapter 4).
- ☐ Air filter clogged. Clean the air filter element or replace it with a new one (Chapter 1).

Compression low

- ☐ Spark plug loose. Remove the plugs and inspect their threads. Reinstall and tighten securely (Chapter 1).
- ☐ Improper valve clearance. This means that the valve is not closing completely and compression pressure is leaking past the valve. Check and adjust the valve clearances (Chapter 1).
- ☐ Cylinder and/or piston worn. Excessive wear will cause compression pressure to leak past the rings. This is usually accompanied by worn rings as well. A top-end overhaul is necessary (Chapter 2).
- ☐ Piston rings worn, weak, broken, or sticking. Broken or sticking piston rings usually indicate a lubrication or fuelling problem that causes excess carbon deposits to form on the pistons and rings. Top-end overhaul is necessary (Chapter 2).
- ☐ Piston ring-to-groove clearance excessive. This is caused by excessive wear of the piston ring lands. Piston renewal is necessary (Chapter 2).
- ☐ Cylinder head gasket damaged. If the head is allowed to become loose, or if excessive carbon build-up on the piston crown and combustion chamber causes extremely high compression, the head gasket may leak. Retorquing the head is not always sufficient to restore the seal, so a new gasket is necessary (Chapter 2).
- ☐ Cylinder head warped. This is caused by overheating or improperly tightened head bolts. Machine shop resurfacing or head renewal is necessary (Chapter 2).
- ☐ Valve spring broken or weak. Caused by component failure or wear; the springs must be renewed (Chapter 2).
- ☐ Valve not seating properly. This is caused by a bent valve (from over-revving or improper valve adjustment), burned valve or seat (improper fuelling) or an accumulation of carbon deposits on the seat (from fuelling or lubrication problems). The valves must be cleaned and/or renewed and the seats serviced (Chapter 2).

Poor acceleration

- ☐ Timing not advancing. The crankshaft position sensor (CKP) or the electronic control unit (ECU) may be defective (Chapter 4). If so, they must be renewed.
- ☐ Engine oil viscosity too high. Using a heavier oil than that recommended in Chapter 1 can damage the oil pump or lubrication system and cause drag on the engine.
- ☐ Brakes dragging. Usually caused by corrosion behind dust seals, ingress of dirt past a deteriorated seal or from a warped disc or bent axle (Chapter 6).
- ☐ Exhaust control valve seized or incorrectly adjusted, or faulty servo. Adjust cables or un-seize butterfly valve. If they are good check the servo motor (see Chapter 4).

3 Poor running or no power at high speed

Firing incorrect

☐ Spark plug socket in ignition coil not making good contact. Make sure that the coils are pushed fully onto the spark plugs.

☐ Spark plugs dirty, defective or worn out. Locate reason for fouled plugs using spark plug condition chart on the inside back cover and follow the plug maintenance procedures (Chapter 1).

☐ Wrongly connected ignition coil wiring.

☐ Incorrect spark plugs. Wrong type or heat range. Check and install correct plugs (Chapter 1).

☐ Ignition coil/spark plug cap defective. Test and renew if necessary (Chapter 4).

☐ Faulty electronic control unit (ECU) (Chapter 4).

Fuel/air mixture incorrect

☐ Fuel tank breather hose obstructed.

☐ Fuel pump faulty or blocked fuel filter. Replace faulty pump - the filter is not available separately (Chapter 4).

☐ Fuel hose kinked. Replace the fuel hose.

☐ Fuel injector clogged. For all the injectors to be clogged, either a very bad batch of fuel with an unusual additive has been used, or some other foreign material has entered the tank. In some cases, if a machine has been unused for several months, the fuel turns to a varnish-like liquid which can cause an injector needle to stick to its seat. Drain the tank and fuel system, ultrasonically clean or replace fuel injectors (Chapter 4).

☐ Intake air leak. Check for loose throttle body-to-intake duct connections and loose or damaged vacuum hoses (Chapter 4).

☐ Air filter clogged. Clean the air filter element or replace it with a new one (Chapter 1).

Compression low

☐ Spark plug loose. Remove the plugs and inspect their threads. Reinstall and tighten securely (Chapter 1).

☐ Improper valve clearance. This means that the valve is not closing completely and compression pressure is leaking past the valve. Check and adjust the valve clearances (Chapter 1).

☐ Cylinder and/or piston worn. Excessive wear will cause compression pressure to leak past the rings. This is usually accompanied by worn rings as well. A top-end overhaul is necessary (Chapter 2).

☐ Piston rings worn, weak, broken, or sticking. Broken or sticking piston rings usually indicate a lubrication or fuelling problem that causes excess carbon deposits to form on the pistons and rings. Top-end overhaul is necessary (Chapter 2).

☐ Piston ring-to-groove clearance excessive. This is caused by excessive wear of the piston ring lands. Piston renewal is necessary (Chapter 2).

☐ Cylinder head gasket damaged. If a head is allowed to become loose, or if excessive carbon build-up on the piston crown and combustion chamber causes extremely high compression, the head gasket may leak. Retorquing the head is not always sufficient to restore the seal, so a new gasket is necessary (Chapter 2).

☐ Cylinder head warped. This is caused by overheating or improperly tightened head bolts. Machine shop resurfacing or head renewal is necessary (Chapter 2).

☐ Valve spring broken or weak. Caused by component failure or wear; the springs must be replaced with new ones (Chapter 2).

☐ Valve not seating properly. This is caused by a bent valve (from over-revving or improper valve adjustment), burned valve or seat (improper fuelling) or an accumulation of carbon deposits on the seat (from fuelling or lubrication problems). The valves must be cleaned and/or renewed and the seats serviced (Chapter 2).

Knocking or pinking

☐ Carbon build-up in combustion chamber. Use of a fuel additive that will dissolve the adhesive bonding the carbon particles to the piston crown and chamber is the easiest way to remove the build-up. Otherwise, the cylinder head will have to be removed and decarbonised (Chapter 2).

☐ Incorrect or poor quality fuel. Old or improper grades of fuel can cause detonation. This causes the piston to rattle, thus the knocking or pinking sound. Drain old fuel and always use the recommended fuel grade.

☐ Spark plug heat range incorrect. Uncontrolled detonation indicates the plug heat range is too hot. The plug in effect becomes a glow plug, raising cylinder temperatures. Install the proper heat range plug (Chapter 1).

☐ Improper air/fuel mixture. This will cause the cylinders to run hot, which leads to detonation. A blockage in the fuel system or an air leak can cause this imbalance (Chapter 4).

Miscellaneous causes

☐ Throttle valves faulty. Check the throttle bodies, particularly the secondary throttle valves and servo (Chapter 4).

☐ Clutch slipping due loose or worn clutch components (Chapter 2).

☐ Timing not advancing. The crankshaft position sensor (CKP) or the electronic control unit (ECU) may be defective (Chapter 4). If so, they must be replaced with new ones.

☐ Engine oil viscosity too high. Using a heavier oil than the one recommended in Chapter 1 can damage the oil pump or lubrication system and cause drag on the engine.

☐ Brakes dragging. Usually caused by corrosion behind dust seals, ingress of dirt past a deteriorated seal or from a warped disc or bent axle (Chapter 6).

☐ Exhaust control valve seized or incorrectly adjusted, or faulty servo. Adjust cables or un-seize butterfly valve. If they are good check the servo motor (see Chapter 4).

4 Overheating

Engine overheats

☐ Coolant level low. Check the level and add coolant (see *Pre-ride checks*).

☐ Leak in cooling system. Check cooling system hoses and radiator for leaks and other damage. Repair or renew parts as necessary (Chapter 3).

☐ Faulty thermostat. Check and renew as described in Chapter 3.

☐ Faulty pressure cap. Remove the cap and have it pressure tested.

☐ Coolant passages clogged. Have the entire system drained and flushed, then refill with fresh coolant.

☐ Water pump defective. Remove the pump and check the components (Chapter 3).

☐ Clogged or damaged radiator fins (Chapter 3).

☐ Faulty cooling fan, relay or ECT sensor (Chapter 3).

Firing incorrect

☐ Wrongly connected ignition coil wiring.

☐ Spark plugs dirty, defective or worn out. Locate reason for fouled plugs using spark plug condition chart on the inside back cover and follow the plug maintenance procedures (Chapter 1).

☐ Incorrect spark plugs. Wrong type or heat range. Check and install correct plugs (Chapter 1).

☐ Faulty electronic control unit (ECU) or CKP sensor (Chapter 4).

Fuel/air mixture incorrect

☐ Fuel tank breather hose obstructed.

☐ Fuel pump faulty or blocked fuel filter. Replace faulty pump - the filter is not available separately (Chapter 4).

☐ Fuel hose kinked. Replace the fuel hose.

☐ Fuel injector clogged. For all the injectors to be clogged, either a very bad batch of fuel with an unusual additive has been used, or some other foreign material has entered the tank. In some cases, if a machine has been unused for several months, the fuel turns to a varnish-like liquid which can cause an injector needle to stick to its seat. Drain the tank and fuel system, ultrasonically clean or replace fuel injectors (Chapter 4).

☐ Intake air leak. Check for loose throttle body-to-intake duct connections and loose or damaged vacuum hoses (Chapter 4).

☐ Air filter clogged. Clean the air filter element or replace it with a new one (Chapter 1).

Compression too high

☐ Carbon build-up in combustion chamber. Use of a fuel additive that will dissolve the adhesive bonding the carbon particles to the piston crown and chamber is the easiest way to remove the build-up. Otherwise, the cylinder head will have to be removed and decarbonised (Chapter 2).

☐ Improperly machined head surface or installation of incorrect gasket during engine assembly.

Engine load excessive

☐ Clutch slipping due to loose or worn clutch components (Chapter 2).

☐ Engine oil level too high. Too much oil will cause pressurisation of the crankcase and inefficient engine operation. Check Specifications and drain to proper level (Chapter 1 and *Pre-ride checks*).

☐ Engine oil viscosity too high. Using a heavier oil than the one recommended in Chapter 1 can damage the oil pump or lubrication system as well as cause drag on the engine.

☐ Brakes dragging. Usually caused by corrosion behind dust seals, ingestion of dirt past deteriorated seal or from a warped disc or bent axle (Chapter 6).

Lubrication inadequate

☐ Engine oil level too low. Friction caused by intermittent lack of lubrication or from oil that is overworked can cause overheating. The oil provides a definite cooling function in the engine. Check the oil level (see *Pre-ride checks*).

☐ Low engine oil pressure. Check the pressure (Chapter 2).

☐ Blocked oil filter or oil cooler (Chapters 1 and 2).

☐ Poor quality engine oil or incorrect viscosity or type. Oil is rated not only according to viscosity but also according to type. Some oils are not rated high enough for use in this engine. Check the Specifications section and change to the correct oil (Chapter 1).

Miscellaneous causes

☐ Modification to exhaust system. Most aftermarket exhaust systems cause the engine to run leaner, which make them run hotter. When installing an accessory exhaust system, always check with the manufacturer/supplier as to whether the ECU requires re-mapping.

5 Clutch problems

Clutch slipping

☐ Clutch plates worn or warped. Overhaul the clutch assembly (see Chapter 2).

☐ Clutch spring broken or weak. Old or heat-damaged (from slipping clutch) springs should be renewed (Chapter 2).

☐ Clutch centre or housing unevenly worn. This causes improper engagement of the plates. Replace the damaged or worn parts (see Chapter 2).

☐ Clutch release mechanism fault or clutch cable wrongly adjusted (see Chapters 2 and 1).

☐ Incorrect type of oil. Use of oils designed for car engines which include friction modifiers can cause clutch slip in a wet clutch application.

Clutch not disengaging completely

☐ Clutch release mechanism fault (see Chapter 2). Clutch cable dry or wrongly adjusted (see Chapter 1).

☐ Clutch plates warped or damaged. This will cause clutch drag, which in turn will cause the machine to creep. Overhaul the clutch assembly (see Chapter 2).

☐ Clutch spring fatigued or broken. Check and renew the springs (see Chapter 2).

☐ Engine oil deteriorated. Old, thin oil will not provide proper lubrication for the plates, causing the clutch to drag. Renew the oil and filter (see Chapter 1).

☐ Engine oil viscosity too high. Using a heavier oil than recommended in Chapter 1 can cause the plates to stick together. Change to the correct weight oil.

6 Gearchange problems

Doesn't go into gear or lever doesn't return

☐ Clutch not disengaging (above).
☐ Gearchange mechanism stopper arm spring weak or broken, or arm roller broken or worn. Replace the spring or arm with a new one (Chapter 2).
☐ Selector fork(s) bent, worn or seized. Overhaul the transmission (Chapter 2).
☐ Selector drum binding. Caused by lubrication failure or excessive wear. Replace the drum and/or its bearing with a new one (Chapter 2).
☐ Gearchange mechanism return spring weak or broken (Chapter 2).
☐ Gearchange lever or linkage broken. Splines stripped out of arm or shaft, caused by a loose linkage arm pinch bolt or from dropping the machine (Chapter 2).

Jumps out of gear

☐ Selector fork(s) worn (Chapter 2).
☐ Selector fork groove(s) in selector drum worn (Chapter 2).
☐ Gear pinion dogs or dog slots worn or damaged. The gear pinions should be inspected and renewed. No attempt should be made to repair the worn parts.

Overselects

☐ Gearchange mechanism stopper arm spring weak or broken, or arm roller broken or worn. Renew the spring or arm (Chapter 2).
☐ Gearchange mechanism return spring weak or broken (Chapter 2).

7 Abnormal engine noise

Knocking or pinking

☐ Carbon build-up in combustion chamber. Use of a fuel additive that will dissolve the adhesive bonding the carbon particles to the piston crown and chamber is the easiest way to remove the build-up. Otherwise, the cylinder head will have to be removed and decarbonised (Chapter 2).
☐ Incorrect or poor quality fuel. Old or improper grades of fuel can cause detonation. This causes the pistons to rattle, thus the knocking or pinking sound. Drain old fuel and always use the recommended fuel grade.
☐ Spark plug heat range incorrect. Uncontrolled detonation indicates the plug heat range is too hot. The plug in effect becomes a glow plug, raising cylinder temperatures. Install the proper heat range plug (Chapter 1).
☐ Improper air/fuel mixture. This will cause the cylinders to run hot, which leads to detonation. A blockage in the fuel system or an air leak can cause this imbalance (Chapter 4).

Piston slap or rattling

☐ Cylinder-to-piston clearance excessive. Cylinder and/or piston worn, usually accompanied by worn rings as well. A top-end overhaul is necessary (Chapter 2).
☐ Piston ring(s) worn, broken or sticking. Overhaul the top-end (Chapter 2).
☐ Piston pin, piston pin bore or connecting rod small-end worn from high mileage or seized due to lack of lubrication (Chapter 2).
☐ Piston seizure damage. Usually from lack of lubrication or overheating. Replace the pistons and upper crankcase, as necessary (Chapter 2).
☐ Connecting rod big-end clearance excessive. Caused by excessive wear or lack of lubrication. Replace worn parts.

☐ Connecting rod bent. Caused by over-revving, trying to start a badly flooded engine or from ingesting a foreign object into the combustion chamber. Replace the damaged parts (Chapter 2).

Valve noise

☐ Incorrect valve clearances – check and adjust (Chapter 1).
☐ Valve spring broken or weak. Check and replace weak valve springs with new ones (Chapter 2).
☐ Camshaft or camshaft journals in the cylinder head worn or damaged. Lubrication failure at high rpm is usually the cause of damage due to insufficient oil or failure to change the oil at the recommended intervals. Since there are no replaceable bearings in the head, the head itself will have to be replaced with a new one (Chapter 2).

Other noise

☐ Cylinder head gasket leaking. Check around the joint for blowing with the engine running.
☐ Exhaust pipe leaking at cylinder head connection. Caused by incorrect fit of pipe(s), loose exhaust flange or damaged gasket. All exhaust system fasteners should be tightened evenly and carefully to avoid leaks (Chapter 4).
☐ Crankshaft runout excessive. Caused by a bent crankshaft (from over-revving) or damage from an upper cylinder component failure. Can also be attributed to dropping the machine on either of the crankshaft ends.
☐ Engine mounting bolts loose – ensure all the bolts are tightened to the specified torque settings (Chapter 2).
☐ Crankshaft bearings worn (Chapter 2).
☐ Cam chain rattle, due to worn chain or defective tensioner. Also worn chain tensioner/guide blades (Chapter 2).

8 Abnormal driveline noise

Clutch noise

☐ Clutch housing/friction plate clearance excessive (Chapter 2).
☐ Wear between the clutch housing splines and input shaft splines (Chapter 2).
☐ Worn release bearing (Chapter 2).

Transmission noise

☐ Bearings worn. Also includes the possibility that the shafts are worn. Overhaul the transmission (Chapter 2).
☐ Gears worn or chipped (Chapter 2).

☐ Engine oil level too low. Causes a howl from transmission. Also affects engine power and clutch operation (see *Pre-ride checks*).

Final drive noise

☐ Drive chain excessively loose/worn or drive sprockets excessively worn. Adjust chain or replace chain and sprockets as a set (Chapters 1 and 6).
☐ Sprocket coupling, dampers or bearing worn or damaged (Chapter 6).
☐ Front or rear sprocket loose. Tighten fasteners (see Chapter 6).

9 Abnormal frame and suspension noise

Front end noise

☐ Low fluid level or improper viscosity oil in forks. This can sound like spurting and is usually accompanied by irregular fork action (Chapter 5).
☐ Spring weak or broken. Makes a clicking or scraping sound. Fork oil, when drained, will have a lot of metal particles in it (Chapter 5).
☐ Steering head bearings loose or damaged. Clicks when braking. Check and adjust or replace with new ones as necessary (Chapters 1 and 5).
☐ Fork yoke clamp bolts loose – ensure all the bolts are tightened to the specified torque (Chapter 6).
☐ Forks bent. Good possibility if machine has been dropped. Replace the inner and outer tubes with new ones as required (Chapter 5).
☐ Front axle or axle pinch bolts loose. Tighten them to the specified torque (Chapter 6).
☐ Loose or worn wheel bearings. Check and replace with new ones as needed (Chapters 1 and 6).
☐ Faulty steering damper (see Chapter 5).

Rear end noise

☐ Shock absorber fluid level incorrect. Indicates a leak caused by defective seal. Shock will be covered with oil. Replace shock with a new one or seek advice on repair from a suspension specialist (Chapter 5).
☐ Defective shock absorber with internal damage. This is in the body of the shock and can't be remedied. The shock must be replaced with a new one or rebuilt (Chapter 5).
☐ Bent or damaged shock body. Replace the shock with a new one (Chapter 5).

☐ Loose or worn swingarm bearings. Check and replace with new ones as necessary (Chapter 5).
☐ Loose or worn suspension linkage bearings. Check and replace with new ones as necessary (Chapter 5).
☐ Loose or worn wheel bearings/sprocket bearing. Check and replace with new ones as needed (Chapters 1 and 6).

Brake noise

☐ Squeal caused by pad shim not installed or positioned incorrectly (where fitted) (Chapter 6).
☐ Squeal caused by dust on brake pads. Usually found in combination with glazed pads. Clean using brake cleaning solvent (Chapter 6).
☐ Pads glazed. Caused by excessive heat from prolonged hard use or from contamination. DO NOT use sandpaper, emery cloth, carborundum cloth or any other abrasive to roughen the pad surfaces as abrasives will stay in the pad material and damage the disc. A very fine flat file can be used, but new pads is the best remedy (Chapter 6).
☐ Contamination of brake pads. Oil or brake fluid can cause the brake pads to chatter or squeal. Fit new pads. Identify the cause of the contamination, especially check the caliper piston seals for leaking fluid. Clean disc thoroughly with brake system cleaner (Chapter 6).
☐ Disc warped. Can cause a chattering, clicking or intermittent squeal. Usually accompanied by a pulsating lever and uneven braking. Replace the disc with new one (Chapter 6).
☐ Loose or worn wheel bearings. Check and replace with new ones as needed (Chapters 1 and 6).
☐ Forks incorrectly aligned on front wheel axle causing caliper or mounting to contact disc. Loosen front axle pinch bolts and re-align.

10 Oil pressure low

Engine lubrication system

☐ Oil level low. Inspect for leak or other problem causing low oil level and add recommended oil (see *Pre-ride checks*).
☐ Oil pump defective, blocked oil strainer gauze or failed pressure relief valve. Carry out an oil pressure check (Chapter 2).

☐ Oil viscosity too low. Very old, thin oil or an improper weight of oil used in the engine. Change to correct oil (Chapter 1).
☐ Camshaft or crankshaft journals worn. Excessive wear causing drop in oil pressure. Abnormal wear could be caused by oil starvation at high rpm from low oil level or improper weight or type of oil (Chapter 1).

11 Excessive exhaust smoke

White smoke

☐ Piston rings worn or broken, causing oil from the crankcase to be pulled past the piston into the combustion chamber. Replace the rings with new ones (Chapter 2).

☐ Plating on cylinders worn or scored. Caused by overheating or oil starvation. Renew the crankcases and pistons (Chapter 2).

☐ Valve stem oil seal damaged or worn. Replace the oil seals with new ones (Chapter 2).

☐ Valve guide worn. Perform a complete valve job (Chapter 2).

☐ Engine oil level too high, which causes the oil to be forced past the rings. Drain oil to the proper level (see *Pre-ride checks*).

☐ Head gasket broken between oil return and cylinder. Causes oil to be pulled into the combustion chamber. Replace the head gasket with a new one and check the head for warpage (Chapter 2).

☐ Abnormal crankcase pressurisation which forces oil past the rings, usually caused by a clogged breather.

Black smoke

☐ Air filter clogged. Clean the air filter element or replace it with a new one (Chapter 1).

☐ Fuel injection system malfunction (Chapter 4).

Brown smoke

☐ Air filter poorly sealed or not installed (Chapter 1).

☐ Fuel injection system malfunction (Chapter 4).

12 Poor handling or stability

Handlebar hard to turn

☐ Steering head bearing adjuster nut too tight. Check adjustment as described in Chapter 1.

☐ Bearings damaged. Roughness can be felt as the bars are turned from side-to-side. Replace the bearings with new ones (Chapter 5).

☐ Races dented or worn. Denting results from wear in only one position (e.g., straight ahead), from a collision or hitting a pothole. Replace the bearings with new ones (Chapter 5).

☐ Steering stem lubrication inadequate. Causes are grease getting hard from age or being washed out by high pressure car washes. Disassemble steering head and repack bearings (Chapter 5).

☐ Steering stem bent. Caused by a collision, hitting a pothole. Replace damaged part. Don't try to straighten the steering stem (Chapter 5).

☐ Front tyre air pressure too low (see *Pre-ride checks*).

☐ Steering damper incorrectly adjusted (see *Pre-ride checks*).

Handlebar shakes or vibrates excessively

☐ Tyres worn or out of balance (Chapter 6).

☐ Swingarm bearings worn. Replace the bearings with new ones (Chapter 5).

☐ Wheel rim(s) warped or damaged. Inspect wheels for runout (Chapter 6).

☐ Wheel bearings worn. Worn front or rear wheel bearings can cause poor tracking. Worn front bearings will cause wobble (Chapters 1 and 6).

☐ Fork yoke clamp bolts or handlebar clamp bolts loose. Tighten them to the specified torque (Chapter 5).

☐ Engine mounting bolts loose. Will cause excessive vibration with increased engine rpm – ensure all the bolts are tightened to the specified torque settings (Chapter 2).

Machine pulls to one side

☐ Frame bent. Definitely suspect this if the machine has been dropped. May or may not be accompanied by cracking near the steering head, swingarm mountings or engine mountings. Replace the frame with a new one (Chapter 5).

☐ Wheels out of alignment. Caused by poor chain adjustment, improper location of axle spacers or from bent steering stem or frame (Chapters 1 and 5).

☐ Forks bent. Disassemble the forks and replace the damaged parts (Chapter 5).

☐ Swingarm bent or twisted. Replace the arm with a new one (Chapter 5).

☐ Fork oil level uneven. Check and add or drain as necessary (Chapter 5).

☐ Fork pre-load adjusters set unevenly (Chapter 5).

Poor shock absorbing qualities

☐ Too hard:
  a) Suspension adjustment incorrect.
  b) Fork oil level excessive (Chapter 5).
  c) Fork oil viscosity too high. Use a lighter oil (see the Specifications in Chapter 5).
  d) Fork tube bent. Causes a harsh, sticking feeling (Chapter 5).
  e) Fork internal damage (Chapter 5).
  f) Shock shaft or body bent or damaged (Chapter 5).
  g) Shock internal damage.
  h) Swingarm bearings or suspension linkage bearings seized (Chapter 5).
  i) Tyre pressure too high (see Pre-ride checks).

☐ Too soft:
  a) Suspension adjustment incorrect.
  b) Fork oil level too low (Chapter 5).
  c) Fork oil viscosity too light (Chapter 5).
  d) Fork springs weak or broken (Chapter 5).
  e) Fork or shock oil leaking (Chapter 5).
  f) Shock internal damage (Chapter 5).

13 Braking problems

Brakes are spongy, don't hold

☐ Low brake fluid level (see *Pre-ride checks*).
☐ Air in hydraulic system. Caused by inattention to master cylinder fluid level or by leakage. Locate problem and bleed brakes (Chapter 6).
☐ Pad or disc worn (Chapters 1 and 6).
☐ Contaminated pads. Caused by contamination with oil, grease, brake fluid, etc. Fit new pads. Identify the cause of the contamination, especially check the caliper piston seals for leaking fluid. Clean disc thoroughly with brake system cleaner (Chapter 6).
☐ Brake fluid deteriorated. Fluid is old or contaminated. Drain system, replenish with new fluid and bleed the system (Chapter 6).
☐ Master cylinder internal seals worn or damaged causing fluid to bypass (Chapter 6).
☐ Master cylinder bore scratched by foreign material or broken spring. Fit a new master cylinder (Chapter 6).
☐ Disc warped. Replace disc with new one (Chapter 6)

Brake lever or pedal pulsates

☐ Disc warped. Replace disc with new one (Chapter 6).
☐ Axle bent. Replace axle with new one (Chapter 6).

☐ Brake caliper bolts loose – tighten the bolts to the specified torque (Chapter 6).
☐ Wheel warped or otherwise damaged (Chapter 6).
☐ Wheel bearings damaged or worn (Chapters 1 and 6).

Brakes drag

☐ Master cylinder piston seized. Caused by wear or damage to piston or cylinder bore (Chapter 6).
☐ Lever balky or stuck. Check pivot and lubricate (Chapter 6).
☐ Brake caliper piston seized in bore. Caused by corrosion behind dust seals or ingress of dirt past deteriorated seal (Chapter 6).
☐ Rear brake caliper slider pins sticking or corroded, preventing full movement of caliper (Chapter 6).
☐ Brake pad damaged. Pad material separated from backing plate. Usually caused by faulty manufacturing process or from contact with chemicals. Fit new pads (Chapter 6).
☐ Pads improperly installed (Chapter 6).
☐ Brake caliper incorrectly installed (Chapter 6).
☐ Forks incorrectly aligned on front wheel axle. Loosen front axle pinch bolts and re-align.

14 Electrical problems

Battery dead or weak

☐ Battery faulty. Caused by sulphated plates which are shorted through sedimentation. Confirm with battery condition check (Chapter 8).
☐ Broken battery terminal making only occasional contact.
☐ Battery leads making poor contact (Chapter 8).
☐ Load excessive. Caused by addition of high wattage lights or other electrical accessories.
☐ Ignition switch defective. Switch either grounds (earths) internally or fails to shut off system. Renew the switch (Chapter 8).
☐ Regulator/rectifier defective (Chapter 8).
☐ Alternator stator coil open or shorted (Chapter 8).

☐ Charging system fault. Check for excessive current leakage (Chapter 8).
☐ Wiring faulty. Wiring grounded (earthed) or connections loose in ignition, charging or lighting circuits (Chapter 8).

Battery overcharged

☐ Regulator/rectifier defective. Overcharging is noticed when battery gets excessively warm (Chapter 8).
☐ Battery faulty. Confirm with battery condition check (Chapter 8).
☐ Battery amperage too low, wrong type or size of battery. Install manufacturer's specified amp-hour battery to handle charging load (Chapter 8).

A

ABS (Anti-lock braking system) A system, usually electronically controlled, that senses incipient wheel lockup during braking and relieves hydraulic pressure at wheel which is about to skid.

Aftermarket Components suitable for the motorcycle, but not produced by the motorcycle manufacturer.

Allen key A hexagonal wrench which fits into a recessed hexagonal hole.

Alternating current (ac) Current produced by an alternator. Requires converting to direct current by a rectifier for charging purposes.

Alternator Converts mechanical energy from the engine into electrical energy to charge the battery and power the electrical system.

Ampere (amp) A unit of measurement for the flow of electrical current. Current = Volts ÷ Ohms.

Ampere-hour (Ah) Measure of battery capacity.

Angle-tightening A torque expressed in degrees. Often follows a conventional tightening torque for cylinder head or main bearing fasteners **(see illustration)**.

Angle-tightening con-rod bolts

Antifreeze A substance (usually ethylene glycol) mixed with water, and added to the cooling system, to prevent freezing of the coolant in winter. Antifreeze also contains chemicals to inhibit corrosion and the formation of rust and other deposits that would tend to clog the radiator and coolant passages and reduce cooling efficiency.

Anti-dive System attached to the fork lower leg (slider) to prevent fork dive when braking hard.

Anti-seize compound A coating that reduces the risk of seizing on fasteners that are subjected to high temperatures, such as exhaust clamp bolts and nuts.

API American Petroleum Institute. A quality standard for 4-stroke motor oils.

Asbestos A natural fibrous mineral with great heat resistance, commonly used in the composition of brake friction materials. Asbestos is a health hazard and the dust created by brake systems should never be inhaled or ingested.

ATF Automatic Transmission Fluid. Often used in front forks.

ATU Automatic Timing Unit. Mechanical device for advancing the ignition timing on early engines.

ATV All Terrain Vehicle. Often called a Quad.

Axial play Side-to-side movement.

Axle A shaft on which a wheel revolves. Also known as a spindle.

B

Backlash The amount of movement between meshed components when one component is held still. Usually applies to gear teeth.

Ball bearing A bearing consisting of a hardened inner and outer race with hardened steel balls between the two races.

Bearings Used between two working surfaces to prevent wear of the components and a build-up of heat. Four types of bearing are commonly used on motorcycles: plain shell bearings, ball bearings, tapered roller bearings and needle roller bearings.

Bevel gears Used to turn the drive through 90°. Typical applications are shaft final drive and camshaft drive **(see illustration)**.

Bevel gears are used to turn the drive through 90°

BHP Brake Horsepower. The British measurement for engine power output. Power output is now usually expressed in kilowatts (kW).

Bias-belted tyre Similar construction to radial tyre, but with outer belt running at an angle to the wheel rim.

Big-end bearing The bearing in the end of the connecting rod that's attached to the crankshaft.

Bleeding The process of removing air from an hydraulic system via a bleed nipple or bleed screw.

Bottom-end A description of an engine's crankcase components and all components contained there-in.

BTDC Before Top Dead Centre in terms of piston position. Ignition timing is often expressed in terms of degrees or millimetres BTDC.

Bush A cylindrical metal or rubber component used between two moving parts.

Burr Rough edge left on a component after machining or as a result of excessive wear.

C

Cam chain The chain which takes drive from the crankshaft to the camshaft(s).

Canister The main component in an evaporative emission control system (California market only); contains activated charcoal granules to trap vapours from the fuel system rather than allowing them to vent to the atmosphere.

Castellated Resembling the parapets along the top of a castle wall. For example, a castellated wheel axle or spindle nut.

Catalytic converter A device in the exhaust system of some machines which converts certain pollutants in the exhaust gases into less harmful substances.

C (column 3)

Charging system Description of the components which charge the battery, ie the alternator, rectifer and regulator.

Circlip A ring-shaped clip used to prevent endwise movement of cylindrical parts and shafts. An internal circlip is installed in a groove in a housing; an external circlip fits into a groove on the outside of a cylindrical piece such as a shaft. Also known as a snap-ring.

Clearance The amount of space between two parts. For example, between a piston and a cylinder, between a bearing and a journal, etc.

Coil spring A spiral of elastic steel found in various sizes throughout a vehicle, for example as a springing medium in the suspension and in the valve train.

Compression Reduction in volume, and increase in pressure and temperature, of a gas, caused by squeezing it into a smaller space.

Compression damping Controls the speed the suspension compresses when hitting a bump.

Compression ratio The relationship between cylinder volume when the piston is at top dead centre and cylinder volume when the piston is at bottom dead centre.

Continuity The uninterrupted path in the flow of electricity. Little or no measurable resistance.

Continuity tester Self-powered bleeper or test light which indicates continuity.

Cp Candlepower. Bulb rating commonly found on US motorcycles.

Crossply tyre Tyre plies arranged in a criss-cross pattern. Usually four or six plies used, hence 4PR or 6PR in tyre size codes.

Cush drive Rubber damper segments fitted between the rear wheel and final drive sprocket to absorb transmission shocks **(see illustration)**.

Cush drive rubbers dampen out transmission shocks

D

Decarbonisation The process of removing carbon deposits - typically from the combustion chamber, valves and exhaust port/system.

Degree disc Calibrated disc for measuring piston position. Expressed in degrees.

Detonation Destructive and damaging explosion of fuel/air mixture in combustion chamber instead of controlled burning.

Dial gauge Clock-type gauge with adapters for measuring runout and piston position. Expressed in mm or inches.

Diaphragm The rubber membrane in a master cylinder or carburettor which seals the upper chamber.

Diaphragm spring A single sprung plate often used in clutches.

Direct current (dc) Current produced by a dc generator.

Diode An electrical valve which only allows current to flow in one direction. Commonly used in rectifiers and starter interlock systems.

Disc valve (or rotary valve) A induction system used on some two-stroke engines.

Double-overhead camshaft (DOHC) An engine that uses two overhead camshafts, one for the intake valves and one for the exhaust valves.

Drivebelt A toothed belt used to transmit drive to the rear wheel on some motorcycles. A drivebelt has also been used to drive the camshafts. Drivebelts are usually made of Kevlar.

Driveshaft Any shaft used to transmit motion. Commonly used when referring to the final driveshaft on shaft drive motorcycles.

E

Earth return The return path of an electrical circuit, utilising the motorcycle's frame.

ECU (Electronic Control Unit) A computer which controls (for instance) an ignition system, or an anti-lock braking system.

EGO Exhaust Gas Oxygen sensor. Sometimes called a Lambda sensor.

Electrolyte The fluid in a lead-acid battery.

EMS (Engine Management System) A computer controlled system which manages the fuel injection and the ignition systems in an integrated fashion.

Endfloat The amount of lengthways movement between two parts. As applied to a crankshaft, the distance that the crankshaft can move side-to-side in the crankcase.

Endless chain A chain having no joining link. Common use for cam chains and final drive chains.

EP (Extreme Pressure) Oil type used in locations where high loads are applied, such as between gear teeth.

Evaporative emission control system Describes a charcoal filled canister which stores fuel vapours from the tank rather than allowing them to vent to the atmosphere. Usually only fitted to California models and referred to as an EVAP system.

Expansion chamber Section of two-stroke engine exhaust system so designed to improve engine efficiency and boost power.

F

Feeler blade or gauge A thin strip or blade of hardened steel, ground to an exact thickness, used to check or measure clearances between parts.

Final drive Description of the drive from the transmission to the rear wheel. Usually by chain or shaft, but sometimes by belt.

Firing order The order in which the engine cylinders fire, or deliver their power strokes, beginning with the number one cylinder.

Flooding Term used to describe a high fuel level in the carburettor float chambers, leading to fuel overflow. Also refers to excess fuel in the combustion chamber due to incorrect starting technique.

Free length The no-load state of a component when measured. Clutch, valve and fork spring lengths are measured at rest, without any preload.

Freeplay The amount of travel before any action takes place. The looseness in a linkage, or an assembly of parts, between the initial application of force and actual movement. For example, the distance the rear brake pedal moves before the rear brake is actuated.

Fuel injection The fuel/air mixture is metered electronically and directed into the engine intake ports (indirect injection) or into the cylinders (direct injection). Sensors supply information on engine speed and conditions.

Fuel/air mixture The charge of fuel and air going into the engine. See Stoichiometric ratio.

Fuse An electrical device which protects a circuit against accidental overload. The typical fuse contains a soft piece of metal which is calibrated to melt at a predetermined current flow (expressed as amps) and break the circuit.

G

Gap The distance the spark must travel in jumping from the centre electrode to the side electrode in a spark plug. Also refers to the distance between the ignition rotor and the pickup coil in an electronic ignition system.

Gasket Any thin, soft material - usually cork, cardboard, asbestos or soft metal - installed between two metal surfaces to ensure a good seal. For instance, the cylinder head gasket seals the joint between the block and the cylinder head.

Gauge An instrument panel display used to monitor engine conditions. A gauge with a movable pointer on a dial or a fixed scale is an analogue gauge. A gauge with a numerical readout is called a digital gauge.

Gear ratios The drive ratio of a pair of gears in a gearbox, calculated on their number of teeth.

Glaze-busting see **Honing**

Grinding Process for renovating the valve face and valve seat contact area in the cylinder head.

Gudgeon pin The shaft which connects the connecting rod small-end with the piston. Often called a piston pin or wrist pin.

H

Helical gears Gear teeth are slightly curved and produce less gear noise that straight-cut gears. Often used for primary drives.

Helicoil A thread insert repair system. Commonly used as a repair for stripped spark plug threads **(see illustration)**.

Installing a Helicoil thread insert

Honing A process used to break down the glaze on a cylinder bore (also called glaze-busting). Can also be carried out to roughen a rebored cylinder to aid ring bedding-in.

HT (High Tension) Description of the electrical circuit from the secondary winding of the ignition coil to the spark plug.

Hydraulic A liquid filled system used to transmit pressure from one component to another. Common uses on motorcycles are brakes and clutches.

Hydrometer An instrument for measuring the specific gravity of a lead-acid battery.

Hygroscopic Water absorbing. In motorcycle applications, braking efficiency will be reduced if DOT 3 or 4 hydraulic fluid absorbs water from the air - care must be taken to keep new brake fluid in tightly sealed containers.

I

lbf ft Pounds-force feet. An imperial unit of torque. Sometimes written as ft-lbs.

lbf in Pound-force inch. An imperial unit of torque, applied to components where a very low torque is required. Sometimes written as in-lbs.

IC Abbreviation for Integrated Circuit.

Ignition advance Means of increasing the timing of the spark at higher engine speeds. Done by mechanical means (ATU) on early engines or electronically by the ignition control unit on later engines.

Ignition timing The moment at which the spark plug fires, expressed in the number of crankshaft degrees before the piston reaches the top of its stroke, or in the number of millimetres before the piston reaches the top of its stroke.

Infinity (∞) Description of an open-circuit electrical state, where no continuity exists.

Inverted forks (upside down forks) The sliders or lower legs are held in the yokes and the fork tubes or stanchions are connected to the wheel axle (spindle). Less unsprung weight and stiffer construction than conventional forks.

J

JASO Quality standard for 2-stroke oils.

Joule The unit of electrical energy.

Journal The bearing surface of a shaft.

K

Kickstart Mechanical means of turning the engine over for starting purposes. Only usually fitted to mopeds, small capacity motorcycles and off-road motorcycles.

Kill switch Handebar-mounted switch for emergency ignition cut-out. Cuts the ignition circuit on all models, and additionally prevent starter motor operation on others.

km Symbol for kilometre.

kmh Abbreviation for kilometres per hour.

L

Lambda (λ) sensor A sensor fitted in the exhaust system to measure the exhaust gas oxygen content (excess air factor).

Lapping see Grinding.

LCD Abbreviation for Liquid Crystal Display.

LED Abbreviation for Light Emitting Diode.

Liner A steel cylinder liner inserted in a aluminium alloy cylinder block.

Locknut A nut used to lock an adjustment nut, or other threaded component, in place.

Lockstops The lugs on the lower triple clamp (yoke) which abut those on the frame, preventing handlebar-to-fuel tank contact.

Lockwasher A form of washer designed to prevent an attaching nut from working loose.

LT Low Tension Description of the electrical circuit from the power supply to the primary winding of the ignition coil.

M

Main bearings The bearings between the crankshaft and crankcase.

Maintenance-free (MF) battery A sealed battery which cannot be topped up.

Manometer Mercury-filled calibrated tubes used to measure intake tract vacuum. Used to synchronise carburettors on multi-cylinder engines.

Micrometer A precision measuring instrument that measures component outside diameters **(see illustration).**

Tappet shims are measured with a micrometer

MON (Motor Octane Number) A measure of a fuel's resistance to knock.

Monograde oil An oil with a single viscosity, eg SAE80W.

Monoshock A single suspension unit linking the swingarm or suspension linkage to the frame.

mph Abbreviation for miles per hour.

Multigrade oil Having a wide viscosity range (eg 10W40). The W stands for Winter, thus the viscosity ranges from SAE10 when cold to SAE40 when hot.

Multimeter An electrical test instrument with the capability to measure voltage, current and resistance. Some meters also incorporate a continuity tester and buzzer.

N

Needle roller bearing Inner race of caged needle rollers and hardened outer race. Examples of uncaged needle rollers can be found on some engines. Commonly used in rear suspension applications and in two-stroke engines.

Nm Newton metres.

NOx Oxides of Nitrogen. A common toxic pollutant emitted by petrol engines at higher temperatures.

O

Octane The measure of a fuel's resistance to knock.

OE (Original Equipment) Relates to components fitted to a motorcycle as standard or replacement parts supplied by the motorcycle manufacturer.

Ohm The unit of electrical resistance. Ohms = Volts ÷ Current.

Ohmmeter An instrument for measuring electrical resistance.

Oil cooler System for diverting engine oil outside of the engine to a radiator for cooling purposes.

Oil injection A system of two-stroke engine lubrication where oil is pump-fed to the engine in accordance with throttle position.

Open-circuit An electrical condition where there is a break in the flow of electricity - no continuity (high resistance).

O-ring A type of sealing ring made of a special rubber-like material; in use, the O-ring is compressed into a groove to provide the sealing action.

Oversize (OS) Term used for piston and ring size options fitted to a rebored cylinder.

Overhead cam (sohc) engine An engine with single camshaft located on top of the cylinder head.

Overhead valve (ohv) engine An engine with the valves located in the cylinder head, but with the camshaft located in the engine block or crankcase.

Oxygen sensor A device installed in the exhaust system which senses the oxygen content in the exhaust and converts this information into an electric current. Also called a Lambda sensor.

P

Plastigauge A thin strip of plastic thread, available in different sizes, used for measuring clearances. For example, a strip of Plastigauge is laid across a bearing journal. The parts are assembled and dismantled; the width of the crushed strip indicates the clearance between journal and bearing.

Polarity Either negative or positive earth (ground), determined by which battery lead is connected to the frame (earth return). Modern motorcycles are usually negative earth.

Pre-ignition A situation where the fuel/air mixture ignites before the spark plug fires. Often due to a hot spot in the combustion chamber caused by carbon build-up. Engine has a tendency to 'run-on'.

Pre-load (suspension) The amount a spring is compressed when in the unloaded state. Preload can be applied by gas, spacer or mechanical adjuster.

Premix The method of engine lubrication on older two-stroke engines. Engine oil is mixed with the petrol in the fuel tank in a specific ratio. The fuel/oil mix is sometimes referred to as "petroil".

Primary drive Description of the drive from the crankshaft to the clutch. Usually by gear or chain.

PS Pfedestärke - a German interpretation of BHP.

PSI Pounds-force per square inch. Imperial measurement of tyre pressure and cylinder pressure measurement.

PTFE Polytetrafluroethylene. A low friction substance.

Pulse secondary air injection system A process of promoting the burning of excess fuel present in the exhaust gases by routing fresh air into the exhaust ports.

Q

Quartz halogen bulb Tungsten filament surrounded by a halogen gas. Typically used for the headlight **(see illustration).**

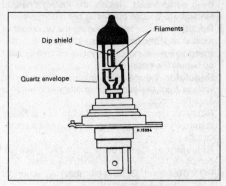

Quartz halogen headlight bulb construction

R

Rack-and-pinion A pinion gear on the end of a shaft that mates with a rack (think of a geared wheel opened up and laid flat). Sometimes used in clutch operating systems.

Radial play Up and down movement about a shaft.

Radial ply tyres Tyre plies run across the tyre (from bead to bead) and around the circumference of the tyre. Less resistant to tread distortion than other tyre types.

Radiator A liquid-to-air heat transfer device designed to reduce the temperature of the coolant in a liquid cooled engine.

Rake A feature of steering geometry - the angle of the steering head in relation to the vertical **(see illustration).**

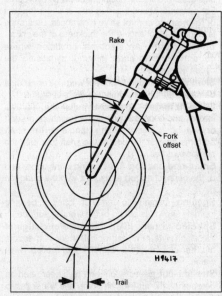

Steering geometry

Rebore Providing a new working surface to the cylinder bore by boring out the old surface. Necessitates the use of oversize piston and rings.

Rebound damping A means of controlling the oscillation of a suspension unit spring after it has been compressed. Resists the spring's natural tendency to bounce back after being compressed.

Rectifier Device for converting the ac output of an alternator into dc for battery charging.

Reed valve An induction system commonly used on two-stroke engines.

Regulator Device for maintaining the charging voltage from the generator or alternator within a specified range.

Relay A electrical device used to switch heavy current on and off by using a low current auxiliary circuit.

Resistance Measured in ohms. An electrical component's ability to pass electrical current.

RON (Research Octane Number) A measure of a fuel's resistance to knock.

rpm revolutions per minute.

Runout The amount of wobble (in-and-out movement) of a wheel or shaft as it's rotated. The amount a shaft rotates 'out-of-true'. The out-of-round condition of a rotating part.

S

SAE (Society of Automotive Engineers) A standard for the viscosity of a fluid.

Sealant A liquid or paste used to prevent leakage at a joint. Sometimes used in conjunction with a gasket.

Service limit Term for the point where a component is no longer useable and must be renewed.

Shaft drive A method of transmitting drive from the transmission to the rear wheel.

Shell bearings Plain bearings consisting of two shell halves. Most often used as big-end and main bearings in a four-stroke engine. Often called bearing inserts.

Shim Thin spacer, commonly used to adjust the clearance or relative positions between two parts. For example, shims inserted into or under tappets or followers to control valve clearances. Clearance is adjusted by changing the thickness of the shim.

Short-circuit An electrical condition where current shorts to earth (ground) bypassing the circuit components.

Skimming Process to correct warpage or repair a damaged surface, eg on brake discs or drums.

Slide-hammer A special puller that screws into or hooks onto a component such as a shaft or bearing; a heavy sliding handle on the shaft bottoms against the end of the shaft to knock the component free.

Small-end bearing The bearing in the upper end of the connecting rod at its joint with the gudgeon pin.

Spalling Damage to camshaft lobes or bearing journals shown as pitting of the working surface.

Specific gravity (SG) The state of charge of the electrolyte in a lead-acid battery. A measure of the electrolyte's density compared with water.

Straight-cut gears Common type gear used on gearbox shafts and for oil pump and water pump drives.

Stanchion The inner sliding part of the front forks, held by the yokes. Often called a fork tube.

Stoichiometric ratio The optimum chemical air/fuel ratio for a petrol engine, said to be 14.7 parts of air to 1 part of fuel.

Sulphuric acid The liquid (electrolyte) used in a lead-acid battery. Poisonous and extremely corrosive.

Surface grinding (lapping) Process to correct a warped gasket face, commonly used on cylinder heads.

T

Tapered-roller bearing Tapered inner race of caged needle rollers and separate tapered outer race. Examples of taper roller bearings can be found on steering heads.

Tappet A cylindrical component which transmits motion from the cam to the valve stem, either directly or via a pushrod and rocker arm. Also called a cam follower.

TCS Traction Control System. An electronically-controlled system which senses wheel spin and reduces engine speed accordingly.

TDC Top Dead Centre denotes that the piston is at its highest point in the cylinder.

Thread-locking compound Solution applied to fastener threads to prevent slackening. Select type to suit application.

Thrust washer A washer positioned between two moving components on a shaft. For example, between gear pinions on gearshaft.

Timing chain See **Cam Chain**.

Timing light Stroboscopic lamp for carrying out ignition timing checks with the engine running.

Top-end A description of an engine's cylinder block, head and valve gear components.

Torque Turning or twisting force about a shaft.

Torque setting A prescribed tightness specified by the motorcycle manufacturer to ensure that the bolt or nut is secured correctly. Undertightening can result in the bolt or nut coming loose or a surface not being sealed. Overtightening can result in stripped threads, distortion or damage to the component being retained.

Torx key A six-point wrench.

Tracer A stripe of a second colour applied to a wire insulator to distinguish that wire from another one with the same colour insulator. For example, Br/W is often used to denote a brown insulator with a white tracer.

Trail A feature of steering geometry. Distance from the steering head axis to the tyre's central contact point.

Triple clamps The cast components which extend from the steering head and support the fork stanchions or tubes. Often called fork yokes.

Turbocharger A centrifugal device, driven by exhaust gases, that pressurises the intake air. Normally used to increase the power output from a given engine displacement.

TWI Abbreviation for Tyre Wear Indicator. Indicates the location of the tread depth indicator bars on tyres.

U

Universal joint or U-joint (UJ) A double-pivoted connection for transmitting power from a driving to a driven shaft through an angle. Typically found in shaft drive assemblies.

Unsprung weight Anything not supported by the bike's suspension (ie the wheel, tyres, brakes, final drive and bottom (moving) part of the suspension).

V

Vacuum gauges Clock-type gauges for measuring intake tract vacuum. Used for carburettor synchronisation on multi-cylinder engines.

Valve A device through which the flow of liquid, gas or vacuum may be stopped, started or regulated by a moveable part that opens, shuts or partially obstructs one or more ports or passageways. The intake and exhaust valves in the cylinder head are of the poppet type.

Valve clearance The clearance between the valve tip (the end of the valve stem) and the rocker arm or tappet/follower. The valve clearance is measured when the valve is closed. The correct clearance is important - if too small the valve won't close fully and will burn out, whereas if too large noisy operation will result.

Valve lift The amount a valve is lifted off its seat by the camshaft lobe.

Valve timing The exact setting for the opening and closing of the valves in relation to piston position.

Vernier caliper A precision measuring instrument that measures inside and outside dimensions. Not quite as accurate as a micrometer, but more convenient.

Wet liner arrangement

VIN Vehicle Identification Number. Term for the bike's engine and frame numbers.

Viscosity The thickness of a liquid or its resistance to flow.

Volt A unit for expressing electrical "pressure" in a circuit. Volts = current x ohms.

W

Water pump A mechanically-driven device for moving coolant around the engine.

Watt A unit for expressing electrical power. Watts = volts x current.

Wear limit see **Service limit**

Wet liner A liquid-cooled engine design where the pistons run in liners which are directly surrounded by coolant (**see illustration**).

Wheelbase Distance from the centre of the front wheel to the centre of the rear wheel.

Wiring harness or loom Describes the electrical wires running the length of the motorcycle and enclosed in tape or plastic sheathing. Wiring coming off the main harness is usually referred to as a sub harness.

Woodruff key A key of semi-circular or square section used to locate a gear to a shaft. Often used to locate the alternator rotor on the crankshaft.

Wrist pin Another name for gudgeon or piston pin.

Note: *References throughout this index are in the form - "Chapter number" • "Page number"*

Haynes Motorcycle Manuals – The Complete List

Title	Book No
APRILIA RS50 (99 – 06) & RS125 (93 – 06)	4298
Aprilia RSV1000 Mille (98 – 03) ♦	4255
Aprilia SR50	4755
BMW 2-valve Twins (70 -96) ♦	0249
BMW F650 ♦	4761
BMW K100 & 75 2-valve models (83 – 96) ♦	1373
BMW F800 (F650) Twins (06 – 10) ♦	4872
BMW R850, 1100 & 1150 4-valve Twins (93 – 06) ♦	3466
BMW R1200 (04 – 09) ♦	4598
BMW R1200 dohc Twins (10 – 12) ♦	4925
BSA Bantam (48 – 71)	0117
BSA Unit Singles (58 – 72)	0127
BSA Pre-unit Singles (54 – 61)	0326
BSA A7 & A10 Twins (47 – 62)	0121
BSA A50 & A65 Twins (62 – 73)	0155
CHINESE, Taiwanese & Korean Scooters	4768
Chinese, Taiwanese & Korean 125cc motorcycles	4781
DUCATI 600, 620, 750 & 900 2-valve v-twins (91 – 05) ♦	3290
Ducati Mk III & Desmo singles (69 – 76) ◇	0445
Ducati 748, 916 & 996 4-valve V-twins (94 – 01) ♦	3756
GILERA Runner, DNA, Ice & SKP/Stalker (97 – 11)	4163
HARLEY-DAVIDSON Sportsters (70 – 10) ♦	2534
Harley-Davidson Shovelhead & Evolution Big Twins (70 -99) ♦	2536
Harley-Davidson Twin Cam 88, 96 & 103 models (99 – 10) ♦	2478
HONDA NB, ND, NP & NS50 Melody (81 -85) ◇	0622
Honda NE/NB50 Vision & SA50 Vision Met-in (85-95) ◇	1278
Honda MB, MBX, MT & MTX50 (80 – 93)	0731
Honda C50, C70 & C90 (67 – 03)	0324
Honda XR50/70/80/100R & CRF50/70/80/100F (85 – 07)	2218
Honda XL/XR 80, 100, 125, 185 & 200 2-valve models (78 – 87)	0566
Honda H100 & H100S Singles (80 – 92) ◇	0734
Honda 125 Scooters (00 – 09)	4873
Honda ANF125 Innova Scooters (03 -12) ♦	4926
Honda CB/CD125T & CM125C Twins (77 – 88) ◇	0571
Honda CBF125 (09 – 12) ♦	5540
Honda CG125 (76 – 07)	0433
Honda NS125 (86 – 93)	3056
Honda CBR125R (04 – 10)	4620
Honda MBX/MTX125 & MTX200 (83 – 93) ◇	1132
Honda XL125V & VT125C (99 – 11)	4899
Honda CD/CM185 200T & CM250C 2-valve Twins (77 – 85)	0572
Honda CMX250 Rebel & CB250 Nighthawk Twins (85 – 09) ♦	2756
Honda XL/XR 250 & 500 (78 – 84)	0567
Honda XR250L, XR250R & XR400R (86 – 03)	2219
Honda CB250 & CB400N Super Dreams (78 – 84) ◇	0540
Honda CR Motocross Bikes (86 – 07)	2222
Honda CRF250 & CRF450 (02 – 06)	2630
Honda CBR400RR Fours (88 – 99) ◇♦	3552
Honda VFR400 (NC30) & RVF400 (NC35) V-Fours (89 – 98) ◇♦	3496
Honda CB500 (93 – 02) & CBF500 (03 – 08) ♦	3753
Honda CB400 & CB550 Fours (73 – 77)	0262
Honda CX/GL500 & 650 V-Twins (78 – 86)	0442
Honda CBX550 Four (82 – 86) ◇	0940
Honda XL600R & XR600R (83 – 08) ♦	2183
Honda XL600/650V Transalp & XRV750 Africa Twin (87 – 07)	3919
Honda CB600 Hornet, CBF600 & CBR600F (07 – 12) ♦	5572
Honda CBR600F1 & 1000F Fours (87 – 96) ♦	1730
Honda CBR600F2 & F3 Fours (91 – 98) ♦	2070
Honda CBR600F4 (99 – 06) ♦	3911
Honda CB600F Hornet & CBF600 (98 – 06) ◇♦	3915
Honda CBR600RR (03 – 06) ♦	4590
Honda CBR600RR (07 -12) ♦	4795
Honda CB650 sohc Fours (78 – 84)	0665
Honda NTV600 Revere, NTV650 & NT650V Deauville (88 – 05) ◇♦	3243
Honda Shadow VT600 & 750 (USA) (88 – 09)	2312
Honda NT700V Deauville & XL700V Transalp (06 -13) ♦	5541
Honda CB750 sohc Four (69 – 79)	0131
Honda V45/65 Sabre & Magna (82 – 88)	0820
Honda VFR750 & 700 V-Fours (86 – 97) ♦	2101
Honda VFR800 V-Fours (97 – 01) ♦	3703
Honda VFR800 V-Tec V-Fours (02 – 09) ♦	4196
Honda CB750 & CB900 dohc Fours (78 – 84)	0535
Honda CBF1000 (06 -10) & CB1000R (08 – 11) ♦	4927
Honda VTR1000 Firestorm, Super Hawk & XL1000V Varadero (97 – 08) ♦	3744
Honda CBR900RR Fireblade (92 – 99) ♦	2161
Honda CBR900RR Fireblade (00 – 03) ♦	4060
Honda CBR1000RR Fireblade (04 – 07) ♦	4604
Honda CBR1100XX Super Blackbird (97 – 07) ♦	3901
Honda ST1100 Pan European V-Fours (90 – 02) ♦	3384
Honda ST1300 Pan European (02 -11) ♦	4908

Title	Book No
Honda Shadow VT1100 (USA) (85 – 07)	2313
Honda GL1000 Gold Wing (75 – 79)	0309
Honda GL1100 Gold Wing (79 – 81)	0669
Honda Gold Wing 1200 (USA) (84 – 87)	2199
Honda Gold Wing 1500 (USA) (88 – 00)	2225
Honda Goldwing GL1800 ♦	2787
KAWASAKI AE/AR 50 & 80 (81 – 95)	1007
Kawasaki KC, KE & KH100 (75 – 99)	1371
Kawasaki KMX125 & 200 (86 – 02) ◇	3046
Kawasaki 250, 350 & 400 Triples (72 – 79)	0134
Kawasaki 400 & 440 Twins (74 – 81)	0281
Kawasaki 400, 500 & 550 Fours (79 – 91)	0910
Kawasaki EN450 & 500 Twins (Ltd/Vulcan) (85 – 07)	2053
Kawasaki ER-6F & ER-6N (06 -10) ♦	4874
Kawasaki EX500 (GPZ500S) & ER500 (ER-5) (87 – 08) ♦	2052
Kawasaki ZX600 (ZZ-R600 & Ninja ZX-6) (90 – 06) ♦	2146
Kawasaki ZX-6R Ninja Fours (95 – 02) ♦	3451
Kawasaki ZX-6R (03 – 06) ♦	4742
Kawasaki ZX600 (GPZ600R, GPX600R, Ninja 600R & RX) & ZX750 (GPX750R, Ninja 750R) (85 – 97) ♦	1780
Kawasaki 650 Four (76 – 78)	0373
Kawasaki Vulcan 700/750 & 800 (85 – 04) ♦	2457
Kawasaki Vulcan 1500 & 1600 (87 – 08) ♦	4913
Kawasaki 750 Air-cooled Fours	0574
Kawasaki ZR550 & 750 Zephyr Fours (90 – 97) ♦	3382
Kawasaki Z750 & Z1000 (03 – 08) ♦	4762
Kawasaki ZX750 (Ninja ZX-7 & ZXR750) Fours (89 – 96) ♦	2054
Kawasaki Ninja ZX-7R & ZX-9R (94 – 04) ♦	3721
Kawasaki 900 & 1000 Fours (73 – 77)	0222
Kawasaki ZX900, 1000 & 1100 Liquid-cooled Fours (83 – 97) ♦	1681
KTM EXC Enduro & SX Motocross (00 – 07) ♦	4629
LAMBRETTA Scooters (58 – 00) ♦	5573
MOTO GUZZI 750, 850 & 1000 V-Twins (74 – 78)	0339
MZ ETZ models (81 – 95) ◇	1680
NORTON 500, 600, 650 & 750 Twins (57 – 70)	0187
Norton Commando (68 – 77)	0125
PEUGEOT Speedfight, Trekker & Vivacity Scooters (96 – 08)	3920
PIAGGIO (Vespa) Scooters (91 – 09) ◇	3492
SUZUKI GT, ZR & TS50 (77 – 90) ◇	0799
Suzuki TS50X (84 – 00)	1599
Suzuki 100, 125, 185 & 250 Air-cooled Trail bikes (79 – 89)	0797
Suzuki GP100 & 125 Singles (78 – 93)	0576
Suzuki GS, GN, GZ & DR125 Singles (82 – 05) ◇	0888
Suzuki Burgman 250 & 400 (98 – 11) ♦	4909
Suzuki GSX-R600/750 (06 – 09) ♦	4790
Suzuki 250 & 350 Twins (68 – 78)	0120
Suzuki GT250X7, GT200X5 & SB200 Twins (78 – 83) ◇	0469
Suzuki DR-Z400 (00 – 10) ♦	2933
Suzuki GS/GSX250, 400 & 450 Twins (79 – 85)	0736
Suzuki GS500 Twin (89 – 08) ♦	3238
Suzuki GS550 (77 – 82) & GS750 Fours (76 – 79)	0363
Suzuki GS/GSX550 4-valve Fours (83 – 88)	1133
Suzuki SV650 & SV650S (99 – 08) ♦	3912
Suzuki GSX-R750 & 750 (96 – 00) ♦	3553
Suzuki GSX-R600 (01 – 03), GSX-R750 (00 – 03) & GSX-R1000 (01 – 02) ♦	3986
Suzuki GSX-R600/750 (04 – 05) & GSX-R1000 (03 – 06) ♦	4382
Suzuki GSF600, 650 & 1200 Bandit Fours (95 – 06) ♦	3367
Suzuki Intruder, Marauder, Volusia & Boulevard (85 – 09) ♦	2618
Suzuki GS850 Fours (78 – 88)	0536
Suzuki GS1000 Four (77 – 79)	0484
Suzuki GSX-R750, GSX-R1100 (85 – 92) GSX600F, GSX750F, GSX1100F (Katana) (88 – 96)	2055
Suzuki GSX600/750F & GSX750 (98 – 02) ♦	3987
Suzuki GS/GSX1000, 1100 & 1150 4-valve Fours (79 – 88)	0737
Suzuki TL1000S/R & DL V-Strom (97 – 04) ♦	4083
Suzuki GSF650/1250 (07 – 09) ♦	4798
Suzuki GSX1300R Hayabusa (99 – 04) ♦	4184
Suzuki GSX1400 (02 – 08) ♦	4758
TRIUMPH Tiger Cub & Terrier (52 – 68)	0414
Triumph 350 & 500 Unit Twins (58 – 73)	0137
Triumph Pre-Unit Twins (47 – 62)	0251
Triumph 650 & 750 2-valve Unit Twins (63 – 83)	0122
Triumph 675 (06 – 10) ♦	4876
Triumph 1050 Sprint, Speed Triple & Tiger (05 -13) ♦	4796
Triumph Trident & BSA Rocket 3 (69 – 75)	0136
Triumph Bonneville (01 – 12) ♦	4364
Triumph Daytona, Speed Triple, Sprint & Tiger (97 – 05) ♦	3755
Triumph Triples & Fours (carburetor engines) (91 – 04)	2162
VESPA P/PX125, 150 & 200 Scooters (78 – 12)	0707
Vespa GTS125, 250 & 300 (05 – 10)	4898

Title	Book No
Vespa Scooters (59 – 78)	0126
YAMAHA DT50 & 80 Trail Bikes (78 – 95) ◇	0800
Yamaha T50 & 80 Townmate (83 – 95) ◇	1247
Yamaha YB100 Singles (73 – 91) ◇	0474
Yamaha RS/RXS 100 & 125 Singles (74 – 95)	0331
Yamaha RD & DT125LC (82 – 87)	0887
Yamaha TZR125 (87 – 93) & DT125R (88 – 07) ◇	1655
Yamaha TY50, 80, 125 & 175 (74 – 84) ◇	0464
Yamaha XT & SR125 (82 – 03) ◇	1021
Yamaha YBR125 & XT125R/X (05 – 13)	4797
Yamaha YZF-R125 (08 – 11) ♦	5543
Yamaha Trail Bikes (81 – 00)	2350
Yamaha 2-stroke Motocross Bikes (86 – 06)	2662
Yamaha YZ & WR 4-stroke Motorcross Bikes (98 – 08)	2689
Yamaha 250 & 350 Twins (70 – 79)	0040
Yamaha XS250, 360 & 400 sohc Twins (75 – 84)	0378
Yamaha RD250 & 350LC Twins (80 – 82)	0803
Yamaha RD350 YPVS Twins (83 – 95)	1158
Yamaha RD400 Twin (75 – 79)	0333
Yamaha XT, TT & SR500 Singles (75 – 83)	0342
Yamaha XZ550 Vision V-Twins (82 – 85)	0821
Yamaha FJ, FX, XY & YX600 Radian (84 – 92)	2100
Yamaha XT660 & MT-03 (04 – 11) ♦	4910
Yamaha XJ600S (Diversion, Seca II) & XJ600N Fours (92 – 03) ♦	2145
Yamaha YZF600R Thundercat & FZS600 Fazer (96 – 03) ♦	3702
Yamaha FZ-6 Fazer (04 – 08) ♦	4751
Yamaha YZF-R6 (99 – 02) ♦	3900
Yamaha YZF-R6 (03 – 05) ♦	4601
Yamaha YZF-R6 (06 – 13) ♦	5544
Yamaha 650 Twins (70 – 83)	0341
Yamaha XJ650 & 750 Fours (80 – 84)	0738
Yamaha XS750 & 850 Triples (76 – 85)	0340
Yamaha TDM850, TRX850 & XTZ750 (89 – 99) ◇♦	3450
Yamaha YZF750R & YZF1000R Thunderace (93 – 00) ♦	3720
Yamaha FZR600, 750 & 1000 Fours (87 – 96) ♦	2056
Yamaha XV (Virago) V-Twins (81 – 03) ♦	0802
Yamaha XVS650 & 1100 Drag Star/V-Star (97 – 05) ♦	4195
Yamaha XJ900F Fours (83 – 94) ♦	3239
Yamaha XJ900S Diversion (94 – 01) ♦	3739
Yamaha YZF-R1 (98 – 03) ♦	3754
Yamaha YZF-R1 (04 – 06) ♦	4605
Yamaha FZS1000 Fazer (01 – 05) ♦	4287
Yamaha FJ1100 & 1200 Fours (84 – 96) ♦	2057
Yamaha XJR1200 & 1300 (95 – 06) ♦	3981
Yamaha V-Max (85 – 03) ♦	4072

ATV's

Title	Book No
Honda ATC 70, 90, 110, 185 & 200 (71 – on)	0565
Honda Rancher, Recon & TRX250EX ATVs	2553
Honda TRX300 Shaft Drive ATVs (88 – 00)	2125
Honda Foreman (95 – 11)	2465
Honda TRX300EX, TRX400EX & TRX450R/ER ATVs (93 – 06)	2318
Kawasaki Bayou 220/250/300 & Prairie 300 ATVs (86 – 03)	2351
Polaris ATVs (85 – 97)	2302
Polaris ATVs (98 – 07)	2508
Suzuki/Kawasaki/Artic Cat ATVs (03 – 09)	2910
Yamaha YFS200 Blaster ATV (88 – 06)	2317
Yamaha YFM350 & YFM400 (ER & Big Bear) ATVs (87 – 09)	2126
Yamaha YFZ450 & YFZ450R (04 – 10)	2899
Yamaha Banshee and Warrior ATVs (87 – 10)	2314
Yamaha Kodiak and Grizzly ATVs (93 – 05)	2567
ATV Basics	10450

TECHBOOK SERIES

Title	Book No
Twist and Go (automatic transmission) Scooters Service and Repair Manual	4082
Motorcycle Basics Techbook (2nd edition)	3515
Motorcycle Electrical Techbook (3rd edition)	3471
Motorcycle Fuel Systems Techbook	3514
Motorcycle Maintenance Techbook	4071
Motorcycle Modifying	4272
Motorcycle Workshop Practice Techbook (2nd edition)	3470

◇ = not available in the USA ♦ = Superbike

The manuals on this page are available through good motorcycle dealers and accessory shops.
In case of difficulty, contact: **Haynes Publishing**
(UK) **+44 1963 442030** (USA) **+1 805 498 6703**
(SV) **+46 18 124016**
(Australia/New Zealand) **+61 2 8713 1400**

Preserving Our Motoring Heritage

> The Model J Duesenberg Derham Tourster. Only eight of these magnificent cars were ever built – this is the only example to be found outside the United States of America

Almost every car you've ever loved, loathed or desired under one roof at the Haynes Motor Museum. Over 300 immaculately presented cars and motorbikes represent every aspect of our motoring heritage, from elegant reminders of bygone days, such as the superb Model J Duesenberg to curiosities like the bug-eyed BMW Isetta. There are also many old friends and flames. Perhaps you remember the 1959 Ford Popular that you did your courting in? The magnificent 'Red Collection' is a spectacle of classic sports cars including AC, Alfa Romeo, Austin Healey, Ferrari, Lamborghini, Maserati, MG, Riley, Porsche and Triumph.

A Perfect Day Out

Each and every vehicle at the Haynes Motor Museum has played its part in the history and culture of Motoring. Today, they make a wonderful spectacle and a great day out for all the family. Bring the kids, bring Mum and Dad, but above all bring your camera to capture those golden memories for ever. You will also find an impressive array of motoring memorabilia, a comfortable 70 seat video cinema and one of the most extensive transport book shops in Britain. The Pit Stop Café serves everything from a cup of tea to wholesome, home-made meals or, if you prefer, you can enjoy the large picnic area nestled in the beautiful rural surroundings of Somerset.

> John Haynes O.B.E., Founder and Chairman of the museum at the wheel of a Haynes Light 12.

> The 1936 490cc sohc-engined International Norton – well known for its racing success

The Museum is situated on the A359 Yeovil to Frome road at Sparkford, just off the A303 in Somerset. It is about 40 miles south of Bristol, and 25 minutes drive from the M5 intersection at Taunton.

Open 9.30am - 5.30pm (10.00am - 4.00pm Winter) 7 days a week, except Christmas Day, Boxing Day and New Years Day

Special rates available for schools, coach parties and outings Charitable Trust No. 292048